SHARING THE EARTH, DIVIDING THE LAND

Land and territory in the Austronesian world

SHARING THE EARTH, DIVIDING THE LAND

Land and territory in the Austronesian world

edited by THOMAS REUTER

E PRESS

Published by ANU E Press
The Australian National University
Canberra ACT 0200, Australia
Email: anuepress@anu.edu.au
Web: http://epress.anu.edu.au

National Library of Australia
Cataloguing-in-Publication entry

Sharing the earth, dividing the land : land and territory
in the Austronesian world.

Bibliography.
Includes index.
For tertiary students.
ISBN 1 920942 69 6 (pbk.).
ISBN 1 920942 70 X (online).

1. Ethnology - Asia, Southeastern. 2. Ethnology - Oceania.
3. Southeast Asians. 4. Pacific Islanders. I. Reuter,
Thomas Anton.

305.800959

Cover design by ANU E Press

Dedication

This book is dedicated to all the people of the Asia Pacific whose land has been alienated in the wake of colonialism, modernity and development, and whose traditional insights into human beings' relationship with their physical environment have rarely received the serious consideration they indisputably deserve.

Table of Contents

List of Figures

Chapter 2

Chapter 3

Chapter 4

Chapter 6

Chapter 7

Chapter 8

Chapter 9

Chapter 11

Chapter 12

Chapter 13

Chapter 15

Acknowledgments

The editor initiated the process culminating in the publication of this volume by organising an invited session at the annual conference of the Australian Anthropological Society in Perth in October 2000. This session was to explore changing concepts of territoriality and patterns of land distribution in the Austronesian world. My thanks go to the conference organisers for providing this initial forum, and to the participants for their contributions.

Preliminary discussions identified land as a central concern in the traditional and modern lives of Austronesian-speaking peoples across the Asia Pacific, and revealed a number of common cultural themes in how the relationship between humans and the land is conceptualised in the region. I therefore proposed for these findings to be explored further in an intensive two-day workshop with a wide range of invited contributions to reflect some of the immense cultural diversity of the Austronesian world. Such a workshop was eventually held at The Australian National University in Canberra, on June 18-19, 2001. I would like to express my gratitude to the Research School of Pacific and Asian Studies (ANU) for hosting this event and contributing to the payment of participants' travel expenses.

The more vital debt to be acknowledged here, however, is of an intellectual kind. The editor would like to thank Professor James Fox, in particular for his advice and support throughout the inception and publication of this volume. More generally, the contributors, many of whom are his former students, are indebted to Prof. Fox for encouraging us to share and deepen our understandings of the varied cultures of the Austronesian world by way of systematic ethnological comparisons. The present volume should be seen as a further contribution to the hugely successful series of edited volumes published as a direct or indirect result of the Comparative Austronesian Project at the RSPAS, of which Prof. Fox was the main initiator.

I would like to thank Monash University for institutional support and the Australian Research Council for two successive fellowships and grants.

Chapter 1. Land and Territory in the Austronesian World

Thomas Reuter

Contemporary societies within the South-East Asia-Pacific Region still maintain a distinctively Austronesian cultural perspective on land and territory. The present volume contributes to the comparative study of Austronesian societies by exploring this important theme of land and territory within their traditional cultures. At the same time, the authors acknowledge that these are cultures in transition and traditional relationships to land are increasingly compromised by the legal and administrative systems of modern nationstates in the region. This volume also contributes to a current debate in anthropology on the conflicting human tendencies of mobility and emplacement. In the context of this debate, many anthropologists have called for a greater focus on mobility to better reflect the increase in human mobility in the current postmodern period. The ethnographic evidence presented herein, however, shows that mobility is not just an issue in the study of contemporary cosmopolitan and migrant populations. A struggle with experiences of displacement and re-emplacement has been central to the historical experience of Austronesian societies for millennia. Many of the presumably 'traditional' models of society that have evolved from this struggle reflect a deep understanding of and appreciation for the formative historical influence of human mobility on society. These local models provide an alternative or, at least, some valuable inspirations for Western theories of society, which are only just beginning to afford a central place to the idea of 'cultures on the move'.

Austronesian-speaking peoples articulate their personal sense of belonging to particular places and lay claim to land or other territorial rights by invoking local histories of ancestral origins and migration. These accounts of human movement and emplacement might be written down but more often they are conveyed as oral histories. Origin histories are also inscribed on the physical landscape in the form of sacred sites, and on the minds of local participants through their shared experience of ritual performances held at these sites. Together these commemorative social practices generate a powerful sense of belonging and emplacement. There is also a strong emphasis on temporality and change. Clusters of settlements or ritual sites are linked through histories of human movement rather than being depicted as static arrays of bounded and separate places. A group and its place of belonging is usually constructed as a station on a pathway of ancestral migrations. People's rights to land or other localised resources and their social identity are thus inseparable, and both are defined by reference to time, or 'precedence'. Status and rights to land are indexed on their relative proximity to the sacred origin place or 'source' of this path, so that the ultimate ritual overlordship of a territory is often vested in the human representative of this source. At the same time, Austronesians also recognise the significance of secular power and the impact of political change on the historical trajectories of their societies and resource economies. Many origin narratives recognise and attempt to reconcile these conflicting value spheres of religious status and secular power within the models of society they create. According to these models, people share a collective ritual responsibility towards the Earth, which requires and promotes social cooperation. At the same time, they acknowledge that, as individuals with a strategic interest in a political economy based on agriculture, people also have a concern for dividing and controlling land. This volume explores these local models through a method of regional comparative ethnology, with the aim of identifying the key insights Austronesian societies have gained in their efforts to address some of the basic existential issues that arise from the relationship between people and land.

Austronesian-speaking societies occupy a vast and fairly cohesive area stretching from Taiwan to Madagascar and across South-East Asia, Micronesia and Melanesia into the Pacific, as far as Hawai'i, Easter Island and New Zealand. Austronesian societies share a common cultural heritage but have become widely dispersed through a long historical process of migration. In the course of this history of geographic dispersion and expansion, an immense diversity of linguistic and cultural forms was produced. This combination of a shared cultural base and a wide range of creative innovations provided a strong foundation for the meaningful comparative study of Austronesian societies. Recognising this comparative potential, a group of anthropologists around Professor James Fox, acting in collaboration with colleagues in archaeology, comparative linguistics and other disciplines, initiated the path-breaking Comparative Austronesian Studies Project at The Australian National University in the 1980s. Researchers attached to this project have published numerous individual papers as well as an important series of edited volumes (Fox 1993; Bellwood, Fox and Tryon 1995; Fox and Sather 1996; Fox 1997; Vischer, in press). Reflecting the unique research experiences of 14 leading Australian ethnographers in as many different Austronesian-speaking societies, from Sumatra to Tonga, the present contribution on land and territory is a further volume in this series.

Traditional ideas about land and territorial entitlements within the region have had to be renegotiated continuously in the past two centuries in response to a tumultuous history of colonisation and an often equally difficult process of incorporation within the legal and administrative structures of modernising, independent nationstates. Local people's traditional relationship to land also has been transformed by a gradual and accelerating process of globalisation, whereby concepts of traditional ownership increasingly come into conflict with the principles of an international, Western-dominated, late-capitalist economic and political system. One common type of conflict resulting from these changes is between indigenous peoples and the development agendas of modernising nationstates. Acting in conjunction with multinational corporations, national governments often have dismissed indigenous people's claims to collective ownership of traditional clan or village land and have legislated to reclassify such land as state-owned or private property. While we may focus on Austronesian traditions, the authors also explore some of these issues of social change. We thus hope to provide a useful resource to readers with an interest in contemporary political conflicts relating to traditional land rights in the Austronesian world and beyond.

In a traditional cultural context, Austronesian-speaking societies have constructed their sense of identity and legitimised their territorial claims to land and other resources by reference to local and sometimes regional origin narratives. These origin histories typically tell a tale either of gradual population growth and associated geographical expansion or of more spontaneous additions to the population with the sudden arrival of immigrants (invaders, refugees, affines or allies). In either case, the narratives tend to treat 'people' and 'land' as mutually constitutive categories within a single, place- and movement-oriented schema of ancestral identity and sacred geography. Place-based identities are commonly ranked in order of precedence, a concept of temporal order that draws precisely on the fact that different places and groups of people are linked through a history of ancestral migrations. The elements or stations in such pathways of identity are often remembered and narrated as long lists of placenames or 'topogenies' (Fox 1997: 8-12), rather than relying on genealogies, which allow people to trace ancestral connections by remembering the names of people. Historical ties between a set of places and resident communities may be commemorated also through complex systems of ritual visiting arrangements and asymmetric ceremonial exchange. Collective ritual performances, in a wide variety of forms, help to reinforce the religious character of this model of hierarchical emplacement by bringing it into the lived experience of the participants.

Their traditional sense of belonging to particular places, however, is much more than just a marker of identity and social status to the agriculturalist peoples of the Austronesian world. Land has also been, and continues to be, a primary economic resource and a matter of great strategic interest in its own right. Although there have been dramatic changes to patterns of land usage in recent times, evidence suggests the overall significance of land has not been declining in the region. The proportion of people engaged in subsistence agriculture may be shrinking, and with it some of the motivation for a religious perspective of land. The scarcity of land is increasing, however, and so are incidents of legal or political contestation of identity-based claims to ownership and usage rights. In this climate of increasing scarcity, old and new ways of thinking about land rights are clashing, sometimes violently. Conflicts frequently arise where village or clan land is appropriated by the State and made available to, for example, timber and mining companies or other development interests. Internal disputes are also common, especially where collectively owned land has been reclassified legally as individual private property and subsequently divided and sold off, to support consumer spending or for reinvestment into new means of production. The case studies in this volume document how Austronesians are attempting to negotiate changing relationships with the land at the nexus between a still relevant traditional way of life and the new rules that come into play as local societies are incorporated within nationalising and globalising political economies.

Local tensions between traditional and contemporary concepts of place raise the more general question of how we should conceptualise the changing relationship between people and land or 'place' within an economic and political context of globalisation and a cultural context often loosely referred to as the postmodern or late-capitalist condition. This condition is said to be characterised by an unprecedented degree of human mobility, migration, displacement and de-territorialisation. The case studies presented herein suggest, however, that many so-called traditional cultures have long and openly recognised human mobility and associated processes of social change as fundamental to the existence and historical development of society. Indeed, the idea of mobility has been central in defining identity and status relationships in the Austronesian world. Movement and migration lie at the very heart of their traditional models of emplacement, and also have been central to the historical experience on which these models are based. At the same time, the way in which place is conceptualised in Austronesian cultures also suggests that, no matter how much displacement they might experience, their relationships with the land, their place of origin and their place of residence are matters of utmost importance to all people, and no less so to a people on the move. Detailed ethnographic research and ethnological comparison is thus an essential step towards developing a better understanding of how different cultures have attempted to solve the fundamental conundrum of reconciling a basic human interest in mobility with a similarly fundamental interest in the security of emplacement.

In the remainder of this introduction, I will explore some of these theoretical and comparative issues in more detail, as well as providing an outline of the case studies in this volume.

Land and Territory in the Context of Human Mobility and Globalisation: A Theoretical Debate and an Ethnological Solution

Contemporary anthropological theorists have moved away from an earlier tendency to view cultures as social systems localised in specific places or territories. Space had sometimes served as a convenient metaphor to articulate a clear and lasting division of the world, assigning to each distinguishable culture its unique and original place—a cultural habitat based on a coincidence of spatial separation and cultural difference. Some authors have directed their critique at the 'incarceration' cultures in fixed places (Appadurai 1988) and others at the metaphor of the 'localness' of cultures (Clifford 1988), or at the latent functionalist search for cultural stability and social equilibrium (Malkki 1995).

One reason why this habitual linking of culture and topology, of nation and territory, became the focus of much critical analysis was the increasing mobility of culture and people on an unprecedented scale in the 20th century. While still appreciating the merits of detailed ethnographic research, most contemporary theorists now insist that cultures need to be understood as systems in motion. An increasing number of ethnographers are following this advice and are turning away from classical, localised fieldwork to conduct studies of human mobility. Some study loosely connected groups of tourists, itinerant workers, asylum-seekers and migrants, while others observe the confluence of cultural traditions in diasporal, expatriate and multicultural communities (e.g. Lavie and Swedenburg 1996). This new body of anthropological research does indeed show that in today's world of electronic communication and mass movement, a culture can no longer be associated exclusively with a single place or assigned a definitive homeland, let alone confined within narrowly conceived territorial boundaries. Studies of transnational and intra-national migration, for example, raise questions about how to assign a spatial referent to groups of people whose identity is situated somewhere in between the places of their origin and current residence.

At the same time, it would seem futile to try to deny the basic localising constraints of the human condition. As embodied individuals, we necessarily operate in specific physical environments wherein many of our most important social interactions must take place. Direct face-to-face interaction is dependent largely on the language and other culture-specific codes operative within such a local setting. Even if we accept the postmodernist hypothesis that there is a global trend towards a hybridisation of cultures, there is as yet no universally intelligible language, and the local use of interactive codes is never arbitrary even where multiple codes have become available. Other than exerting an influence on how we satisfy our immediate social and communicative interests, the human condition of situated embodiment also tends to propel us to look locally for resources to satisfy some of our most immediate material interests. One of these interests is to own, borrow or lease a territory or 'socially demarcated place' that provides shelter, security and perhaps a source of income.

There are numerous studies on the social construction of place and landscape and on the symbology and politics of space, which all suggest that territory is still very much something humans are prepared to contest, no matter whether the claims to the territory are material or symbolic, political or religious, historical or mythological. Ironically, new research with a focus on movement—whether it has looked at cases of voluntary displacement or forceful eviction—has raised our awareness of the importance and cultural process of constructing spaces, localities and associated identities (Gupta and Ferguson 1992). The image of a place or country of origin is often vigorously cultivated by, for example, people living in a diaspora setting. Memories of home are carefully maintained, and not just as a matter of nostalgia. Access to social networks created by transnational emigration, for example, can serve as an economic resource or as a means for generating influence and power in relation to the nation state (Marcus 1993). Ever-new places of mythical origin and pathways of migration are thus being imagined and lived in, and they are often the subject of disputes within and across local social contexts.

The debate about changing relationships between people and places in anthropology reflects on a number of important political issues, trends and events of global importance. The new trend towards research on the mobility of cultures may in part reflect our own lived experience of a postmodern condition of de-territorialisation, which has been brought about by increased mobility, information exchange and a new political economy, incorporating a global system of finance, production, promotion and consumption. To point out how physical displacement through mass migration, social atomisation and the rise of fluid, consumption-based identities have changed our lives, however, is to tell only one half of the story of what might constitute the typical contemporary experience of culture. In this same historical period, we have witnessed a series of conflicts in the Balkans, the Middle East, Africa, the former Soviet Union and elsewhere, which have highlighted the enduring importance of culture and ethnicity in the legitimisation of claims over territories and localised resources. The so-called 'War on Terror', the largest of these contemporary conflicts and the one most likely to preoccupy the world for decades to come, likewise draws on ideas of cultural or religious difference. While it is not portrayed as a territorial war, the underlying struggle in this presumed 'clash of civilisations' seems to be for the control of localised material resources such as oil reserves. Similarly, the enduring appeal of a defensive territorial attitude is also evident in the recent political history of many Western nations, including Australia, Denmark and Italy, where a 'tough stance' on refugees and on other immigration issues has delivered a succession of election victories to conservative governments in the first decade of this new millennium.

These global political trends illustrate the resilience of ethnic and cultural ideas of difference and their strategic function in resource conflicts. Even authors who strongly advocate the study of human mobility and displacement in a globalising world have commented on this stubborn persistence of territorial conflicts (e.g., Olwig and Hastrup 1997: 4). One obvious reason for the resilience of cultural constructs of emplacement is the paramount value of such constructs as a means of legitimising exclusive or privileged control over land and other important material resources. In my view, however, the mere fact that strategic discourses of identity can be useful in resource conflicts does not support the radical constructivist argument that such conflicts are entirely a product of ideology. Resource competition is not contingent on cultural constructs. And, in any case, cultural constructs of place and identity can be just as important for conflict resolution. Despite their strategic legitimising function, shared concepts of identity and emplacement can help to regulate the distribution of local resources among different groups of people and can thus reduce the potential for violent conflict among them. This more positive aspect provides an additional incentive for the cross-cultural study of discourses of emplacement and associated systems of local resource distribution—assuming we accept the basic anthropological idea that there is something we can learn from other societies by looking at how they have attempted to resolve a perennial existential challenge that we too must face.

This volume thus has much to contribute to the debate in current anthropology on the mobility and territoriality of human cultures. It does so by exploring how for centuries people in 14 of the numerous historically and linguistically related societies of the vast Austronesian world have dealt with the very same underlying issues that seem to so concern the postmodern world. The most fundamental of these issues are: first, the dynamic tension between the simultaneous human tendencies towards mobility and emplacement, and second, the link between territorial claims for material resources and the social identity constructs that legitimise and regulate these claims. I will refer to these two as 'the mobility issue' and 'the legitimacy issue' respectively.

Austronesian social categories of land and discourses about land claims exemplify how the basic issues of mobility and legitimacy have been negotiated in the societies of this region. Like all social systems, Austronesian societies have devised a system for accommodating the inevitable conflicts to do with 'carving up the land' while simultaneously allowing people to 'share the earth', by finding ways to avoid or reduce violent confrontations in the context of resource competition. By exploring the nuanced strategies Austronesian societies have developed over many centuries, the papers in this volume illustrate that mobility is not really a new issue at all. In the Austronesian world, at least, migration has long been a standard response to tensions arising from population change and resource scarcity in a given locality, and to the allure of finding more abundant resources elsewhere through migration.

Austronesians have always been remarkably mobile, as is evident from their history of continual migration, originating in southern China and moving in numerous waves via Taiwan across the far-flung islands of the Indian and Pacific Oceans. Perhaps it is this remarkable mobility that has inspired them to turn human mobility into the conceptual backbone of a social philosophy wherein concepts of 'origin' and 'precedence' are the most central constructs.

The concepts of origin and precedence reflect the fact that people on the move will necessarily encounter others who have preceded them and already lay claim to the land to some degree. Various local origin narratives acknowledge that there are different ways in which these earlier settlers can respond to the arrival of newcomers, ranging from assimilation at the margins to accommodation into the very centre of local society. They also illustrate how widely the outcomes of such encounters can range depending on the attitude and power of the newcomers, who might seek a culturally mediated agreement on how to share the land and other material and symbolic resources with earlier settlers, or who might violently or treacherously usurp the precedence claims of the latter.

All in all, Austronesian ideas about people and land show an appreciation that society is the sediment of human movements and, indeed, that life itself is predicated on movement. An example of this celebration of movement in a social context is the appreciation Austronesians tend to show for the 'flow of life' that occurs in the context of marriage exchanges between exogamous groups (see Fox 1980). The idea of culture-in-motion, arising from the interplay between time, place and human action, is thus the central idiom of Austronesians' 'models of' their own societies, and of the cosmos as a whole. At the same time, these are also 'models for', insofar as they are designed to cope with the potential for conflict over land and other local resources.

A detailed discussion of the comparative ethnology of Austronesian models of movement and emplacement is provided in the postscript of this volume. In order to better appreciate the thematic connections between the papers, however, some of the main features and implications of these cultural models of social space need to be identified in advance.

The Social Construction of Land, Place and Territory in the Austronesian World: From Ethnography to Comparative Ethnology

Although they are dispersed widely, from Sumatra in the west to Tonga in the east, the 14 societies discussed in this volume share a common cultural and historical heritage. Linguistic, biological, archaeological and anthropological evidence shows that contemporary Austronesian-speaking societies have a common origin and history of dispersion. This history can be traced back some 6,000 years, to when their ancestors began a long series of migrations from southern China via Taiwan to South-East Asia and onward to Madagascar, Micronesia, Melanesia, Polynesia and New Zealand (Bellwood, Fox and Tryon 1995). This history of migration was accompanied by continuous cultural adaptations and transformations. There were also long-term interactions with earlier inhabitants and their cultures—in Halmahera and Melanesia, for example—which sometimes led to the assimilation of Austronesian languages and culture by other populations. Today more than 1,000 different Austronesian languages are spoken by an estimated 270 million people in this vast region.

The linguistic diversity of these societies is matched by their cultural diversity, and the preceding volumes in the Comparative Austronesia Project series since 1993 have illustrated some of this staggering variety of social forms. The shared Austronesian heritage of these societies is, however equally evident. Two of the most important dimensions of this shared cultural heritage were described in the first volume of this series, *The Austronesians: Historical and Comparative Perspectives*, as a common tendency towards

> the tracing of local origins and the reliance on a variety of narratives for the construction of a shared past. Thus the sharing of a journey may be used to define relatedness whereas claims to precedence, often based on the order of events in particular narratives, figure prominently as a means of defining social difference. (Bellwood, Fox and Tryon 1995: 10)

Social history tends to be depicted as a temporal sequence of events identified with named locations, which are all part of the pathway of an ancestral journey and can be ranked according to their proximity to the point of origin. This often gives rise to place-based models of human relatedness or 'topogenies', to use a term introduced by James Fox in another of these earlier volumes, *The Poetic Power of Place* (1997). Rather than or in addition to using genealogies in which named personal ancestors are used to establish connections between the living, many Austronesian societies rely on lists of placenames or topogenies to establish historical links between groups of people within and across different localities in a region. Topogenies are thus narrative accounts of a complex history of human movement and emplacement. Topogenies are used to explain (and often also to contest) how contemporary societies came to be grouped and status differentiated as they are today.

In Austronesian-speaking societies, the most salient social categories are often based on cohabitation or shared usage of a named area of residential or agricultural land by a particular group of people. One reason why place is such a common, convenient and powerful marker of identity, in the Austronesian world and beyond, is that the membership of place-based groups need not be homogenous. Whether they are ancestral origin houses, named settlements, domains or regional ritual federations, place-based social categories are very useful to societies with a complex history of human migration and relocation. The complexity created by movement demands a social capacity for maintaining unity in the face of diversity at the local level. At the same time, co-residents will usually compete for the control of local resources to some degree. This creates a tendency to construct a system of social differentiation by stressing diversity of origins in other contexts to serve as a status marker. The Austronesian model for this simultaneous sharing and dividing of the land focuses on human movement and utilises associated ideas of precedence as the main classificatory principle for regulating access to land.

The topogenies of Austronesian societies are therefore valorised as 'moral' spaces wherein individual locations are not simply distinguished but are ranked in order of precedence, as are the people whose identities are indexed to these locations (Fox 1997: 4). This suggests that—although it may often be owned collectively within localised groups—the way land is shared is neither free and unproblematic nor necessarily equitable in Austronesian societies. Land has indeed been the single most important material resource, and land rights have constituted a primary privilege in the predominantly agriculture-based political economies of this region.

The balance between the value of the privileges and the cost of the obligations attached to land usage rights is variable across different communities depending on demographic and other factors. A need to restrict access to land ownership or usage rights has been felt most frequently in cases where population growth within an expanding system of segmentary social organisation has led to a local scarcity of agricultural land and a corresponding increase in value. Maintaining privileged access to land through claims of precedence was not only about securing land for personal use. Even under conditions of relative abundance, land was still valuable because any excess could be distributed profitably to client newcomers in return for ritual or political allegiance. In future, land scarcity seems set to become a more or less continuous condition and will reach an unprecedented pitch as land values continue to increase across the South-East Asia-Pacific region. The discursive space between place and identity is likely to become more and more contested and politicised as a result.

Variations in resource scarcity are an important aspect of the operating conditions of all human societies, and Austronesian societies are not unique in this sense. As far as these fluctuations are concerned, Austronesian societies can differ more from one another, and vary more within themselves over time, than they differ from many non-Austronesian societies at any given time. What makes human societies unique are not fluctuations in the existential problems they face in managing finite resources but the distinctive cultural strategies they develop for distributing these resources and for mediating resource conflicts whenever they arise.

The Austronesian model of emplacement through narratives of movement is one such strategy. The distinguishing feature of this model is that it typically creates a fluid and evolving system of social differentiation based on a principle of precedence ranking which, in turn, is predicated on a fundamental assumption of human mobility in a context of segmentary expansion or migration. The main task of this comparative volume, then, is to spell out how this basic concept of emplacement through growth and movement plays out in different Austronesian societies—under a variety of different operating conditions and as a result of continual cultural innovation—to produce a wide range of comparable social formations of variable size and character.

Most of the papers in this volume were first presented at a workshop held on June 18-19, 2001 at The Australian National University in Canberra, Australia, entitled 'Sharing the Earth, Dividing the Land: Territorial Categories and Institutions in the Austronesian World'. The aim of the workshop was to identify and discuss common categories, organisational principles and historical processes of innovation among related populations in different parts of this region. Participants were asked to describe territorial institutions of varying size in the societies they had studied, from house or longhouse territories to the more extensive lands belonging to a hamlet or village, and to look at how these different layers of territorial organisation interrelated conceptually and institutionally. Special attention was to be paid to larger, regional institutions such as domains, chiefdoms or polities, which tended to be composed of several of the smaller territorial units and might, in turn, have provided the building blocks for early state formation in the region.

Four important dimensions for the comparison of Austronesian models of emplacement could be identified in subsequent discussions, and each of these were exemplified by several of the case studies in this volume. These comparative dimensions concern: 1) the territorial categories of Austronesian languages; 2) the specific metaphors that characterise Austronesian models of emplacement and social identity; 3) how ceremonial domains have been transformed by, and also contributed to, the formation of more complex polities, and 4) how traditional ways of relating to the land are being challenged within the context of modern nationstates and their globalising economies.

Austronesian Territorial Categories

The terminology we use to designate different territories and social relations to land in Western societies—words such as 'estate', 'village', 'domain', 'territory', 'proprietor', 'tenant' and their reflexes in other European languages—are not suitable to serve as universal categories for the purposes of cross-cultural comparison. The meanings of these terms are embedded irrevocably in a distinctly European political history and legal tradition, and even within that tradition there is much heterogeneity. It may be impossible to avoid completely the use of these loaded terms in the act of translation. It is possible and indeed imperative, however, to develop an appreciation for the semantics and pragmatics of local categories.

The meaning of key terms within a society arises from their conceptual relation to the local cosmology and idiom wherein they are embedded, and their pragmatic use is revealed in relation to local behavioural models for the pursuit of communicative and strategic interests. 'Territorial categories' in Austronesian societies thus need to be understood in the context of a culture-specific perception of land and a rationale for legitimising land ownership, which, in turn, is associated with a specific pattern of social organisation. These considerations have prompted the authors to approach the task of comparative analysis by exploring the relevant indigenous Austronesian categories, rather than imposing a set of alien categories derived from a European tradition of political history and social science.

Comparison has revealed that, with few exceptions (see below), words used by speakers of contemporary Austronesian languages to designate named tracts of land are reflexes of just three Proto-Austronesian reconstructions. Variations in the actual meaning of these related terms are somewhat more pronounced. For example, the size of the units of land referred to by the same set of reflexes differs across cultures, as does the relative emphasis placed on centres versus boundaries in defining these units. Their meaning within the general local model of relations—between humans and the land, and among 'emplaced humans'—however, remains fairly consistent. At a more pragmatic level, finally, the comparison has exposed substantial variation in the practical significance these traditional territorial terms carry across contemporary Austronesian societies, particularly in view of major political and economic changes in their recent history.

Three sets of reflexes are of particular interest in exploring categories of people and land due to their wide distribution and pivotal social significance in Austronesian languages and societies. The first set are reflexes of the Proto-Austronesian (PAN) reconstruction **banua* (*banua, banwa, wanua, vanua, fanua, panua, manua, banuah, banuwa, banwa, binua, bonua, menoa, nua, knua, fua, whenua, hena, fena*). The reflexes of **banua* are variable in their meaning across different languages and contexts, but generally refer to a designated 'stretch of land', 'territory' or 'dwelling place' of varying size, and/or to the inhabitants of such a place. Two other sets of reflexes that carry a similar meaning are reflexes of the reconstructions **tanah* (*tana, tanaq, taneq, taneh, tano, 'ano*) and **daya* (*darat, dare, dae, rae, rai*). James Fox considers these sets of reflexes and their variable semantic contents in more detail in his postscript. It is important, however, to discuss in advance some of the implications of these linguistic family resemblances among Austronesian populations.

It would be easy to succumb to a sense of frustration as one tries to pinpoint the actual significance and limits of the link between linguistic and cultural similarities within this region and in general. The problem with the idea of a comparative ethnology based on comparative linguistics, as so often in social theory, is not really that the link between language and culture is intrinsically ambiguous or indeterminate. It is simply extremely complex. Without delving into the depths of communication theory, and for the specific purposes of this present discussion, one way to account for a good part of this complexity is to adopt a socio-historical perspective to comparative ethnology. This approach assumes, first, that the link between words and their meaning is fundamentally arbitrary, and, second, that the link, such as it is, is socially constructed over time among populations of regularly communicating individuals. Once constructed, the link can be very durable, so that contemporary reflexes of a word may retain much of the original meaning for centuries, even millennia. A total loss or reassignment of meaning is also possible, however, and subtle fluctuations occur all the time. An incentive for changing the meaning of words might arise, for example, from gradual or sudden changes in a people's way of life, their environment, economic activities and relations with other populations.

The relationship between language and social history is clearly significant insofar as systematic similarities between languages, and even loan words, are always the sediment of historical connections or interactions, including migration, conquest, trade and individual travel. At the same time, the use of similar terms in different societies is insufficient in itself to serve as a predictor of specific cultural similarities because there is a constant drift in the local meaning of terms, which is a function of their embeddedness within ever-evolving social contexts. This drift may explain why the social performance of cultural meaning is often less conservative than the social performance of words as signs in a given language.

What does this entail for the present set of Austronesian case studies? By definition, linguistic connections can be traced between any two Austronesian languages, and this reflects the historical fact that the speakers of these languages are related populations and the sociological fact that language tends to be conservative. This does not provide a guarantee that the two societies will also show cultural similarities. Nevertheless, it is very likely indeed that they will, given that the link between words and their meanings is also quite conservative, especially with very basic words such as 'land' or 'house'. Similarly, there can be no guarantee that societies whose members speak closely related languages are culturally more similar than speakers of more distantly related languages within the same family. Looking at the case studies in this volume, for example, one could point out that the languages of Buru, Seram, Banda, Sikka, Keo and Timor all fall within the Central Malayo-Polynesian Group, those of Bali and Sumatra within the Western Malayo-Polynesian Group, and those of North Mekeo, North Pentecost, Ambrym and Tonga in the Oceanic Group of Austronesian languages. I would argue, however, that the comparative evidence so far is insufficient to support a claim that cultural similarities are greater among societies within than across these language groups. Other factors, such a geographic proximity and ease of interaction between populations, are as, or more, important in this context.

It also needs to be considered that throughout the region new terms with initially quite foreign meanings were introduced to refer to territorially defined administrative units within early Indic states, coastal trading polities, colonial states or independent modern nation states. The local meaning and social significance of an introduced term, such as the Sanskrit word *desa* ('village') in Indonesia, for example, can match that of earlier, local Austronesian terms (*banua* in this case) more closely than it matches the meaning and social significance of the same term in the original language and society from which it is derived. This semantic localisation of introduced terms can be a complex historical process. In the part of the region that came under the influence of Indic kingdoms, for example, terms first introduced as Sanskrit loan words (*desa, kuta, negara*) were later adopted and heavily reinterpreted by modern nation states such as the Republic of Indonesia. Their usage has spread correspondingly, within the new boundaries of these nation states and far beyond the geographic reach of the early Indic kingdoms that first adopted them. Thus the term *desa* (*dinas*), for example, reached West Papua only in the 1950s, and only as the designation for a modern, Indonesian administrative structure. In Bali the situation is more complicated (Reuter 1999). Here the classical Indonesian adaptation of the Indic term *desa* still exists, referring to the '*desa adat*', an institution that has survived from the times of Bali's early Hindu polities. This more traditional *desa* coexists and competes for significance with the same modern Indonesian administrative unit we now also find on Buru. The latter is referred to as the *desa dinas* in Bali in order to distinguish it from the *desa adat*.

In many contemporary Austronesian societies, modern territorial terms and associated administrative units thus coexist with earlier schemata for the social construction and division of space. The physical boundaries of these old and new categories may or may not coincide, though there is often some degree of continuity. Conflicts tend to arise when new administrative boundaries divide people who consider themselves historically related and part of a social whole or, conversely, throw together people who do not have any recognised traditional connections.

Metaphors of Socio-Spatial Relations

Metaphors of socio-spatial relations, like all metaphors, are figures of speech whereby a thing is spoken of as being that which it only resembles. The metaphors Austronesians use to imagine and reflect on the social structure of a domain or similar socio-territorial unit show striking similarities. Again, this suggests that the usage of such metaphors tends to be rather conservative, notwithstanding the fact that their meaning and social implications will vary from one society to the next.

Botanic metaphors are among the most commonly used metaphors for social relationships in the Austronesian world. The source ancestor of a clan or founding clan of a village, for example, may be referred to as the 'trunk' or 'root' and his descendant or newcomer clients as the 'leaves' or 'tips' of the same tree. Similarly in a topogeny, the place of origin is usually the ritual centre or 'trunk' of the domain, to which a path of origin is ceremonially traced back along one or several 'branch' villages, beginning from the newest settlements or 'tips'. The people who reside at, or in some other way can lay claim to, the origin site tend to maintain a position of ritual precedence or of political authority in the domain, but rarely both. Botanic metaphors generally suggest a segmentary process of spatial expansion due to organic growth from within, but can and are applied also within local societies featuring a population with multiple origins.

Body metaphors are also used widely for the imagery of social space in the Austronesian world. In highland Bali, for example, differently ranked members of the village council of elders are associated with specific body parts of sacrificial animals, which are divided among them to be consumed during ritual meals. Indeed, some of the titles of elders are derived from body parts, especially from the divisions of the forelegs (Reuter 2002a, 2002b). The 'head' of domains is often associated with the most upstream inhabited locations at the source of river systems. Left and right body halves are often associated with ceremonial moieties or other forms of dual social categories. The four extremities of sacrificial animals, finally, tend to be associated with some form of fourfold division of space and society (see Mosko, this volume), which is also a common pattern within the region.

Of all the metaphors used to conceptualise socio-territorial units in Austronesian societies, the most important is that of a 'path' or 'journey'; a trajectory of human movement through space and time. The significance of mytho-historical movements through space is evident particularly in the cosmological organisation of larger, regional socio-territorial units, including ritual domains and pre-colonial kingdoms. Such domains and polities tend to be composed of smaller units linked together by a history of ancestral migration, beginning at a shared point of origin or, sometimes, ending at a shared destination, which is then transformed into a point of origin for all future purposes (see Winn, this volume).

An idiom of relatedness based on kinship and marriage is also used frequently to conceptualise the unity and divisions of local society, along with the boundaries and divisions of land claimed by various groups. Among highland Balinese, for example, historical ties between villages are often expressed figuratively by postulating asymmetric kinship relationships between village ancestor deities. Often the physical landscape contributes to, and is subsumed within, the imagery of a more complex socio-physical totality that is attributed with a numinous quality. In such an integrated world, the land and its people are so tightly interwoven that it is futile to try to discuss social categories without reference to categories of land, and vice versa.

From Ritual Domains to States: Scales of Complexity

There is considerable variability in the relative complexity of land-related categories and land tenure arrangements in Austronesian societies. Among other factors, these variations seem to depend on: a) the relative abundance of land and the general conduciveness of ecological and climatic conditions to intensive agriculture on that land; b) the population density; c) the social diversity, especially in terms of the presence or absence of immigrants (in small or large numbers; with or without a separate ethnic identity, language or religion; with or without colonial or modern state sponsorship); d) the degree of local access to regional or international trade networks; and e) the degree of direct foreign intervention in local affairs. More complex social and political systems might have evolved first in areas that could sustain large and dense populations through intensive agriculture, division of labour or trade, or where an influx of migrants necessitated more complex models of emplacement.

It is likely that some of the larger, regional systems of Austronesian socio-territorial organisation provided a foundation for the formation of polities and early states. While local developmental processes might have been enough to create social systems of considerable size and complexity in their own right, it is evident that the first major states did not build on the logic of an indigenous Austronesian social system and cosmology alone. This is true particularly for the greater part of South-East Asia, which has been subject to Indic influence at some time.

A number of the large Hindu-Buddhist polities emerging in the region from the fifth century onward employed Indic notions of divine kingship in order to generate an inter-local form of organisation for the first time in a particular area. Others appear to have utilised and transformed pre-existing, though perhaps hitherto predominantly ritual, forms of regional organisation in order to create a more cohesive and centralised political system or 'state' (*negara*), though still with a strong ritual component (Geertz 1980). In other cases again, there might have been hostility, avoidance or some kind of truce between people with a stake in an earlier system of regional socio-territorial organisation and encroaching Hindu-Buddhist (and later Muslim) polities that were seeking to establish some degree of sovereignty over their territory (Reuter 2002a). The polities that developed in Tonga and elsewhere in the Pacific, finally, appear to have evolved initially without any direct foreign influence.

All of the case studies presented in this book, however, provide evidence of how people's traditional ways of categorising and regulating access to land were profoundly transformed, once again or for the first time, by their incorporation into the political, administrative and legal systems of colonial empires and/or, more recently, independent modern nation states. The transformations tended to be more incisive than those of earlier periods. Earlier Indic and Muslim states grew out of trade links accompanied by the importation of foreign religions and associated concepts of sovereignty, but essentially had to be built on local foundations to some degree. Colonial states, while they too might have begun as trading ventures, were ultimately built on military conquest or control, and involved the establishment of a government apparatus led by foreigners. Nevertheless, local forms of social and political organisation were maintained as a support structure in many cases, due to the limited resources of the expatriates in many colonial states. This kind of collaboration eventually produced Western-educated local elites who later led the anti-colonial struggle and put themselves at the head of the newly emerging independent states in the region. In cases where such collaboration was limited and colonial rule was more direct, earlier models of land tenure might have all but disappeared.

In many contemporary societies in the Austronesian world, one therefore finds a complex layered patchwork of territorial and other social institutions that can be traced to various stages in a historical movement towards ever-increasing complexity. I will later return to the question of how relevant Austronesian territorial categories still are in the context of complex modern nation states with rapidly globalising economies.

Outline

The ethnographic case studies in this volume are presented in geographical order from the west moving eastward. Each paper contributes to several of the comparative themes identified above. A brief description of the content of each case study is provided in advance in order to identify which of these themes they are most relevant to. These descriptions also reveal some of the unique variations and less obvious commonalities in the ways different Austronesian societies have approached the basic social issue of regulating the relationship between people and land.

In the first paper, Minako Sakai discusses the '*Kute*' as an indigenous territorial category and institution in South Sumatra (Chapter Two). The Sanskrit-derived Old Malay word *kute* ('a fortified town or palace') was used widely in the highlands of South Sumatra. The author examines how the term and the category '*kute*' survived by looking at the case of the Gumai. At a level of state administration, *kute* has been replaced with a succession of other terms, including *marga*, *dusun*, and finally, *desa*. Like *kute* itself, these newer terms have acquired some of the meaning of an underlying Austronesian territorial concept that envisages a shared social identity based on a specific 'foundation event'. Many Gumai villages in the South Sumatran highlands are thought to have been established by, and thus trace their 'origin' to, a single ancestor, the *Puyang Ketunggalan Dusun*. Villages contained a small ancestor house (*lunjuk* or *rumah puyang*) for the spirits of the founding ancestors, where rituals would be held to commemorate the village origins. The morpheme *pu* in *puyang* could be a reflex of *puqun*, which is a Proto-Malayo-Polynesian reconstruction meaning 'tree', 'trunk', 'base' or 'source'. Villages are inhabited by the descendants of the *puyang* and their affines. The population is divided into origin groups called *jungkuk* which are ranked in order of precedence based on birth order and ritual seniority.

My own paper (Chapter Three), Ritual Domains and Communal Land in the Highlands of Bali, explores the significance of ceremonial domains (*banua*) among highland Balinese. *Banua*, in Bali, are ritually defined regional territories of variable size. About 15 of these domains have been identified, studied and compared by the author. Each is under the spiritual protection of the deified ancestors who first cleared the forest and established settlements. These ancestral deities are located in village temples. The temple of the oldest settlement in a domain is gradually transformed into a regional temple where the most senior ancestors are venerated by people from all branch villages within the domain. Origin myths and rituals retrace the path of the first ancestors, their emigrating descendants or new immigrants, thus creating the image of a complex land- and time-scape that has been inscribed and is perpetually re-inscribed by human action. Despite their focus on origin histories, regional ritual alliances among villages are voluntary associations, and the status distribution among participants is fluid and contested.

Status relations among villages in a domain are defined by notions of precedence and are thus asymmetric. This has few economic implications in contemporary *banua*. Ritual status differences between households within a village do, however, have such implications. Only village-founder households have access to land owned collectively by the village (*tanah desa*) and administered by a council of elders (*kerama desa*), who are seated in order of precedence in the village longhouse (descending in rank from the 'tip' to the 'trunk' end). Claims to village-founder status, furthermore, necessarily draw on the origin narratives of the domain of which the village is a part.

A case study of a local origin myth is used to show that the historical transformation of a village into a much more complex regional domain coincides with a shift from material to symbolic resources as the object of primary concern. The idea of a shared land or territory is retained and commemorated in a ritual context, even when individual villages have already gained independence in all practical matters in the course of this transformation. The shift to a predominant concern with symbolic resources is underpinned by a desire to participate in a regional process of status competition among Bali Aga villages, and also reflects their efforts to establish a degree of political unity among themselves vis-a-vis the outside world.

Graeme MacRae's paper (Chapter Four) complements this account of highland Balinese domains by exploring how such domains were built on in processes of state formation. MacRae examines inter-village networks of ritual association that have been brought into the context of a traditional Balinese state, the Kingdom of Ubud. South Balinese traditional culture tends to be seen, in the mainstream of local society and in scholarly studies, as originating in Majapahit Java and ultimately in Indic culture. A close examination of ideas and practices to do with land and landscape, however, suggests greater commonalities with other Austronesian societies. The paper examines the interface between these Austronesian and Indo-Javanese dimensions of southern Balinese ideas of land and landscape. MacRae also considers transformations of this landscape in the wake of Dutch colonialism, Indonesian independence and the more recent internationalisation of Bali's political economy.

In his paper (Chapter Five), Phillip Winn describes a rather unusual case. He shows how the idea of a 'blessed land' (*tanah berkat*) has helped to define the Banda Islands as a 'shared destination' for migrants from different ethnic origins, rather than as a 'shared origin' site with a set of indigenous custodians. Despite the diverse historical origins of the contemporary population—who were brought to the Banda Islands by the Dutch after their original inhabitants had been killed or dispersed—a similar sense of shared identity and moral community is conveyed by such narratives of immigration. In a conjuncture of land (*tanah*) and local tradition (*adat tanah*), the roots of moral community are envisaged as existing in place. *Tanah* itself is viewed as eliciting, endorsing and enforcing moral practice through the actions of Muslim founder-spirits and through people's membership of a traditional village (*negeri adat*). This model of society has facilitated social participation irrespective of ethnic divisions.

In her paper 'Mapping Buru: The politics of Territory and Settlement on an Eastern Indonesian Island' (Chapter Six), Barbara Dix Grimes begins by exploring small territorial units known as *fena*, which she identifies as a reflex of the Proto-Austronesian **benua*. On Buru, there is a strong relationship between particular *fena* and the 'origin group' (*noro*) considered to be the traditional owners of that land. In any one settlement, one clan is usually dominant numerically and socially. Thus the territorial concept *fena* and the social category *noro* become almost interchangeable, even though, usually, some *fena* residents are immigrants. There is no evidence for any territorial organisation larger or more complex than the *fena* in the sparsely populated interior of Buru, except for some references to regional clusters such as the seven *fena* (*fenar pito*) that comprise the regency of Masarete. The island was dominated politically by the small coastal kingdoms of Muslim immigrants who were later recognised by the Dutch as the rulers of Buru as a whole. More recently, much confusion has arisen from a lack of correspondence between *fena* and the territorial unit '*desa*' which was introduced by the Indonesian Government.

Still within the Moluccas, Christine Boulan-Smit's paper looks at the structure of the *hena* among the Alune of West Seram (Chapter Seven). The 'Wele Telu Batai' ('Three Rivers') upland region of West Seram is divided into a number of territorial units occupied by Alune or Wemale communities of shifting cultivators. In modern Indonesia, these are designated as *desa* (villages) and *kecamatan* (subdistricts). In Alune, however, the smaller units are called *hena*, and alliances of several *hena* along a river system are called *batai* (literally, 'tree trunks'). The paper describes how a *hena* is organised internally, particularly in relation to the origin group (*nuru*) who were its founders. As a territorial unit, the *hena* is a single body or entity, no section of which may be fenced, divided or sold. It is also a social unit aware of its origin, history and ritual duties, all of which are supported by narratives of origin. Boulan-Smit then describes how *hena* are linked together within the larger domain-like institution of the *batai* in a complex order of precedence. This status order is articulated through the seating order of *hena* representatives at customary meetings (*nili ela*), as they sit in a row from the trunk to the tip end of a ritually felled tree trunk (compare with Reuter, this volume, on orders of seating on the main beam of longhouses). The *batai* network as a whole is envisaged as a tree-like shape. Botanic metaphors are thus used as a signifier of precedence relationships. Batai also belong within even larger named regional clusters such as Wele Telu Batai.

In a seminal paper entitled 'From Domains to Rajadom: Notes on the History of Territorial Categories and Institutions in the Rajadom of Sikka' (Chapter Eight), Douglas Lewis discusses a historical process that is of general relevance to eastern Indonesia, whereby some societies gave rise to local states while others did not. For example, the Ata Tana Ai in the eastern part of Sikka in Flores never formed a secular polity but maintained a traditional division into five *tana* or 'ceremonial domains', which closely resembles the social organisation of highland Bali, Buru and Seram (see above). Central Sikka, however, developed a local state: a single polity under the rule of a royal house that originated in the Portuguese era and continued as a semi-autonomous state under the Dutch, not unlike the Kingdom of Ubud in Bali. Before the advent of the rajadom, Sikkanese lived in a domain-based society similar to the Ata Tana Ai. Lewis discusses what the domains of Sikka were like before the rajadom, how the Sikkanese rulers established their hegemony over central Sikka and what changes in territorial categories and institutions resulted from the evolution of domains into a rajadom. He concludes that Europeans played a significant role in, but did not cause, the development of local states in the region. Large-scale states such as Srivijaya,

Majapahit and Mataram predated the arrival of Europeans in South-East Asia, and the societies of eastern Indonesia had long been involved with these kingdoms through maritime trade.

The merger of a large number of domains into a single polity required the people of Sikka to reconceptualise categories of territory. The scale of *tana* in central Sikka was small. Perhaps as many as 45 discrete *tana* coexisted in an area of no more than 700 square kilometres, and the *tana, negeri* and *natar* of the older Sikka had no boundaries. The shift to a new idea of territory as bounded landscape was thus significant. In the place of many centres of local, ritual authority, a polity was created in which the raja bore a singular political power over the older, more local centres. A new system of status and prestige came into being within which the authority and power of officers and ministers in the raja's government eclipsed those of the ritual leaders of the domains. The old offices of *tana pu'ang* and other ritual specialists survived, but—similar to the priests of some Bali Aga temples (Reuter 2002a)—their function came to be the legitimation of the new order.

Still concerned with Flores and with a case reminiscent of the Ata Tana Ai, Philipus Tule's paper is entitled 'We are Children of the Land: A Keo Perspective' (Chapter Nine). Tule describes Keo as a 'house-based society'. As in several of the preceding cases, the status of a clan house (*sao*) is defined by its positioning relative to other houses within a settlement or hamlet (*nua*, a reflex of **banua*) and area of land (*tana*). The paper explores social and cosmological interconnections between *tana, nua* and *sa'o* among the Keo. Local participants speak of these interconnections in ritual speech as essential to maintaining a state of harmony, whereby 'the land is not shaky and stones are not trembling'. In keeping with this ideal, disputes over agricultural land and house land (*dae sao*) are mediated by the Lord of the Land (*'ine tana ame watu*) or other, lower-ranking leaders (*mosa daki*). Since Keo regard land as their mother and stone as their father, they reject the idea of individual ownership of ancestral land (*tana ine embu*, or *tana suku*). Only an individual affiliated with a source house (*sao puu*) and settlement (*nua oda*) has the right to cultivate such land. The social bond between people who share ancestral land is maintained through active participation in rituals related to the ancestral house and land.

In his paper 'Contending for Ritual Control of Land and Polity: Comparisons from the Timor Area of Eastern Indonesia' (Chapter 10), James Fox compares traditional categories of 'land', 'territory' and 'domain' across three closely related societies, and describes the ritual and political offices and ceremonies associated with these categories. The first case study examines categories of land and domain among the Rotinese, and is focused on the island's central domain (*nusak*) of Termanu. Termanu's elaborate origin narrative establishes a separation of political power and ritual authority by drawing a distinction between its newcomer ruler and a particular clan lord who holds the title of Head of the Earth (*dae langak*). The narrative illustrates a common Austronesian mythological theme whereby an 'outsider' is installed 'inside' and granted the right of rule. This theme is important in that it shows how Austronesians have mediated the land-related or other (material or symbolic) resource conflicts that frequently arose between earlier and later groups of migrating peoples.

The second case study concerns the Atoni Pah Meto of West Timor. Land (*pah*) is primary within the Atoni concept of identity and prominent in many of their traditional titles. Like the people of Flores and Roti, they have a long history of European contact but their political formations predate this period. Amanuban is the most important domain and became the dominant Atoni state in West Timor for a significant period during the 18th and 19th century. Houses (*ume, uem*) represent Atoni origin groups (*kanaf*) at the level of the local settlement. Settlements (*kuan* > Tetun, *knua* >PAN/PMP **banua*) are significant not as ordered space but as a local stage for an ordering of precedence among particular *kanaf*.

Both cases are then compared with the Tetun of West Timor, whose major domain, Wehali, is regarded by many as the sacred centre of Timor as a whole. Wehali is *rai feto*, 'female land', as opposed to *rai mane*, 'male land', and is the traditional site of the *Nai Bot/Kukun*, 'The Great/Dark Lord'. The authority of this lord was once acknowledged through harvest rituals attracting delegations from a large area of Timor, including many Atoni domains. Similar to the botanic imagery of the origin myth mentioned in Boulan-Smit's paper on Seram, according to its origin myth, Wehali is a great banyan tree that offers shade to its constituent groups. The ordering of subgroups within this confederation follows a fourfold division, as among the highland Balinese. Wehali itself is known as the *Rai Lidun Hat, Rai Sikun Hat*: 'Four Corner Land, Four Section Land.' As on Roti and Bali, the land is envisaged as a body with its 'tail' to the west and its 'head' to the east. The general term for 'earth', 'land' or 'territory' among the Tetun is *rai*. An alternative term is *rae*, which is related to the Rotinese for earth, *dae*. On its own, *rae* has the sense of uncultivated 'land' rather than 'earth'. Within this scheme, Wehali is the *rai hun, leo hun*: 'Land of origin, *Leo* of origin.' Whereas among the Rotinese, a *leo* is a clan-like origin group defined by its position within a particular *nusak* or domain and thereby confined to that *nusak*, a *leo* among the population of Wehali is a named residential group—a hamlet—comprising specific named houses. The Tetun term for 'settlement' or 'village' outside of Wehali is *knua* (> **banua*). Wehali has no *knua* and the term is used only in a metaphoric sense.

Andrew McWilliam's paper stays within the same region, and discusses Fataluku Forest Tenures and the Conis Santana National Park in East Timor (Chapter 11). McWilliam explores customary tenures and land-management practices in the context of an emergent government land policy in East Timor's most easterly district, Lautem. During the period of Indonesian rule in East Timor (1975-99), much of the forested zone was classified as a 'natural conservation reserve'. On paper at least, this prohibited logging and other forms of extractive activity. Under the United Nations Transitional Administration in East Timor (UNTAET) from 1999, the area was reclassified as a 'Protected Wild Area', and, in 2002, through its Directorate of Forestry, the independent East Timor Government initiated a program to demarcate the area as the country's first National Park. The prospects for the successful establishment of the park are in question due to the contested status of the region. This ownership issue arises because the greater part of the forested zone in this proposal is not composed of old-growth forest. Rather, the forest is a mosaic of former swidden gardens and settlement sites. Customary tenures and local claims of Fataluku-speaking populations to the forestry zone remain intact. As a result of consultations with community leaders, government forestry staff informally acknowledge the existence of 'traditional land' (Bahasa Indonesia: *tanah adat*) in the park area, but there is no formal agreement, at this stage, on the prospective status of their ownership claims. Nor has there been any sustained study of the ethnographic context within which these claims emerge. This paper offers a preliminary contribution towards this end.

The focus moves beyond Indonesia with Mark Mosko's paper (Chapter 12), entitled Self-Scaling the Earth: Relations of Land, Society and Body Among North Mekeo, Papua New Guinea'. The territorial categories in the language of North Mekeo (the PNG/Western Papua Tip cluster of Western Oceanic) are *pangua* or *paunga* ('village') and *ango* ('land' or 'territory'). The paper investigates these terms in relation to indigenous conceptualisations of society that employ body metaphors and a systematic fourfold pattern of 'inside–outside' (*aongai-fangai*) distinctions. Such spatial metaphors and associated fourfold divisions of society are widespread in the Austronesian world. North Mekeo classify land, body and society through analogous classificatory and procedural (temporal) mechanisms in terms of inside/outside distinctions and transactions, which consist formally of relations of self-similar or fractal scaling. Consequently, the three contexts of 'land', 'body' and 'society' can be seen as constituting a single semantic domain.

John P. Taylor's paper, 'The Ways of the Land-Tree: Mapping the North Pentecost Social Landscape' (Chapter 13), examines concepts of land and place, and their relationship to land-use practices, in the region of North Pentecost, Vanuatu, which belongs to the Raga language group. The paper begins by identifying important local delineations of territory and geography (*vanua*, *tano*, *uma*) and related concepts of social or personal emplacement (*bwat*) and movement (*hala*). Such concepts are pivotal for defining kinship-related patterns of settlement, land use and social organisation. As in Seram, Wehali and elsewhere in the region, botanic metaphors are used to describe relationships between places. This is illustrated beautifully with a tree-like map drawn by a local informant to show how territories are connected through a history of human movement. With reference to the hamlet cluster of Gelau, the paper describes the emergence of such patterns from their early beginnings, through colonial transformation to the present.

Mary Patterson's paper (Chapter 14) is entitled 'Finishing the Land: Identity and Land Use in Pre and Post-Colonial North Ambrym'. Land and place categories in northern Vanuatu show a distribution that tends to feature one or the other of the *vanua* and *tan* terms. Both words might be present, but if *vanua* is prominent in local discourse then *tan* is not, and vice versa. In Ambrym and South Pentecost there appears to be no reflex of *vanua*. In Vao Island north-east of Malakula, however, *venu* and *vanu* refer to a 'village' or 'place' and in mainland Malakula *vene* appears as part of clan names. Similarly in Malo, *tan* appears as part of clan names. In East Ambae, *vanue* is important but *tano* less so. *Vanue* is not just land (*tano*), it is lived space in which place and people are part of each other.

In North Ambrym, conflict over land use and alienation at the local and national level has given rise to a new rhetoric of connections to land that employs Austronesian territorial categories with a complex history, now refracted through the lens of post-colonial identity politics. The paper examines the North Ambrym context, where novel ways of making status claims are in effect a dynamic refiguring of autochthonous and reticular connections to territory near and far, which appear in mythological and ritual contexts.

Steve Francis's paper 'People and Place in Tonga: The Social Construction of *Fonua* in Oceania' (Chapter 15), provides an important comparison with a society in Polynesia. The author examines the usage of the term *fonua* ('land/people') as a territorial and social category in the Kingdom of Tonga. *Fonua*, a reflex of the Proto-Austronesian reconstruction **banua*, is an important marker of local belonging as well as regional identity in Tonga. Francis shows how modern Tongans employ this social category in varying political, economic and social contexts; political in the sense of elite-commoner relations, economic in the context of land use and landownership, and social within the framework of village, island, regional and national identities. *Fonua* is used as an inclusive social and territorial concept, which incorporates links between local and global scales, the physical and metaphysical, the land and the sea. These links are illustrated through an examination of myth, history, social relations and local boundaries.

In sum, the papers in this volume illustrate the wealth of cultural diversity and important recurrent themes in how Austronesians have conceptualised the dynamic relationships between people and land. Local models of human movement and emplacement reveal a reflexive awareness of the conflicting human tendencies towards mobility and localised interests. They address issues of legitimacy in relation to territorial claims by linking them to cultural constructs of social identity, which, in the Austronesian world, are focused primarily on narrative histories of human movement. These models of society are not prone to primordialism but are instead founded on a celebration of the historicity of human society as a living, growing entity. In this world view, territorial and social categories are often closely interlinked. Founders and newcomers (who are often also affines) are afforded a place in Austronesian cosmological models, and their harmonious interaction is seen as no less integral to society than male and female is to the perpetuation of life itself.

Contemporary Issues and New Directions in Comparative Austronesian Studies

The continuing relevance of Comparative Austronesian Studies for understanding the way of life of contemporary Austronesian-speaking populations cannot be taken for granted. Are Austronesian societies still similar and, at the same time, diverse enough in this 21st century to permit a meaningful comparison? And, if so, is their similarity still based predominantly on a shared cultural heritage or is it on account of their having been similarly subjected to the presumably homogenising influences of colonialism, modernity and globalisation? Or, alternatively, are there any thematic issues in the contemporary Austronesian world that are best understood in terms of an interaction between the influences of a regional cultural heritage and a new, global form of cultural homogeneity?

The evidence suggests that 'traditional' organisational and conceptual patterns derived from a common Austronesian heritage have not become irrelevant. Nor should we ignore the growing dependence of Austronesian-speaking societies on a global capitalist economic system, which does have a homogenising influence on culture, or at least on consumer culture and technology. Both factors seem to be exerting an influence on the cultural trajectory of the Austronesian world. The difficulty, however, lies in the fact that they might do so in fundamentally different ways. Extending Norbert Elias's (1969) historical theory on the rise of modernity, one could argue that the postmodern form of cultural similarity is based no longer on a common heritage, which assumes a process of branching out from a common historical origin, but, quite to the contrary, on an ever-tightening web of socioeconomic interdependencies drawing different cultures inward into the whirlpool of a centrifugal and homogenising world system.

There is no debating the rapid internationalisation that is taking place in the world today. Anthropologists and others with an appreciation for cultural diversity, however, may often feel dismayed at examples they encounter in the public domain of an extreme globalisation perspective on current affairs. As

Friedman (1997: 269) points out, 'Notions of globalisation, hybridisation, and creolisation are socially positioned concepts that in their classificatory thrust say very much about the classifiers and much less about those classified." For example, many political commentators seem to be looking at places like Indonesia once again through Western eyes, as still imperfect replicas of Western democratic nation states, destined to become more and more 'perfect' and hence more transparent to our understanding in the course of globalisation, either naturally or, if need be, with some benevolent intervention here and there. In adopting this new universalist model of a singular future for humanity, the presumably culture-less Western centre of the global system regards 'culture' as a non-Western phenomenon that is increasingly and quickly becoming irrelevant. And whenever the 'locals' provide evidence to the contrary by asserting their tradition, the response is to classify their self-representations as neo-traditionalism, primordialism or some other futile revivalist attempt at reimagining and reinstating a long-lost past. And if they assert their right to be different violently, the problem must be contained by force. 'We', who are already posturing as the defining force of 'their' past—by reducing that past to a history of colonial domination—are now projecting our vision of ourselves into their future, by casting ourselves as the carriers of the universal model of a global, postmodern way of life to which they must inevitably conform. If there is some truth to this popular perspective on globalisation at all, then the process of cultural and political imperialism it alludes to is not necessarily one that should be further encouraged in social science by depicting it as natural and inevitable.

Anthropologists need to challenge reductionist perspectives on globalisation and associated assumptions about cultural homogenisation by highlighting the contrary, localising and diversifying forces that also shape trajectories of socio-cultural change. The preceding comparative analysis has shown some of these contrary forces at work among related societies across a vast region. It has done so by highlighting how changes in local, historical and situational conditions over several millennia have contributed to the cultural diversity of the Austronesian world. At the same time, several of the case studies also allude to the centrifugal or homogenising force of growing interdependence—from complex village societies with clan groups of variable origins, to early state formation, to the rise of modern nations—suggesting that these centrifugal processes are not a new phenomenon. In order to remain viable well into the future, the Comparative Austronesian Studies Project will need to develop methods to identify emergent and centrifugal forms of similarity as well as trends towards new patterns of variation among contemporary Austronesians. This volume is taking some important first steps in this direction.

References

Appadurai, A. 1988. 'Putting Hierarchy in its Place.' *Cultural Anthropology,* 3. pp. 36-49.

Bellwood, P., J.J. Fox and D. Tryon (eds). 1995. *The Austronesians; Historical and Comparative Perspectives.* Comparative Austronesian Studies Project. Canberra: The Australian National University.

Clifford, J. 1988. *The Predicament of Culture: Twentieth-Century Ethnography. Cultural Anthropology* 7. pp. 6-23.

Elias, Norbert. 1969. *Über den Prozess der Zivilisation: Soziogenetische und psychogenetische Untersuchungen.* 2 Volumes. Bern (Switzerland): Francke AG.

Gupta, A. and J. Ferguson. 1992. *Beyond 'Culture': Space, Identity, and the Politics of Identity.* Durham and London: Duke University Press.

Fox, James J. 1980. 'Introduction.' In J.J. Fox (ed.), *The Flow of Life: Essays on Eastern Indonesia,* Cambridge (Mass.): Harvard University Press. pp.1-18.

Fox, James J. (ed.) 1993. *Inside Austronesian houses: Perspectives on domestic designs for living.* Comparative Austronesian Studies Project. Canberra: The Australian National University.

Fox, James J. (ed.) 1997. *The Poetic Power of Place: Comparative perspectives on Austronesian ideas of locality.* Comparative Austronesian Studies Project. Canberra: The Australian National University.

Fox, James J. and Clifford Sather (eds). 1996. *Origins, Ancestry and Alliance; Explorations in Austronesian ethnography.* Department of Anthropology, Research School of Pacific and Asian Studies, Comparative Austronesian Studies Project. Canberra: The Australian National University.

Friedman, Jonathan. 1997. 'Simplifying Complexity: Assimilating the global in a small paradise.' In Karen F. Olwig and Kirsten Hastrup (eds), *Siting Culture: The shifting anthropological subject,* London and New York: Routledge.

Geertz, C. 1980. *Negara: The Theatre State in Nineteenth-Century Bali.* Princeton (N.J.): Princeton University Press.

Lavie, S. and T. Swedenburg (eds). 1996. *Displacement, Diaspora, and Geographies of Literature, and Art.* Cambridge: Harvard University Press.

Malkki, L. 1995. 'Refugees and Exile: From 'Refugee Studies' to the National Order of Things'. *Annual Review of Anthropology,* 24. pp. 495-523.

Marcus, G.E. 1993. 'Tonga's Contemporary Globalizing Strategies: Trading on Sovereignty Amidst International Migration.' In V.S. Lockwood, T.G.

Harding and B.J. Wallace (eds): *Contemporary Pacific Societies. Studies in Development and Change*, Engelwood: Prentice Hall. pp. 21-33.

Olwig, Karen F. and Kirsten Hastrup (eds). 1997. *Siting Culture: The shifting anthropological subject*. London and New York: Routledge.

Reuter, Thomas A. 1999. 'People of the Mountains—People of the Sea: Negotiating the Local and the Foreign in Bali.' In L.H. Connor and R. Rubinstein (eds), *Staying Local in the Global Village: Bali in the Twentieth Century*, Honolulu: University of Hawai'i Press.

Reuter, Thomas A. 2002a. *Custodians of the Sacred Mountains*. Honolulu: Hawai'i University of Hawai'I Press.

Reuter, Thomas A. 2002b. *The House of Our Ancestors*. Leiden: KITLV Press.

Vischer, Michael P. (ed.) In press. *Precedence: Processes of Social Differentiation in the Austronesian World*. Canberra: Comparative Austronesian Studies Project, Research School of Pacific and Asian Studies. Canberra: The Australian National University.

Chapter 2. The Origin Structure of *Kute* Among the Gumai: An Analysis of an Indigenous Territorial Institution in the Highlands of South Sumatra

Minako Sakai

This chapter examines indigenous territorial categories in the highlands of the Province of South Sumatra, by focusing on Gumai villages. While *desa* is the official term for villages, conceived as administrative units of the modern Indonesian State, and while most people will name their *dusun* or 'hamlet' when asked about their place of residence, local ritual specialists still use *kute* as the traditional term to refer to a residential territory (from Sanskrit and Old-Malay *kuta*, 'fortified town' or 'palace'). They do so primarily in the context of the rituals to commemorate the origin of the *kute*.

The Gumai are a Malay-speaking people who reside in the highlands of South Sumatra (Jaspan 1976). Their population across three major residential areas in the Regency of Lahat is approximately 10,000 people, who derive their livelihood largely from the cultivation of rubber and coffee. In terms of language, appearance and customs, the Gumai have much in common with neighbouring Malay speakers. Historically, South Sumatran highland societies consisted of groups who defined themselves by descent from common ancestors and by reference to the specific area of land they inhabited (Andaya 1993: 17). The distinctive identity of the Gumai, for example, derives from the belief that their people are all the offspring of a magical founding ancestor, Diwe Gumai, who descended on Mt Segungtan in Palembang on the night of a full moon (Sakai 1997 and 1999). The descendants of Diwe Gumai then spread along the river system, known as Batang Hari Sembilan, which flows across the region and founded numerous villages. Relocation of some of these villages took place at the turn of the last century in accordance with the replacement of the river system as the main means of transportation by a network of roads.

Presently, most villages in the South Sumatran highlands are located neatly along the main roads. There are three main clusters of villages, all in the Regency of Lahat, namely Gumai Ulu, Gumai Lembak and Gumai Talang. *Jurai Kebali'an* is a title carried by a male heir who represents the most authentic successor of the founding ancestor in terms of genealogical connections. The house of the *Jurai Kebali'an* is located in the regency of Lahat of South Sumatra Province, and serves as a most important ritual place to commemorate the common origins of the Gumai in a ritual attracting hundreds of Diwe Gumai's descendants every month (see Sakai 2003).

Map 1: Ethnic groups in South Sumatra province

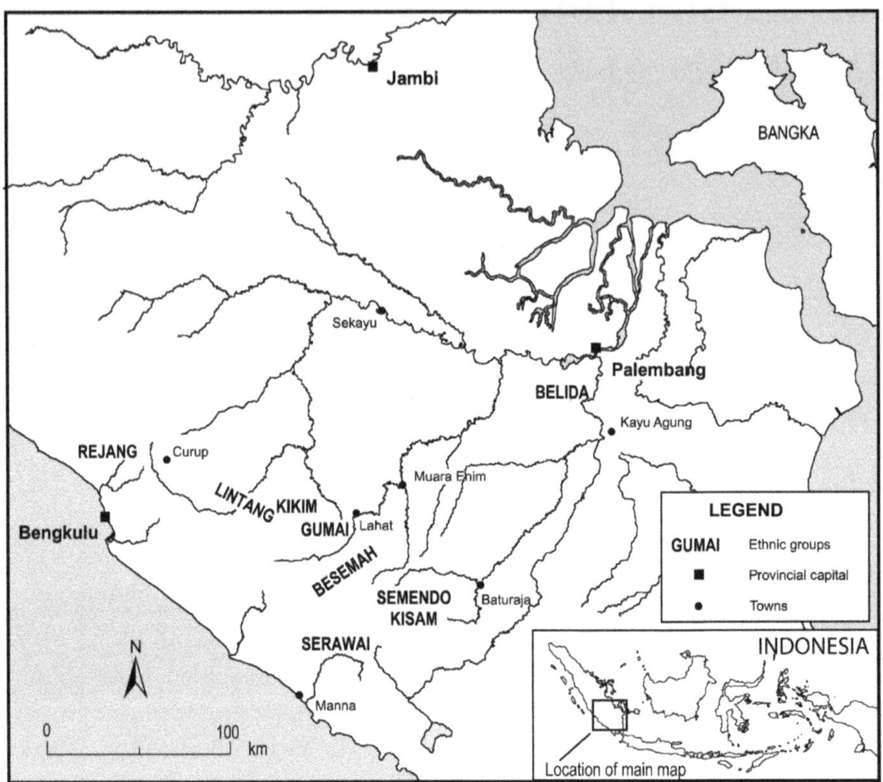

A knowledge of village origins is most important for understanding social structures and associated ritual practices among the Gumai, as well as other Malay-speaking highlanders in South Sumatra. I will therefore begin by examining some village origin stories, collected from settlements in the Gumai Talang region. Gumai Talang consists of 14 villages along the Trans-Sumatra Highway near the town of Lahat. I will show how the village origins are reflected in social and ritual structures. I will then show how Gumai ritual and social practices have contributed to the maintenance of links to a common origin. As a result, Gumai traditional villages, particularly a ritual unit known as *kute*, have maintained themselves as an indigenous territorial category, based on common origins, despite intervening government administrative policies and frequent relocations of villages.

Village Origin Structure

Many Gumai villages are thought to have been established by a single ancestor, the *Puyang Ketunggalan Dusun* (the Founding Ancestor of the Village), and have been inhabited by his descendants and their affines. Narratives I obtained about the origin of Mandi Angin village from the ritual specialist of Mandi Angin in 1994 are a good example to illustrate the importance of a single village founder as the ultimate origin point, and to show the subsequent process of subgroup formation in this village.

Figure 1: Genealogy of Mandi Angin village

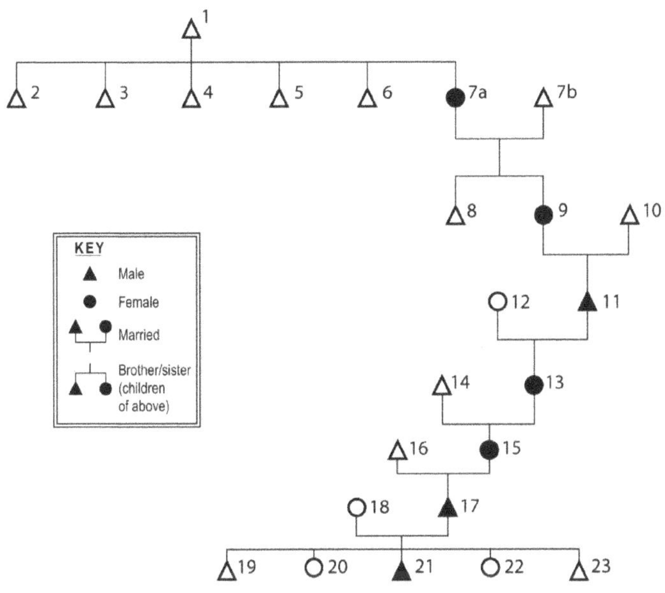

1 Puyang Kerie Tingal (*Puyang Ketunggalan Dusun*)
2 Raje Ringkeh (*Tue Jurai*)
3 Raje Kuhus
4 Raja Dali
5 Raje Bungkuk
6 Pengiran
7a Rebiah (*Jurai Tue*)
7b Name unknown (from OganUlu)
8 Artanan
9 Yamani
10 Name unknown (from Mandi Angin)
11 Tikus Kuning
12 Sudiya from Mandi Angin
13 Majenon
14 Raden Ali from Muara Cawan, Kikim
15 Retipa
16 Perajin from Ngalam Baru
17 Nagajin
18 Name unknown
19 Kosim
20 Name unknown (living in Tebing Tinggi)
21 Mimha (living in Mandi Angin), current *Jurai Tue* in Mandi Angin
22 Siti Robia (living in Tanjung Karangan, Lampung)
23 Ibrahim (living in Mandi Angin)

Note: Black indicates the succession order of the *Jurai Tue*.

> The founding ancestor of Mandi Angin village, Puyang Kerie Tingal, was the eldest son of Puyang Gune Raje, who was the *Jurai Kebali'an* in Lahat. Kerie Tingal had five sons, Raje Ringkeh, Raje Kuhus, Dali, Pengiran and Raje Bungkuk in that birth order. The youngest [child] was a daughter called Rebiah.

Subgroups in Mandi Angin village are known as *jungkuk* ('subgroup') and derive from each of these six children. Each *jungkuk* is responsible for passing on the title *Jungkuk* to one of its members. The appointee needs to reside in his/her villages, to maintain the genealogical knowledge about the ancestors of his/her *jungkuk* and to undertake rituals to remember those ancestors. *Jungkuk* refers to a subgroup formed by the children of the founding ancestor and the family or the person who inherits this role. To differentiate these two, I will refer to the subgroup as *jungkuk* and the title as the *Jungkuk* title. [1]

Each *jungkuk* of Mandi Angin village takes its derivation from the ultimate origin point of the village, Puyang Kerie Tingal, the *Puyang Ketunggalan Dusun*. Figure 1 shows the succession of the *jungkuk* of the *Jurai Tue* of Mandi Angin village. The main task of the person with the title of *Jungkuk* is to reside in his or her native village and to have offspring to continue the genealogical linkage to the village founder. The office needs to be carried on by a successor, who remains in his or her natal village. The succession of this title is through a daughter or a son, and birth order is irrelevant. Currently there are six people, each of whom represents a *jungkuk* in Mandi Angin village. The successor to the *Jungkuk* title is assumed to be the closest living descendant of the founding *jungkuk* ancestor. All the *Jungkuk* titleholders and other *jungkuk* members are expected to undertake a series of rituals to commemorate its origins. [2]

Precedence and Village Ritual Specialists

Despite the fact that each *jungkuk* has derived from a common ancestor, the status of *jungkuk* is not equal. One of the *jungkuk* carries the title of *Tue Jurai* (elderly subgroup) and another holds the title of *Jurai Tue*. The notion of *jurai* is elusive and hazy; it refers to a particular person as a holder of such titles as *Jurai Tue, Tue Jurai* and *Jurai Kebali'an*. On the other hand, *jurai* refers to any number of people who trace their origin to particular ancestors who in turn share a common ancestry in the distant mythological past. The idiom *putus jurai* means the 'severing or disappearance of legitimate successors'; it does not mean the extinction of an ethnic group. [3]

The following account from Mandi Angin village, which I obtained during my fieldwork in the mid-1990s, will illustrate how *jungkuk* are differentiated based on birth order and ritual seniority.

> The *jungkuk* of Raje Ringkeh, the eldest son of the founding ancestor, is paid homage. It is because he is the eldest child of the family and his *jungkuk* is called *Tue Jurai*. After growing up, all the male children of Kerie Tingal wanted to leave their natal village and to go to new places. Therefore, Rebiah, the youngest daughter, was asked to remain in the village permanently and took over the house of her parents as the place to which other descendants could return. She was given the title of *Jurai Tue*, which enabled her to become the village ritual specialist. At the time of the village ritual known as *Sedekah Rame*, the *Jurai Tue* invokes ancestral spirits including the *Puyang Ketunggalan Dusun*. This duty of the *Jurai Tue* includes keeping the knowledge about genealogies traced to the founding ancestor and having offspring in order to transmit this knowledge. Her husband acted as the caretaker of the village and was called *Jurai Tue*, as women were not allowed to perform this role. Since then, the title of *Jurai Tue* has also been inherited among the members of the *jungkuk* of Rebiah, and the current *Jurai Tue* remains in Mandi Angin village.

This account explains the way some *jungkuk* are ranked higher than others. Based on his position as the firstborn, the *jungkuk* which was headed by Raje Ringkeh is ranked higher than the others and is called *Tue Jurai* or 'elder descendant group'. The eldest child is seen as temporally closer to the village founding ancestor and is therefore paid homage by the other *jungkuk* members.[4] People express respect to the descendants of *Tue Jurai*. In the past, at the ritual to commemorate the village origins known as *Sedekah Rame*, the seating arrangements and the nature of the offerings to be prepared were determined by the status and titles of each *jungkuk*. [5] Traditionally, however, no political or economic prerogative is given to the *Tue Jurai* or *Jurai Tue*. [6]

The account also shows how the *jungkuk* of Rebiah was chosen as the successor line of the village ritual specialist, *Jurai Tue*. Since none of the male children stayed permanently within their natal village, the last-born daughter was asked to remain there and to attend to the Gumai customs. In the past, it was customary to allow a daughter to inherit the office of the *Jurai Tue* and let her husband perform the role. [7]

The *Jurai Tue* is to reside in the village and to keep knowledge of genealogies that connect the *Jurai Tue* with the *Puyang Ketunggalan Dusun*. If there are any regalia handed down from the *Puyang Ketunggalan Dusun*, the *Jurai Tue* is responsible for looking after them. [8] The *Jurai Tue* is regarded as the most direct descendant of the village founder, and his or her *jungkuk* as a group is believed to be the closest to the *Puyang Ketunggalan Dusun* as the ultimate origin point.

The title of *Jurai Tue* is associated not only with the person who inherits the title, but with the village location in which he or she is designated to live. Outside the boundaries of that village, that person can no longer act as the *Jurai Tue* or bear the office of the *Jurai Tue*, but is considered an ordinary individual.

When no member of the *jungkuk* of the *Jurai Tue* is considered suitable for the office, it can be transferred temporarily to a member of another *jungkuk*. Since *jungkuk* titleholders are considered close to the village founder, temporary transfer of the title of *Jurai Tue* to another *jungkuk* titleholder is considered appropriate. This custom of temporary transfer is known as *menyandung* (temporary transfer), and whenever there is an appropriate successor among the members of the *jungkuk* of the *Jurai Tue*, the office should be returned.

Figure 2 presents the genealogy of the two *Jungkuk* of Tanjung Karangan village, who share in rotation the office of *Jurai Tue*. When Puyang Pageran died, Senang Irah succeeded to the office of the *Jurai Tue*, and her husband, Setiarap, performed the role. The title of *Jungkuk* was then transferred (*menyandung*) to Lamit, a nephew of Senang Irah. [9] Since Lamit was busy with gardening, the office was transferred to Resek, Lamit's sister. Thereafter, the office was transferred to a daughter of Lamit, Sari, and performed by her husband, Dahlan. Since Dahlan often left the village for work, the office was eventually returned to a grandchild of Senang Irah, Bidin. [10] Bidin is a son of Ren Tasim, who is a son of Senang Irah.

Figure 2: Genealogy of two *Jungkuk* of Tanjung Karangan village

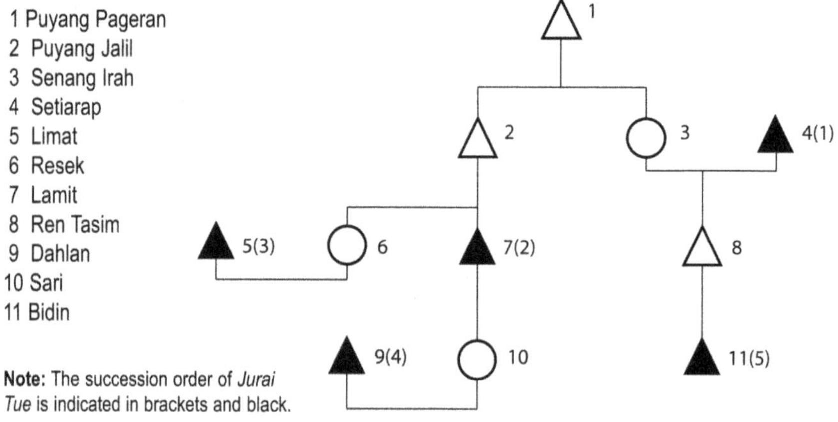

The Division of a Village

While the *jungkuk* is a subgroup within a village, which maintains its relations with the *Puyang Ketunggalan Dusun*, it can also become a point of division at the time of the establishment of a new village. The following example of the bifurcation of Mandi Angin village and the creation of Batay village will illustrate this process.

> Initially the name of Mandi Angin was Cugong Berangin and it was located at Muara Ayer Batay when it was founded by the founding ancestor, Kerie Tingal. Relocation of the site of this village took place several times and its name was changed to Cugong Keramai and eventually to Mandi Angin. When Mandi Angin village was relocated in 1925, it split into two parts. Some *jungkuk* members of Raje Ringkeh, *Tue Jurai*, created *talang* or a temporary residence near their gardens. It was named Talang Batay. The rest of the village moved to a new location and was named Mandi Angin village. When the Japanese army came to Lahat in 1942, Talang Batay was asked to move to a site along the Kikim Raya road. Since new Mandi Angin village was not spacious enough to accommodate the residents of Talang Batay, the residents bought some of the rubber garden areas of Tanjung Beringin and converted them into a village. Since 1944, this new village is known as Batay village. One person from the *jungkuk* of Raje Ringkeh who lives in Batay now assumes the role of the *Jurai Tue* in Batay village.

The *jungkuk* is a good example of what Fox (1988, 1996a) calls an origin group. Origin groups share and celebrate some form of common derivation including a common ancestor, a common cult and a collection of regalia (Fox 1996a: 132). The morpheme *pu* in the word *puyang* could be a reflex of *puqun*, which is a Proto-Malayo-Polynesian reconstruction meaning tree, trunk, base or source (Fox 1995: 36). *Yang*, in turn, may be related to words such as *eyang* (Java), meaning grandparent, or *hyang* (Bali), meaning ancestor/deity. As a subgroup within a village, each *jungkuk* traces a chain of linkages to the village founder as source. *Jungkuk* are not 'lineages' in the classical sense because the succession of the *Jungkuk* titleholder is neither patrilineal nor matrilineal, but is comprised of any descendants as long as they continue to reside within the village of origin.

Multiple Village Origins and Subgroups

Most Gumai villagers can trace genealogical or affinal relations to the *Puyang Ketunggalan Dusun*. In the past, those who did not have genealogical connections to the *Puyang Ketunggalan Dusun* were allowed to reside in a village by forming a separate subgroup (*sungut jurai*) apart from the village's *jungkuk* groups. [11]

It is said that it was common to have *sungut jurai* composed of Semidang descendants. Based on the origin narratives in which Diwe Gumai and Diwe Semidang cooperated with each other to let Diwe Gumai emerge from the shell of a fruit on the Bukit Siguntang, descendants of Diwe Semidang were asked to be members of Gumai villages. Despite the explanations by the *Jurai Tue* and other elders about the existence of *sungut*, I was not able to identify who formed the *sungut* of the Semidang in any Gumai village. This is partially because the status of those who were initially accommodated as strangers and allowed to form a subgroup is not differentiated after three generations of continuous residence in that locality. [12] Furthermore, younger generations, in general, do not pay much attention to the *sungut* or *jungkut*, and the transmission of knowledge related to village origins is difficult to discover. [13]

A person who still claimed foreign descent and was able to tell me an account of his foreign origin was the *Mimbar* of Mandi Angin village, Pak Amat Solek. *Mimbar* is another village ritual specialist who, in times of crises, must support and protect the *Jurai Kebali'an*. Solek owns coffee gardens near Pagaralam and looks after them diligently, and is a relatively wealthy coffee farmer residing in Mandi Angin village. In 1995, he told me the following story, which explains how his ancestor was accepted in Mandi Angin village:

> Siatong Ali was a descendant of Bengkulu, who was at that time living in Rebakau. He held a wedding reception for his child and invited Puyang Gune Raje and his son, Kerie Tingal, went as his father's representative. At the wedding ceremony, Kerie Tingal was not offered food, rather he was ridiculed. So he went home and reported this incident to his father. Gune Raje then advised Kerie Tingal to return to the reception and to carry a dagger named Santan Tekuku with him and advised him to kill all the people with the dagger if he was ridiculed again. Kerie Tingal returned to Rebakau, and Siatong Ali noticed the dagger and asked its name. Upon learning that the dagger called Santan Tekuku was named after a bird, Siatong Ali said, 'So we shall give your bird some food.' [14] This time Kerie Tingal killed all the guests and all the inhabitants of the Rebakau with the dagger. After this incident, Siatong Ali and Kerie Tingal compromised and the former offered his daughter as evidence of submission. She became a wife of Gune Raje and gave birth to a son called Sialam. The family of Siatong Ali was allowed to live in Mandi Angin village as *Mimbar* of Mandi Angin village, whose duty is to fight at the front line in a war and help the five grandchildren of the *Jurai Kebali'an* in Mandi Angin village. Siatong Ali made a vow that he and his descendants would accept this duty and the title of *Mimbar* was inherited by his son, Puyang Demang. Sialam is believed not to be dead, but to have ever-lasting life in the mountain. He said, 'My children, if you are facing difficulty, just burn benzoin resin and bring a goat and call me.' Usually those who ask for assistance are able to achieve their wishes.

The narratives explain that the descendants of Siatong Ali did not share a common ancestry with the rest of the *jungkuk* members in Mandi Angin, who were descendants of Puyang Kerie Tingal. Siatong Ali was a stranger accepted into Mandi Angin village. Since he was trusted by Gune Raje, the title of *Mimbar* was given to Siatong Ali and has been inherited by one of his descendants ever since (see Figure 3).[15]

Figure 3: Genealogy of the origin of the *Mimbar* of Mandi Angin village

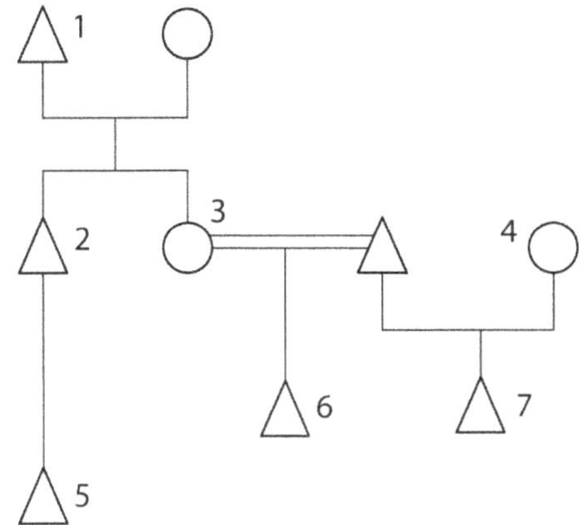

1 Siatong Ali
2 Demang
3 Putri Ratu Rebakau
4 Puyang Gune Raje
5 Ahmad Soleh, *Mimbar* of Mandi Angin
6 Sialam
7 Puyang Kerie Tingal (*Puyang Ketunggalan Dusun* of Mandi Angin)

The Merging of Two Villages

Some villages in Gumai Talang were created by more than two founding ancestors who had no genealogical connections or whose genealogical connections were not known or remembered. For instance, Tanjung Baru village has three *Jurai Tue,* a result of acknowledging three village founders. However, details about how the three ancestors collaborated in establishing one village were not known to any of the current *Jurai Tue.*

Sugih Waras village has two *Jurai Tue, Jurai Tue palak tanah* and *Jurai Tue ujung tanjung.* The latter, Pak Zainal Kisam, a driver in his fifties operating in Lahat, was able to give me an explanation.[16] Consulting some notes he had kept to refresh his memory, he explained to me that the current Sugih Waras village was a result of two villages that had merged into one.

> Puyang Kebah, whose ancestry was traced back to an ancestor in Gumai Ulu, had three sons, Pati Kelam, Pati Tua and Pate Langit. Pati Kelam, the eldest son, was given the title of *Jurai Tue.* At that time, they were living in a place called Talang Kapuk along the Kikim Kecik River. But there never was peace in this village. Fighting among the villagers was a regular feature. So the *Jurai Tue* of Talang Kapuk, Puyang Pati Kelam, consulted Puyang Tuan Raje, the *Jurai Kebali'an,* who advised that Puyang Pati Kelam should ask a descendant of Puyang Pangeran Raje Depati in Lubuk Sele village, in Gumai Ulu, to establish a new village together.
>
> Puyang Raje Depati was the *Jurai Tue* in Lubuk Sele village, who had two sons, Mas Agung and Kebile Agung. Mas Agung succeeded to the

office of the *Jurai Tue*. This office was then inherited by his son, Cahaya Raden, and by his grandson, Puyang Tudakan Dalam. When Puyang Pati Kelam came to Lubuk Sele village, the *Jurai Tue* was Puyang Jikmat, who was a son of Tudakan Dalam. Upon consultation, Puyang Jikmat agreed to establish a new village in Tanah Kemiling with Puyang Pati Kelam. After establishing the new village in Tanah Kemiling, Puyang Pati Kelam, *Jurai Tue* of Talang Kapuk, became the *Jurai Tue palak tanah* and Puyang Jikmat became the *Jurai Tue ujung tanjung* in order to represent each origin. *Palak tanah* literally means 'the top of the land' and refers to 'upstream', while *ujung tanjung* literally means 'the tip of a cape' and refers to 'downstream'. Since then, Tanah Kemiling has become prosperous and peaceful. When this village was moved to another location, both *Jurai Tue* held discussions and created a new name, Sugih Waras. In the local language, *sugih* means rich and abundant, and *waras* is healthy. As this name suggests, residents of Sugih Waras village were rich and healthy by that time. After World War II, Sugih Waras village was moved again to its present location.

Figure 4: Genealogy of Sugih Waras village

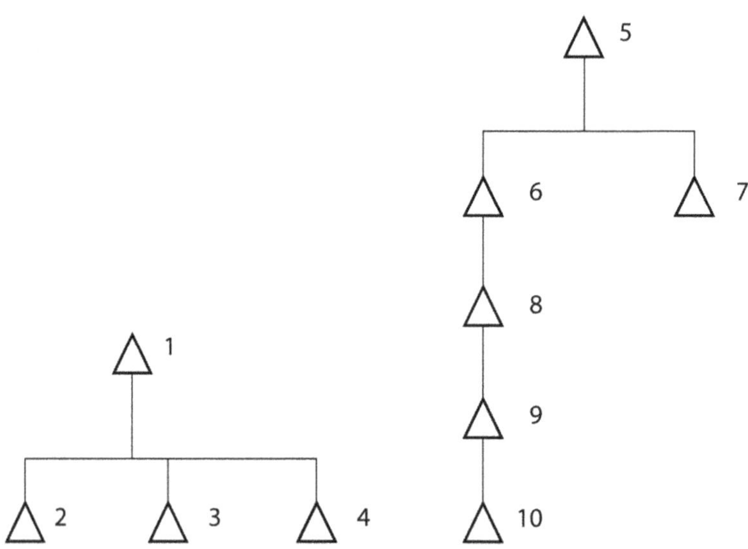

1 Puyang Kebah
2 Puyang Pati Kelam, eldest son, (*Jurai Tue palak tanah*)
3 Puyang Pati Tua
4 Puyang Pati Langit
5 Puyang Raja Depati,
6 Puyang Mas Agung
7 Puyang Kebile Agung
8 Puyang Cahaya Raden
9 Puyang Tudakan Dalam
10 Puyang Jikmat, (*Jurai Tue ujung tanjung*)

Until the present, Sugih Waras village has retained two *Jurai Tue*, to represent the two founding ancestors, each of whom is replaced from within his own *jungkuk* line. Despite the ritual titles, there is no spatial division for residence among the descendants of the two *jungkuk* within the village. The existence of their two *Jurai Tue* illustrates that descendants of Sugih Waras village remember the two ancestors, Puyang Jikmat and Puyang Pati Kelam, as village founders, each represented by a *Jurai Tue*.

Continuity of Person

Marriage Contracts and Residential Rules

Until early this century, as in many regions of the South Sumatran highlands, villages in Gumai Talang did not accept strangers unless they were officially accepted as a subgroup or as in-laws. Two modes of marriage contracts, *jujur* (*belaki, kule*) and *tambi anak* (*ambil anak*), operated to regulate the residence of conjugal couples and contributed to maintaining exclusive village membership. [17]

Jujur or *belaki* was a virilocal marriage that involved the payment of bride wealth. *Belaki* literally means 'to have or follow a husband' (*laki*). The bridegroom had to pay a sum of money to the father of the bride as bride wealth to formalise his marriage. In return for this payment, the tie between the wife and her native village was severed and she moved into the village of her husband. All the children she bore were then regarded as descendants of the husband's side. In other words, children regarded themselves as descendants of the village founder on their father's side, and regarded their natal village as *asal* or an 'origin place'. The payment of bride wealth meant the purchase (*kule*) of the wife's reproductive capacity. If she was widowed, she was not allowed to return home, and was expected to remarry a brother of her deceased husband; a practice known as *nungkat*.

Tambi anak is an uxorilocal marriage, which does not include the payment of bride wealth. In other regions of South Sumatra, such as among the Rejang and the Besemah, this mode of marriage was called *ambil* (*ambel*) *anak* or 'to take a child'. Due to the absence of bride wealth payments, the status of the husband was low and he became a member of the wife's family and had to sever ties with his native village. The children the wife bore were regarded as descendants of the wife's side. Children therefore regarded themselves as descendants of the village founder on their mother's side, and regarded their natal village as their origin place. Marriage between the same village members was said to have been by *tambi anak* marriage form. [18]

Marriage was not always between Gumai. Marrying a non-Gumai affected the status of children. In the past, all the people who were children of a conjugal union between two Gumai were differentiated from the children with one non-Gumai parent, who were known as *jurai muda* ('young descendants') and ranked lower than those born from Gumai parents. The descendants of non-Gumai couples who resided in a village were called *anak tawan* ('children of the captured') and ranked lowest in the village origin structure. [19] After three generations of continuous residence, descendants of *anak tawan* or *jurai muda* were given equal status to those born of Gumai parents. [20]

Through the practice of *jujur* and *tambi anak* marriages, Gumai villages remained groups with largely shared genealogical and affinal relations, with a single founding ancestor or multiple founding ancestors. The Dutch and British authorities, however, believed that these two modes of marriage deprived individuals of their freedom, were humiliating and degrading and equated them with slavery. [21] Supposedly when reformist Islamic movements reached the South Sumatran highlands, the penetration of Islamic marriage commonly known as *nikah* gradually replaced Gumai traditional marriage rules.

Islam taught that marriage should be a bond between a wife and a husband, and did not support the custom of *nungkat*. Along with this change, the selection of a spouse came to be regarded as a personal choice. Relations with the families of both parents should be maintained equally, and a couple should be free to choose a location for their new residence. According to the memories of elderly people in Gumai Talang, a meeting was held among the Gumai in 1944 to decide to abolish *jujur* and *tambi anak* marriages, and to replace them with *tambi anak jurai sesame* marriage. [22] As its name suggests, this new form of marriage is similar to *tambi anak* marriage as it results in uxorilocal residence and has no bride-wealth payment. A husband may live with his wife's family but may leave the house of the wife's father after the couple construct their own. The difference is that this marriage form ensures bilateral relations with parents-in-law after marriage and that descendants are recognised as belonging equally to both the husband's and wife's group of origin.

Marriage is now regarded as a personal arrangement between two people, and *nungkat* is not usually practised or expected to take place any more. [23] Table 1 shows that 67 percent of marriages that took place in villages in Gumai Talang during the period between 1994 and 1995 were uxorilocal. The three cases of neo-local marriage involved couples who moved from Gumai Talang villages to Jakarta or Palembang in relation to their work.

Table 2.1. Residential patterns of newly married couples in Gumai Talang between 1994 and 1995 (%)

Types of marriage	Virilocal marriage	Uxorilocal marriage	Neo-local marriage	Total
Marriage cases	16	38	3	57
Per cent (%)	28	67	5	100

Source: Marriages which took place between the period of 1994 and 1995 surveyed during fieldwork.

With the prevalence of *jurai sesame* marriage, old terms related to the previous marriage systems have begun to be used with new meanings. *Tambi anak* and *belaki* now indicate post-marital residence patterns: the former refers to uxorilocal marriage and the latter to virilocal residential arrangements. [24] Marriage contracts determine the status of descendants and restrict village membership to those who can trace their origins to village founders through genealogical or affinal relations.

Petunggu Dusun

The Gumai mention the name of their natal village to indicate their place of origin. The natal village is called *dusun laman.* [25] The house in which one is born is regarded as an important place that connects the individual to a native village. Therefore, one member of the family is expected to inherit the family house to live in. The person who inherits the house is called *petunggu dusun,* which literally means 'the one who waits in the village'. This person is expected to reside in the house and to have his/her own descendants maintain and represent genealogical connections to the founding ancestor of their village. [26] Gumai ritual specialists, *Jurai Tue, Mimbar* and *Jurai Kebali'an,* are all appointed as *petunggu dusun* among their family members and are asked to stay in their *dusun laman.*

Under the custom of the *petunggu dusun,* the village members consist largely of the households of *petunggu dusun,* who are regarded as the legitimate successors to their ancestors. In ritual language, [27] which is used to invoke ancestral spirits, the residents of a village who are mostly *petunggu dusun* are referred to as *bilang gagang jurai bilang batang nyawe* ('each stem of a descendant, each trunk of a soul'). The *petunggu dusun* is the group who reproduces the next generation of the Gumai. In other words, each *petunggu dusun* is the trunk of life that derives from the ancestors as source and becomes an origin point from which the next generation of descendants is created. [28]

Leaving a house without an occupant in a natal village means losing connections with one's natal village as the point of origin. This is explained as *lupe asal* or 'forgetting origins'. Ancestral spirits are benevolent and will help their descendants to achieve their goals in life if they are remembered properly. Having derived from their ancestors, Gumai should not forget their ancestral origins. Forgetting one's origins can enrage ancestral spirits who can cause a series of misfortunes. Not having a *petunggu dusun* could make a member of a household mentally ill.

Except for the child appointed as *petunggu dusun,* the other children are free to live elsewhere. More than 50 percent of the parents in Gumai Talang surveyed during my fieldwork encouraged their children to leave the village to make their living. Yet, these emigrants should not forget their native village and should pay regular visits to their *dusun laman* with their spouses and descendants. At the time of their visit, the *petunggu dusun* should accommodate the returning siblings at his/her house and offer a place to hold a gathering. [29]

Continuity of Place

Despite a series of village relocations over time, each village retains some physical continuity to the old village sites that are associated with village founders. When a Gumai village needs to be relocated, members of that village cannot simply take up residency in any existing village due to the restrictive residential rules. This requires the Gumai to create a new village at a new site. At present, due to the shortage of land, a village relocation rarely takes place, yet in the past, a series of relocations took place. At these times, it was common to create a new village with village members at a new site, or to create a new village with other Gumai from a different village, or to split into two villages. In any case, having a physical link to the old site is essential for a new village site. No village has been relocated in the past 40 years, but an outline given by the *Jurai Tue* of Mandi Angin highlights the association between old and new village sites:

> The *Jurai Tue* needs to carry a handful of soil from the old site and plant it in the centre of a new village site, where a *lunjuk* or *balai desa* was formerly built. In addition to the soil, a coconut tree and an areca nut tree need to be moved from the old site to the new site. These are also to be planted in the centre of the new village. Village ancestral spirits are to be informed of this relocation through the burning of benzoin and the presentation of offerings which include a goat as a sacrificial animal. [30]

Through the replanting of trees and soil by the most authentic living descendants of the village, the *Jurai Tue*, the new site of a village is connected physically to the old village site.

Lunjuk, Balai Desa and Mosque

In the past, many villages in the South Sumatran highlands contained a small house that was a venue for the reverence of ancestral spirits (*arwah puyang*) and for performing a series of rituals commemorating village origins. These houses were known as *lunjuk* or *rumah puyang* (ancestors' house), and were constructed in the centre of a village, which was linked symbolically to the old sites. [31] In Gumai villages, they are known commonly as *lunjuk*. [32] The *Jurai Tue* of Mandi Angin told me the following story of why such a house was called *rumah puyang*.

> Along the Lematang River, there existed five villages whose ancestry could be traced back to the king of Majapahit in Java (*Ratu Majapahit*). Because of this ancestry, Dita, Muara Siban, Selawi, Pagar Batu and Muara Temiang villages are known as Suku Lima (the five tribes), and

are differentiated from the Gumai. [33] The Gumai established affinal relations with them by marrying a younger sister of Gune Raje, a daughter of Remanjang Sakti, to the eldest son of Ratu Majapahit, Kerie Tabing. However, Kerie Tabing and Kerie Tungkal Diwe, a younger brother of Gune Raje, did not get along well and eventually Kerie Tungkal Diwe was murdered by Kerie Tabing. Gune Raje and his brother Pegeh (Bigeh) went to see Ratu Majapahit and demanded his son be punished for the death of Kerie Tungkal Diwe. Ratu Majapahit answered that he would surrender his son if Gune Raje and Bigeh successfully defeated Sunda Kelam, which was a part of Majapahit. Sunda Kelam is a territory which was sometimes visible and sometimes invisible, thus it is difficult to fight with. Gune Raje and Bigeh arrived at the site of Sunda Kelam but were unable to see anyone in the country. Therefore, they had to return home in vain. Remanjang Sakti ordered that another son of his, Betelak, should accompany the other two sons for this expedition to Sunda Kelam. Betelak was a great coward and he was not willing to come along. So it was suggested that his soul (*nyawe*) should be kept in a bamboo cigarette container called *telak* so that he would not feel timid or scared. When the three arrived in Sunda Kelam, Betelak performed *solat* twice. After his bowing, the heads of the residents of Sunda Kelam became visible; it looked as if the people of Sunda Kelam were floating in the sky. When Gune Raje prayed, the kingdom of Sunda Kelam then fell to the ground. The three Gumai men easily defeated Sunda Kelam. Gune Raje and his two brothers demanded evidence of their victory from Sunda Kelam and they were provided with two princesses and heirlooms. One of the two princesses was a daughter of Ratu Majapahit called Putri Dimengkute, and the other was a fairy (*dayang*) called Putri Kedayang. It was later decided that the two princesses would marry Gune Raje. Their heirlooms consisted of a cannon called Guruh Kemarau, a betel nut box called Bun, a gong known as Gong Pamor Sunda, and a dagger called Betak Sepamah. [34] They took a boat and went up the Musi River. During their voyage, the marriage between the two princesses and Gune Raje took place. When they arrived at the Lematang River, Putri Dimengkute said, 'I cannot continue this journey since I cannot drink dirty water. So I shall return home.' Then she explained the secrets of the heirlooms: Bun needs to be washed in the river for a rain-making ritual. When the Guruh Kemarau roars, it is a sign that misfortune such as cholera is approaching. So a ritual to ward off the coming misfortune needs to be undertaken. Then she asked that all the heirlooms should safely be brought back to the place of Gune Raje. Putri Dimengkute then added that she wished to have a small house constructed in each Gumai village so that she could visit her descendants. This house was called *lunjuk* and

> was usually built in the middle of a village and used as a site of rituals to ward off misfortune.

The penetration of Reformist Islam into the interior led to the disappearance of *lunjuk* in the 1930s. Hoop (1932), who travelled around the South Sumatran highlands in the 1930s to investigate megalithic remains, photographed *lunjuk* located in Karang Dalam village of Gumai Lembak, currently located in the Pulau Pinang Subdistrict of the Lahat District. His comments show that Islam was then rapidly penetrating the highlands and replacing traditional customs.

> In the middle of the *doesoen* stands a small spirits-house, '*roema dewa*' or '*roema pojang*' [sic], of the kind formerly found in all *doesoens*, but which are now disappearing rapidly under the influence of Islam. [35] (Hoop 1932: 13)

This *lunjuk* remains at the site as an example of local cultural heritage, but it no longer functions as a ritual venue. I was able to visit this *lunjuk* with the *Mimbar* of Karang Dalam village during my fieldwork. It was a small house made of wood, with a zinc roof placed on top of four wooden pillars, each of which were two metres high. The house was big enough for two to three people to sit in after they had climbed up a ladder to enter. Inside the *lunjuk* was empty space with only a mosquito net, which was rolled and placed on the floor. I was told that the *Jurai Tue* and *Mimbar* used to go inside the *lunjuk* at times of *Sedekah Rame* to burn benzoin and invoke ancestral spirits there.

After the demolition of *lunjuk* in many villages in the 1930s, *balai desa* were constructed on the same sites to cater for the needs of village meetings and *Sedekah Rame*. *Balai desa* consisted of a small room with a roof, and two long benches, both of which were made of bamboo. The room was a place for the *Jurai Tue*, *Mimbar* and the head of a village (*Rie Punggawa*) to sit, and was set half a metre higher than the benches. Each of the long benches was able to accommodate 40 people.

The *balai desa* in Mandi Angin village is said to have been demolished in 1944, when the Japanese Army organised a party and criticised the practice of differentiating seating and offering arrangements depending on status. *Balai desa* in other villages were also gradually demolished and replaced by village mosques along with the continuing Islamisation. In Mandi Angin, the village mosque stands on the old site of the *balai desa* and is vaguely associated in the minds of the villagers with the old site of their *balai desa*. There is a stone next to the village mosque called *Tapak Puyang Dimengkute*, which indicates the remains of the *lunjuk* at that site. Since the demolition of *lunjuk* and *balai desa*, the ritual venue of *Sedekah Rame* has been moved to the house of the *Jurai Tue* or to the newly constructed village mosque. There remains little in the layout of the current village that might provide a clue to Gumai belief in ancestral and natural spirits.

Graveyard

Not only does a village in Gumai Talang consist of the living who share their ancestry, it comprises the ancestral spirits. Thus a graveyard (*kuburan*) is considered an essential part of a Gumai village. The significance of a graveyard as part of a village was expressed in the following incident, which occurred during my fieldwork:

> In August 1995, students of the University of Sriwijaya came as a part of Kuliah Kerja Nyata (KKN) and stayed in five villages in Gumai Talang for two months. KKN is a social project whose aim is to send the highly educated university students to underdeveloped areas of Indonesia where they are expected to learn from their rural experience. In this case, the students organised village seminars about nutrition and how to purify drinking water. Before they leave, it is customary for students to produce something as a souvenir of their stay. In Endikat Ilir village, some students prepared house number plates which showed addresses within the village, and distributed one to each household for display. [36] Students also decided to produce a souvenir by erecting two posts to show the boundaries of the village. Students consulted with the village heads of Endikat Ilir and Muara Tandi regarding the boundaries. One post was placed between Endikat Ilir and Mandi Angin, and the other was placed between Endikat Ilir and Muara Tandi along the Kikim Raya Road. The post which demarcated Endikat Ilir village from Muara Tandi village was placed at a site which did not include the graveyard of Endikat Ilir village. It was located behind the first house in Muara Tandi village through a lane from Kikim Raya Road. According to the view of the village head of Muara Tandi, the graveyard of Endikat belonged to Muara Tandi village and the space was only lent to Endikat Ilir village. From the point of view of legal status, the graveyard of Endikat Ilir village was located within Muara Tandi village. The village head of Muara Tandi therefore asked the students to put the post so that it excluded the graveyard from Endikat Ilir village. Soon after this post was placed, the *Jurai Kebali'an* asked the village head of the Muara Tandi village to relocate it so that the lane to the graveyard should be regarded as a part of Endikat Ilir village. He explained that even though the graveyard is officially located within the territory of Muara Tandi village, those buried in the graveyard are all from Endikat Ilir village, including the previous *Jurai Kebali'an*. If the graveyard is not considered to be a part of Endikat Ilir village, the village does not have a graveyard and the deceased members of the village would be buried in Muara Tandi

> village. The *Jurai Kebali'an* insisted that the boundaries of Endikat Ilir village should include the village and its own graveyard, and this was approved by the village head of Muara Tandi. After this negotiation, the post was moved to a location which showed that the lane as well as the graveyard could be regarded as a part of Endikat Ilir territory.

In the past, each *jungkuk* and *sungut* had its own burial site. Due to a series of relocations and a shortage of land, however, many Gumai villages now have a single graveyard. Even when a village member dies outside South Sumatra, it is common to transfer the body of the deceased person to his/her village graveyard. The previous *Jurai Kebali'an* passed away in Jakarta in 1999 and his body was taken back to Endikat Ilir village to be buried. This is despite the fact that, according to Islamic teaching, a body should be buried as soon as possible.

Each village in Gumai Talang has its own graveyard. An exception is the graveyard shared by Suka Rame and Tanjung Dalam villages. Since the founding ancestors of the two villages were brothers, villagers regard the two villages as one unit and find no problem in sharing a common graveyard. [37] All the villagers who were born and raised in a village expect to be buried in its graveyard, and access to burial in a village graveyard is restricted strictly to village members.

In a Gumai village graveyard, there are a series of mounds of earth or spots marked by circles of big stones which indicate burial sites. The mound is often decorated with flowers. Relatively wealthy people convert the mound of soil into a rectangular coffin made of ceramics or cement. A village graveyard is always associated with the spirits of the deceased, and people dare not go there alone at night. Spirits of the ancestors believed to reside in the graveyard can be seen at night.

Due to a series of village relocations from the original village site, village founders' graves are located in old village sites, and not in the current village graveyard. In a current village site, however, it is common to find a memorial place called *tapak* ('site') related to a village ancestor. A relatively new *tapak* exists in Tanjung Beringin village, which is believed to have been constructed in the 1940s. It takes the form of a rectangle, framed by stone and cement and raised 60 centimetres from the ground. It is approximately three metres wide and five metres long and has two poles, which are said to represent the head and the legs. This *tapak* is surrounded by a fence made of wood. The *tapak* was constructed because the old site of the ancestral grave had been chosen for a planned railway track. I was told that the spirit of the *Puyang Ketunggalan Dusun* was asked to move from the old site to the new site on the completion of the new *tapak*. Even though the body of the ancestor was not buried there, the spirit is believed to reside in the new site. Villagers occasionally visit this *tapak*, clearing grass and sprinkling water around it, particularly in the month of

Ruwah. [38] Some bring a set of offerings consisting of rice cakes and betel nuts, and recite *Yasin*, the 36th surah of the Qur'an.

Despite its geographical detachment from the village settlement, the graveyard of each village constitutes an extension of a Gumai village, which consists of the living and the dead. A Gumai village is an entity of linkages to village origins represented by the descendants and important sites.

The *Marga* System and its Impact

Let me finally examine the impact of an external administrative unit, the *marga* system, on the succession and continuity of a Gumai village. The *marga* system was used originally by the Sultanate of Palembang, and then was made into a rigid administrative unit by the Dutch Administration in the highlands of South Sumatra in the 19th century.

In order to rule indirectly in an efficient manner, the Dutch concentrated administrative power in a single person, the head of a *marga*, a territorial unit, and appointed him as *pasirah* (Galizia 1996: 136-8). A *pasirah* was a representative of the people of a *marga* and important decisions were always made through discussions among elders within his *marga* unit. In contrast, the Dutch-appointed *pasirah* was made to assume the role of the centralised ruler of a *marga*, with more power in his hands. Only his family members were allowed opportunities for Western education, which provided close connections with the Dutch Colonial Government. [39] A *marga*, in turn, consisted of several villages (*dusun*), each of which was headed by a local *Proatin* with the title of *Krie*, *Lurah* or *Ginda*. Through this indirect control and manipulation of their power at the *marga* level, the Dutch succeeded in directing their administrative power into the lower levels of political organisation in the highlands. [40]

A consequence of the implementation of the *marga* system was that, by 1930, the Gumai were divided into several *marga* located in various parts of Southern Sumatra. According to Wellan's report (1932: 194-8), Marga Gumai Talang and Marga Gumai Lembak were located in Lematang Ulu Subdistrict, while Gumai Ulu and Pagar Gunung were located in the Pasemahlanden Subdistrict. These four *marga* were located in the Palembang Highlands. Other *marga* in which the Gumai were the main population group included Marga Rambang Ampatsuku in the Ogan Ilir Subdistrict, and two *marga* in the Bengkulu Residency: Marga Anak Gumai in the Manna Subdistrict and Marga Semidang Gumai in the Kaur Subdistrict.

In this process of institutionalising the *marga* system, non-Gumai villages were also incorporated into Gumai *marga*. For instance, the people of Jati village in Marga Gumai Lembak claim descent from Suku Lima, who were descendants of the legendary Javanese Kingdom of Majapahit, but Jati village became a part of Marga Gumai Lembak. The creation of Marga Semidang Gumai in South

Bengkulu was the result of combining Gumai villages and Semidang villages into one *marga*.

The *marga* and *pasirah* system continued after the independence of Indonesia until the implementation of the *Law on Village Administration No. 5* of 1979 (*Undang-Undang* 5/1979) under which each *marga* was divided into various villages known as *desa*.

Despite the implementation of the *marga* system, the aim of which was primarily for administration by the outer authorities, it did little to interfere with the social structure and ritual practice of each village. For example, the Gumai did not consider *marga* as a unit sharing origins nor did they develop rituals for the *marga*. *Marga* was perceived as a unit of political administration and knowledge about each village was transmitted by a ritual specialist from each village. There were some discussions on the revival of the *marga* system as a result of regional autonomy in 2000-01, but the idea did not gain any political momentum.

Conclusion

I have examined origin structures and the related roles of ritual specialists among the Gumai of South Sumatra. I have noted that a majority of Gumai villages have to date maintained their distinctive nature as territorial units and maintain a range of rituals to commemorate the origins of their villages. As I have described elsewhere (Sakai 1999, 2002, 2003), they also undertake rituals commemorating their family origins and the origin of the founding ancestor through a monthly ritual, despite the penetrating influence of Islam.

This does not mean Gumai tradition has remained intact and free from challenges. Outside the three settlements of the Gumai there are in fact many villages where a large number of newcomers have settled, which is blurring the definition of village membership. In the case of the neighbouring Besemah people, the influence of reformist Islam has been such that rituals associated with origins have been abandoned. Along with the abandoning of knowledge and rituals, definitions of village membership are no longer as restricted and outsiders are increasingly accepted. Other challenges arise from the migration of younger residents to big cities such as Palembang and Jakarta, which can leave their villages depopulated. People can no longer guarantee a member of the family to serve as *petunggu dusun*. A critical situation arises when there is no one who is prepared to reside in a designated village and act as the *Jurai Tue* or even the *Jurai Kebali'an*. Knowledge about the origins of the Gumai is no longer considered particularly important by many younger Gumai. Since the death of the previous *Jurai Kebali'an* in November 1999, the successor to the office has not been properly appointed. An elder brother of the deceased is assuming a role temporarily. Whether this is merely an example of traditional *menyandung* or another indication of a demise of Gumai tradition remains to be seen.

References

Andaya, Barbara Watson. 1993. *To Live As Brothers: Southeast Sumatra in the seventeenth and eighteenth century*. Honolulu: University of Hawai'i Press.

Bellwood, Peter. 1996. 'Hierarchy, founder ideology and Austronesian expansion.' In J.J. Fox and C. Sather (eds), *Origins, Ancestry and Alliance: Explorations in Austronesian ethnography*, Canberra: Department of Anthropology, Research School of Pacific and Asian Studies, The Australian National University.

Collins, William. 1979. 'Besemah Concepts: A study of the culture of a people of South Sumatra.' Unpublished PhD Thesis, University of California, Berkeley.

Collins, William. 1998. *The Guritan of Radin Suane: A study of the Besemah oral epic from south Sumatra*. Leiden: KITLV Press.

Encyclopaedie van Nederlandsch-Indië 1919 (2nd edition). 's-Gravenhage: Martinus Nijhoff.

Fox, James J. 1971. 'Sister's child as plant: Metaphors in an idiom of consanguinity.' In R. Needham (ed.), *Rethinking Kinship and Marriage*, London: Tavistock. pp. 219-52.

Fox, James J. 1980a. 'Introduction.' In J.J. Fox (ed.), *The Flow of Life: Essays on eastern Indonesia*, Cambridge (Mass.): Harvard University Press. pp. 1-18.

Fox, James J. 1980b. 'Models and metaphors: Comparative research in eastern Indonesia.' In J.J. Fox (ed.), *The Flow of Life: Essays on eastern Indonesia*, Cambridge (Mass): Harvard University Press. pp. 327-33.

Fox, James J. 1988. 'Origin, descent and precedence in the study of Austronesian Societies.' Public lecture in connection with De Wisselleerstoel Indonesische Studien in Leiden, The Netherlands, March 17, 1988.

Fox, James J. 1995. 'Origin structures and systems of precedence in the comparative study of Austronesian societies.' In P.J.K. Li, Cheng-hwa Tsang, Ying-kuei Huang, Dah-an Ho and Chiu-yu Tseng (eds), *Austronesian Studies Relating to Taiwan*, Symposium Series of the Institute of History and Philology, Academia Sinica 3, Taipei: Academia Sinica. pp. 27-57.

Fox, James J. 1996a. 'The transformation of progenitor lines of origin: Patterns of precedence in eastern Indonesia.' In J.J. Fox and C. Sather (eds), *Origins, Ancestry and Alliance: Explorations in Austronesian ethnography*, Canberra: Department of Anthropology, Comparative Austronesian

Project, Research School of Pacific and Asian Studies, The Australian National University. pp. 130-53.

Fox, James J. 1996b. 'Introduction.' pp. 1-17. In J.J. Fox and Clifford Sather (eds), *Origin, Ancestry and Alliance: Explorations in Austronesian ethnography*, Canberra: Department of Anthropology, Comparative Austronesian Studies Project, Research School of Pacific and Asian Studies, The Australian National University. pp. 1-17.

Galizia, M. 1995. *Aufstieg und Fall der Pasirah: Zentralstaatliche Vereinnahmung und lokale Machtstrategien*. Berlin: Reimer.

Galizia, M. 1996. 'Village institutions after the Law No. 5/1979 on village administration. The Case of Rejang-Lebong in South-Western Sumatra.' *Archipel*, 51. pp. 135-60.

Hayatuddin. 1992. *Sumatra Selatan Propinsi Peleburan Suku Bangsa, Proyek I: Identitas dan Etnis di Sumatra Selatan*. Palembang: Pusat Penelitian Universitas Sriwijaya.

van der Hoop, A.N. 1932. *Megalithic Remains in South Sumatra*. Zutphen: W.J. Thieme & CIE.

Jaspan, M.A. 1976. 'Redjang complex.' In Frank LeBar (ed.), *Insular Southeast Asia: Ethnographic studies*, Vol. II, New Haven: Human Relations Area Files.

Lewis, E. Douglas 1996. 'Origin structures and precedence in the social orders of Tana 'Ai and Sikka.' In J.J. Fox and C. Sather (eds), *Origins, Ancestry and Alliance: Explorations in Austronesian ethnography*, Canberra: Department of Anthropology, Comparative Austronesian Studies Project, Research School of Pacific and Asian Studies, The Australian National University. pp. 154-74.

Marsden, William. 1986. Reprint of 3rd ed. *The History of Sumatra*. Singapore: Oxford University Press.

Sakai, Minako. 1997. 'Remembering Origins: Ancestors and Places in Gumai Society of South Sumatra, Indonesia.' In James J. Fox (ed.), *The Poetic Power of Place: Comparative perspectives on Austronesian ideas of locality*, Canberra: Department of Anthropology, Research School of Pacific and Asian Studies, The Australian National University. pp. 42-66.

Sakai, Minako. 2000. 'The Nut Cannot Forget Its Shell: Origin Rituals among the Gumai of South Sumatra.' Unpublished PhD thesis. The Australian National University: Canberra.

Sakai, Minako. 2002. 'Modernising Sacred Sites in South Sumatra? Islamisation of Gumai Ancestral Places.' *In The Potent Dead*, Anthony J.S. Reid and

Henri Chambert Loir, (eds). ASAA series, Allen & Unwin, University of Hawai'i Press. pp. 103-16.

Sakai, Minako. 2003. 'Publicising Rituals and Privatising Meanings.' In N. Tannenbaum and C. Krammerer (eds), *Founder's Cults: Ancestors, Polity and Identity in Southeast Asia*, Yale University Press. pp. 159-83.

Skeat, William. 1967 [1900]. *Malay Magic*. New York: Dover Publications, Inc.

Wellan, J.W.J. 1932. *Economisch overzicht van de gewesten Djambi, Palembang, de Lampoengsche Districten en Benkoelen*. Wageningen: H. Veenman & Zonen.

ENDNOTES

[1] Sometimes the title is known as *pejungkuk*, but in many cases people just used the word *jungkuk* to refer to the social unit and the title.

[2] See Chapter Five of Sakai (2000) for rituals related to village origins.

[3] The Gumai often comment on the Besemah, a neighbouring ethnic group, saying that the Besemah have severed their descendants (*putus jurai*). It does not mean that the Besemah have become extinct; in fact, the number of the Besemah population is far larger than that of the Gumai. *Putus jurai* refers to their view that the succession of legitimate descendants among the Besemah has been broken. Collins (1998: 487) translates it as 'to have one's line extinct'.

[4] Lewis (1996: 155) provides a similar interpretation of older houses in Tana 'Ai of Flores. Older houses exert more social and ceremonial precedence due to their temporal proximity to the source.

[5] The manifestation of this precedence system is said to have been abolished in 1944 during the Japanese military occupation, which forbade differentiation of the people based on rank and encouraged cooperation among the villagers.

[6] Bellwood (1996: 24) states that 'high rank derived from genealogical closeness to an important founder would give access to the economic rights usually associated with chiefs.' However, the ranking of *jungkuk* does not involve any economic prerogatives.

[7] As women are responsible for the organising of an elaborate set of offerings at times of rituals to commemorate origins, it is reasonable to allow a daughter to succeed to the title of *Jurai Tue*, and let her husband perform the role. Women were and still are not allowed to perform the role of the *Jurai Tue*.

[8] Regalia include weapons such as *kris* and *tombak*. Some of the regalia were said to have been taken by the Dutch at the time of the Fort Jati War.

[9] The reason for this transfer was not remembered. Ren Tasim, who was expected to assume this role, might have been too young to carry out the task.

[10] I came to know some cases of disputes over the succession of the *Jurai Tue*. For an example of contestation of precedence see Sakai (2000, Chapter Five).

[11] The residential rule still operates in the 14 villages in Gumai Talang but is no longer observed in villages located in the lowland area of South Sumatra.

[12] After three generations, distinctions are no longer made. In fact, I did not encounter any person who claimed his or her origin from Diwe Semidang in villages in Gumai Talang during my fieldwork.

[13] The Besemah consist of six subgroups called *sumbai*, but Hayatuddin (1992: 19) reports that the significance of the *sumbai* was so minimal that its meaning was not known to his Besemah informant.

[14] Not offering food to guests is considered rude among the Gumai. The fact that Kerie Tingal was not offered food indicates that he was not treated as a guest.

[15] The acceptance of Siatong Ali and his descendants is still remembered and their status as a part of the origins of Mandi Angin village is expressed at *Sedekah Rame* ceremonies in the village.

[16] The *Jurai Tue palak tanah*, Pak Hasan Basri, had lived for a long time in Palembang and had hardly any knowledge about the village origins of Sugih Waras.

[17] One of the early references regarding the practice of these two modes of marriage is Marsden (1986: 225-9, 235-7), who described the two practices among the Rejang.

[18] First-and second-cousin marriage was prohibited and still is strongly discouraged among the Gumai. This was because cousins share the same origin and relationships between them were considered incestuous. This made marriage among members of the same village rather difficult.

[19] According to Collins (1998: 311), *anak tawan* were normally women and children who were captured from enemy villages among the Besemah or became captives due to debt. They were often kept as sex slaves. The Besemah are reluctant to talk about who are the descendants of these women.

[20] All these classifications functioned until the middle of last century but no longer feature in the daily life of the Gumai.

[21] For a summary of the Dutch view on South Sumatran marriage modes, see Collins (1979: 125-51).

[22] Another name for this marriage is *semendo*, which became widely practised after the prohibition of *jujur* and *ambil anak* marriage (Collins 1979: 144-45).

[23] Marriage arranged by parents was known as *rasan tue,* in contrast with the marriage decision made by a couple based on their romantic feelings (*rasan mude*). In the past, *rasan tue* was a common practice among the Besemah elites (Collins 1998: 19). Since *rasan tue* is no longer popular, an expression, *ade rasan,* is often used among the Gumai today when parents announce the engagement of their children. It means that there is a mutual agreement between a young man and a young woman to marry.

[24] In daily conversations with Gumai men and women regarding the whereabouts of other family members, I often received these replies: '*Kerawai aku udem belaki*' — My sister has taken a *belaki* marriage' or '*Jemetu, milu binie, ibarate sini tambi anak*'—'That person has followed his wife to live in his wife's village'. This practice is called *tambi anak* here.

[25] *Dusun laman* is an equivalent of the Indonesian term *kampung halaman,* 'birthplace' or 'natal village'. *Laman* means yard.

[26] The person who is chosen as *petunggu dusun* normally inherits gardens too so that he or she can make a living from agriculture.

[27] See Sakai (2000, Chapter Five), on the ritual language used by the Gumai.

[28] Botanic metaphors of life are used widely among Austronesian speakers as a discourse on origin and as kinship terms. For linguistic analyses of metaphorical botanic expressions, see Fox (1971, 1980a, 1980b, 1996b).

[29] For details of rituals related to individual origins, see Sakai (2000, Chapter Six).

[30] Classifications of sacrificial animals are of great importance for the Gumai. The sacrificial goat for this occasion is *kambing irang,* which is a red-haired goat.

[31] The Besemah, the Gumai and the Kikim are known to have possessed small houses for ancestral spirits. In addition to the *lunjuk* in Karang Dalam village that I have mentioned, there is another *lunjuk* located in Pagardin village of the Bunga Mas Subdistrict of the Lahat District. People say that this *lunjuk* glows in the dark on every 13th night according to the lunar calendar.

[32] Among the Besemah this building was called *rumah poyang* (ancestors' house) and was replaced by a mosque (Collins 1979: 173).

[33] These villages were administered as a part of Marga Gumai Lembak.

[34] Guruh Kemarau was believed to have been taken to the Netherlands after the Fort Jati War. Skeat (1967:373) reports that *bun* in the Malay Peninsula refers to *bun* in Dutch, which means 'a large tin or copper box for tobacco or *sirih* leaves'. Among the Gumai, the pronunciation of *bun* is close to *bon;* the *bon* is kept in the house of the *Jurai Tue* in Mandi Angin village. Gong Pamor Sunda is kept at the house of the *Jurai Tue* of Lubuk Sepang. Betak Sepamah is located in the house of the *Jurai Kebali'an.*

[35] *Doesoen* is an old spelling of *dusun,* a hamlet.

[36] Residents in a village all know who lives where, and a mailman delivers all the mail to a stall along the road or the house of the village head, hence number plates in the village do not have any practical value in daily life.

[37] They used to share a village mosque, but now each village has its own.

[38] Another name of this month is Sya'ban. In this month, spirits of the dead are believed to return to their native places and people visit the graveyard.

[39] Only the *Pasirah* was allowed to use stamps for documents to show his authority.

[40] Local administrative officers such as *pasirah, proatin* and *penggawa* were nominated by people in the *marga* and then appointed by Dutch authority. The Dutch exerted influence and manipulated

nominees in their favour. In order to represent the administrative hierarchy among native administrators, the Dutch granted distinctive titles such as *Depati* and *Pangeran* upon appointment, and demonstrated these titles by providing distinctive caps and buttons (*Encyclopaedie van Nederlandsch Indië* 1919: 267-8). Extensive *marga* were divided into smaller units to decrease their power, and a non-cooperative *marga* was joined with another *marga,* which was close to the Dutch authority. For a case study of the *pasirah* system in Bengkulu Residency, see Galizia (1995).

Chapter 3. Ritual Domains and Communal Land in the Highlands of Bali

Thomas Reuter

Introduction

The central highlands and some coastal areas of Bali are home to a little-known indigenous minority group, the *Bali Aga* or 'Mountain Balinese'. This paper focuses on ritual domains formed by clusters of Bali Aga 'villages' (*desa adat* or *desa ulu apad*). These regional, spatially bounded and historically conceived networks are known as *banua*. The *banua* and its constituent *desa* form a sacred landscape inscribed by the memory of a continuous history of human settlement and migration, and re-inscribed through origin narratives and ritual performances at sacred sites of origin, which are marked by shrines or temples. This multi-layered process of inscription defines how different groups of participants relate to the land in terms of spiritual ownership or obligation but also in terms of their practical ownership of land as a primary material resource.

I will argue that many agriculturalist peoples in the Austronesian world, such as the Bali Aga, define their social identities as well as rights of access to particular pieces of arable land by creating a hermeneutic circle of reciprocal mapping between social and physical landscapes. I further suggest that there is a historical movement of emphasis from material to symbolic resources as spatially defined entities grow in size or complexity. Because actual land rights tend to be negotiated locally, in the village or the 'house', the nature of people's claims to a relationship with an area of land tend to become more distant and detached from practical concerns with material resources in the much larger structure of a regional, ritual-political organisation such as the *banua*. At this level of social organisation, status and other forms of symbolic resources tend to become the primary concern instead. [1]

Highland Bali and Comparative Austronesian Studies: Historical and Linguistic Considerations

My ethnographic research has revealed a confluence of Austronesian and Indic influences in highland Balinese culture. Annual ceremonies at the regional temples, which form the ritual centres of *banua*, for example, contain some elements of classical Hindu religion alongside other important rites, such as buffalo sacrifices, which are more commonly associated with cultures of the Austronesian region of which Bali is a part. In short, the cultural history of the *banua* of the Balinese highlands is in many ways typical of societies in the Indian-influenced part of the Austronesian world.

Megalithic stone carvings and other archaeological evidence suggests that some major contemporary regional temples of highland Bali have been places of worship from prehistoric times (Bernet-Kempers 1991). The earliest Indic kingdom on Indonesian soil was established in Kutai (Borneo) in the fifth century AD and others soon after in Java and Sumatra, while Indian trade and cultural influence in the region, including Bali, probably dates back to the first century AD at least (Ardika and Bellwood 1991).

The earliest written sources of local cultural history are ninth-century royal edicts from the first Balinese Hindu kingdoms (*negara*), which might have been centred in the region of the highlands and northern coast. These edicts depict several important and ancient temples that are the ritual centres of contemporary *banua* already at the heart of regional ritual organisations (Reuter 2002a). The prehistoric significance of these same sacred sites makes it seem very likely that ritual domains preceded the formation of early Hindu kingdoms on Bali as well as providing an organisational platform for their establishment, not just in the highlands but on the island as a whole (for evidence of similar ritual networks with royal patronage in southern Bali, see MacRae, this volume). By the same token, there is no doubt that the evolution of highland domains took a new direction under the influence of local Hindu kingdoms and again after their collapse in the 14th century, when Javanese invaders established new Hindu dynasties centred in the south.

Bali Aga society provides an ideal contemporary vantage point from which to explore some of the Austronesian foundations of Balinese culture that have become less visible in the polities and communities of the southern lowlands (Reuter 2002a). Highland people actively resisted the influence of Javanese-descended royal courts of southern Bali and the orthodoxies of the Brahmana priesthood affiliated with these courts for more than half a millennium (Reuter 2003). Studies of Austronesian traditions in highland Bali and in Balinese culture generally are also exceptionally valuable to comparative Austronesian studies because they were and still are better protected under the umbrella of Hinduism, with its great tolerance of local diversity, than societies in other parts of Indonesia and beyond whose local religious practices and belief systems have been devalued and abandoned under the influence of proselytising, monotheistic world religions. [2]

Many societies in the Austronesian-speaking world show patterns of regional and local organisation wherein a category of 'place'—the kingdom, domain, village or house—serves as a key idiom of social identity in its own right, though often also in combination with a notion of common ancestry or 'name'. In the Balinese case, and probably in other societies too, there are recurrent metaphors, idioms and concepts in how the idea of 'place' is defined across different levels of social organisation. Indeed, the distinctions house-village, village-domain, and domain-kingdom are all more or less fluid (see Reuter 2002a). In part, this conceptual similarity and fluidity is a reflection of historical processes. A house with a cluster of branch houses could grow into a village, which in turn could acquire branch villages and grow into a domain, which could—alone or in conjunction with other, allied domains—become the ritual foundation for the formation of a Hindu polity. [3]

Of the four most important terms for territorial categories in Bali, '*desa*', the term for village, and *negara*, the term for a kingdom or its capital town, are of Sanskrit origin while *umah*, 'house', and '*banua*', the contemporary designation for a regional ritual domain, are Austronesian words. My main focus in this paper will be on the regional institution of the *banua*, given that regional forms of social organisation in the Austronesian world remain relatively under-explored. There is a large body of literature on the comparative ethnology of much smaller social forms, namely the 'house' (**rumaq*, **balay*, but occasionally also **banua*) and there has also been much research and debate on very large institutions, such as the classical Indic polities of South-East Asia (*kerajaan*, *negara*). The comparative lack of studies on regional organisation is regrettable especially because it is rather difficult to imagine how states or large chiefdoms in the Austronesian world could have been built directly on a foundation of localised houses and in the complete absence of ritual alliances between houses within villages, domains, or other, similar social structures of intermediary size.

Any comparison of the social organisation of a number of Austronesian societies inevitably leads to the discovery that speakers of Austronesian languages use similar metaphors and related words to describe their ideas of and relationship to a particular stretch of land, even though the meaning and social implications of the reflexes may vary widely. In this case, reflexes of the Proto-Malayo-Polynesian reconstruction **banua* in the contemporary languages of this language family all tend to convey the general idea of a 'place' of varying size, namely, the ancestral territory of a 'longhouse', 'hamlet', 'village' or 'domain'. For example, in Old Javanese, the term *wanua* connotes a 'village'; in Iban, *menoa rumah* is the 'territorial domain of a longhouse'; in Ngada (Sara-Sedu), a *nua* is a 'village' or 'ritual territory'; and in Lio, *nua* is a 'ritual territory, domain or polity'. Similarly, in Goodenough, *manua* connotes a 'village' or 'dwelling place', while in Vanuatu (East Ambai) and Fiji *vanua,* is a 'land' or 'territory'. More sporadically, reflexes of **banua* are used to refer to (the territory of) a 'house', as in Toraja, Banggai, Wolio, Molima and Wusi-Mana. Two other sets of terms with a similar emphasis on 'place' in this group of languages include reflexes of the contructs **tanah* (*tana*, *tanaq*, *taneq*, *taneh*, *tano*, *'ano*), of which the Balinese reflex is *tanah*, and **daya* (*darat*, *dare*, *dae*, *rae*, *rai*).

Similarities and differences in the cultural meaning and social implications of these terms need to be established through detailed ethnographic and ethno-historical research, followed by ethnological comparison. This volume is dedicated to the task of an ethnological comparison of social categories based on the idea of a place or territory. As a contribution, this paper will unpack the meaning of the Balinese reflex *banua* by describing in some detail what a *banua* is or can be in the highlands of Bali.

The Ritual Domains of Highland Bali

Balinese communities at the time of the early royal edicts appear to have been organised around a council of seniority-ranked elders, who were paired and grouped into ceremonial moieties. This pattern of precedence-based village organisation is still a defining characteristic of contemporary Bali Aga communities (Reuter 2002b). The edicts refer to the localised communities represented by these elders as *banua* (Old Balinese) or *wanua* (Old Javanese), rather than *desa*. Most likely the meaning of the term *banua* in Bali at that time referred to something more like a 'village' than a 'domain'. It is possible that the newer term for village, *desa*, was introduced later in order to distinguish between a single village community and territory (*desa*) and a very old settlement (*banua*), which once had a very large 'territory' on which a whole cluster of newer hamlets were established as the population grew, naturally or by immigration. When these newer settlements became independent villages, the original village lost direct control over the land that fell within their respective 'village territories' but retained a special status as ritual overlords in the domain as a whole. In historical perspective, therefore, the term *banua* in Bali has consistently carried the meaning of 'a unit of land or territory shared by a community', while the size and complexity of the unit of land and community thereby designated appears to have changed over time in the direction of greater complexity. This trend is evident in the contemporary situation.

Bali's central highlands and northern coast today are home to about 100 Bali Aga villages. These villages form at least 13 distinct *banua* or 'ritual domains' of varying size, clustered around regionally important temples (*pura*). These ritual alliance clusters are depicted in Figure 1.

Each domain is a bounded space in that all of the villages within certain boundaries normally partake in the one encompassing ceremonial order. While domains are named after and are socially oriented to a centre, the boundaries, while not emphasised very much in ritual, are quite clear. This is because the participating villages have definite boundaries nowadays, and probably always did. The royal inscriptions of classical Bali already mention streams and ridges as village boundaries. In any case, *banua* networks, figuratively speaking, do not have any gaps or outliers.

Figure 1: Ritual networks in the highlands of Bali

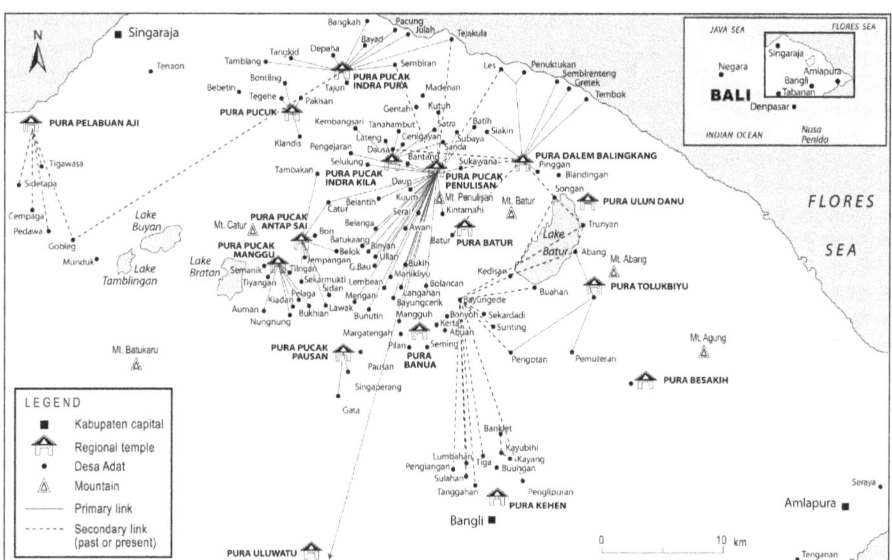

It is a common feature of most of the larger domains, however, that they incorporate smaller subsidiary domains, each with its own regional temple of lesser status. Such complex layered networks are nevertheless conceived as single *banua* with a common origin rather than overlapping, historically unrelated domains. There are a few cases where two distinct domains do share part of the same network of villages. However, this usually means that one of the two was formerly a sub-domain of the other, has attempted to break away from it to become an independent domain in its own right, and has had only partial success in doing so.[4]

From the perspective of local participants, the term *banua* designates a bounded 'spiritual territory'. More specifically, a *banua* is conceived as a large and clearly defined area of agricultural land whose fertility, along with the prosperity (*rahayu*) of its human occupants, depends on the ancestral deities enshrined at the domain's paramount temple or *pura banua*. Likewise, the smaller divisions of land *within* a domain are under the protection of the lesser and more local ancestor deities of 'village temples' or *pura desa*. These lesser village deities are often identified in narratives of origin as the children or children-in-law of the domain's paramount founder deity. The congregation of a *pura banua* is thus a network of otherwise autonomous villages, just as the congregation of a *pura desa* is a group of otherwise autonomous households (*umah*, 'house', or *kuren*, 'hearth'). This raises the question of why these independent villages would find it desirable to continue to recognise the precedence status of the origin village.

A *banua* is a self-evident fact to its participants; a paramount natural (*sekala*) and supernatural (*niskala*) reality with a social character. The force of this social reality is vested in the agency of post-human or non-human agents—the local ancestral and non-local Hindu deities. The relationship with ancestral and other deities is enacted dramatically in a ritual setting. A ritual domain is thus experienced in ritual as a given and is described officially as non-negotiable. Simultaneously, from an ethnographic perspective, the spiritual territory or domain of a temple is a socially constructed reality, a man-made and negotiated boundary and a set of internal relations inscribed on the land by the narrative and ritual performances of a temple's human congregation.

I would like to reconcile these two perspectives. Participants, speaking from a position of individual lived experience, are quite correct in their perception of the *banua* as a non-human facticity. First of all, the land itself is part of a self-evident material reality that predates human occupation, although land is also transformed by human beings for the purpose of agriculture or house-building; land is thereafter classified, respectively, as *tanah ladang* or *tanah pakarangan*. It is also self-evident that nearly all land is visibly occupied and claimed by someone—agricultural land by means of regular cultivation and the construction of garden huts and fences, and house land by means of regular habitation. Given that particular people will argue a claim to the right to occupy particular pieces of farm and house land, this land cannot easily be taken away from them. The *banua* and its subsidiary *desa* therefore are not only a material given, but also a 'supernatural' or rather 'post-human' facticity, in the sense that contemporary society is encountered as a reality that was created by now-deceased and invisible others in the past, namely, by one's own historical predecessors or 'ancestors'.

From the point of view of an interactionist social theory, this still may not seem like an entirely satisfying explanation of the status quo in a *banua*. Although a particular land tenure arrangement, once it has been established, may constitute a self-evident social fact, the more important questions are how such arrangements were established in the first place, and by what means they are maintained or changed. Indeed, local participants are immensely interested in the same questions, though their intuitive answers may be phrased in an unfamiliar idiom.

The Bali Aga are always keen to discuss how relationships between particular people and places came to be. Each domain has its origin narratives, and so does every village within it. Often enough, these narratives exist in different and competing versions. Ritual performances aimed at maintaining good relations with the 'supernatural', which are regular, frequent and elaborate in the highlands of Bali, serve to commemorate this origin history. As are the narratives that inform them, these rituals are subject to variation and can also become a means of contesting origin-based status claims. For the Bali Aga, the answer to the question of how a village or domain came to be in the hands of particular people is, 'history', and as for the means by which this claim to the land is maintained or challenged, the answer is 'commemorating [or forgetting] particular ideas about history in a ritual context'. If I am to convey accurately what a *banua* is or can be, my two principle tasks therefore are to do justice to the regulated practices by which the Bali Aga conceive of the present as a self-evident product of the past, while at the same time acknowledging that the present is also the not-so-self-evident product of a strategic remembering or reconstruction of the past.

Let me begin by looking at regulated practice. Usually, when it is not in (com-) motion, a *banua* 'rests', so to speak, on a shared conviction among participants that the founders of all the villages in the domain originated from a single source village, namely, the village where the domain's paramount temple is now located. Origin narratives retell how these founders left the source village, cleared land somewhere nearby to establish gardens and hamlets, and how these hamlets eventually became independent villages with their own local temples. In these temples, the branch village founders are now enshrined to be venerated by their many descendants. These deified founders still own the land because death is not the end of life, of rights and obligations, but simply the beginning of a gradual transformation from a human to a post-human state of being.

There are different degrees of post-humanisation or sacredness on a temporal scale of precedence. This means that the ancestral founders of a branch village, even though they are local deities in their own right, still have ritual obligations towards their own ancestors, who are enshrined in the origin temples of the domain's source village. (Their obligations in fact mirror those of members of a small kin group around a branch house temple towards the older, larger temple of their clan or local clan segment.) In practical reality, of course, the ritual obligations from junior to senior ancestors have to be met by the living descendants of the junior ancestors in the branch villages. As a consequence of this remembering of ancestral relations, the *pura desa* of the source village is transformed into a regional *pura banua*, which is thereafter maintained collectively from regular contributions (*peturunan*) paid by every household in every one of the branch villages.

Figure 2 depicts the logical pattern of these relationships in schematic form. The diagram is based loosely on the internal organisation of the very large *banua* of the regional temple Pura Pucak Penulisan, which has four major sub-domains centred on the temples of the ancient villages of Bantang, Selulung, Kintamani and Sukawana (Reuter 1998). Each of these secondary ritual centres has its own following of subsidiary villages. What the figure does not show and as we shall see later, the sub-domain of Kintamani, for example, contains yet another, smaller

Figure 2: The path of origin and the ritual order of a domain (*banua*)

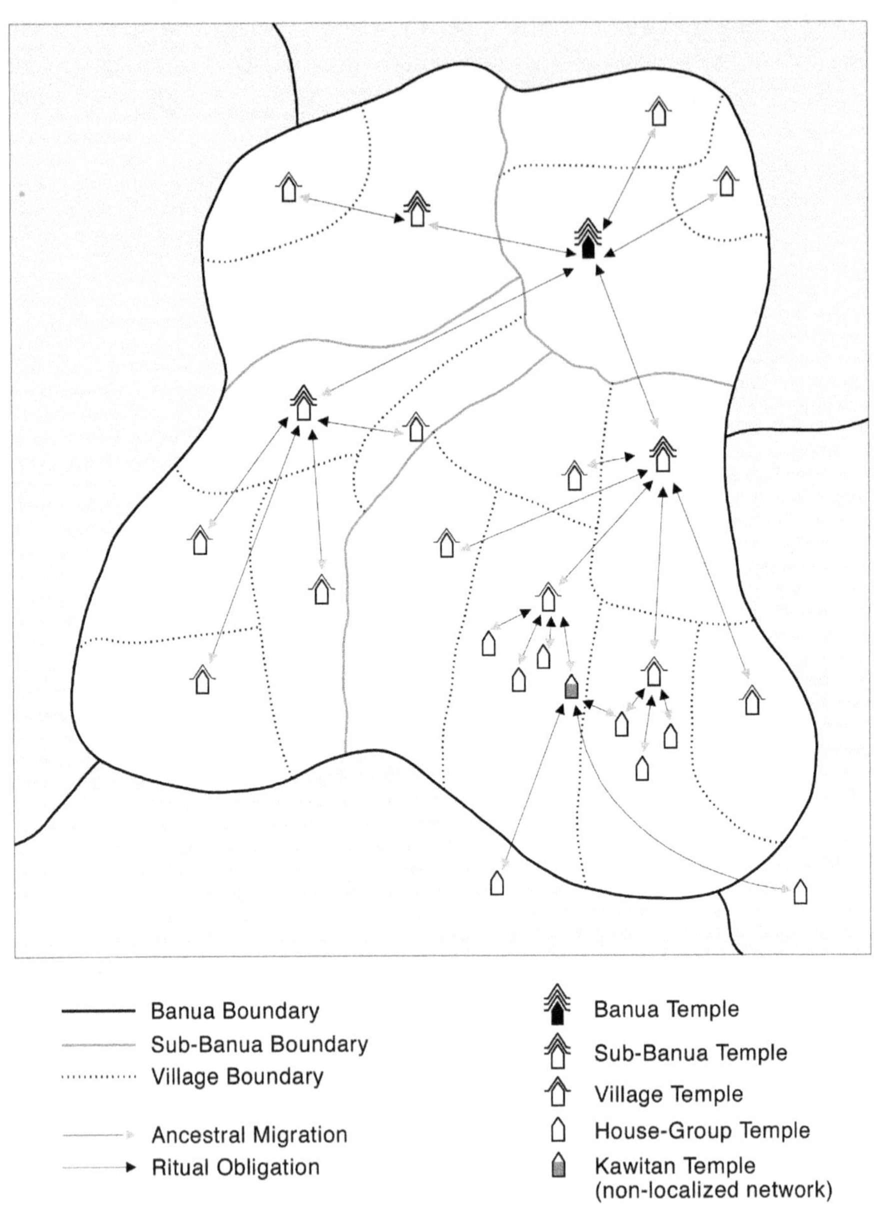

sub-domain consisting of a cluster of villages around the small regional temple Pura Tebenan. In short, the logic of the status relationship that gives an origin village ritual precedence over its branch villages can be applied recursively wherever people recognise an extended sequence of historical migrations and settlement foundation events. The length of such a historical sequence of migrations may seem unlimited theoretically, but in ritual practice connections of precedence are restricted within the more narrow confines of a socially recognised history. My research has shown that the depth of ancestral origin and migration connections in a domain usually amounts to only two layers (origin and branch), and rarely exceeds three layers, as depicted in Figure 2 (see Reuter 2002a). Four layers are very rare, and I have no example of a five-tiered domain.[5] The pattern shown in Figure 2 may look much like a network of ancestor temples, and in some ways it is. However, what we are dealing with here is not a simple kinship system nor a complex one, but a Lévi-Straussian house society in a ritualised modality (see Reuter 2002b). The organising principle is a sequence of inhabited places represented symbolically by sacred ancestor houses or 'temples'. These sacred houses are ranked in order of their foundation. In short, the contemporary order of ritual obligations maps and retraces a path of origin through a socio-historically inscribed landscape.

The emphasis in this system of social relations lies on a series of place names within a landscape rather than on personal names in a genealogy. Villagers in the highlands are unable to recount a genealogy of named predecessors from themselves all the way back to either the clan or village founders, let alone the domain founders. People's genealogical memory usually spans no more than four generations, and rights to an inheritance as well as duties to ritually post-humanise recently deceased predecessors are serious issues only within that range. Beyond four generations, what serves as a means of connecting people within kin groups are once again links between sacred places, rather than named ancestors. The connections in this case are between older and newer ancestral 'origin temples' or *sanggah kamulan*, the private temples of groups of agnates whose individual houses are usually located within a single compound. The older temples in a sequence of source and branch *sanggah* become *sanggah gede* (great *sanggah*) and the oldest *sanggah* within a clan is elevated eventually to the status of a so-called *pura kawitan* ('temple of the source, beginning, or trunk').[6] One reason for this reliance on place markers and forgetfulness of personal ancestor names was that despite their agnatic ideology and patrilocal residence, members of Balinese kin groups in fact often chose to incorporate male outsiders through uxurilocal marriages (*nyentana*) and strategic adoptions.

This openness of place-based categories is even more evident at a village or domain level. Villages may afford a special status to members of the houses of the founding emigrants who originated from an older source village. In most villages, however, there are also newcomer houses founded by more recent immigrants from elsewhere. At a domain level, flexibility about ancestry is manifest in the fact that sometimes entire villages are said to have been founded by immigrants who were not at all related to the source of the domain by descent. Their relationship to the source was established on the basis of their use of domain land, which incurred a ritual debt that had to be paid in accordance with the customs of the domain. In this way, newcomer settlements were culturally and ritually incorporated to such an extent that they soon became difficult to distinguish from genuine branch villages that were founded by emigrants from the source village (Reuter 1999).

On whatever level of organisation they may operate, models of human relations that are based on 'place' rather than 'name' have the advantage of greater inclusiveness, of being able to accommodate a diversity of people within its folds. This is all very well, but encounters with newcomers also need to be regulated. People will tend to protect their land and other resources from new claimants unless they have a good reason for sharing. This problem returns me to my second task, that is, to analyse processes of memorising and reconstructing the past which serve as a strategy for negotiating and contesting the distribution of land and other resources.

I will approach this analytical task first at the village level. The most important aspect of history to be either actively remembered or conveniently forgotten in this context is that certain people are the agnatic descendents of the village founders, or literally, 'the people of the trunk' (*wedan*), while others are not. This distinction is almost universally necessary given that village founders were nearly always joined by unrelated immigrants later on, by 'newcomers' or, literally, 'people of the leaf' (*pendonan*). In an agrarian society such newcomers required land and as long as vacant land was still available it was freely given. Indeed, newcomers were rather welcome because together with a share of land, they were also given a share of the fixed cost of celebrating the festivals of the village temples in honour of the founding ancestors and spiritual owner-caretakers of that land. In most highland villages, though not in all, land was thus given to the newcomers outright rather than being leased to them as dependent clients or sharecroppers.

In most cases, the botanic metaphor-based distinction of trunk and leaf people thus has limited significance when it comes to controlling access to land. While members of the villages founder group tended to have larger landholdings overall, newcomers had to be given villages land or sufficient other land to be able to make a living. The twofold social classification of *wedan* and *pendonan* is still very important, however, due to a distinction between two types of land, namely 'village land' (*tanah ayahan desa*) and 'owned land' (*tanah milik*). [7] Only the men who farm classificatory village land are represented in the community's seniority-ranked council of elders and priest-leaders, while others are not. The council (*ulu apad*) consists of the male heads of eligible households and meets on new and full moons in the village longhouse. Divided into ceremonial moieties, the men sit in order of precedence (depending on when they became married householders) on the massive side beams of the longhouse floor, with the ranks decreasing from the tip (and uphill) to the trunk (downhill) end of the beam (compare with the *nili ele* councils of Seram, Boulan-Smit, this volume).[8]

Belonging to the people of the village trunk or an early, now fully integrated immigrant group that has been admitted into the village council thus signifies access to political and ritual authority. In short, material resources, in the form of land, were given away for two reasons: to share the material costs of ritual with others and to acquire symbolic resources in relation to these others. These symbolic resources take the form of ritual and political authority over a group of client households which are economically independent.

Contemporary *banua* have much less relevance for land usage rights than *desa*. A ritual domain is not at all definable as a landowning corporation, whereas a *village* can be, or at least formerly could be, classified as such. Prior to Indonesian independence, village land was often owned by residents collectively and in many cases individual plots of land were rotated continuously from recently defunct households of older, retired or widowed couples to the households of newly married couples, irrespective of any relationship by descent between them. After following a shift from subsistence agriculture to cash crops such as coffee, which require long-term labour investments, this rotation system was abandoned in many villages in favour of a de facto inheritance system, whereby the special character of 'communal land' became more and more nominal (see also Waelty 1993). In other villages all land has been classified as 'privately owned' for as long as anyone can remember, and is passed on by inheritance within kin groups.[9] In both types of villages, the introduction of new legal codes by the Dutch and Indonesian governments has encouraged a shift to more modern notions of landownership, especially from the 1970s onwards. Nevertheless, there is no such thing as individual landownership free of ritual obligations in highland Bali.

There is evidence that the *banua* was still relevant for maintaining land claims until the 1930s and the *desa* has remained important until today. Occupants of classificatory village land can be dispossessed if they fail to meet their ritual responsibilities to the *desa* and, theoretically at least, to the *banua* of which it is a part. Individual ownership of so-called 'private land' (*tanah milik pribadi*) is also contingent on meeting ritual obligations towards the village (*desa*) or the hamlet (*banjar*), or both, as well as social obligations towards one's extended kin group (at least for as long as the older generation can delay a formal transfer of land certificates to their heirs). Even the non-resident owners of land used for commercial purposes are subject to a ritual levy for village and local domain temples.

This evidence suggests a historical process whereby land as a material resource always remained under the control of relatively small units of social organisation. In addition, as I have argued earlier, there has been a longstanding principle of allowing or even encouraging the alienation of material resources for the sake of gaining symbolic resources, namely in the course of accommodating immigrants and newcomers into a house, village or domain. Indeed, even the more regular mode of *banua* expansion, through a process of emigration, is posited quite explicitly on a granting of material autonomy to branch villages while the source village retains a privileged access to symbolic resources. In short, the apparent tendency towards a gradual devolution of material resource control to smaller, subsidiary social units is in fact the result of the growth of originally small units of ritual organisation, such as single villages, into larger units, which are concerned increasingly with the distribution and control of symbolic resources rather than land usage rights or other material resources.

The ritual process of a gradual post-humanisation or deification of ancestral founders follows a similar logical pattern, in that gains in spiritual status are accompanied by the loss of material bodies, in successive layers of decreasing density (from *kasar* to *halus*). One possible explanation for this historical process of ritual alliance-building might be that alternative coercive means, which would have allowed for a similar expansion of the social order by an accumulation of material power, were never available to any group within Bali Aga society, which has been politically marginal as a whole for centuries.

Within a village, to control symbolic resources means to have ritual status as well as political authority. The people of the trunk who man the village council are not only the ritual leaders, they make and amend local customary regulations, settle disputes, impose sanctions and take political decisions on behalf of the community as a whole. In a domain, by contrast, the source village does not wield any such power in relation to branch villages outside the context of the annual ritual of the domain temple and perhaps in a number of other ritual matters. There is a political link between *desa* and *banua*, however, insofar as any claim to village founder status and associated rights is a local historical claim embedded in a wider domain history. The *banua* as a whole may be said to have a political dimension as well, but the orientation of this politics is toward participants' relationships with the outside world rather than an internal politics of land rights. Ritual domains have served as a powerful means for organising Bali Aga responses to a wider world beyond the highlands, a world that, I believe, would have long swallowed them up if it had not been for their intricate ritual networks of regional integration and cooperation. [10]

I would now like to retell the origin narrative of a particular *banua* in order to illustrate that local participants themselves also reflect on this shift in significance in historically expanding place-based social categories, as they are transformed from material into symbolic resource pools. The example I have chosen is a narrative that describes how the village of Tebenan is transformed into the depopulated ritual centre of a sub-domain.

Once a group of subjects approached the king of Bali at his residence near the ancient regional temple of Penulisan to ask leave for establishing a new settlement 'downhill' or *teben*. He granted their request for land, but also warned that disaster was sure to befall them if their village council were to grow beyond a membership of 33 household heads. The new village was called Tebenan to commemorate its origin from upstream Penulisan. Its rice fields were fertile, people's lives were leisurely, and soon the population grew until the village council had a membership of 200 heads of households. It then happened that a ritual was planned in which a deer was to be sacrificed, offered to the gods, and divided among the council members. But much of the forest had been cleared and deer were hard to find. On the day of the ritual, the hunting party finally returned with a small animal. Once the victim had been sacrificed and divided, the meat portions obtained were fewer than the number of eligible members. Arguments began, a fight broke out, even brothers killed one another, and the survivors were scattered in the eight directions of the compass as leaves blown by a wind. They founded eight new villages: Ulian, Gunung Bau, Bunutin, Langahan, Pausan, Bukhi, Bayung Cerik and Manikliyu, closest to the old Tebenan. The land was plentiful, but their lives were short, their labour hard and fruitless. Then the senior priest-leader (*kubayan*) of Manikliyu had a dream in which he learned that their lot would improve if only they remembered their common origin and resumed the cult of the village temple of the abandoned Tebenan. He enticed people to search for the foundations of the forgotten temple in the forest, and they uncovered nine [i.e., eight around a centre] sacred xylophone 'leaves' (*don selunding*), indicating that they had found the precise site of the old temple. The former village temple was then rebuilt to become a sub-regional temple. Ever since, the *banua* of eight villages has gathered there for an annual joint ceremony to honour their deified ancestors and to ask for a blessing upon their crops. Until today there may not be more than 33 elders in the 'village council' of Manikliyu. Before these elders take their ritual meal after a new moon meeting, they speak these words: 'King's men, insiders, elders of the heart, shoulder, elbow ... [and so forth in order of rank]. Come together, there are more food portions than people!'

The present origin narrative confirms Desa Manikliyu's role as a ritual leader among the eight villages of this sub-domain. The origin point of the sub-domain is identified as Pura Tebenan. The reference to the higher authority of the ancient kings of Penulisan, as the ultimate and now deified overlords of the land, reflects the fact that all villages in this sub-*banua* also participate within the larger ritual order around Pura Penulisan.

When their usage in specific social contexts is taken into consideration it becomes evident that the origin narratives of a domain cannot be interpreted as disembodied texts. A structural analysis might reveal their intrinsic logic and the pattern of relations between their conceptual constituents, but even these elements have a contingent or non-intrinsic meaning. As Paul Ricoeur (1981: 217) has argued, narratives of origin bear reference to a cultural world per se but also to particular situations within that world.

Bali Aga origin narratives are rarely written down, they are not recited formally in ritual contexts, nor are they told in a ritual language marked by distinct formal characteristics. Most often origin narratives are retold spontaneously among a group of priests, elders and ordinary participants during the quieter moments of a festival at a *banua* temple. Their conversation can be described as a 'discussion' insofar as there is much room for polite disagreement about the narrative's content and interpretation. Therefore each narrative must be seen not as a monolithic text but as a tentative consensus reached by particular people at a particular time and place.

At the same time, such narratives also refer to a shared material world and a shared way of life, and thus contain non-ostensive references that bear meaning beyond any of the specific contexts in which the narrative might be retold and discussed. I agree with Ricoeur that origin narratives are not only the focus of a conflict of interpretations but may also depict important existential conflicts or 'boundary situations' in the world, which are of general relevance. A compromise approach towards the interpretation of myths of origin may thus be: to *hear* them, as the spoken discourse of specific authors with specific intentions, and simultaneously to *read* them, as the textual testimony of a collective world of shared experience and knowledge.

The tale of Pura Tebenan, if it is read rather than heard, illustrates how the social unity of a domain is contingent on the symbolic labour of recollecting and re-enacting a common origin. The path of origin is marked first by a lateral expansion, by the growth of a new branch domain out of the unity of the Penulisan domain. Then a second expansion is caused by the violent rupture of the village unity represented by what is now the Tebenan sub-domain temple. Processes of lateral expansion or sudden fission establish relationships between parts and a whole embodied as a sacred origin point. With each progressive differentiation, the degree of 'social unity' is diminished in the more immediate sense because the people involved no longer share the same, finite material resources of a single village. The idea of a social unity, however, is reintroduced simultaneously at a broader, more symbolic level by bringing several villages together in the ritual context of the origin temple and its ceremonial order.

The idea that only a finite number of people can derive a reasonable share from a single sacrifice may be taken as a metaphor, suggesting that in any given place there is a natural limit for sustainable solidarity on a material plane. This limit is often violated. The narrative hints at a golden mean, to be achieved by avoiding a practical condition of scarcity that arises from the togetherness of too many people in one place, and an equally undesirable condition of social isolation, which would arise if one were to define the small world of a single village as the only relevant sphere of social interaction. The problem of negotiating this balance is the archetypal 'boundary situation' in the world, which this origin narrative addresses. The proposed solution is to allocate material and symbolic concerns to separately conceived levels of social interaction. Thus, the narrative can be read as a culture-specific commentary on a general dilemma of social cooperation and competition in agrarian communities with finite land and expanding populations. It also illustrates some of the historical processes involved in the evolution of larger, regional social institutions, which in turn may have facilitated the emergence of small states (*negara*) in South-East Asia and in other parts of the Austronesian world.

Concluding Remarks

The highlands of Bali are divided into *banua* or ritual domains. These domains are spatially bounded alliances of several or even dozens of villages around a ceremonial centre in the oldest or source village, which signifies their common point of origin. *Banua* are said to have been established as emigrants from the source village or immigrants from elsewhere founded new settlements within its existing territories. Participating in the ceremonial life of village and domain temples, in the cult of the guardian spirits of the land, was and to some extent still is a way to assert the right to use that land. It is also much more. Domains, and the villages and houses within them, are not just stretches of usable land to people, they are sacred places of meaning. Temples are the markers of such sacred places and help to map complex identities arising from a complex history of migration.

The more distant events in this history, especially, are no longer concerned with the assertion of land rights but with the distribution of non-material resources within regional symbolic economies. The *banua*, from a historical perspective, is situated well beyond the boundary condition where material resource scarcity began to outweigh the benefits of practical cooperation. *Banua* temples are the spatial markers of the most distant events in origin history, the abode of the most completely disembodied or post-humanised beings, and the social stage on which struggles for the most refined, symbolic resources become the paramount theme.

I should add here that participants' personal concern with spiritual obligation is a powerful motivation independent of their concerns about relative status. People have a very immediate and highly personal bond to the ancestral land that keeps them physically alive, and to the history inscribed on it, the ritual path of origin that one day will lead them also to a post-human state of immortality. They also very much enjoy their participation in the larger ritual community of a domain. For the time being, these sentiments and associated local regulations have helped to preserve people's spiritual relationship to their land despite significant changes to the official, legal conceptualisation of land ownership that has occurred in Indonesia under Dutch rule and in the course of a number of land reforms since independence.

References

Ardika, Wayan and Peter Bellwood. 1991. 'Sembiran: The Beginnings of Indian Contact with Bali.' *Antiquity*, 65 (247). Pp.221-32.

Bernet-Kempers, A.J. 1991. *Monumental Bali: Introduction to Balinese Archaeology*. Berkeley: Periplus Editions.

Geertz, Clifford 1980. *Negara: The Theatre State in Nineteenth-Century Bali.* Princeton (N.J.): Princeton University Press.

Howe, Leo 2001. *Hinduism & Hierarchy in Bali.* Oxford: James Currey.

Ramstedt, Martin. 1997. *Weltbild, Heilsprakmatik und Herrschaftslegitimation im vorkolonialen Bali.* Frankfurt: Peter Lang Verlag.

Reuter, Thomas A. 1998. 'The Banua of Pura Pucak Penulisan: A Ritual Domain in the Highlands of Bali.' *Review of Indonesian and Malaysian Affairs,* 32 (1).pp.55-109.

Reuter, Thomas A. 1999. 'People of the Mountains - People of the Sea: Negotiating the Local and the Foreign in Bali.' In L.H. Connor and R. Rubinstein (eds), *Staying Local in the Global Village: Bali in the Twentieth Century,* Honolulu: University of Hawai'i Press.

Reuter, Thomas A. 2002a. *Custodians of the Sacred Mountains.* Honolulu: University of Hawai'i Press.

Reuter, Thomas A. 2002b. *The House of Our Ancestors: Precedence and Dualism in the Highlands of Bali.* Leiden: KITLV Press.

Reuter, Thomas A. 2003. 'Mythical Centres'. In T.A. Reuter (ed.), *Inequality, Crisis and Social Change in Indonesia: The Muted Worlds of Bali,* London: Routledge-Curzon Press.

Ricoeur, Paul. 1981. 'The Model of the Text: Meaningful Action Considered as a Text.' In J.B. Thompson (ed.), *Paul Ricoeur: Hermeneutics and the Human Sciences,* Cambridge: Cambridge University Press.

Waelty, Samuel. 1993. 'Gemeinschaftsland und Aeltestenraete in den Bali Aga Gemeinden von Kintamani.' *Geographica Helvetica,* 1993 (1). pp.19-26.

ENDNOTES

[1] One could argue generally that in political institutions a concern with symbolic resources combines with a concern for material resources, such as having the technical means to exercise coercive force or surveillance, and that both forms of resources are needed in order to generate political power. The *banua* of highland Bali are not political institutions, however, except insofar as they create a degree of protective solidarity among the Bali Aga in relation to external threats (Reuter 2002a). Most likely these domains were de-politicised after the fall of highland kingdoms in the 14th century because the new kings in the southern lowlands would not tolerate a highland kingdom nor did they ever have the reach fully to incorporate and control the highlands. These kingdoms, while they did make use of military forces to sort out issues of competition among themselves, were also heavily reliant on the symbolic resource of ritual status as an underpinning of royal authority so as to stop dissent within the kingdom. This symbolic resource was generated either by way of the king's own involvement in ritual or by his patronage of Brahmana priests as ritual specialists (Geertz 1980; Ramstedt 1997). Similar observations could be made about small polities on other islands in the region.

[2] I am not denying that Hinduism has had a levelling influence on Bali and on the cultures of South-East Asia in general, however, there has not been any systematic campaign against local religious diversity in Bali until recently. Brahmana-dominated government Hindu organisations like Parisada Hindu Darma Indonesia have had a strong vested interest in standardizing the practice of Hinduism in Bali since Indonesian independence (Howe 2001). This agenda was largely a response to the pressures on Hindus to develop a standard code of belief and worship and some form of monotheism in order to gain recognition for Hinduism as a State-endorsed religion under the Indonesian Constitution, alongside Islam and Christianity.

[3] Hindu kingdoms, of course, have long ceased to be bona fide political institutions in modern Bali, and the historical process of traditional state formation no longer applies. Nevertheless, this change is relatively recent. Many of Bali's kings had survived colonialism as regents under Dutch indirect-rule policy, and some of their descendents still command considerable influence and wealth. MacRae's paper (this volume) further shows that traditional forms of power arising at the ritual domain-'kingdom' interface are still relevant in Bali today.

[4] For example, while there is an overlap between the domain of Pura Pucak Penulisan and that of Pura Balingkang, the reason is that the two were still one single domain until quite recently, and are still connected through ritual interactions. The domain of Pura Pucak Indrakila and the network of Pura Batur were also previously part of the domain of Pura Penulisan, whose supreme prominence probably derives from the fact that it was a major state temple for Bali's early Hindu dynasties.

[5] Note that the (branch) villages' temples are themselves origin sites and ritual centres in relation to the numerous houses or extended house groups that make up a village. The relationship between *umah* and *desa* could therefore be considered as an additional layer in an overall pattern of territorial organisation.

[6] Networks of more exclusive or kinship-oriented temples are few and not very well formed in this part of Bali. These essentially inter-local networks seem to be more or less a southern Balinese innovation, which spread from aristocratic circles to commoners and has found its way into the highlands only in very recent times. Note the use of botanic metaphors to express the notion of origin and precedence.

[7] The word *ayahan* is the noun form of Balinese *ngayah,* to work. This refers to the right of working a piece of communally owned land and the duty to perform a substantial amount of ritual labour in the context of village temple festivals, as well as paying a share of the ritual expenses incurred. Note that 'owned land' often refers to forested land that was cleared by newcomers who did not receive village land.

[8] Botanic and body metaphors are used prolifically by the Bali Aga in reference to village councils, *banua* and many other aspects of their social organisation.

[9] In villages where all land is privately owned, the distinction between founders and newcomers is maintained simply by forbidding the sons of newcomers to join the village council. In a way, newcomers are kept out even more systematically in these communities because land ownership as such is not enough to be a full citizen of the village. In other villages, newcomers gained entry into the council because they were given a plot of classificatory 'village land'. In some cases, *tanah milik* owners also became integrated. In those cases the distinction between the two types of land was eventually ignored to allow a recruitment of new village members, which reduced the cost of temple rituals per household. There is some historical evidence to suggest that such open recruitment tended to follow sudden population losses caused by a short-term famine or an epidemic.

[10] An argument could be made that the ritual order of the *banua* is more specifically religious and less political in its character than the *desa*. It is difficult to say, however, whether this is yet another manifestation of a principle whereby larger social categories become concerned with more and more 'refined' (more exclusively symbolic) types of resources. It could well be that the lack of a stronger political dimension in the *banua* is simply the result of a wider Balinese political scenario in which the highlands were unable to establish a more highly developed form of political unity.

Chapter 4. *Banua* or *Negara*? The Culture of Land in South Bali

Graeme MacRae

Land has always been a critical resource in the successive political economies of south Bali, and not surprisingly, it has also been deeply embedded in a rich matrix of cultural meanings. [1] This ,was evident to the earliest foreign observers—'There is a ... correlation of the ... people with ... the land' (Covarrubias 1994: 11, see also pp. 59, 84)—and has remained so until relatively recently. In the past generation, however, land has been relocated substantially from this matrix of meaning into something increasingly resembling the universal capitalist commodity hidden in the misleading term 'real estate', with all the attendant emptying-out of traditional meaning. This has happened primarily through its massive revaluation and inflation as a primary resource in an economy dominated by tourism as well as systematic attempts by the National Government, aided and abetted by foreign agencies, to 'free' it from the bonds of traditional forms of tenure and make it available to the widest possible market.

This process has been further aided at a more subtle psycho-cultural level by the phenomenological effects of various technologies that have progressively diluted and obscured the once-powerful and awe-inspiring daily (and particularly nightly) experience of landscape. Roads have connected places, such as the mountains or distant kingdoms, once awesome for their sheer remoteness. Motor vehicles have reduced distances of days to a matter of hours and their omnipresent noise, smell and sheer mechanical power have annulled much of the direct sensory experience of landscape, which was integral to the knowledge of previous generations. Kerosene lamps, battery-powered torches and more recently electric lighting penetrate the veil of darkness that once obscured the *sekala* (natural world), allowing people to glimpse the *niskala* (supernatural world) beyond. Radio, television and electronic amplification have pushed aside the sounds of bamboo rustling in the wind, the fading notes of a distant gamelan or even the stately creak of an ancient Dutch bicycle. People born since about 1970 have little or no experience of the landscape unmediated by these technologies, and when I ask them for directions they reply in terms of gas stations and hotels rather than *waringin* trees or temples.

I have discussed elsewhere some political-economic aspects of land in south Bali (MacRae 2003). The purpose of this chapter is to consider the matrix of meaning and customary practices in which land was and to some extent still is embedded. As with the political-economic dimension, from which they can never be entirely separated, these occur in the context of concrete historical processes.

The land has always been there, a primary element of human experience, and successive cultural and political orders have made their own sense and inscribed their own meanings on it. Some recent transformations of these have been touched on above, but the primary axis around which this discussion revolves is the extent to which 'traditional' ideas and practices to do with land might usefully be seen in terms of ancient, pre-Indic forms, common to a degree throughout the Austronesian world and evident especially in the Bali Aga forms described by Reuter (this volume).

The Cultural Landscape of South Bali

The south-central quarter of Bali is a wedge of land, sloping down and out from the central mountains, steeply at first, then flattening onto a coastal plain several kilometres wide. The soil is predominantly volcanic ash (*paras*), fertile and soft, allowing the rivers flowing down from the mountains to cut deep gorges, dividing the land into long tapering radial strips. In these gorges are remnants of the original rainforest that once covered most of the island while the strips between, some little more than ridges, others relatively flat and a kilometre or more wide, are terraced, irrigated and planted with rice and secondary crops such as sweet potato, interspersed with rows of coconut palms.

This landscape is divided, in traditional Balinese thinking, into two primary categories: wild forest (*alas* or [BI] *hutan*) and land that has been brought into human cultivation and ritual order (Boon 1977: 99). [2] *Alas* is inhabited by all manner of unseen (*niskala*) beings that are potentially disruptive and even dangerous to human life. When it is occupied by humans, the forest is cut, social and spatial institutions are established and ritual processes initiated to maintain harmony between human and *niskala* inhabitants. [3]

A well-known origin story in this part of Bali concerns Rsi Markandeya, a holy man from East Java, who came, with followers, to establish a community in the wilderness of Bali. They began cutting (*marabas*) forest by the River Wos at Campuan near Ubud, but were attacked by wild animals and diseases and the expedition was abandoned. Back in Java, Markandeya, received supernatural advice that he had neglected to establish the proper ritual relationships with the *niskala* inhabitants of the place. He tried again, this time taking appropriate ritual precautions, the most important of which was the burial of five elemental metals (*panca datu*) in the soil of the new land. This time he was to be rewarded with success. They cleared the forest, divided the land into dry and irrigated fields and established the primary institutions of social, ritual and economic organisation—*banjar*, *desa* and *subak*. [4] *Banjar* is the local community organisation oriented to essential social tasks, especially the disposal of the dead. *Subak* is the organisation responsible for the collective management of irrigation water, essential to material subsistence. *Desa* is the organisation responsible for the maintenance of ritual harmony between human and *niskala* communities in a particular spatial/ecological zone. [5]

While it can be argued that *banjar* is the primary secular social unit (Guermonprez 1991), *desa* is the primary spatial and ritual unit (commonly, but somewhat misleadingly, translated as 'village')—binding local community to local landscape through collective responsibility to local deities. [6] Land is understood to belong to these deities. Humans occupy and use it on what may be described as a leasehold basis, perpetual but subject to the regular performance of collective ritual obligations. It is the *desa*, rather than individuals, which is party to this arrangement with the gods, and individual households maintain their right to occupy *desa* land (*tanah ayahan desa*) by contributing to collective ritual obligations (Boon 1977: 100-2; Covarrubias 1994: 59,84; Reuter 2002b; Stuart-Fox 2002: 42-4; Warren 1993: 38-42). These obligations take the primary form of maintaining two (or more) main temples and performing in them regular ceremonies, which the various deities associated with the *desa* are invited to visit and are then plied with offerings of music, dance, food, flowers, incense and sacrificial animals.

The two main temples are the *pura puseh* ('navel', 'centre' or 'origin' temple) and the *pura dalem* (temple of the 'great deity' of death). The *pura puseh* is associated with the origins of the *desa*, in the form of founding ancestors and life-giving water from the mountains, and is located ideally and usually towards the uphill (*kaja*) end of the *desa* territory. It usually contains, in its middle courtyard (*jaba tengah*), a pavilion known as *bale agung* (great pavilion), in which all the gods of the *desa* assemble periodically. The *pura dalem* is associated with the spirits of the dead, but not yet fully purified and deified members of the *desa*. It is located ideally and usually near the graveyard and cremation ground (*setra*) at the downhill (*kelod*) end of the *desa* territory. [7]

The walled compounds (*pekarangan*) occupied by households of the *desa* are strung along either side of the uphill-downhill road (and sometimes parallel secondary streets) between these two temples. Each house yard is occupied by a household (or set of related households) in perpetuity but subject to prescribed contributions to collective ritual (*ayahan*, literally 'work'). Such land (*pekarangan desa* or *karang ayahan desa*) might not be bought or sold. [8] Spatially, each house yard replicates the fundamental uphill-downhill orientation of the *desa* itself. [9] *Desa* are bounded laterally (east-west in this part of Bali) by the untamed space of the parallel river gorges and in the uphill-downhill direction by a neutral zone of cultivated land, which is owned by individuals and managed by *subak*.

Figure 1: Typical *Desa* layouts

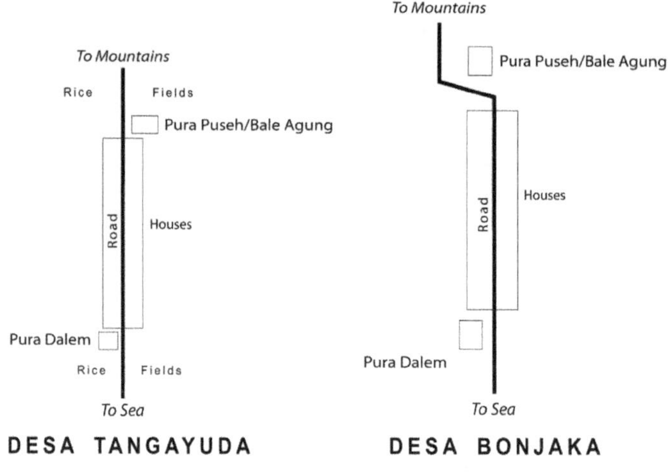

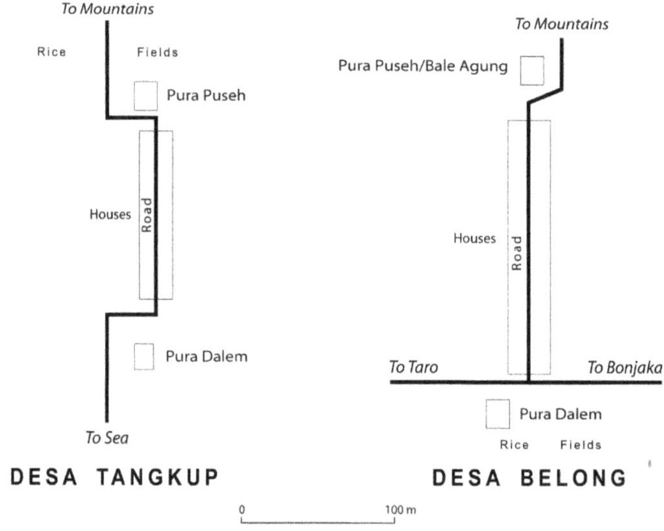

Land Tenure

While household land is held in trust by the *desa*, articulating the ritual-economic relationship between humans and gods, there are also other kinds of collectively held land. *Laba pura* is productive land reserved for the material support of particular temples. Many *desa* and temples also have land (*tanah bukti*) reserved for the support of *desa* officials (*klian, bendesa*) or temple priests (*pemangku*). Streets, pathways and other public spaces including *setra* are collective property and are maintained by *banjar*, as are local community halls (*bale banjar*).

Productive land, on the other hand, is generally privately owned, a right established initially by clearing and cultivation, later by capture and redistribution by local rulers and currently by sale and purchase.

Across this mosaic of *desa* and agricultural land are overlaid the historical designs and ambitions of a series of ruling elites, many of them descended from noble warriors of the Hindu-Javanese empire of Majapahit whose forces invaded Bali in the 14th century. They brought with them more hierarchical modes of social and political organization, which were also inscribed onto the landscape. A proportion of *desa* in this part of Bali thus have, superimposed on the linear/axial spatial organisation described above, a centric, *mandala* form, focused on a central crossroads, where rulers built *puri* (palaces), markets and temples. In most of these *desa*, the *bale agung* has been relocated to a *pura desa* in this central complex. [10]

As well as appropriating and reconfiguring the ritual (or *niskala*) landscape of *desa*, new or invading *puri* took control of substantial areas of productive land, which they allowed their subject populations to continue to cultivate through various arrangements. The most distinctive and widely used in this part of Bali was a system known as *pecatu* or *tanah ayahan puri*, by which land was made available to farmers for their subsistence in exchange not for a portion of the crop but for certain services to the *puri*. The nature of *pecatu* has been the subject of considerable debate since the attempts of the first Dutch administrators to make sense of it (Gunning and van der Heiden 1926; de Kat Angelino 1921).The debate essentially concerns the extent to which it was a system of forced labour, of patronage or a variation on traditional *desa* obligations (Boon 1977: 56; Geertz 1980: 176; Hobart et al 1996: 55; Schulte-Nordholt 1996: 60; Warren 1993: 63). It is my impression that the divergence of interpretations probably reflects as much local differences of practice and terminology as it does the relative correctness of the authors. What is significant here is that it is a system in which rights to productive land are exchanged for labour obligations. As a result, just as residential land was occupied subject to ritual obligations to the gods via the *desa*, use of much productive land became increasingly subject to corresponding obligations to *puri*. [11]

Trans-local Organisation

It is unclear what, if any forms of socio-spatial organisation larger than *desa* existed in this part of Bali before or independent of the multiplication and expansion of *puri* in the 18th century. On the one hand it is reasonable to expect that 'ritual domains' along the lines of the Bali Aga *banua* described by Reuter (this volume) might have existed, but on the other, the evidence of local oral history suggests that the settlement of much of the area coincided with rather than predated *puri* expansion.

The anthropological record is also somewhat ambiguous on this subject. While the Dutch scholarly colonial orthodoxy that 'the village forms a closed, self-contained unit' (Goris 1984: 79) has long since fallen from favour, subsequent writers continued to take for granted the village as the natural unit of analysis.[12] This focus has been at the expense of recognising modes of organisation beyond and between villages. The existence of such modes of organisation is, however, evident in the literature. This evidence includes:

1. Seasonal migrations of *barong* and performing art troupes between villages and/or temples (Lansing 1983; Mead 1970).
2. The formation of links between villages through temples (Bateson 1970; Boon 1977: 100).
3. Groups of 'mother-daughter' villages in East Karangasem and Batur-Kintamani areas (Boon 1997: 104-5; Covarrubias 1994: 58, Goris 1969: 107-8, 1984: 96, Stuart-Fox 2002: 49-51).
4. Royal patronage of local temples and systems of 'state temples' at central, uphill and seaward extremities of kingdoms.
5. The travels of Rsi Markandeya (Howe 1980: 13, Stuart-Fox 2002: 261-3) or other mytho-historical connections (Boon 1977: 100).
6. Market networks (Hobart 1979: 69-74).

Despite such widespread evidence, the implications have not been pursued systematically with the exceptions of Lansing's (1991) work on water temples, Schulte-Nordholt's (1988a, 1991a,1991b) on pre-colonial state temples, and Reuter's (1998, 2002a) more recent work on Bali Aga *banua*. None of these refer to the ordinary villages and temples of south Bali. Recent ethnographic evidence, however, indicates traces of *banua*-like forms, especially the further one moves uphill from the *puri* centres of Ubud, Tegallalang and Payangan, towards the more unequivocally Bali Aga areas documented by Reuter.[13]

For example, Desa Sebatu, according to local tradition never subject to *puri* control, is the centre of a network of some five *desa* linked by reciprocal ritual ties. They are not, however, referred to as a named collective entity. The ritual cycle in these *desa* is, as in mountain *banua*, tied to the old lunar calendar (*sasih*) rather than the Hindu-Javanese one (*wuku*). On the other hand, they utilise the services of Brahman high priests (*pendeta*) in some of their rituals, which is evidence of influence from the Majapahit lowlands.

In nearby Pųjung (Talepud), Leo Howe (1980: 13-27) reports a similar blend of lowland and highland customs, as well as local oral traditions including a version of the Rsi Markandeya story, which link Talepud to nearby *desa*. Unfortunately, he gives little detail of contemporary practices of trans-*desa* organisation. According to my inquiries in Pujung in 1996, however, it is the centre of a group of nine ritually linked *desa* but these are not referred to as a *banua*. *Pendeta* do not officiate at temple rituals here and the ritual cycle is tied neither to the lunar nor *wuku* calendars, but to the local cycle of the traditional rice crop. The form and seating arrangements of *desa* meetings likewise appear to be a fusion of elements characteristic of mountain and lowland forms. Local opinion, however, sees it more as the transplantation of the forms of their village of origin in Karangasem (East Bali), forms that are themselves more consistent with those Reuter characterises as Bali Aga.

Immediately downhill of Pujung and Sebatu are a number of small *desa* (e.g, Kebon, Tangkup, Cebok), which have no *bale agung* of their own but share that of the older village from which they originated (e.g, Kedisan)—a mode of relationship consistent with processes of linkage in both the mountains and East Bali (Reuter 2002: 38-41; Stuart-Fox 2002: 46-51). At roughly the same elevation and a couple of ridge/valley systems to the west, near Payangan, is yet another group of eight *desa,* linked to a shared temple, known as Pura Banua, in Desa Bukian. Unlike the category of Bali Aga temples of the same name (*pura banua*), this Pura Banua is not understood as the centre of a ritual domain so much as a regional temple with a unique history. According to local oral narratives, its origin lies not in a ritual alliance but a defensive one, at the time of the Payangan wars of 1843, with the temple being a place of assembly in times of crisis. However, the term and metaphor of *banua* was chosen, which suggests familiarity with the concept, and, as Reuter (2002: 80) notes, this area is one of the few *puri*-dominated areas with strong ritual links to Bali Aga temples. [14]

The evidence of all of these examples consists merely of traces of various kinds, and there is no evidence of systematic organisation or a sense of collective identity as in the mountain *banua*. David Stuart-Fox (2002: 46-51), writing of similar but different groupings of villages further east in Bali, reminds us, however, that no matter how ancient and timeless they may appear, all these groupings of villages are the result of concrete historical processes. I would suggest furthermore that it is to these processes that we need look if we are to understand their contemporary forms; a point to which we will return later.

If we look further downhill, where the political and ritual dominance of *puri* increases there is progressively less evidence of such forms or of 'ritual domains' (*banua*) other than pre-colonial 'kingdoms' (*negara*). This would suggest that *banua* are either a form distinctive to the mountain regions for some reason, or that they have been eliminated or obscured in the areas subject to Majapahit *puri* domination. There remains, however, the evidence listed above, even in relatively downhill areas, of elements of inter-*desa* organisation, articulated through links between temples. Are they *negara* or *banua* or something else? The remainder of this paper considers this question by summarising and examining my own ethnographic evidence of a more substantial network of linkages in the upper Wos Valley.

The 'Ritual Domain' of the Wos Valley

> Village temples ... are linked together in a given area by hereditary ties or because of allegiance to a princely house or to that of a Brahmana high priest. Thus to the head temple on the day of its yearly festival will come the members and the priests from a number of tributary temples round about, bearing their gods in procession, accompanied by their gamelan orchestras, with spears and banners and all ceremonial regalia, and bringing also the Barong and the Rangda. *(Jane Belo 1949: 40)*

At Campuan, in the gorge just west of Ubud, above a fork in the River Wos, is the temple Pura Gunung Lebah. The name means literally 'low mountain', 'below the mountain' or 'the mountain below'. It is held in local lore to be especially sacred but it does not fit unambiguously into the conventional scheme of local temples. It is specific neither to *desa* nor to any one clearly defined group. The *ayahan* is performed by a group of *subak* around Ubud and the people of Banjar Taman Kelod, working on behalf of Puri Ubud. [15] Its major *palingih* (sitting-places for visiting deities) are two pagoda-like towers (*meru*)—a seven-tiered one for the resident deity of Gunung Lebah and a five-tiered one for Bhatari Sri Batur (the goddess of Mt/Lake Batur).

At the beginning of anniversary ceremonies (*odalan*), processions arrive from Ubud and from a circle of villages approximately centred on the temple. These people bring their *barong* (gods in the form of large animal puppets) and other sacred objects, most of which were made, donated by, or in some other way connected to the *puri*. In explaining their relationship with the temple, they refer to these connections and also to Rsi Markandeya and his travel up the Wos Valley.

Pura Gunung Lebah has a range of associations and meanings, constituted in different ways. It is (a) the *pura masceti* (regional irrigation temple) for a group of *subak*, (b) a royal temple of the *puri*, and is associated (c) with a group of villages, including Ubud, and their *barong*, (d) with the travels of Rsi Markandeya, (e) with the Wos Valley as far as Taro, and is finally (f) a visiting place (*pasimpangan*) for the goddess of Mt/Lake Batur. These connections are articulated through the temple but are not organised around a single consistent set of ideas. They are constituted variously through more or less defined groups of people, through the static form of land and the dynamic of flowing water and through hazily remembered mythologies and the regular visits of gods. [16]

Figure 2: The Pura Gunung Lebah network

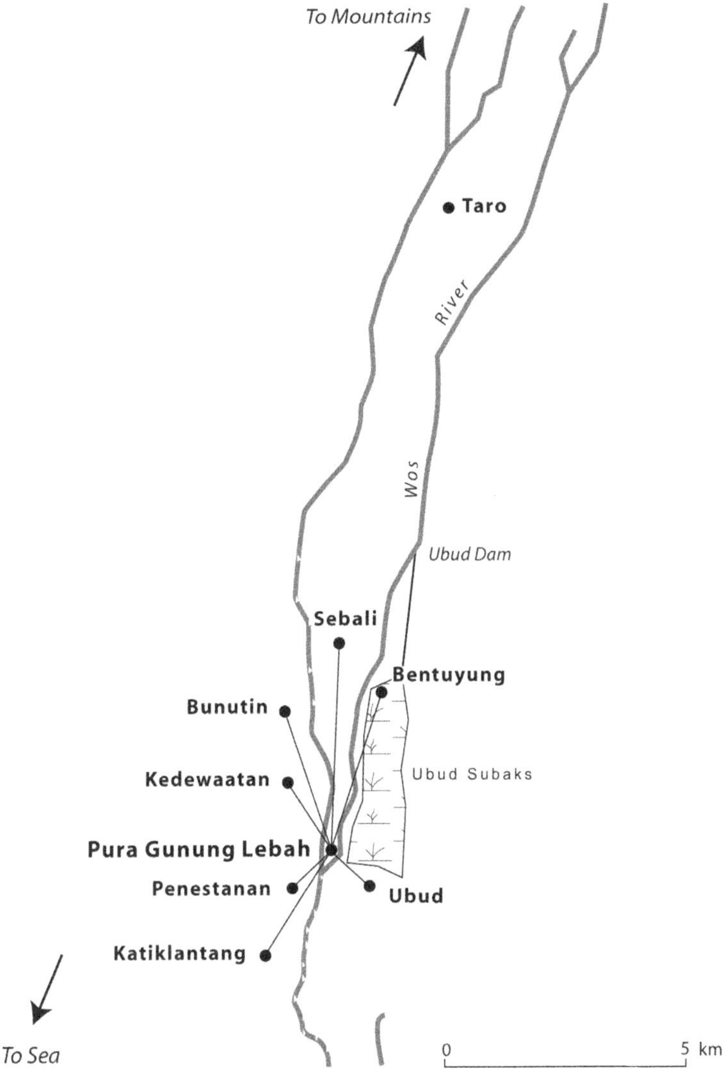

Many of the *desa* connected to Pura Gunung Lebah are themselves linked in similar ways to others around Ubud and eventually to others all the way up the Wos Valley. The net result of these linkages may be described as a network of villages and temples within a more or less defined region. This network takes the form not of a single grid but of several imperfectly overlapping ones constituted variously in the dimensions of topography, hydrology, irrigation, mythology, history, *barong* migrations and temple connections. The following sections summarise these 'layers' of linkage.

Figure 3: The Wos Valley

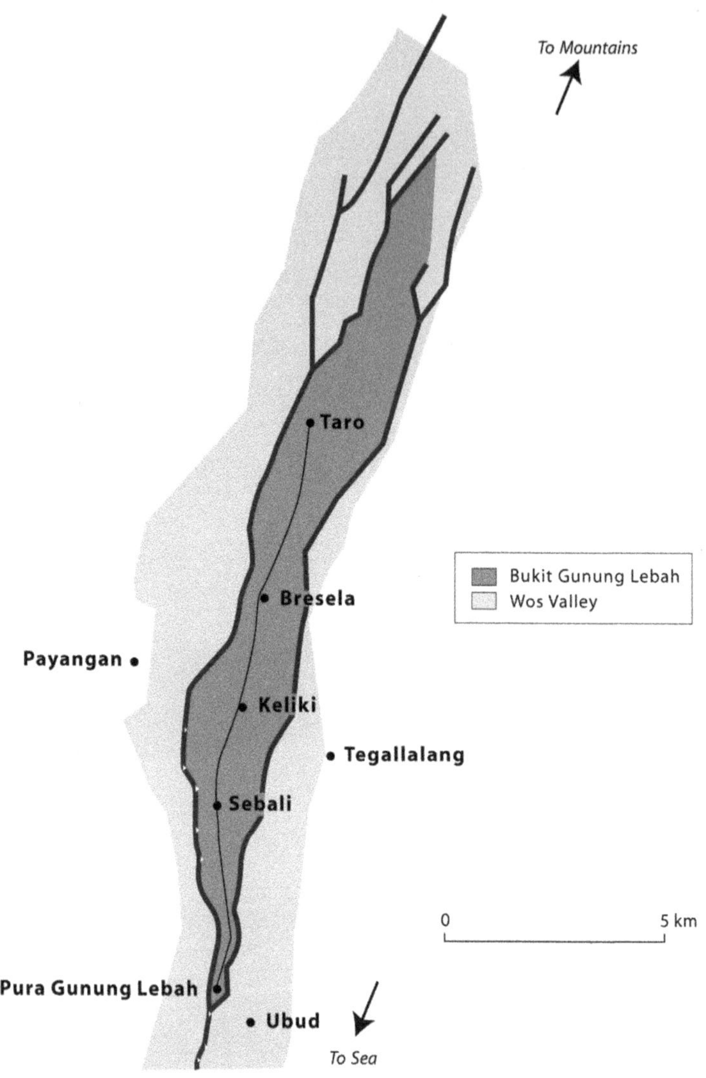

Irrigation

Pura Gunung Lebah sits on the lower end of a ridge (*bukit*). This narrow ridge, never more than two kilometres across, runs uphill, between two deep, forested ravines in which flow the east and west arms of the Wos, until it flattens out onto the plateau flanking the crater of Gunung Batur. On either side of this double valley run the parallel ridge roads through the major villages and court centres of Peliatan-Tegallalang-Pujung and Sayan-Kedewatan-Payangan.

Figure 4: The Upper Wos Valley: irrigation

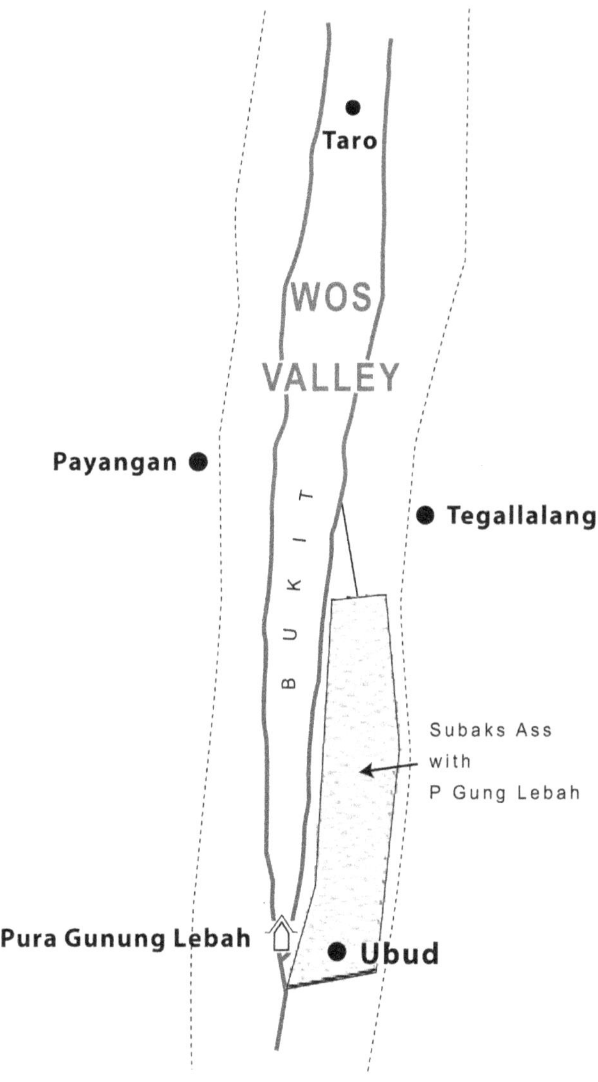

Along the central ridge are a series of villages strung along a narrow road. The gradient is gentle and easily traversed and the distances between settlements are generally no more than a kilometre. The intermediate *sawah* (irrigated rice fields) are traditionally worked by families of both, or even other, villages, and there are few obstacles to up-down-*bukit* travel. Irrigation and *sawah* ownership tend to cross village boundaries and collective maintenance and management of the irrigation system necessitates a degree of cooperation between upstream -downstream neighbours.

Figure 5: The Upper Wos Valley: Rsi Markandeya's journey

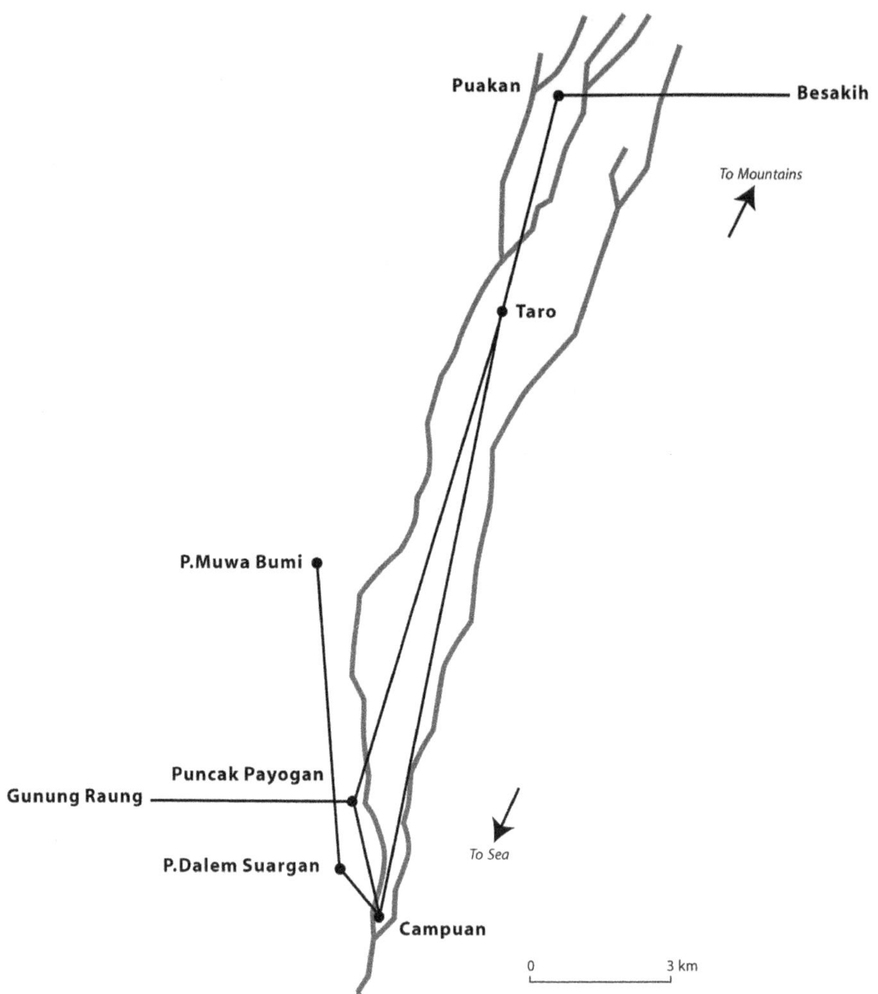

Balinese irrigation is gravity-fed and flows from mountain lakes and springs. Because of the depth of the river gorges, water is channelled from sources far upstream of the fields it irrigates and can be used only within the valley in which it originates. This basic hydrological form configures irrigation, like the land itself, into a set of long, narrow systems that depend on cooperation between upstream and downstream users of the system. [17]

Within the Wos Valley, the rice fields along the *bukit* from Bankiangsidem to above Taro are irrigated from dams on the two inner arms of the Wos. Although these *subak* are within the area associated with Pura Gunung Lebah, they do not relate to it as their *pura masceti*. Conversely, the primary congregation of the temple in its function as *pura masceti* are *subak*, which are physically located outside the *bukit* but draw their water from a dam on the Wos. Land and irrigation are separated ritually and the area served by Pura Gunung Lebah in its function as an irrigation temple does not correspond physically with the area with which it is connected in other ways.

Rsi Markandeya

Throughout the Wos Valley, the Markandeya story is trundled out routinely in response to questions about the foundation of local villages and temples. The details vary and village people frequently refer to Puri Ubud or to published versions for the 'complete' or 'correct' story. [18]

Although not all the places mentioned in these stories are confined, even in the most parochial versions, to the *bukit*, the story serves to identify the poles of Campuan and Taro and an axis between them and to identify these with the foundations of Balinese civilisation. To its inhabitants, this area is known by such names as Ujung Taro, Bukit Taro, Gunung Taro, Gunung Raung or Bukit Gunung Lebah and is replete with material evidence of Rsi Markandeya's exploits, mostly in the form of temples.

The Migratory Habits of Barong

Barong, 'at once the most familiar and the most obscure' figures in Balinese tradition (Spies and de Zoete 1973: 93) are known to everyone but understood only in contradictory ways by relatively few people. [19] They are essentially creatures of place, associated with *desa* and their territories, which they patrol seasonally to prevent the entry of unwanted influences. As Mead (1970) observed, they are subject also to a season of migration during which they might wander promiscuously performing as their will or habit takes them. They also practice a third, more regulated kind of migration: mutual visiting, along with other sacred objects (*pretima*), at temple ceremonies. It is through these visits that contemporary ritual links between villages in the Wos Valley are most readily traced.

For example, at the *odalan* of Pura Jemeng in Sebali, in addition to three *barong* from local temples, others are (usually) brought from Keliki, Lungsiakan, Ubud and Bentuyung. Likewise, reciprocally, the resident *barong* at Pura Jemeng attends *odalan* at the home temples of all these *barong* and at Pura Gunung Lebah. Keliki is immediately up-*bukit* of Sebali, with which it has close historical links. Some of these *barong* also travel, along with others from the area, to Pura Sabang Dahat, on the lonely plateau above Puakan. Every Manis Galungan, many *barong*, mostly from Bukit Taro/Gunung Lebah, present themselves at this temple and report to other local temples before making their own ways back down the *bukit*.[20] For the month after Galungan, reciprocal visiting continues between *barong* in the area.

Figure 6: The Upper Wos Valley: *barong migrations*

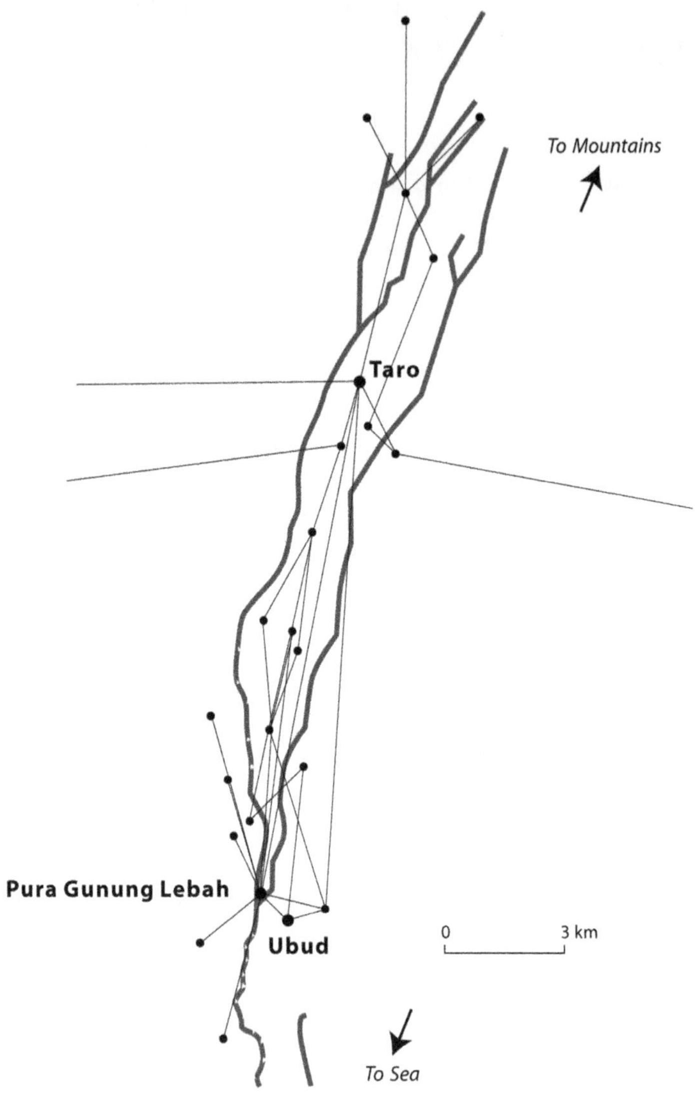

Most other *desa* have similar networks of related villages and temples which, can be traced by the travels of their *barong*. Taken together, the dominant pattern of connection is along the *kaja-kelod* axis within the *bukit*, but there are also some trans-*bukit* links to Ubud and others to apparently random temples elsewhere.

Figure 7: The Upper Wos Valley: *bale agung* orientations

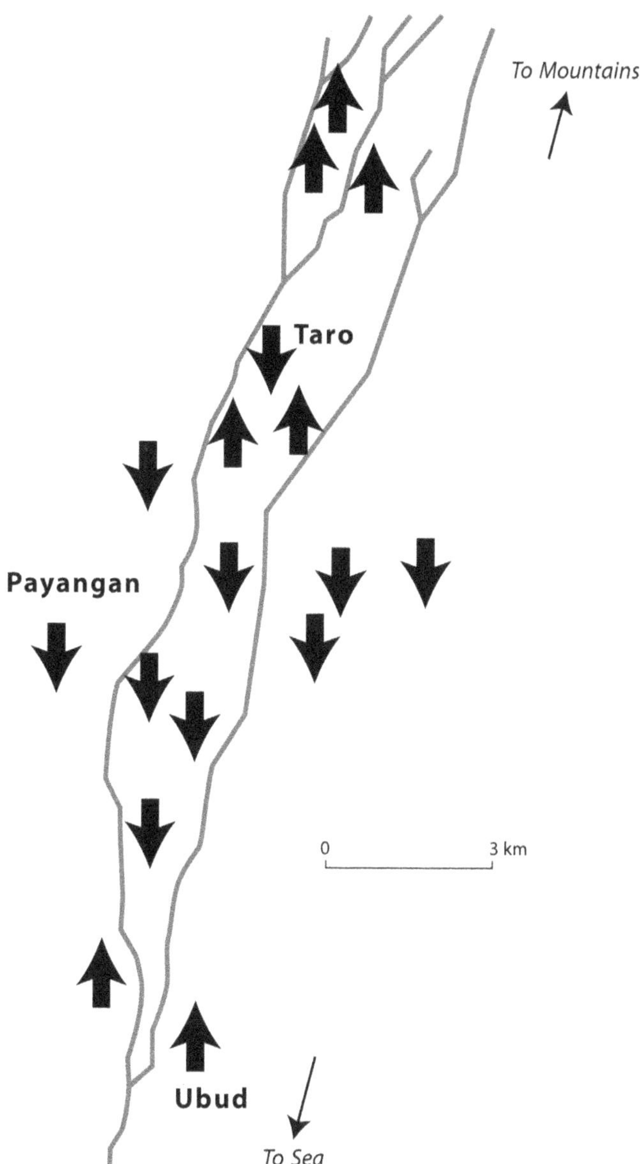

Bale Agung and Reversals of Orientation

A *bale agung* (lit: 'great pavilion') is a raised pavilion in which the gods associated with a village assemble. In old-style villages, it was oriented along the central *kaja-kelod* axis in the centre of the village and was large enough for living village members to occupy together with their deified ancestors at monthly meetings.[21] In new-style villages, it is large enough only for the gods and is situated in the middle courtyard (*jaba tengah*) of one of the village temples. In either case, it is linear in form and oriented *kaja-kelod.* [22] Furthermore, it is directional, having a head (*ulu*), which may consist of an enclosed timber cabinet containing sacred objects, a seat, or a (usually painted or carved) timber panel. The most important offerings are placed at this end and in old-style *bale* senior members of the village sit at this end. In the majority of *bale*, this head is oriented, like the heads of other entities of higher status or purity, *kaja*, uphill. [23]

The *bale agung* that forms part of the Pura Agung Gunung Raung complex in Taro, widely believed to be the longest and the oldest in Bali, is oriented in the opposite direction, with its head downhill, towards the sea! So also are the *bale agung* of Sebali/Bankiangsidem, Keliki Kawan, Keliki/Yehtengah, Kelusa and Bresela. This is an extraordinary reversal of convention, affecting the majority of *bale* within the *bukit*, although there are significant exceptions. [24] So, while within the area of Bukit Taro-Gunung Lebah there is a dominant pattern of reversal of normal orientation of *bale agung* there are also sufficient exceptions and anomalies to cast doubt on any easy generalisation.

Local explanations of this pattern of reversal are confusing but reflect a certain logical consistency. [25] *Bale agung* in this area, associated with Rsi Markandeya and Gunung Raung, are oriented not to the central mountains but to Gunung Lebah, which is the *pusat* (BI: centre), *puseh* (navel, origin) or *puncak* (peak, summit) of this area. When I pointed out to local people that 'Gunung' Lebah seemed to me to be at the lowest rather than the highest point of the *bukit*, I was referred to the mystery contained in the name 'Gunung Lebah': the low mountain or the mountain at the bottom.

On what grounds can Gunung Lebah be described as a *puncak*? According to some, because Rsi Markandeya appeared first at Campuan and then travelled *kaja* along the *bukit* this was the *pusat* and therefore also the *puncak.* [26] There is, however, sufficient uncertainty and contradiction in accounts of the direction of his travels that this explanation seems incomplete at best.

More philosophically sophisticated exegeses, by priests and princes, invoked the principle of the unity of high and low, mountain and sea, Brahma and Visnu. Just as the waters may be seen flowing from the mountains down to the sea, they also return, unseen to the mountain lakes (Schulte-Nordholt 1991: 157). The orientation to Gunung Lebah thus reflects the reversal at a *niskala* level of ordinary *sekala* orientation. [27] A further variation of this explanation was that the location of Gunung Lebah is at the central point on the whole mountain-sea axis and was thus the *pusat* or *puncak* of the whole (inherently reversible) system.

Figure 8: Upper Wos Valley: Puri Ubud patronage

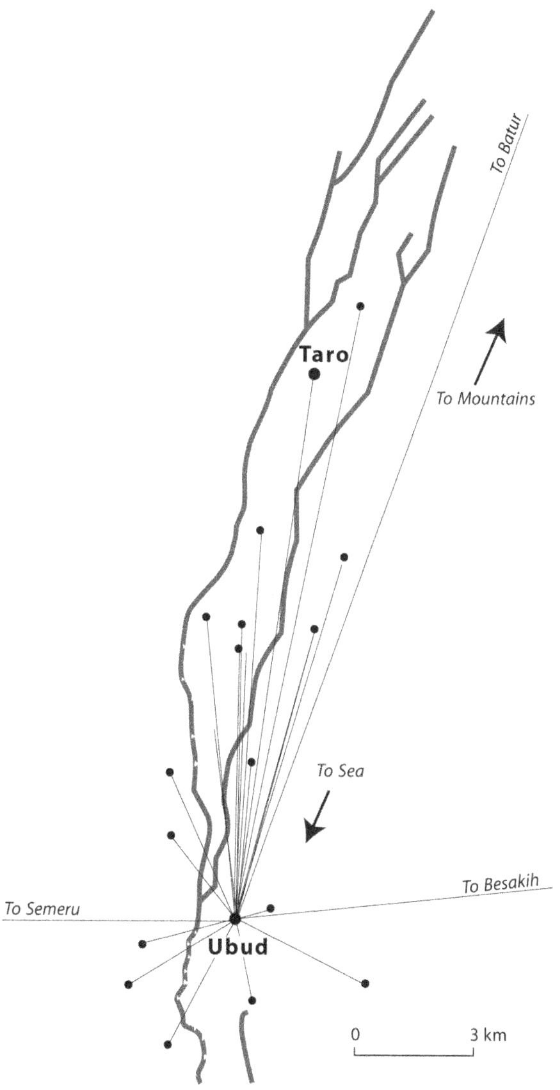

Logically unsatisfying as these explanations might be, the point in each case is clearly that within the boundaries of Bukit Gunung Lebah, ordinary *sekala* topography is in certain respects subordinate to a localised *niskala* topography of which Gunung Lebah is a peak or summit.

Puri Ubud

Throughout my inquiries, wherever *bale agung* were oriented *kelod*, wherever Rsi Markandeya was said to have been, wherever *barong* were linked, and especially throughout Bukit Gunung Lebah, there was evidence of the patronage and influence of Puri Ubud. This involvement took forms such as renovation of temples, support of local dance/music groups, advising on matters of tradition and providing rationalised interpretations of local mythical history. In return, the *puri* were deferred to on matters of tradition and invited to ceremonies in local *pura*. They also called on such villages to provide ritual labour or performances at Ubud temples or *puri*.

Local people speak of this relationship as an appropriate continuation of long tradition. Members of the *puri* regard it as their hereditary obligation: leadership, guidance of the community and protection and sponsorship of traditional cultural forms. The geographical spread of this involvement does not, however, correspond with any precision to the area controlled by the *puri* in pre-colonial times.

Puri Ubud also assume a central position in the network through their controlling role at Pura Gunung Lebah. It is not uncommon for local *puri* to take over responsibility for *pura masceti* within their area of politico-ritual jurisdiction (Lansing 1991: 131). Pura Gunung Lebah is, like other irrigation temples, a visiting place (*pasimpangan*) of Pura Batur, whose principal deity has jurisdiction over all water flowing through this part of Bali (Lansing 1991: 74). Although the *puri* (and the local *subak*) have links with this temple, other aspects of the network described however do not extend directly to Batur.

Networks and Layers

Such are the more obvious dimensions or 'layers' of interconnection between places in this landscape. They are mutually connected by virtue of a degree of overlap, spatial and conceptual, hinging around the axis of Bukit Taro/Gunung Lebah. This overlap, however, is less than perfect and exceptions and anomalies abound.

It is perhaps timely at this point to remember two things. The first is that, as James Fox (1993: 23) reminds us, the 'symbolic orders' of Austronesian space tend to be 'multiple' and are 'constantly created and recreated' though ritual practice. The second is that these 'networks' and 'layers' are, unlike the mountain *banua* recorded by Reuter, not local categories of speech and thought, much less institutions of systematic practice, but abstractions created from my observations of a corpus of local practices and stories, which establish relationships between places and institutions. The analytical question would thus appear to be whether these systems and their correspondences are coincidence, figments of an overheated anthropological imagination, manifestations of normal Austronesian symbolic pluralism, residues of Austronesian *banua* or 19th-century *negara,* or whether they reflect an order of some other kind.

Knowledgeable local people with whom I discussed my work recognised the direction of my inquiries but were unable (or perhaps unwilling) to formulate it in any clearer terms. I sought therefore to 'explain' my findings by reference to some underlying order at a further level of abstraction. Neither Lansing's 'systems' of 'water temples' nor any other structural logics provided this. Every case has its own explanation, unique and sometimes seemingly quixotic. These local explanations are instructive: when I inquired about relationships between villages, temples or *barong,* I was frequently answered with vague reference to Rsi Markandeya or Gunung Lebah or simply the self-evident '*ada hubungan*' (there is a relationship). If I pressed the matter harder, there was usually someone who could provide an explanation specific to the case in question. Such explanation inevitably took the form not of logical structural relationship but of a story relating specific mytho-historical causes: *barong* made from wood from the same tree, a king who had received divine inspiration at this spot and had founded a temple that the local village looked after on his behalf. Things are said (and seen) to be the way they are 'because' of the story of their origin. Likewise, the exceptions to the dominant pattern of reverse-oriented *bale agung* discussed above are all explained not by logical default to the status quo but by reference to their specific historical origins. This led me to look more seriously at the historical processes at work (and seen to be at work) in the area. [28]

Negara and *Banua*

What are known in the historical literature as 'kingdoms', to Balinese as *kerajaan* and to some writers (Geertz 1983; Schulte-Nordholt 1996) as *negara,* were indeed a form of trans-*desa* politico-ritual organisation, albeit imposed from the top down and fluid and unstable at the best of times. They were, however, based on an (at least implicit) ideology of 'ritual domains'. This ideology is re-packaged in Indic political-religious thought, embedded architecturally in the forms of centric *mandala* village plans and linguistically in terms such as *jagat* ('world/universe') and *bhumi,* but what gives such legitimating power to this ideology is the fact that it resonates with older Balinese ideas of what I call *niskala* landscape. These seem to me to be not unlike the ideas embedded in the *banua* of highland Bali: 'sacred landscapes inscribed by a continuing history of human action and re-inscribed through narrative and ritual performances' (Reuter, this volume). Let us consider briefly the history of Negara Ubud in this light.

Negara Ubud

In the orthodox history of Bali, Ubud was a minor *puri,* at best secondary to the eight subdued by the Dutch and subsequently immortalised as modern administrative districts (*kabupaten*). [29] In fact, at the time of the Dutch takeover, the ruler (*punggawa*) of Ubud was arguably the most powerful person in this part of Bali (A. Agung 1991: 134; Mahaudiana 1968: 97; Vickers 1989: 75, 140). Together with his allies, he controlled a vast tract of land between the Rivers Ayung and Petanu, from the coast at Ketewel to near Taro in the mountains.

Puri Ubud's claim to this area was, and still is, made firstly on the basis of descent from the former kingdom of Sukawati, which, from the early 18th century held nominal jurisdiction over the entire land between the Ayung and Pakerisan rivers, from the sea to Mt Batur (G. Agung 1983; Sanggra 1971). This jurisdiction was based not on conquest or physical occupation, but on transactions with the invisible custodians of this territory: it was, in other words, essentially a *niskala* domain rather than a political one. [30] Because of the subsequent dissolution of Sukawati and absorption of its scattered satellite *puri* into the emergent kingdom of Gianyar in the late 18th century, the Sukawati descendants had to wait more than a century and resort to warfare to reclaim their inheritance in political or *sekala* form.

This occurred in a confused series of rebellions within and wars between kingdoms towards the end of the 19th century. In the midst of this turmoil, the Prince of Ubud and his neighbouring relatives combined forces to take control of much of this territory in 1891 (A. Agung 1991; G. Agung 1983; Mahaudiana 1968: 82-85; Sanggra 1971). The details of the subsequent redistribution of land are not entirely clear but Ubud, as the strongest (if not senior) partner in the alliance, gained control of the western half of the Wos Valley from the sea to around Bresela. [31] This formed the basis of an area over which Puri Ubud held power until Gianyar came under Dutch protection in 1900 and, even after this, a residue of political-economic and moral-spiritual authority, which is by no means defunct today.

The ruler of Ubud played an important role in the King of Gianyar's decision to place the kingdom under Dutch protection, and throughout the colonial period members of Puri Ubud successfully cultivated relationships of mutual benefit with the Dutch (Hilbery 1979; Schulte-Nordholt 1996: 200; Vickers 1989: 140). They also cultivated relationships with other foreigners, which were to provide the contacts, reputation and skills on which the tourist industry was subsequently built (MacRae 1992; Vickers 1989: 140-2). Although the relationship between *puri* and people remained close, with *puri* members assuming active roles in government (*dinas*) and customary (*adat*) institutions, internal tensions within the *puri* (Hilbery 1979: 12-15), followed by the political and economic instability of the years from 1940 until 1965 (Bagus 1991; Robinson 1988; Hilbery 1979: 2; Vickers 1989: 146-73), diverted the interest and resources of the *puri* away from matters of tradition, especially in areas remote from Ubud. By the time tourism began again in the late 1960s, Ubud was poor and divided and the *puri's* relationship with the further reaches of its former kingdom was at a low ebb.

Figure 9: Ubud territory in the late 19th century

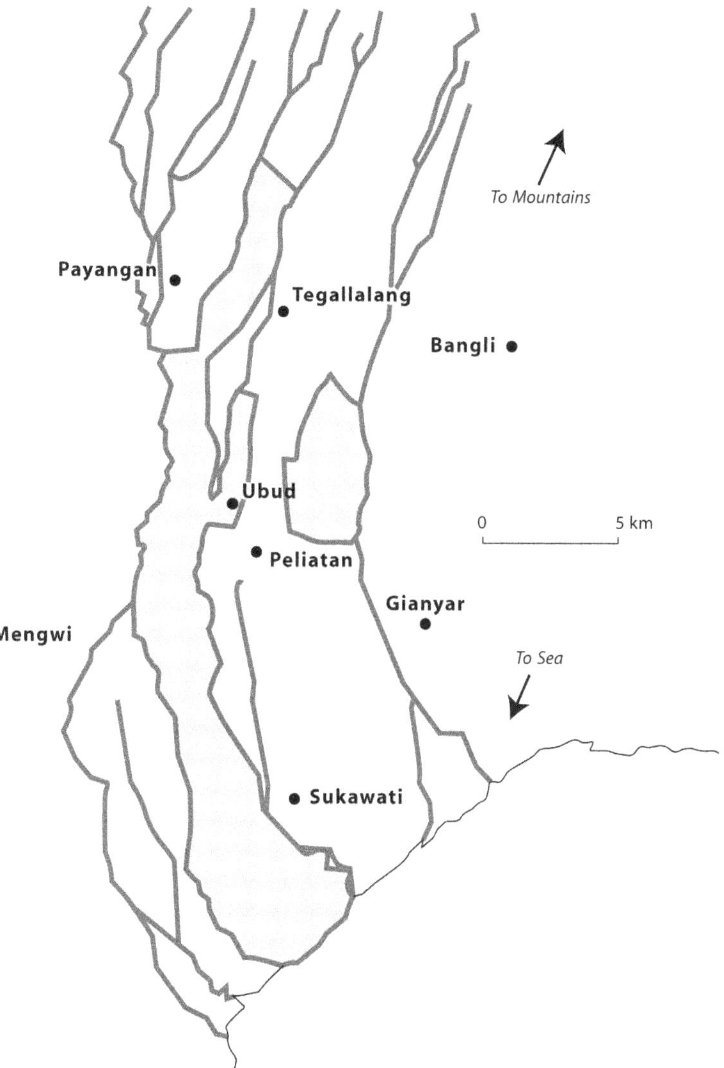

During the 1970s and '80s, as Ubud prospered through tourism, the *puri* prospered too through extensive sales of land and development of its own tourism interests. Unlike other *puri* which concentrated on politics and business (C. Geertz 1963: ch.4; Hanna 1976: 122-8), Puri Ubud sought also to re-establish their role as guides and guardians of local tradition as well as taking prominent positions in the local administration (MacRae 1999).

Outside Ubud, where such avenues were not open to them, especially in areas such as Bukit Gunung Lebah, which is part of another administrative district, Puri Ubud reverted to the old standby of royal patronage to reclaim their kingdom. During the 1960s, Ck. Agung Sukawati involved himself in the restoration of temples and *pretima* (sacred objects) all over Bali (Hilbery 1979). Upon his death, this mantle was taken up by his nephew, Ck. Agung Suyasa, who, since the late 1980s, has embarked on a program of sponsorship of ritual and culture around Ubud, up the Wos Valley and in other places. This program is based on restoration of temples, organising of and contributing to ceremonies, renovation of dance and music troupes and especially *barong* as well as researching and interpreting local history and tradition. Much of the evidence of *niskala* landscape and *negara* recorded above are in fact the fruits of this programme.

So while the history of Negara Ubud is at one level a conventionally politico-military one, it has at various crucial points been built and rebuilt on ideas of sacred landscape—successive political domains have been built on underlying assumptions of a ritual domain.

The Network as a System of Knowledge

It is the program of sponsorship by the *puri* that today draws together the diverse layers into what I have described as a network: a *barong* sponsored here, a temple restored there, a ceremony organised or an interpretation of the Rsi Markandeya story somewhere else. Some of these establish or reinforce direct links between villages and temples, all increase a sense of common 'shelter under the umbrella (*payung*)' of the *puri*.

This umbrella is, however, just one more image local people use to talk about an aspect (layer) of what I have been labouring to systematise into a network. What the *puri* are doing is systematising this same something but with an assurance that obviates any need to name it as such. Rather than a tangible network that can be plotted unambiguously on a map, what they are really working with is a set of ideas dispersed among a diverse corpus of practices and stories, a proto-theory of regional identity, a system of local knowledge integrated with the forms of ritual practice and narrative. It was the systematic nature of these ideas that people recognised when I spoke to them about my project and it is this basis of recognition also which provides the cultural material that the *puri* are recycling, developing and ordering.

Negara or *Banua*?

The conclusions I have drawn previously from this evidence have tended to emphasise the way in which the *puri* has utilised this *niskala* landscape as a symbolic resource in a contemporary political economy dominated by tourism (MacRae 1997, 1998, 1999), namely by reconstructing, inventing (Hobsbawm and Ranger 1983) or imagining (Anderson 1991) a neo-*negara*, a new kingdom constructed in symbolic terms, through material practices of temple construction and ritual sponsorship. Seen through the lens of comparative Austronesian ethnography, however, it is instructive to consider the ways and extent to which this is built on foundations of appropriated local and inter-local organisation which predate and appear to exist independently of the *puri* and resonate with ideas more common to the Austronesian than the Indic world. [32]

Firstly, the idea that the landscape has, as well as its physical aspect, a subtle, inner magico-ritual aspect is common in India as well as throughout the Austronesian world. Some aspects of this landscape, however, take forms either more Indic or more Austronesian. Secondly, while sacred mountains are (literally) central to Indic sacred landscape, the primary level of spatial organisation in Bali—the linear uphill-downhill axis—corresponds directly to a well-documented Austronesian pattern as do the practices of orienting buildings and their component elements to this axis (Fox 1993: 14-15). The centric, *mandala*-type *desa* forms on the other hand, are unknown elsewhere in the Austronesian world and are in fact found in villages clearly dominated by *puri* of Hindu-Javanese descent. Thirdly, despite the absence of clear trans-*desa* levels of organisation such as the *banua* of the mountains, there is considerable evidence of an embryonic, residual or perhaps simply different form of inter-linkage between *desa*, articulated especially through temples. Fourthly, the programs of *negara*-building carried out by *puri*, while referring to aspects of Indic kingship, are based on mobilising relationships with and ideas about land, which are congruent with Austronesian ones in general and Bali Aga ones in particular.

Twentieth-Century Transformations

It was residues of some of the *kerajaan* of the 19th century that formed the basis of the considerable inequalities of land tenure that have continued in Bali to the present day. While some raja lost considerable amounts to the Dutch, others were able to retain and even consolidate their holdings (Mortimer 1972; Utrecht 1969). This inequality, combined with population increase, led to intensified competition for scarce productive land and facilitated systems of crop-sharing that favoured the interests of the landowners over those of their tenants. Dutch taxation policies placed considerable hardship on small farmers, which was intensified by the fall of commodity prices during the Great Depression. As a result, many farmers lost some or all of their land, further exacerbating existing inequalities. During the first decade of independence, in the 1950s, access to productive land was one of the burning political issues throughout Indonesia and was a major factor in the rise of the Communist Party (PKI), which lobbied strongly for a program of land reform. This was initiated in the early 1960s but landlords were able to retain significant amounts of land, by using strategies of obstruction and evasion (MacRae 1997: 383-5). The destruction of the PKI in the massacres of 1965-6 put an end to any further land reform program, although the original process has continued, slowly and incrementally, until the present (MacRae 1997: 386-7).

The primary piece of legislation (UUPA 1960) on which land reform was based also provides a set of legal tools for extricating land from the constraints of traditional collective tenure and enabling privatisation and alienation of land through a process of registration of title (*sertipikat*) in a manner essentially similar to Western models of private ownership.

Since then the economy has been transformed by tourism and associated export industries and the value of land has escalated exponentially (MacRae 1997: 70-8). People have come to think increasingly of land in terms of its exchange rather than use value, or ritual value. A generation ago it was considered highly inauspicious to sell rice fields, let alone convert them to non-agricultural use. Now owners of farm land regularly sell or convert land. The decline in incomes from farming has made this increasingly attractive, especially in major urban and tourist centres where often the least productive but strategically located land fetches astronomical prices. Others have lost their land as a result of compulsory acquisition for hotel construction. This commodification of land has led to new forms of wealth, but also to landlessness and poverty. The process has been aided and abetted by government programs providing the legal basis and moral encouragement to register land under individual, alienable title (*sertipikat*)—ostensibly to protect people from the depredations of former landlords, but simultaneously facilitating the sale and purchase of such land. *Tanah pekarangan desa* is also subject to registration in this way, but to date no one, in Ubud at least, has dared to sell such land. There are, however, partial exceptions and stories of it having happened elsewhere.

Conclusion

While the rituals of *desa* and *bhumi* linking people, land and gods continue on a scale not dreamt of by previous generations, the very land to which they refer is being steadily registered, subdivided, alienated and sold, often to foreigners. Austronesian ideas and practices of land belonging to the gods and of collective ritual responsibilities, transformed but reinforced by Indo-Javanese ideas and practices are now again being transformed but this time also eroded by the replacement of collective *adat* stewardship with private individualised ownership, commodification of the value of land and the transformation of the phenomenological experience of land by new technologies. Likewise the residual *banua*-like forms in this part of Bali are being progressively appropriated by processes of aristocratic control and harnessed to struggles for power in the tourism-dominated economy. While the land is being carved up; the ideologies embodied in ritual perpetuate the belief that the earth is still being shared.

References

Agung, A.A.G. 1989. *Bali Pada Abad XIX*. Yogyakarta: Gadjah Mada University Press.

Agung, G. 1981. 'Babad Dalem Sukawati.' Typewritten manuscript in latin script of Balinese, in possession of Puri Kaleran Sukawati.

Agung A. 1983. 'Sejarah Awal berdiri dan Berkembngnya puri Agung & penataran Agung Tegallalang.' Photocopied typewritten Indonesian manuscript.

Anderson, B. 1991. *Imagined Communities: Reflections on the origins and spread of nationalism*. London: Verso.

Bagus, G.N. 1991. 'Bali in the 1950s: The role of the Pemuda Pejung in Balinese Political Process.' In H. Geertz (ed.), *State and Society in Bali*. Leiden: KITLV Press.

Bateson, G. 1970. 'An old temple and a new myth.' In J. Belo (ed.), *Traditional Balinese Culture*, New York: Columbia University Press.

Barnes, R.H. 1974. *Kedang: a study of the collective thought of an eastern Indonesian people*. Oxford: Clarendon.

Belo, J. 1953. *Bali: Temple festival*. Seattle and London, Washington: University of Washington Press.

Boon, J. 1977. *The Anthropological Romance of Bali*. Cambridge, London, New York, Melbourne: Cambridge University Press.

Budihardjo, E. 1986. *Architectural Conservation in Bali*. Yogyakarta: Gadjah Mada University Press.

Covarrubias, M. 1994. *Island of Bali*. New York: Knopf.

Creese, H. 1991. 'Balinese *Babad* as Historical Sources: a reinterpretation of the fall of Gelgel.' *Bijdragen tot de Taal-, Land-, en Volkenkunde*, 147. pp. 179-210.

Davies, P. 1991. 'The Historian in Bali.' *Meanjin*, 1 (1991). pp. 63-80.

Fox, J.J. (ed.) 1993. *Inside Austronesian Houses: Perspectives on domestic designs for living*. Canberra: Research School of Pacific and Asian Studies, The Australian National University.

Fox, J.J. (ed.) 1997. *The Poetic Power of Place: Comparative perspectives on Austronesian Ideas of Locality*. Canberra: Research School of Pacific and Asian Studies, The Australian National University.

Geertz, C. 1959. 'Form and Variation in Balinese Village Structure.' *American Anthropologist,* 61. pp. 991-1012.

Geertz, C. 1980. *Negara: the theatre state in nineteenth century Bali*. Princeton: Princeton University Press.

Goris, R. 1969. 'The Decennial Festival in the Village of Selat.' In J. van Baal et al. (eds), *Bali: Further Studies in Life, Thought and Ritual,* The Hague: Van Hoeve.

Goris, R. 1984 (1960). 'The Religious Character of the village community.' In Swellengrebel (ed.), *Bali: Studies in Life, Thought and Ritual,* Dordrecht: Foris Publications.

Grader, C.J. 1969. 'Pura Meduwe Karang at Kubutumbuhan.' In J. van Baal et al. (eds), *Bali: Further Studies in Life, Thought and Ritual,* The Hague: Van Hoeve.

Guermonprez, J.F. 1990. 'On the Elusive Balinese Village: Hierarchy and values versus political models.' *Review of Indonesian and Malaysian Affairs*. 24. pp. 55-89.

Gunning, H. and A. van der Heiden. 1926. 'Het Petjataoe-en Anstveldenprobleem in Zuid-Bali.' *Tijdschrift voor Indische Taal-, Land-en Volkenkunde,* 66. pp. 329-94.

Hanna, W.A. 1976. *Bali Profile*. New York: American Universities Field Staff.

Hilbery, R. 1979. 'Reminiscences of a Balinese Prince.' *S.E. Asia Paper No. 14*. Honolulu: University of Hawai'i Press.

Hobart, A., U. Ramseyer and A. Leemann. 1996. *The Peoples of Bali*. Oxford, Cambridge (Mass.): Blackwell.

Hobart, M. 1979. 'A Balinese Village and its Field of Social Relations.' Unpublished PhD thesis, School of Oriental and African Studies, London.

Hobsbawm, E. and T. Ranger. 1983. *The Invention of Tradition*. Cambridge, New York: Cambridge University Press.

Howe, L. 1980. 'Pujung: The foundations of Balinese Culture.' Unpublished PhD thesis, University of Edinburgh, Edinburgh.

Howe, L. 1983. 'An Introduction to the cultural study of traditional Balinese Architecture.' *Archipel*, 26. pp. 137-58.

de Kat Angelino, P. 1921. 'De Robans en Parekans op Bali.' *Kolonial Tijdschrift*, 10. pp. 590-608.

Lansing, J.S. 1991. *Priests and Programmers*. Princeton: Princeton University Press.

MacRae, G.S. 1992. 'Tourism and Balinese Culture.' Unpublished M.Phil. thesis. University of Auckland, Auckland.

MacRae, G.S. 1997. 'Economy, Ritual and History in a Balinese Tourist Town.' Unpublished PhD thesis. University of Auckland, Auckland.

MacRae, G.S. 1999. 'Acting Global, Thinking Local in a Balinese Tourist Town.' In R. Rubinstein and L. Connor (eds), *Staying Local in the Global Village: Bali in the Twentieth Century*, Honolulu: University of Hawai'i Press.

MacRae, G.S. 2003. 'The Value of Land in Bali: Land-tenure, land reform and commodification.' In T.A. Reuter (ed.), *Inequality, Crisis and Social Change in Indonesia: The muted worlds of Bali,* London, New York: Routledge-Curzon Press.

Mahaudiana. 1968. *Babad Manggis Gianyar*. Gianyar: Thaman.

Mead, M. 1970. 'The Strolling Players in the Mountains of Bali.' In J. Belo (ed.), *Traditional Balinese Culture*, New York: Columbia University Press.

Mortimer, R.A. 1972. *The Indonesian Communist Party and Land Reform 1959-1965*. Melbourne: Centre for South-East Asian Studies, Monash University.

Reuter, T.A. 1998. 'The Banua of Pura Pucak Penulisan: A Ritual Domain in the Highlands of Bali.' *Review of Indonesian and Malaysian Affairs*, 32 (1). Pp. 55-109.

Reuter, T.A. 2002a. *Custodians of the Sacred Mountains: Culture and society in the highlands of Bali*. Honolulu: University of Hawai'i Press.

Reuter, T.A. 2002b. *The House of Our Ancestors: Precedence and Dualism in Highland Balinese Society*. Leiden: KITLV Press.

Robinson, G. 1995. *The Dark Side of Paradise: Political violence in Bali*. Ithaca, London: Cornell University Press.

Sanggra, M. 1971. *Babad Timbul Sukawati*. Sukawati: Yayasan Loka-Phala Budhaya (photocopied typewritten manuscript).

Schulte-Nordholt, H. 1991. 'Temple and Authority in South Bali, 1900-1980.' In H. Geertz (ed.), *State and Society in Bali: historical, textual and anthropological approaches,* Leiden: KITLV Press.

Schulte-Nordholt, H. 1996. *The Spell of Power: a history of Balinese Politics 1650-1940*. Leiden: KITLV Press.

Schwartz, H.J.E.F. 1906. 'Aanteekeningen Omtrent het Landschap Gianjar 1.' *Tijdschrift voor het Binnenlands Bestuur, 1901-1906*. pp. 166-89.

Stuart-Fox, D. 2002. *Pura Besakih: temple, religion and society in Bali.* Leiden: KITLV Press.

Utrecht, E. 1969. 'Land Reform in Indonesia.' *Bulletin of Indonesian Economic Studies* 3. pp. 71-88.

Ubud. 1983. 'Monografi Kelurahan Ubud, tahun 1983-1984.' Typewritten manuscript. LKMD, Ubud.

UUPA. 1960. *Undang-Undang No. 5 Tahun 1960 tentang Peraturan Dasar Pokok-pokok Agraria.* Government of the Republic of Indonesia.

Valeri, V. 1991. 'Afterword.' In J.S. Lansing, *Priests and Programmers,* Princeton: Princeton University Press.

Vickers, A. 1989. *Bali: A paradise created.* Ringwood: Penguin Books.

Warren, C. 1993. *Adat and Dinas: Balinese communities in the Indonesian state.* Oxford, Singapore, New York: Oxford University Press.

Waterson, R. 1997. *The Living House: An anthropology of architecture in South-East Asia* London: Thames and Hudson.

Wiener, M. 1995. *Visible and Invisible Realms: power, magic and colonial conquest in Bali.* Chicago, London: Chicago University Press.

de Zoete, B. and W. Spies. 1973. *Dance and Drama in Bali.* Kuala Lumpur: Oxford University Press.

ENDNOTES

[1] For a discussion of the political economy of land in south Bali, see MacRae (2003).

[2] Translations are Balinese unless indicated as Indonesian (Bahasa Indonesia, BI).

[3] The model presented here is based on understanding developed in the course of field research conducted in and around Ubud predominantly in 1993-94, 1996, and shorter visits in 1998 and 1999. This research is documented in detail in my PhD thesis (1997) and partially in previously published articles (1999, 2003).

[4] Amongst the parade of great holy men, bearers of culture and religion from Java and beyond, who dominate early Balinese mytho-history, there is no mention (in English at least) of Markandeya until Howe (1980). He appears in old Indian texts and, according to Stuart-Fox (2002: 261) in old Javanese ones, but he has become widely known in Bali only in recent times. In the past couple of decades, a series of published versions of the story have appeared. Several of these refer to a 'Lontar Markandeya Purana', but Stuart-Fox was unable to locate any such original manuscript. One is said also to exist in the possession of Puri Ubud. In some cases, local oral versions have also been written and stored in private collections. For a more detailed discussion see MacRae (1997: 233).

[5] For variations on this formulation, see Boon (1977: 94) and Geertz (1959).

[6] The relationship is, as Guermonprez (1990) argues, more complex than this, and he offers a sophisticated, if contestable interpretation of it, but for the present purpose a 'social vs. ritual' is sufficient. For other interpretations, see Geertz (1959: 991), Stuart-Fox (2002: 31-4) and Warren (1993: 21-2).

[7] The well-known *kahyangan tiga* (three temples) model, is an ideological construct of relatively recent invention. It entered Western discourse in 1935 (Goris 1960: 80-90) and has been recycled ever since with varying degrees of (mis) understanding and dogmatism in local, popular and academic forms. Empirically, however, it is—in this part of Bali at least—the exception rather than the rule (see also Stuart-Fox 2002: 23-4).

[8] This terminology, and the arrangements they refer to, varies somewhat in different parts of Bali (Stuart-Fox 2002: 43; Warren 1993: 39).

[9] For descriptions of Balinese house yard layouts see Budihardjo (1986: 60-4), Covarrubias (1994: 90), Howe (1983) and MacRae (1997: 185-7).

[10] Obvious examples of such *desa* include Ubud, Tegallalang and Payangan, but there are also less obvious ones such as Kedisan, Kebon and Sayan. For a detailed account of the establishment of such a 'royal centre', see Schulte-Nordholt (1991).

[11] The landholding practices of Puri Ubud were something of an exception to this pattern, with the majority of land retained by the *puri* and sharecropped by local farmers, a system that has been of considerable commercial advantage to the *puri* in the tourism-driven inflation of land values during the late 20th century. For a detailed discussion of Ubud land tenure, see MacRae (2003).

[12] See, for example, Covarrubias (1994), C. Geertz (1959), Guermonprez (1990), Hobart (1979), Schulte-Nordholt (1991) and Warren (1991).

[13] Evidence presented here, unless referenced otherwise, is from my own fieldwork in Ubud and the areas immediately uphill during the years 1993-99.

[14] Reuter (2002a) mentions a network of five villages around a temple, which is also called Pura Banua, located in the nearby village of Margatengah. Temples known as Pura Banua are not in fact uncommon in Bali. There is one in the Besakih complex (Stuart-Fox 2002: 400-1), and Grader (1969: 134-41) documented several in North Bali, which he believed to be associated primarily with dry-field agricultural ritual.

[15] *Puri* means 'palace' or 'noble house' in the English multiple sense of a building, a family and a sociopolitical institution. Puri Ubud refers here to a cluster of some 40 households descended from the pre-colonial rulers of Ubud and who still occupy a prominent role in the public life of Ubud. I refer here to 'the *puri*' as if it were a single monolithic institution. In fact, this is far from the case and internal differences within the *puri* are an important part of the wider picture. For the purposes of this paper, however, I use it as a convenient shorthand for the collective interests of a cluster of related households descended from the original Puri Ubud.

[16] James Fox (1993: 23), citing Roy Ellen and Clifford Sather, reminds us that the 'symbolic orders' of Austronesian space tend to be 'multiple' and 'constantly created and recreated in ritual.'

[17] Liefrinck (1969) and Lansing (1991) describe this system in some detail.

[18] Knowledge of the elements of the story is widespread in this area, especially among men of all ages. Confidence in retelling it and knowledge of details is surprisingly rare and is limited to a few, usually older men, not necessarily priests or leaders but with acknowledged expertise in matters of religion and history. These are precisely the people who tend to be least fluent in Bahasa Indonesia, so the fact that I initially worked entirely in this language probably left me with an impression of less knowledge than there actually is.

[19] *Barong* are, in a material sense, giant puppets animated by men inside them. The most common forms represent animals, usually tigers or a vaguely leonine species of mythical beast known as *ket(et)*, possibly descended from the dragons indigenous to the Far East (Belo 1949: 32-3) and related to similar creatures elsewhere in Indonesia. In *niskala* terms, they are a kind of deity resident periodically in this material body and/or the bodies of the men animating it. For a more detailed discussion, see MacRae (1997: 235-40).

[20] Manis Galungan is an important day in the 210-day cycle of the Balinese calender and the beginning of the 35-day month during which most *barong* customarily make their travels.

[21] The old/new terminology refers to differences first noted by Dutch scholars between the physical forms and social organisation of the Bali Aga villages found mostly in the mountains and those in the court-dominated lowland areas. In fact, many villages in the area discussed here display combinations of elements of the two ideal types. For recent discussions of this classification, see C. Geertz (1980), Guermonprez (1992), Lansing (1977: 217) and Warren (1991: 18).

[22] There are around Bedulu and reportedly in Karangasem also a number of Bale Agung oriented east-west, the logic of which I have not yet investigated.

[23] On the term *ulu* and its significance, see Howe (1980: 59).

[24] The exceptions consist of *bale* within the *bukit*, which are oriented conventionally or split into sections oriented each way. In all cases there are specific historical reasons for the difference. The anomalies consist of *bale* outside the *bukit*, such as those at Payangan and in a group of villages east of

Tegallalang, which are oriented downhill. The explanations of these are more complex and are beyond the scope of this essay.

[25] These explanations were obtained from a wide range of local people in the villages concerned and were subsequently supplemented by the more impartial opinions of people of acknowledged expertise in Ubud and other places.

[26] Michael Vischer has suggested (personal communication) similarities to materials from further east in the archipelago, where orientation to a 'point of origin' is common and cultural ideas are frequently expressed in the form of 'couplets' conjoining mutually contradictory concepts. See also Barnes (1974: 78-80) and Valeri (1991: 136-8) on this subject.

[27] Pura Sang Hyang Tegal, a large temple dedicated to dry and wet agriculture and to Brahma and Wisnu, located between Taro and Puakan, and recently renovated by Puri Ubud, is also associated with this concept. A similar concept is embodied in the construction of mountain *bale agung*, said to represent 'divine unity and the passage ... through the circle of life, afterlife and rebirth' (Reuter 1996: 156).

[28] The subject of 'history' in Bali is inherently problematic (see Bateson 1970 [1937]; Creese 1991; Davies 1991; Grader 1960: 163; Hobart 1979: 35; Schulte-Nordholt 1992; Vickers 1986, 1990; Wiener 1995: 76-96) and beyond the scope of this essay. I am concerned here less with verification of factual accuracy than with the use of history as a charter explaining and legitimating the present. The accounts I present here are assembled from the published material referred to in the text, most of which repeats, in more systematic form, oral accounts of people in and around Ubud.

[29] I speak of orthodox history advisedly. History in Bali is no less contestable than anywhere else. There is, however, a broad consensus as to the overall outline, of which the various versions of the Babad Dalem are the primary source, aristocratic recitations the second and academic interpretations the third layer. These layers have become an orthodoxy enshrined in common knowledge, tourist guidebooks and academic publications.

[30] For details of these transactions see MacRae (1997: 271-83.

[31] Evidence of this division of territory can be found in Controleur Schwartz's report of 1900—the moment at which Gianyar came under Dutch protection. There is no reason to suppose that this represents any Dutch rearrangement. Local oral history, patterns of land ownership that survived even the land reform of 1961, and patterns of royal sponsorship of temples all confirm this picture.

[32] It is perhaps appropriate to acknowledge, somewhat belatedly, that Thomas Reuter has long sought to remind me of how my material looked from the vantage point of the mountains of the Bali Aga and comparative Austronesian ethnology, and that Mark Mosko has likewise recognised this aspect of my material and urged me to develop it.

Chapter 5. *Tanah Berkat* (Blessed Land): The Source of the Local in the Banda Islands, Central Maluku

Phillip Winn

> Within this archipelagic area a variety of ethnic groups meet which originate from a range of regions in Indonesia alongside those whose origins are in Maluku alone ... Of course they arrived with their own cultural backgrounds ... Nevertheless if the customs and traditions that take place are examined closely, it is clear that indigenous cultural elements are certainly dominant. So that here outside cultural features have dissipated in the context of indigenous culture.[1]
> Uneputty et al (1985:27-8)

Introduction

The Banda Islands in central Maluku have long been a site of historical transformations. As a consequence, human relationships to land and place in the Bandas need to be understood in terms of dynamic processes of culture and history. In the pre-colonial period, the islands formed a key part of extensive trading networks reaching across the archipelago to link Maluku with the northern seaports of Java, the cosmopolitan city-state of Malacca in peninsular Malaysia, and ultimately to the Middle East, China and Europe. By the arrival of the first Europeans, the population of the islands included numbers of resident Malay and Javanese merchants, with significant socio-cultural changes in progress. In particular, autochthonous structures of authority had been transformed through the acceptance of Muslim practices and the burgeoning importance of local trade functionaries.

Military conquest of the Banda Islands in 1621 by the Dutch East India Company or VOC (*Verenigde Oost-Indische Compagnie*) resulted in more radical change: the destruction or displacement of much of the existing population of the islands followed by the imposition of the *perkeniersstelsel* or 'nutmeg-planter system'. Among the world's earliest plantation enterprises, this venture relied on several centuries of importing captive labour—in particular, slaves—from regional and extra-regional sources. The VOC's decimation of indigenous-language speakers, in combination with the diverse origins of the colonial-era population, can certainly be linked to the emergence of a shared and distinctive Malay language that has been referred to as Banda Malay. [2] It still forms the main contemporary vernacular spoken in the Banda Islands.

It is against this background that representations of the land (*tanah*) itself is prominent in shaping an ontological topography within which the contemporary significance of locality and the legitimacy of local identification take shape. [3] The current population acknowledge descent from immigrants of diverse origins and generally engage in what Carsten (1997) characterises as a 'future orientation', where genealogical reckoning is relatively shallow in historical depth but extremely broad in contemporary reach. Unlike the island Malay population Carsten describes, contemporary Bandanese valorise traditions of knowledge concerning the past, in particular, those that relate to the Banda Islands. This knowledge (known as *adat Banda*) represents the islands as possessing profound religious significance—in fact, as a blessed land or *tanah berkat*.

By engaging in collective ritual practice (known as *kerja adat*), local residents enact obligations to social collectivities that derive their meaningfulness from narratives of place, rather than genealogically based visions of ancient shared relatedness. Participation in collective ritual occasions was understood as communicating and reinforcing the moral commitments and goals of religion alongside idealised visions of sociality. Ritual practices additionally confer legitimacy to contemporary assertions of authentically local identity.

The Blessed Land

The small archipelago of the Banda Islands is envisaged by its local inhabitants as a unified landscape in a sense that exceeds the administrative standing of the island group as a *kecamatan* or sub-regency. The islands are often referred to collectively as *tanah Banda*, 'the land of Banda', an expression that simultaneously marks the Bandas as a distinct locale and emphasises the earth that physically constitutes the islands. *Tanah Banda* was popularly understood as possessing a singular significance, that of being a 'blessed land' or *tanah berkat*. The source of this special status was envisaged in terms of the islands having played an important historical role in significant religious events.

An example of this perspective appears in a document dated 1922. Purportedly the transcription of an ancient origin narrative obtained in the settlement of Lonthoir on Banda Besar Island, it begins with Noah and the flooding of the Earth:

> At the end of the flood the lands all rose above the water, in the West, in the South and in the East. The land Andare in the East, that is Banda, was raised first, after that Tidore and Ternate, and Java and Bali, followed by the other lands. (Van Ronkel 1945: 124)

A similar account, also attributed to Lonthoir but dated 1924, contains additional details. [4] Noah's craft is described running aground on Mount Ararak, after which he releases a dove in order to ascertain whether the flood has truly ended. The dove journeys to another mountain where it alights on a pomegranate tree and pecks off the terminal sprout, carrying it to the ark. Convinced, Noah releases animals back into the world. The dove, for its part, is depicted as returning to the pomegranate tree, which the text then reveals as growing on the peak of Mount Lewerang—a still-active volcano in the Banda Group.

In the late 1990s, this volcano-island was generally known by the more ubiquitous title Gunung Api (literally, 'volcano'). [5] The peak, and the Banda Islands as a whole, were no longer given such a prominent part in tales of the flood, but a motif of religious significance continued. The islands' special status was attributed widely to the actions of several male siblings in the archaic past (*jaman dulu*), who journeyed from the islands seeking religion. They are said to have returned with Islam, obtained from its source in Mecca. Both the historical texts cited previously provide descriptions of the siblings' journey that closely parallel contemporary accounts. [6] Crucially, among local Muslims (who formed the bulk of the population) there is a common assertion that the Bandas were in fact the first location in Indonesia to receive Islam. The rest of the archipelago—and in some local accounts, the rest of the non-Arab world—encountered Islam after this.

Such narratives clearly evoke powerful claims for the islands: the first dry land after the flood, the first place visited by Noah's dove, the first Indonesian location to receive Islam. It is notable too that the repetitive theme, in addition to being religious, involves an assertion of precedence. This cultural motif has been highlighted throughout Austronesian populations, often associated with claims to ritual authority or other status (Fox 1995). In this case, there is a vision of peculiar potency attached to the islands in a physical sense—to the very land or earth itself.

The tiny uninhabited outlier of the Banda Group is called Suanggi Island, a title that is described as marking it as the boundary of *tanah Banda*. The *suanggi*—a malevolent witch-figure—is a common image throughout Maluku; in the Bandas its range of powers are said to include invisibility and the ability to fly. Suanggi Islands name is said to stem from the fact that any flying *suanggi* who passes the island would be robbed of its powers as a result of crossing into the Banda Groups zone of influence, plummeting to earth on the island or into the sea. [7] Similarly, soil or sand from the Bandas was frequently incorporated into amulets by Banda residents that were designed to provide safety against the influence of *suanggi* (and all evil intent) while one was travelling outside the islands. Many residents even suggested that the mere fact of their personal association with the Bandas could be sufficient to ward off the machinations of *suanggi* encountered elsewhere.

Other more tangible evidence of the blessed nature of *tanah Banda* existed in the form of sites known as *keramat* that dot the landscape of the islands. *Keramat* were viewed as ancient locations associated with the journeying male siblings and other early autochtonous figures in the islands. Sometimes the sites are described as *tempat sakti*, i.e. 'places which are *sakti*', a term generally translated into English as 'sacred' or 'supernaturally powerful' (Grimes 1996).[8] They may also be referred to as *tempat suci*, 'holy places'. *Suci* generally refers to matters more specifically religious, much as the term 'holy' does in English—partaking of God/godliness.

These sites then are regarded as both powerful and holy, a significance connected directly to the early Muslim founder-figures with which they are associated. Most are viewed as graves and have this appearance (with single or double markers, sometimes of decoratively carved coral-stone blocks); others comprise enduring physical features such as springs, large boulders or caves associated with specific activities of these individuals in the distant past. Many of the sites are linked to placenames, establishing a close connection between the landscape and local origin narratives. The Banda *keramat* form a continuous mnemonic suggestion to island residents of a dense inscribing of hidden significances in the land, particularly of important historical events and religious figures, and of their coexistence in the Bandas with these figures who continue to exist in spirit form (see Winn 2000). The figures themselves (which include, but are not limited to, the journeying siblings) are often referred to collectively as *datu-datu*.

In standard Indonesian, the term *datuk* can be translated as ancestor or forebear, but the expression has cognates in local languages across Indonesia, Malaysia, Brunei and the Philippines that also form titles of respect or recognition linked to Islamic religious scholars, shamans and/or high-ranking officials attached to a local rulers court (Federspiel 1995: 47). Such was the emphasis in the Banda Islands, where they were also sometimes referred to variously as *wali* and *imam besar*—Islamic saints and holy figures, as Islamic or religious teachers (*guru Islam*; *guru agama*) and as religious experts or scholars (*tokoh agama*; *ahli agama*; *kiai*).

The Banda *datu* figures were seen as possessing immense religious knowledge, particularly of the esoteric and mystical elements of Islam, a realm viewed by local Muslims as enormously powerful but difficult to access for the ordinary person in the contemporary world. In the words of one informant: '[Their] Islamic knowledge is far greater [than ours]' (*'pengetahuan agama Islam jauh lebih tinggi'* [Hatta]). This was a result of the *datu* being close to God (*dekat Allah*). Informants also described them as the beloved (*habib*) or grandchildren (*cucu*) of the prophet Mohammed, who were elevated or glorified by God. Their special status is manifest in their association with *keramat*: 'people who give rise to *keramat* have received honour from the All-Powerful' (*'orang yang terjadi keramat dapat mulia dari yang Maha Besar'* [Lonthoir]). It is this closeness to God and to

Mohammed that is popularly considered as providing them with the capacity to intercede on behalf of those who visit a *keramat* site.

It is important to note that a repetitive emphasis in *adat* narratives is on the status of *tanah Banda,* rather than the agency of the *datu.* Narratives stress the prominence of the islands in God's view as giving rise to the siblings and their journey to Mecca. The actions of the siblings do not create the island's prominence—they are vehicles for the operation of God's intent. In this respect, the origin of the siblings is popularly linked to a miraculous emergence from a pomegranate fruit, through God's will. In the 1924 text, this fruit emerged on the same tree encountered by Noah's dove, later inhabited by Gabriel (Jibrail), the archangel Mohammed met in a cave while meditating and who carried the Qur'an for recitation. In the 1922 text, the pomegranate tree arose through the prayer of a holy woman who desired to eat that particular fruit, and as a result became pregnant. [9] Some informants even maintained that the Banda Islands were considered by God as the birthplace for the prophet Mohammed himself. As evidence, one *adat* specialist repeated part of a ritual verse that explicitly brings Banda into relation with Mecca: 'the land of Mecca is heavy, the land of Banda is light; therefore the Prophet was born over there'(*'tanah Mecca berat, tanah Banda ringan; padahal Nabi melahirkan di sana'*[Selamon]). He illustrated this using his hands to mimic a set of scales, tipping down in Meccas favour.

The *datu* and their immense religious knowledge in a sense personify the islands and ultimately remain attached to them. A widespread view suggested that *keramat* sites were not constructed by human effort but rather appeared miraculously on the death of the holy figure linked to the site. This would occur even if the *datu* died away from the islands: 'in speaking of *keramat*, he dies in a different place, afterwards a *keramat* appears here by itself'(*'dikatakan keramat, dia mati di tempat lain, nanti keramat jadi di sini sendiri'*[Lonthoir]).

This emphasis on the mystical providence of *keramat* sites works against their representation as 'shrines', a term applied to similar sites elsewhere in the Muslim world. [10] The expression tends to carry suggestions of a formally bounded or enclosed sacred precinct, relying overmuch on the salience of a profane-sacred opposition. Rather than marking a boundary separating the realms of the sacred and the profane, the Banda *keramat* bear witness to the generalised significance of the islands to Islam. Where humanly sponsored elements appear at Banda *keramat* such as tiles, concrete borders, roofs or fences, these were understood as respectful gifts or additions to the site, enhancing its visibility, not as somehow containing sacred substance. Neither were *keramat* used as repositories for relics or iconic symbols. Many Banda *keramat* are certainly isolated—located on promontories, cliff-sides and mountaintops relatively remote from homes or human activity. But others are situated within areas of settlement, or adjacent to gardens and well-used paths.

Rather than enclosures, the *keramat* constitute foci for the potency that imbues the islands more generally. As obvious centres of this force, they attract human attention, but there is no local vision of a sacred precinct, absolutely demarcated or contained by physical boundaries of some form. Though the entire landscape could be regarded as sacred (*tanah berkat*), in a practical everyday sense some places will of necessity be more revered than others. As Hubert has suggested, 'not every stone or plot of earth can be treated with the same degree of respect'(1994: 18). The *keramat* thus can be understood as complex ontological toponyms, specific places that act as potent signifiers of a larger whole. The key perspective in the islands is that *adat* is fundamentally emplaced: 'it belongs to the earth/ground, not to people'('*tanah punya, bukan orang punya*'[Lonthoir]).

Linked to the *keramat* sites and essentially grounded in the islands, the *datu* spirits were unable to leave *tanah Banda* with the fleeing population after the Dutch conquest in 1621 but continued to exert a watchful presence and active influence over their original territory. The *datu* were not considered the ancestors or biological founders (i.e. apical ancestors) of existing populations in the islands. [11] The *datu-datu* of the Bandas were associated with place rather than personal origins. They were the figures who founded human community in the islands ('*mulai membuka kampung ini*"). It is through their ritually based engagements with these figures and their sites that a population acknowledging its immigrant status is also able to argue that it has become demonstrably local. This identification is grounded literally in their presence on the *tanah berkat*. In the local view, populations elsewhere that continue to trace origins to the pre-conquest Banda Islands and who might even declare a form of contemporary identification as Bandanese must also recognise that the inability of themselves and their displaced ancestors to continue an intimate connection to the Banda *keramat* over several centuries has compromised any claims they may wish to assert regarding prior rights in the islands. The legitimacy of the 'newer' residents is evident in the relations they have successfully maintained with *keramat* and *datu*, a relation intrinsic to the influence that the founder-figures are understood as exerting over general wellbeing in the islands, including the fecundity and accessibility of resources.

A narrative concerning the origins of Hatta Island illustrates this close connection, but also the agency of Allah working through the land, to which the founder-figures are themselves subject. The island was said to have come into existence as the result of a catastrophic event linked to the flooding of another nearby island named Skaru, whose people were *bikin kotor* (behaving immorally). [12] Only two people were *orang bersih* (righteous, good, literally 'clean'), a conjugal couple. Their deliverance and the punishment of the others coincides with Hatta Island's creation:

> There was a large celebration ... an elderly person asked for water, wanted to drink. All the households refused ... those in one home, husband-wife, they provided it. The person told them: 'Do not go to sleep before twelve o'clock midnight. Shortly, a white chicken will come; climb onto it, shut your eyes; the chicken will fly. Don't open your eyes until the chicken's feet bump dry ground.' The chicken carried the couple to Hatta, on top of Fleeing Mountain. Hatta was newly risen from the sea. Skaru was drowned, the evil population all died. Therefore on Hatta Island, everyone is unsullied. [13]

The place where the righteous spouses landed in Hatta, Gunung Lari (Fleeing Mountain), has a *keramat* near the peak, said to mark the spot where they first touched the earth. Another less widespread version involved two chickens (male and female) who worked together to save husband and wife respectively. In this case, they did not land on the top of Gunung Lari, but rather at two other important local *keramat*—*keramat tanjung kenari* and *keramat tanjung buton*. These sites were about one kilometre apart on the northern coastline immediately in front of the site of the original *negeri* (ie the current *Kampung Lama*). The male landed first at that *keramat* closest to Skaru because the man was heavier, and the chicken became tired. Those who adhere to the first version tended to see the coastal sites as the two graves of the couple. Conversely, those embracing the second pointed to the mountain-top as their grave.

In any case, the role of the coastal *keramat* illustrates the close relation between these morally exemplary founder-figures and the land itself. They were linked to the erection of two *sasi* poles (*tiang sasi*) in the tidal zone (*maiti*) at either end of the same northern beach and tidal flats stretching for about one kilometre inbetween. Widespread in Maluku, *sasi* refers to periodic restrictions on the harvesting of a local resource – in this case, focused on trochus-shell—controlled by ritual action that is linked in turn to the sanction of ancestors and/or spirit figures. [14] The placement of these poles effectively closes community access to the resource while their removal permits it. Both actions were simultaneous with the fundamental ritual activity associated with *adat* practice throughout the islands—the collective construction of *sirih* containers (*tempat sirih*) by men and women, which were then carried to several *keramat* for placement on their surface, along with Muslim prayer. [15] On the island of Banda Besar, the placement of *tempat sirih* on *keramat* was sometimes associated with ensuring the supply of water in wells, the abundant fruiting of nutmeg and kenari trees, the successful growth of gardens and their protection from the depredations of wild pigs.

Banda *adat* practice is revealed here as (re-)inscribing an intimate connection between place, locality and ideas of community and their moral state. Not only was an entire population erased in the past because of the scale of impure action, but the land itself descended under the waves. At the same time, the salience of such forces remained vivid in the contemporary period through the control they exercised over the fruitfulness of the local environment. Indeed, ritual procedures are deemed necessary not only to make particular sought-after resources available, but to ensure their abundance and the safety of those who gather them. The ultimate cause of local catastrophes throughout the Bandas (for example, the 1988 eruption of Gunung Api) were widely interpreted in terms of moral explanations, particularly the conduct of the communities most affected. The practice of *adat* rituals provides collective opportunities to acknowledge the character of locality and reaffirm and enact the ideals of moral community. A key point is that this concern with local founder figures and locally derived *adat* was not simply portrayed as an end in itself (i.e. obtaining some direct benefit) but represented as an engagement with the principal terms of locality itself. In a general sense, informants explicitly affirmed a shared perspective of the islands' importance and their now-obscured pre-colonial history. The *datu-datu* are not simply magically powerful or religiously potent figures—their autochthonous origins exemplify their closeness to the *tanah berkat*. They represent a compelling ontological source of localness, a relationship with the cultural terms of belonging to the Banda Islands as place.

The *Negeri Adat*

If the *keramat* themselves testify to the claim that the islands are blessed ground, then the practices occurring at these sites actively enact this perspective and provide a concrete expression of connection to place. *Keramat* played a central part in the context of regular (though infrequent) collective ritual action involving the residents of particular settlements. Concentrations of important local *keramat* offer legitimation and focus within such collective practice, providing evidence of the existence of a pre-colonial polity known as *negeri adat* occupying the same location as contemporary settlements. These *negeri adat* in turn provide the social boundaries of ritual participation, in addition to providing a source of more specific communal identification within the embracing notion of *orang Banda* (being *orang Lonthoir* or *orang Hatta*, for example).

The expression *negeri* is likely an archaic one. The *Hikayat Tanah Hitu*, an indigenous narrative chronicle concerning the Muslim polity of *Tanah Hitu* on the north coast of Ambon, uses the terms *negeri* and *tanah* interchangeably in referring to the Banda Islands—'*Tanah Bandan*' and '*Negeri Bandan*' (Manusama 1977: 193). Geertz (1980: 4) posits the term *negeri* as a variation of *negara*, a loan word derived from the Sanskrit *nagara*, originally meaning 'town' or 'city'. The Indonesian terms *negara*, *nagari* and *negeri* developed to encompass such diverse ideas as 'palace', 'capital', 'state' and 'realm' in addition to 'town' (Wisseman-Christie 1986: 67). Reflecting on the Malay use of *negeri*, Milner

(1982: 123) suggests: '[It] denotes a fairly large community ... an entrepot for foreign merchants, with some political influence over the surrounding territory.'

Certainly the Banda Islands were an important trading entrepot in Central Maluku, perhaps the most important in a local network of trade that included the island groups of Aru and Kei and the small archipelagic chain off eastern Seram (Ellen 1987). Early European traders recorded dealing with several distinct polities located throughout the islands, many of which directly paralleled the locations of named *negeri adat* in the contemporary Bandas. Geertz (1980: 121) also notes, however, that *negara* 'catches up a various field of meanings, but a different field than *state*, leading to the usual misconnections of intercultural translation when it is thus rendered'. As a case in point, Geertz notes the existence in Bali of a 'custom community' or '*negara adat*', which he depicts in part as

> a stretch of sacred space ... all those living within its bounds, and therefore benefiting from its energies, were collectively responsible for meeting the ritual and moral obligations those energies entailed. (Geertz 1980: 128-9)

Traube (1986: 13) makes the Durkheimian-inspired observation that ritual obligations may be viewed as synonymous with social obligations—not simply an adjunct to relationships but rather constituting them as meaningful social forms. There are areas of important congruence here with local perspectives in the Banda Islands concerning *adat* obligations to the *negeri adat* and its *datu-datu*. These obligations were rarely expressed in the idiom of 'life' itself or couched in the idioms of derivation involving biological substance, as is widespread in eastern Indonesia. [16] As noted, the *datu-datu* were not envisaged as ancestors, and neither did social groupings (such as 'houses') defined by systems of marriage exchange have a presence in the contemporary Banda Islands. But ancestry and marriage exchange are far from being the only form ideas of relatedness might take. In the Bandas, concerns of social derivation tended to emphasise instead the source of productive social relations, the physical and moral conditions understood as underpinning and enabling community existence.

In this respect, informants regularly interpreted the cooperation and mutual assistance inherent in *adat* practice as providing a model for contemporary life: 'following the example of the *negeri* people from the past'('*mengikuti jejak daripada orang negeri dari dulu*'[Waer]) or 'similar to the way people behaved in the distant past, doing what is good, what is right'('*semacam orang dulu-dulu punya cara, bikin baik, bikin bersih*'[Lonthoir]). [17] Despite the absence of social groups defined in relation to apical ancestors, the Banda *negeri adat* can nevertheless be viewed as constituting origin groups of a kind, but one that emphasises concerns with the origins of community itself and the sustaining characters of communal life rather than personal derivation. This is reflected vividly in the greater local salience of moral metaphors linked to religious ideals—particularly *bersih* and *kotor* (clean-pure vs. soiled-impure)—rather than biological or botanical idioms of (e.g. blood or roots-tips).

My research showed that the depth of an individual's personal genealogical knowledge usually comprised two or, more rarely, three prior generations. Very few individuals could recall genealogical detail of any kind beyond this. The origin of ancestors who came to the Bandas from elsewhere tended to be conceived in extremely general terms, such as 'Java', rather than involving specific locations. [18] Many people simply stated that they did not know the geographic origins of personal forebears, and little systematic attempt was made to maintain the memories of distant ancestors. Carsten (1997: 271) describes a similar situation among an island-coastal community of Malay immigrants and stresses that this should not be interpreted solely in terms of the loss of important knowledge, as implied, for example, in descriptions such as 'structural amnesia'.

Instead, the absence of genealogical knowledge may play a critical positive role in the production of sociality among populations comprising a high level of impoverished immigrants. In this reading, analytical focus is given to the downward or forward-looking kinship practices that do exist as a productive orientation to social relations which work to integrate and cohere an otherwise diverse group: 'it may be more important to create kinship out of new ties than to remember ancestors whose identity has become largely irrelevant' (Carsten 1997: 270). It is unsurprising then that traditions associated with multiple points of ancestral origin should disappear over time, particularly as low-status groups or commoners regularly form the most mobile segments of a population. Under such conditions, 'kinship—or a sense of connectedness to place and people—is not derived from past ties but must be created in the future' (Carsten 1997: 272).

This kind of kinship orientation appears likely to have arisen also in the Bandas, where the bulk of colonial era immigrants were slaves, convicts and indentured labourers. As with Carsten's Malay-based study, Bandanese kinship is cognatic and tends to be 'wide' rather than 'deep': 'it stretches outwards, following degrees of siblingship, rather than backwards into the past' (Carsten 1997: 272). [19] She notes also that the long-term process of creating relatedness under such circumstances might rely on strongly asserted elisions of difference: 'the emphasis is on absorbing and blending, rather than maintaining regional and cultural difference'(Carsten 1997: 270). In the Bandas, this insight also appears applicable. Social differentiation based on issues of origin within *negeri adat* was considered impossible because the entire population was described as the descendants of immigrants, a perspective often put with some insistence: 'we are [all] immigrants, there are no truly autochthonous [people] left ... where can you find them? They are gone ... [people of] truly autochthonous origins – there are none'(*'katorang pendatang, asli betul su tarada lai ... mo dapat orang asli di mana? Su habis ... asal asli betul—tarada'* [Lonthoir]). A general principle of equality of origin appears almost axiomatic: all are *pendatang* (immigrants) and *campur* (mixed).

For the bulk of contemporary Bandanese, this overt rejection of social differentiation based on personal derivation has not eliminated the possibility of valorising the past. In emphasising the narratives of Banda as *tanah berkat*, the theme of incorporation and inclusion is given greater productive possibilities than the mere absence of ancestral detail. It facilitated a resiling from the kind of ethnic, religious and status differentiations that characterised colonial social life in the Banda plantations. In the post-colonial era, earlier distinctions that are still part of living memory between longer-term residents residing in hamlets outside the walled plantation compounds and more recent immigrants (many of whom were indentured labourers) who formed the bulk of the plantation workforce have fallen away, as a legacy of revolutionary-era nationalist sentiment and intermarriage.[20] In this context, the *negeri adat* emerged as an embracing ritual entity and a moral community, capable of cutting across religion and providing a vehicle of commonality rather than differentiation.

At the same time, informants suggested that their immigrant ancestors were obligated to become members of the *negeri* where they took up residence (*'musti masuk warga negeri'* [Lonthoir]), an act that involved adapting themselves to the *adat tanah* (*'sesuai diri dengan adat tanah'* [Lonthoir]) and, in so doing, joined the ritual activities associated with the existence of the *negeri* (*'ikut keadaan, kerja negeri'* [Selamon]). This principle remained predominant in thinking about *negeri* membership and identification. Local birth and local residence were the primary factors in allowing participation in the important ritual practices of the *negeri adat*, which in turn conferred and substantiated claims of local identification, being of the *negeri*—a *negeri* person (*orang negeri*).

An important enabling factor was undoubtedly an absence of social stratification based upon landownership. *Negeri adat* in the Banda Islands clearly express a mode of territorial ordering in the existence of the frontiers seen as separating different *negeri*. The significance of *negeri* membership for access to local resources was considerable, in particular for tree crops such as nutmeg and kenari nut, and also in some instances to marine biota (see, for example, Winn 2002). But the relation of the *negeri* to landownership was slight. A general recognition existed that much of the land was officially owned by the Government (*tanah negara*), a consequence of being formerly part of colonial plantation holdings. Nonetheless, a perspective I encountered frequently among ritual specialists suggested that no formal agreement existed between the Bandanese and the Dutch that involved passing ownership of the land to the latter, rather the use of the land only. In this view, the Indonesian Government has misconstrued what occurred historically and therefore, in taking possession of Dutch property in the 1950s, erroneously included areas of extant traditional holdings within its general declaration of the plantation areas as *tanah negara*. There was a persistent hope that former plantation land currently used for individual residences, garden cultivation and tree-planting would at some future point be converted officially into individual *hak paki* (exclusive right of use), if not *hak milik* (exclusive right of property).

Nonetheless, state law did not determine local practices of landholding. While taking account of the regulatory regimes of the State (or, at least, local conceptions of what these might involve), landholding practices were less involved with normative concepts of property consisting of 'jural typification' and much more concerned with constellations of social relationships and the distribution of property among living people (von Benda-Beckmann and Taale 1996: 39-40). A general area of emphasis involved the recognition of effort, in particular clearing and planting. These acts set in motion a constellation of local views akin to those described as '*perusah*' (von Benda-Beckmann and Taale 1996: 45) and customary 'pioneer's rights' (White 1999: 244), established in the first instance by a person's efforts in clearing and cultivating or house-building. Ownership of trees and use-rights to gardens was viewed locally as constituting part of an individual's estate (*warisan* or *pusaka*), passed on to their heirs after death. This was in turn shaped by varied interpretations of Islamic inheritance law, the most prevalent being that sons should receive twice the portion of daughters. People often noted that in practice the land had been used and passed on to descendants over many years without interference from the Government, a situation they hoped would continue.

Adat and Being Muslim

The accessibility of the founder-figures through ritual practice, and through them, *tanah Banda*, existed as the centre and focus of the Banda *negeri*, acting in ontological terms as the personification and source of the link between land and territory, place and people. Participation in collective ritual practice not only constituted the *negeri* as a social-territorial unit—a ritual polity—but provided the basis for a population of predominantly diverse immigrant ancestry to claim a legitimate sense of Bandanese identification. *Adat* fundamentally offers the legitimate terms of access to and engagement with local place and identification. In this instance, this is achieved not through articulating lines of precedence and their outcomes in social organisation but by stressing the continuity of *adat* and the enduring and active presence of the *datu*, depicted not only as the source of autochthonous *adat*, but importantly also as Muslims. As Muslims, residents can construct a direct identifying link with the founders that is able to transcend questions of personal derivation and origins, particularly in the absence of local claims of autochthony.

The key mark of 'deeper understanding' in local terms was to speak about the religious meanings of *adat*. Among *adat* specialists (*orang adat*), *adat* practice was often represented as incorporating symbolic elements (*lambang*) relating to religion or, as one informant suggested, 'reminders of religious matters' (*'peringatan hal-hal agama'* [Hatta]). After completion of one significant, involved and lengthy *adat* ritual I spoke with the Lonthoir ritual leader about his approach to *adat* practice and its relation to *agama*. He stressed that they were in essence the same; the motivation and method followed the same indistinguishable path (*'jalan bersama, bersatu'*[Lonthoir]). He stated that *adat* must not be understood as the forerunner to religion but rather as the *pembawa*, the 'carrier' or 'bearer' of religion. *Adat* practices contained and communicated religion and religious thought. He locked the index fingers of each hand around the other and pulled fruitlessly—there was no separating the two. A local healer (*dukun*) in *Negeri* Selamon offered the same image, saying that *adat* 'carries religion' (*'membawa agama'*), and stated firmly that it was not possible to speak of them as distinct or different (*'tarbisa bilang beda atau lai''*).

The substance of these kinds of interpretations was not confined to *adat* experts. A doxic, taken-for-granted quality existed in the broader community with respect to the fundamental commonality of Islam and *adat*. On the day of an important *adat* event in Lonthoir I woke early to hear the mosque playing Muslim songs through loudspeakers as it did on Islamic feast days such as *Maulud*, *Hari Korban* (*Hari Raya Haji*), *Lebaran* (*Idul Fitri*/*Hari Raya*) and *Isra Mi'Raj*.[21] I asked a neighbour why the mosque was playing music. He answered: 'because there's a celebration in the *negeri* ... to make our place lively ... aren't you aware of the festivities?' (*'Karna ada ramai di negeri ... supaya bikin katorang pung kampung ramai ... tarlihat ada ramai?'*). When I suggested the celebration was an *adat* occasion rather than a *hari raya*, he replied: *'Adat*, religion—it's the same thing. When practising *adat* you have to use incense, don't you?' (*'Adat, agama—sama. Kalau kerja adat musti paki kamanyan ka?'*). In pointing to the use of incense, he was identifying one of the defining elements of sacred action which applies equally to occasions of house-based gatherings for the recitation of Muslim prayers and various contexts of *adat* practice. This was true also of numerous other features, such as men and women wearing articles of attire locally defining of Muslim affiliation while engaging in *adat* ritual practice. The participation of the local imam was viewed as necessary, as was Muslim prayer involving Qur'anic readings.

Wherever it occurs in Indonesia (or Malaysia) the notion of *adat* rarely possesses a determinate meaning—its significance is highly contingent and potentially broadly embracing. *Adat* often signifies far more than 'conduct' or 'custom' (both of which are common glosses), frequently emphasising local ideas of a sacral code that provides a focus for the identity of a particular community (Milner 1982: 95). Indeed, early dichotomised representations of local *adat* versus global Islam have been effectively undermined, for example, by Peletz (1981: 151) who characterises *adat* as 'a unitary, all-embracing concept encompassing an expansive set of institutions governing the conduct of all personal, kin, and local affairs'. Interpretations of *adat* as 'rules that constitute a way of life' (Bowen 1991: 25) or 'socio-culturally regulated behaviour' (Rousseau 1998: 7) far more clearly open the way for religious thinking to occur within the rubric of *adat*, in that rules or regulations operate in a moral universe that draws its legitimacy from some source. Warren (1993: 3), for example, agrees that *adat* must be understood as incorporating the moral idea of social consonance and the behavioural imperative of propriety (viz. Geertz 1983: 207-14). She maintains this involves an underlying religious-social vision involving the necessary correspondence of cosmic and human relationships towards which it is directed.

This view effectively serves to evoke the potential of *adat* as itself constituting a source of governance, in the sense that Government can be understood as heterogeneous and pervasive rather than emanating from a single controlling source such as the State. This perspective is akin to Foucault's 'Governmentality' neologism, which places stress on aspects of the relationship of the self to the self (Foucault 1988: 19) and the modes through which the individual establishes their relation to a rule and recognises themselves as obliged to put it into practice (Rabinow 1997: xvii). Though stopping short of a detailed elaboration of a generalised link between religion and Governmentality, Foucault does trace the power of religious subjectivity in the shaping of human life. Such analysis is developed throughout Foucault's explorations of the nature of power, religion and the subject, where Carrette (2000: 150) suggests religion emerges as a politics of self; for example, in describing processes of subjectification 'the way in which people are invited or incited to recognise their moral obligations' whether divine law revealed in a text, rational rule, natural law, a cosmological order (Foucault 1997: 264). The religious self is always a part of the historical technology that produces and maintains the self. Indeed, religion can be viewed as a politics of self, revealing the truth of what we are by the practices we perform. To paraphrase Ricoeur (1995: 70), sacred practice is a continuing interpretation of the substance regarded as grounding the community—for the community to address itself to a substantially different notion of the sacred would be to make a decision concerning its social identity.

In the case of the Bandas, local interpretations of *Banda adat* in terms of idealised discourses concerning morality and religion involves thinking about *negeri* communities as (in ideal terms) moral communities. This perspective incorporates local concern with issues of correct practices, Islam itself and identification as Muslims—indeed, it is through 'Islamic' discourse that the particular moral community regarding itself as 'Muslim' appears:

> We should not assume that religion and culture make up any a priori system of meaning, and we should not look for what is essential in Islam; rather than that we should look for historical social formations within which Muslims themselves engage in discourse on what should be central to Islam. (Manger 1999: 9)

In the Bandas, ideas of the moral governance of Islam drew on a local vision involving the spirits of place—the Muslim *datu* who carried Islam to the islands, and the islands themselves as *tanah berkat*. The *negeri adat* find their raison d'être in these representations, so that *adat* (and ritual practice in particular) becomes a way of collectively preserving, transmitting and renewing the morality seen as inherent to Islam. In this sense *adat* practice in the Banda *negeri adat* could be said to act 'on behalf of the source'(viz. Lewis 1996: 167) with the notion of 'source' combining three dimensions that together effectively constitute a local moral community: the source of land, the source of sociality, the source of legitimacy (Lewis 1996: 167). In the Banda case, the source of the local was also the local source of Islam. This is the full significance of thinking about the idiom of *tanah berkat*.

Conclusion

The contemporary population of the Banda Islands ultimately embraces its status of being non-autochthonous (*bukan orang asli Banda*) while affirming the veracity of its claim to be truly local—authentically of the islands (*orang Banda asli*). This claim is rooted in their presence and engagement with the blessed land of Banda (*tanah Banda tanah berkat*) through membership of a *negeri adat* and participation in its defining ritual activities, a participation that for the bulk of residents is enhanced and deepened through their identification also as Muslims.

In Banda, representations of the islands as *tanah berkat* draw on understanding the islands as physically embodying the religious foundations of moral order that inform the locally cogent terms of moral community. As such, they appear as capable as nationalism in 'linking fraternity, power and time meaningfully together' (Anderson 1991: 36), and of doing so with considerable ontological potency with respect to locality and community. The implications for identification are summarised cogently by Battaglia (1999: 119): 'The struggle for identity reveals itself as based in claiming *a distinctive moral order*, rather than in maintaining national, ethnic or any other sort of mappable boundaries.'

References

Battaglia, Debbora. 1999. 'Towards an ethics of the open subject: Writing culture in good conscience.' In H.L. Moore (ed.), *Anthropological Theory Today*, Cambridge: Polity Press. pp.114-50.

Carrette, Jeremy R. 2000. *Foucault and Religion. Spiritual Corporality and Political Spirituality*. London: Routledge.

Carsten, Janet. 1997. *The Heat of the Hearth. The Process of Kinship in a Malay Fishing Community*. Oxford: Clarendon Press.

Chambert-Loir, Henri and Anthony Reid. 2002. 'Introduction.' In H. Chambert-Loir and A. Reid (eds), *The Potent Dead: Ancestors, Saints and Heroes in Contemporary Indonesia,* Sydney/Honolulu: Asian Studies Association of Australia in association with Allen and Unwin and University of Hawai'i Press. pp. xv-xxvi.

Ellen, Roy. 1977. 'The trade in spices.' *Indonesian Circle*, 12: pp. 21-15.

Ellen, Roy. 1983. 'Social theory, ethnography and the understanding of practical Islam in South East Asia.' In M.B. Hooker (ed.), *Islam in South-East Asia*, Leiden: E.J. Brill. Pp. 50-91.

Ellen, Roy. 1984. 'Trade, environment, and the reproduction of local systems in the Moluccas.' In E.F. Moran (ed.), *The Ecosystem Concept in Anthropology*, Boulder (Colorado): Westview Press. pp.163-204.

Ellen, Roy. 1987. 'Environmental perturbation, inter-island trade, and the relocation of production along the Banda Arc; or, Why central places remain central.' In T. Suzuki and R. Ohtsuka (eds), *Human Ecology of Health and Survival in Asia and the South Pacific*, Tokyo: University of Tokyo Press. pp. 35-61.

Foucault, Michel. 1988. 'The ethic of care for the self as a practice of freedom.' In J. Bernauer and D. Rasmussen (eds), *The Final Foucault*, Cambridge, Massachusetts: MIT. pp. 1-20.

Foucault, Michel. 1997b. 'On the genealogy of ethics: an overview of work in progress.' In P. Rabinow (ed.), *Michel Foucault. Ethics: Subjectivty and Truth. The Essential Works,* Volume One. London: Allen Lane/The Penguin Press. pp.255-80.

Fox, James J. 1989. 'Ziarah visits to the tombs of the wali, the founders of Islam on Java.' In M. Ricklefs (ed.), *Islam in the Indonesian Social Context*, Annual Indonesian Lecture Series No. 15, AIA-CSEAS. pp. 19-36.

Fox, James J. 1995. 'Origin structures and systems of precedence in the comparative study of Austronesian societies.' In P.J.K.Li, C. Tsang, Y. Huang,

D. Ho and C. Tseng (eds), *Symposium Series of the Institute of History & Philology*, Taipei: Academia Sinica 3. pp. 27-57.

Fox, James J. 1997. 'Place and landscape in comparative Austronesian perspective.' In J. Fox (ed.), *The Poetic Power of Place: Comparative Perspectives on Austronesian Ideas of Locality*, Canberra: Department of Anthropology Comparative Austronesian Studies Project, Research School of Pacific and Asian Studies, The Australian National University. pp. 1-21.

Fox, Robin. 1967. *Kinship and Marriage*. Middlesex: Penguin.

Geertz, Clifford. 1973. *The Interpretation of Cultures*. London: Fontana Press.

Geertz, Clifford. 1980. *Negara: The Theatre State in Nineteenth Century Bali*. Princeton (New Jersey): Princeton University Press.

Geertz, Clifford. 1983. *Local Knowledge*. New York: Basic Books.

Grimes, Barbara. 1991. 'The development and use of Ambonese Malay.' *Pacific Linguistics*, A-81. pp. 83-123.

Grimes, John. 1996. *A Concise Dictionary of Indian Philosophy*. New York: State University of New York Press.

Hubert, Jane. 1994. 'Sacred beliefs and beliefs of sacredness.' In D. Carmichael, J. Hubert, B. Reeves and A. Schanche (eds), *Sacred Sites, Sacred places*, London: Routledge. pp. 9–19.

Kaartinen, Timo. 2001. "Moments of Recognition: Truth, evidence and the visiting stranger in Kei (East Indonesia)" In J. Sikala (ed.), *Departures: How Societies Distribute Their People*. Transactions of the Finnish Anthropological Society No. 46, Helsinki: the Finnish Anthropological Society. pp. 107-25.

Lewis, E.D. 1996. 'Origin structures and precedence in the social orders of Tana 'Ai and Sikka'. In J. Fox and C. Sather (eds), *Origins, Ancestry and Alliance: Explorations in Austronesian Ethnography*. Canberra: Department of Anthropology, and Comparative Austronesian Studies Project, Research School of Pacific and Asian Studies, The Australian National University. pp. 145-74.

Manger, Leif. 1999. 'Muslim diversity: local Islam in global contexts.' In L. Manger (ed.), *Muslim Diversity Local Islam in Global Contexts*, Surrey: Curzon. pp. 1-36.

Manusama, Z.J. 1977. 'Hikayat Tanah Hitu: Historie en Sociale Stuctuur van de Ambonse Eilandens in het Algemeen en van Uli Hitu in het Bijzonder tot het Midden der Seventiende Eeuw. Unpublished PhD thesis, University of Leiden.

Meilink-Roelofsz, M.A.P. 1962. *Asian Trade and European Influence in the Indonesian Archipelago Between 1500 and About 1630*. The Hague: Martinus Nijhoff.

Milner, A.C. 1982. *Kerajaan: Malay Political Culture on the Eve of Colonial Rule*. Tucson, Arizona: University of Arizona Press.

Peletz, Michael Gates. 1981. 'Social history and evolution in the interrelationship of adat and Islam in Rembau, Negeri Sembilan.' *Research Notes and Discussions Paper*, No. 27. Singapore: Institute of Southeast Asian Studies.

Peletz, Michael Gates. 1988. *Share of the Harvest. Kinship, Property, and Social History Among the Malays of Rembau*. Berkeley: University of California Press.

Pemberton, John. 1993. *On the Subject of 'Java'*. Ithica: Cornell University Press.

Rabinow, Paul. 1997. 'Introduction.' In P. Rabinow (ed.), *Michel Foucault. Ethics: Subjectivty and Truth. The Essential Works,* Volume One, London: Allen Lane/The Penguin Press. pp. xi-xlii.

Ricoeur, P. 1995. *Figuring the Sacred. Religion, Narrative and Imagination*. Minneapolis: Fortress Press.

Traube, Elizabeth. 1986. *Cosmology and Social Life. Ritual Exchange Among the Mambai of East Timor*. Chicago: University of Chicago Press.

Uneputty, T.J.A., Usman Thalib; M. Nanlohy; B. Berhitu and A. Batkunda. 1985. In H.A. Yunus and Suradi (eds), *Upacara Tradisional yang Berkaitan dengan Peristiwa Alam dan Kepercayaan Daerah Maluku*, Jakarta: Departemen Pendidikan dan Kebudayaan Proyek Inventerasi dan Dokumentasi Kebudayaan Daerah.

Villiers, John. 1981. 'Trade and society in the Banda Islands in the sixteenth century.' *Modern Asian Studies,* 15 (4). pp. 723-50.

Villiers, John. 1990. 'The cash-crop economy and state formation in the Spice Islands in the fifteenth and sixteenth centuries.' In J. Kathirithamby-Wells and J. Villiers (eds), *The Southeast Asian Port and Polity Rise and Demise*. Singapore: Singapore University Press. pp. 83-105.

Warren, Carol. 1993. *Adat and Dinas: Balinese Communities in the Indonesian State*. Oxford: Oxford University Press.

Winn, Phillip. 2000. 'Graves, groves and gardens: Place and identity in central Maluku, Indonesia.' *The Asia Pacific Journal of Anthropology,* 1 (2). pp. 24-44.

Winn, Phillip. 2002. 'Violence, sovereignty and moral community in Maluku.' In M. Sakai (ed.), *Beyond Java: Regional Autonomy in Indonesia*, Adelaide: Crawford House.

Winn, Phillip. 2002. ' "Everyone searches, everyone finds": moral discourse and resource use in an Indonesian Muslim community.' *Oceania*, 72 (4). pp. 275-92.

Winstedt, R.O. 1924. 'Karamat: sacred places and persons in Malaya.' *Journal of the Malayan Branch of the Royal Asiatic Society*, II. pp. 264-79.

Woodward, Mark R. 1989. *Islam in Java: Normative Piety and Mysticism in the Sultanate of Yogyakarta*. Tucson (Arizona): University of Arizona Press.

ENDNOTES

[1] *'Di daerah kepulauan ini ditemukan berbagai jenis golongan etnis yang berasal dari berbagai daerah di Indonesia disamping mereka yang berasal kepulauan Maluku sendiri ... Sudah barang tentu mereka datang dengan latar belakang budaya sendiri-sendiri ... Walaupun demikian kalau diamati dengan teliti adat istiadat yang berlaku, maka nampaknya unsur budaya asli tetap dominan. Jadi di sini anasir-anasir budaya pendatang telah terlebur dalam konteks kebudayaan asli.'* (Uneputty et al. 1985: 27-8)

[2] Non-English words appearing in italics, particularly those appearing in direct quotes, reflect this form of Malay as spoken in the Banda Islands. Worthy of study, it varies in numerous respects from Indonesia's standard national Malay (known as Bahasa Indonesia) and also from Ambon Malay, which forms something of a lingua franca throughout central and increasingly also south-east Maluku (see Grimes 1991).

[3] This paper is based on 20 months of field research in the Banda Islands conducted between 1996 and 1997 and in 1999 under the auspices of the Indonesian Institute of Sciences (LIPI) Jakarta, in cooperation with Pattimura University Ambon and with support from the Department of Anthropology, Research School of Pacific and Asian Studies, The Australian National University, Canberra.

Direct quotes from local informants in the Bandas can be dated to this period (i.e. between 1997-99). The location of each interlocutor concerned is provided in square parenthesis immediately after the quote.

[4] I am indebted to Tom Goodman for bringing this text to my attention, located among the papers of the late Swedish anthropologist John-Erik Elmberg at the National Museum of Ethnography in Stockholm.

[5] Based on fieldwork in 1996-97 and in 1999. Knowledge of the name Lewerang was restricted to ritual specialists who described it as the original or authentic name (*nama asli*) and reserved it for use on ritual occasions.

[6] Kaartinen (2001) notes a version of this narrative occurring within a group in the Kei Islands tracing descent from refugees that fled the Banda Islands during the Dutch conquest in 1621.

[7] As a result, some informants claim that the Bandas are entirely free of *suanggi*. Others suggest they are able to arrive by more conventional means such as inter-island shipping.

[8] Geertz (1980: 106) defines *sakti* in its original Sanskrit as 'the energy or active part of a deity' and notes of the cognate *sekti* in Bali that it is a term used for "the sort of transordinary phenomenon that elsewhere is called mana, baraka, orenda, kramat ... a divinely inspired gift or power, such as the ability to perform miracles'. The terms *sakti* and *keramat* were not equivalent in the way that they were used in the Bandas. In daily use in Lonthoir, *keramat* was a noun, not an adjective. It referred to a particular kind of site, but not to descriptions of the qualities of that site (as the term often did elsewhere, particularly in the Malay Peninsula). Common statements such as 'I am going to a *keramat'* (*'mo pi keramat'*) are not possible using *sakti*—one can go to a *sakti* place (*tempat sakti*) but not to a *sakti*. Objects could be *sakti* (such as the heirloom objects of the community) but are never described as *keramat*. Nevertheless, *keramat* were referred to occasionally as *'tempat keramat'*, suggesting this might once have been the common usage.

[9] The idea of conception through partaking of a certain food is a widespread motif throughout the Austronesian-speaking world. In a Malay context, a pomegranate-related conception story occurs in

the *Hakiyat Salindong Lima*, recorded by Overbeck (1924: 280-1). Carved pomegranates adorn the wooden *mimbar* or sermon-platform of one Banda mosque; another has a carved pomegranate at a central point in the internal ceiling immediately below the central external minaret.

[10] *Keramat* in peninsular Malaysia are described regularly as shrines (e.g. Linehan 1951: 151; bin Mohd. Yatim 1985: 20; Peletz 1988: 113). The Javanese *kramatan*, as among the better-documented sites of this kind in Indonesia, has also been described as a shrine (Woodward 1989: 170). The expression 'tomb-shrines' has been used to refer in general terms to holy places associated with holy people that attract building, renovation or financial support from ruling figures—a practice described as widespread from Morocco to Indonesia (Renard 1996: 179). In Bangladesh, Gardener provides an account of *pir* (Sufi saint) cults whose graves are 'venerated as shrines' (1999: 40). Chambert-Loir and Reid (2002: xxii) note that 'the worship of saints is so common that it can be regarded as a characteristic of Islamic praxis'. Given disputes among Muslims concerning the practice (Wahabists are particularly vehement in their opposition to this practice, which they view as a near-definitive feature of the Sufist traditions they reject), the term 'veneration' is probably less potentially pejorative than 'worship'. Even among Indonesian Sunni Muslims, the issue of the ability of Muslim holy figures to intercede directly on behalf of a petitioner either with Mohammed or God is frequently controversial.

[11] In discussing the latter, Banda interlocutors would speak of *nenek moyang, moyang-moyang* or *nenek-nenek*.

[12] Skaru becomes quite accessible at neap tides, and attracts Hatta residents as a site for gathering marine biota.

[13] *'Ada pesta besar ... jadi satu orang tertua minta air, mo minum. Semua rumah tarkasih ... dorang satu rumah, laki-bini, dorang kasih. Dia bilang: "tarboleh tidur sampai jam duabelas malam. Nanti, ayam putih datang; naik di atas, tutup mata; nanti ayam terbang. Tarboleh buka mata sampai ayam pung kaki tonka di tanah kerin." Ayam bawah orang ke Hatta, di atas Gunung Lari. Hatta baru tumbu di laut ... Skaru tinggilam, rakyat jehat semua mati. Jadi di Pulau Hatta, semua bersih.'* (Hatta). Some informants suggested the old man was Mohammed in disguise.

[14] Zerner (1994: 81) describes the term *sasi* as originating in 'Makassar Malay'. In the Banda Islands, the term is associated with a notion of Maluku Malay (Bahasa Maluku) and sometimes Ambon Malay (Bahasa Ambon).

[15] *Tempat sirih* are usually circular containers woven from the leaves of immature coconut palm fronds, though on Hatta they are more often fashioned as flat layered 'plates' made from banana leaves. Both contain flower petals, cigarettes, loose tobacco, coins and the ingredients required for betel-nut chewing. In the Bandas, as is common throughout Indonesia, the latter includes powdered lime or *kapur*, betel leaf or *daun sirih* (from the climbing vine *Piper betle*), slivers of areca nut known as *pinang* or *pinang sirih* (the seed of the palm *Areca catechu*) and crumbled *gambir* (an astringent extract obtained from the leaves and shoots of the tropical shrub *Uncaria gambir*). Generally, men obtain the fronds, construct the containers and carry them to the *keramat*, while women prepare the ingredients and fill the containers. All these actions tend to be prefaced with prayer.

[16] In Traube's East Timor context, for example, these obligations are rooted in idioms of indebtedness, reciprocity and balance between groups identified as life- (or wife)-givers and life- (wife)-receivers that parallel and iterate an asymmetric dependency characterising human relations with cosmic beings: 'The debt that is owed to the various social sources of life and well-being is also the debt that is owed by society as a whole to the encompassing cosmos. Social and cosmological obligations intermingle in ritual contexts' (Traube 1986: 14).

[17] For a comparative linguistic discussion of closely related cognates of the Banda causative *'bikin'* (also *biking, beking*) in Ambonese, Ternate and Menado Malays, see Litamahuputty (1997).

[18] An exception to this is that component of Banda's population that traces their origins to the Tukang Besi Islands, who are generally able to point to a specific island in this group as their ancestors' point of origin.

[19] The greater breadth and flexibility of affiliation provided by cognatic modes of relatedness offer another positive advantage in small island settings, such as the Bandas. It facilitates emigration as a response to local population pressures through providing abundant ties to kin residing elsewhere. The Banda Islands produce a constant flow of more or less permanent migrants to numerous areas, especially Ambon, Tual (Kei Islands) and Dobo (Aru Islands) in Maluku Province and Fak-Fak in Papua Province.

[20] This is not to suggest, of course, that other post-colonial stratifications are not present in the Banda Islands as exist elsewhere in Indonesia.

[21] *Maulud*: Mohammed's birthday; *Hari* (*Raya*) *Korban* (or *Hari Raya Haji* or *Idul Adha*): celebration of the Mecca pilgrimage; *Lebaran* (or *Idul Fitri*): the end of the fasting month of Ramadan; *Isra Mi'Raj*: Mohammed's miraculous night ascension to heaven.

Chapter 6. Mapping Buru: The Politics of Territory and Settlement on an Eastern Indonesian Island

Barbara Dix Grimes

> In terms of most communication theories and common sense, a map is a scientific abstraction of reality. A map merely represents something which already exists objectively 'there.' In the history I have described [of Siam], this relationship was reversed. A map anticipated spatial reality, not vice versa. In other words, *a map was a model for, rather than a model of, what it purported to represent.*
> Thongchai (1988:110, cited in Anderson 1991:173, my emphasis)

On the most up-to-date maps of the Indonesian Province of Maluku, one will find Buru Island labelled 'District of Buru Island' (*Kabupaten Pulau Buru*). Buru's attainment of district status in 1999 was the result of several years of effort by delegates in the Provincial Assembly in Ambon. Before this, Buru appeared on maps merely as three 'subdistricts' (*kecamatan*) in the 'District of Central Maluku' (*Kabupaten Maluku Tengah*), governed from the district centre at Masohi on the island of Seram. [1]

The need to update maps of Buru is nothing new. In the 16th century, the island of Buru was claimed by the Sultan of Ternate as one of his 'dependencies'. By others, it was identified as a 'vassal' of Portugal. After the Dutch East Indies Company (*Verenigde Oost-Indische Compagnie*, hereafter VOC) arrived in the early 17th century and replaced the Portuguese as the predominant European power in the region, the Dutch took advantage of an earlier Portuguese-Ternate alliance to claim their own sovereignty over Buru because it had been 'land that sat under the crown of Ternate'. Later, in 1824, a colonial law resulted in the division of Buru into regencies (*regentschap*) as Dutch officials sought to incorporate local political systems into an overarching administration. For the next 100 years the map of Buru again changed repeatedly as the number of regencies declined gradually from 14 to seven.

For centuries foreigners have made claims and drawn maps of Buru as 'models for' their political aspirations. From Ternate, Ambon, Jakarta and other places across the sea, notions such as 'vassal', 'dependency', *regentschap*, *kecamatan* (subdistrict), *desa* (administrative village), and now *kabupaten* (district), have been mapped onto Buru. The people of Buru, however, have not always embraced these foreign concepts nor the political relationships they imply. In the mid-1980s when I first went to Buru, I was hosted by the late Raja of *Regentschap* Masarete.

One of the first tasks I set for myself was to ascertain what contemporary significance was attributed to the notion of *regentschap*, and specifically to *Regentschap* Masarete. A dusty old *regentschap* map hung respectfully in a subdistrict office in recognition of Buru 'tradition' (*adat*), even though there was no correlation between the *regentschap* boundaries and the boundaries of the subdistrict map. I did not have to spend long, however, to realise that a territorial concept existed that was far more salient than *regentschap*, or even *kecamatan* or *desa*. It was the Buru concept of *fena*. This paper discusses how Buru discourses of territory are centred on the concept of *fena*, and how Buru people draw on this concept from their Austronesian heritage to interact with alternative models for territory that have been mapped onto their island.

Noro and *Fena:* Clan and Land on Buru

Etymologically, *fena* comes from the Proto-Austronesian word **benua*. Blust (1987: 100) proposed the meaning of this proto-term to be 'an inhabited territory that includes not only the human population and dwellings, but also all plant and animal forms that contribute to the maintenance of the human community'. Like many other cognates of **benua*, *fena* is primarily a territorial concept, and a very useful concept for sharing the land. On Buru, however, the *fena* is associated so closely with the *noro*—the Buru origin group or 'clan'—that the two terms not only imply each other, they can represent each other.

The inhabited or domesticated aspect of *fena* can be seen clearly in the Buru opposition between *fena* and *mua*. *Mua* is a term used primarily to refer to the vast tropical rainforests that dominate much of the island. When contrasted with *fena*, *mua* can also include open grasslands or any other uninhabited, uncultivated space, regardless of whether it would be classified by Western categories as jungle. Thus, the dichotomy of *fena* versus *mua* brings out the distinction between domesticated land versus wild or undomesticated land. People use these terms to distinguish, for example, between *fafu fena*, 'village or domesticated pigs' and *fafu mua* 'jungle or wild pigs'.

So while *fena* delineates the sphere of socially or humanly controlled land, the agents who control that land are a particular *noro*. On the basis of its origin account, each Buru clan is linked to a well-defined 'place' or 'territory' (*neten*) and the members of the clan are considered to be 'custodians of the territory' (*geba neten duan*). Such a link exists between every Buru clan and a specific territorial area on the island. These places are well defined by boundaries such as stream beds, rivers, mountain ridges, large rock formations and other topographical features. This relationship between clan and land was described by several different colonial officials who studied land tenure on Buru in the 19th century, carefully noting down the Buru term *rah isin fena*, 'land of the *fena*' (Willer 1858: 100; Wilken 1875: 12). One wrote:

> The ownership of all the lands, from the tops of the mountains to the seaside, belong, thus to the different *fena;* the Alfuru is very specific about this, when he says, that the *fena* is *neten duan,* that is, master of the land. The rights to the land belong to the members of the *fena.* (*De eigendom van all de gronden, van de toppen der bergen tot aan het zeestrand, behoort dus aan de verschillende fenna's; de Alfoer drukt zich heiromtrent vrij bepaald uit, wanneer hij zegt, dat de fenna is 'nettin doean', d. i. heer (eigenaar) van de grond. Het bezit van den grond berust bij de leden der fenna.*) (Wilken 1875: 12).

Later on, in the early 20th century, a Dutch missionary-scholar wrote several articles on Buru including one titled *Noro en fena op Buru* (Schut 1921). He also described the relationship between these two Buru concepts, arguing as we would say now, that *noro* refers to a kin group or clan, while *fena* refers to the territory of a clan.

Thus, *fena* is polysemous and can refer to the 'territory' (*neten*) of a clan, to a settlement of that clan, or to the clan itself. For example, *noro Masbait* refers unambiguously to the people in the Masbait clan; while *fena Masbait* can refer to the specific territory linked to the Masbait clan who are considered to be its 'custodians' (*geba neten duan*), to a settlement in which many Masbait clan members reside, or to the people in the Masbait clan. In this final sense, *fena* is interchangeable with *noro.*

Living on the Land: Residence and Settlement on Buru

When *fena* is compounded to *fen-lale* (inside a *fena*) this refers unambiguously to a settlement rather than the clan or the total *fena* territory. The link between clan and land is not contingent on custodians living on their *fena* land. In fact, many Buru people live on land belonging to another clan. If men 'request with respect' (*laha tu hormat*) to hunt, make gardens, or even to build villages on the land of others, particularly the land of their mother's brothers or brothers-in-law, their request should be granted. Since the land belonging to a clan is also constructed as the clan members' place of origin, there may be a difference between place of origin and place of residence. In any given *fen-lale,* there will be people from the clan considered to be 'custodian of the territory' residing in their place of origin. In addition, people from other clans will also be residing there, usually by agreement with the custodial clan.

The following table shows the number of households found in six south Buru villages and the clan affiliation of those households:

Table 6.1. Clan affiliation of households in six Buru villages

Fen-lale --------- Noro	Kudil Lahin	Mngeswaen	Wae Nama Olon	Fakal	Wae Katin	Wae Loo
Mual	9*	25*	7*	3	10	-
Gebhain	1	5	7	5	26*	20*
Gewagit	-	-	8	2	9	1
Masbait	-	14	-	22*	1	1
Biloro	-	2	-	5	1	2
Liligoli	-	1	-	-	-	5
Tasane	-	1	-	-	-	-
Leslesi	-	-	-	-	-	1
Migodo	-	1	1	-	-	-
Outsiders	-	1	1	-	1	1
Total	10	49	24	37	48	35

* Indicates the founding clan of each village.

In spite of the permanence associated with English terms such as 'village', Buru villages or settlements are not fixed centres of population concentration; they are continually impacted by a semi-nomadic lifestyle, which needs to be understood in light of several different factors. First, various seasonal activities tend to either disperse people or gather them together. Activities associated with hunting and gathering alternate with more intensive periods of agricultural activity. Buru men seek to gain a reputation as good hunters and considerable food comes from their hunting activities, particularly during the peak of east monsoon (June and July) when men 'enter the jungle' (*rogo mua*) to hunt the small marsupial cuscus and wild pig as an exclusively male activity. Women also gather wild vegetables and tubers from the jungle whenever possible. During the west monsoon (November to April), the activities of men and women focus on agriculture and they prefer to be in or near their gardens most of the time.

Swidden agriculture also contributes to mobility on Buru. Typical of non-volcanic islands in equatorial regions, Buru soil is relatively infertile (Bellwood 1985: 12), and shifting agriculture is needed to allow for soil replenishment. The need to make new gardens on a fairly regular basis means that village-to-garden distance increases as people remain in the same settlement over time and new gardens must be made further and further away. The further gardens are from settlements, the more days or weeks people tend to spend in their gardens without returning to the village, particularly in labour-intensive periods of clearing, planting and harvesting. After 20 years or so, it is not uncommon for entire Buru villages to move to a new location, where primary forest is available for new gardens, typical of how settlements are sometimes 'forced to move to keep up with swiddens' (Dumond 1969: 337).

This means that people might alternate between a 'village house' (*hum-fena*), a 'garden house' (*hum-hawa*; usually just a hut) and sometimes a 'hunting house' (*hum-tapa*; a forest hut usually associated only with men). The best way of viewing Buru residence is in terms of these several options which people have available to them. At certain times they might live for extended periods in their garden or in the jungle, and at other times they might return to a house in a village. These options are then multiplied, because it is possible to have several hunting huts or garden houses in different gardens several days' walk apart. In addition to the possibility of living with relatives in other villages, all this provides people with numerous options for residence and with socially significant ways to avoid conflict and asymmetric relations. A common pattern in Christian villages is for people to return to the village from their gardens on Saturday afternoon and leave again on Sunday afternoon or Monday morning after the Sunday church service.

Studies of swidden agriculture have pointed out how this type of agriculture usually requires that relatively large amounts of land per capita be available for agricultural use, and that settlements cannot remain permanently in place (Meggers 1957: 82; Dumond 1969: 337). Both these factors occur on Buru where population density is about 11 people/km^2. In addition to having limited permanence, the composition of Buru settlements varies significantly with none being very large. [2] The smallest type of settlement is a single isolated garden or jungle hut for a single family or hunting party. The term 'circle of houses' (*hum-lolin*) can refer to a small settlement of three to 10 houses (20 to 50 people). This term refers to the settlement and the social group that lives there, as households in this type of settlement usually belong to a single lineage or sub-clan, which is also called *hum-lolin*. Larger settlements may have 30 to 50 households (150 to 300 people) belonging to several clans (*noro*). The term *fen-lale* (inside a *fena*) can be used to refer to these multi-family settlements. On the coast there are a few multi-ethnic settlements such as the subdistrict centres with more than 200 househoulds.

Table 6.2. Buru settlement patterns

Single family garden house (*hum-hawa*)
Single hunting hut of a male hunting group (*hum-tapa*)
Single sub-clan 'circle of houses' with 3-12 dwellings (*hum-lolin*)
Multi-clan settlement with 15–50 households (*fen-lale*)
Multi-ethnic coastal towns of 200 or more households (BI: *ibu kota kecamatan*)

Several colonial accounts (Willer 1858; Wilken 1875; van der Miesen 1908, 1909a, 1909b) reveal how terminology to describe Buru settlements posed a dilemma to European administrators. Many settlements in the 19th century were recorded as having about 20 or 30 inhabitants although some had as many as 174 inhabitants (Willer 1858: 194). In these reports, settlements were often referred to with the Buru term *hum-lolin*, and one official (Willer 1858: 100) made it a point to translate *hum-lolin* as 'hamlet' (Dutch: *gehucht*) rather than 'village' (*dorp*) because of the small size. Others referred to them inconsistently as *gehucht* or *dorp*.

In many places in Maluku it is commonly said that people did not live in villages until they were forcibly resettled, usually on or near the coast, by the Dutch or Indonesian Governments. It is not obvious that this occurred on Buru. In colonial accounts there is no discussion of resettling people into larger villages nor is there any oral history from that time suggesting villages were formed by forced resettlement. In fact, small villages (*hum-lolin*) on Buru Island today are very similar to those described in the last century. And the larger villages (50 houses) of today are not limited to areas of government intervention. Several large villages in the interior of the island remain outside the scope of government contact and service.

A more significant change in regard to Buru settlement in the past century than village size is the fact that a more sedentary lifestyle has been promoted by the Government as a prerequisite for 'national development'. Cement and tin roofing create more permanent structures than those built from traditional jungle materials and in some villages these items have been carried up the mountains with great difficulty to build schools, churches and a few individual houses. Government officials as well as imported pastors and schoolteachers encourage sedentary living and more permanent houses as a sign of modernity.

But even cement, tin roofing, churches and schools have limited impact on mobility. Explanations of why villages continue to move often have to do with sickness and multiple deaths. If too many deaths occur in a short time, it is often deemed time to abandon the village. [3] New villages form as a founder, called a 'village custodian' (*negri duan*), gathers people together. The number of people living in a village is thus partly a reflection of an individual village custodian's charismatic ability to gather people together and to maintain a sense of solidarity. Some of the mountain villages in which churches were established by Dutch missionaries in the early 20th century still exist at the same location, although not without having endured various problems that would usually be resolved in Buru society through migration. In certain cases the pressure has become too much and even villages with Dutch churches have migrated. During my fieldwork in 1990, a large village near the lake with a prestigious reputation for having several cement houses, was abandoned and dispersed after internal disputes, with one clan returning four days' walk, halfway across the island, to their land of origin.

'Where They Marry Each Other': Territory as Localised Networks of Affinity

With the *noro* as the highest form of traditional political organisation and *fena* as the most inclusive territorial unit, at its most encompassing level Buru society is a multiplicity of localised networks of affinity. *Noro* are exogamous and, with high value placed on the symmetrical exchange of women between two patrilineal *noro*, sister exchange is an ideal marriage arrangement. It is desirable for a *noro* to have affinal relations with numerous other *noro*, but this does not mean every *noro* has such relations with every other *noro*, for in reality, marriage relations correlate highly with place. Clans who live near each other, frequently intermarry, while clans who live far from each other do so with far less frequency. This correlation is acknowledged openly such that places are, at least in part, defined by the marriages that occur there. A common way to explain a distant unfamiliar place is to contextualise it as the place where two specific *noro* 'marry each other'.

The correlation between place and marriage relations can be seen by taking an example from the Gebhain *noro*. Around the territory of the Gebhain *noro* in south Buru are two villages a day's walk apart, Wae Katin and Wae Loo. Each village has approximately 200 inhabitants or 40 households. In the village of Wae Katin, 50per cent (24/48) of the households are affiliated with the Gebhain *noro* and in the village of Wae Loo 65 per cent (28/43). In many of the other households there are wives who came from the Gebhain *noro*, so that in total, 83 per cent (40/48) of the households in Wae Katin and 88 per cent (38/43) of the households in Wae Loo have one Gebhain spouse. Yet in these two villages, the main Gebhain marriage exchange partners are not the same *noro*.

Table 6.3. Noro of the spouses of Gebhain clan members in the villages of Wae Katin and Wae Loo

Gebhain men whose wives are from *noro*	In village of Wae Katin	In village of Wae Loo
Gewagit	11	3
Mual	10	5
Masbait	1	0
Hangwasit	2	3
Nalbessy	0	1
Wae Dupa	0	11
Wae Eno	0	4
Wae Kolo	0	1
TOTAL	24	28

Natal Gebhain women married to men in *noro*	In village of Wae Katin	In village of Wae Loo
Gewagit	7	1
Mual	8	0
Hangwasit	1	2
Nalbessy	0	4
Wae Dupa	0	3
TOTAL	16	10

The best way to see the relation between place and the frequency of marriage relations is to interpret these figures with reference to local geography (see Map 1). Wae Loo is further north than Wae Katin, and thus closer to Lake Rana. More than half of the marriages in Wae Loo are with *noro* whose origin places are around Lake Rana: Nalbessy, Wae Dupa, Wae Eno and Wae Kolo. The village associated with the Hangwasit *noro*, called Unet (a migration from the former village located at Ena Biloro), is located roughly equidistant from Wae Katin and Wae Loo. Correspondingly, there are equal numbers of Hangwasit spouses in Wae Katin and Wae Loo. The village of Wae Katin is near the 'ancestral stream' (*wae moyang*) of the Mual noro, at Wae Brapa, as well as being near Mngeswaen, a village associated with the Muals. Wae Katin is also near Fakal, a village associated with the Masbait *noro*. The numerous marriages with the Gewagit *noro* in Wae Katin can be explained with reference to the Gewagit origin place, a stream called Erwagit, which is near the (now former) village of Wang Karang Fatan. Between Wang Karang Fatan and the Wae Brapa River, there are several small Gewagit settlements as well.

Map 1: Wae Katin, Wae Loo and surrounding villages

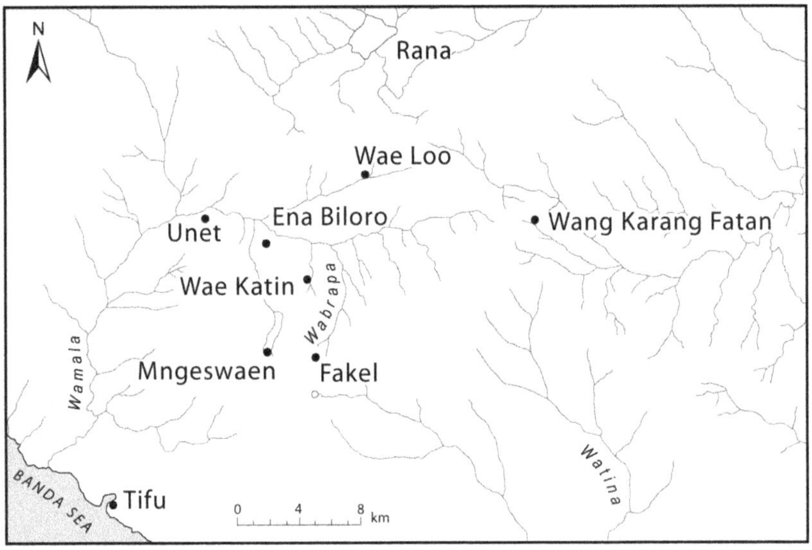

From the perspective of Buru people, there is thus a strong correlation between place and marriage relations of *noro*. Even larger areas are conceived of in terms of the *fena* land of a *noro*. When I asked people in the interior of Buru about the meaning of Masarete, there was no attempt to identify it as a former *regentschap* or as a territory with a raja. To them, Masarete was a large area but an area defined as 'seven villages/lands, seven clans' (*fenar pito noro pito*).

People of the Mountains and People of the Coast: Sharing the Land with Outsiders

Although I have focused largely on indigenous Buru society up to this point, Buru is a multi-ethnic island and Buru people share their island with others whom they classify as 'people from across the sea' (*geba fi lawe*). In fact, more than 65 per cent of Buru's 110,000 inhabitants are 'immigrants' in this sense, making Buru predominantly an 'immigrant' island. Many living on the north and west coasts of Buru originate from the island groups of Buton and Sula. Some have carefully kept track of their family history on Buru through the generations, but today still maintain their Buton or Sula identity, language and Muslim religion. Furthermore, almost all the immigrants live at or within easy access of the coast. [4] In contrast, indigenous Buru people refer to themselves as 'people of the mountains' (*geb fuka*) and most self-identify as Christians in the contemporary Indonesian religious context. [5] As a result, the population distribution on Buru reflects multiple layers of dichotomous pairs for which central Maluku is famous: inside/outside; native/immigrant; mountain/sea; Christian/Muslim.

Map 2: Coastal immigrant communities on Buru

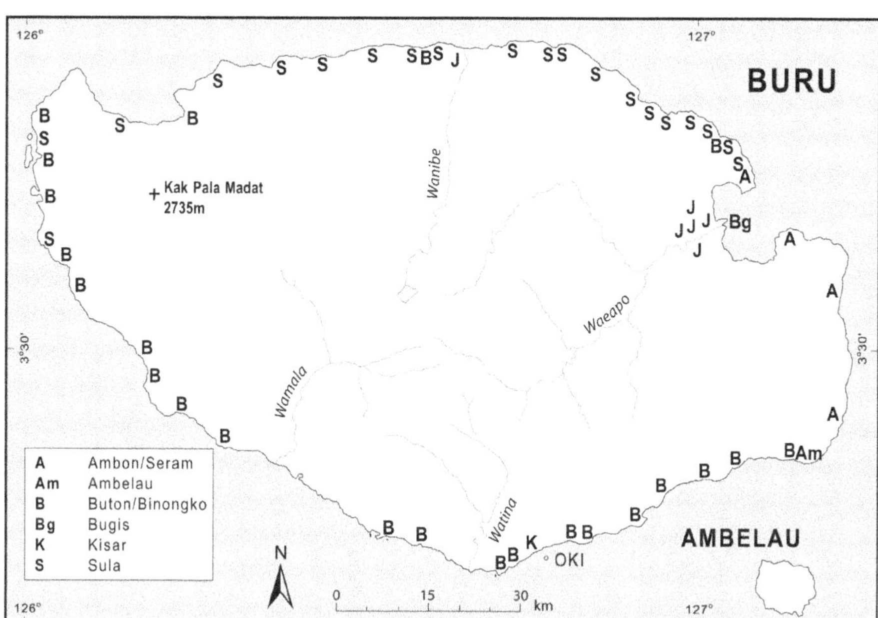

Many of the outsiders on Buru are familiar with clans or have clans as part of their own social organisation. According to the Buru people, these immigrants may have a *fam* (the Ambonese Malay term for clan), but they have no *fena* and therefore are not 'people of Buru Island'. The possession of a *fena* is thus the critical marker of Buru identity, distinguishing people of 'Buru mountain/island' (*geb fuk Buru*) from 'people from across the sea', even though some Buru clans also came from across the sea. Some Buru clans claim autochthonous origins with a founding ancestor arising from a spring or sacred place on the island. The founding ancestors of other clans came from across the sea, and when they arrived were given land by the autochthonous clans, making them custodians of a *fena* and, as a result, 'people of Buru island'.

But even though some clans claim autochthonous origins and predated the clans who arrived later and were given *fena* land, Buru people see this as relatively unimportant and do not use it as a basis for creating asymmetrical relationships between *noro*. Instead, a strong discourse of equality between *noro* is created through the practice of sister exchange and symmetrical marriage alliances.

The Colonial Creation of Raja and *Regentschap*: Making the Outsider King

Buru was of no economic interest to the Portuguese or the Dutch when they arrived in Central Maluku, as there were no native clove or nutmeg trees on the island. The VOC aimed to gain a world monopoly on the trade of cloves, but it offered such low prices that people often sought out other traders (Chinese, Javanese, Makassarese) offering better prices. Cloves were a profitable enterprise for growers and traders and, by the middle of the 1600s, production was in excess of world consumption (Meilink-Roelofsz 1962: 218, 224; Chauvel 1990: 19). To make a profit, the VOC decided to curtail clove production by designating Ambon and the Lease Islands (Saparua, Haruku, Nusa Laut) as the only clove-producing areas. Each household on these islands was ordered to plant 10 new clove trees a year. To ensure that no clove trees were grown in prohibited places, each year the VOC carried out inspections throughout Central Maluku using conscripted labour for rowing services in what came to be referred to as *hongi* fleets.

Nevertheless, there was considerable resistance to this control. The growing of cloves and trade with other traders continued and Buru became involved. Due to its geographical position and the local terrain, which provided many excellent shelters in river mouths, Buru became an excellent place to hide boats coming from Makassar. Buru thus became a 'problem' to the VOC. Several warnings were given until, in 1648, a Dutch lieutenant and a small force were sent to south Buru where they destroyed 3,000 productive clove trees and pulled up countless smaller ones. They also managed to capture and burn down a Makassarese fort up a river and to burn several Makassarese boats (Rumphius 1910, II:50).

The VOC eventually concluded that it needed not only to expel the Makassarese from Buru and destroy the 'illegal' cloves trees there, it needed to do something about the people whom it saw as unruly and untrustworthy rebels. After capturing leaders of coastal Buru, on October 2, 1658, the VOC Governor made a treaty with them, promising pardon if the remained legal allies of the VOC and made no trading contracts with any other people. They were to move all their villages from around the entire island to a fort to be built at Kayeli in order to live under the supervision of the VOC. In addition, all clove trees on Buru were to be destroyed and these leaders were to assist the VOC in locating them. And finally, as they were Muslim, the VOC assured them that they would not be harassed because of their religious beliefs.

Map 3: Approximate location of coastal villages removed to Kayeli Fort in 1658

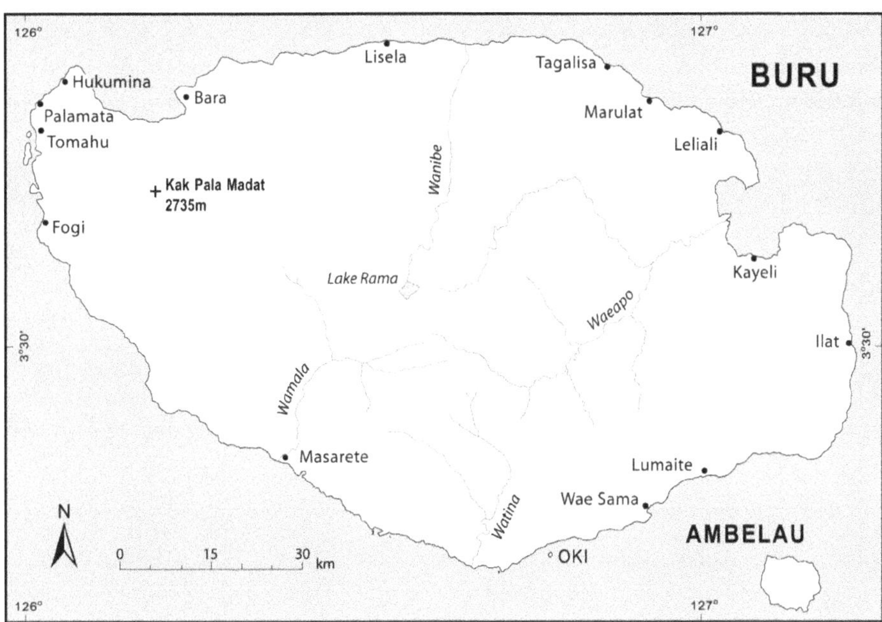

The same month the contract was signed, the Governor went to Kayeli Bay where a temporary fort was built, manned by 24 soldiers with four cannons. Thirteen separate villages were made around the fort, one for each of the villages from around the island which came to the fort: on the east side of the fort were the villages of Lumaite, Hukumina, Palamata, Tomahu and Masarete; Waisama lay to the south; and on the west side of the fort were Marulat, Leliali, Tagalisa, Ilat, Kayeli, Bara and Lisela (Rumphius 1983: 205). Each village had its own leader (Rumphius 1910, II: 118-21; Valentijn 1856, II: 197, 618). The coastal people of Buru were thus forced into a mixed community with the Dutch as their ever-present overlords, cut off from their former overseas allies and deprived of their local source of revenue from cloves.

Once the fort was established to keep an eye on the rebels, the next 150 years were ones of little change on Buru while the focus of VOC activity in Maluku was on the controlled clove-producing areas of Ambon and Lease. By the middle of the 19th century, approximately 2,000 people were living around the fort at Kayeli. Most of these people were Muslim villagers, still organised in their original villages from 200 years earlier.

During this time, Kayeli was the only place of significance on Buru for the Dutch, who often equated Kayeli with all Buru. The Dutch consistently used the term *orang Boeroe* or 'Buru people' to refer to the Muslim villagers living around the fort, in contrast with the *Alfuru*, the natives living in the interior of the island.

A law passed as *Staatsblad 19a* of 1824 sought to reorganise local political systems with the goal of incorporating them into the colonial system. To do this on Buru, where there were only clans and no overarching political system, the Dutch had to appoint rajas and create regencies (Dutch *regentschap*). Because of the history of VOC involvement on Buru, they were able to find 14 raja in one convenient location—Kayeli.

With the passing of *Staatsblad 19a* in 1824, Buru was incorporated into the colonial administrative system by dividing the island into territories (*regentschap*) named after the former villages that had been removed to the fort at Kayeli in 1658. The current leader from each village in Kayeli was designated as regent for the *regentschap* of his ancestral village. With all the regents (who soon came to be referred to as raja) living there, Kayeli was the colonial capital of Buru just as it had been for the VOC.

Map 4: *Regentschap* of Buru circa 1850

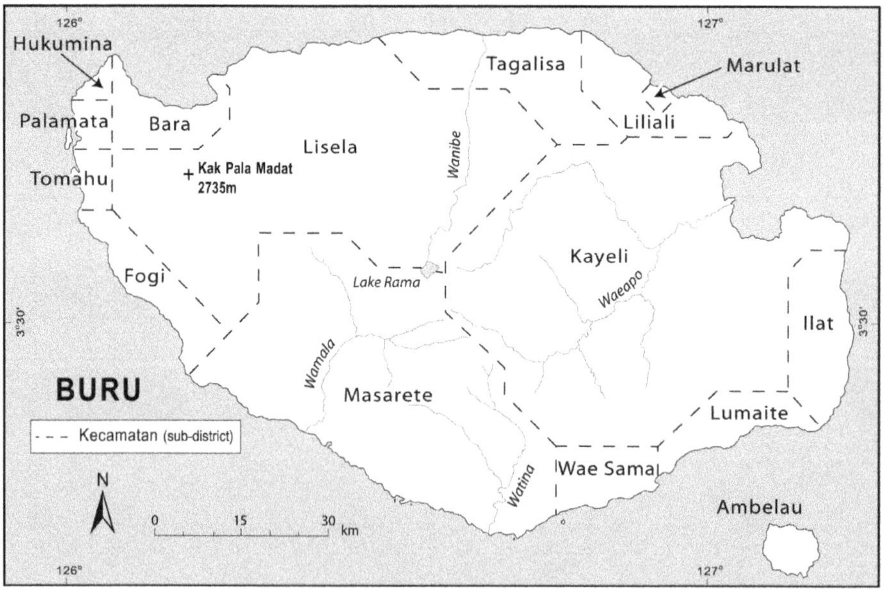

In this way, the *Alfuru* or indigenous people of Buru were officially mapped into the colonial system as subjects of the Muslim rajas at Kayeli. In the second part of the 19th century, however, some colonial officials began to express concern about this arrangement, claiming that the Buru rajas acted like despots in their treatment of the *Alfuru*, demanding large amounts of 'tribute' (*enati*) from each Buru clan in their *regentschap*. The tribute included baskets of rice, millet, coconuts, sago, sweet potatoes and tobacco, in addition to services requiring each clan to supply a given number of men on a periodic basis to work exclusively for the raja. Wilken (1875: 6, 7) noted that the tribute system was not an indigenous *Alfuru* idea, but had been introduced by the Muslim rajas who legitimated their authority over the *Alfuru* as coming from the supremacy of Ternate and Islam. For the *Alfuru*, the arrangement was unpleasant (the burden of tribute is still remembered today), but it was legitimated by their own notions that allowed rulers to be outsiders, illustrated by the following *Alfuru* explanation of why the Hentihu clan was raja of Lisela.

> Once there was a Patti Buton, a leader of the Butonese immigrants to Buru whose family name was Hentihu, and a Patti Bessy, who was a local leader of the native Buru Nalbessy *noro*. The Patti Buton said to the Patti Bessy: 'Let's decide who will be the raja. We will each get a bucket of sand and whoever has the heaviest bucket will be the raja.' The Patti Bessy agreed and then the Patti Buton added: 'Because you are from the land, you walk landward to get sand, and because I am from the sea, I will walk seaward to get sand.' So that's what they did and of course the wet sand of the Patti Buton was heavier. This is why the raja of Lisela is an outsider, and why the Hentihu family from Buton has been raja for many generations. [6]

Some Kayeli rajas were well supplied with tribute from the *Alfuru* in their *regentschap*, but the *Alfuru* were not distributed equally in every *regentschap*. In fact, in some *regentschap* there appear to have been no or very few *Alfuru*. This might have been due partially to migration of the native people in the interior of the island as discussed above, but for whatever reason, the varying capacities of rajas to draw tribute from *Alfuru* created significant differences among them. As time passed, the rajas without *Alfuru* subjects faded away and their *regentschap* dropped off the maps of Buru as the boundaries were redefined to include only *regentschap* with *Alfuru* subjects (and wealthy rajas). In 1847, the *regentschap* of Maro, Hukumina, Palamata and Tomahu had no *Alfuru* (Willer 1858); by 1875, this included Bara and Ilat as well (Wilken 1875: 10).

Kayeli gradually began to decline. In the 1880s, the rajas of Leliali, Wae Sama and Fogi, along with most of their people, returned to their ancestral homes on coastal Buru after more than 200 years at the fort. About the turn of the century, the rajas of Leliali and Tagalisa did the same. By that time, the villages of Maroelat and Bara were extinct, and the ruling families of Hukumina, Tomahu and Lumaiti had died out. In their concern about the Muslim rajas' treatment of *Alfuru*subjects, in *regentschap* Masarete the Dutch appointed a new raja from an *Alfuru* clan who lived at Tifu on the coast of south Buru. By 1907 there were only 231 Muslims at Kayeli, compared with 1,400 50 years earlier (van der Miesen 1908: 836, 837). Today Kayeli is largely abandoned, and the old Dutch fort is half-sunk in a malarial swamp. Across the bay, the town of Namlea has replaced Kayeli as the major population centre, and is the new centre for the District of Buru Island (*Kabupaten Pulau Buru*).

In 1906, colonial laws were passed that changed the administrative system of governance in Java and Madura and then, in 1938, similar laws were passed for other areas. After independence, early Indonesian laws regarding administrative structure were based on the Dutch laws. While the *regentschap* system was no longer the official system of governance, rajas continued to be acknowledged, and several rajas were influential individuals serving in the Provincial Legislature in Ambon in the 1950s and 1960s.

Map 5: Indonesian subdistricts (*kecamatan*): North-West Buru, North-East Buru and South Buru

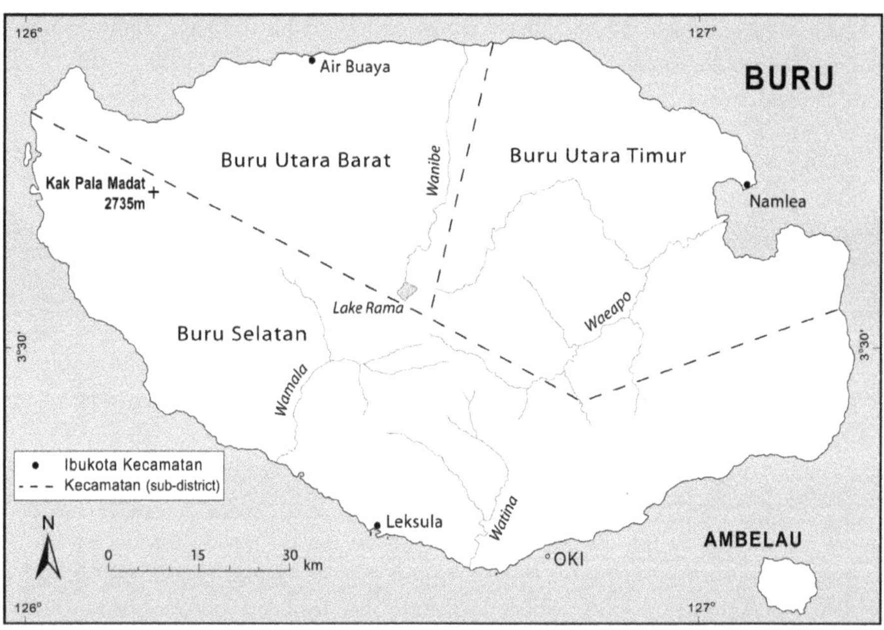

To Buru people, rajas were seen as 'guarding the doors to Buru', meaning their role was to interact with the outside, not the inside of society. To the Government, on the other hand, rajas (and *regentschap*) came to be seen as vestiges of Buru 'tradition' (*adat*). In the Government discourse of modernisation, however, tradition is antithetical to progress, so rajas and *regentschap* came to be seen as not relevant (and in some instances, hindrances) to the modern administrative system of *camat* (subdistrict head) and *kecamatan*. In the past few years, regional autonomy and traditional rights have been coming to the forefront of legislation and social debate in Indonesia. In Buru, as in Ambon and other places in Central Maluku, the beginning of a return to the authority of tradition has evoked a return to the authority of rajas, through a strong social forgetting that rajas were in fact colonial creations.

It still remains to be seen whether the recognition of Buru rajas will continue long term, partially because there are problems in regard to succession. Among the Muslim rajas, heredity is an established criterion for succession and the title passes from father to son or uncle to nephew. In *regentschap* such as Masarete, however, where the Dutch eventually appointed a native Christian rajas, heredity is not assumed, just as it is not assumed in the traditional Buru political system where *noro* members appoint *noro* leaders through consensus. In the past, the Dutch took an active role in appointing a new raja each time an old one died, but since the raja of Masarete died in 1986, the Indonesian Government has taken no such initiative, claiming it must come from the 'people'. The district head (*bupati*) was reported to have been willing to write a letter supporting whomever he was convinced had local support as raja. But from the perspective of Buru people in Masarete, rajas have always been entitled by outsiders, not by people inside Buru society. So with neither the government nor the local people seeing it as their responsibility to come up with a new raja, the system attenuates. A few individuals have had clear ambitions to be raja (including the former raja's eldest son), but no one can appoint himself, and so far no one has been successful in getting himself appointed by others.

Another reason for questioning the longer term survival of rajas on Buru is because egalitarianism between clans is very strong and there is no traditional space for political leadership higher than the clan. This egalitarianism is predicated largely on symmetrical marriage alliances. As is common in Austronesian societies, marriage creates an inherently asymmetric relationship with wife-givers superior to wife takers. On Buru this is expressed as the *kori* (the bride's parents and clan elders) holding the machete handle over the *sanat* (the groom's parents and clan elders). Sister exchange, however, referred to as the 'exchange of maidens' (*emhuka eptukar*), is arranged in a single set of marriage negotiations where the asymmetrical relationship is cancelled, as both parties are *kori*. The two bridegrooms in this case are said to be *wali-tal-dawet* (reciprocally both BW and ZH to each other) and their relationship reflects the ideals of friendship based on equality. Even without simultaneous sister exchange, the reciprocal exchange of women over time allows not just specific men but entire *noro* to see their overall relation as one of symmetry and equality. From this foundation of equality, Buru people stress that each clan should govern only its own clan, leaving no role for a raja inside society.

Map 6: *Regentschap* of Buru perceived as historical vestiges of Buru 'tradition' (*adat*) in 1991

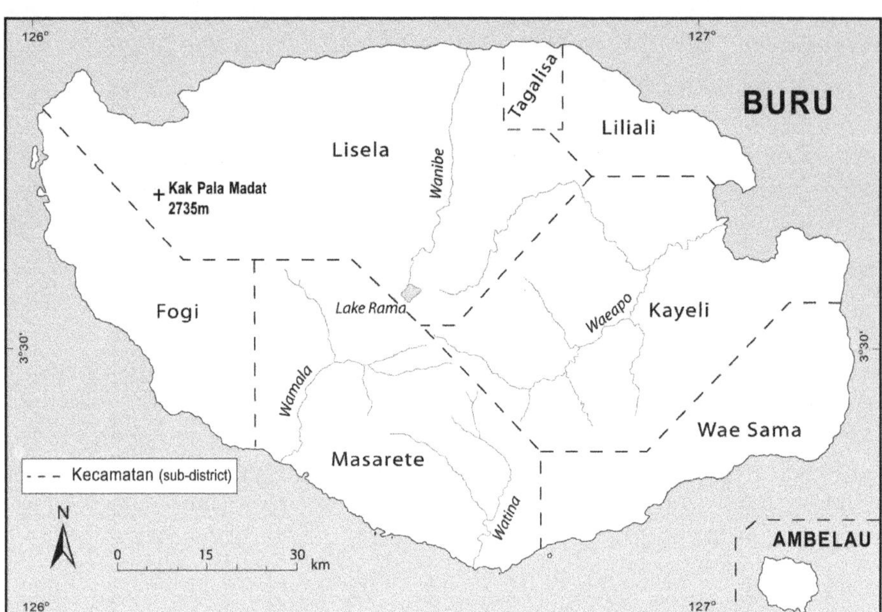

The Indonesian Creation of *Desa*: Making the Outsider Village Head

Another territorial construct that has been fraught with recent conflict on Buru is the Government's concept of *desa*, or administrative village. Concern for stronger mobilisation of forces for development at the *desa* level began to appear in the mid-1970s with the Government's five-year plan in 1978 stating:

> It is important to ensure the success of development in all areas throughout Indonesia in order to achieve the desired national characteristics based on the *Pancasila*, that is, a just and prosperous society, both materially and spiritually for all people of Indonesia. So it is necessary to strengthen *Desa* government to be better able to mobilise the people in their participation in development and to carry out a broader and more effective village administration. (*Yang penting adalah mensuksekan pembangunan di segala bidang di seluruh Indonesia, guna mencapai cita-cita Nasional berdasarkan Pancasila, yaitu masyarakat adil dan makmur, baik material maupun spiritual bagi seluruh rakyat Indonesia, maka perlu memperkuat pemerintah Desa agar makin mampu menggerakkan masyarakat dalam partisipasinya dalam pembangunan dan menyselenggarakan administrasi Desa yang makin meluas dan efektif.*) (GBHN 1978)

On December 1of the next following year, the law known as *UUPD* (*Udang-Udang Pemerintahan Desa—Laws of Village Governance*) 1979 was passed by the Parliament. A major concern expressed in the preamble was that the old laws were no longer adequate because

> in accord with the goals of national unity of the Republic of Indonesia, as far as possible the arrangement of *Desa* government needs to be made uniform as much as possible, by paying attention to the diversity that exists among *Desa* and the established local customs that still exist, in order to strengthen *Desa* government so that it is increasingly able to motivate the people to participate in development and to carry out *Desa* administration which is increasingly broad and effective. *(bahwa sesuai dengan sifat Negara Kesatuan Repulik Indonesia maka kedudukan pemerintahan Desa sejauh mungkin diseragamkan, dengan mengindahkan keragaman keadaan Desa dan ketentuan adat istiadat yang masih berlaku untuk memperkuat pemerintahan Desa agar makin mampu menggerakan masyarakat dalam partisipasinya dalam pembangunan dan menyelenggarakan administrasi Desa yang makin meluas dan efektif.)* (UUPD 1979)

The *UUPD* sought a uniform structure of village government throughout the nation whereby the lowest level of government in urban areas was to be the *lurah* and in rural areas the *desa*. The latter was defined as follows:

> A *Desa* is an area in which is located a number of inhabitants as a social unit/unit of society including among it a legal unit of society which has the lowest governmental organization immediately below the *Camat* and has the right to organise its own households within the network of the national unity of the Republic of Indonesia. (*Desa adalah suatu wilayah yang ditempati oleh sejumlah penduduk sebagai kesatuan masyarakat termasuk di dalamnya kesatuan masyarakat hukum yang mempunyai organisasi pemerintahan terendah langsung di bawah Camat dan berhak menyelenggarakan ruma tangganya sendiri dalam ikatan Negara Kesatuan Republik Indonesia.)* (UUPD)

Among other things, the *UUPD* clearly laid out the requirements for each office-holder. For example, a village head had to be between 25 and 60 years old and a graduate of middle school (nine years of schooling) or have equivalent experience. It also detailed the oath the *kepala desa* and *lurahs* were to take on entering office, and how the election process was to be carried out. But many details and variables were still left to the discretion of various government officials.

To clarify some issues, in 1981, the Minister of Domestic Affairs (*Mentri Dalam Negri*) put out several letters of decision with more details about the structure of village government, the decisions that could be made by village governments (including how to type the letter of decisions), and how *desa* were to be formed, divided, joined and deleted. Of particular importance for Buru and Central Maluku were the requirements laid out for *desa*: a *desa*needed to have a population of at least 2,500 people or 500 families. In creating *desa*, religious and socio-cultural factors needed to be considered, as well as the way of life of the inhabitants. And *desa* were to be created by decision of the Governor based on suggestions from district heads, after getting the agreement of the minister.

Map 7: The boundaries of *desa* territories on Buru Island

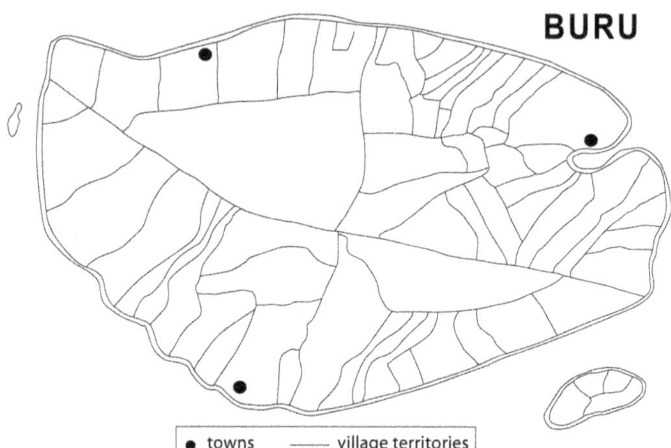

Given the size of the country, there is some common sense in the desire of the Indonesian State to have a uniform system of governance to facilitate development down to the village level (in 1983, there were 63,058 *desa* in Indonesia). However, the way *desa* were mapped onto Buru and elsewhere in Central Maluku created numerous problems. First, the large population size stipulated by the minister meant that in a place such as Buru, with a relatively low population density, a *desa* had to incorporate a huge area if it was to include 2,500 people or 500 families. [7] Second, even though the minister stipulated that religious and ethnic factors should be considered, most *desa* boundaries were mapped onto Buru in total disregard of religion and ethnicity. *Desa* in Buru were drawn as parallel strips running inland from a small coastal area where an immigrant settlement was located. This meant that each *desa* encompassed coastal Muslim immigrants and interior Christian natives. Since it was far more convenient to reach settlements on the coast by boat (there are very few roads on Buru), candidates for village head were almost always selected by the *camat* from the coastal Muslim settlement rather than the interior. Buru people in the interior had learned to share their land with immigrants for many centuries, having only minimal interaction. But with the creation of these *desa*, more interaction was demanded. The Government policy of distributing cash to poor *desa* became particularly contentious, with people in the mountains repeatedly complaining that the money always stopped at the village head and none of it went upstream to them. [8]

Conclusion: Mapping as Power

Like many Austronesians, Buru people believe that land can and should be shared. They do this through the concept of *fena*, recognising the people who are the custodians of a *fena*, and those who have requested respectfully to live on a *fena*. Yet there is considerable conflict in Buru about boundaries and territories, not because land is a scarce resource, but because of the power relationships associated with different concepts of land. In the past two centuries, *regentschap* and *desa* have been mapped onto Buru. Both have proven to be disadvantageous to the native people of the island, by defining them as subjects liable for tribute to Muslim immigrant rajas, and by excluding them from government services, opportunities and aid, because they live in the remote interior rather than on the coast.

As I realised long ago, the map that is lacking is the map of Buru *fena*. Some on Buru also realise this lack as they are beginning to recognise the power of maps and land titles to legitimate land claims within the Indonesian national context. I was once requested to be a scribe for men from a Buru *noro* as they recited from memory the boundaries of their *fena* from a named river bed, to a named rock, to a mountain peak and so on. To them, *fena* is not just tradition handed down from their ancestors in the past, it is a valuable resource they hope to secure for their grandchildren in the future.

References

Anderson, Benedict. 1991. *Imagined Communities: Reflections on the Origin and Spread of Nationalism*. London: Verso.

Bellwood, Peter. 1985. *Prehistory of the Indo-Malaysian Archipelago*. New York: Academic Press.

Biro Pusat Statistik Buru. 1997. Buru Dalam Angka 1997 Namlea.

Blust, Robert. 1987. 'Lexical reconstruction and semantic reconstruction: the case of the Austronesian "house"'. *Diachronica: International Journal for Historical Linguistics*, 4 (1-2): pp. 79-106.

Chauvel, Richard. 1990. 'Nationalists, soldiers and separatists: the Ambonese islands from colonialism to revolt, 1880-1950.' *Verhandelingen van het Koninklijk Instituut voor Taal-, Land- en Volkenkunde*, 143. Leiden: KITLV Press.

Dumond, D.E. 1969. 'Swidden Agriculture and the Rise of Maya Civilization.' In Andrew Vayda (ed.), *Environment and Culture Behavior*, Austin: University of Texas Press. pp 332-49.

Grimes, Charles E. 1991a. 'The Buru language of eastern Indonesia.' PhD dissertation, The Australian National University.

Grimes, Charles E. 1991b. 'Central Malayo-Polynesian: A critical evaluation.' Paper presented at the Sixth International Conference of Austronesian Linguistics' Honolulu.

Jansen, H.J. 1933. 'Gegevens over Boeroe (1928).' *Adatrechbundels*, 36. pp. 463-89.

Kantor Statistik Kabupaten Maluku Tengah. 1987a. Kecamatan Buru Selatan dalam angka. Leksula.

Kantor Statistik Kabupaten Maluku Tengah. 1987b. Kecamatan Buru Utara Barat dalam angka. Air Buaya.

Kantor Statistik Kabupaten Maluku Tengah. 1987b. Kecamatan Buru Utara Timor dalam angka. Namlea.

McWilliam, Andrew R. 1999. 'From lord of the earth to village head; Adapting to the nation-state in West Timor.' *BKI*, 155-1. pp. 121-44.

Meggers, B.J. 1957. 'Environment and culture in the Amazon basin: An appraisal of the theory of environmental determinism.' In *Studies in Human Ecology*, Pan American Union, Social Science Monographs, No. 3, Washington.

Meilink-Roelofsz, M.A.P. 1962. *Asian trade and European influence in the Indonesian archipelago between 1500 and about 1630*. 's-Gravenhage: Martinus Nijhoff.

Rumphius, G.E. 1910. 'De Ambonsche historie, behelsende een kort verhaal der gedenkwaardigste geschiedenissen zo in vreede als oorlog voorgevallen sedert dat de Nederlandsche Oost Indische Comp. het besit in Amboina gehadt heeft.' 2 parts. *Bijdragen tot de Taal-, Land- en Volkenkunde*, 64.

Rumphius, G.E. 1983 [1674-78]. *Ambonsche Landbeschrijving*. Edited by Z.J. Manusama. Jakarta: Arsip Nasional.

Schut, J.A.F. 1921. 'Noro en fena op Boeroe.' *Bijdragen tot de Taal-, Land- en Volkenkunde van Nederlandsch-Indië*, 77. pp. 615-22.

Thongchai, Winichakul. 1988. 'Siam Mapped: A History of the Geo-Body of Siam.' Unpublished PhD thesis, University of Sydney, Sydney.

Valentijn, F. 1856-58 [1724-26]. *Oud en Niew Oost-Indiën*. 8 Vols. Amsterdam: Dordrecht.

van der Miesen, J.W.H. 1908. 'Een tocht langs de noordoostkust van Boeroe.' *Tijdschrift van het Koninklijk Nederlandsch Aardrijkskundig Genootschap te Amsterdam*, 25/2. pp. 833-71.

van der Miesen, J.W.H. 1909a. 'Tochten op het eiland Boeroe.' *Tijdschrift van het Koninklijk Nederlandsch Aardrijkskundig Genootschap te Amsterdam*, 26/1. pp. 214-63.

van der Miesen, J.W.H. 1909b. 'Niewe tocht naar het eiland Boeroe.' *Tijdschrift van het Koninklijk Nederlandsch Aardrijkskundig Genootschap te Amsterdam*, 26/2. pp. 578-97.

Wilken, G.A. 1875. 'Bijdrage tot de kennis der Alfoeren van het eiland Boeroe.' *Verhandelingen van het Bataviaasch Genootschap van Kunsten en Wetenschappen*, 38. Batavia: Bruining and Wijt. pp. 1-61.

Willer, T.J. 1858. *Het eiland Boeroe, zijne exploitatie en Halfoersche instellingen.* Amsterdam: Frederik Muller.

www.websitercg.com/ambon/Buru.htm

ENDNOTES

[1] This also predated the recent separation of North Maluku into a separate province.

[2] Population is not distributed evenly on the island. About 70 per cent of the population lives on or near the coast, making the population density in the vast interior of the island much lower.

[3] In the past, warfare also encouraged mobility. The mobility of Buru people in the vast interior of their island has been a significant survival strategy not only in the past, but also during the religious warfare between Muslims and Christians that spread to Buru from Ambon after January 1999.

[4] This includes former political prisoners (referred to as *tapol* or *tahanan politik* in Indonesian) from the aftermath of 1965, who were interned in the Wae Apo River Valley. Years later, most were reclassified as transmigrants.

[5] Official government statistics from 1997 list the religious affiliation of the population on Buru as 48 per cent Muslim, 41 per cent Christian and 11 per cent Other. These statistics are not disaggregated according to ethnicity, and do not explain the meaning of 'other' religion (Buru Dalam Angka 1997).

[6] This story was told to C. Grimes on the north coast of Buru in 1989 and is almost identical to one that was told to Jansen in 1928 (Jansen 1933), explaining why the regent of Lisela was a 'Butonese usurper' (*Boetonneeschen usurpator*).

[7] In some places in Indonesia, *desa* were formed with populations smaller than the official requirement. The relevance for Buru is that, although smaller *desa* would have been more appropriate socially, Buru social structure and residence patterns were ignored, and Buru people had little voice in the formation of these 'outside' political units.

[8] In contrast with Buru where government positions such as village head (*kepala desa*) are filled largely by 'outsiders', see McWilliam (1999) in which he describes how traditional leaders in West Timor have been subsumed into the *desa* system as village heads. Given this scenario, a West Timorese village head/traditional leader 'emerges as a mediator between the competing demands of government and tradition'. On Buru, however, the competing demands of 'government' (*pemerintah*) and 'tradition' (*adat*) lack such a degree of mediation and the indigenous people continue to view 'government' largely as an outside system with outside agents attempting to exert control over their lives.

Chapter 7. Traditional Territorial Categories and Constituent Institutions in West Seram: The *Nili Ela* of 'WELE Telu Batai and the Alune *Hena* of Ma'saman Uwei

Christine Boulan-Smit

Introduction

Seram, the largest island of the Moluccas, lies only a few hours by boat from the regional capital city of Ambon. According to tradition, Seram is referred to as Nusa Ina, the 'Mother Island'. An Alune narrative, collected by A.D.E. Jensen, recalls that at one time in the past Seram, Ambon and the Uliase Islands (Saparua, Haruku and Nusalaut) formed a single island where warfare was constant. So, the people of Ambon cut off a large parcel of land, tied it with human hair and dragged it to where it lies nowadays. Later, those of Saparua, Haruku and Nusalaut did the same and they have been separated from their Mother Island ever since. However, all know that once upon a time they were part of Seram and this is why they call Seram Nusa Ina and why the members of the same origin groups are spread out over all of these islands. [1]

Seram is now divided administratively into three regions: West, Central and East Seram. This paper focuses on Seram's western region, which is called 'Wele Telu', the 'Three Large Rivers', and encompasses roughly one-fifth of the island (about 35,000km2). It examines how West Seramese traditionally envisioned their land at the regional and domain level. The first part of the paper considers the categorical divisions of an ancient inter-domain institution, the *Nili Ela* (or *Saniri Ela*, 'Large Assembly') of 'Wele Telu Batai (The Three Large River Valleys), now mostly a feature of the past. This ancient league [2] linked the highland domains of the 'Wele Telu area and their coastal allies or 'rulers'. These loose and changing networks of political and ritual alliances seem to have been in place as far back as the 14th century. The Nili institution was abolished by the Dutch Colonial Government in 1914, but still operated informally and in secret at least until the middle of the 20th century. [3]

The highland valleys of West Seram are settled by two linguistically related groups, the Wemale in the east and the Alune in the west. Their modern *desa* or villages usually correspond to former traditional territorial units or domains. The second part of the paper focuses on such a traditional Alune domain, or *hena*. The paper investigates how Hena Ma'saman Uwei (by metathesis, Manusa Manuwe), a semi-autonomous highland domain previously part of 'Wele Telu Batai, conceived of itself in the early 1990s and how particular categories or groups of people were allocated rights and responsibilities for specific divisions of its land.

Map 1: West Seram, Ambon and Uliaser

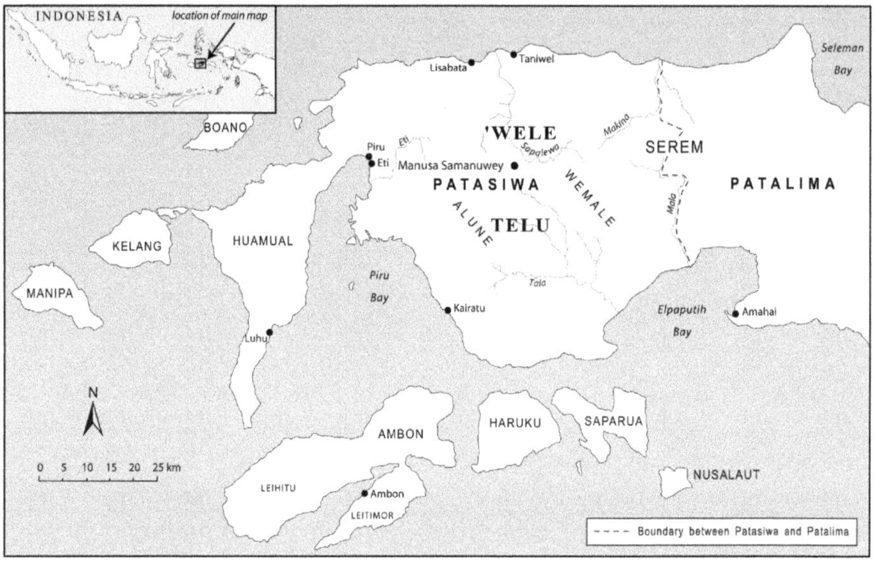

The Setting

Because of its reputation for inaccessibility, Seram was for centuries the refuge of sizeable communities of pirates, dissidents and separatists groups from neighbouring islands who brought in new knowledge and goods. [4] Traders and migrants from Sulawesi and Java also settled along the coasts. In the second half of the 20th century, they were joined by sizeable communities of transmigrants and resettled families.

In the 1990s, the majority of the population was concentrated in the low hills and along the coast but a handful of villages still clung to their ancient highland traditional territories. [5] The trend to 'modernity' promoted an ideology of uniformity, but the mountain and coastal populations lived in different environments and had distinct modes of subsistence, social organisation and cultural values. Mountain groups were essentially forest farmers who hunted and gathered forest products to complement their diets or to trade at the coast. The diverse populations established along the coasts and in the low hills were involved in sedentary agriculture, fishing, trade, the plywood industry, or belonged to the sizeable military and administration posts established there.

With the influx of migrants, the coastal population was, in majority, Muslim with interspersed Christian settlements. The highlanders, converted by the Dutch-Ambonese Protestant mission at the beginning of the 20th century, were all registered as Christians. In times of peace, many highlanders journeyed to the coast where education, health care, jobs and commerce were centralised.

The history of Seram is difficult to retrace. Although at the geographical centre of the Moluccas and the largest island of its archipelago, Seram holds a peripheral position in the official history of the region. The groups living inland can seldom trace their own history back more than 100 years. In pre-colonial times, West Seram was a sparsely populated area, located at the periphery of a large trading operation controlled by the north Moluccan sultanates. At least since the 14th century, the Ternatan, Bacanese and Tidorese sultanates had established alliances with coastal groups in the north and the south. West Seram, a halt along the trading routes, became a small producer of cloves (mainly on the peninsula of Huamual) and an exporter of sago. In the first half of the 17th century, Luhu, a vassal of Tidore on Huamual, became a prominent trading centre and a producer of cloves. [6] No domain on Seram, however, could establish a realm of influence powerful enough to become a salient political centre in the Moluccas.

Between the 17th and the 19th century, the intervention of the Dutch East Indies Company (VOC) and the reorganisation implemented by the colonial administration progressively altered the situation on the coasts of Seram. Meanwhile, the more isolated western highlands retained most of their territorial and political autonomy until the end of the 19th century. Early reports sketch small independent domains with loose and changing alliances. Coastal and mountain communities were known to trade and intermarry but a general state of tension, enmity and warfare was reported between them. Indeed, the oral traditions of the Alune and Wemale who still occupy the western highlands recall numerous movements of population seeking land in the mountains as well as on the coast or migrating because of quarrels, illnesses or warfare. Such a state of affairs justified the intensive military 'pacification' campaigns and the administrative re-configuration of the highlands that took place in the early 20th century and continued during the post-colonial era.

As a result of this assimilation within the colonial and later national administrations, the region has been, during the past 100 years, subjected to ruthless and erratic changes. For the past four or five generations, its indigenous people have been implicated in warfare, guerilla activities and military occupation, and submitted to drastic 'modernisation' and relocation policies. They have also been confronted by intense deforestation of their environment and a massive influx of transmigrants. Since 1999, many more communities, old and new, have been displaced or dismembered. [7]

'Wele Telu Batai

'Wele Telu Batai takes its name from the three large river systems it encompasses.[8] These three rivers flow from the Ulateina (*ulate*: 'mountain'; *ina*: 'mother'), a central mountainous watershed that bisects the highlands along an east west axis. The Eti River flows westward away from this central area to the sea, the Tala flows southward and the Sapalewa follows the divide for half of its course before flowing northward (see Map 1).

The traditional eastern boundaries of 'Wele Telu Batai correspond with the ancient partition of the island into *Patasiwa*, the 'Group of Nine', in West Seram, and *Patalima*, the 'Group of Five', to the east of it. This boundary was retained as the colonial administrative subdivision (*onderafdeeling*) for West Seram until the 20th century. [9] The highlanders of West Seram were black *Siwa* (*Patasiwa Hitam*), initiated in the male brotherhood of the *Kakehan* to which most adult men belonged. [10] The coastal settlers were white *Siwa* (*Patasiwa Putih*).

The Wemale and the Alune who occupy the highlands of 'Wele Telu refer to their river valleys and to the people who inhabit them as a single *batai*. Nowadays three administrative subdistricts, the *Kecamatan* of Seram Barat, Kairatu and Taniwel, correspond roughly with the traditional political divisions in these three *batai*, each regrouping the mountain domains and coastal settlements of a river valley. [11] In the highlands, most modern *desa* correspond to a former traditional territorial unit or domain, the *hena*, some of which had ritual and/or political duties in the *batai* of their valleys. [12]

Until the beginning of the 20th century, small-scale warfare and headhunting were frequent in the mountains and on the coast and everybody lived in mutual suspicion. Yet exchanges were vital and alliances, even temporary ones, were indispensable. [13] Furthermore, the idea of a common origin linked to a central Mother Mountain and to a sacred cosmic banyan tree, the *Nunusaku*, was largely shared throughout West Seram, even among coastal newcomers. In this central Moluccan tradition, Seram is Nusa Ina the 'Mother Island', and *Nunusaku*, a giant and invisible banyan tree, stands on the Ulate Ina the 'Mother Mountain', of West Seram, which is the first abode of mankind and the symbolic centre of the region. [14] Spreading its branches to the Heaven (*Lanite*) and its roots into the Hearth (*Tapele*), *Nunusaku* is also the source of the three rivers, which give the area its name. The cosmic banyan is said to extend its river trunks (*batai*) over the area, encompassing all the people of the region. [15]

Nunusaku sama ite	Nunusaku has distributed us
Sama ite 'Wele Telu	Allotted us to the Three Rivers

Periodic assemblies of elders were called *Nili*. These councils facilitated relationships within this heterogeneous society. This widespread institution gathered the elders of small and large units, at the level of domains (*nili hena*: 'domain council'), river valleys (*nili ela*: 'large assemblies') and region (*Nili 'Wele Telu Batai*: the 'Assembly of the Three Large Rivers'). [16] Although each small unit remained fiercely independent, these councils maintained some communication and coordination between the various coastal and highlands groups. Matters of regional interest and precedence were settled at the legislative and judicial level and later registered within the oral tradition. Thus the narrative of origin of Hena Ma'saman Uwei recalls various *nili ela* and bases several of its claims on decisions taken by these assemblies.

The *Nili Ela* Organisation

Large *nili* were held at the main coastal domains, alternating between the three rivers. Numerous animals were sacrificed and buildings constructed for guests since debates sometimes lasted several weeks. [17] The felled trees on which the *nili batai* elders sat to deliberate were ritually felled in the forest. The logs were brought in procession by the participants and ceremonially placed on the ground. The representatives sat on them from base to tips according to the seniority of their office. The assembly started with the *Tapea*, [18] a greeting chanted by the Herald. This greeting chant set out the order of precedence that applied for the specific meeting. Having called *Tapele 'ai Lanite*, 'the Earth and the Heaven', as witnesses, the herald welcomed the representatives of each river, chanting the full name of each domain, its position in the organisation and the title of its dignitary. The high-ranking dignitaries of the host coastal domain were greeted first, followed by the upstream coastal and highland domains of the same river. The same procedure (from coast to mountain) was repeated for each river *batai*.

Nili ela were primarily assemblies where conflicts between domains were brought for arbitration. Matters such as land disputes, murder or inter-domain feuds and corresponding compensation claims were discussed at length. The parties in conflict were assisted or pressured to reach an agreement, which was witnessed by the representatives of the whole region. The *nili* of one river was the point of convergence for highland and coastal groups to meet, interact and debate. A core group arbitrated these large conciliatory coastal meetings, which contributed to preserve some form of regional cohesion. *Nili* provided an arena in which wise and respected men could reassess the precedence of their domains and their own prestige.

At the beginning of the 20th century, the same model (probably modified over centuries) was replicated roughly in each of the three rivers' *batai*. The core group of the *nili ela* consisted of seven main positions per river *batai*. Each position was held by a specific domain and represented by its dignitary. The dignitaries changed (titles were usually hereditary) but the positions remained in the same domain, which had received that function in ancestral time. [19] A domain could hold two positions, or two domains could hold one position jointly.

The seven positions were the following:

1 and 2. The *Inama* or *Inama Latu* ('Lord Mother Father') was the most senior position. [20] In each of the rivers' *batai*, that position was held jointly by a large coastal settlement, as formal vassal of Ternate, and by a low hill settlement, supposedly representative of the highland domains: for example, *Lisabata* (coastal) and *Nuniali* (mountain) in the Sapalewa River *Batai* or *Piru* (coastal) and *Eti* (mountain) in the Eti *Batai*.

3. The duty of the *Sarimetene* ('Black Machete') was to present the cases to be arbitrated by the assembly. In each river, this position was held by the representative of the domain in charge of that duty.

4. The position of *Anakota*, the implementer of the decisions or sanctions of the assembly in each region, was filled by high dignitaries from one or two domains per river, who were called *Anakota Mawena*. [21]

5. The coastal domains designated in Alune as *Inama Sariwei* (*Sari*, *Sali* or *Sael Uwei*: 'the base/handle of the machete') held the positions of senior judges. Wemale used the metaphor of pole and flag to refer to the same position: *Bandera Ehuwei* ('the staff/pole of the flag'). [22] These coastal dignitaries sat on the base of the felled trees used as benches by the council of arbitrators.

6. The position of *Inama Saribubui* (*Sali* or *Sael Bubui*: 'the tip, blade of the machete') was held by highland domains. [23] Their representatives sat (in a junior position) on the tip end of the felled trunk of their river. The highland *Inama Saribubui* were the counterpart arbitrators of the coastal *Inama Sariwei*. The first one was the 'handle' and the later the 'blade' of the machete, which was the symbol of the arbitration.

7. The domains holding the position of *Kapitan* were in charge of summoning the members of their river *batai* to the assembly and their representatives were the envoys in charge of that duty. The role of interpreter and herald (*alamanane*) was also part of that duty. [24]

Most but not all domains belonged to this alliance. [25] When greeted and seated in front of the whole assembly, the domains were positioned in their *Batai* in an order of precedence from coast to mountain. 'The *nili* of one *batai* forms a tree,' explained a mountain elder. 'It gathers the riverine domains of one valley as the people and the land of one resting tree.' This tree lies with its 'base' (*uwei*), the 'core' of the tree, at the coastal centre, its branches (*sanai*) and tips (*bubui*) extend over the region and encompass the coastal and highland domains of the league. Figure 1, for example, depicts the tree-like pattern of alliance of Nili Sapalewa Batai, circa 1903.

Figure 1: The tree of Nili Sapalewa Batai (circa 1903)

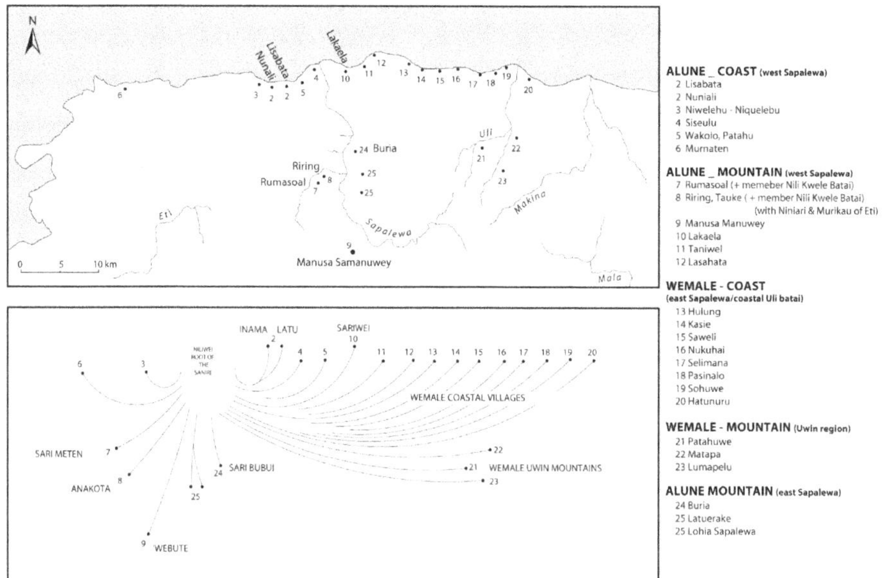

In each *batai*, the representative of a powerful coastal Muslim domain and his highland counterpart held the senior position (*Inama Latu*). Regarded as female and male (*ina ama*, 'mother father'), this dual position was given ultimate precedence as the *Niliwei* the 'core', 'base', 'source of continuity', of the *nili*. Other positions/duties were shared between coastal and highland domains. Seniority was accorded to larger and stronger domains, the seating position of these dignitaries reflecting this precedence. The most respected men of the region, and the resting trees on which they sat, together epitomised the *batai* as a political entity.

The league of the Three Rivers *Batai* held assemblies at a regional level. Yet, it had no strong centralised authority and was not bound by a single treaty. Domains were held together by their affiliation in a political organisation of elders and representatives, the *nili*, and in a men's brotherhood, the *kakehan*.[26] The first provided a forum for arbitration (a court of justice); the second gathered them in a ritual brotherhood. [27]

In each river *batai*, the domains were centred on a coastal 'core', their *niliwei*. It also situated them in an order of precedence that was oriented roughly from coast to mountain, from core/base *uwei*, to branches (*sanai*) and tip (*bubui*) and from elder/first (*a mena*) to younger/after (*a muli*). [28] However, in the ritual matters of the *kakehan*, this precedence was reversed. Highland domains were Black *Patasiwa* and considered as the elders (*a mena*) and the coastal domains were the younger, White *Patasiwa*, who followed behind (*a muli*).

At the end of the 19th century, the necessity of relinquishing what was no longer a lucrative trade in spices gave rise to new colonial policies in the Central Moluccas. The first aim of the Dutch was to achieve full administrative control of the region, and the second to evaluate its economic potential for European free trading entrepreneurs. Accordingly, the exploration of the remote regions and their 'pacification' became a priority. [29] The Colonial civil, military and religious administrators at the beginning of the 20th century attributed headhunting and the resistance against colonisation in West Seram to the *kakehan* and to the *nili ela*, to which almost all the coastal and mountain domains belonged. In 1914, after all attempts to transform these organisations into administrative instruments of the colonial bureaucracy had failed, the *kakehan* was banned, the *saniri ela* was officially abolished and their assemblies prohibited. [30] The traditional leaders of political and religious organisations who were an obstacle to the colonial control of the region were converted or evicted; those who resisted were arrested or exiled and replaced by approved candidates. Smaller assemblies continued to be held secretly in the highlands until the 1950s but the modern subdistrict division, carved out of the 'Wele Telu, further diffused all *batai* unity.

Nuru and *Hena*

Before colonisation there was little restriction on mobility. The oral narratives give the impression that most communities experienced some division as they expanded, quarrelled or were defeated by a neighbour. Those who departed opened new regions, joined another group or took over some of its territory. Some domains had renowned war leaders (*ama lesi*, 'war father'). They were able, if required, to call on and obtain the support of other allied domains against a predatory neighbour, or to enrol them as a raiding partner. [31] These authoritative and respected men were active members of the *nili* and the *kakehan* of their river, where followers (wife-takers) were coopted.

Among the Alune and the Wemale, origin groups are called *nuru*. Alune *nuru* perpetuate themselves by reference to a genitor line of derivation and Wemale *nuru* by reference to a genitrix one. Large *nuru* expand into new territories and set forth branches (*sanai*) over the whole region, establishing Houses (*Luma*) that can be found in more than one domain. [32] Residency determines linguistic affiliation and mode of derivation of these *Luma* units. What all the members of a *nuru* have in common is a name. To this name is attached a narrative recalling the deeds of an ancestor and/or a place of origin.

The people regarded as the descendants of the initial 'core' of a *nuru* constitute its *nuruwei*, its elder or 'initial trunk' (*sumber, pohon*). The claim to that prestigious position might be disputed between the 'branches' (*sanai*) of a *nuru*. *Nuru* order their 'branches' in different, sometimes combined orders of precedence. Thus a 'branch' might call itself *a mena*, the 'elder' ('firstborn', 'the one who walks ahead'), while another 'branch' might be *a muli*, in a junior position ('last born', 'the one who came after/follows'). Between them, a 'female branch' (*bina*) might have developed among various collateral 'branches'. As 'branches' grow and diversify, some keep their core name, recognising a common origin without necessarily keeping in contact with the initial 'core' (*nuruwei*). Other units take an additional name to distinguish their 'branch' and might forget their name of origin. 'Branches' might also sever the link with their initial *nuruwei* and initiate a new *nuru* (of which they become the *nuruwei*).

As *nuru* generate influential members and rich Houses, it is not so much a hierarchy that is established between them as a fluctuating competition. Renown and value are the objects of regular evaluation and readjustment. Thus claims for prestige and precedence apply between *nuru* and within them, between their 'branches' and Houses established in the various domains. However, there is little interaction between the various 'branches' of a *nuru* unless their Houses are in the same or a nearby domain. There is no *nuru* head, nor any authority that can be applied over a branch, a House or an individual by the *nuru* as a jural body. As some *nuru* become extinct, while the 'branches' of others transform themselves into a new core, it is difficult to make a precise count of the *nuru* and of their branches and Houses distributed across all Wemale and Alune domains and on other islands.

All *nuru* consist of 'Houses' or *Luma*. The first House to arrive in a domain is the *Luma inai*, the 'mother House', of its *nuru* in a domain. The Houses of the same *nuru* who arrived afterward, or decided to branch out from their *Luma inai* but remained in the same domain, are differentiated and called *Luma sanai*, 'branch Houses'.

The various Houses of a *nuru*, in one or several domains, are usually distinct and unrelated; however they do not intermarry. Sharing a common *nuru* name implies exogamy. It is by the intermediary of their Houses, which are exchanging units, that different *nuru* give and return brides to each other within or beyond a domain. Remote communities such as Hena Manusa Manuwe are essentially endogamous at domain level. Within the domain, the 'rich and famous' (*hena upui*: 'Grandfathers of the *hena*'), the elder and ruling lines, which have gained founding positions, exchange brides largely among themselves. But, through strategic marriages, proper behaviour and multiple descent, any House or any of its lines, including those perpetrated by women, may achieve status and wealth, enhance its renown and eventually fuse with, or replace, an older line or a declining House.

An Alune *hena* is a territorial, sociopolitical, economic and ritual unit standing in its own right. [33] The members of this community have joint assets and interests. They also share a sense of common identity and similar values, which derive from a strong awareness of the spiritual duties associated with their historical domain in the region. The entity called the *hena* comprehends the group, its settlements, its land, hills, rivers, forest and gardens, all named and narrated. It also includes all the dead and living beings dwelling within it.

Narratives depict how supra-human ancestors explored the region, marked territorial boundaries and assembled families (*Luma*), leading them through warfare and alliances to found a community. These founding ancestors established the position of their domain within the river *batai* and its institutions (the *nili ela* and *kakehan*). The following generations had to maintain these rights and gather enough followers to preserve a strong community and a large territory. As elders say: 'who adds people adds land.' [34] Nowadays, under the administration of the modern State, maintaining the number of their members remains a matter of survival for the highland communities.

One of these ancient domains is the Alune Hena Ma'saman Uwei, now called Desa Manusa Samanuwey (or Manusa Manuwe).

Hena Ma'saman Uwei

Ma'saman Uwei	The place which is/the people who are at the origin/centre of the distribution/allotment

As one is told on first entering the *hena* of Ma'saman Uwei, this is 'the place from which everything in the world, land, people, tools, were distributed'. [35] This initial deed of its founding ancestor, Samai, 'the one who distributes', gave this domain a permanent and special status within the region as the ultimate source of wealth and fecundity to all the groups of the area. [36] Because of this position, epitomised in its name and proven by its narrative of origin, this *hena* claims a central ritual position at the level of the entire 'Wele Telu Batai (and beyond). Similarly, the other domains make various claims, some of which are conflicting. Only strong groups can maintain such claims on their rights. Samai is renowned for having welcomed many people, building up a powerful domain that could defend and extend itself.

A topogeny is an ordered recitation of placenames, similar to a genealogy of people. [37] The topogeny of Hena Ma'saman Uwei describes how the founding ancestors departed from their place of origin and followed a path of successive differentiation and bifurcations (between *Patasiwa* and *Patalima*, Black and

White, Alune and Wemale, older brother at the coast and younger brother in the highlands). The ancestors finally delimited a territory and established the *hena* as a group of seven founding *nuru* (*nuru itu*). [38] Nuruitu is the name given to the final site of the topogeny. There, the founding ancestors laid down seven stones, one for each of the seven unnamed *nuru* to establish the foundation of the *hena*. By doing so, they established the ritual centre that legitimises the social order of the *hena* and its territorial claims. The hill of Nuruitu overlooks the confluence of the Tau and the Sapalewa rivers. The Tau is the *'wele wei*, the sacred 'water of origin', of the *hena*. At Nuruitu, through its origin river, the *hena* unites with the whole of the river *batai*. Downstream, it leads to the other groups of the Sapalewa *batai*, upstream to the *Nunusaku*. [39]

With time, the Houses of various *nuru* came and went. Some settled and expanded, others left, declined or became extinct. Ten years ago, Manusa Manuwe was made up of Houses from 15 different *nuru*, a number that fluctuates. However, while their identity might have changed, the number of founding *nuru* has remained fixed at seven. Seven is also the number of positions that order the ancient social organisation of the *Hena* and make it a complete body. These dignitaries hold the title of *Hena Upui*, 'Domain's Grandfathers' (or 'Ancestors').

These seven positions were: 1) *Latu Ela Mena*, 'Great Lord at the Front', the leader, ruler or head; 2) *Upu Tapele*, 'Grandfather of the Earth', the lord of the land; 3) *Maeta'e*, 'the One who Feeds the Stones', the ritual performer (the *kakehan* officiant); 4) *Ama Lesi*, 'Father of the War', the warlord; 5) *Ama Nili*, 'Father of the Nili', the leader of the village elders' assembly (and chief negotiator); 6) *Alamane*, the 'Spokesman', interpreter and herald, also called 'The Left Hand'; and 7) *Ama Tita*, 'Father Bridge', the liaison agent, also called 'The Right Hand'. [40] The Great Lord, the Lord of the Land and the Ritual Performer were honoured by the title of *Latu*. These positions can be paired. Great Lord and Lord of the Land have complementary duties, so have the Warlord and the *Nili* Leader as well as the Left and Right Hands. The duty left out is the position of ritual performer, whose spiritual role extends over but also beyond it. These functions were superseded or altered under the colonial and new order administrations. However, most still carry a ritual or symbolic significance as modern position bearers perform comparable duties.

In Manusa Manuwe, most duties have remained consistently in the same *nuru* for several generations, thus the founding *nuru* and the founding duties of the *Hena Upui* mostly coincide. [41] The Houses that do not hold one of the seven *Hena Upui* positions are *Ana Mulini*: the 'Younger Children' those who came after. [42] However, the history of the *Hhena* shows that some 'Younger Children', have through time and appropriate alliances grown to be 'Domain's Grandfathers'. Since the narrative does not specify any *nuru* name as *Hena Upui*, in principle virtually any line can achieve the prestige and power to claim (or buy) such a position.

The seven duties implied in the name of the domain's ritual centre establish an ordered but flexible social organisation. It allows the indispensable insertion of new members in the community. The territorial groups of the *nuru* are their Houses. Groups recall coming from specific places, but after leaving this place of origin, each group became a landless family welcomed into another community. This insertion in a domain provides new groups with access to land and entry into a close-knit network of exchange and alliances in which to prosper. The *hena* is a territorial unit and only residence establishes someone's full membership in the community.

The *nuru*'s Houses that claim the position of *Hena Upui*, the 'Domain's Grandfathers', are also those who claim the largest sections of the *hena* land. The order of precedence organised around these positions is still visible on the land and in the social organisation of the domain. The *Ana Mulini* have claims on smaller areas, however, they can receive communal land from the *hena* or land from another *nuru*, if their group increases. [43]

Land Allocation in Hena Ma'saman Uwei

The *hena* is a territorial unit. The elders insist on the inalienability of its land as a whole. Segments of it can be allocated for farming and other purposes but no section may be taken away, sold or even fenced. The community claims traditional rights over some 3,500 thousand hectares of land, a claim supported by narratives and the uninterrupted customary use of this territory for numerous generations.

The whole territory is called *tape lale*, the 'land within' ('inside', 'in the middle'). At its centre is the new settlement (*desa*). [44] The land is distributed between the powerful *Hena Upui* and the junior *Ana Mulini*. The *Hena Upui*'s claims to a substantial share of this 'land within', are embedded in the village history and in their own narratives. Also included in the 'land within' is the *tape malenete*, 'empty land' which no one occupies. The *tape malenete* is part of the historical territory claimed by the domain but not by individual Houses. [45] This 'empty land' also comprises the land of extinct Houses, which has not yet been redistributed. It is a common hunting, trapping and collecting ground but may also be used for communal projects. Outsiders, refugees or newcomers may receive access to the *tape malenete* to make gardens or plantations.

Figure 2: The land and settlements of Hena Ma'saman Uwei

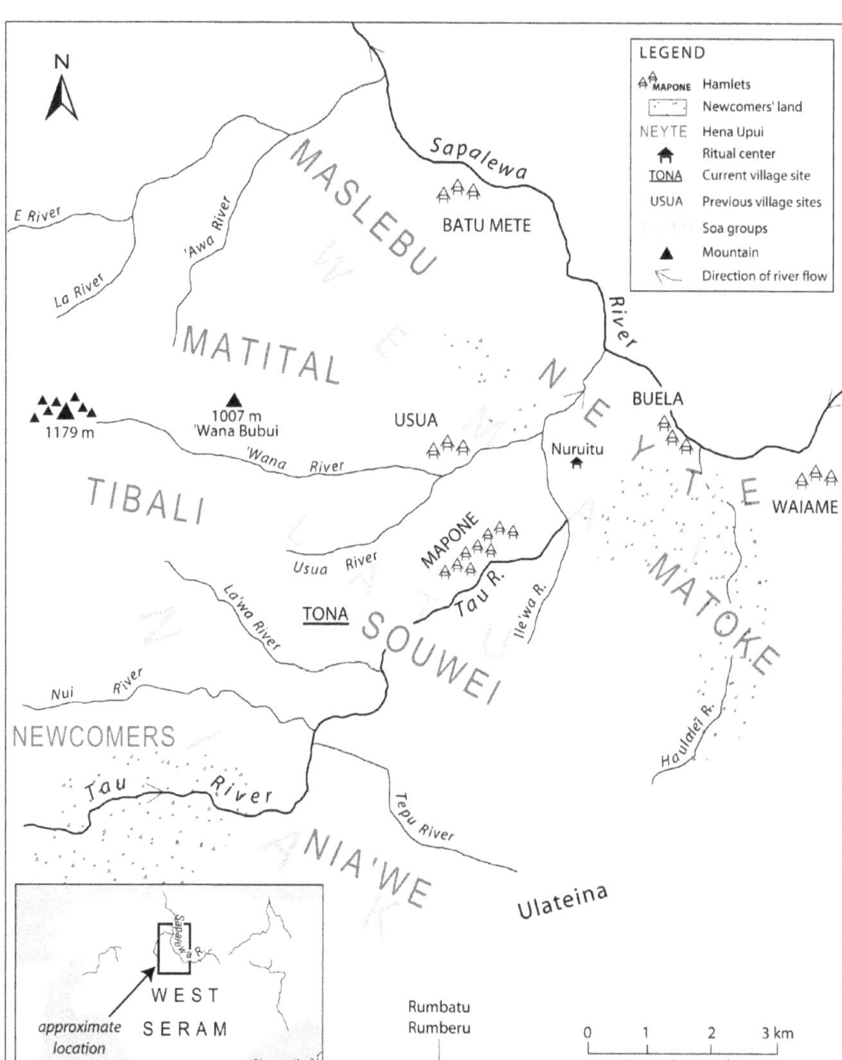

The Tau, the ancestral river, flows south-west to north-east across Hena Ma'saman Uwei before reaching the Sapalewa at Nuruitu, the ritual centre. At the centre of the *hena*, alongside the Tau and encompassing the new settlement and the ancient *kakehan* house, is the land of Souwei, the *nuru* of the *Latu Upu Tapele*, the Lord of the Land. In the north-east, besides Nuruitu, is the land of Matoke, the *nuru* of the *Latu Maeta'e*, the former Ritual Performer. Further north, on the path to the rival Wemale domain of Abio, is the land and post house of Neyte, the *nuru* of the former *Ama Nili*, renowned for negotiating a peace treaty with Abio. In the north-west, on the path to the powerful allied domain of Riring, is the land of Maslebu, the *nuru* of the *Ama Lesi*, the former Warlord, once marked by a large post house and the graves of prominent warriors. On the path to the north coast is the land of Matital, the *nuru* of the *Ama Tita*, 'The Right Hand'. Guarding the entry of the village to the south is the land of Nia'we, the *nuru* of the *Alamane*, 'The Left Hand'. The seventh *nuru* on the land is Tibali. [46] The land of the newcomers, the *Ana Mulini*, is along the northern and southern paths to the *hena*'s 'children' villages which developed from early garden houses closer to the coast. The position of 'Great Lord', village leader, alternates between different *Upu Hena*, hence there is no land for a ruler in the *hena*. [47]

One initiated elder described the land as a body. Other elders were unsure or denied this. In this model, the *nuru* carrying out the duty of *Latu Upu Tapele*, Lord of the Land, watches over the body of the land and the sacred river. The *nuru* of the *Latu Maeta'e*, Ritual Performer, is near the head of the ritual centre. The four members of the body are represented by the land occupied by the *nuru* of the *Ama Lesi*, the Warlord, the *nuru* of the *Ama Nili*, the *nuru* of the *Alamane*, or 'Left Hand', the Herald and the *nuru* of the *Ama Tita*, or 'Right Hand', the Liaison Officer. Of these four, the first two are more prominent, the latter more ancient in the area.

All the territory of the domain is under the corporate care of the *hena*. The *tape malenete*, 'empty land', is administrated collectively. Portions of the *nuru* land are under the custody of individual households. In Manusa Manuwe, most Houses have corporate rights over the land they use for gardens (*mlinu*), long-term plantations, orchards and groves (*lusune*, *lusun*, or *lusu*), hunting grounds and fishing pools. One says that a House 'sits' *due* on a portion of land and watches over its plantations (*da'a lusune*: 'to care for a plantation'). A portion of domain land that is claimed for its exclusive use by the House(s) of a *nuru* is called a *lusun mena* ('primary plantation'). The term *mena* marks precedence in space and/or time. The *lusun mena* is the common estate of all the associate members of a House. Unrelated branches of the same *nuru* have separate claims. Each *lusun mena* is administrated by a *ntuane lusu*, 'elder of the plantation', who must be consulted before new gardens are opened or plantations established on this common land. Households inherit rights to specific shares of the collective *lusun mena* of their House through the male line.

The portions of *lusun mena* land claimed by each household (often shared with a brother or a nephew) are referred to as 'personal plantations' (*lusu are 'ue*: 'plantation my work'), but individuals own only the usufruct of their own and inherited plantations. [48] The land on which someone's trees are planted remains in the custody of his/her House. Ultimately, however, all land belongs indivisibly to the community of the *hena* and no one possesses exclusive title or has the right to sell any segment of land. [49]

A person's plantations (not the land itself) are his/her *lusun dati*. Every *lusune* has a name and belongs to a *dati*, unit. Typically, a *dati* (the term is widespread in Central Moluccas) is an administrative unit of people (relatives or allies) in relation to service, tax and commitment on the one hand, and the use of the land on the other. In the highlands, it is usually the members of one or several Houses of the same *nuru* who form a *dati* under the arbitration of an elder, the *ntuane dati*. A *dati* might include one or several *lusun mena*. [50] *Lusun dati* are planted by successive generations for themselves and their descendants. Theoretically, outsiders cannot 'eat' (*ane*) from these plantations, but newcomers or followers may be integrated. Some Houses have little *lusune* land, and if their households increase, they might quarrel over the use of the usufruct of the trees of their common *lusune*. Elders say that if a man is wise, he will plant as many separate *lusu* plantations as he has sons so that each of them may add to his own *lusu* and pay for schooling or buy what he needs. Thus an individual has access to the *lusun mena* of his House and may nominally own some trees privately in *lusun dati*. Relatives can collect some products from this land but there are restrictions.[51]

Long established Houses (*hena upui*) that have access to a large portion of land might allot a section of it to a landless family of newcomers (*ana mulini*) securing them as followers. Alternatively, a *ntuane dati* might allow someone of the village or a newcomer to make a garden (*mlinu*: short term plantation and forest farming) on the land of his group. It might be advantageous for all to do so as no outsider can settle on a parcel of land that is already worked by someone. In such cases, the *dati* group always maintains precedence on that land and the *ntuane dati* dictates the terms of its use. Once given, this right of use is hereditary and need not be requested again. The *dati* group, however, retains the right to recover the land at any time. [52] Reclaiming a parcel of land can produce tension or hostility so groups are cautious in taking the decision to allow an outsider to work on their *dati* land.

Land is transmitted through males, but an unmarried daughter who resides in her father's house with her children might be given custody of his land until her son is of an age to care for it by himself. [53] A woman who marries still has limited access to the *lusune* of her House of origin but she cannot plant long-term plantations on it. Most widows regard themselves as dispossessed and landless;

however, they are usually cared for by one of their children or by relatives who allow them to make a garden and take a share in the usufruct of their plantations.[54]

There is no market in Manusa Manuwe and forest gardens are sometimes at several hours' walk. For generations, people have planted edible leaves and fruit trees along the paths to sago groves, gardens, fishing and hunting grounds so that no one will go hungry on the way to and from the forest. As they go hunting or sago-beating together, brothers-in-law also plant trees on each other's land for their children as a sign of conviviality. Nowadays, the *dati* group usually discusses which parcel each member will farm that year, but *mlinu*, annual gardens (mountain rice interspersed with corn, cassava and vegetable), are planted and tended individually. [55] A garden is planted twice or a maximum of three times after which it is left fallow for about 25 years before the caretaker or his/her descendant returns to clear the land again. Meanwhile, fruit and other useful trees mark boundaries and signal occupancy.

Conclusion

This paper has examined the organisation of 'Wele Telu Batai, the League of the Three Large Rivers, and its *batai*. It has also examined one constituent riverine valley subdivision of this *batai*, the Hena Ma'saman Uwei and the institutions associated with territoriality and land usage within it.

The *nili ela* and *nili batai* supported a wide network of alliances and economic exchanges. The institution acted as a political arena as well as a court of arbitration. Its members acknowledged the *Nunusaku* as the central feature of the common cosmic order organising their relationships. Men were bound by the brotherhood of their initiation cult, its rules, ritual practices and celebrations. Gathering the domains of the Three Rivers and their most noted dignitaries, the *nili* assemblies preserved a form of cohesion between the domains of the Three Rivers, the strength of this coalition offsetting the region's general instability.

Once all attempts to use or transform these assemblies into administrative instruments of the colonial bureaucracy had failed, the *nili ela* and *nili batai* were officially abolished, their meetings prohibited, non-compliant dignitaries eliminated and harsh punitive expeditions launched against any form of resistance. At the dawn of the 21st century, cohesive modern institutions have yet to replace the Nili Ela 'Wele Telu or the riverine *nili batai*. [56]

In contrast with the *nili ela* organisation, the *hena* successfully incorporated various formative influences and successive transformations imposed by the centralised administrations in the past two centuries. The capacity to adapt according to context, while still keeping the core principles of its initial structure, has served and preserved a traditional form of social order within the *hena*. The living body of narratives that constitute and continuously update the origin structures of the domain supports this social order. This flexible and semi-openestructure allows the insertion of newcomers (and new ideas) that are essential to ensure the continuation of the community.

Each domain (*hena*) in its river valley and each House in the *hena* is a custodian of a share of common land, its history and its natural and spiritual environment. The social identity of these units is embedded in the land. It translates continually into action, ritual and political duties, ordering the interactions of constituent groups and their precedence within the domain, its river valley and within the League of the Three Rivers.

References

Blust, R. 1980. 'Early Austronesian Social Organisation: The Evidence of Language.' *Current Anthropology* 21 (2). pp. 221-47.

Boulan-Smit, C. 1998. 'We of the Banyan Tree: Traditions of Origin of the Alune of West Seram.' Unpublished PhD thesis, Department of Anthropology, RSPAS, The Australian National University, Canberra.

Boulan-Smit, C. 2001. 'Founding Communities: Departure, Arrivals, Returns and Resettlements in West Seram.' In J. Sikala (ed.), *Departures: How Societies Distribute their People*, Helsinki: The Finnish Anthropological Society TAFAS 46. pp. 7-21.

Fox, J.J. 1989. 'Categories and Complement: Binary Ideologies and the Organisation of Dualist in Eastern Indonesia.' In D. Maybury-Lewis and Uri Almagor (eds), *The Attraction of Opposites: Thoughts and Society in a Dualistic Mode*, Ann Arbor: University of Michigan. Pp. 33-56.

Fox, J.J. 1994. 'Reflection on "Hierarchy" and "Precedence".' In M. Jolly and M. Mosko (eds), *Transformations of Hierarchy: Structure, History and Horizon in the Austronesian World*, Special issue of *History and Anthropology* 7 (1-4). pp. 87-108.

Fox, J.J. 1995a. 'Origin Structures and Systems of Precedence in the Comparative Study of Austronesian Societies.' In P.J.K. Li, Cheng-hwa Tsang, Ying-kuei Huang, Dah-an Ho and Chiu-yu Tseng (eds), *Austronesian Studies Relating to Taiwan*, Taipei: Symposium Series of the Institute of History and Philology, Academia Sinica, No. 3. pp. 27-57.

Fox, J.J. 1995b. 'Austronesian Societies and their Transformations.' In P. Bellwood, J.J. Fox and D. Tryon (eds), *The Austronesians: Historical and Comparative Perspectives*, Canberra: Department of Anthropology, Comparative Austronesian Studies Project, RSPAS, The Australian National University. pp. 214-28.

Fox, J. J. 1997. 'Genealogy and Topogeny: Toward an Ethnography of Rotinese Ritual Place Names.' In J.J. Fox (ed.), *The Poetic Power of Place: Compar-*

ative perspectives on Austronesian ideas of locality, Canberra: Department of Anthropology, Comparative Austronesian Studies Project, RSPAS, The Australian National University. pp. 91-102.

Jensen, A.D.E. 1977. 'Indigenous Classification Systems in the Ambonese Moluccas.' In P.E. de Josselin de Jong (ed.), *Structural Anthropology in the Netherlands*, The Hague: Martinus Nijhoff (KITLV Traduction Series, 17). pp.101-15.

Jensen, A.D.E. and H. Niggemeyer. 1939. *Hainuwele: Volkserzählungen von der Molukken-Insel Ceram*. Frankfurt am Main: Klostermann.

Knaap, G.J. n.d. 'The Saniri Tiga Air (Seram): An Account of its "Discovery" and Interpretation between about 1675 and 1950.' In *B.K.I. Deel*, 149 (2). pp. 250-73.

McWilliam, Andrew. 1989. 'Narrating the Gate and the Path: Place and Precedence in Southwest Timor.' Unpublished PhD thesis, The Australian National University, Canberra.

Sachse, F.J.P. 1907. *Het eiland Seran en Zijne Bewoners*. Leiden: Brill.

Sachse, F.J.P. 1922. 'Seran: Mededeelingen van her Bureau voor Bestuurszaken der Buitengewesten.' *Encyclopaedisch Bureau*, No. 24.

Tauern, O.D. 1918. *Patasiwa und Patalima. Vom Molukkeneiland Seram und seinen Bewohners*. Leipzig: Voitgelander.

Traube, E.G. 1980. *Cosmology and Social Life: Ritual Exchanges amongst the Mambai of East Timor*. Chicago: University of Chicago Press.

van Wouden, F.A.E. 1968 [1935]. *Type of Social Structure in Eastern Indonesia*. (English translation by R. Needham). KITLV Translation Series 11. The Hague: Nijhoff.

ENDNOTES

[1] Jensen (1938: No. 73,126; Summarised translation).

[2] League: (Lat. *ligare*: to bind) an association of nations or other political entities for a common purpose; an association of people or groups united by a common interest or goals; an informal alliance (*Webster's Ninth New Collegiate Dictionary* 1991).

[3] In 1990, elders remembered that assemblies were held secretly in the forest if important inter-domain matters such as war or a land dispute had to be arbitrated.

[4] Some went far inland. Thus, Tauern (1918: 29-30) attributes a Halmaherese origin to the Alune, a highland group of West Seram who are also credited with introducing the loom and the knowledge of woven fibres.

[5] The paper is based on several fieldwork trips carried out in the area in 1983, 1985 and 1991-92.

[6] Luhu, a large coastal settlement, was referred to as a *kota*, 'town'.

[7] The inter-communal violence that rocked the Moluccas between 1999 and 2003 tore apart dozens of communities, killing an estimated 15,000 people and displacing more than half a million as refugees. In the process, communal and individual lands have often been appropriated and redistributed. People are returning slowly to rebuild their shattered communities, but as witnessed in the history of the area, unresolved land issues could constitute a significant obstacle to securing a lasting peace.

[8] The traditional name of West Seram is 'Wele Telu Batai, the Three Large Rivers Trunks: '*Wae'we, kwae, kwe* means river; *le, ela*: large; *telu*: three; and *batai* is a classifier for large oblong objects such as a log or the trunk of a felled tree. *Batai* is also used to refer to a river valley or a mountain range and to the people who inhabit it. ''Wele Telu Batai is adjacent to but excludes the westernmost peninsula of Huamual.

[9] It is delimited by the Makina River in the north and the Mala in the south.

[10] The *kakehan*, about which we know very little although much has been written, was described as a masculine secret society acting as a large regional association of male initiation groups. The brotherhood was characterised by initiation practices, secret paraphernalia, ritual seclusion of boys in men's houses, warfare and ritual murder (headhunting).

[11] Their three coastal *ibu kota* (administrative centres) are Piru, a few kilometres north of the mouth of the Eti River, Kairatu, south-west of the Tala, and Taniwel, east of the Sapalewa.

[12] Domains can be referred to as *kota, inama* or *anakota* in relation to their position within their *batai*.

[13] The highlanders depended on the coast to obtain goods such as salt, weapons or heirloom objects; the coastal settlers traded these goods for forest products and services.

[14] The name Seram ('frightening') evokes a dark, mysterious passive and powerful source of life.

[15] According to M. Sijauta S.J.M., a prominent Ambonese Alune elder in 1983, *Ulate Ina*, is recalled as the 'Mother Mountain, mother of all *Uli*' (territorial groups).

[16] In Ambonese, *Saniri Besar* or *Saniri Hutu*. In Alune, used as a verb, the word *nili* means 'to mix' or 'to arouse'. Mixing people and ideas and stirring them into actions was a purpose of the *nili*.

[17] The early colonial civil servants and administrators regarded these *nili ela* (or *nili batai*) as a waste of resources and as potentially dangerous political gatherings.

[18] *Tapele*: the land, the Earth, as opposed to *Lanite*: the sky, the Heavens.

[19] People believed in a form of metempsychosis along family lines. Thus one might say that the function was also regarded as staying with the 'same' persona.

[20] Following Blust's reconstruction (1980: 217), the Proto-Malayo-Polynesian **datu* offers four possible components: 1) political leader, chief; 2) priest; 3) aristocrat, noble; and 4) ancestor, grandfather, elder. According to Belwood (1996: 19), the *datu* is probably a lineage- (or clan-)like official. Traditionally in Seram, the title of *Latu*, Lord, suggests a leading position rather than a specific duty. A Lord of the Land, a ruler, a high priest or a warrior may all be honoured by the title of *Latu*.

[21] Authors usually translate *Mauwen* or *Mawene Anakota* ('captain of a boat') as 'High Priest' because the *Mauwena* were also leading dignitaries of the *kakehan*. Indeed, the brotherhood was also ensuring that traditional law was implemented among its members.

[22] In Bahasa Indonesia: *Pohon Bandera*.

[23] Wemale: *Bandera Erui*: 'Tip of the Flag'; Bahasa Indonesia: *Udjung Bandera*. 'The imagery [of flag and pole, base and tip] evokes a paradigm of objects that stand fixed in place and reach upward toward the sky. Like such *axis mundi* as the cosmic mountain, the world tree, and the origin house, the union of the pole and flag expresses a hierarchical distinction between one who plants, grips and steadies the foundations of a structure and one who keeps it upright and erect' (E.G. Traube 1980: 57).

[24] The title of *kapitan* evokes a war leader (*Kapitan Perang*). It was first given by the crews of Portuguese ships who visited the region to the spokesmen with whom they had contact and who seemed to lead their groups since they came forward. These *kapitan* (the title was incorporated in various local languages) were the dignitaries in charge of the relationships of their domain with the outside. By extension, the envoys of the *nili* received the title of *kapitan*. The ancient Alune highland name for the same function was *alamanane*. *Alamanana* means 'to intone', *alamanane*, a 'ritual chant', and the *alamanane* or *ma'a alamanane* was 'the one whose office is to chant', the other duty of the *kapitan* or *alamanane*.

[25] Thus, the Wemale domains of Abio Batai, Walokone and Waraloin in the upper Uli and Sapalewa Rivers area do not seem to be mentioned anywhere in relation to the Nili 'Wele Telu Batai. Other coalitions were also formed within or outside the *nili*. For example, the domains of Rumasoal and Riring respectively, *Sarimetene* and *Anakota* of the Sapalewa River *batai*, were also part of another independent alliance called Nili Kwele Batai (the 'Assembly of the Big River') with three other highland domains of the upper Eti River (Niniari, Murikau and Lumoli). This coalition had its own representation in the regional assembly (Nili 'Wele Telu Batai). As an indigenous highland association, it counterbalanced the influence of the rich and powerful Muslim coastal domains of Kaibobo (Eti) and Lisabata (Sapalewa), both former vassals of the Ternatan governor of Luhu (Huamual). The Nili Kwele Batai later played an important role in the resistance against the Dutch colonisation of the highlands.

[26] Authoritative members of the *kakehan* were prominent elders in the *nili*. Throughout the region, groups and their allies received each other in large men's houses, built semi-buried deep in the forest, to perform ancestral rituals, duties, and to celebrate and debate local politics.

[27] In 1914-16, the league had attained enough cohesion to propagate a succession of uprisings, from domain to domain along each river valley, in a last attempt to resist colonisation.

[28] *Mena* means: 'first', 'primary', 'earlier', 'in the front' or 'before', as opposed to *muli*: 'after' or 'behind', 'in the back', 'last'. The distinction between 'core' and 'tips' or 'branches' and between those who are 'in the front' and those who are 'in the back' is used to construct the recursive asymmetric relational categories that mark precedence (see Fox 1994, 1995).

[29] *Pacificacie*: the ruthless military repression of any form of rebellion (including peaceful flight) against the imposition of colonial rule.

[30] *Kakehan* and *nili ela* were undoubtedly related, if only because prominent elders and political leaders assembled in both councils. However, the *kakehan* was of the order of *adat agama*, a 'religious tradition', now disappeared, while what remains of the *nili* (at village scale) is still concerned with *adat pemerintah*, a 'traditional administration', that was regarded by the colonial and new order Indonesian administrations as cumbersome remnants of a past to be disposed of.

[31] The renown of an important individual or his personal wealth in ceremonial objects enhanced the prestige of his domain, re-enforcing its position within the *batai*.

[32] House and *Luma* with a capital 'H' and 'L' are used to distinguish these social units from the 'house' (*luma*), the building of the same name.

[33] The domains of 'Wele Telu Batai were called *hena inama kota* or *anakota* in relation to their position in the *nili* of their river.

[34] In Bahasa Indonesia: *tamba jiwa tamba tanah*.

[35] *Ma'a* is an agentive, locative or genitive noun forming a prefix, which is affixed to the verbal root. Thus it conveys the triple idea of 'the people who', 'the place where', and 'the origin of'. *Sama* means 'to share', 'divide', 'split up', or 'allot' (Bahasa Indonesia: *bagi*); *ne* is the nominative marker. The word *uey*, *wei* or *uwei* can be translated as 'origin', 'beginning', 'centre', 'source of continuity' and also 'junction point' (Bahasa Indonesia: *pusat*: 'centre', 'navel').

[36] Samai is also referred to as Latu Pati Ama Samane: 'The Lord Dignitary Father (who) Distributes'.

[37] 'An ordered succession of place names' that establish precedence in relation to a particular starting point—a point of origin. Generally these topogenies assume the form of a journey: that of an ancestor, an origin group or an object' (J.J. Fox, 1997: 91).

[38] In the *ilmu* 999, a numerical system widespread in the region and beyond, the number nine is used to represent any totality, and seven is one of the combination of numbers used to represent social units, clans, rulers, bodies, etc. In that system elements are grouped to form units. Each complete unit is counted as one element of its sub-units for it represents the totality of them (a body represented by its head). There is only one totality per unit. As a result, when units merge the final combination shows only one totality.

[39] The realm of the dead is upside down and the opposite of the world of the living. While the fecundating river waters flow downstream, the ancestral substance returns upstream via the three rivers to the Nunusaku. Those of Manusa Manuwe follow the Sapalewa.

[40] *Tita*: 'to cross over', 'to visit' and, by extension, 'to trade'.

[41] In the modern *desa* too, members of *nuru* still regarded as *Hena Upui* often hold administrative functions. This is not so much the remnant of 'feudal practices' but merely the fact that some representatives of these Houses have the experience, the authority and the network of allies that allow them to perform their tasks. These positions are challenged by newcomers, particularly the position of 'Great Lord' (now *Kepala Desa*), one of the most accessible.

[42] Because the *hena* regards itself as the origin of all the groups in the area, all newcomers finds themselves in the position of one who 'returns' (*leu*) to Manusa Manuwe.

[43] Who is someone else's land giver and who was *a mena* (elder) on a piece of land is forgotten only if the group who watched over it becomes extinct.

[44] The ancient hamlets were amalgamated in three *soa* in the 1920s and the whole population regrouped in one village in 1977.

[45] In Bahasa Indonesia, it is referred to as *tanah sejarah*.

[46] The topogeny of the Hena Ma'saman Uwei recalls the bifurcations and differentiations of the first ancestors as they follow the path that leads them down and away from the undifferentiated place of

origin (the *Nunusaku*). While Samai, the founding ancestor of the *hena*, and his followers established the ritual centre of Nuruitu, his elder brother Latuelamena (the 'Big Lord in the Front') left with the regalia that testified to the history of origin. He settled at the coast with his followers and found the powerful Alune low hills domain of Eti along the river of the same name. Eti was the *Inama*, the 'Mother-father', of the Eti River's *nili* and was allied with Ternate through its relationship with Piru, the political centre of the south west coast. At that time, says the narrative, Latuelamena took the *nuru* name of Turukai. The small 'shots' of his *nuru* who remained with Samai in Hena Ma'saman Uw*e*i were nicknamed *anasosi*, 'ignorant children'. Their descendants are the Houses of *nuru* Tibali. They still insist on their 'ignorance' but their *nuru* controls a substantial portion of the *hena* land near the path to the south coast, where newcomers are welcomed to settle (see Fig. 2).

[47] Between 1916 and 1990, the position of Great lord (variously called regent, *Radja*, *Pesawat* and *Kepala Desa*) was held successively by elders who belonged to the *nuru* of the *Upu Tapele*, the *Latu Maeta'e*, a follower of the *Ama Lesi*, and the *nuru* of the *Ama Nili*.

[48] Even the rights on this usufruct are not exclusive in as much as everyone is expected to share and nothing is fenced (except by traps and prohibition signs).

[49] During the New Order, this system became vulnerable to manipulation and abuse. In Manusa Manuwe, a lumber company was granted the rights to fell large sections of forest on the land of several Houses by 'the community', i.e. the civil servants put in place by a corrupted regional government. These Houses were never adequately compensated.

[50] At the beginning of the 20'th century, the highlanders who lived in hamlets on their respective House land had to register themselves with the Dutch Colonial Administration and regroup in larger settlements along a path to the coast. In Manusa Manuwe, the *dati* system was probably introduced during this period and integrated by the people into the local *lusu* system.

[51] Closer relatives have more rights than others, but all should apply restraint.

[52] The *Ntuane dati* might signal to the user family that the group is claiming the parcel back by planting long-term plantations on it.

[53] In Manusa Manuwe, the rights of one line can be transferred through unmarried women for several generations until a suitable male heir is born.

[54] A man who cares for his wife will leave instructions for her care to his children.

[55] In the past relatives, allies and friends harvested and celebrated jointly with the ancestors. The New Order Government and the Church discouraged the practice of this 'wasteful' and 'backward' thanksgiving ritual.

[56] It remains to be seen if the *nili hena* ('village council') will be revived in a new form within the LMD (*Lembaga Masyarakat Desa*: Fellow Villagers' Association).

Chapter 8. From Domains to Rajadom: Notes on the History of Territorial Categories and Institutions in the Rajadom of Sikka

E.D. Lewis

Introduction [1]

Two forms of Sikkanese society can be distinguished in contemporary Kabupaten[2] Sikka of eastern Flores on ethnological grounds. One is that of the Ata Tana 'Ai in the eastern region of the *kabupaten*. The other is that of central Sikka, which includes the villages of the central hills and mountains and the north and south coasts of the regency. [3] The main difference between the two societies that will concern me here is this: whereas no secular polity ever developed in Tana 'Ai, by the beginning of the 20th century, the society of central Sikka constituted a local state, a single polity under the rule of a Sikkanese royal house, which traced its origins through 18 rajas and at least 16 generations. [4] The Rajadom of Sikka dated at least to the Portuguese era in eastern Indonesia, evolved into a semi-autonomous state under the Dutch policy of *zelfbestuur* (self-rule) in the 19th and 20th centuries, and reached the apex of its power and independence in the absence of the Dutch Colonial Government in the decade immediately after World War II. Tana 'Ai came under direct Sikkanese rule only in the last three decades of the history of the Rajadom of Sikka. Indeed, Sikkanese rule had so little practical effect in Tana 'Ai that contemporary Ata Tana 'Ai still recognise five *tana*, or 'ceremonial domains', in their region today (see Map 1) and remember very little of the rajadom or its Sikkanese rulers.

In these two societies we thus see, recapitulated on the scale of a single Florenese region, a pattern characteristic of eastern Indonesia generally, whereby some societies gave rise to local states while others did not. In the case of Sikka, on a relatively local scale, the question becomes: how did Sikka become a state while the Ata Tana 'Ai retained a society founded on ceremonial domains? This is an ethnological and a historical question. Any advance towards an answer should contribute to solving two general problems in eastern Indonesian ethnology and history. Firstly, how did local states arise in eastern Indonesia? Secondly, why did some societies in eastern Indonesia develop into local states while others did not?

Map 1: Settlements and domains (tana) of Tana 'Ai

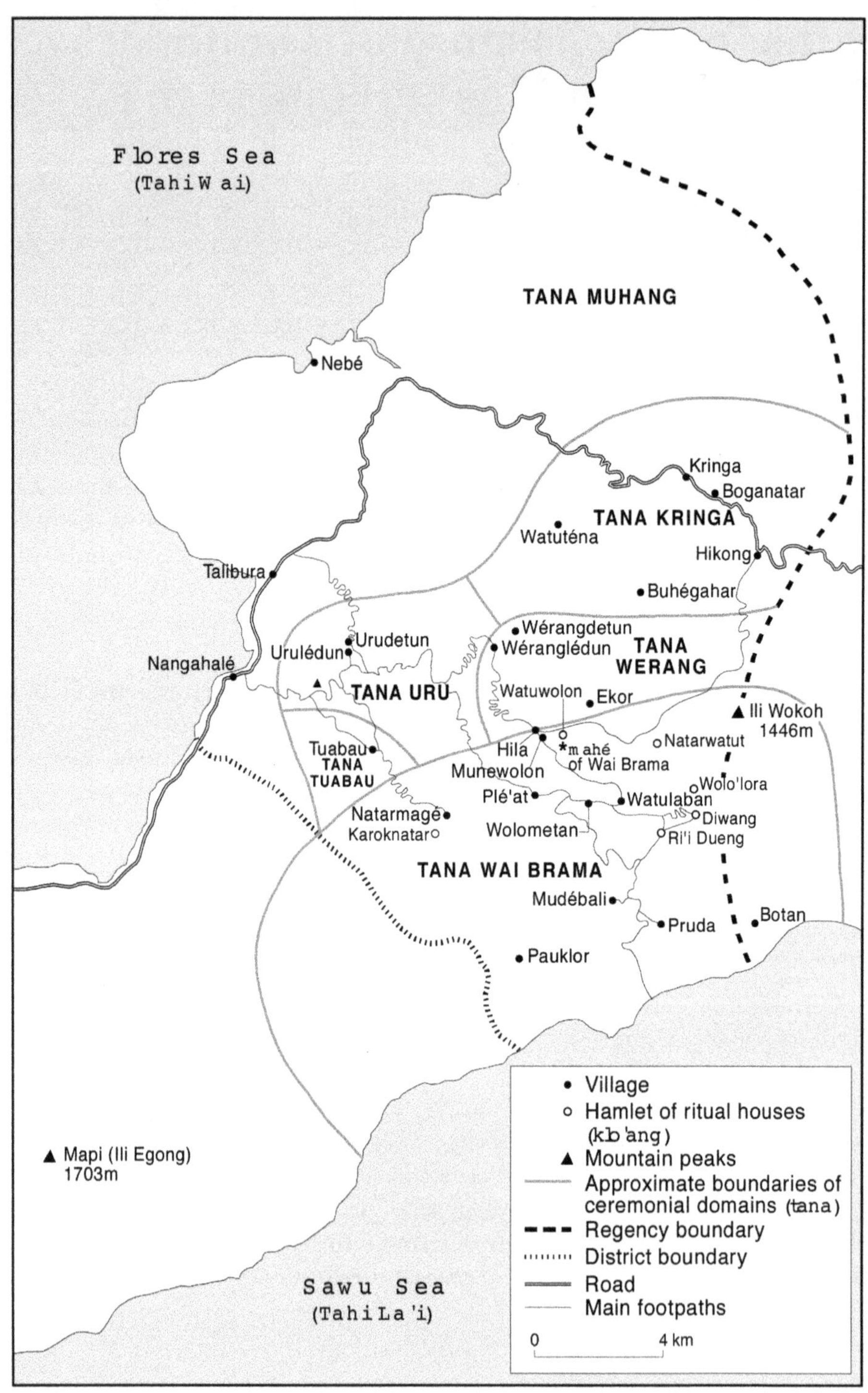

In examining the specific case of Kabupaten Sikka, I will make the following ethnological assumptions: 1) the nature and organisation of the Tana 'Ai domains did not change greatly during the two or three centuries in which the Sikkanese Rajadom evolved; and 2) despite differences between the societies of Tana 'Ai and Sikka, before the advent of the rajadom, Sikkanese communities were domain-based societies similar to those of Tana 'Ai. These assumptions are justified on the evidence of contemporary ethnographic research in Sikka, which includes oral histories of people in Sikka Natar (the village of Sikka on the south coast of Flores from which the rajadom and the contemporary *kabupaten* took their names), the myths of origin of the rajadom, and the origin myths of the immigrant groups who make up Sikka Natar.

I shall approach the Sikkanese case by addressing three questions: 1) What were the domains of Sikka like before the rajadom and the arrival of the Dutch? 2) How did the Sikkanese rulers establish their hegemony over central Sikka? And 3) what changes in territorial categories and institutions resulted from the evolution from domains to a rajadom in central Sikka?

I shall begin with a brief, comparative reference to the domains of Tana 'Ai in far eastern Sikka. I do this because I assume that the basic features of *tana* ('domains', in Sara Sikka [SS], the language of Sikka) in the area of Tana 'Ai were in the past also those of the *tana* of central Sikka.

Tana as a Territorial Category in Tana 'Ai

Domains (*tana*) in Tana 'Ai are the highest order of the classificatory categories of Tana 'Ai society. They are, in the broadest sense, religious in nature and ceremonial in manifestation. Leadership in a *tana* is, or was until recently, exercised mainly in the realm of sacred authority and ritual performance and the *tana* had no single secular authority. The Tana 'Ai pattern is best illustrated by features of the domain of Wai Brama, the largest of the *tana* of Tana 'Ai. In Wai Brama the most important decisions affecting the secular affairs of the domain's clans and houses are taken by the *ina geté* ('great mothers') of those clans and houses while men, as ritual specialists, carry out domain rituals on behalf of their sisters and mothers. As a society, Tana Wai Brama is defined by the relations of the clans which provide their members with land in the domain by virtue of the clans' positions in a system of precedence set out in the domain's myths of origin. [5]

Tana Wai Brama is a ceremonial domain headed by a *tana pu'an*, a 'source of the domain', who is always of the central house of the central clan in terms of the precedence of clans in the domain and houses in the clan. The central clan is credited with founding the domain in the mythic past. The *tana pu'an* is the head of a ceremonial system within which the clans of the *tana* must help organise, provision and conduct rituals of the domain. These rituals are the *gren mahé* and the rituals to open and close the dry and wet seasons. [6] It is important to note that it is clan membership that entitles, indeed, requires, a person to discharge obligations in *gren mahé*, regardless of whether he or she resides at a place clearly within the domain's territory. Given that the clans are not themselves associated with demarcated territories, neither the clans of the domain nor the *tana* as a whole can be described strictly as territorial institutions. A *tana* is instead a loosely organised region defined by a centre, whose peripheries form no clear boundary. A *tana*'s centre is defined ritually (if not geographically) by its *mahé*, the domain's central ceremonial site, and socially by the ceremonial office of the *tana pu'an*. Notwithstanding the delimitation of domain boundaries in Map 1, the domains are best thought of as social spaces defined by ritual centres whose influence and power extend radially and outwards until overshadowed by the power of neighbouring domains radiating from their centres. Thus, a person living on the frontier of two *tana* might have obligations in one *gren* by virtue of clan membership while participating in the *gren* of the other *tana* as a way of hedging his or her bets with respect to the fertility of gardens (which the *gren* ensures) or because he or she traces ancestral origins to a clan of that *tana*.

Territorial Categories in Central Sikka

Tana (SS), *natar* (SS), and *negeri* (BI) are three commonly used markers of territories in central Sikka but they are slippery words in Sikkanese discourse.

The word *tana* in Sara Sikka encompasses the following meanings:

1. *niang tana* : 'the earth, the world'. For example, *ata teri niang 'era tana* are 'the people who live (sit) on the land and arise (stand up) from the earth', and *ata tawa tana* , 'people who arose from the earth', are autochthons (BI *orang asli*).
2. territory, district, region: *tana Sikka* is the 'region of Sikka', which is innately ambiguous insofar as Sikka refers variously to the village of Sikka, the Regency of Sikka, and the aggregate of domains that demarcated central Sikka from its neighbours to the east and west.

The word *natar* in Sara Sikka means:

1. *kampung* (BI: village). Thus Sikka, Natar is specifically the village of Sikka.
2. *desa* : 'village' in Bahasa Indonesia, but note that Wilkinson defines the word in Malay as 'region; country; country-village' and comments, 'a word used rather loosely, viz.: (i) of a territorial unit of any size ... (ii) of the country in contr[ast] to the townships ... (iii) in Java, a country hamlet; = (Mal[ay]) kampong' (Wilkinson 1959: 277-8). While not wishing to suggest that the Sikkanese speak Malay (much less an old form of Malay) rather than Bahasa Indonesia, use of the word *desa* in contemporary Kabupaten

> Sikka accords as well with Wilkinson's definitions as with modern Bahasa Indonesia, in which *desa* means 'village'. [7]

The word *negeri* is Malay and Bahasa Indonesia, but is used commonly in Sara Sikka and is used frequently in certain Sikkanese texts. Here matters become truly confused. In contemporary Bahasa Indonesia, *negeri* means 'country, land' (Echols and Shadily 1989: 386), but Echols and Shadily note that in Malay and in eastern Indonesia the word denotes 'village', an observation supported by recordings of Sikkanese speech and the word's use in early Sikkanese manuscripts. Noting the origin of the word in Sanskrit, Wilkinson defines *negeri* as

> settlement; city-state ... used loosely (Mal[ay]) of any settlement, town or land ... more specifically (Min[angkabau]) of an autonomous area or group of villages under a penghulu andeka ... or other territorial chief, e.g. Negeri Sembilan (the 'Nine States', each autonomous though collectively under a suzerain). (Wilkinson 1959: 802)

I belabour the reader with these definitions because they are of key terms and because they warn us to take care about usage in context. The 'looseness' in usage that Wilkinson notes is firstly a matter of variation in the meaning of a single word across the Malay-Indonesian Archipelago and, secondly, a matter of lexical polysemy in the context of a single linguistic community. The pairs *tana* and *natar* in Sikkanese and *negeri* and *desa* in Indonesian are used commonly in Kabupaten Sikka and, more importantly for my purposes here, occur frequently in the Sikkanese texts from which I will draw evidence for territorial categories in central Sikka. It is thus crucial to be as certain as possible about the multiple meanings of the terms in the context of Sikkanese usage.

The inhabitants of some of the villages of central Sikka have preserved the ritual sites (*mahé*) which, in Tana 'Ai, would mark the centres of *tana*, ceremonial domains (Plates 1, 2 and 3), with this difference: whereas the *mahé* of Tana Wai Brama is in a clearing hidden within a stand of primary forest some distance from human habitation, the *mahé* of central Sikka are located in the centres of villages in public spaces reminiscent of the ritual sites of the societies of central and western Flores. These central Sikkanese sites can be taken as direct evidence for past ceremonial systems in central Sikka and as indirect evidence for the location of the centres of *tana*, which were perhaps similar to those of contemporary Tana 'Ai. [8]

Plate 1: Remains of *Mahé* Mo'ang Hi'eng at Héwoklo'ang (1979)

Plate 2: Remains of the *Mahé* at Baomékot (1979)

Plate 3: Remains of the *Mahé* at Kangae (2000)

Plate 4: The organisation of the Rajadom of Sikka in the era of Mo'ang Don Alésu da Silva (Pareira unpublished [2002]: 12-13)

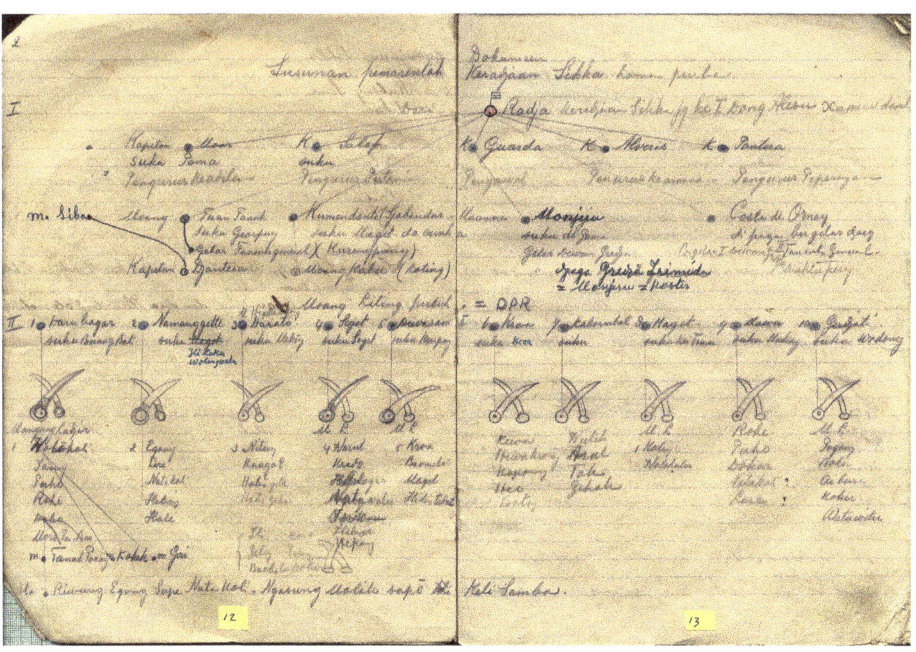

Additional evidence for territorial categories effective in Sikka's past designated by the terms *tana, natar* and *negeri* in central Sikka can be found in interviews with Sikkanese informants in the years 1977-2002 and, of particular value, in the narratives of the foundation myth and subsequent history of the Rajadom of Sikka, written by Mo'ang Alexius Boer Pareira and Mo'ang Dominicus Dionitius Parera Kondi, two Sikkanese authors of the first half of the 20th century. [9]

One of Mo'ang Boer's notebooks (Document 001, Sikka Manuscripts Collection; Pareira unpublished [2002]) includes a rough chart (Plate 4 and Figure 1) [10] of the organisation of the Rajadom of Sikka in the era of the first raja, Mo'ang Don Alésu Xamenes da Silva, a time undated in the history of the rajadom.

Figure 1: The Organisation of the Rajadom of Sikka in the Era of Mo'ang Don Alésu da Silva (after Pareira unpublished [2002]: 12-13)

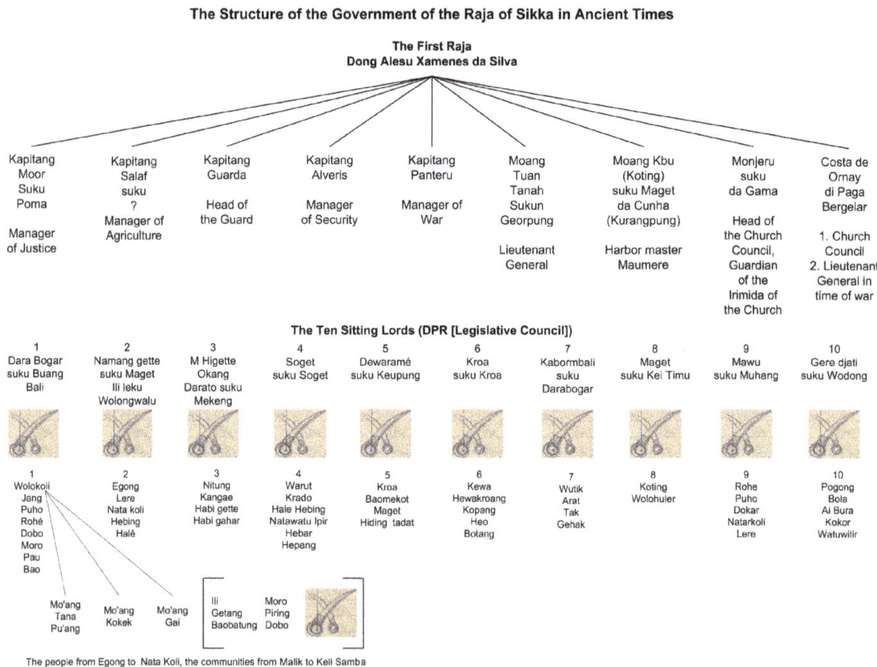

Mo'ang Boer's depiction of the structure of the Rajadom of Sikka 'in ancient times' indicates two levels of organisation. The first shows the relation of the first raja to eight office-holders called *kapitang* (captains) and indicates their responsibilities. Most of the *kapitang* were drawn from groups that Boer identifies as *suku* (SS 'clans') of Sikka Natar and from clans outside Sikka Natar that were allied closely with *lepo geté* (SS 'great house'), the royal house of Sikka. This is an interesting point because the people of contemporary Sikka Natar deny that they belong to clans and that *suku* are categories of Sikkanese society. [11] They point out that Sikka Natar is divided into *'wisung wangang*, which are extended family groups. The people of each *'wisung* bear a Portuguese (P) name and are associated with households and territorial homesteads within the village.

In Boer's chart, the eight *kapitang* are shown as holding offices labelled by two Malay titles and six Portuguese titles. Five of the offices are identified as being associated with clan names or villages. Boer's list of the *kapitang* under Don Alésu, the first of the Sikkanese rajas, and explanatory notes about the meaning of the titles (from left to right in Boer's chart) are given below. [12]

Kapitang Moor: Pengurus Keadilan (Manager of Justice)	From *capitão mor* (P): until the beginning of the 20th century, the commander of a Portuguese village militia.
Kapitang Salaf: Pengurus Pertanian (Manager of Agriculture)	The origin of the title *salaf* is obscure, but three possibilities can be identified. 1) from *capitão de sala* or *capitão de salas* (P), possibly a captain in charge of bureaucracy, provisions, supply, ordnance. 2) *Salaf* is not an Arabic word but might derive from *safra* (P), 'harvest'. It is possible that in borrowing this word the Sikkanese first changed it to **safara* or **safala*, which was further altered by metathesis (**salafa*) and the loss of the final vowel (*salaf*). An alternative evolution might have involved a metathesis first (*safra* **serafa*, **sarafa* or **salafa*) followed by the loss of the final *a*. Dr A.N. Baxter (personal communication) notes that the loss of the final vowel is curious since Sara Sikka allows both vowels and consonants at the end of syllables. A third possibility is that, in drawing on oral history as his source, Boer might have mistranscribed the word in his manuscript.
Kapitang Djantera, Source of the Earth, Clan Georpung: Tanenti General (Lieutenant General)	*Djantera* might derive from *dianteira* (P), 'vanguard'. Boer wrote in Malay and used the orthography common in Indonesia in Dutch times in which /j/ was written *dj* and /y/ was written *j* (*sadja* 'only', *saja* 'I'). *Djantera* would have been pronounced /jantera/ in speech, but Boer might have intended that the *ja* in the word (which in the Dutch orthography has the sound /ia/) be pronounced as /ia/, the *j* replacing the *i* in *dianteira*. If this were the case, then the Sikkanese word would be pronounced /diantera/, but if he intended the *dj* to be pronounced /j/, then the word would be pronounced /jantera/ and would have been altered from the Portuguese when it came into the Sikkanese language.
Kumandanti Sjabandar Maumere	*Syahbandar* (Malay) is a harbour master.

Kapitang Guarda: Pengawal ('First', of people) (First Minister?)	*Kapitang Guarda* from (P) *capitão da guarda* or 'captain of the guard'. Boer identifies this *kapitang* as '*monyeru*' and with the *Irimida*. An *irimida* (SS) is *erimida* (P), a chapel or small church usually built outside and some distance from a village. The word *monjeru* (in Boer's writing, pronounced /monyeru/) is somewhat puzzling. It might be related to *monge* (P), 'friar, brother of a Christian order'. Boer equates *monjeru* with *koster* (Dutch), 'sexton, verger' (*Küster* in German; Latin *custos*, 'guard, keeper'). Boer notes that this officer '*Gelar dewan gredja [sic] jaga gredja irimida*', that is, 'holds office on the church council and looks after the church's chapel'.
Costa de Ornay of Paga, '*bergelar djrey*', 'holds the office of *djrey*'	*Djrey*: the combination of consonants *djr* (*jr* in modern orthography) does not exist in Malay or Bahasa Indonesia. However, the change from /di/ to /ji/ is common in Portuguese itself and in Portuguese creole languages and this term is almost certainly from *de rei* (P: 'of the king'). Boer describes the holder of this office as responsible for the church council and for serving as '*Tanenti General waktu perang*', that is, 'lieutenant general in time of war'. The sense of the term might be that of a minister plenipotentiary.
Kapitang Alveris: Pengurus keamanan (Manager of Safety, Security)	In the Portuguese military, *alferes* was a rank between *sargento* and *tenente*. Boer equates *kapitang alveris* with *pengurus keamanan* (BI), 'manager of safety, security'.
Kapitang panteru: Pengurus peperangan (Manager of War)	The shift from /p/ to /f/ is common in Portuguese words borrowed by speakers of Malay and Tagalog and if this happened in Sikka, *panteru* might well derive from *infante* (P: 'infantry soldier'). Baxter (personal communication) has suggested that in a purely local formation, *infante* (P) acquired the Portuguese agentive suffix *-ero* (which became *eru* in Sikkanese) to form a local Sikkanese word, *panteru*, meaning 'infantry' or, better, 'one who is involved with the infantry'. *-Ero* is highly productive in South-East Asian creole varieties of Portuguese, such as that of Malacca, and such a change in Sikka would not be surprising. In his chart, Boer equates *kapitang panteru* with '*pengurus peperangan*' (BI), 'manager of war'.

Below these *kapitang*, or ministers, Boer identifies the *Mo'ang Liting Puluh*, Ten Sitting Lords, whom he describes as constituting a 'DPR' (BI: *dewan perwakilan rakyat*), a legislative council or legislative assembly. The Sitting Lords are identified further by clan and the *negeri* (villages and village clusters) which were their responsibilities.

The word *'liting* (SS) means 1) 'base, foundation' and 2) 'chair', and in Sikkanese ritual speech there are references to

du'a deri é'i 'liting pulu	the *du'a* (honorific for women) who sits at the seven foundations;
mo'ang 'er é'i 'ler walu	the *mo'ang* (honorific for men) who stands at the eight leaning places. [a]

[a] *Du'a mo'ang* are leaders and ritual specialists.

Boer identifies each of the Ten Sitting Lords not by name, but by clan affiliation. This identification is highly significant because the people of Sikka Natar are not, strictly speaking, divided into clans, whereas the people of the central hills of Sikka are. Below each Sitting Lord, Boer drew a pair of crossed elephant tusks. Ivory tusks were one of the main goods with which, according to the mythic histories of the rajadom, the early rajas secured alliances with the leaders of local communities in the central hills and mountains of Sikka (see Lewis 1998b, 1999). Below each of the 10 pairs of crossed tusks and clan names, Boer lists a number of villages in the following groupings:

1. Wolokoli Iang
Puho Rohé
Dobo Moro
Pau Boa [= Baot?]
2. Egong Lere
Nata Koli
Hébing Halé
3. Nitung
Kangae Habi
Geté Habi
Gahar
4. Warut Krado
Halé Hébing
Nata Watu
Ipir Hébar
Hepang
5. Kroa
Baomékot
Maget Hiding
Tadat
6. Kéwa
Héwaklo'ang
Kopang [Kopong] Héo
Botang
7. Wutik Arat
Tak [Tok?]
Géhak
8. Koting Wolo
Huler
9. Rohé Puho
Dokar Natar
Koli Lere
10. Pogong Bola
'Ai Bura
Kokor Watu
Witir

An 11th group of villages has been pencilled in below the main list:

11. Ili Gétang
Baobatung
Moro Piring
Dobo

If duplicate names are ignored [13] and the placenames are drawn onto a map of central Sikka, these 11 groups of villages form territorial clusters (Map 2). Although Boer does not do so in the document I have cited, I am strongly inclined to view the territories delimited by these clusters as *tana*, domains with which the early Sikkanese rulers treated during the era in which they created the rajadom.

Map 2: Clusters of placenames and villages identified with the Ten Sitting Lords

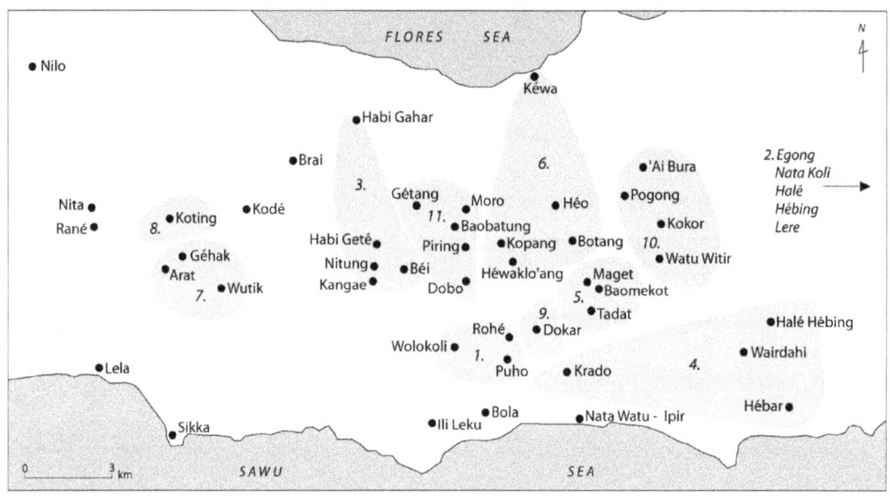

Towards the end of the notebook, Boer makes the following observation and appends a list of villages with which Raja Don Alésu made alliances (Pareira unpublished 2002):

Nora Don Alésu balong wawa Malaka mai dadi ratu é'i Niang Sikka te neti nora bala bala gawang gu mai bano néte natar baké na'i mangung ore na'i lajar. E'i Nuhang Ular tana lorang té'i é'i bahagian Tahi La'i sebela selatan molé é'i Tahi Wai sebela utara é'i natar natar wawa ba'u te'i.

When Don Alésu returned from Malaka and became Raja of the Land of Sikka he brought many elephant tusks which he then placed in the villages to raise up masts and sails. [a] This he did on Snake Island [Flores], in the land between the Male Sea to the south and the Female Sea [b] to the north, in many villages here.

There were Masts and Sails in the villages of:

1. Mudebali
2. Runut
3. Warut

16. Pora Nelu
17. Mage Panda
18. Manu Kako

31. Béi Nara
32. Ili Getang
33. Dobo Baobatung

4. Egong
5. Waidaki
6. Kroang Popot
7. Warut Krado
8. Rohe
9. Wolo Koli
10. Ili Leku
11. Mbengu
12. Molik
13. Rangga Se
14. Wolowaru
15. Nggéla
19. Wolosoko
20. Nua Lolo
21. Natawulu
22. Nilo
23. Rane
24. Koting
25. Wutik
26. Kailiwu
27. Kode
28. Brai
29. Habi Weko
30. Nitung Kangae
34. Kéwa Héwo Klo'ang
35. Ngalupolo
36. Kota Ndona
37. Masebewa
38. Kroa Baomekot
39. Ngalu Poto Pogong Bola
40. Wolomari (Lio)
41. Wolotopo
42. Molik (Ndori)
43. Kota Jogo
44. Wolo Mage Feondari

[a] The gift of twin elephant tusks, *mangung lajar* (mast and sail), to cement alliances between the rajas of Sikka and the *negeri* (villages) of the district, is a recurring theme in Boer's and Kondi's texts of the mythic histories of the Sikkanese rajadom.

[b] Tahi La'i (the Male Sea) and Tahi Wai (the Female Sea) are the Savu Sea and the Flores Sea, respectively.

Although much can be made of these lists, what should be noted immediately is that the structure of the raja's government depicted in Boer's diagram (Plate 4 and Figure 1) is not that of the raja's government under the Dutch. The arrangement of government in Dutch times was territorial: the *kerajaan* (BI: rajadom) was divided into a number of districts, each headed by a *kapitang*. The captaincies came to be (more or less) the first *kecamatan* [14] in the early years of the Indonesian administration of Sikka, but note that the *kecamatan* have changed over the years since the introduction of the *kabupaten* system of government in the late 1950s and early 1960s. Boer's diagram does not mention districts, but depicts a unified and hierarchical system of government. The raja is at the apex. Next is the level of the ministers, who were drawn largely from the Sikkanese nobility. Below the ministers are the Ten Sitting Lords, who were the heads of villages or clusters of villages and who are depicted as an advisory council to the raja. At this level the system begins to appear territorial, but note that the territories were not headed by *kapitang*, who were appointed by the raja and were not necessarily from the districts over which they had authority, but by locals who might (in some instances) have been *tana pu'ang*.

In 1982, Dr J.K. Metzner published a detailed study of the geo-ecology of agriculture in central Sikka. That work includes a section on 'Traditional Land Tenure' in which Metzner provides a map of 'the chief traditional territories (*tana*) of the 'lord of the earth' (*tana puang*)' [15] (Metzner 1982: 110; Map 3 below). The map is a reconstruction of the *tana* of Sikka in the 'pre-contact era—that is until about the end of the nineteenth century' (Metzner 1982: 110). Metzner's reconstruction requires correction on many points, but the pattern he identifies can be taken, for the purposes of this paper, to be correct in its essentials. Metzner writes:

> The size of a *tana puang* territory was essentially contingent upon population density. As [Map 3] shows[,] the *tana puang* territories were clearly smaller in densely populated Central Sikka than in eastern and western Sikka. The boundaries of these territories ... are not official, although they are sufficiently accurate in Central Sikka. ... [The map] thus serves to convey an approximate idea of former *adat* [16] territories. In one of the most densely populated portions of central Sikka—at the saddle of Nita and around Maumere—however, it was not possible to delineate unequivocally the borders of such territories. (Metzner 1982: 111–3). [17]

Map 3: Metzner's reconstruction of the *tana* of Central Sikka. [18]

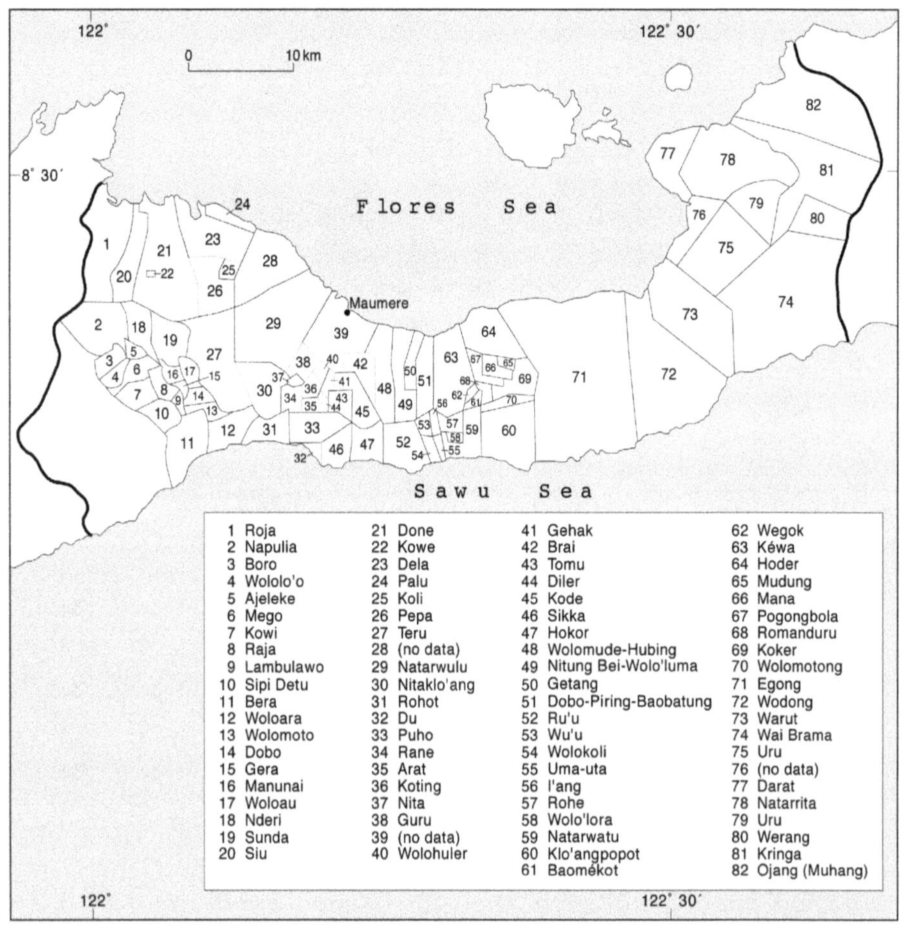

If we somewhat arbitrarily exclude the mainly Lionese regions of western Sikka and Tana 'Ai in the east from consideration and limit our focus to the *tana* of the central region of Metzner's map, [19] we find 48 *tana*. Comparing the names of *tana* on Metzner's map with the 44 names provided by Boer in his list of *mangung lajar* villages, we find the concordance between Metzner's and Boer's enumerations of places likely to have been considered *tana* is only 13 names. Despite confusion about the names of the *tana* and some errors in Metzner's spelling of *tana* names, it is striking that the numbers of *tana* listed by Boer and Metzner (44 and 48, respectively) are very nearly the same.

Metzner's suggestion that the number of *tana* in the densely populated central region of Sikka was strikingly greater than in the eastern and western reaches of the rajadom was justifiable. As Metzner implies, it might well have been the case that as the population and population density of the central region increased through time, older and larger *tana* might have fragmented into smaller domains with the result that the number of *tana* in the region increased in the course of Sikka's history. If this were the case, we glimpse a dynamic and changing array of domains, which is in marked contrast with the situation in Tana 'Ai, whose oral histories represent the domains of the region as unchanged since their creation.

Tana and the Creation of the Sikkanese Polity

There is an old idea in the ethnology of South-East Asia about the differences between lowland or coastal peoples and the peoples of the interior highlands. This distinction between lowland and highland peoples is condensed in the title of Robbins Burling's book on South-East Asian cultures; *Hill Farms and Padi Fields* (1965). In Burling's conception,

> ... each country in southeast Asia has both hill people and plains people, and the contrast—and sometimes conflict—between the two ways of life can provide a theme which helps to bring order into our understanding of the area. (Burling 1965: 4)

The peoples of the relatively densely populated lowlands are culturally homogeneous wet-rice cultivators who are adherents to one of the universal religions; the hill people, 'who are always far more heterogeneous', speak different languages, have no political unity among themselves, and practice shifting cultivation (ibid.). [20] With due respect to Burling, in Kabupaten Sikka, lowland and coastal people tend to view their highland cousins as just that: somewhat coarse, not completely Catholic, uneducated, a bit simple, and barefoot, but nevertheless their cousins. As an educated Sikkanese man once told me in the course of a conversation about the differences between his people and the Ata Tana 'Ai, 'They are still what we once were.' [21]

We can distinguish, as do the coastal Sikkanese themselves, three varieties of Sikkanese people: the Ata Tana 'Ai of the eastern valleys, the Ata 'Iwang (the phrase means *orang udik* [BI: person from a rural village; hillbilly] or, somewhat less pejoratively, *orang pedalaman* [BI: person of the back country] [22]) of the central hills, and, roughly, the southern and coastal Sikkanese, that is the people of the skewed crescent-shaped region from Nita in the west southward to Léla on the south coast, through Sikka Natar, to Bola in the east. Of these ethnonyms, the Ata Tana 'Ai call themselves Ata Tana 'Ai (at least, they acquiesce when others call them that) and the Sikkanese call themselves Ata Sikka (but, then, so does everyone in the district); but the Ata 'Iwang do not call themselves Ata 'Iwang: who, after all, refers to himself by saying, 'I am a heathen hillbilly'?

There is a small, fourth group: the ruling Sikkanese. In the district of Sikka, a ruling house arose on the south coast of Flores, in the village of Sikka. The house was Lepo Geté, the Great House, and its people used the name da Silva. The rulers it produced were known as *ratu* (rajas). This designation 'ruling Sikkanese' is easily quarrelled with because just who these early Sikkanese rulers were is something of a problem. All of the people of Sikka agree that the people of the ruling house are Sikkanese, but according to their own myth of origin, they are not. That myth tells the story of how, long ago, a sailing ship was wrecked on the south coast of Flores near Sikka Natar. Its crew, who were from 'Siam' (or 'Sailan', depending on the version of the myth one has to hand), could not repair their vessel, and so they took up residence on Flores. They met the *orang asli* (BI: 'aboriginal people') in the hills, with whom they made alliances. The myth relates the subterfuge by which, later on, the immigrants seized Sikka Natar from its aboriginal inhabitants and how immigrants from other parts of Flores and from farther away settled in Sikka to create a confederation of immigrant houses from which the whole of the region came to be ruled. In other words, the 'ruling' Sikkanese were immigrants; they were all 'new' Sikkanese.[23]

In one of the most important episodes in the myth, one of the descendants of the marooned ship's crew, Don Alésu, travelled to Malaka, where he 'studied *ilmu politik* [BI: 'political science']' and became a Christian. On his return, he and a travelling companion brought Catholicism to Sikka and founded the Rajadom of Sikka. If we jump forward to the end of the 19th century, we find Alésu's descendants ruling Kerajaan Sikka with authority delegated by the Dutch. [24] This Alésu's descendants did until 1954. Sikka is thus a good example of the process of formation of a state which incorporated rulers on the coast who had direct links to the outside world and people of a hinterland who, while absorbed into the state, were not at its political centre.

Whereas the Ata Tana 'Ai preserved much of their *hadat* and have continued practising the rituals of their ceremonial system, which are the essence of their *tana*, during the past two or three centuries, the *tana pu'ang* of central Sikka lost their power and Christian symbols were added to the *mahé* of the region (see Plates 1, 2 and 3). In the same centuries, the people of Sikka Natar took Portuguese names and developed a state; 1) whose office-holders took titles that reflected Sikkanese perceptions of Portuguese organisations in eastern Indonesia, including ranks of the Portuguese military hierarchy; 2) whose efflorescence coincided historically with the rise of Dutch dominance in Flores; 3) whose foundation, as recounted in the mythic histories of the rajadom, coincided with the introduction of Catholicism in Sikka; and 4) whose development paralleled that of the Catholic Church on Flores. But more is required to understand what happened to Sikka's *tana*.

The *tana* of central Sikka (and their *tana pu'ang*) were not displaced entirely under the rajas' rule. Boer's diagram of the structure of the rajadom under Don Alésu is crucial evidence bearing on this question. The chart identifies localities and clusters of villages which were allied to the new rulers. Boer's and Kondi's histories tell us how these allegiances were secured and how the alliances were formed. The diagram also depicts graphically the imposition of a hierarchical system of governance over what theretofore had been autonomous local domains, a system imposed (according to Boer and Kondi) by an alien, immigrant people, according to an alien, Portuguese system of organisation, and, later, condoned by the alien, Dutch Colonial Government.

A central clue to what happened to the *tana* of Sikka is to be found not in what is in Boer's diagram, but what is not. Boer connects the raja and his ministers with lines that indicate their relationships. He connects the *tana pu'ang* to the villages under their authority with vertical lines, but there are no direct connections between the offices of the rajadom and the *tana pu'ang* identified on the chart. Furthermore (and somewhat puzzling), the crossed elephant tusks of the diagram, which indicate alliances, are not placed between the rajadom and the *tana*, but between the clans named as *pu'ang* and the territories associated with them.

This evidence points to a simple hypothesis: the rajas did not directly interfere with Sikkanese *tana* but, through time, usurped the *tana pu'ang* by incorporating them as lowest-level functionaries in the rajadom's government. As the Church and rajadom grew in power and influence in the district, the ritual importance of the *tana pu'ang* and thus their *tana* as territorial institutions simply withered away, although the concept of the *tana* as a ceremonial domain that bound its people together in a small-scale community remained. This progression was in most respects complete by the time the rajadom came to an end in 1954, and the *tana* as a territorial institution did not survive the transition to the modern government in the regency.

Not only did the immigrant rulers of Sikka usurp whatever local authority might have existed among the indigenous Sikkanese, the origin myth of the

Sikkanese ruling house makes the claim that the immigrant rulers created the *tana* and *tana pu'ang* of central Sikka. Three key passages from the *Hikayat Kerajaan Sikka* (*The History of the Rajadom of Sikka*) illuminate this claim:

> In the beginning, because of his wise policy, his majesty the Raja of Sikka ordered every tribe of the interior, those who were wealthy and brave, to a meeting in which they were given offices by his majesty the Raja along with the titles Mo'ang and Kapitan; each tribe had such an officer and they lived continually in the nation of Sikka. Thus the nation's origins were in the interior and outside and as each became an ally of the nation, they were governed by the Raja and the Raja took decisions about matters to make the nation safe and its allied villages in the interior with their Tana Pu'ang … and Kapitan whom he had appointed in the interior. (Kondi 2001: 7)

Secondly,

> In his lifetime, Mo'ang Bata Jawa sailed here and there, obtaining on his journeys large plates which he then brought home to his country. [25] After returning, he visited all the inhabitants of his territory, telling them: 'We human beings must have a God, from whom we ask assistance. Thus there must be a place for making offerings. So the plates which I have brought I must divide among all the *negeri* [i.e., *tana*] and designate in each a *tana pu'ang* (Source of the Earth).' (Kondi 2001: 27)

Finally, as recounted in Kondi's *Hikayat Kerajaan Sikka,* Mo'ang Baga Ngang, the third of Sikka's 'proto-rajas', appointed *tana pu'ang* and created *tana*. Kondi tells how Baga Ngang went around central Flores making alliances with the 'tribes' of the interior of the island:

> Mo'ang Baga asked: 'Who is your leader?' They replied: 'We here do not have a leader.' Mo'ang Baga said: 'When you have a dispute, who unravels and decides the matter?' They replied: 'There is no one. Whoever happens to be present mediates our quarrels. And if we do not accede, it is just left so and whoever is strongest is the one who wins.' Mo'ang Baga said: 'In that case, there is no order. I will choose a person for you who will be your leader.' … After that Mo'ang Baga praised them, saying that 'I along with my companions have come from Nata Gahar [High or Great Village] wishing to visit you here … Perhaps you know who among you is the most respected and who was the first to come and open a garden and to live here?' Then two men stepped forward and faced Mo'ang Baga, saying: 'We are the two who originally came here and we are also the two who are most respected.' Mo'ang Baga replied: 'Good. This one is appointed as Source of the Earth and is to be called by the title *tana pu'ang*; he is the one who will make offerings on

> the altar (*watu mahé*) whenever you make a feast for opening a new garden, require the healing of illness, marry, build a new house, and for other things. You must bring offerings and when there is a dispute, just go to him.' ... Then Mo'ang Baga took a little of the heart of a pig, some rice, and gin and placed them atop the altar, which Mo'ang Baga had ordered constructed as an example for the Source of the Earth [*tana pu'ang*]. After finishing these things mentioned above, the people began serving food to entertain Mo'ang Baga and his companions. (Kondi 2001: 31- 2)

The most curious thing about these passages is that these mythic proto-rajas are credited with creating something that must already have existed: the ceremonial domains and the *tana pu'ang* who headed them.

Portuguese Missions and Administrative Territories Created by the Dutch

The earliest European presence on Flores was that of the Portuguese, who established missions around the contemporary town of Larantuka at the eastern end of Flores and on the islands of Adonara and Solor. [26] Not long afterward, at least seven Portuguese mission stations were established on the island of Ende and on the coast of Ende Bay. [27] Between Larantuka and Ende, the Portuguese presence was sparser, but Visser (1925: 292) locates two stations on the north coast of central Flores, at Dondo on the western end of Maumere Bay and at 'Krove' on the north coast near contemporary Nebé. [28] According to Visser, the station at Krowé was founded between the years 1561 and 1575.

In addition, Visser cites evidence that Paga in the south-western reaches of Kabupaten Sikka and Sikka Natar itself were the sites of such stations on the south coast. While there is only a vague tradition among the contemporary people of Sikka Natar that their village was the site of a Dominican mission station, as Visser reports, it is possible that the village was, if not a Dominican station, then at least a place visited more or less regularly by Dominicans embarked on the Portuguese ships that passed along Flores's south coast. Visser's source [29] identifies the station at Sikka as a 'parochie' bearing the name Saint Lucia, and as a congregation numbering 1,000 souls in 1598. [30]

The earliest mention of Sikka I have found in the literature is that in an unattributed description of the first Christians of the islands of Solor and Timor, which de Sá includes in his compilations of documents from the period 1568-79 relating to the history of Portuguese missions in the Orient:

Map 4: Dominican mission stations on Flores, Adonara and Solor in the 16th century (after Visser 1925: 292)

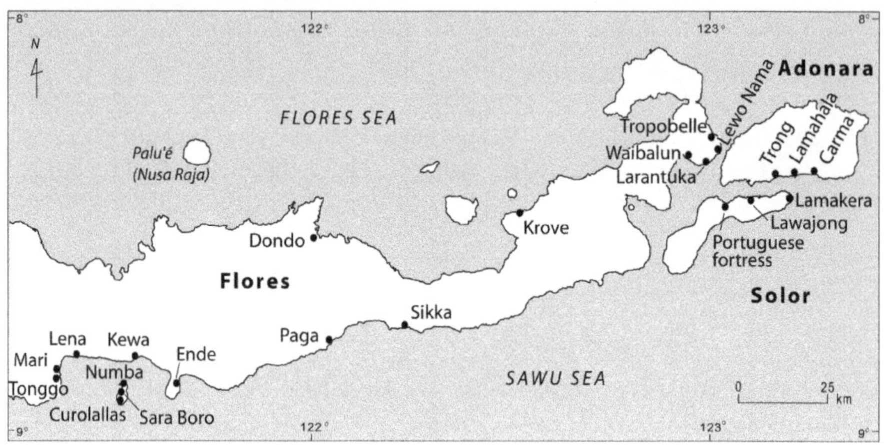

On this island of Larantuka, there would be fifteen leagues between the main settlement, that is referred to by the same name [i.e., Larantuka], and another that is further ahead on the island, called Siqua [Sikka], and another called Pagua [Paga]. Ende is another fifteen leagues beyond. All are Christian settlements, of one thousand firearms, and the majority, in addition to many other Christians and pagans, are our friends, having the aforesaid weapons. [31]

Just how frequent and intense was the contact between the Sikkanese and the Dominicans in the 16th and 17th centuries is an important question for which I have no answer. But it is likely that the contacts, and thus the direct influence of the Portuguese on the locals, were mainly on the coasts. Having said this, surely some Portuguese must have ventured inland from time to time (as from Krowé south into Tana 'Ai?) and surely people from the interior must have travelled to the coasts, if only to have a look at the foreigners—no place in east central Flores being more than a day's walk from the north or the south coasts. Evidence for at least indirect Portuguese influence in the interior is strong. For example, a small number of not-too-mangled Portuguese words turn up in transcriptions of ritual speech I recorded in Tana Wai Brama in the 1970s and 1980s.

The Dutch acquired Flores from the Portuguese in 1859 but it was some years before they became sufficiently interested in the region of Sikka to send a government official there. When that happened in the 1870s, the official settled not in Sikka Natar, the Village of Sikka on the south coast and the home of the rajas, but at Maumere on the north coast. Maumere was then a low-lying, hot, malarial place, sodden in the rainy season and smoky and dusty in the dry. It has since grown into one of the largest towns on Flores, a centre of education, and, with its excellent harbour and landing strip, a major port of entry for Flores and a commercial centre.

According to Dutch records and the *hikayat* of Kondi and Boer, much shuffling of allegiances and shifting of local *negeri* (villages, but in the *hikayat*, clearly the Malay equivalent of *tana*, 'domains') between the two (and for a while, three) rajadoms of Sikka went on in the two centuries before 1925. One effect of the shifting of *negeri* (each of which was probably a *tana* with its own *tana pu'ang*) and the rise of Sikka as a secular polity under the rajas of Sikka was to erode the importance of what the early Dutch records call *tana pu'ang-schappen* (*tana pu'ang*-ships). Once this process of incorporation into the rajadom and erosion of the *tana pu'angs*' authority was complete—by about 1950—the local *tana pu'ang* retained respect in their communities, but no longer exercised any real power.

Here we encounter the limitations of the scarce historical sources on the early culture and history of Sikka and a peculiarity of the voluminous later manuscripts written by Sikkanese authors. Briefly, the problem is this: the authors of the first texts written by a few men of the first or second literate generation of Sikkanese were all officials in the government of the Rajadom of Sikka. The two major texts from that era, one by D.D.P. Kondi and the other by A. Boer Pareira, treat the history of Sikka in detail, but from the distinctive point of view of Lepo Geté, the 'Great House', the Royal House of Sikka. Since the people of Lepo Geté are, according to their own myth of origin, immigrants to Flores and by no means indigenes, their history cannot be taken to be the history of the indigenous Sikkanese peoples, which remains a subject about which we know very little. Furthermore, even the main outlines of the internal divisions of the Sikkanese people into communities is obscured, firstly by the Dutch, who created the administrative districts of the rajadom, and then by the early Sikkanese authors, who were little concerned with explaining the territorial categories and institutions of the indigenous social landscape but were concerned centrally with the creation of the Sikkanese rajadom and the legitimation of its rule.

Although information about early Dutch activity in Sikka is sketchy at best, we can get at least a general idea of what was going on in the old rajadom between about 1860 and 1942. Indeed, the picture becomes a bit more detailed once the Dutch, with their penchant for archiving the *memories van overgave* of their officials, arrived in Sikka. [32]

The Dutch administrative divisions of Flores, which must quickly have become territorial categories in the minds of the Florenese ('I am of Ende', 'He is from Sikka Maumere', 'They are Larantukans'), changed often in the years from 1879 until 1942, when the Dutch flag over Flores was replaced briefly with the Japanese rising sun. From 1879 to 1907, these were the administrative divisions of Flores (Map 5):

Map 5: Dutch administrative divisions of Flores, 1879-1907

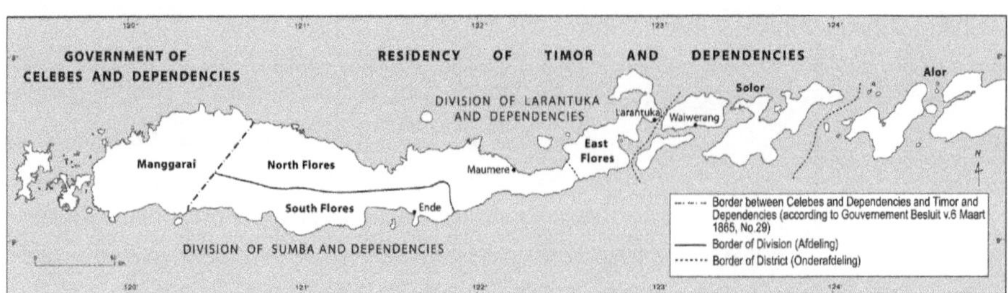

Note that this was before the Dutch had adjusted administrative boundaries to coincide with the rajadoms they later recognised on the island. Manggarai in the west was part of Gouvernement Celebes en Onderhorigheden (Government of Celebes [Sulawesi] and Dependencies) while the rest of Flores was administratively part of Residentie Timor en Onderhorigheden (Residency of Timor and Dependencies). Within the Residency of Timor, South Flores (*Zuid Flores*), which included Ende, most of Nage Keo and some of Ngada, was part of the Division (D: *Afdeling*) of Sumba and Dependencies while the rest of Flores was the Division of Larantuka and Dependencies. Larantuka was divided into the subdivisions or districts (D: *Onderafdelingen*) of North Flores (which included Sikka and Maumere, which the Dutch had made the administrative centre of the subdivision), East Flores, Solor and Alor. This administrative division of the island did not work too well, as a brief glance at the map might lead us to suspect, and so, in 1907, the lines were redrawn as follows (Map 6):

Map 6: Dutch administrative divisions of Flores, 1907-09

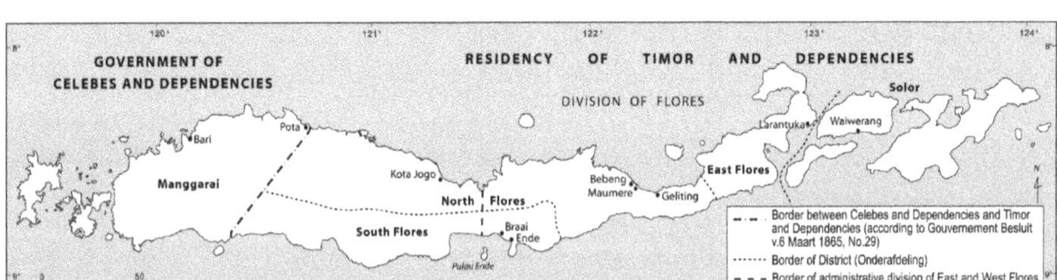

In these years (1907-09), Manggarai remained part of the Government of Celebes, while the rest of Flores was the Division of Flores and was included in the Residency of Timor. South Flores was removed from the Division of Sumba and made part of the Division of Flores, which was divided into the Subdivisions of South Flores, North Flores, East Flores and the Solor Islands. This arrangement should have worked all right, except that, in 1908, an administrative division between West Flores and East Flores was created. The new division crosscut South Flores and North Flores and must have been the source of innumerable headaches for the officials assigned to the island. But those headaches lasted only two years.

In 1909, the divisions of the island were shuffled once again, in such a way as to bring the administrative divisions into accord with at least some of the rajadoms on the island (Map 7).

Map 7: Dutch administrative divisions of Flores, 1909-31

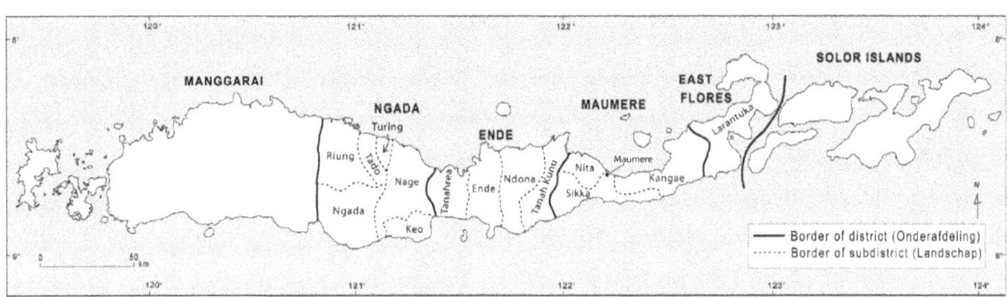

Manggarai was removed from the Government of Celebes and made a subdivision (*onderafdeling*) of the Division of Flores. The old divisions of South Flores, North Flores and East Flores disappeared and were replaced by subdivisions (*onderafdelingen*) that took greater account, though roughly, of the linguistic, social, economic and, perhaps most important, the political realities of the island. These were (in addition to the Subdivision of Manggarai) the Subdivisions of Ngada (including Nage Keo), Ende (including Lio), Maumere, East Flores (including Larantuka) and the Solor Islands. The subdivisions were further divided into districts (*landschappen*). Most of the names of the districts corresponded with the names of socio-linguistic groups on the island. The new district and administrative arrangements were comparatively rational, since they took account of the native rajadoms the Dutch had either recognised or created in the previous 50 years. In particular, the three rajadoms of the District of Maumere, Sikka, Nita and Kangae, were clearly demarcated. This arrangement of administrative divisions survived until about 1930, when some of the rajadoms were amalgamated.

Joachim Metzner has given us the following reconstruction of the political divisions of eastern Sikka towards the end of the 19th century. This would have been some 20 years after the earliest entries in the *Dagboeken van het Controleuren van Maoemere*, which were kept, more or less faithfully, by the *posthouders* assigned to Maumere, beginning in 1879, but before the dispute between the rajas of Sikka and Larantuka over Tana 'Ai was settled (Map 8). [33]

Map 8: Political divisions of Sikka towards the end of the 19th century and before Dutch intervention in the border dispute between Sikka and Larantuka

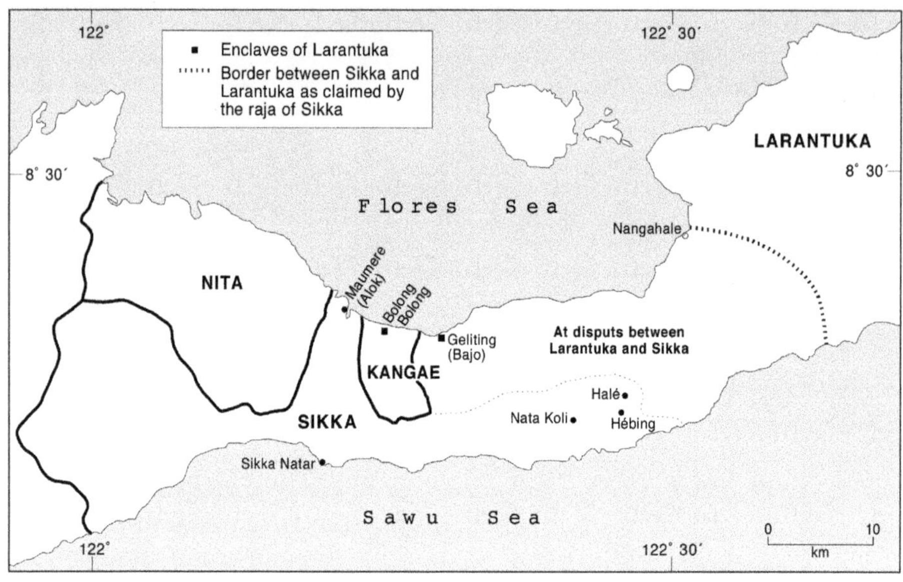

Map 9: Political divisions of Sikka in the early 20th century after Dutch intervention

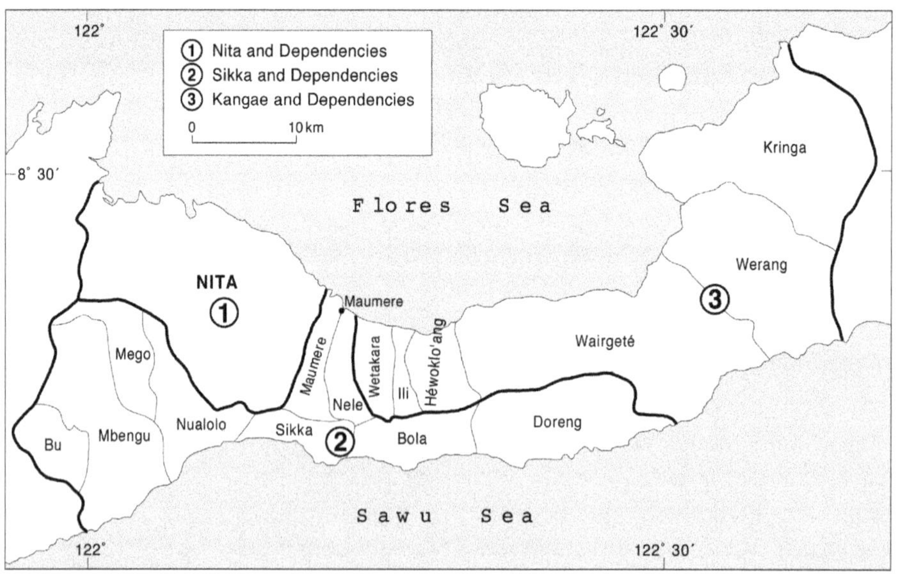

More certain are the political divisions of the District of Maumere after the boundaries established by the Dutch after they settled the Tana 'Ai dispute at the beginning of the 20th century. The settlement placed Tana 'Ai within the Rajadom of Kangae (Map 9).

Here we see plainly the way the Dutch, by 1904, recognised the indigenous polities of the Sikka region, which were ruled by the Raja of Sikka, the Raja of Nita and the Raja of Kangae. The Raja of Kangae ruled a region created by the Dutch when they could find no other way to control the subversive and overtly hostile activities of one Raja Nai against the authority of the Raja of Sikka. These boundaries—around what the Sikkanese called *kapitan-schappen*—correspond roughly to the *kecamatan* into which the *kabupaten* is divided today.

By 1929, the Dutch acceded to the amalgamation of the Rajadoms of Nita and Kangae into the Rajadom of Sikka, whose raja, Mo'ang Ratu Thomas Ximenes da Silva, ruled the whole of the region of Sikka until his death in 1954. The dissolution of the Rajadom of Kangae, which had been born of a rebellion against the Raja of Sikka in the first decade of the 20th century over a question of taxation, followed the enforced settlement by the Dutch of the dispute between the rajas of Sikka and Larantuka over sovereignty over Tana 'Ai, which became firmly part of the Rajadom of Sikka. The Rajadom of Nita, whose rulers were kinsmen of the Raja of Sikka, was also dissolved and its territory placed under the rule of Sikka, partly as an administrative convenience for the Dutch but also in response to the political activity and persuasiveness of Raja Don Thomas, the last of the Sikkanese rulers.

After 1931 and until the beginning of the Japanese occupation in 1942, the administrative map of Flores was as depicted in Map 10: [34]

Map 10: Administrative divisions of Flores, 1931 to early 1950s

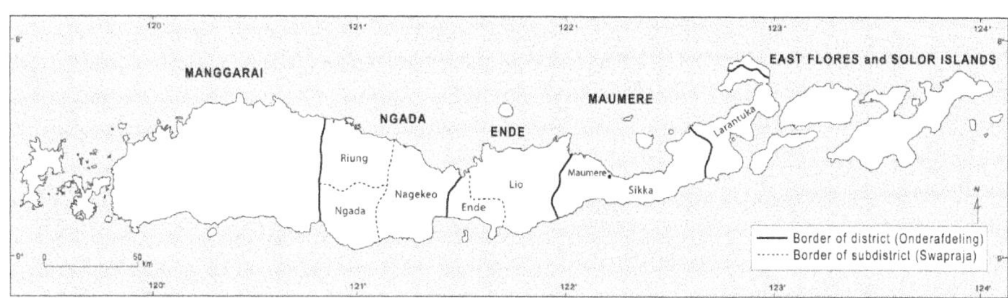

These boundaries were those of the rajadoms of Flores within the Division of Flores. Under the government of the newly independent Indonesia, the rajadoms were abolished in the early 1950s, after which the old divisions, and their boundaries, were retained as *kabupaten* in the new system of government.

The Reconceptualisation of Territorial Categories in Central Sikka

It would be simple enough, but somewhat facile, to assume that local states and the territorial categories and institutions that attend them arose on Flores—and elsewhere in eastern Indonesia—when and where local communities came into sustained contact with Europeans. Certainly Europeans played significant roles in the development of local states in the archipelago of Nusa Tenggara Timur. Officers of the Dutch Government, for example, intervened in local affairs to nominate one house or another as a ruling house. But it is less clear that Europeans caused the rise of states. In any case, attributing the advent of states to the influence of Europeans does not answer the question of why it was that states arose in some places but not in others (even though those non-state regions came at some stage in their histories under the influence of or were incorporated into states). It is the case that places that experienced long and continuous contact with Europeans came to have local rulers. Examples in eastern Indonesia include Larantuka (Portuguese and Dutch) and Roti and parts of south-western Timor (Dutch). But it is less clear why communities such as Sikka, which had occasional but probably not continuous contact with the Portuguese and Dutch before the Dutch established a permanent governmental presence on the island, would have developed state structures.

In considering this question we should bear in mind two facts. Firstly, there were large-scale states in Indonesia that predated the arrival of Europeans in South-East Asia. Secondly, while the societies of eastern Indonesia were to some degree remote from the western Indonesian archipelago and mainland South-East Asia, where such states thrived in pre-European times, they were not cut off from communication with those ancient centres. Indeed, through maritime trade, courts and kingdoms such as Srivijaya, Majapahit and Mataram exerted profound and lasting influences on quite distant communities, which were neither part of their territories nor under their direct rule. In a most useful work on trade and state development in South-East Asia between 1000 and 1500 AD, Hall commented:

> By the thirteenth century this Western demand [for South-East Asian spices] had greatly enhanced the commercial importance of Southeast Asia as a source of trade goods in Western eyes and as the source of valuable spices in particular. … During this time merchants based on the Java coast carried on two kinds of external trade, a trade with East and West (primarily with India and China) in spices and other luxury goods, and an export-import trade in rice to the Moluccas and to other parts of the eastern and western archipelago in exchange for spices and cloth. … Java's success as the intermediary of the international spice

> trade was based on a mutual dependency that came to exist between Java and the islands of the eastern archipelago. (Hall 1985: 209-10)

Hall identifies a trade network in the Java Sea as one of five South-East Asian trade zones that arose between 1000 and 1500 AD, one that 'included the Lesser Sunda Islands, the Moluccas, Banda, Timor, the western coast of Borneo, Java, and the southern coast of Sumatra' (Hall 1985: 226). He goes on to say: 'The new east Java-based state of Majapahit that came into existence at the end of the thirteenth century established a loose hegemony over the eastern and western archipelago' (ibid.).

In other words, models for local states in eastern Indonesia predate the European era in eastern Indonesia. Trade networks would have served not only as media for the exchange of goods, but also of ideas. While Sikka itself may not have played a central role in these networks, its location near the epicentre of an arc from south Sulawesi through the Banda Sea to Timor, which was part of those networks, would have guaranteed that its people were exposed to the people and ideas of other parts of Indonesia. When exploring the histories of eastern Indonesian states it may be fruitful to keep in mind that, whatever influence the Europeans might have had on the development of eastern Indonesian states, their origins and underlying structures might have been Indonesian.

In central Sikka, the evolution of a large number of village domains into a single polity under the rule of a raja from Sikka Natar would have required the Ata Sikka to reconceptualise categories of territory. This reconceptualisation, like much culture change in Sikka, involved not so much the redefinition of *tana* and *negeri* as the addition of a new concept of territory and new territorial categories. Thus, in 200 years of history, the Ata Sikka acquired *kampung* (BI: 'village'), *kerajaan* (BI: 'rajadom'), *desa* (BI: 'village-based municipality'), *kecamatan* (BI: 'district'), and *kabupaten* (BI: 'regency'), all of which were coeval with new institutions of government and administration. The *tana*, *negeri* and *natar* of the older Sikka had no boundaries; none, at least, until the first map-makers arrived on the scene. Although the scale of *tana* in central Sikka was small—perhaps as many as 45 discrete *tana* coexisted in an area of no more than 700 square kilometres—the reconceptualisation of the idea of territory by the addition of the concept of territory as bounded landscape to the early concept of territory as places within the fluctuating realm of a local centre of ritual power would have been considerable. It involved a shift from a social world made up of many centres of local, ritual power to that of a polity in which the raja bore a singular power that, while delegated through new institutions of government, overrode the powers of the old local centres. In those centuries, the Sikkanese brought about a profound shift from a polycentric and polycosmic to a monocentric and monocosmic culture.

Unlike the older domains, under Dutch administration, the rajadom came to be bounded. The boundaries of the rajadom necessarily implied territories of similar constitution beyond those boundaries, and thus a sense of Sikka as a part of Flores and as a part of a larger political entity. The rajadom introduced new institutions that evolved mutually with the new concepts and a new hierarchy of officeholders whose authority encompassed all the old domains. Thus a wholly new system of status and prestige came into being within which, in later years, the authority and power of district officers and ministers in the raja's government all but completely eclipsed those of the ritual leaders of the domains. The old offices of *tana pu'ang* and ritual specialists survived, but their main function came to be the legitimation of the new order. It may be worth quoting here an observation I made in one of my earliest publications on Sikka:

> There is a striking similarity between the character of the ritual office of *tana pu'ang* in Sikka [Natar] and the Dae Langgak of the Rotinese domains. In Sikka, as on Roti, the *tana pu'ang* claims priority of authority because of earlier presence. The present *tana pu'ang* of Sikka Natar recounts that his forebears actually created the Sikkanese rajadom by nominating one Sikkanese lineage as that of the *ratu* [raja].[35] As on Roti, the Sikkanese *tana pu'ang,* except in his role as ritual lord of the earth, is treated by members of the community (especially by those of the noble lineages) as socially inferior and something of a buffoon (Fox 1980: 109). To be sure, the office of the *tana pu'ang* in Sikka Natar has survived the institution of the rajadom by many years. (Lewis 1988: 318, footnote 9)

Although there are men in the villages of central Sikka who still claim the position, few modern Sikkanese can identify the *tana pu'ang* of their home villages. Yet it is the case that, in modern Maumere, events occasionally occur in which it is necessary for someone to act in the capacity of *tua adat* (ritual specialist). When such an event occurs it is rare for anyone with a link to one of the old ceremonial systems of central Sikka to serve. Most frequently, a knowledgeable retired schoolteacher or other student of Sikkanese history and culture assumes the role of *tana pu'ang* on occasions such as the funerals and marriages of influential people.[36] Thus the concept of the *tana pu'ang* as efficacious ritualist who personifies the order of a domain persists in modern times among the most sophisticated Sikkanese and in a society whose contemporary political and economic structure is that of a *kabupaten* derived from a rajadom.

Acknowledgment

Map 3 is redrawn from Metzner (1982: 112), and Maps 5-10 are redrawn from Metzner (1982: 72, 73, 79 and 82).

References

Burling, Robbins. 1965. *Hill Farms and Padi Fields: Life in Mainland Southeast Asia*. Englewood Cliffs (New Jersey): Prentice-Hall.

da Franca, A. P. 1970. *Portuguese Influence in Indonesia*. Jakarta: Gunung Agung.

de Sá, Artur Basílio 1956. *Documentaçã para a Histõria das Missões do Padroado Português do Oriente. Insulíndia 4.º Vol. (1568-1579)*. Lisboa: Agência Geral do Ultramar, Divisão de Publicações e Biblioteca. P. 480.

Echols, John M. and Hassan Shadily.1989. *An Indonesian-English Dictionary*. Third Edition. Ithaca: Cornell University Press.

Fox, James J. 1980. 'Obligation and Alliance: State Structure and Moiety Organisation in Thie, Roti.' In J.J. Fox (ed.), *The Flow of Life: Essays on Eastern Indonesia*, Cambridge (Mass.): Harvard University Press. pp. 98-133.

Hall, Kenneth R. 1985. *Maritime Trade and State Development in Early Southeast Asia*. Honolulu: University of Hawai'i Press.

Kondi, D.D.P. Unpublished [2001]. 'Hikayat Kerajaan Sikka (History of the Rajadom of Sikka).' E.D. Lewis and Oscar Pareira Mandalangi, editors and translators.

Lewis, E.D. 1988. People of the Source: The Social and ceremonial Order of Tana Wai Brama on Flores.' *Verhandelingen van het Koninklijk Instituut voor Taal-, Land- en Volkenkunde*, 135. Dordrecht: Foris Publications.

Lewis, E.D. 1996a. 'Origin Structures and Precedence in the Social Orders of Tana 'Ai and Sikka.' In James J. Fox and Clifford Sather (eds), *Origins, Ancestry, and Alliance: Explorations in Austronesian Ethnography*. Canberra: Monographs of the Department of Anthropology, The Australian National University.

Lewis, E.D. 1996b. 'Invocation, Sacrifice, and Precedence in the *Gren Mahé* Rites of Tana Wai Brama, Flores.' In Signe Howell (ed.), *For the Sake of Our Future: Sacrificing in Eastern Indonesia*, Leiden: CNWS Publications, Vol. 42.

Lewis, E.D. 1998a. 'The Tyranny of the Text: Oral Tradition and the Power of Writing in Sikka and Tana 'Ai, Flores.' *Bijdragen tot de Taal-, Land- en Volkenkunde*, 154 (3). pp. 457-77.

Lewis, E.D. 1998b. 'Don Alésu's Quest: The Mythohistorical Foundation of the Rajadom of Sikka.' *History and Anthropology*, Vol. 11 (1). pp. 39-74.

Lewis, E.D. 1999. 'The Encyclopædic Impulse: Accounts of the Origin of the Rajadom of Sikka by Two Sikkanese Authors.' *Bijdragen tot de Taal-, Land- en Volkenkunde*, 155 (3). pp. 543-78.

Lewis, E.D. In press. 'Precedence and Hierarchy in the Formation of Tana Wai Brama and the Rajadom of Sikka.' In Michael P. Vischer (ed.), *Precedence and Social Differentiation in the Austronesian World*, Canberra: Monographs of the Department of Anthropology, Research School of Pacific and Asian Studies, The Australian National University.

Lewis, E.D., Timothy Asch and Patsy Asch. 1994. *A Celebration of Origins*. 16mm film. Watertown, Massachusetts: Documentary Educational Resources, Inc.

Meersman, A. 1967. *The Franciscans in the Indonesian Archipelago, 1300-1775*. Louvain: Nauwelaerts.

Metzner, Joachim K. 1982. *Agriculture and Population Pressure in Sikka, Isle of Flores: A Contribution to the Study of the Stability of Agricultural Systems in the Wet and Dry Tropics*. Development Studies Centre Monograph No. 28. Canberra: The Australian National University.

Pareira, Alexius Boer. Unpublished [2002]. 'Notes on Hadat Sikka from the 1940s and 1950s by Mo'ang Alexius Boer Pareira.' Transcribed, translated and edited by E.D. Lewis and Oskar Pareira Mandalangi.

Pareira, M. Mandalangi. 1992. *Kerajaan Sikka, Nita, Kangae Masa Lampau*. Maumere: Mimeograph by author.

Sejarah Gereja Katolik Indonesia, Jilid 1. 1974. Ende-Flores: Percetakan Arnoldus.

Visser, B.J.J. 1925. *Onder Portugeesch-Spaansche Vlag: De Katholieke Missie van Indonesië 1511-1605*. Amsterdam: N.V. de R.K. Boek-Centrale.

Wilkinson, R.J. 1959. *A Malay-English Dictionary (Romanised)*. London: Macmillan.

ENDNOTES

[1] Some of the research material on which this paper is based was first presented in the Comparative Austronesian Studies Workshop, *Sharing the Earth, Dividing the Land: Territorial Categories and Institutions in the Austronesian World*, June 18-19, 2001, Canberra, The Australian National University, Research School of Pacific and Asian Studies. The version published here was drafted in 2003 and completed while I was Visiting Professor of Anthropology in the Department of Social Anthropology, University of Bergen, Norway, in 2004. I wish to thank Professors Edvard Hviding and Bruce Kapferer and Associate Professor Olaf H. Smedal for arranging my visit to Bergen and for the support I received while I was a member of their department.

[2] *Kabupaten* is an administrative division of the Indonesian State below the level of province. The word translates as 'regency.'

[3] I exclude the communities of Lamaholot-speaking people in the north-eastern region of the regency, which the Sikkanese refer to as Muhang, and the Lionese population of the far western and south-western region of the *kabupaten*.

[4] See Lewis (1996a) for a genealogy of the rajas of Sikka.

[5] See Lewis (1996a and in press) for discussions of precedence in the social orders of Tana 'Ai and Sikka.

[6] The *gren mahé*, or celebration of the *mahé*, is the culminal rites of the ceremonial system of a Tana 'Ai domain. The *gren* requires the sacrifice of animals by all of the domain's clans and houses and, thus, the participation of all of the domain's people (see Lewis 1988, 1996b; and Lewis, Asch and Asch 1994).

[7] Note also the Sara Sikka word *klo'ang*, which is a small village or hamlet in Sikka and, in Tana 'Ai, a hamlet composed of clan and ritual houses.

[8] Note the modern graves bearing Christian symbols interspersed with the stones of the *mahé*s at Héwoklo'ang (Plate 1) and Baomékot (Plate 2) and the juxtaposition of a cannon (provenance unknown) and the stones of the small *mahé* in the village of Kangae (Plate 3).

[9] These works (Kondi unpublished [2001] and Pareira unpublished [2002]) are two of more than 90 manuscripts that make up a collection of works by Kondi, Boer and other Sikkanese authors. The collection and the histories of the Rajadom of Sikka, which are their principal subject, are described in Lewis (1998a, 1998b and 1999).

[10] The text of the chart is incomplete: the *suku* (clan) affiliation of the Kapitang Salaf is not specified (although space has been left for it to be added) and the original diagram, which was written in pencil, has been amended at least twice, once with writing in blue ink.

[11] Sikka contrasts with the communities of the Tana 'Ai domains, in which *sukun* (clans) are the major social groups.

[12] I am indebted to Dr Alan N. Baxter of the University of Macau, an authority on Portuguese linguistics and Portuguese creoles in Africa, South America and South-East Asia, for assistance with these notes and for pointing out to me the linguistic significance of the borrowings from Portuguese that are found in Sara Sikka.

[a] *Du'a mo'ang* are leaders and ritual specialists.

[13] Puho and Rohé, for example, appear in group 1 and group 10 while Nata Koli appears in groups 2 and 9.

[a] The gift of twin elephant tusks, *mangung lajar* (mast and sail), to cement alliances between the rajas of Sikka and the *negeri* (villages) of the district, is a recurring theme in Boer's and Kondi's texts of the mythic histories of the Sikkanese rajadom.

[b] Tahi La'i (the Male Sea) and Tahi Wai (the Female Sea) are the Savu Sea and the Flores Sea, respectively.

[14] In the modern system of government divisions, a *kecamatan* is a district within a *kabupaten*.

[15] In places, Metzner uses the old representation *tana puäng*, whereby the intervocalic umlaut represents a glottal stop, for *tana pu'ang*. Elsewhere he spells the words *tana puang*, but note that *puang* and *pu'ang* are different words in Sara Sikka.

[16] *Adat* (BI), 'custom, tradition; customary law'.

[17] Metzner carried out his field research in Sikka in the 1970s, shortly before I began my fieldwork in Sikka Natar and Tana 'Ai in late 1977. He notes that he based the *tana* boundaries depicted in his map on oral and written information provided by informants who included A. Boer Pareira at Bola. I have been unable to locate copies of the unpublished documents he cites in this section of his book.

[18] This map is redrawn from Metzner (1982: 112). A few corrections have been made, but otherwise the *tana* names are as Metzner recorded them. As will be argued below, it is likely that the *tana* of Sikka changed through time, which means the enumeration of *tana* and reconstruction of *tana* centres and possible boundaries is extremely difficult and, at best, speculative. I hope to publish another map of Sikka's *tana* and a tentative reconstruction of their evolution in the future.

[19] That is, the *tana* from and including Egong to the east and those east of and including Natarwulu (which is properly Natarwalu), Teru and Wolo'lora to the west.

[20] Burling's formula holds true for Sikka, except that the linguistic differences among the Sikkanese are those of dialects rather than languages.

[21] I.e., 'matriarkal' rather than patrilineal, pagan rather than Catholic, simple rather than educated and sophisticatedly cosmopolitan, and rather easily snookered in their dealings with the outside world. The gentleman went on to outline how Tana 'Ai might have a fence built around it and be set aside as a 'cadangan budaya dan sejarah,' a 'culture and history reserve'. His thinking was this: since we Sikkanese have become modern, and since the Ata Tana 'Ai are the way we used to be and have not changed, we Sikkanese can preserve our history and traditional culture by preserving Tana 'Ai as a kind of living museum.

[22] 'Iwang Geté was (and still is) the region of Kecamatan Kéwapante on the north coast and to the east of Maumere, including the coastal town of Geliting and the *negeri* of Watublapi, Héwoklo'ang, Baomékot, Ohé, Klo'ang Popot, Halé, and Hébing. Krowé is another name for the hill region of central Sikka, including the *negeri* of Nita, Koting, Nele, Tilang, Ribang, Dokor, Ili, Kéwapante, Habi and Bola. Ata Krowé are also called the Ata 'Iwang by the Sikkanese. 'Iwang Geté (Greater 'Iwang) included Watublapi, Héwoklo'ang, Baomékot, Ohé, Klo'ang Popot, Halé, and Hébing.

[23] See Lewis (1998b and 1999) for treatments of the origin myth of the ruling Sikkanese and Lewis (1998b) for details of this episode in the myth.

[24] References to Kerajaan Sikka as Swapradja Sikka are found occasionally in the literature on Sikka in the first half of the 20th century. *Swapradja* (*swapraja* in the new spelling) were autonomous areas or regions.

[25] The genealogy of the rajas of Sikka account for 18 rajas, beginning with Don Alésu. Before Don Alésu there were 13 generations of Sikkanese leaders, the last three of which can be described as proto-rajas. These were Mo'ang Bata Jawa, Mo'ang Igor and Mo'ang Baga Ngang, Mo'ang Alésu's father (see Lewis 1998b).

[26] See Franca (1970) for references to the Portuguese influence in Sikka.

[27] Meersman (1967: 37) documents the arrival of three Franciscan friars at Ende in 1589.

[28] That is, Krowé; see footnote 25. Dondo is not a placename in contemporary Kabupaten Sikka.

[29] The information Visser cites derives from a compilation by Joao dos Santos OP, a Dominican missionary who worked in Mozambique and elsewhere and who died in 1622 in Goa. The data were published in a book entitled *Ethiopia Oriental*, which dos Santos completed ca. 1599 and to which he added notes as late as 1606. The book was reprinted in 1891 in Lisbon and from it another priest, P. Bierbaum, published a summary of information about the Solor missions in *Zeitschrift für Missionswissenschaft* (1924: 19) (*Sejarah Gereja Katolik Indonesia* 1974: 377).

[30] The mythic histories of Sikka attribute the first conversions of Sikkanese to Catholicism to a Malaccan named Augustinu (or Augustinus) Rosario da Gama, the son of a Malaccan ruler identified as Raja Worilla. Da Gama accompanied the first Raja of Sikka, Alexius Don Alésu da Silva, on his return to Sikka after a stay in Malacca, where Alésu converted to Christianity and studied religion and government. In a mimeographed essay on the rajadoms of Sikka, Nita and Kangae, M. Mandalangi Pareira (1992) summarises the arrival of Catholic missionaries in Sikka. Pareira cites a Dominican report that mentions a church named Santa Lusia (Lucia) with a congregation of 1000 souls at Sikka in 1598 and identifies the church at the station at Dondo on the north coast of Flores as Santa Maria da Boa Virgem. This information is found in Visser (1925), but Pareira does not cite Visser and the source of his information is unclear.

[31] '*Averá nesta ilha de Larantuca, entre a provoação prinçipal, que se chama deste proprio nome, e outra está pella ilha adiante, quinze legoas, a que chamão Siqua, e outra que chamão Pagua, e o Ende, que está outras quinze adiante; todas de christãos, obra de mil espingardas, e melhoria dellas, allem de outras muitos christãos e gentios, amigos nossos, com as armas que assima fica dito*' (Sa 1956: 480). It is worth noting that the people of Sikka Natar themselves assert that their ancestors converted to Catholicism in 1552.

[32] *Memories van overgave* (D: memoranda of handing over or transmission) were reports written by Dutch civil servants who had served in a district as sources of information for officials newly appointed to the district. These reports contained social, political, geographic and economic information compiled by an outgoing official on the district for which an incoming official would assume responsibility.

[33] The *Dagboeken* were diaries kept by the leading Dutch officials (*posthouders*) in Maumere from 1879.

[34] It is unclear to me whether the Japanese altered in any way the administrative territories elsewhere on Flores, but the boundaries of the Rajadom of Sikka were not changed under Japanese occupation.

[35] Recall that Kondi's manuscript history of the rajadom includes episodes of the origin myth of the Sikkanese rajadom in which the earliest rajas are credited with creating the region's *tana* and *tana pu'ang*.

[36] A striking example of such an event occurred in 1994 when a ceremony was held in Maumere to repair a 50-year-old rift between two branches of the Royal House of Sikka. On that occasion, a retired school teacher, an elderly man from Sikka Natar who is recognised widely as one of the regency's leading authorities on the history and *adat* of Sikka, presided over the agenda and performed the animal sacrifices by which the rift was healed. Officials of the regency government were seated among the scores of invited onlookers in the house yard rather than with the parties to the ritual on the verandah of the house where the ritual was performed, an arrangement the significance of which was missed by no one present.

Chapter 9. We Are Children Of The Land: A Keo Perspective

Philipus Tule

Introduction

This paper explores traditional forms of land tenure in the Worowatu subdistrict of the Keo region in Central Flores, Indonesia. The focus is on the communal attachment of community members, Muslims and non-Muslims, indigenous people and newcomers, to their inherited clan land (*tana ko'o 'ine 'embu*). [1] The organisation of land tenure is tied to a number of traditional offices, reaching down from the 'Lord of the Land' (*'ine tana 'ame watu*) and the 'Overseers of the Land' (*'ine ku 'ame lema*) to the 'individual cultivators' (*nio tiko éu tako*).

Keo people believe that individuals do not own the land, rather the land owns them, in the same sense as a mother can be said to own her children. This philosophy is reflected in a number of traditional expressions. 'Mother land, father stone' (*'ine tana 'ame watu*) is the title for a Lord of the Land, and 'mother plain, father field' (*'ine ku 'ame lema*) is how the lower ranking Overseers of the Land are referred to. This sense of being children of the land leads Keo people to regard land certificates issued by the Government for any clan land as invalid and as not binding in any way.

Every individual community member can gain access to ancestral land by observing various rituals and social-political obligations. Incorporated members within a clan, such as war migrants (*tama dia kono ondo*) and invited warriors (*kéu mére kambe déwa*), are also given land to cultivate and settle on (*tau koe nua kadi 'oda*) on the proviso of observing a particular, local charter of propriety (*adat*). If migrants violate this *adat* charter, their land rights can be cancelled.

The paper will also explore land disputes. Disputes over land rights frequently require resolution, and may concern such issues as the extension of land boundaries (*pi singi rete ra'i*) or the right to claim the office of Lord of the Land. The people of 'Udi and Worowatu, for instance, once struggled to prevent the usurpation of their authority over the land by the neighbouring villages of Witu and Giriwawo. They had to fight, since they believed that if they were to lose their authority over the land to which they properly belonged as the Lord of the Land, they would lose their sense of identity and their rights to speak out.

The Keo region is located in the south of Central Flores, an island in the Nusa Tenggara Timur (NTT) Provinces of Indonesia (see Map 1). As a distinct ethnic or cultural group in the context of Central Flores ethnography, the name Keo still retains currency on Flores largely by virtue of its former recognition as a separate administrative sub-unit (*Onderafdeeling NageKeo*) within the system of Dutch colonial government, even though NageKeo was later merged with the Nage region (Forth 1994a: 95). [2] In the modern administrative structure of the Indonesian State, Keo society incorporates Mauponggo, Keo Tengah and Nangaroro, three subdistricts (kecamatan) within the district (kabupaten) of Ngada with a total population of 46,313 people and a territory of some 300 square kilometres (BPS, Ngada 1995: 131).

Map 1: The Keo Region of Central Flores

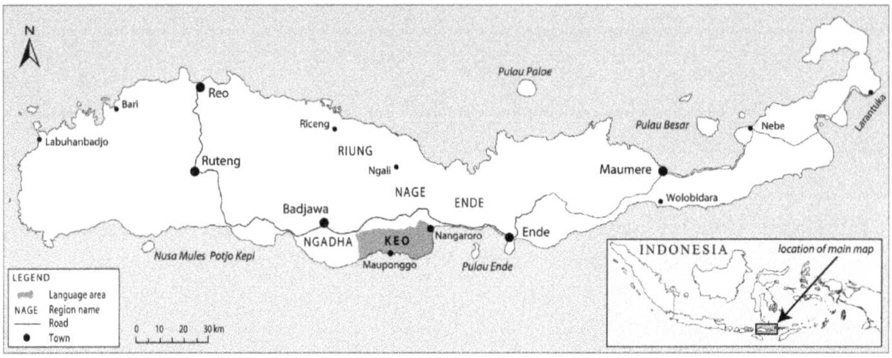

Source: *Antropologi Indonesia*, 56 (XXII): 70

While Keo is identical to its neighbour Nage in many details of culture, language and society, these two regions do display a number of general differences as compared with the neighbouring regions of Ngada and Ende. In terms of religion, nearly 93 per cent of the Keo are Catholics, and the remainder are Muslim fishermen and traders who live along the south coast between Maumbawa and Nangaroro. Catholicism was introduced to Keo in the 1920s, when Fr. Y. Ettel (SVD) started to visit several government schools and baptise students in Tonggo, Wajo and Sawu (Muskens, 1974: 1171). Most of the Catholic Keo nese are subsistence farmers and stock raisers. Today only a few Keo people practice their earlier, local religion in its entirety, but many do retain some elements thereof in their beliefs and ritual practices.

The History and Development of Tana Worowatu

The 'secondary district' (*kepala mére*) or 'domain' (*tana*) of Worowatu is named after the village (*nua*) of Worowatu (from, *woro* 'hill'; *watu*, 'stone'). According to a local myth, people established this settlement after a tsunami and inundation forced them to take refuge on the south slope of Mt Koto. This flood is blamed on the cancellation of a marriage between a Keo girl from Wondo village and a whale. Before the flood, the founding ancestor of Worowatu, a man called Taku Nuru, had resided at Tudiwado and had married the mythical girl 'Embu Tonga from the So'a region. When Worowatu was established as a secondary district (*kepala mére*) by the Dutch in 1917, the man appointed by the Dutch as subdistrict head (*kepala mére*) was Séme Rau, a direct descendant of Taku Nuru. [3]

It is interesting to note that the villages within Tana Worowatu are named on the basis of distinguishing features including natural or strategic features of their location. Worowatu village is named as such because it is located on a stony hill. Tudiwado (*tudi*, 'drop in or stop over';*wado*, 'return') refers to the strategic location of this settlement and the legendary hospitality of its people to travellers passing through. The name of the village, 'Udi, means 'rudder'. Kodinggi (*kodi*, 'lontar palm';*engge*, 'clusters') refers to the plenitude of lontar palms in this particular village. Its previous name, Bedo, which referred to an area at the southern end of 'Udi village, might derive from a word *belo*, which means 'to make a turn' as the result of a rudder's function. Tonga Tonggo (*tonga*, 'to watch, supervise';*tonggo*, 'the people from Tonggo') indicates a strategic position in which the people of Tonggo guard and supervise the coming of the people to an open market in Ma'undai. Ma'undai (*ma'u*, 'coast'; *Ndai*, name of a tribe) means the strip of coastline belonging to the Ndai people.

Land Tenure in Worowatu

Land tenure in contemporary Keo and in adjacent domains within the district of Ngada shows considerable variation, and there have also been a number of historical changes. Moreover, my study of the origin myths of 'Udi-Worowatu in conjunction with local oral history has convinced me that the region's land tenure system was never fixed and stable, but has been open to contestation from the beginning. Perhaps the most well-remembered case within living memory that demonstrates this openness is a dramatic conflict between the Worowatu and Witu-Ma'uara villages that occurred in 1937, and is known as *léto laka witu*. [4]

One of the more important historical changes came at the end of the 1950s, when the Indonesian Government introduced a new notion of the 'village' (*desa*) as an administrative unit within the structure of the State, or what locals refer to as 'new-style villages' (*desa gaya baru*). Until Indonesian independence, and for some time thereafter, the Keo men recognised and employed by the Dutch Colonial Administration to serve as local political leaders had invariably been their traditional leaders or 'lords of the land' (*'ine tana 'ame watu*).

The size of different communities' overall landholdings, and the amount of land accessible to individuals, has always varied greatly from one *nua* to another. My informants in 'Udi-Worowatu insisted that in other places a certain area of land, perhaps 10 hectares or more, was the informal minimum holding required if a person wanted to be a village leader (*Kepala Mere* or*Kepala Gemeente*) under the Dutch. Control over extensive landholdings as such, however, was insufficient grounds to make someone a 'Lord of the Land' in 'Udi-Worowatu. Locals believe that this office is inherited from a powerful, named founding ancestor.

Taku Nuru was the founding ancestor of Worowatu, and his male-line descendants hold the right to the office of Lord of the Land over the area that includes Worowatu as well as 'Udi, Bedo, Witu and Ma'uara. This claim is supported by an oral history of origin:

> The girl Tonga Mbu'e So'a was found as an infant by 'Embu Nderu in So'a, lying on a liana tree (*tadi kada*). 'Embu Nderu took the girl home and brought her up. When Tonga grew up into a beautiful young lady, she suggested to her adoptive mother, 'Embu Nderu. that they should go to the coast. 'Embu Nderu and Tonga Mbue Soa then moved down to the south coast of Flores through Ma'umbawa. They arrived at Seko Nangge, near 'Ae Tolo and Ma'umbawa. They stayed at the home of 'Embu Paja Wae. Tonga then left for Ma'undai to search for a tree without leaves (*do kaju wunu mona*). She met Taku Nuru, a local leader from Worowatu under the tree. They married. From that marriage, Tonga Mbue Soa gave birth to Waja 'Ake, Waja De'e and Waja Sébho, who were the grand ancestors of the people in Worowatu and Ma'undai.

The story further claims that from the beginning the Lord of the Land for the whole territory of Worowatu, including the villages Witu and Ma'uara, was always a descendant of Taku Nuru. His descendants claim that he is their founding ancestor. However, another group claims that Taku Nuru came from Koto Mountain and settled in Tudi Wado village before the others arrived. His wife, 'Embu Tonga Mbu'e So'a, is said to have been sent from afar, from outside, from a place called So'a near the town of Bajawa. She met Taku Nuru under 'a tree without a name and without leaves' (*do kaju ngara mona ne'e wunu mona*) in Ma'undai. [5] An informant, Jamaludin Husein, a man from Ma'undai, even called them the Adam and Eve of Worowatu.

So'a, as the place of origin of 'Embu Tonga, seems to be referred to in myth but is not linked to any contemporary practices. For example, there is no evidence today to suggest a relationship between the two places (So'a and Worowatu) that may be framed as a wife-giving group (*'embu mame*) and wife-taking group (*'ana weta*) relationship. So'a, the home of the progenitor mother of the Worowatu people, is used here as a common place of origin. This seems to fit with a common idea among the Ngadha, that So'a (and Naru) are primeval places where earth and sky used to be connected with a liana tree. Gregory Forth also mentions that throughout the Nage and Keo regions one continually encounters the idea that the present population originally came from So'a, as did important items and traditions such as the areca palm and the practice of palm tapping(Forth 1998: 235-6).

A second issue that would seem relevant to land tenure relates to the question of individual access to agricultural land. With remarkable unanimity of opinion, however, the people of Worowatu and Witu-Ma'uara proclaimed to me that they had few problems with regulating individual access to land. The real problem in contemporary Keo is how to maintain the idea that Worowatu and Witu-Ma'uara share the same land and belong to the same ritual confederacy, given that the creation of new style villages (*desa gaya baru*) such as 'Udi Worowatu and Witu Romba 'Ua has introduced a new pattern of territorial division and authority and is producing a widening gap between the two traditional groups. The new pattern of land tenure and land cultivation introduced under the administration of the two *desa gaya baru* seems to be creating a separation of Witu and Ma'uara from Worowatu. The modern administration has also challenged the office of Lord of the Land (who is from Worowatu), prompting a serious decline in his political and ritual authority. [6] Before discussing these more recent conflicts, I will first describe traditional perceptions of land among the Keo in more detail.

The Land is Our Mother

In 'Udi-Worowatu, the land is considered the mother of the people. This is evident in ritual language discourse about death and in the honorific titles of*adat* leaders. In metaphoric ritual language, those who have died are said to have 'returned to the mother's womb' (*ta négha tama tuka 'ine*) or to be 'under the soil and the stone' (*ta négha wena tana 'au watu*). [7] Some informants elaborated further by adding the titles mother (*'ine*) to the land, and father (*'ame*) to the stone. The complete ritual speech couplet thus runs as follows: *ta négha wena 'ine tana, ta négha 'au 'ame watu*, 'those who are under mother soil and father stone'. The Keo believe that while the physical body may be destroyed, the soul (*mae*) continues to live, staying forever in the womb of its mother land. Such a belief leads people to make various kinds of offerings (*wésa léla*) to the ancestral spirits who dwell in their land.

The feeling of awe and respect for the land, as their parent and as a living body, takes shape as a sacred geography. For the 'Udi-Worowatu people, this geography is not limited and extends into the territory of their neighbours, because they tend to represent themselves as being at the centre of a wider universe:

1. *Tana mére Ende*	The great land extends to Ende.
2. *Watu déwa Jawa*	The long stone extends to Java.
3. *'Udu mbe'i kédi*	The head leans to the mountain (Koto).
4. *A'i ndeli mesi*	The feet reach to the sea (Sawu).

5. *Puru wundu mbudu wutu*	Stretching the fishing snare 40 x 40 arm lengths. [a]
6. *Négha mona dhu*	Cannot reach far enough.
7. *Tana ha bhabha*	(Our) land is one piece.
8. *Watu ha di'e*	(Our) stone is one unit.
9. *Dange wai toko pale*	The boundary is marked by clumps of rice.
10. *Bhondho wai toko odo*	The boundary is marked by clumps of sorghum.

[a] *Wundu* is a local variety of fishing line made from hand-spun cotton. *Puru wundu mbudu wutu negha mona dhu* means to extend 40 times 40 arm-lengths of cotton fishing line into the deep sea; and still it cannot reach the furthest reach of the border of their marine territory.

Worowatu ritual leaders tend to extend the idea of a sacred unity of the land to the domains of related neighbours, in Jawawawo, Wuji and Giriwawo villages to the north, on the slope of Mt Koto. At the same time, the southern boundary reaches into the Sawu Sea, to a distance greater than 40 rolls of traditional fishing snare (*wundu*).

My experience working with the locals and the ritual leaders on opening up the inter-village road from Ma'undai to Giriwawo in 1997, further illustrates the significance of this sacred geography. Locals argued that the new road should not run through the centre of their villages (*nua*) because each village, with its various cultural monuments and functioning as a ritual site, is a sacred site. Even an abandoned village (*nua 'odo*), such as Nua Ora, is sacred because there people still find the ritual sites of founding ancestors such as Rangga 'Ame 'Ari. Another sacred site outside the village of Worowatu, which is called Watu Dia Meo (Stone of the Cat's Cave), is also protected from violation. People also say that the blood of the ancestors has wet the territory. [8] When the road construction passed the site, the Worowatu ritual leader, 'Ameka'e Muwa, had to perform a special ritual with chicken blood to wet the stone and ask permission from the ancestral spirits who dwell there.

The following two examples of rituals also illustrate the notion of Worowatu sacred geography. The first has to do with 'extending the boundaries of someone's land' (*pi singi rete ra'i*). It is considered a criminal action to thus annex another's property; as well as a negation of, or false claim to parenthood. In order to settle a subsequent boundary dispute, a ritual specialist (*'ata madi*) recites an oath, witnessed by both parties:

1. *Ke ko'o pata kita peka mena*	Our words have reached the eastern end

2. *Ko'o seru kita rembu rade*	Our conversation has reached the western end
3. *Ngara poa né'e wengi rua*	If it happens in the future
4. *Sai ta pi singi rete ra'i*	Someone wants to extend his boundaries
5. *Tau bhora ko'o pata seru 'ine 'embu*	Someone brings down the words of the ancestors
6. *Ta negha wedu*	Who have decided
7. *Mo'o dako kiki tuka*	The dog will bite his belly
8. *Mo'o manu kale 'ate 'imu.*	And the chicken will peck his liver
9. *Mota kau bhida koja*	You will be exterminated like a canary
10. *Membu kau bhida ra'u*	You will become extinct like a*ra'u* tree
11. *Mota pu'u ridi dolo jeka réde dudu*	Your extermination starts from the corner (near the hearth) up to the back of the house
12. *Mata kau pi rua*	Your death will be in two (generations)
13. *Re'e kau tenda tedu*	Your misfortune will be in three generations.

After the oath has been recited, both parties eat the livers of a chicken and a dog while drinking toddy. A false claim to landownership can result in deaths, famine, drought, earthquake and disharmony in the family and society, because the 'mother land' (*'ine tana*) does not stand firm but 'becomes shaky'. That is also why a *pala* ritual should be undertaken in the village with the slaughtering of buffaloes at certain times, so the meat will be shared and the blood wet the earth, 'so that the soil does not shake and the stones do not tremble'.

A second ritual concerns theft. If community leaders cannot identify the thief, an oath of eating soil is undertaken to invite the spirit of 'mother land' to be present and to witness. To prove that someone has not stolen something, the suspect has to eat a certain amount of soil, witnessed by the community and a ritual leader. The accused must also recite a particular oath: [9]

1. *Ngara ja'o naka tu'u mbé'e mbé'e*	If I have really stolen
2. *O ngara ja'o pi singi rete ra'i*	or annexed someone's land
3. *Tana mo'o ka ja'o*	the land will swallow me
4. *Watu mo'o pesa ja'o*	the stone will eat me
5. *Ngara mona, ja'o mona apa-apa*	If not, I will be all right

The religious appreciation of the land's motherhood in eastern Keo society is distinct from Western or modern Indonesian ideas of land as a privately owned commodity. The 'Udi-Worowatu people believe that their 'ownership' of land is intrinsically linked to their mythological knowledge of the ancestors' places of origin and paths of migration. The paths that have been travelled by their ancestors, for instance, from So'a through Ma'umbawa and Ma'undai or from Paulundu through Ngera, or from Sumbawa through 'Eko Kota and Paga, seem to provide a map of identity. Keo people understand their country and link themselves with specific places. The travels of the ancestral beings, and the power they left at specific locations, bind together those people who claim to be their descendants. This linking of place with mythology in a sacred topogeny provides an important key to understanding why rituals to do with the land are so fundamental to the stability of Keo society.

An incident involving the destruction of a sacrificial post (*léto laka*) in the village of Witu in 1937 provides a pertinent example. A whole generation from Witu had neglected their past and their topogeny, which resulted in continuing conflict and violence. Another conflict in 1962, between the villages of Ma'uara and Bedo, was also caused by a denial of the past. At that time, the village of Bedo was transferring its cultural monuments from 'old Bedo' to 'new Bedo', a village now known as Kodinggi. The people of Ma'uara, who used to be members of a traditional alliance, Bedo-Dokarea, refused to be involved in the ritual. They claimed that their ancestor, Tai, was older than Bedo's ancestor, Seso. That is why they further claimed that the whole ritual should belong to 'Embu Tai (*'oda tau ko'o 'Embu Tai*). The subsequent dispute over ritual precedence required police involvement to calm down the two parties.

Certification of land is still very rare among the eastern Keo people, and the so called 'Seri A Letters' issued by the Indonesian Government nowadays seem to show an appreciation of the past links between ancestors, land and mythology. A 'Seri A Letter' indicates that the clan lands belong to a named ancestor or an*'embu*, and acknowledges the existence of collective land-ownership of clan land among the *'embu*'s descendants. The descendants are believed to be the children of the land (*'ana tana*) and can obtain access to their ancestral land by performing rituals and fulfilling various social-political and religious obligations related to their 'large house' (*sa'o mere*) or 'source house' (*sa'o pu'u*) and to their village life (*nua 'oda*).

Guardians of the Land

At the domain and village level, we can identify at least three different levels of authority dealing with the organisation of Land cultivation and land rights; the Lord of the Land (*'inetana 'amawatu*), the Overseers of the Land (*'ine ku, 'ame lema)* and individual cultivators (*nio tiko éu tako*). The honorific title 'Lord of the Land', and other titles like it, are common in traditional eastern Indonesian societies. Arndt briefly describes the role of clan leader (*kepala woe*) among the Ngada tribe in dealing with clan land. Although clan land is divided between smaller groups, it still belongs to the clan (*woe*) and its cultivation is never free from the intervention of the clan leader (Arndt 1954: 353-4). Among the Endenese, the central position of the*rhaki pu'u* or the *rhaki tana* (man of the source/land) is still recognised by other traditional leaders such as *rhaki ria bewa* or 'speaking lord' and the *ndetu 'au* or 'village head' (Nakagawa and Aoki 1993: 69; Suchtelen 1921: 69-70, 79, 83). Forth records the honorific title *mangu tanangu* or 'owner of the land' in Rindi, eastern Sumba. The full title in ritual speech is *ina mangu tanangu, ama mangu lukungu*, 'mother of the land, father of the river' (Forth 1981: 249). Among the Kedang of Lembata, Barnes also records the existence of the Lord of the Land (*leu-auq wala*), who possesses the authority to alienate individual fields (*etang*) because all land in cultivation is the communal possession of the clan (Barnes 1974: 90).

In 'Udi-Worowatu, which is typical of Keo and even of Nage, the full title for a Lord of the Land is *'ine tana 'ame watu*, 'mother land, father stone', and refers to someone who represents a group descended from a common male ancestor or*'embu*. A Lord of the Land had significant power in organising land tenure and in settling various land disputes, and he even had the authority to take away a man's fields and excommunicate him from village life if he did not fulfil his social obligations. For example, while there was initially land available for so-called war migrants and 'invited warriors' (*topo todo dé'e taka todo nga*), he had the right to prevent any individual from cultivating certain pieces of land. Once, in 1937, the Lord of the Land of Worowatu even abolished the right of the Witu people to erect a sacrificial post (*léto laka*) and undertake a*pala* ritual in their own village of Witu. Nowadays, however, the authority of the *'ine tana 'ame watu* seems to be rather nominal. He has no final power of decision in land disputes, but still possesses a moral authority that is binding in the context of *adat* assemblies.

In the domain of 'Udi-Worowatu, there are lesser village leaders under the Lord of the Land who are called the 'heads of the fields' (*'ine ku 'ame lema*). [10] In actuality, these men are leaders or overseers of the ancestral land of specific kin groups or extended families. They are also sometimes referred to as 'village leaders' (*mosa nua daki 'oda*). [11] Indeed, every named village has its own leader, who will support the Lord of the Land by taking on some of his responsibilities, or by 'passing on warnings and instructions to the members of his kin group or extended family' (*wuku 'udu 'énga 'éko*). Usually, this position is held by a lineal descendant of the apical male ancestor (*'embu*). For Worowatu village, the *'ine tana 'ame watu* also functions as the *'ine ku 'ame lema* (always chosen from the descendants of Taku Nuru, the joint-office was most recently held by 'Ameka'e Wea, a descendant of 'Embu Waja 'Ake). For the village of 'Udi, this position is filled by the descendant of 'Embu Rangga 'Ame 'Ari; for the village of Bedo or

Kodinggi by the descendant of 'Embu Je Lendo; while in the village of Tudi Wado the position is filled by the descendants of 'Embu Sambu Mite. [12] The village leader of Ma'undai, a Muslim village, does not hold the title*'ine ku 'ame lema* because he belongs to a group of 'invited warriors' (*keu mere kambe dewa*).

Individual fields cultivated by a personal cultivator are termed *nio tiko éu tako*. Boundaries are generally demarcated by a line of coconut or areca palm trees. Since no one actually 'owns' the land, a person can obtain rights to the land he cultivates as long as he is actively engaged in exploiting the land, belongs to an indigenous male ancestral lineage and respects various aspects of village life *(ndi'i nua mera oda)*. Aspects of village life that should be respected include the rights of other members to gain access to ancestral land, and the obligation to give contributions of food and animals during the ritual ceremonies held in the village (*pebhu tindu ndou mapi*).

Each individual field of ancestral land (*tana 'ine 'embu*) is under the supervision of an overseer of the land (*'ine ku ame lema*). The individual rights to the cultivated fields can never amount to full ownership or possession but only to a right of cultivating the land for one's livelihood and for feeding one's children (*tau tuka pagha 'ana*). This idea might be reminiscent of a concept of usufruct, as Hooker suggests:

> Van Vollenhoven and later writers, particularly Ter Haar, denied that the rights of an individual could amount to 'ownership' in the European sense by which they meant the availability of the right of a free and unrestricted alienation. Ter Haar indeed went further and refused to distinguish between an individual right of possession and the right of usufruct. (Hooker 1978: 119)

Apart from considering the rights and responsibilities associated with the three levels of guardians of the land, we must also understand the distribution of a sacrificial pig's head in relation to leadership. In 'Udi Worowatu, apart from the Lord of the Land and his Overseers of the Land, other 'elders' (*mosa daki*) are also considered worthy of receiving special portions at a communal meal (*nado mére*). [13] That these leaders must be aware of their responsibilities towards the whole of society is well indicated in the adage; 'The elders should warn after eating and drinking' (*mosa ta 'odo ka waka, daki ta 'odo minu na'u*), which means that they are responsible for encouraging others to follow the path of virtue in order to obtain harmonious relations within society and with the ancestral spirits. This seems equivalent to the task of *mosa laki* among the Lio, that is, 'to ensure a reproduction of cosmogonic conditions within the limits imposed by the social conditions in contemporary life' (Howell 1996: 102).

The *mosa daki*'s powers are limited to their own village (*nua*). Within their village they are known as*mosa nua, daki oda*. Even the Lord of the Land (*ine* *tana ame watu*), who also has the title of 'land and stone' leadership (*mosa tana daki watu*), cannot intervene in any matters of daily governance in other villages (*nua*). Each *nua* is a completely independent body in political terms. Hence, when disputes or conflicts arise between the inhabitants or *mosa daki* of two different villages (*nua*), then the two parties will meet under the supervision of a *mosa daki* from a third *nua*, who is respected and can function as an impartial judge. According to Keo ideology, a judge is the one who acts as a measurer, and who functions by measuring with a device consisting of a long bar and a counterweight which can be moved back and forth along the longer arm of the bar (the person and the device are called *tuka timba mata dasi*). [14] In Tana Worowatu, the *mosa daki* of Nua Bedo (Kodinggi) is called on to act as *tuka timba mata dasi* whenever Worowatu village is in conflict with either 'Udi or Witu.

A careful examination of ritual speech and practice shows subtle differences in the roles of traditional leaders, and we can identify at least three levels of *mosa daki*. The highest level is the Lord of the Land, who carries the honorific title *'ine tana 'ame watu*. Because he is simultaneously a community leader (*mosa daki*), he also accepts the title of 'Lord of the Land and stone' (*mosa tana daki watu*). His moral and political leadership used to extend over a wider territorial space known in the ritual language as *mosa gége mére, daki danggo déwa*, which literally means 'a big leader who guides in the floods, an influential chief who shepherds in the plain'; that is, someone who has power and authority extending over a wide territory. At the middle level are the Overseers of the Land. As*mosa daki*, they receive the honorific title of 'village leaders' (*mosa nua daki 'oda* or *mosa 'udu daki 'éko*) or the title of leader of a smaller social unit, such as 'leader of the baskets' (*mosa mboda daki wati*). A third group are *mosa kamba daki wéa*. This type of leadership is attained by means of material wealth (*kamba wéa*: buffaloes and gold) or some form of prestige associated with the outside world.[15]

These categories of leaders, especially the first two, have existed for centuries in'Udi Worowatu society, but colonial intervention also introduced new types of leadership that did not fit the local context. The Dutch Colonial Government introduced the notion of kingdom (*radjaschap*) under a raja and a number of lower-ranking supporters (*kepala mére,kepala nua* and*Mandoor*). The Indonesian system of government then introduced another set of leadership positions, such as *bupati,kepala camat* and *kepala desa*, with various subordinates such as *sekretaris,kepala urusan*, *kepala rukun tetangga* and *kepala rukun warga*.

Concerning the rights and obligations of traditional leaders, my informant, Severinus Rangga, once explained that they 'put the bad things on their head, and carry the difficulties on their shoulder' (*woso su'u ta re'e, wangga ta amba*). This statement implies that *adat* leaders have obligations more than rights. Personally, *'ine tana 'ame watu* never receive any material gift from farmers in exchange for receiving land to cultivate. During rituals, however, those land cultivators who are immigrant newcomers have to pay contributions in cash and kind, which is referred to as 'adding to and overfilling a half-full basket' (*tutu mbotu, penu mbora*). These payments are not for the Lord of the Land and the *adat* leaders as such, but for the whole society.

During communal meals (*nado mére*), the local leaders alone have the right to 'sit cross-legged' (*bhodhu pémba jawa*) at the centre of an *adat* assembly (*mbabho ngasi*). At the same time, they have obligations to solve problems in the assembly and to instruct the people of the village by way of 'calling the people from the head and the tail of the village' (*tau wuku 'udu 'énga 'éko*). Only then, during the concluding meal, do they 'receive the head of the pig' (*simo 'udu wawi*). The social and moral status associated with traditional leadership has nevertheless been sufficiently desirable to create competition among various descent lines for the title of Lord of the Land and other local offices.

In the case of Worowatu, only descendants of the so-called 'three ancestors' (*'embu tedu*) are candidates for the office of Lord of the Land and are allowed to receive sacrificial animal heads (pig, goat or dog) at communal meals. The gift and subdivision of an animal's head in a village ceremony thus functions as the symbolic representation of a social order of precedence. [16] The 'three ancestors' are three siblings: Waja De'e, her younger brother, Waja 'Ake, and the youngest brother, Waja Sébho, as depicted in Figure 1. [17]

Figure 1: The founding ancestors of Worowatu and their descendants

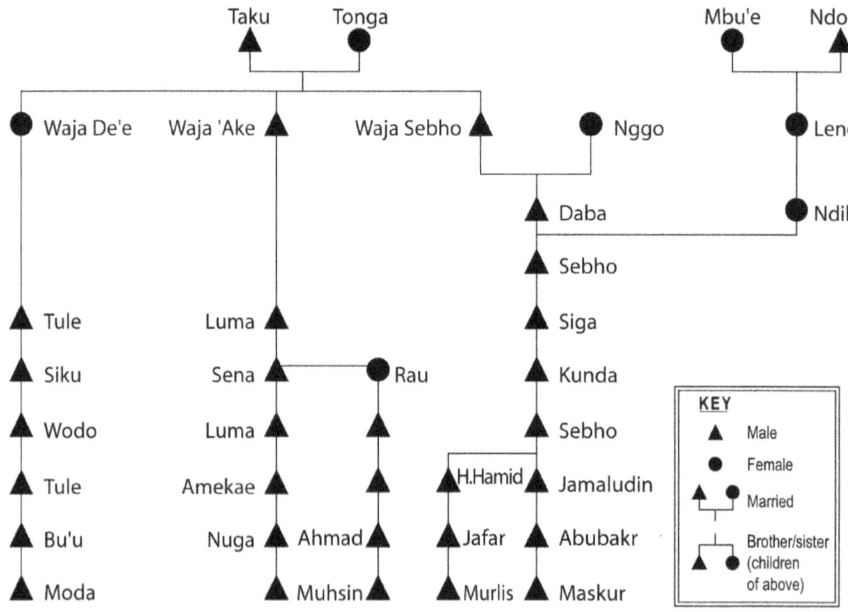

The real authority as*kepala mére* belongs to a descendant of the elder brother, Waja 'Ake, and the man who currently holds this office is Amekae Wea. He is the one who 'sits silently like a basket' (*eta kemu, bhodhu jotu bhida ko'o sondu*) and never speaks in *adat* assemblies. The right to speak (*mbabho ngasi*) falls to a descendant of the youngest brother, Waja Sébho, namely to Jamaludin Husein. My informant explained that the upper part of the pig's head including the ears should be offered to Amekae Wea, who sits, leading and listening, while the snout of the pig should be offered to Jamaludin Husein, because he is the one who speaks. [18] The eldest female line is not considered in the distribution of power among origin houses. There is a right associated with her seniority as the eldest, namely the right to speak, but this right is passed on to the house of the youngest brother, Waja Sébho. This type of diarchy, or dyadic structure of speech and silence, is encountered in other eastern Indonesian societies as well.[19]

A pig's head is most commonly given to someone as the acknowledgment of his authority and leadership as Lord of the Land or Overseer of the Land. These offices are based on communal acceptance (*'ata mbé'o*). Consequently, to ask for a pig's head at a communal meal without entitlement is an insult to the whole community and a violation of the social order. For example, an incident related to a pig's head occurred in the early 19th century, which demeaned the Lord of the Land of Worowatu and caused a serious tribal war between 'Udi-Worowatu and the Niondoa and Giriwawo villages. [20] The oral history is as follows:

> Once upon a time, 'Embu Daki Tonggo from Sa'o Mere Doka Ora (central large house) in the village of 'Udi invited the neighbouring village leaders (*mosa daki*), relatives, friends (*minda woe ka'e ari*) and people in the village to participate in clearing a garden (*songga*) in Dandu. The leaders from the neighbouring villages were 'Embu Nanga Medi from Niondoa, 'Embu Jawa Wonga from Giriwawo, 'Embu Siga Dalo from Worowatu and 'Embu Tiko Embo from Bedo. At breakfast time (*pesa 'uta poa*), Nanga Medi and Jawa Wonga asked for the pig's head, but Daki Tonggo did not give it to them. This degenerated into a dispute. The work did not go well. The leaders from 'Udi, Worowatu and Bedo with their people abandoned their work and left the leaders of Giri Wawo and Niondoa behind. They brought their food down to Ku Dhema, near the village of 'Udi, where they had their communal meal (*nado ka*) on their land. Nanga Medi and Jawa Wonga did not come along. The conflict went on and resulted in a tribal war between the two parties. Tiko 'Embo sided with and helped the 'Udi-Worowatu group. Nanga Medi and Jawa Wonga's group sent a courier to seek help from Tiko 'Embo from Bedo. Unofficially, Tiko 'Embo sent several men under the guard of 'Embu Wenggu Wonga as peacekeepers (*koe timbo né'e tuki 'api*). The main support was received from the Lio people (*'Ata Aku*) led by 'Embu 'Epu

> Kojo. The 'Udi-Worowatu party sought help from 'Embu Nggawa Ende and Kala Ende. Both parties used guns and black magic (*kadha*), and the war is said to have lasted for 12 years.

At the end of the war, it was announced that Pi'o Bhoko, a man from 'Udi, and the invited war leader from Lio, Epu Kojo, had both been killed. Finally, a Bedo peacekeeping team was able to bring about a truce. As a reward, Bedo village received seven pieces of land from the Niondoa and Giri Wawo parties.

Incorporated Groups

The following categorisation of incorporated immigrant groups provides an understanding of the rights of newcomers to cultivate the land on the basis of various traditional contracts. The newcomers are incorporated into or installed inside a local group.

One category of newcomers are 'war migrants' (*'ata tama dia, kono ondo*). An example are the people of lower Worowatu (*Worowatu Wena*), who are descendants of people from Ndai (*'Ata Ndai*) who had left Ndai after being invaded and defeated by the people of Noli. The refugees were protected by the people of Worowatu and made members of the community through a contract, which states that they are 'free to chop with axe and cutlass in clearing the land' (*topo todo dé'e, taka todo nga*). From the beginning, however, there was a condition stipulating that 'the daughters you bear will be our son's wives' (*'ana ta miu dhadhi, tau fai 'ana kami*). Thus the migrant group has been a wife-giving group for the indigenous people of Worowatu, although their social rank is still differentiated from that of other wife-givers to the village. Their contribution to ritual ceremonies is not a 'main contribution' (*pebhu tindu*) but an 'additional contribution to make up any shortfall' (*tutu mbotu penu mbora*). [21]

A second incorporated group in Worowatu are the so-called 'supportive neighbours' (*'ata ta ndi'i 'ipi mera kemo*). [22] This group includes the descendants of 'Embu Tai from the *nua* of Witu. According to oral history, 'Embu Tai came to settle in *'Udu Sambi Rupu*, on Worowatu territory, without asking permission. He then committed a crime by stealing a goat from the Lord of the Land. 'Embu Waja 'Ake wanted to chase him away but 'Embu Tai promised to be a loyal supporter. In the oral history of Worowatu, the subsequent sharing of land with Tai's descendants has created a ritual confederacy, which implies mutual assistance in working the land, in the installation of cultural monuments and in enacting ritual performances. The newcomers have to ask for the presence of the Lord of the Land at their own major rituals, and are obliged to contribute *tutu mbotu penu mbora* to Worowatu rituals.

A third group is that of the 'invited warriors' (*'ata kéu mére kambe déwa*). Belonging to this group are descendants of a number of Muslim pioneers: Nggawa Ende in Ma'undai, and Susu 'Ele Terpase in Ma'unori. [23] Nggawa Ende (from

Ende) was invited by 'Embu Siga and 'Embu Sena from Worowatu to join in a tribal war between Daki Tonggo and Jawa Medi. He and his descendants in return received a gift of some land in Ma'undai.

The incorporation of Nggawa Ende, the Hadramis and other migrant groups seems to be similar to the process of 'naturalisation' in modern nations in some ways. It involves an individual or a group giving their voluntary allegiance to a certain local group on the basis of a contract, which specifies the 'primary goods' (Rawls 1971) associated with citizenship. In the Keo context, the outsiders are incorporated and seen as an inner group because of their ancestral service as participators and helpers (*to'o jogho mbana daka*) in a war.

Such traditional contracts have been challenged by recent social changes in the region. Economic competition has forced the Hadramis to find other locations which are more promising for their businesses. At the same time, population growth has led to land scarcity in Ma'unori, and has caused the indigenous people to reclaim their clan land. These changes have resulted in a conflict over house sites (*da'e sa'o*) between the Hadramis and the descendants of 'Embu Mite Pale in Ma'unori.

The structure of precedence concerning traditional leaders and various categories of indigenous and newcomer groups in *tana* Keo is depicted below in Figure 2.

Figure 2: Structure of precedence in dealing with Keo land cultivation

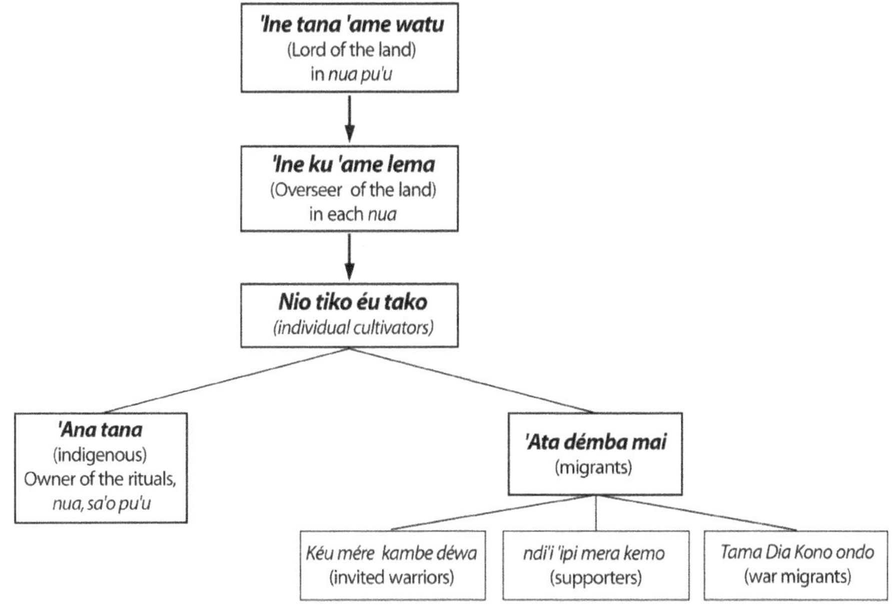

The relationships between local and newcomer groups is not predetermined but is always the outcome of a specific history. Newcomers can gain rights similar to those of earlier settlers, as the following case study will illustrate.

On October 11, 1997, I had an opportunity to speak with Al-Hadat from a Hadramis family in Ma'unori. I was accompanied by Ignas Isa and Severinus Rangga. We discussed various topics including social, religious and cultural problems. The main topic of our discussion was Sayyid Habib Idrus Al-Hadat, who was a pioneer and leader of Islam in Ma'unori. We also discussed why the Hadramis family occupies a piece of land in Ma'unori as their house site.

An oral history shared by various local leaders, including Ignas Isa, states that the occupation of the land by the Hadramis family was based on the involvement of 'Embu Susu Ele Terpase from Ende in a tribal war between the Noli and Ndai tribes. In that war, the exact date of which is not known, the Noli tribe, assisted by Susu Ele Terpase, succeeded in destroying the Ndai tribe by using the fire-gun known as*Meriam Se Ndai,* brought by Susu Ele Terpase. As a reward for his contribution, he was given a piece of land in Ma'unori for his family to settle on (*tau koe nua kadi 'oda*). That land later passed to his daughter, No'o Lalo, whose daughter, 'Ine 'Ipa Ende, married Habib Idrus Al-Hadat, whose father, Habib Umar Al-Hadat, was a Hadramis from a city called Terim. [24] Habib Idrus landed and settled in Ma'unori in 1914 and built the mosque Bait al-Rahman there (see Figure 3). Until now, the imam and khatib in the mosque are mostly from Habib Idrus's family.

The most interesting point that came up in my discussion with Al-Hadat in July 1997 was the historical process of their incorporation into a large house (*sa'o mere*) in the village of Nuamuri, and how this incorporation agreement was cancelled after a house site dispute. According to *adat* law, the family members and the descendants of Susu Ele Terpase, by consanguinal and affinal derivations, are eligible to inherit that piece of land. Hadramis are commonly seen as outsiders who have been made insiders (see also Fox 1995).

The Hadramis are regarded as members of the 'large house' of 'Embu Mite Pale in Nuamuri. Their membership in this ritual house was as a reward for Susu Ele's war service (*to'o jogho mbana daka*), which is described in ritual language as 'a gift which is never taken back' (*ti'i mona wiki pati mona dai*). It is obligatory for the Hadramis family to provide ritual contributions known in ritual language as 'additional contributions' (*tutu mbotu penu mbora*) or 'green beans and resin torches' (*mbue kaju api ida*) to the 'house' of Mite Pale. In return, Hadramis are no longer regarded as foreigners or migrants, but as people who own the right to cultivate and to settle on clan land in Ma'unori.

Figure 3: The genealogy of the Hadramis in Ma'unori

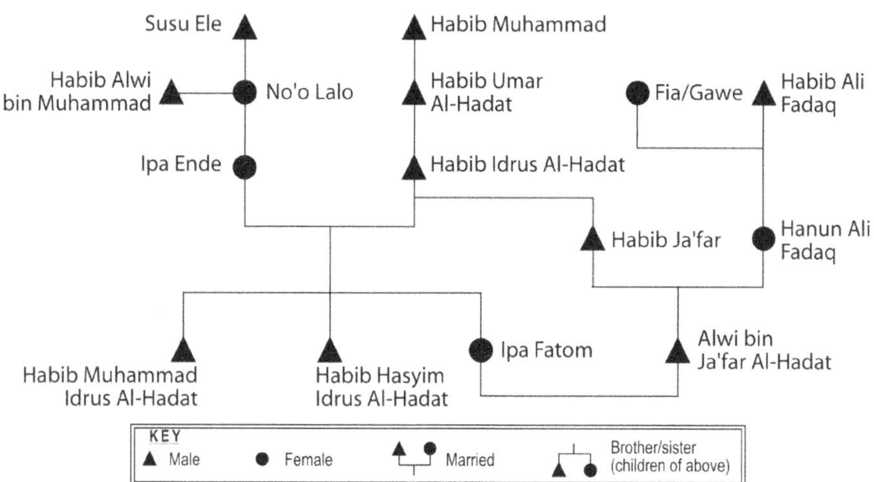

A Conflict Over Land

Since 1997 the Hadramis family in Ma'unori has been accused by a group in the large house (*sa'o mére*) of Mite Pale of violating the common philosophy of land motherhood by 'certifying' their land claim through the government land registration office. This led to a serious conflict with Gabriel Wundu, an 'Embu Mite Pale descendant. The conflict reached its peak when the government authorities in the subdistrict of Ma'uponggo became involved. The story runs as follows:

> After the death of Habib Idrus and his oldest son, Taha Idrus in the 1970s, the Hadramis family left their inherited house site and rented a new house about 20 metres in front of their old house site. The only Hadramis family living in Ma'unori nowadays is Ipa To, one of Habib Idrus's daughters who married Al-Hadat from Waingapu. Other sons and daughters of Habib Idrus live in Surabaya, Ende and Bajawa. Because the house site had been deserted for 20 years, Gabriel Wundu started to build a permanent house on it in 1996, with the involvement of local people and several *adat* leaders. On January 17, 1997, when one-quarter of the construction was completed, Alwi Jafar Al-Hadat brought the case to the Government at the subdistrict level of Ma'uponggo on behalf of the Hadramis family, reporting that Gabriel Wundu had built a house on their house site, which had been certificated and registered in the National Land Office (*Badan Pertanahan Nasional*) with a serial number AG 731606 24. 09. 06. 11. 1. 00007, dated March 26, 1997. As proof of their claim, the Hadramis family attached a copy of the land certificate

with the witness signatures of the village leader (*kepala desa*), Mbae Nuamuri, and landowners including Gabriel Wundu himself. Eventually an agreement was reached in the subdistrict office (*kecamatan*) of Ma'uponggo that Gabriel would hand back the land to the Hadramis because the land was 'a gift which is never taken back' (*ti'i mona wiki pati mona dai*). However, as recompense for the construction that had already taken place, the Hadramis family was ready to pay 3,000,000 rupiah. Both parties agreed formally to resolve the conflict in front of a special assembly of traditional leaders from Mbae Nuamuri, which is known in ritual language as 'the head waits for the Endenese, the tail waits for the Javanese or the outsiders' (*'udu kére Ende, 'éko napa Jawa*). The police from the subdistrict resort of Ma'uponggo, based on this agreement, went to stop Gabriel Wundu continuing his construction. However, Gabriel stirred up trouble again by questioning the validity of the certificate, saying that even though his signature was apparently on it, he had never signed any document for certification of that piece of land. The conflict resumed and was brought to the court in Ma'uponggo, where both parties were urged to find a peaceful and amicable solution (*secara kekeluargaan dan damai*) under the auspices of the local leaders and legal traditions (*hukum adat*). After they came back from Ma'uponggo, neither party put the agreement to put the problem before the *adat* assembly into practice. Gabriel Wundu spread the news that he had been pushed to accept such an option to solve the conflict by the subdistrict government and the Hadramis family. Gabriel Wundu and his family then took the case to court at the district level in Bajawa.

Before the juridical court hearing in Bajawa took place, I visited the District Head, Dr. John Samping Aoh, and discussed the case with him. In our conversation, two important issues were raised in relation to the conflict over the housesite (*da'e sa'o*): first, the act of certifying the clan land by the Hadramis family in Ma'unori and, second, the usefulness of traditional principles such as *ti'i mona wiki pati mona dai* ('a gift that is never taken back'). However, when I revisited the field site in Ma'unori in July 1999 and spent time with Gabriel and his sons, they showed me a bundle of documents in relation to the house site dispute written by both parties for the court in Bajawa. Both parties supplied the court with information on the basis in *adat* law of their respective claims to possession of the land. The parties created conflicting versions of their ancestral history and of the events that brought the great cannon (named *Meriam Se Ndai*) into the large house (*sa'o mere*) of 'Embu Mite Pale. 'Embu Mite Pale's descendants (including Gabriel Wundu) contested the claim that a traditional installation had taken place, and explained the presence of the cannon in their house as a reward given by Susu Ele Terpase for the participation of the grandfathers of Mite Pale and Dhae Pale ('Embu Jona and Ndoa) in a tribal war in Ende. Apart from the cannon, Susu Ele also gave a piece of land of about four and a half hectares, known as *Tanah Sabadeo Tana* Kéo, near Ndao, in the town of Ende. According to this party's version, the occupation of the disputed house site by the Hadramis family started with No'o Lalo (Susu Ele Terpase's daughter) and her daughter, Ine Ipa Ende, in the 1920s, after getting permission from 'Embu Isak Ado, Mite Pale's son. Then, Habib Idrus married Ine Ipa Ende and settled there too. Later in 1938, Habib Idrus brought his second wife, Ine Ipa Pulo, from Pulau Ende to Ma'unori.

The Hadramis have their own version of their settlement on the disputed house site, as stated earlier. They claim that the house site was a reward for Susu Ele Terpase for his participation in the tribal war between Noli and Ndai. The land was then inherited by No'o Lalo and her daughter, Ine Ipa Ende, and her husband, Habib Idrus, then by Thaha Idrus and his family until they recently obtained the certification.

From my observation, the *adat* assembly had not been sufficiently consulted in this dispute. The court in Bajawa, which might have been able to mediate between the two parties, did not listen to the testimony of the traditional leaders of Mbae Nuamuri (*'udu kére Ende, 'éko napa Jawa*). The Hadramis had violated the philosophy that 'no one owns clan land' by obtaining government certification. In daily practice, such a principle is applied strictly to the clan lands that are cultivated as the source of people's livelihood. For clan lands categorised as house sites and settlements (*da'e sa'o* and *nua 'oda*), such a certification is necessary due to the requirements of national civil laws and regulations. Anyone who wants a permit to construct a permanent construction (*Surat Ijin Mendirikan Bangunan*) must first provide a land certificate. However, the certification by the Hadramis had not been carried out with the permission of the *adat* assembly.

In a conversation with Gabriel Wundu during my return to the field on July 29, 1999, he explained that the Hadramis (c.q. Al-Hadat) had violated the traditional contract between 'Embu Mite Pale and 'Embu No'o Lalo, Susu Ele Terpase's daughter. He claimed that the legal status of the disputed house site was captured by the following traditional saying:

1. Kami ti'i mona ka wiki	We give and never take back,
2. Kami pati mona ka dai	we share and never recollect,
3. Asa miu to'o ma'e ndi'i	but you have to wake up without staying,
4. Mbangga ma'e mera	you get up without restraint,
5. Miu pana ma'e todo dangga	you send an arrow, never passing the limit,
6. Poke ma'e todo ndore	you throw never passing the border,

7. Miu wiwi ma'e isi	your lips (words) must never overact,
8. Dema ma'e de'e	your tongues never be sharp.
9. Ngara to'o ndi'i mbangga mera	If you get up with restraint,
10. Ko'o kami, wado 'ena kami	ours will be ours.
11. Ngara miu pana todo dangga	If you send an arrow passing the limit,
12. Poke todo ndore	if you throw a stone passing the border,
13. Ne'e wiwi isi dema de'e	if your words overact and are sharp,
14. So'o ria miu lela	it would be better for you to go.

In Gabriel Wundu's view, this Hadramis family had overacted in their words and behaviour by certifying the house site and claiming that it was their personal inheritance from their grandmother, No'o Lalo, which had been owned for 100 years and passed on for generations before it was certified on March 26, 1997.

In dealing with this issue, the District Head, Ngadha, seemed to adopt a different view from the court. In a personal conversation with me, he explained that the Indonesian national civil law still recognises the values of *adat* law. In his opinion, the agreement that was contracted by the ancestors was characterised by the principle of *ti'i mona wiki pati mona dai* and such traditional principles are a valuable inheritance to be passed down to the next generation. A one-sided negation of the agreement and its principles is really a violation of the *adat* law, and therefore should be solved by the local *adat* assembly. That is why the District Head thought the ideal solution for the conflict between the Hadramis family in Ma'unori and 'Embu Mite Pale's people in Nuamuri would be to return the case to the *adat* assembly of the village of Nuamuri.

On April 28, 1999 the court made a temporary decision that the Hadramis' claim to the land was dismissed (*niet onvankelijk verklaard*). Gabriel Wundu interpreted the decision as a victory. The Hadramis, however, saw hope therein for a further case if they could provide new evidence. In the meantime, the Hadramis family decided to leave Ma'unori and move to Ende. This move amounted to a cancellation of the longstanding *adat* contract of their incorporation as newcomer settlers, and resulted in this Muslim Arab family having to abandon their ancestral tomb located in the backyard of the Bait al-Rahmat Mosque in Ma'unori, which is another matter for concern.

Oral History and Land Tenure

Why is it that there are two versions of oral history about the great gun or cannon, *Meriam Se Ndai*? From a literary point of view, there are two reasons that should be taken into account to understand why Mite Pale's descendants deconstructed and reconstructed their version, which is different from the version of the Arab's family and the whole society of *'udu kére Ende 'éko napa Jawa*. The first reason is the gradual erosion of oral culture by written tradition in Flores. In the everyday discourse of a non-literate people such as the Keo, the storytellers are not merely entertainers and literary artists. They are at once scholars, jurists and custodians of the traditions of their society in the original sense (Sweeney 1991: 22-3). When written traditions were introduced, the new repositories of traditional knowledge were educated storytellers and writers who could more effectively store, retrieve, transmit and sometimes reconstruct the traditions of their people. The dependence on the memory and oral recitation skills of *adat* leaders was no longer absolute. Eventually, a whole set of new criteria was used as a legal basis in modern disputes: 1) land certificates, 2) evidence of who holds the sacred paraphernalia in dispute, and 3) logical and historical relationships between any group and the disputed object. This seems to be the start of an erosion of the traditions of oral history (Sweeney 1987: 284).

The second reason for there being two versions of this history concerns the relationship of the text to issues of power and knowledge. In modern literature, a text is viewed commonly as a written communication enmeshed in a context and environment—historical, cultural, political and religious. Although the father of structuralism, Lévi-Strauss, studied mainly unwritten texts or oral traditions, most of the structuralists perceive the text rather as a series of forms produced by the institution of literature and the discursive codes of a culture. However, the postmodernists argue that every text is related to every other text, and this makes for 'intertextuality' (Foucault 1972; Kristeva 1980: 36) and emphasises the relationship of the text to power and to the many forces that influence its production and its final form (Rosenau 1992: 36). The reinvention of the story about *Meriam Se Ndai* by Mite Pale's descendants should be viewed in line with Foucault's theory.

The abuse of power by the Government-appointed village head (*kepala desa*) of Mbae Nuamuri was one basic reason why Mite Pale's descendants created a new version of the story. The village head seemed to have acted in collusion with the subdistrict leader (*camat*) and the Hadramis in recommending to the BPN (*Badan Pertanahan Nasional*) that it should issue a certificate for the disputed house site. At the same time, the power of the *adat* assembly seems to have declined and was therefore not taken into account by either the *kepala desa* or the*camat*. Decisions made by functionaries of President Suharto's New Order State (*Orde Baru*) were challenged retrospectively by 'Embu Mite Pale's descendants, as is evident in the following letter, which they sent to the Juridical Court of Bajawa:

> It is clear that the certification on behalf of Thaha Idrus (an Arab) is false because it has been issued by the New Order Government in a manner categorised as an act of corruption, collusion and nepotism. The New

> Order Government pretended to issue mass certification on the basis of a program known as the National Project of land certification (*PRONA*) for the government's benefit as well as the people involved in it. This [mass land certification scam] should be taken into consideration in this court-case (in the current Reformation Era) in order that [the court decision] should not be accepted as valid, and [the defendants] should not be tried as criminals. (*Tangkisan serta Eksepsi*, February 17, 1999, p. 17) [25]

Conclusion

On the basis of oral tradition and mythical history, I would conclude that under the Dutch, the size of a landholding might have played an important role in political leadership in some parts of eastern Flores. The people of 'Udi-Worowatu, however, based their Lord of the Land position on the authority passed down from generation to generation from the founding ancestor, Taku Nuru. Although this traditional office was more pertinent to the ritual sphere than to modern politics, recent democratic elections have given descendants of the Lord of the Land a new opportunity to gain political office by using their traditional prestige, their newly acquired educational qualifications and a knack for charismatic leadership.

The people of 'Udi-Worowatu clearly still hold to the philosophy that 'no one owns the land, but people belong to the land'. This philosophy depicts a notion of the land as mother, as is implied in the metaphors of ritual speech. Every individual cultivator (*nio tiko eu tako*) has a right to a share of ancestral land (*tana suku* or*tana 'ine 'embu*) under the supervision of the guardians of the land, namely the Lord of the Land (*'ine tana 'ame watu*) and the Overseers of the Land (*'ine ku 'ame lema*). In proportion to their land usage rights, they have socio-religious obligations to participate in various rites dealing with the sacred land that is under the control of the ritual domain (*tana*) of Worowatu, a federation that consists of the villages of Witu and Ma'uara. Groups of Muslims and indigenous migrants have been incorporated into a particular source house, and are all part of this ritual confederacy.

Every village (*nua*) in the domain (*tana*) of Worowatu consists of a constellation of dwelling houses (*sa'o ndi'i*) derived from a single source house (*sa'o pu'u*). Each village has its own elders (*'ine ku, 'ame lema*) and can be categorised as a unit of customary law (*'uku 'ada*), underwritten by a very strong link of kinship and co-residence. In reality, this extended kin group has the right to cultivate and control certain pieces of land through the office of the *'ine tana 'ame watu*. Moreover, the daily cultivation of the land is carried out by particular individuals or families. Continuous cultivation of a certain piece of land or even several pieces of land tends not to create or produce personal rights over the land. In dealing with the rights and authority of *'ine ku, 'ame lema,* some of the sociopolitical and religious authority given to the Lord of the Land is also invested in the sub-lords of the land, who operate at the level of the *nua*. The authority to receive a pig's head, to lead an *adat* assembly (*mbabho ngasi*) as a legal and executive leader, and to place the first corner stone for a new construction are all invested in the *'ine ku, 'ame lema.*

Although narratives of origin are designed to establish an order of precedence for each person or house group, conflicts over power and status are continually played out in disputes between neighbouring groups, between the descendants of the younger brother and the elder brother, between the Lord and the Overseers of the Land. The most controversial case of conflict recorded was between the indigenous people and Muslim migrants, the Hadramis, in Ma'unori. The Hadramis were outsiders but had been accepted as insiders for generations until their recent violation of the*adat* contract with the indigenous people caused tension. Thus, the notion of installing outsiders on the inside has not proven to be an absolute transformation in this case. The relative ease of contestation for land claims based on oral history may well provide a basis for future conflict between indigenous people and migrants, between the commoners and the Lord of the Land. In the context of current national politics, religion is becoming more important as compared with other forms of identity construction. However, the idea that the indigenous people are 'children of the land' (*'ana tana*) remains central, as does the idea of indigenous groups entering relationships with newcomers by incorporation into a common source house and by subsequent sharing of the same ancestral land (*tana 'ine 'embu*).

References

Arndt, Paul. 1954. *Gesellschaftliche Verhältnisse der Ngadha*. Freiburg: Studia Instituti Anthropos, No. 8.

Barnes, Robert H.*Kedang: A Study of the Collective Thought of an Eastern Indonesian People*. Oxford: Clarendon Press.

BPS Ngada. 1995. *Ngada Dalam Angka 1995*. Bajawa: Central Bureau of Statistics.

Clarence-Smith, W.G. 2001. 'From horse trading to commercial supremacy: Arabs in the Lesser Sunda Islands, c1800 to 1940.' Unpublished paper.

Forth, Gregory. 1981.*Rindi: An Ethnographic Study of a Traditional Domain in Eastern Sumba*. The Hague: Martinus Nijhoff.

Forth, Gregory. 1998. *Beneath the Volcano: Religion, Cosmology and Spirit Classifications Among the Nage of Eastern Indonesia*. Leiden: KITLV Press.

Forth, Gregory. 1994a. 'Keo Kin terms.'*Anthropos*, 89. pp.95-109.

Forth, Gregory. 1994b. 'Consideration of Keo as an Ethnographic Category.' *Oceania,* 64 (4). pp. 302-15.

Foucault, Michel. 1972.*Histoire de la Folie*. Paris: Gallimard.

Fox, James J. 1977. *Harvest of the Palm*. Cambridge (Mass.): Harvard University Press.

Fox, James J. 1995.*Installing the Outsider Inside: The Exploration of an Epistemic Austronesian Cultural Theme and its Social Significance*. Leiden: Leiden University.

Hooker, M.B. 1978. *Adat Law in Modern Indonesia*. Kuala Lumpur: Oxford University Press.

Howell, Signe. 1996. 'A Life for Life: Blood and Other Life-Promoting Substances in Northern Lio Moral Discourse.' In S. Howell (ed.), *For the Sake of our Future: Sacrifice in Eastern Indonesia,* Leiden: Research School CNWS. pp. 92-109.

Kristeva, J. 1980.*Desire in Language*. Oxford: Basil Blackwell.

Langan 1921. 'Endeh (Flores).' *Mededeelingen van Het Bureau Voor De Bestuurszaken der Buitengewesten, Bewerkt Door Het Encyclopaedisch Bureau,*No 26.

Sweeney, A. 1987.*A Full Hearing*. California: University of California Press.

Sweeney, A. 1991. 'Literacy and the Epic in the Malay World.' In J.B. Fueckiger and L.J. Sears (eds), *Boundaries of the Text*, Michigan: Universtity of Michigan Press.

Therik, Tom G. 1995. 'Wehali: The Four Corner Land: The Cosmology and Traditions of a Timorese Ritual Centre.' Unpublished PhD thesis, The Australian National University, Canberra.

Tule, Philipus. 2001. 'Longing for the house of God, Dwelling in the house of the Ancestors: Local Belief, Christianity and Islam Among the Keo of Central Flores.' PhD thesis, The Australian National University, Canberra.

ENDNOTES

[1] This paper is based on the author's ANU PhD thesis (Tule 2001), which was published in 2004. Note that the term*'embu* refers to male ancestors.

[2] Forth has explored some of the various meanings of the term 'Keo' (1994). I prefer to understand Keo as the name of a territory that was merged with the Nage region by the Dutch (1923). The name Keo may have originated from a village named Keo Belo, or Nua Keo, near Maukeo and Mauponggo. Keo came to be used as a designation for the whole domain, comprising 10 subdistricts, unified into Kerajaan Kota Keo under Muwa Tonga. The 10 secondary districts were Tonggo, Riti, Lewa, Wajo, Wuji, Pau Tola, Kota, Sawu, Lejo and Worowatu (Forth 1994b: 309-10).

[3] Note, however, that Séme Rau was not born in Worowatu village. He was a 'returning child' (*'ana mera*) from the village of Witu. The term *'ana mera* is commonly translated into Indonesian as 'adopted children' (*anak angkat*), but this translation does not capture its exact meaning among the Keo. A better translation would be 'incorporated children' or 'returning children'. The implication is the incorporation of a person back into his/her mother's natal group or source-house. Filiation, or quasi-filiation by nurturing, is the main criterion. Such incorporation provides access to inherited leadership positions in a source house and its territory, and the right to claim land even if one is not a resident (Langness 1964: 170).

[4] *Leto laka* is related to the destruction of the sacrificial post (*laka*) in the village of Witu in 1937 because the people of Witu did not wait for the presence of the Lord of the Land of Worowatu.

[5] Jamaludin explained that the tree is also believed to be the source of richness and prosperity (*bhanda ngawu*). The people of Worowatu are unlucky because it fell down with its tip seaward. This meant that the people from overseas (*'ata tana dau*), the outsiders or 'people of Java' (*'ata Jawa*), would always be rich while the people of 'Udi-Worowatu are poor. According to local interpretation, the tip should have fallen uphill (pointing towards the 'head' of the mountain) and the trunk or roots downhill (towards the 'tail' or 'feet' of the mountain).

[6] A recent political movement (1997) wants to split the sub-district of Ma'uponggo into East and West Ma'uponggo. The new East Ma'uponggo subdistrict is to have its headquarters in Ma'undai, on about 4.5 hectares of land donated by several land cultivators from Worowatu, Bedo and Ma'uara villages. Although this movement could lessen the previous conflict between both parties (Worowatu and Ma'uara), those land-cultivators who are from Ma'uara have not yet expressed their agreement.

[7] *Tuka* literally means belly or stomach. The people of 'Udi-Worowatu are limited in their knowledge of anatomy and the physiology of pregnancy, however, and hence they equate the womb and stomach.

[a] *Wundu* is a local variety of fishing line made from hand-spun cotton. *Puru wundu mbudu wutu negha mona dhu* means to extend 40 times 40 arm-lengths of cotton fishing line into the deep sea; and still it cannot reach the furthest reach of the border of their marine territory.

[8] A story tells that Daba Nggo (a leading figure from Worowatu) and Juju 'Ari were both murdered in Nua Ora by Rangga 'Ame 'Ari when they were found committing adultery.

[9] In Keo language, this sort of oath is called *Supa Ka 'Awu* (soil-eating oath).

[10] *Ku* means a small piece of land cultivated by an individual or family, a plot, or a parcel of land.*Lema* is synonymous with *ku*. The term *lema* rarely stands alone, nearly always occurring together with*ku*.

[11] This level of leadership is equivalent to the*tulaku paraingu* of Rindi (Forth 1981: 257).

[12] The recent village leader of 'Udi Worowatu (*Kepala Desa* 1998) is Mathias Ndiwa, one of 'Embu Sambu Mite's descendants.

[13] *Mosa daki* literally means 'mature male'. *Mosa* also means 'mature' in reference to male dogs, buffaloes, horses or cattle, but not other animals. *Daki* means 'male'. It seems to be a synonym of *aki* in Keo and a metathesis of*laki* in Indonesian and Malay.*Daki* is also used in describing a man as monogamous (*ha daki*) or bigamous (*daki rua*) or polygamous (*daki rua tedu* or*daki séwe*).

[14] Among the people of Mbae Nuamuri village, another terminology is used for this *adat* judge: 'the leader who has a stick which is not sharp, but has a long cloth to cover' (*mosa bubu nusu, débha duka déwa*). The office is vested in the sub-clan Sina Jai.

[15] This newer type of leadership has come to dominate the others to some extent. Belonging to this group are successful traders and others with material wealth, such as 'buffaloes and gold'. Another local term is 'people who are rich' (*'ata ta bhanda ngawu*). Recently, even the Catholic priests, retired government officials and teachers are included in this type of leadership.

[16] Instead of the head, in other parts of Flores they offer the tail and the back or the foot.

[17] There is a new version that claims that the three founding ancestors who received the title '*waja*' (honourable) were not real siblings. One informant claimed that 'Embu Sena 'Ea was a classificatory brother (*ka'e ari sa'o tenda*) from Mbeku, a village four kilometres further north. Because 'Embu Waja 'Ake lacked house members (*weki weni do todo*), Sena 'Ea was adopted to be a house chief instead of 'Embu Bajo Dhéma, a migrant worker (*tae mbene*) from Bajawa. Another source mentions that 'Embu Waja Sébho was originally a *ka'e ari sa'o tenda* from the village of Jawa Wawo. He was incorporated into and inherited from the female house of Waja De'e. Through an *adat* process, 'Embu Waja De'e gave her authority back to her brother, Waja 'Ake, and then he handed over to Waja Sébho, because Waja De'e was only a female (*kote one*). Through that process, Waja Sébho was elevated to the status of a real sibling (*ka'e 'ari*) and given authority to be a 'spokesman' (*dipi wiwi déu dema*). Thus the status of lord of the land (*'ine tana 'ame watu*) should really go to the descendants of Waja 'Ake.

[18] Because Jamaludin Husein is a Muslim, the pig's snout will be taken by his delegate. If a goat is slaughtered, he will receive the goat's nose himself.

[19] Such a dyadic structure is encountered in Wehali, where the male *Liurai* is authorised by the female *Liurai*, known as*maromak oan*, to do the speaking. The*maromak oan* remains silent in the ritual centre (Therik 1995: 81, 101). In the case of Daja village, the three founding ancestors (*'embu tedu*) still retain the female as eldest because she is considered wise and an eloquent speaker.

[20] Based on the reconstruction of life stories and genealogies of several local leaders (*mosa daki*), it is estimated that the war began about 1813 and ended in 1825.

[21] In Ma'unori and Nuamuri, the same type of contribution is known as 'green bean and resin torch' (*mbue kaju 'api 'ida*).

[22] *Ndi'i 'ipi mera kemo* literally means 'those who live close to someone's hip'.

[23] My informant in Ma'unori mentioned that before the Noli and Ndai war, Mite Pale was invited by Susu 'Ele Terpase to Ende to help in the war between Mbonga Wani and Ndao. The people of Mbonga Wani under the leadership of Susu 'Ele won the war and were given a piece of land in Ende known as *tana saba déo tana Kéo*.

[24] Habib Umar Al-Hadat was born in the city of Tarim (Hadramaut) and migrated to Kupang in the 1850s. Another Hadrami in Sumba (Waingapu), Habib Ali Fadaq, was also a migrant from Medina. He married a girl from Ende, Fia Gawe, a relative of Susu 'Ele. Habib Idrus Al-Hadat, who was born in Kupang (1880s), migrated to Ma'unori in 1913 and died in Ma'unori on April 16, 1951 (see Plate 3.2). Habib Muhammad Idrus Al-Hadat was born in Ma'unori, where he became the imam of the local mosque until the 1970s. He moved to Kupang where he died in 1994 and was buried near the tomb of Sayyid Abd al-Rahman bin Abu Bakr al-Qadri, who used to live on Sumba. Related to the Hadrami sultan of Pontianak in West Borneo, the Sayyid was exiled from his native city in 1829, for reasons that remain unclear. He built up a friendship with a Dutch official in Batavia, D.J. van den Dungen Gronovius, and went to Kupang when Gronovius was appointed Resident there in 1838. After working for the Dutch customs authorities for a while, Sayyid 'Abd al-Rahman went as Gronovius's commercial and political agent to Ende (Flores), where he married a daughter of the Muslim sultan. Gronovius lent Sayyid 'Abd al-Rahman 14,000 Dutch florins and gave him permission to settle in 1842 on Sumba, where he became the leading horse trader until his death in 1878. His horse-trading business expanded so rapidly and extensively that it radically affected the political economy of the island. By 1879, the main traders in Sumba consisted of 13 Arabs and three indigenous Indonesians (Clarence-Smith 2001: 6; Forth 1981: 8; Fox 1977: 163; Parimartha 1995: 174-6).

[25] In the Indonesian original the text runs as follows: '*Jelaslah, bahwa sertifikat atas nama Thaha Idrus [an Arab] itu adalah palsu, karena dibuat dengan cara yang tergolong perbuatan KKN (Korupsi, Kolusi dan Nepotisme) dimana Orde Baru dengan berdalihkan Proyek Nasional (Prona) Penyertifikatan Tanah secara masal demi keuntungan pribadi pula dari pihak pembuatnya, sehingga perlu mendapat perhatian utama dalam perkara ini (di Era Reformasi) untuk tidak dibenarkan, ataupun dipidanakan*' (*Tangkisan serta Eksepsi, 17 Februari 1999, hal. 17*).

Chapter 10. Contending for Ritual Control of Land and Polity: Comparisons from the Timor Area of Eastern Indonesia

James J. Fox

Defining a Focus

The first task in this paper is to locate the problem at hand within a theoretical framework that identifies its significance.[1] I begin with an examination of the idea of land and domain among the Rotinese. My specific focus is on the central domain (*nusak*) of Termanu on the island of Roti itself. Although there is considerable linguistic and cultural variation among the domains of the island, the Rotinese share a basic understanding about the nature of their domains. They have all been subjected to similar formative influences. Among the domains of Roti, Termanu was the domain selected by the Dutch East India Company to establish its strategic presence in the second half of the 17th century and, as a consequence, through much of the 18th and 19th centuries, it was politically and socially paramount in developments on the island.

Nearly one third of the Rotinese population now lives on the island of Timor, having begun migrating there in the early 19th century. Although the Rotinese have brought to Timor many ideas of identity based on the particular domain from which they originated, they have not formed new domains (*nusak*) on Timor. This fact is itself significant and suggests that the *nusak* was a particular historical formation. Such a formation could not be replicated culturally in the new conditions the Rotinese encountered on Timor in the 19th century.

Having considered Rotinese ideas of land and territory, I will extend my analysis to two societies on the island of Timor: the Atoni Pah Meto who are also known as the Dawan, the dominant population of West Timor, and the Tetun, particularly the southern Tetun, whose centre in Wehali is regarded by many Timorese as the ritual centre of the island. For purposes of comparison, I focus on the domain of Amanuban among the Atoni. This domain rose to considerable political prominence, particularly in the 19th century, when it successfully resisted Dutch colonial incursions into the mountains of West Timor. For the southern Tetun, I consider Wehali itself, whose ritual head was regarded by the Dutch as Kaiser (*Keizer*) and by the Portuguese as Emperor (*Imperador*) of the island of Timor. Wehali was the ritual centre of a network of tributary states, which the Dutch and Portuguese regarded as paramount to the political organisation of the island.

At the outset of this paper, it is important to note that land and territory in eastern Indonesia are oriented space. On Timor, this orientation is based on two primary axes: an east-west axis (in line with the 'path' of the sun) and another crosscutting axis, which is, depending on the lie of the land, generally north-south. Thus the 'head' of the land is to the east; the 'tail' to the west. These axes and the values associated with them are part of the origin structures of the societies of Timor and are implicit in the local understanding of origin narratives. What constitutes the idea of the 'centre', however, varies among these societies and is usually constructed by reference to the categories of up/down or inside/outside. Subtly but invariably, the centre is given either a 'male' or 'female' symbolic valency. Wehali insists on an emphatic self-definition as 'centre' and 'female.'

In the communicative context of eastern Indonesia, to focus on any category prompts consideration of the dyadic sets within which that category occurs. Critical knowledge in the societies of the region is invariably encoded in formal pairs of semantic terms whose relation to one another provides an understanding of the cultural sense of both terms. [2] The ritual languages relied on to recount the most fundamental cultural knowledge are expressed in dyadic, profoundly poetic forms of speaking (see Fox 1988).

Land and Domain on Roti

The key terms to consider here are the Rotinese words *dae* (Proto-Austronesian **daReq*), meaning variously 'earth', 'land' and 'territory', and *nusa(k)* (Proto-Austronesian, **nusa*) which can be translated, in different contexts, as 'island', 'land' or 'domain'. I begin with an exegesis of the word *dae*.

In ordinary language, *dae* refers to the earth. In ritual language, *dae,* 'earth', pairs with *batu,* 'stone'. Thus the formal expression for the earth is *dae bafak ma batu poin,* 'Land's Mouth and Rock's Point', in contrast with the 'Heavens and Heights', *poin do lain,* and the 'Depths of the Sea', *liun do sain.* (*Dae* can also have the meaning of 'below' as in the phrase, *ndia neme lain leo dae*: 'it goes from above to below.)'

One can refer to the 'land of Roti' as *dae Lote* but Roti itself is described generally as a *nusa,* an 'island'. Thus Roti is simply Nusa Lote. Nusa, however, also forms the semantic basis for designating the named territories or domains (*nusak*) that form the local polities of the island: *Nusak sanahulu falu lai nusa Lote a*: 'There are eighteen domains (*nusak*) on the island (*nusa*) of Roti.'

Each *nusak* was headed by a ruler whose title was that of *Manek* or 'Male' Lord. Rule was centred on the site of the ruler's residence, which was designated as the *nusak lain,* the 'high domain'. The power of the ruler was based in, and emanated from, this 'high domain'. The ruler presided at a court in the 'high domain'. The symbolic ordering of this court centre was intended to reflect the state of the domain as a whole. In Rotinese, *nusak* thus denotes court and court centre as well as the domain as a whole (See Fox, in press a).

Each *nusak* ± was composed of a number of *leo*. These *leo* are the clans or 'origin groups' of the domain. The existence of each *leo* was acknowledged by a position in the 'high domain', by representation at the Lord's court and by assignment of a role in the performances of the origin rituals of the domain. Each *leo* was thus represented at court by its own *Mane Leo*.

Leo, in turn, are generally divided into smaller named lineages or *-teik* ('wombs', 'stomachs'), which can be distinguished further into *bobongik* ('birth groups'). Houses (*uma*) are the basic units of Rotinese society but rarely encompass more than two generations. Unlike other societies in eastern Indonesia, there are no houses that represent an entire 'origin group/clan' (*leo*) or even an entire lineage (*-teik*). Clans make general claims to ancestral areas—different parts of a particular domain associated with ancestral actions or earlier historic residence—but ownership of productive land—fields, gardens, portions of an irrigated rice complex—is maintained at the level of the household (*uma*) or among closely related households that derive from the same immediate ancestor.

Marriage rules for the *leo* of Roti vary. In some domains of Roti, *leo* are strictly exogamous. In others, such as Termanu, small *leo* are generally exogamous, whereas large *leo* permit marriage among individual *teik* or lineages (see Fox 1979a for a comparison between the domains of Thie and Termanu).

Clans (*leo*) have no existence outside their particular *nusak*; hence, there is no system of island-wide clan connections nor any clan network that transcends a particular *nusak*. The rulers of different domains intermarried but each ruler retained his own dynastic line based on a distinct genealogical origin. Thus no form of comprehensive nobility emerged on Roti. The *nusak* established strict (physical) boundaries for definition of all origin groups.

In ritual language, *nusa* pairs with *ingu*, another term for 'land', 'territory', 'place of residence'. Thus one can refer to *nusa no tola-non, ingu no ka'a-fadi*: 'a domain of relatives, a land of lineage mates.' In some dialects of Rotinese, such as Bilba, the term *ingu-lain* is used with the same sense as *nusak lain* in the dialect of Termanu. *Ingu*, however, also forms a pair with *leo*, meaning 'clan's or 'origin group'. *Ingu* is also a common element in the name of various origin groups: Ingu-Beuk, Ingu-Fao, Ingu-Nau. There are thus, linguistically and culturally, close linkages between the concepts of *nusa*, *ingu* and *leo*. A key point that needs to be emphasised is the fact that there is no presumed size to any of these categories. Some *nusak* on Roti are large units, either in terms of land or population, and are comprised of many *leo*; others are much smaller and are only a fraction of the size of the larger *nusak*.

In present-day Roti, members of different origin groups (*leo*) tend to cluster in different parts of a domain but the *leo* itself has lost most of its associations as a residential group. The origin narratives, however, describe the *leo* as if they were originally residential groupings: as separate small *ingu* or independent *nusak* that were, by conquest or deception, brought under the power of the high domain (*nusak lain*) of the ruler.

In Roti, residence is scattered. There are no discrete 'villages' and only limited evidence of a period when there might have been such discrete villages. The Rotinese terms for village are *taduk* or *nggolok* (*nggolo-taduk*), which imply a 'promontory' or headland. Generally, settlements are designated by specific names and names change as one moves through any particular settlement.

The existence of the various domains on Roti was acknowledged formally by a succession of contracts between their individual rulers and the Dutch East India Company beginning as early as 1662 (Fox 1971). As local polities, they continued to be recognised until 1968 when they were subsumed within the bureaucratic structures of the Indonesian Government. Warfare among these polities, especially over issues of land, continued well into the 19th century when the Dutch Colonial Government asserted the right to determine and maintain fixed borders between states. [3]

Each domain possesses its own narrative of the origin of the *nusak*, whose foundation and initial formation is regarded as having occurred before the arrival of the Europeans. The narratives provide an account of the ancestral foundation of the state, of the dynasty of its rulers and of the precedence and prerogatives of its origin groups. These state narratives, as told from the point of view of each ruling line, also recount the conquest, assimilation and absorption of other origin groups as the state expanded. This process of state incorporation allowed for the inclusion of other outsider groups within the domain.

The Domain of Termanu

Termanu was recognised by the Dutch East India Company as the foremost domain on Roti in 1662. [4] It might already have been in the process of growth at the time of its recognition. Dutch recognition and the location of a small Dutch post on the coast of Termanu contributed to a period of expansion. In the 18th century, this expansion was curtailed and territory that Termanu appears to have subjugated was granted separation and returned to other rulers. Thus Termanu was initially advanced and then eventually disadvantaged by its relations with the Company. Because of these continuing relations, the archival records of developments in Termanu are particularly revealing.

Termanu possesses an elaborate oral history that is concerned primarily with the establishment and development of the domain. In the telling of the history of the domain, the first important narrative recounts a division of the domain between its ruler and a particular clan lord who holds the title of *dae langak*, Head of the Earth. In the narrative, the ancestor of what is to become the ruling clan of Termanu arrives in the domain and challenges the resident ancestor of the Head of Earth's clan to a series of contests, which he wins by cunning and deception. This narrative establishes a separation between political power on the one hand and ritual authority on the other. The narrative is an example of a common Austronesian political charter myth whereby an 'outsider' is installed 'inside' and thus granted the right of rule (Fox 1995; Sahlins 1985). According to this narrative,

> the first person to settle in the territory (then known as Pada) was Pada Lalais. One day the ancestor of what was to become the ruling line of Termanu, Ma Bulan, wandered through Pada and met Pada Lalais. They immediately began to argue over who was first to arrive in Pada and agreed to test each other's claims by planting trees to see whose tree would flourish. Pada Lalais planted a quick-growing *damar* tree while Ma Bulan planted a slow-growing *bubuni* tree. After the trees were planted, however, Ma Bulan went back and switched the trees in each hole. When the two inspected the trees, the tree in Ma Bulan's hole was alive and well and he thereby claimed to be the winner. Pada Lalais would not accept this outcome so they agreed to have another contest.
>
> This time, they vied with each other over who could call the sea. Ma Bulan knew the sea, having come from over the seas, whereas Pada Lalais had an autochthonous knowledge of the earth. Ma Bulan therefore told Pada Lalais to call the sea as the tide was about to go out. He called but the tide continued to recede. Ma Bulan then waited until the tide was about to come in; he then called the sea and it came to him. Thus Ma Bulan was able to claim victory in the second contest.
>
> The two then agreed to have a third contest by examining each others's houses to see whose showed signs of being older. Ma Bulan immediately rethatched his house with eucalyptus leaves and then lit a fire that quickly turned the eucalyptus thatch soot-black. When the two ancestors came to inspect each other's houses, Pada Lalais' lontar leaf thatch was not as black as the eucalyptus thatch of Ma Bulan's house. Ma Bulan once more claimed victory.
>
> In the end, Ma Bulan, who had demonstrated the deceptive cleverness required of a ruler, offered the following solution to divide their functions. Thus he made the following proposal: 'It would be good if I became Lord and you became Head of the Earth for succeeding generations. When men have filled this domain, I will rule them and you may levy a tribute on the domain and take a portion of lontar syrup from

> each person who lives in the domain. And for all times, since you were the first to settle in this domain, this domain will be given the name Pada, in keeping with your name, Pada Lalais, and your grandchildren and descendants.

The narrative of this ancestral division of land and polity ends, however, with an additional narrative observation based on a folk etymological link between the personal name of a later ruler and the name of the domain. This is recounted as follows:

> In the time of Lord Tolamanu Amalo, a descendant of Ma Bulan, the company asked Tolamanu: 'What is the name of your domain?' So Tolamanu said: 'It is called Tolamanu in recognition of my name.' So it was called Termanu but the name Pada did not disappear. The domain is called by both names, Pada and Termanu, to the present time.

The chief elements of this narrative consist of: 1) the arrival of the stranger from the sea; 2) a set of contests between the stranger and the indigenous inhabitant; 3) the eventual installation of the stranger as ruler; and 4) a division of the realm in which the indigenous inhabitants retain rights over the earth. The displacement that occurs in this narrative is regarded as irreversible. Ritual authority over the land or earth is vested in a particular clan within the domain, whose priority of residence is acknowledged but whose precedence is superseded by that of the ruler.

Termanu is not alone in possessing a narrative account of similar opposition between an outside ruler and indigenous ancestral group. Each domain has its own narrative recounting the origins of this opposition—which, in some cases, amounts to implacable enmity—between ruler and 'head of the earth'. In some domains, such as Thie, this basic structure is more complicated: the function of 'head of the earth' is vested in one clan but various rights to harvest produce are disbursed among several clans associated with the 'head of the earth' (see Fox 1980b: 120-5).

Several critical points are important to note here. Dual structures occur at different levels in different societies in eastern Indonesia. On Roti, the primary diarchy in relation to the earth occurs at the foundation of the *nusak*. The *nusak* thus locates the rituals of the earth and sets a boundary to their functioning. No rituals of the earth extend beyond the boundaries of the *nusak*. All *nusak* have this primary diarchy, which may well be the most critical feature of a *nusak*.

A *nusak* as a structural entity is expandable. In line with the oral narratives, a *Manek* can incorporate the *ingu/leo* of another *manek* within his realm and bring the individual rituals of those incorporated *ingu/leo* into the cycle of his own rituals.

The significance of these features of Rotinese society should become apparent in a comparative analysis of other societies in eastern Indonesia.

Comparison with the Atoni Pah Meto of Timor

The Atoni are a large and distinct ethnic population of more than 750,000 people, who inhabit more than two-thirds of West Timor. They refer to themselves as the 'people of the dry land' (*atoni pah meto*). Land (*pah*) is primary in their definition of themselves and in a great number of Atoni titles: *Atau-pah, Ana'-pah, Afen-pah, Abain-pah*. Like the Rotinese, they have a long history of European contact. They have been subject to longer and more intensive contact than the Rotinese with both the Portuguese and the Dutch. Their political formations date back to a period well before the coming of the Europeans (Fox 1988) and although there are similar patterns of political structure among the Atoni states or domains, differences among these states are greater than among Rotinese domains. For the purpose of this paper, I draw comparisons between Termanu, the largest domain on Roti and Amanuban, the domain that became the dominant Atoni state in West Timor for a significant period during the 18th and the 19th centuries.

One of the chief differences between the Rotinese and the Atoni is in the structures of their origin groups. Atoni origin groups are known as *kanaf*. Each *kanaf* designates a named clan group, all members of which bear the same name. Members of a *kanaf* claim the same origin and are said to derive from the same source, whose site is (or is regarded as) a physical location. A *kanaf* is predominantly exogamous in that most members marry with members of other *kanaf* but it is possible for 'female' lines to form within local settlements and for 'male' lines of the same *kanaf* within these settlements to marry with these 'female' lines (Fox 1999).

'Houses' (*ume, uem*) are important social units but, as on Roti, there are no houses that represent an entire *kanaf*. Houses represent members of a *kanaf* at the level of the local settlement. Settlements (*kuan* > Tetun, *knua* > PAN/PMP **banua*) are significant not as ordered space but as a local ordering of precedence among particular *kanaf*.

A recurrent theme in Atoni narratives is the need for land: *Pahat maklen leuf, nifu maklen leuf*: 'Land too limited, water too limited.' This quest for land has scattered members of the different *kanaf* throughout West Timor. The expansion of *kanaf*, as related from the perspective of any one *kanaf*, is described as a journey of a single being or a single name. These narratives, recounted in ritual language, describe the significant encounters of the *kanaf* in its passage through the Timorese landscape.

States among the Atoni are seen as a coming together of a cluster of *kanaf* as a single domain. The recurrent formula for this clustering is always that of a group of four lords (*usif*), four 'fathers', each representing a separate *kanaf*, subject to and thus supporting a single lord (*usif*) of a ruling *kanaf*. The pattern is recursive. The domain can be built up of circles of four clans. Any lesser lord can also order groups around him in a cluster of four.

The demographic strength of a *kanaf* and its authority as a ruling *kanaf* may be confined to a single domain; yet members of most *kanaf* are not confined to a single domain but can be found in many domains. Thus, unlike Roti, *kanaf* identity transcends the boundaries of any domain or state.

Any domain is an 'ordering' of the land. Thus, for example, the great ruler of Amanuban was known by the personal title *Ta mes pah*: 'We Unify the Land' (see Schulte Nordholt 1971: 310), or *Ek pah*: 'To Enclose the Land' (McWilliam 1989: 39).

Among the Atoni, anyone who claims local authority can be called a *pah tuaf*, 'lord of the land'. The title has many of the connotations of that of *dae langak* on Roti. For example, a *pah tuaf* generally has the right to claim harvest tribute.

The Domain of Amanuban

There are a variety of versions of the narrative of the founding of Amanuban. Here I will summarise the narrative account told by the late Raja of Amanuban, K. Nope, to A.D.M. Parera (1971: 127-9). The narrative links the ancestor of the ruling line of Amanuban to Roti and its traditions.

> According to this narrative, the ancestors of the Nope and Isu lines came from Roti. After spending some time in Kupang, these ancestors became goat herders for Lord Abineno in Oekabiti. At the time, each night a goat would disappear. Ancestor Nope therefore took up guard at night and discovered that a great snake with a shining jewel in its head was stealing the animals. He and Isu stole the jewel and fled from Oekabiti with their treasure along the southern coast of Timor to a place at Tun'am in Amanatun. There they met the ancestors of Nitbani and Nomleni to whom they became wife-takers in return for a tribute of the harvest. This arrangement failed and so the two ancestors left Amanatun and moved on to Tunbesi in Amanuban where Tenis and Nubatonis were lords of the land (*pah tuaf*). Nope and Isu assisted Tenis and Nubatonis in trading sandalwood.
>
> In time, these ancestors quarrelled over who was to become Raja and they agreed to resolve the issue by various contests. The first contest involved the planting of a banana tree that had been cut in two. Tenis and Nubatonis planted the tip of the banana, which failed to take root and grow; Nope, however, planted the base of the banana, which grew. The second contest involved the planting of sugar cane. This time Tenis

> and Nubatonis planted the base of the sugar cane while Nope planted the tip. Again, Nope's plant grew. In their third contest, the ancestors lit torches to see which one would burn longest. Tenis and Nubatonis' torch went out during the night when it became damp with dew. Instead of burning his torch, Nope took the jewel he had taken from the great snake and placed it into his torch. This jewel shone through the night until dawn. Thus Nope became ruler using both the name of Nope and that of Nuban (from Nubatonis). He elevated Isu and Fina as his male lords and Saé and Bako as his female lords, with Sole, Nome, Nabuasa and Teflopo as his *meo*-warriors. This created the first structure of the domain of Amanuban. Nope was installed at the centre of the domain surrounded by circles in groups consisting of four lords with different functions.

This narrative has various parallels with the foundation narrative for the domain of Termanu. Nope is an 'outsider' who triumphs over the local lords of the land by a series of contests, supplants these lords, and installs himself at the centre the domain. In analogous founding charters, the new lord drives out the previous lords of the land. Here, as is the case in Termanu, the previous 'heads of the earth/land' remain as subordinate lords in the domain.

As with the Rotinese narrative, the name of the domain is considered crucial. In Roti, the compact between the two ancestors initially establishes the name of the domain as Pada, after the head of the earth. Only later is the ruler's name adopted as a second name. In the Amanuban narrative, there is a similar compromise. The ruler takes two names, one of which is that of the lord of the land. In effect, therefore, the domain retains the name, Nuban (Ama—Nuban: 'Father(s)—Nuban') of the supplanted lord of the land. As in the Termanu narrative, the Amanuban contest between the ancestors determines precedence among the constituent clans of the domain. The ordering of the domain follows the recurrent formula of four lords around a centre with a second group of lords (*meo* = warrior lords) around these inner lords.

The Tetun of Timor

Analysis of Tetun society requires an investigation like that directed to Atoni society. The Tetun are a large group who straddle both sides of the East/West Timor border. In West Timor, the Tetun are divided into a northern (*foho*: 'mountain') and a southern (*fehan*: 'coastal') group. The northern group reckons relations within its origin groups through males; the southern group reckons its origins through its women. The coastal Tetun also extend across the border into East Timor and another group of Tetun is located in the central south of the territory as well. There are more than 400,000 Tetun who speak the Tetun language as a first language. (Others in East Timor have adopted a simplified dialect of the language as a lingua franca, which is on its way to becoming the national language of the country.)

This paper will concentrate on the coastal Tetun of West Timor and, more specifically, on the Tetun of Wehali. Wehali is regarded as the sacred centre (*laran*) of the entire Tetun population. Wehali is considered *rai feto*, 'female land', as opposed to *rai mane*, 'male land', and is the traditional site of the Maromak Oan, 'The Child of the Luminous', who is also described as the *Nai Bot*, 'The Great Lord', or *Nai Kukun*, 'The Dark Lord'. The authority of this lord was once acknowledged through the presentation of harvest offerings from groups from a large area of Timor, including many of the domains of the Atoni themselves.

Wehali's authority still encompasses a wide area that acknowledges Wehali as its centre. According to its origin myth, Wehali is a great banyan tree that offers shade to its constituent groups. The ordering of its groups follows a fourfold division. Wehali itself is known as the *Rai Lidun Hat, Rai Sikun Hat*: 'Four Corner Land, Four Section Land.'

In linguistic terms, the Tetun are the population related most closely to the Rotinese. Both peoples share similar seeming categories of social organisation. Yet the differences between these categories are profound.

The general term for 'earth', 'land' or 'territory' is *rai*. As on Roti, the land is oriented with its 'tail' (Tetun: *ikun*; Rotinese: *iko-k*) to the west and its 'head' (Tetun: *ulun*; Rotinese: *langa-k*) to the east. Another term used among the Tetun is *rae*. (This is the term that relates—by sound change of r > d—to the Rotinese for earth, *dae*.) The term *rae* among the Tetun is most often used in opposition to the (directional) term for sea, *lor*. In the coastal Tetun cosmology, north is the *rae ulun* ('head land'); south is *lor ain* ('foot land'). On its own, *rae* has the sense of (uncultivated) 'land', rather than 'earth'.

Within this scheme, Wehali is the *rai hun, leo hun*: 'Land of origin, *leo* of origin.' The critical term here is *leo*. Whereas among the Rotinese, a *leo* is a clan-like origin group defined by its position within a particular *nusak* or domain and thereby confined to that *nusak*, a *leo* among the population of Wehali is a named residential group—a hamlet—comprised of specific named houses. Just as Wehali is the source and centre of the whole population, the houses in the named hamlets surrounding the central hamlet of Wehali are the origin of individual members of society. Houses and the land associated with them are inherited by the eldest of a group of sisters in each generation. Thus continuity is maintained at the centre, whose purpose has long been to export its population, particularly its male population.

Inner Wehali's formal structure consists of four hamlets (*leo*) around a single central hamlet known as *Laran*, 'centre'. Within this centre, however, is an inner complexity of 12 named houses (*uma*). (See Therik 2004 for a remarkable study of the domain of Wehali.)

Contemplating Categories: Comparisons of 'Male' and 'Female'

At its centre, in Wehali, was the *Nai Kukun*, 'The Dark Lord', who represented the earth. He was 'The One who eats reclining, who drinks reclining' (*mahaa toba/mahemu toba*). He was also known as 'The Female Lord' and as a representative of the female attributes of the Earth. As such, he was—as is everything in Wehali—'feminised'. In contrast with this 'Dark Lord' was the lord who spoke and acted on behalf of this shrouded, silent presence. This speaking lord was referred to as the *Nai Roman*, 'The Visible Lord'. In historical terms, this figure was the Liurai of Wewiku. As *Liu-Rai*, this personage stood visibly 'above the earth', as 'male' (*mane*) on the 'periphery' (*molin*) of Wehali. This idiom is capable of continual, recursive extension: the *Liurai*, in turn, could be seen as 'centre' and 'female' in relation to the next sphere of rule, which was 'male' and 'exterior'.

Wehali is a totally matrilineal area: all land, all property, all houses belong to women and are passed from one generation of women to the next. In contrast, most other Timorese societies (including other Tetun groups as well as the Rotinese and Atoni) are patrilineal in political orientation (although not necessarily in their total social organisation). In Wehali, men are exchanged as husbands in marriage, never women. And in legend as in reality, Wehali is the 'husband-giver' to other areas of Timor. Thus, whereas Wehali traces its origins within its sphere exclusively through women, surrounding realms trace their relations of origin through males, some of whom are said to have come from Wehali. The founder of the Sonba'i Dynasty among the Atoni peoples, for example, is recognised as having come as a lone male from Wehali.

In terms of the comparisons set out for discussion in this paper, *Rai Wehali* is conceived as the centre of Timor (*Rai Timor*) and of the Earth itself (*Rai Klaran*). It is a 'female' centre and extends without limit. As a centre, it represents the Earth itself. By comparison, the domains of the Rotinese and Timorese are bounded entities. The ruler of Amanuban, for example, held the title of 'he who enclosed the land'. In contrast with Wehali, Termanu—and all the other *nusak* on Roti—are 'male' centred domains. The lord or lords concerned with the rituals of the earth are subordinate to the ruling male power of the domain. Amanuban—and other Atoni domains—are a curious halfway house. Amanuban's formal structure is like that of Wehali: a central lord with four protecting lords, then four warrior lords. But Amanuban's central lord displaced earlier lords of the earth and was distinctively 'male'. However, once installed as ruler within a structure that implied (indeed required) a female centre, the authority of that ruler was 'feminised' and the rulers around him took on evident formal male characteristics as guardians of the centre.

It is interesting that the Tetun term for 'settlement' or 'village' outside Wehali is *knua* (> **banua*). Wehali has no *knua*. The term *knua*, however, is used for Wehali in a specific metaphoric sense. In this sense, it refers to the 'sheath' of a sword. Wehali is that 'sheath'. In regard to Wehali, it is said, *Mola isin e mela knuan*: 'Take the sword but leave the sheath.' According to the Wehali view of itself, as a centre, it can only give; it can never take. As permanent 'giver', Wehali cannot be subordinate. Hence in Timor there is only one polity like Wehali.

Conclusions

Comparison is the critical task of anthropology. A controlled comparison sets forth as precisely as possible the framework within which a particular comparative effort is undertaken. In this paper, the general framework has been provided within a comparative Austronesian context but with a specific focus on three linguistically distinct cultural groups—the Rotinese, the Atoni Pah Meto and the Tetun—in the Timor area of eastern Indonesia. The concern has been with each cultural group's categorical conception of land and territory and how these categories are defined within specific historically formed, ritually defined, (state-like) structures—Termanu, Amanuban and Wehali.

Such comparisons lead to wider issues fundamental to each of these societies—ideas of rule and authority, of precedence and derivation, of encompassed and encompassing, of subordination and superordination—all linked intimately to conceptions of 'male' and 'female'. Each of these societies possesses its own variant understanding of the world and has articulated this understanding within specific, historically bound, socially constructed polities. Comparison allows us to appreciate how these various articulations relate to one another and how they may relate to other Austronesian societies.

Based on present linguistic and archaeological evidence, it would appear that Austronesian-speaking populations have been on Timor for more than 4,000 years. Timor, as a rich source of precious aromatic sandalwood, has been the target for long-distance traders for at least 1,000 years (see de Roever 2002) and its populations have been subjected to European influences for more than 500 years. These factors—a long-resident population that has had time to differentiate and to settle the diverse environments of a relatively large island, that has been open to a steady flow of trade goods including weapons, seeds and tools and that, as a result, has been able to develop and elaborate a variety of related, yet competing polities—have given the Timor area a distinctive cultural signature within the wider Austronesian-speaking world.

Similar configurations of categories and ideas define the Timor area in ways that can be seen to differentiate Timor from other parts of eastern Indonesia and, more broadly, from other parts of the Austronesian world. At the same time, many of the basic categories on which these configurations are constructed are common (or at least similar) throughout the Austronesian-speaking world. Perhaps it is only when we have clearly defined the categories of one area of the Austronesian world and come to understand their historical variation that we can move on confidently to wider comparisons.

References

de Roever, Arend. 2002. *De jacht op Sandelhout: De VOC en de tweedeling van Timor in de Seventiende Eeuw*. Proefschrift: Leiden University.

Fox, James J. 1971. 'A Rotinese dynastic genealogy: structure and event.' In T.O. Beidelman (ed.), *The Translation of Culture*, London: Tavistock. pp. 37-77.

Fox, James J. 1979a. 'A tale of two states: ecology and the political economy of inequality on the island of Roti.' In P. Burnham and R.F. Ellen (eds), *Social and Ecological Systems*, London: Academic Press. pp. 19-42.

Fox, James J. 1979b. 'Standing in time and place: the structure of Rotinese historical narratives.' In A. Reid and D. Marr (eds), *Perceptions of the Past in Southeast Asia*, No. 4, Kuala Lumpur: Heinemann Educational Books (Asia) Ltd. pp. 10-25.

Fox, James J. 1980a. 'Introduction.' In J.J. Fox (ed.), *The Flow of Life: Essays on Eastern Indonesia*, Cambridge (Mass.): Harvard University Press. pp. 1-18.

Fox, James J. 1980b. 'Obligation and alliance: State structure and moiety organisation in Thie, Roti.' In J.J. Fox (ed.), *The Flow of Life: Essays on Eastern Indonesia*, Cambridge (Mass.): Harvard University Press. pp. 98-133.

Fox, James J. 1983. 'The Great Lord rests at the centre: The paradox of powerlessness in European-Timorese relations.' *Canberra Anthropology*, 5 (2). pp. 22-33.

Fox, James J. 1988a. *To Speak in Pairs: Essays on the Ritual Languages of Eastern Indonesia*. Cambridge: Cambridge University Press.

Fox, James J. 1988. 'Historical consequences of changing patterns of livelihood on Timor.' In D. Wade-Marshall and P. Loveday (eds), *Northern Australia: Progress Prospects* (*Vol. 1: Contemporary Issues in Development*), Canberra: Research School of Pacific Studies, The Australian National University. pp. 259-79.

Fox, James J. 1995. 'Installing the "Outsider" Inside: The Exploration of an Epistemic Austronesian Cultural Theme and its Social Significance.' First Conference of the European Association for Southeast Asian Studies, Leiden University.

Fox, James J. 1999. 'Precedence in Practice among the Atoni Pah Meto of Timor.' In L.V. Aragon and S. Russell (eds), *Structuralism's Transformations: Order and Revisions in Indonesia and Malaysia*, Tucson (Ariz.): Center for Southeast Asian Studies, Arizona State University. pp. 1-36.

Fox, James J. In press a. 'Traditional Justice and the "Court System" of the Island of Roti.' In Dionisio Babo Soares et al (eds), *Traditional Justice and Conflict Resolution in Timor*, Asia Society.

Fox, James J. In press b. 'The discourse and practice of precedence.' In Michael Vischer (ed.), *Precedence*, Canberra: Research School of Pacific and Asian Studies, The Australian National University.

McWilliam, Andrew 1989. 'Narrating the Gate and the Path: Place and Precedence in South West Timor.' Unpublished PhD thesis, The Australian National University.

Parera, A.D.M. 1971. *Sedjarah politik pemerintahan asli di Timor*. Kupang: University of Nusa Cendana.

Sahlins, Marshall. 1985. 'The stranger-king; or Dumezil among the Fijians.' In M. Sahlins, *Islands of History*, Chicago: the University of Chicago Press. pp 73-103.

Schulte-Nordholt, H.G. 1971. 'The Political System of the Atoni of Timor.' *Verhandelingen van het Koninklijk Instituut voor Taal-, Land- en Volkenkunde*, No. 60. The Hague: Martinus Nijhoff.

Therik, Gerzon Tom. 2004. *Wehali: The Four Corner Land: Traditions of a Timorese Ritual Centre*. Canberra: The Australian National University.

ENDNOTES

[1] For at least two decades, I have been engaged with colleagues and students in the comparative study of the societies of eastern Indonesia (see Fox 1980a for an early formulation of this comparative project). Approximately a decade later, through the Comparative Austronesian Studies Project initiated in the Research School of Pacific and Asian Studies, these comparative interests in eastern Indonesia became subsumed within a wider comparative framework. This framework offers a perspective on what may be considered the distinctive features of the societies of eastern Indonesia and on how they relate to the wider Austronesian-speaking world. From the outset, this comparative study has focused on cultural categories, their 'metaphoric' elaboration and their social expression. An array of common Austronesian categories provides a 'starting point' for a combination of cultural and social analysis. Insofar as it relies on the evidence of historical linguistics to provide an initial defining point, this kind of analysis is essentially historical.

[2] Since the early 1980s, researchers have focused on the 'house' (*uma, soa, fada*) as a key social and symbolic component in the structuring of the societies of eastern Indonesia (Fox 1980a: 10-12). Equally important in the analysis of eastern Indonesian societies has been the focus on 'clans' as 'origin groups' represented, in various ways, by their constituent 'houses'. The particular problematic concern of this

comparative examination will be on the relationship between 'origin groups', the house or houses that represent them, and the territory they occupy.

[3] Eastern Indonesia is an area of early European contact and historical records offer considerable, often detailed, accounts of local developments. In some cases, these records date back to the 16th and 17th centuries; in others, the records begin only in the 19th or as late as the early 20th century. Generally, as these records become particularly informative, they signal a transformation in local societies as a result of the European encounter. It is often possible to chart these transformations: the coalescence of groups, the rearrangement of relations among territorial entities, the creation of polities and the beginnings of an administrative structure. These changes are of direct relevance to concepts of 'land', 'territory' and 'domain'. In eastern Indonesia, history looms large in another sense. Virtually all of the societies of the region maintain accounts of the past. These narratives are called on to explain, confirm and justify relations among groups within specific territories. Some recount the formation of the land, others the journeys of the ancestors and their arrivals, the founding of domains and the development of relations within them. I have referred to these narratives and the accompanying commentaries, together with the implicit rules by which these narratives are utilised as 'origin structures'. They present an image of the past and define precedence in the present. To gain an understanding of local ideas of land and territory, it is necessary to locate these fundamental categories within their particular 'origin structures'.

[4] I have already written various accounts of the domain of Termanu (see Fox 1971 on the dynastic genealogy of the domain; Fox 1979b on its historical narratives; and Fox In press b. on the order of precedence among origin groups established by the combination of genealogy and narrative). Here I wish merely to sketch an outline of the domain and its historical narratives for purposes of comparison.

Chapter 11. Fataluku Forest Tenures and the Conis Santana National Park in East Timor

Andrew McWilliam

Introduction [1]

Fataluku society of Lautem, the most easterly district of East Timor, has attracted comparatively little detailed ethnographic research. [2] This paper aims to contribute to a better understanding of this region by exploring Fataluku customary tenures and cultural land management practices in the context of emergent land administration policy in East Timor. Fataluku land and forest tenures will be examined from a comparative perspective, placing them within the wider context of eastern Indonesian ethnology.

The district of Lautem contains one of the finest contiguous blocks of dense lowland tropical and monsoon forest on the island of Timor. Covering an area of some 300 square kilometres and incorporating the heavily forested Paichao Range of low mountains (to 925m), this forest zone extends from the eastern extremity of East Timor (Jaco Island) in a narrow band (7-10km) westwards following the unpopulated southern coastal hinterland. As a region with great ecological value and complex biodiversity, the area has long been accorded special significance. [3] During the period of Indonesian rule in East Timor (1975-99), much of the forested zone was classified as a natural conservation reserve (*kawasan suaka alam*). [4] This category of protection, on paper at least, prohibited logging and other forms of extractive activity within its boundaries. Subsequently, under the United Nations Transitional Administration in East Timor (UNTAET) from 1999, after the truculent withdrawal of Indonesian forces, the area was reclassified and declared one of 15 so-called 'Protected Wild Areas' (UNTAET Reg. 19/2000). This sentiment and commitment to recognize and conserve the heritage and resources of the Tutuala-Paichao Reserve has continued under the new government of the independent East Timor. In 2002, through its Directorate of Forestry, the Government initiated a program to formally demarcate and legislate the area as the country's first 'National Park'.

As part of this program of development, the East Timorese Administration has formalised a memorandum of agreement with the NSW National Parks and Wildlife Service (Australia) to collaborate in developing effective park management strategies and resource inventories. Although conservation is the primary objective in the establishment of the park, this does not preclude complementary development possibilities including eco-tourism, bio-exploration and/or carbon credit trading. [5]

The concept of the park also serves other government agendas, especially the broader 'nation-building' task of post-conflict East Timor. A recent proposal to name the park 'The Conis Santana National Park' honours the sacrifice of a former, highly revered Falantil commander (1993-98), and thus commemorates the nationalist struggle for independence from Indonesian and Portuguese colonial rule. The fact that the forested region of the proposed park provided shelter and refuge over many years for armed Falantil guerillas, including then resistance leader, Xanana Gusmao, gives the region a special standing in the history of East Timor

Without denying the importance of these sentiments and values and the evident enthusiasm in government for its formal creation, the prospects for the successful establishment of the park and the development of effective management regimes are highly dependent on the future regulatory framework and ownership status of the region. This issue arises because, contrary to perceptions of a would-be wilderness of natural heritage values, the greater part of the forested zone in this proposal is not composed of ancient old-growth primary forest. Rather, the forest reflects a highly enculturated mosaic of aged and long-fallowed secondary regrowth of former swidden gardens and settlement sites. Its very existence as a canopy forest is, to a significant degree, the result of a particular history of disengagement by local 'traditional owners' due to coercive external pressures applied by successive colonial governments, especially in the form of resettlement policies and restrictive security arrangements. Although long ignored and subsumed within government regulations, customary tenures and local claims of Fataluku-speaking populations to the forestry zone remain substantially intact. They form the historically asserted and contested grounds on which any negotiation and determination of land title and management authority within the forested park would seem to rest.

As a result of preliminary consultations with selected community leaders, government forestry staff informally acknowledge the existence of a right to 'traditional land' (BI: *tanah adat*) and interests to the resources of the park area. They accept the need to incorporate continuing low-level extractive activities undertaken by customary users into the park management policy. However, there is no consensus or agreement, at this stage, over the prospective formal status of their practical interests and ownership claims. Nor has there been any sustained attempt to systematically investigate the ethnographic context within which these claims emerge.

This paper offers a preliminary contribution to that exercise and explores elements of continuing Fataluku customary attachments and affiliation to the proposed national park. What emerges from these insights is a forest environment inscribed with complex and layered social meanings and memories. Local forest tenures are constituted and embedded as much in the sacred geographies and spiritual connections that people retain with specific localities, as they are in the histories of personal engagement with and economic exploitation of the forest environment. The proposed national park is, for many Fataluku groups, a wholly local preserve and the vital inheritance of their ancestors. In this context, nationalist and public claims for control and 'management' of the forest tend to be viewed with a mixture of scepticism and mistrust by local groups with a landed interest in the outcome.

Locating Fataluku

The indigenous Fataluku-speaking population of East Timor, currently numbering about 35,000 speakers, forms the largest linguistic community of Lautem district. Lautem itself is composed of five subdistricts (*posto*) and Fataluku speakers form the dominant population group in the three most easterly areas (Tutuala, Fuiloro and Lautem). [6] Among Fataluku native speakers there are numerous dialect forms, reportedly up to seven varieties, which are nevertheless mutually intelligible. The term Fataluku can be translated as 'plain' or 'straight' speech. Although the Tutuala dialect in the eastern extremity of the region is generally considered to express the purest form of the language, the most popular and widely spoken version of Fataluku centres on the district capital, Los Palos, and the more populous central subdistrict of Fuiloro. [7]

Fataluku is one of the principal non-Austronesian languages of East Timor classified as part of the Trans-New Guinea phylum with strong West Papuan substratum features (see Hull 1998: 22). [8] While linguistic differences distinguish Fataluku populations from their more numerous Austronesian-speaking neighbours in East Timor, it is by no means obvious that the different phylogenetic origins of Fataluku as a language have produced a corresponding degree of cultural distinction (see Bellwood et al. 1995: 3-4). As Hull has observed, Fataluku society reflects a hybrid cultural identity, being more 'Proto-Malay than Melanesian in racial type' and possessing the 'most typical Austronesian material culture in Timor' (1998: 165). [9] In this regard, the existence of a remnant Austronesian linguistic island of Lovaia or Makwa [10] within the dominant Fataluku language area suggests a long-term engagement with Austronesian social and cultural ideas and practices, however these might be defined.

A predominantly agrarian society, Fataluku people have for centuries pursued systems of smallholder dry-land swidden agriculture combined with irrigated rice production in favourable areas, as well as extensive systems of animal husbandry focused on buffalo, domesticated pigs and goats. Hunting in the forests and coastal margins is also undertaken regularly and most of the population relies on a wide variety of forest products for domestic and household use.

At the present time, settlements in Lautem tend to form concentrated residential groupings and linear developments along arterial roads. Residential populations are grouped administratively into villages (*suco*), [11] a legacy of Portuguese colonialism, and usually contain a varied number of constituent hamlet (*aldeia*) settlements within the wider land area of the village. These patterns of settlement, however, are, for the most part, comparatively new. By and large, they reflect the policies of successive Portuguese and Indonesian administrations to concentrate and spatially contain Fataluku sociality in the interests of facilitating administration and control. More traditional patterns of residence were dispersed. People tended to live in small clusters of family based households (*otu*) in swidden gardens, moving with the rhythm of forest clearing and fallow, and affiliating to one or another larger settlement and ritual centres known as *lata*.

Origins and Inscriptions of Place

One of the first comments I recorded in my investigations into Fataluku land tenure was that all the land had long been divided among the respective resident and named *ratu*, which comprise key social institutions in Fataluku society. Subsequent enquiries identified dozens of named *ratu* groups historically resident within Lautem, the names often recurring in different localities. It is at the level of the patrifilial *ratu* that forms of communal or common property ownership to clearly defined blocks of arable land are asserted and organised. Evidently the evolution of these patterns of customary land tenure are the result of complex historical engagements between congeries of *ratu* defined variously as allies and enemies, and their mutual interaction with external, colonising powers. At the present time borders between *ratu* lands remain clearly demarcated, although not recognised officially by government. Nevertheless, across Lautem, there is apparently no land to which authoritative customary claims of tenure do not apply.

The name '*ratu*' for the key social institution of Fataluku society is an example of the thoroughgoing Austronesian influences on the cultural patterning of social practice and formation. The term means 'ruler' or 'lordly', and its cognates, *datu*, *dato* and *datuk*, are familiar status terms in Austronesian-speaking contexts. Membership of a *ratu* group in Lautem consists of a core of male kinsmen, their in-married spouses, and children from these marriages. Although in the past it is likely that individual *ratu* formed close-knit, largely co-residential and localised groupings, over time membership has dispersed across Lautem and regions beyond. Nevertheless, the unity of the *ratu*, its shared and emplaced ancestral origins, spiritual and ritual obligations, and the areas of land to which it lays claim, represent a key set of values reproduced over time. Social and personal identities of individuals are intimately connected and reproduced through the discursive frames of *ratu* ritual practices and relation. These markers of affiliation are expressed in a variety of ways; from the use of certain inherited indigenous names, [12] ritual knowledge and practice, [13] to *ratu*-specific textile designs, and inherited animal ownership brands and food proscriptions. Normative social relationships are formulated around continuing and complex systems of exchange and marriage alliance between the exogamous *ratu* affiliations.

Within this broad pattern of social organisation, Fataluku distinguish a series of clearly defined class or caste-like divisions which have been reproduced over many generations. [14] *Ratu* identity is accorded the senior, classificatory 'elder sibling' status (*kaka*) and appears to include a majority of the population. A junior and socially subordinate grouping, referred to as *paca*, is accorded a 'younger sibling' status (*noko*). *Paca* groups form an integral part of the wider *ratu* social collectivity, their status linked to social differentiation in the mythic past. A third group of people are known as *akanu* and are defined as descendants of former slaves and war captives. *Akanu* are aligned notionally with different *ratu* groups but their ascribed social status is weak and their rights limited and constrained. By definition, they are severed from their origins and therefore maintain no direct connection with their ancestral land. Intermarriage between the social levels was uncommon traditionally and, although the divisions carry less weight in contemporary politics and society than before, tensions between the social levels are still evident especially in relation to contracting marriage.[15] For the purposes of this discussion, however, it is sufficient to know that all land is traditionally vested in the *ratu*, and there are no higher order structures of customary landownership. Within the *ratu* jurisdiction, rights to parcels of land follow the segmentary houses of classificatory siblings, with overall authority in land matters vested in the senior male agnates of the *ratu*.

The historical division of Fataluku lands and the development of common property regimes over specific areas are constituted in and through ancestral histories and itineraries. Careful and privileged preservation of narratives of origin (*nololo, sau*) are combined with continuing practices of sacrificial communication with ancestor spirits that link individual members of the *ratu* with sites of ancestral origin. Although there appears to be wide variation in the specificities of cultural and ritual practice between different Fataluku *ratu* groups, a number of common sites for sacrificial communication and commensality can be discerned. All are designated as sacred or taboo (*tei*) and for that reason must be approached with caution and respect.

Four principal categories of 'sacred places' (*lata teino*) are recognised. They comprise a network of interlinked sites for members of the agnatic kin group. Every *ratu* group recognises a *calu ia mari* ('ancestor footfall/footprint') site, located at different points along the coast, which represents the mythic landing place of the original ancestor/s of the group. Customarily, *ia mari* sites are marked by an altar post (*sarapua*) erected on a base of flat stones in the characteristic and iconic image of sacrificial sites in Timor and elsewhere in the eastern Indonesian Archipelago. [16]

A second focal site of sacrifice is referred to as *ete uru ha'a* (heartwood). These places are marked conventionally by two carved figurines of a man and a woman. They represent the first ancestral couple and often, simultaneously, the site of the first settlement of the group. [17] They are said to guard the path of ancestors and are placed facing the direction of their origins.

Complementing the sites of ancestral arrival and origin are a variety of massive stone graves (*calu lutur tei*) that contain ancestral remains. Typically these are situated within the former walled settlement sites (*lata paru*) that are found in large numbers throughout the region. [18] Often located in strategic defensive positions on hilltops and cliffs, *lata paru* and their ancestral graves represent important sites for worship and sacrifice by members of a *ratu* experiencing difficulties and seeking guidance or relief from severe chronic illness, barren marriages and other challenges.

The fourth main component of this complex of cultural belief and practice is house altars and sacrificial shrines (*aca kaka*) [19] that are maintained to provide protection and spiritual assistance for constituent households of the *ratu*. Each shrine contains a stone hearth (*aca pata*) and a small forked post (*sikua*—from the sikua tree [*Bridelia ovata*]), [20] which serves to mediate communication with the ancestors. Ideally, married male members of the *ratu* maintain a separate *aca kaka* in their newly created households. These days, however, it is more typical for *ratu* house segments to utilise one central shrine that serves as the focus for extended household rituals. Sacrificial household rituals are directed to lineage ancestors. [21] They are conducted for all manner of life-cycle transitions and as a source of spiritual protection for the health and wellbeing of its members. [22] Rituals typically involve the sacrifice of domestic animals, 'feeding' (*fané*) the ancestors with offerings of offal and rice, and the shared consumption of the 'sacred meat' (*leura tei*) among male kinsmen within a *ratu* segment. [23] The use of auguries (*ari toto*) and divination (*lonia, mu'ufuka totole*) to determine the efficacy and messages conveyed through rituals are also common features of Fataluku sacrifice and collective knowledge.

Despite the high levels of avowed Catholicism and the depredations of Indonesian rule of Lautem for many years, indigenous religious belief and ritual practice remains fundamentally important in Fataluku social life. Close attention to ancestral obligations and fear of the consequences of their neglect condition the rhythm of social life and link domestic rituals with the sacred landscape of ancestral origins across the region.

Forests, Settlements and Dislocation

The historical vesting of ownership in land by a particular *ratu* group is denoted by the title *mua ho cawaru*, which may be translated as 'lord of the land'. In more formal language, the parallel phrase is: *Mua cao vele ocawa :: horo cao vele ocawa* (land head skin lord :: gravel head skin lord). [24] This phrase speaks to the Fataluku idea of a conceptual distinction between the 'body' of the earth and its 'skin' (*vele*), which is cultivated for staple food crops. The title of 'lord of the land', held by a particular *ratu* group in relation to a defined area of land, is one that confirms and honours their status as founder settlers. Their claims to precedence of origin provide the cultural basis for asserting ownership over tracts of land within their ancestrally defined jurisdiction. Their status is also maintained through their ritual custodianship of spirit forces and entities associated with particular territories (part of the pre-existing *tei* sphere).

Ideally, the communally inherited land of the *ratu* may not be sold or alienated. It forms part of the 'sacred land and sacred garden' of the group (*mua tei ho pala tei*). [25] However, marriage and long-term alliance relationships between *ratu* groups moderate this perspective. Alliance allows for complex sharing arrangements concerning forested swidden garden land that may be sustained over many generations. Fataluku designate marriage alliance relationships with the terms *arahopata* and *tupurrmoko*. These metaphors encode a cultural and status asymmetry between affines. The *arahopata*, the 'base and post', represent the symbolically 'male' wife-givers and are contrasted with their symbolically 'female' wife-takers, or *tupurrmoko* or 'little women'. Under Indonesian rule, when many populations were relocated and restricted to cultivating defined areas, practices of temporary use rights to *ratu* land also developed. These people as newcomers are said to be 'passengers' (*micani horune*) on the land of resident *ratu*, with limited rights of cultivation for seasonal food crops but without claims to ownership or inheritance.

Preliminary explorations of the forested zone with local claimants to traditional land have revealed something of the scope and character of continuing traditional tenures within the proposed national park. I present them here as two case studies. To my knowledge, there has never been any sustained attempt to map *ratu* clan land boundaries in Lautem. Their status was formally ignored within state-based administrative regimes of the Indonesian Government and the Portuguese before them. [26] As a result, traditional titles to land reside for the most part in the minds and narrative memories of *ratu* elders, but they are no less significant or important to the integrity and reputation of the *ratu* for this.

The first case study is based on several days' walking in the dense undulating forest around the western foothills of the Paichao Range. The second explores something of the indigenous attachment to land in the Vero River Valley, which lies to the south of the settlement area of Tutuala and drains into the sea to the east of the Paichao Range (see Map 1). The studies illustrate both the reality of population displacement from these areas and the continuing reproduction of symbolic and practical attachment to ancestral country.

Map 1: Lautem showing approximate location of the conservation zone

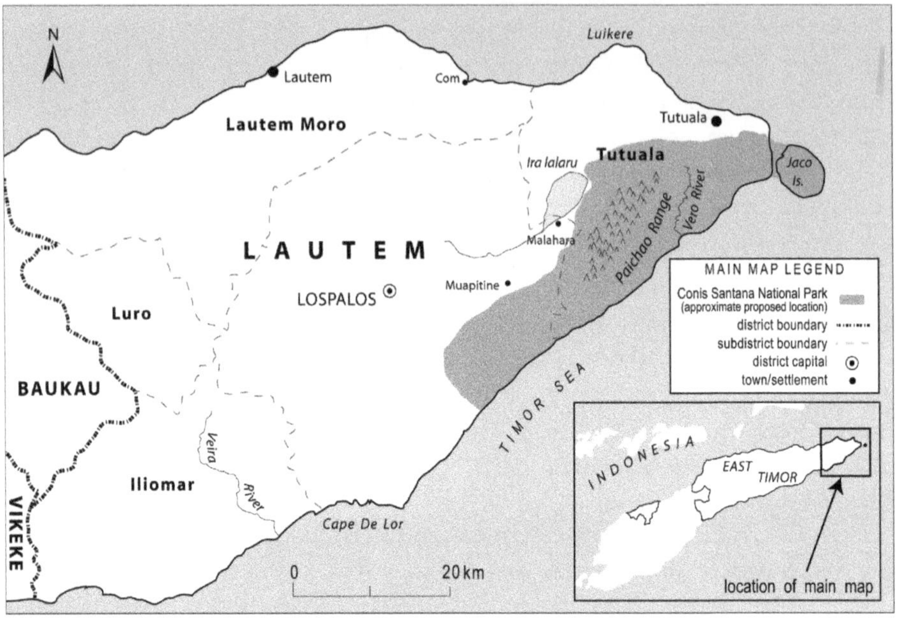

Perspectives from the Paichao Range

Contemporary members of the patrifilial Paichao *ratu* group currently reside in the hamlet (*aldeia*) of Malahara, located on the southern shores of the shallow lake, Ira Lalaru. The forested mountains of the Paichao Range border to the south and extend east in a series of forested peaks. The residents of Malahara cultivate the adjacent hillsides with seasonal maize, cassava and secondary food crops. Malahara comprises one of the constituent communities of the village (*suco*) of Muapitine.

Formerly, the Paichao *ratu* community lived in and around their historical forest settlement, Veteru (*lata paru*), some 6km to the south towards the coast. Historically, Veteru formed a distinct administrative hamlet in the village of Muapitine. After the Indonesian occupation of East Timor in 1975, the community of 36 households fled and dispersed, with a small group eventually being resettled in Malahara on land owned by Ponu Ratu.[27] They still live in the settlement but their numbers have dwindled to six households. Nevertheless, they still hope to return home to cultivate their own land if their numbers increase, as their present circumstances preclude inheritance of land cultivated by permission from Ponu Ratu.

I was invited to join a senior member of the *ratu* and his nephew in visiting ancestral origin sites of Paichao *ratu*, prompted by their concerns over the proposed establishment of the national park and the uncertainty of future tenure arrangements. With sufficient food and camping supplies, our party of three plus hunting dog left Malahara and followed a track into the nearby forest, passing through a complex of fallowed swidden fields and secure timber garden fences. Entering the forest proper, my guide, Umberto Rakupua, left the path and picked out his own track through the dank undergrowth littered with coralline rubble, negotiating the dense undulating forest terrain with consummate and barefooted ease. Walking under closed canopy forest, my companions pointed out a diverse range of tree species and vines, along with their various practical uses for building, consumption and medicinal purposes. We passed through extensive areas of lowland forest with networks of remnant limestone garden walls and sites of former habitation. As distinctive cultural markers, these intersecting walls provided objective historical evidence of former occupation and land claims; all associated with former members of the Paichao *ratu* community, according to my guides.

By the late afternoon, in light rain, we reached the first of three historical settlement sites (*lata paru*) located at high points in the forest and characterised by distinctive and substantial stone-walled fortifications with strategically guarded entrance ways. Although long abandoned as a settlement site, possibly for more than 100 years, the social history of the *lata paru* of Pariloho *ratu* (or one version of it) was quite familiar to my guides. According to this view, Pariloho *ratu* had been granted permission from the original landowner, Paichao *ratu*, to settle temporarily in the area. Over time, relations had soured between the two groups and Pariloho *ratu* was pushed out and forced to seek a new settlement site outside the region. Although a number of old graves remain untended in the defensive walled complex, members of the Pariloho *ratu* are not known to return for ceremonial activities, and the Paichao *ratu* group has reasserted its ownership over the area.

As night fell, we camped in a spacious limestone rock shelter on the eastern face of the old settlement, a site used by former Falantil and Indonesian Army troops alike. The next morning we walked for another three hours through the forest to the principal origin site for Paichao *ratu*. Further numerous useful tree and plant species were identified, [28] including a massive *Pua ara* forest tree, which for generations has housed 'honey-bee hives' (*wani le*: lit. 'bee house') with their white wax head (*ucu pacu*) structures hanging off the upper branches.[29] Beeswax was formerly a lucrative commodity sold by the kilo and recognised as *ratu* property. [30]

By midday, we arrived at the massive elongated limestone outcrop of Veteru, heavily overgrown with large fig trees (*hama*) and tangled vines, and barricaded with metre-wide limestone walls. Culturally, Veteru is understood to be a fossilised seagoing stone boat (*loiasu matar*), which carried the Paichao *ratu* ancestors to Timor and lodged in the foothills of the Paichao Range. It is oriented on an east-west axis, with the head (*cao*) of the boat to the east and the tail (*irik*) to the west. The centrepiece of the *lata paru* complex is a large double stone grave believed to be that of the first Paichao *ratu* ancestor and his wife (a woman from Tutuala). Cleaned of invading vegetation, the grave is oriented with its headstone to the east towards the mountain of Paichao (*Paichao ili*). It forms the key sacrificial site for the group in times of illness and misfortune.

At the time of the Indonesian Army invasion of East Timor in 1975, the Paichao *ratu* and their resident affines (*vaianu*) lived in scattered households around the base of Veteru, then classed as an administrative *povoção* (hamlet) by the Portuguese Colonial Government. Remnant areca and coconut palms still grow scattered among the rubble of abandoned swidden garden walls, but otherwise secondary forest regrowth has obliterated most evidence of prior settlement.

From this vantage point, the forest land of Paichao *ratu* extends in all directions. To the west is the River Karo'o, the boundary with Reme Latu Loho *ratu*, whose contemporary members now live in the main settlement of Muapitine near Malahara. [31] To the east is the boundary known as Vekase Vero'o, the border of Tutuala lands and the senior patrifilial owner, Renu Ratu (see following case study). Formerly, on Mt Paichao itself were the traditional lands of another group, Huamai *ratu*. Their members are said to have all died out and their lands remain unclaimed to the present.

Little more than 500 metres to the west of Veteru on a ridge overlooking a steep slope to the forested stone country of the coastal lowlands lies another abandoned *lata paru*. Known by the placename Lamira, the old fort was formerly occupied by an allied group known as Kanaluri *paca*. According to oral tradition, this group fell into enmity with their western neighbours, Reme Latu Loho *ratu*, from the *lata paru* Voviara. In the murderous hostilities that ensued, Paichao *ratu* went to the aid of Kanaluri Paca, but lost two of its members in the fighting. The survivors of the settlement, unable to pay the compensation demanded for the deaths of their allies, agreed to abandon their site and gift their lands to Paichao *ratu* as payment. They subsequently sought refuge with Serelau *ratu* on lands near Lake Ira Lalaru where their descendants live today.

From the crumbling ruins of Lamia, our party continued west and then north on a circuitous return route to Malahara. At a certain point, we joined a major footpath that links Malahara to the beach, *Vaiara*, on the southern coast. This site provides the location for the annual gathering of sea-worms (*meci*; *Eunice virides*), which assemble in massive numbers in late February and early March. All households from Malahara reportedly make the trek to the beach on the appointed full moon for this ceremonial harvest of the sea's bounty (see McWilliam 2003).

Perspectives from the Vero River Valley

The upper reaches of the Vero River lie close to the contemporary settlement area of Tutuala. The single constituent village (*suco*) of Pitilete comprises four hamlets (*aldeia*), namely Pitilete, Cailoro, Iyoro and Vero. Extensive areas of dry monsoon forest and fallow swidden gardens surround the settlements, which are located about 400m above the coast with commanding views over the surrounding seas. For the most part, the location of current settlements is an artefact of recent colonial history reflecting, in particular, the dictates of the Indonesian Government and its policy of containing Fataluku populations in closely supervised proximity. This included former residents of the Vero Valley, who were forced to relinquish their swidden fields and tree crops in the lowland forests in favour of concentrated settlements adjacent to the sealed road. Here, their movements were restricted and monitored closely by local government staff and military commanders.

The small hamlet of Vero is a case in point. Staunch supporters of the resistance struggle and the Falantil guerillas who continued a cat and mouse insurgency in the surrounding forests for more than 20 years, most of the households of the hamlet had little opportunity to maintain their swidden gardens on ancestral lands. [32] During this period they gained access and cultivation rights to nearby garden lands from allied local *ratu* groups, usually strengthened through marriage alliances and the lifelong reciprocal obligations that characterise these relationships. With the achievement of independence, however, residents of Vero are once again considering the possibility of returning to their ancestral country and re-establishing their attachments to the area. [33] While not opposed to the idea of a national park that would incorporate their lands within a conservation zone, many have expressed concern over the future of their inherited rights or resource use and ownership under a new management regime.

My visit to the valley and subsequent insights into its cultural landscape was facilitated by the political leader of Vero hamlet and a patrifilial member of Serelau *ratu* that maintains entitlements in the Aleara Lafae area of the Vero River Valley. A kilometre or so from the main Vero settlement, Mario dos Santos Loyola cultivates a block of dry-land swidden maize garden with members of his extended family. [34] The southern garden fence marks the contemporary edge of cultivated land and it was from here that we entered the forest proper and joined the well-trodden path that leads down through the hills to the coast. At this point the mouth of the Vero River lies some six kilometres to the south-east, with the dense coastal forest rising into the Paichao mountain range extending into the western distance.

Though evidently drier than the forests of the western Paichao Range, the path descends through dense-canopy forest, broken occasionally with patches of open grassy knolls and fields. In the upper reaches, evidence of former cultivation is less apparent and lends credence to Mario's claim that there remain extensive areas of old growth-forest. [35] Along the way, he pointed out numerous plant species used for traditional medicine and remedies that people continue to rely on in the absence of alternatives. Like many of his kinsmen, Mario has spent periods of time living in the forests and has a keen eye for edible plants, fruits and leaves. One specimen he described as 'presidential food', the leaves of which, eaten raw with fresh coconut, were a preferred forest food of former guerilla leader Xanana Gusmao, during his days secreted in the area.

Although the specifics of Fataluku land and forest tenures to the Vero River Valley require further research and articulation, a general consensus of the broad outline is readily accepted. In this view, the mythic original immigrant settlers of the area arrived in seagoing boats (*loiasu*) at the mouth of the river. At this location is an *ia mari tuliya* (ancestral footprint) commemorative site known as *Telu'o*. [36] Collective sacrificial ceremonies are regularly undertaken at this location, which also still forms the focus for the annual sea-worm (*meci*) gathering festivals among contemporary descendants affiliated with the site.

The origin ancestors to the area are referred to as two named pairs of *ratu*: Renu/Paiuru and Marapaki/Keveresi. Mythically, they are distinguished from the time of their ancestral maritime arrivals. After a period of intense feuding, they are said to have divided the land along a common border following the Vero River inland. Over time, other immigrant boats arrived and sought rights of settlement from these founder groups. The subsequent history of the Vero Valley, including its population dynamics, the impact of warfare and marriage alliance has seen the land become consolidated under the authority of a range of *ratu* groups with defined boundaries and claims, all lying within the historical administrative jurisdiction of Suco Pitilete.

West of the Vero River and extending to the border (*Vekase Vero, Ili Mimiraka*) [37] with Paichao *ratu* mentioned earlier, all groups agree that Renu *ratu* is the senior authority. [38] Renu *ratu* is referred to as the *nalu lafae*, the 'great mother', by virtue of the continuing marriage of its daughters to in-marrying settler *ratu* groups (*tupurrmoko*). This accords them a 'progenitor' status for subsidiary groups that maintain received and nested rights to land in this process. In other words, Renu *ratu* maintains the status of a wife- and life-giving group (*arahopata*: 'base and post') in relation to their subsidiary allies (*tupurrmoko*). These allies include members of Paiuru *ratu*, Pae Lopo *ratu*, Aca Cao *ratu*, Pai *ratu*, Tana *ratu* and Serelau *ratu* among others, all of whom were allocated settlement rights in the forested hinterland of the western Vero River Valley and maintain connections to former settlements and grave sites in the area.[39]

In the present day, these ancestrally constituted relationships are recalled and reproduced in continuing alliance relationships between descendants of the founding ancestors. Although long displaced from the forested Vero Valley, members of these *ratu* maintain a vital link to their origins in the narrative histories and emplaced mythologies of settlement, made manifest in the sacred geography of the land. The former fort (*pamakolo*) and barricaded settlement (a *lata paru* named Haka Paku Leki) of Renu *ratu*, situated midway between the sea and the upper reaches of the Paichao Range, is a case in point. Along with the ritual landing site of *Telu'o*, the former settlement with its ancestral graves provides a key site for the sacrificial enactment of attachment by members of the Renu *ratu* group. Allied *ratu* maintain their own sacrificial and culturally significant sites in the area. They include the identification of the mythic 'fossilised' boats of immigrant ancestors across the valley, numerous abandoned walled settlement sites (*lata paru*) and aged cultivars such as coconut and lontar palms, which mark earlier swidden gardens. Upstream from the mouth of the Vero River is the 'stone boat' of Marapaki, standing in an area of grassy flats and covered with a tangle of vegetation. Nearby, I was shown the imprint of the 'boat' of Serelao *ratu*, a shallow elongated dry waterhole, marked by a sacrificial post (*ete uruha'a*) where the ancestral boat was said to have rested before moving higher up to its current position at Alaera Lafae. The subsequent move was prompted, reportedly, because of its overly close proximity to the 'boat' of Marapaki. Nevertheless, the site remains a defined location for ritual sacrifice and prayer among members of the *ratu* owning group. Like its mythic counterparts emplaced across the cultural landscape of the lower Vero, the imprint of the ancestors attests to the continuing cultural connections that contemporary Fataluku people maintain with this area, lying deep within the proposed boundaries of the national park.

For all the intense connections to the lower Vero, however, the forested landscape remains 'unsettled' and generally uncultivated, a condition thatappears to have existed for about 50 years since the end of Japanese wartime occupation in 1945 and the reinstatement of Portuguese colonial rule in East Timor. According to local memories, this period saw the displacement, relocation and concentration of Vero Valley farming communities north to the main settlement area of Tututala. Before 1945, the population of the Vero community in the forest is said to have numbered more than 150 households dispersed along the coastal hinterland, and was seeking to be recognised as an autonomous village (*suco*) in its own right. The depredations of World War II, and the postwar history of East Timor, meant that the population of Vero community suffered demographic decline and still remains less than one-third of its earlier size.

Despite this displacement of the former settled population, the proximity of contemporary settlements in Tututala means that there remains a continuing and comparatively intensive utilisation of resources. Timber and rattan vines, as well as medicinal trees and plants are gathered, and hunting for a wide range of species is undertaken regularly. The use of spears (*choro*), hunting dogs (*iparu*), traps and blow-pipes (*tutufa*) represent the main hunting implements. Favoured forest species include monkeys (*lua*), deer (*vaca*), marsupial cuscus (*acuru, lo*), feral pigs (*pai hoto*) and bats (*maca*), along with a range of bird species (*olo*), freshwater fish (*api*), prawns, lizards and snakes. All provide a rich and varied supplement to rural diets. In the lower Vero River Valley, I was introduced to my guide's father's younger brother (kin term: *Palu noko*). At the time, he and his wife were busy curing fleshy strips of a large sea turtle (*ipitu*), which he had caught on the beach and was intending to take back to the settlement for consumption and sale. [40]

The importance of forest fauna is also highlighted in ceremonial practices associated with the dry-season cultivation of maize gardens and associated food crops, the so-called *temuru pala* ('eastern gardens'; cultivated from June to early September). As part of the ritual management of cropping and the successful gathering of an abundant yield, maize harvest rituals (*cele sakawahine, cele masule* and *cele sipile*) are accompanied by the hunting and shared consumption of 'forest meat' along with quantities of locally produced sugar-palm wine (*tua piti*) and spirits (*tua haraki*). The collective nature of harvesting with participating family groups means that a significant 'harvesting' of local forest species occurs at this time and undoubtedly contributes substantially to rural diets as well as periodic pressures on forest fauna.

For the resident populations of Tututala with ancestral links and attachments to the Vero and Paichao Ranges, the forest and its resources represent a region of abiding socioeconomic value. Simultaneously, an 'archive of past habitation and sociality' (Fairhead and Leach 1996: 113) and 'landscape of memory' (Hviding and Bayliss-Smith 2000), the forests also form a complex ecological arena for practical resource exploitation and a rich store of arable land, which may yet be brought back into production in the future. Although its potential value as a conservation area of national importance and the location for eco-tourism or bio-research might be appreciated and understood, it is by no means obvious to local Fataluku that these prospects will prove to be consistent with local interests and inherited rights.

On Fataluku Customary Tenures and Forest Management

The proposal to develop a national conservation park in East Timor, the first in the context of national independence, has created the requirement for a better understanding of customary Fataluku land tenures within the forest reserve. This paper has highlighted something of the emplaced significance of Fataluku customary attachments to the area and the structure of social relationships within which land tenures are embedded. Further research and cultural mapping will undoubtedly provide a more detailed perspective on the complex networks of engagement with the forested landscape. [41] Arguably, such studies are critical to the development of strategic approaches to effective park management and a more informed basis for negotiating management agreements. Nevertheless, these preliminary observations are perhaps sufficient to indicate something of the character of Fataluku attachments to ancestral lands; attachments that appear to have much in common with neighbouring ethno-linguistic groups in the wider region. These attachments also highlight something of the complexity of and challenges for incorporating customary tenure regimes within national land administration structures.

The comparative ethnography of eastern Indonesia, and particularly the Lesser Sunda Islands of which East Timor is a constituent part, has focused on the predominantly Austronesian-speaking language communities of the region. Many of these studies have highlighted a range of common cultural features and conceptions about locality and landscape that are thought to reflect aspects of a shared Austronesian heritage (see Fox 1997; Fox and Sather 1996; Bellwood, Fox and Tryon 1995; Atkinson and Errington 1990). These shared characteristics are varied and numerous but may be thought to minimally include the following aspects. Firstly, there is an attention to the valorising of space through symbolic coordinates. Two axis systems are prominent in eastern Indonesia, whereby the primary orientation follows the east-west axis with a secondary orientation utilising an upstream-downstream, or right-left axis. Secondly, there is a common indigenous focus on 'discourses of origin' and the relative precedence of origins as a basis for structuring social relations. This orientation to the past is expressed frequently through the reproduction of narrative topogenies (discourses of place) for the encoding of social memory in cultural landscapes. [42] All these societies have also been demonstrated to share an abiding interest in the representation of relationships and processes by paired metaphors of complementarity and difference. Social meanings are constructed culturally through such 'symbolic operators' as trunk and tip, male and female, elder and younger, right and left, hot and cold. Typically, too, these culturally significant asymmetric categories are applied recursively and thus generate orders of difference or precedence within social contexts. These combinations of elements, applied creatively, have been shown to be highly illustrative of the dynamic and often contested relationships characteristic of eastern Indonesian and wider Austronesian societies (see Fox and Sather 1996; Vischer forthcoming).

Although clearly of non-Austronesian linguistic origins, the schematic outline of Fataluku land and forest tenures presented in this paper appears to share many of these characteristics of Austronesian ideas of place and landscape. The principal coordinate of orientation among Fataluku is ordered along the east-west axis. Typically this is expressed as an associated distinction between head and tail: *mua cao, mua ulafuka* 'head of the land, tail of the land'. A second-order orientation is marked in relation to the seas to the north and south. The terms *tahi tupurru—tahi calu* ('female' sea—'male' sea) represent a composite linguistic construction of Austronesian and Papuan terms. [43] We can also identify a strong and continuing focus on ancestral origins and the complex locating of mythic narratives and ancestral itineraries within the Fataluku landscape. Moreover, there is evidently a persistent emphasis on such classificatory binary categories as male/\female (*nami tupurru*), younger/elder (*noko kaka*), small/large (*moko lafae*) among numerous other key organising distinctions. The systematic use of ritual speech couplets is also marked, as in the phrases *hitu ho coro* (sword and spear), *ete ho taru* (tree and vine), *ira ho oco* (water and tree crops), *iniku ho poku* (fine-grained sand and course sand), among others. Seen in these terms, Fataluku society shares much in common with its Austronesian speaking neighbours, both in terms of cultural principles of social order and relation, as well as in the forms of attachment they reproduce in relation to their ancestral lands. As a non-Austronesian-speaking language community with clear evidence that they have borrowed extensively from Austronesian registers and concepts over many generations, their example highlights the limitations of the linguistic distinction—Austronesian/non-Austronesian—to define the scope of cultural comparison in the region. This is not to deny the utility of what may be termed 'Austronesian cultural characteristics'. Rather, as the example of Fataluku and other proximate non-Austronesian-language communities indicates, significant cultural overlap and hybridity offer the prospect for extending comparative analysis beyond the linguistic boundary (see also Platenkamp 1984 and 1988). Recent studies arguing for thematic comparison across this language boundary offer directions for future research (Strathern and Stewart 2000).

While these academic questions are unlikely to trouble policy-makers in East Timor, the more practical issues of integrating Fataluku common property regimes within a park management regime are of central concern. To its credit, the Government appears to have recognised the strong and continuing attachment to and dependency on the diverse resources of the proposed park of local Fataluku communities. Under the present government structure of Timor Leste, the Ministry of Agriculture, Forestry and Fisheries (*Ministerio de Agricultura, Floresta e Pesca*) has, to date, taken the formal responsibility for park management. An indication of their intentions can be seen in a 2002 draft 'letter of agreement', which seeks to establish a mutually agreed framework for management between the Government and local communities bordering the forest boundaries. Under this agreement, the park will be accorded a 'Category 5' status, following the guidelines of the International Union for Conservation of Nature and Natural Resources (IUCN), which establishes the region as a multi-use landscape permitting a range of extractive activities within its boundaries. These activities include limited cultivation of fallowed former swidden fields along the park boundary as a temporary concession recognising the impoverished economic circumstances of farmers in the region. Hunting and gathering is to be confined to two months a year with restrictions covering protection of habitat and types of animals available for consumption. Some limited extraction of trees for construction purposes is allowed subject to an agreed permit system. To monitor and coordinate these arrangements, the agreement also envisages the creation of a management commission combining Government and community representatives to promulgate a regulatory framework. Perhaps most significantly, the government offers the possibility of recognising the existence of customary rights in land (*tanah adat*) as well as sites of cultural importance (*tei, lata paru* and *calu lutur teino*) within the park (Surat Kesepakatan 2002, Direccão Geral de Floresta [draft, Bahasa Indonesia version]).

The draft document requires the signatures of the leadership of the three Fataluku villages (*suco*) bordering the park. [44] Taken at face value, this agreement represents a realistic understanding of the continuing significance of customary claims and this practical use made of the forest. It also concedes the reality that without active local engagement in the management of the national park, the Directorate of Forestry on its own is ill-equipped to undertake the multiple tasks of managing the region. However, by way of proviso, it is worth noting that the 'letter of agreement' remains in draft form (as of December 2002) and subject to parliamentary and ministerial approval. Until formal ratification of the document and its legal intent is established, the status of the proposed park and the respective rights of individuals, *ratu* groups and the National Government remains uncertain. The question of the future legal status of customary land (BI: *tanah adat*) is particularly unclear given that this form of tenure is not recognised explicitly under the East Timorese Constitution, nor has there been any administrative agreement governing the question of customarily claimed land (see Fitzpatrick 2002).

The prospect of recognising a range of customary attachments and interests within the park boundaries is one that needs to be translated into a workable division of respective rights and responsibilities; one that acknowledges the importance of history in policy practice. In the development of a formal regulatory arrangement there would appear to be at least two prospective avenues for government action. Firstly, and perhaps most likely, the National Government will legislate to assume direct ownership of the park and the primary responsibility for management. Arguably, this is consistent with the recently adopted Constitution, which allocates sovereignty over natural resources to the State. Local communities might be encouraged to participate in management, and specific places of heritage significance within the park such as *lata paru* and ritual sites (*calu lutur, ia mari, ete uru ha'a*) could be protected under law. [45] The main difficulty with this approach is the constrained financial capacity of the Government to develop its own effective system of management with all the monitoring and protection services it requires. Moreover, the assumption of full government control may give rise to feelings of disenfranchisement among customary rights-holders who will have little interest or legal recourse to maintain the forest as a forest. Economic opportunism and increased exploitation are the likely consequences, if the experience of regional autonomy in Indonesia is any guide (see Potter and Badcock 2001).

An alternative or compromise approach is one that recognises and legally supports the tenurial rights of the customary common property-holders, and accords them a form of collective customary ownership of their ancestral lands within the park, under a broad framework of government supervision. While not without its own set of challenges, many of which could be resolved through greater research and public consultation, the existing Fataluku customary tenure arrangements and understandings within the park arguably represent the only consistent and historically legitimate forms of claim over the forested domain. Recognition of common property rights to the forest, as McKean (2000: 42) and others have argued, gives owners the incentive to husband their resources, to make investments in resource quality and to manage them sustainably and efficiently. Moreover, if legal recognition of Fataluku forest tenures was offered on the basis that the park would then be leased back to the nation for the purposes of managed conservation, the basis for a mutual framework of shared interests could be established. Such an approach offers the possibility of building an effective system of joint or co-management that combines the intimate local knowledge and ancestrally sanctioned attachment of local communities with the authority, technologies and financial assistance of external agencies. It is also one that permits a much stronger role for customary rights-holders in decision-making than if principal control and decision-making resides in the central corridors of national government.

The decision about the locus and distribution of legal rights and responsibilities in relation to the park is likely to emerge in the near future, and it represents a necessary condition for developing an effective management regime, but not a sufficient one. As much of the literature on common property rights and community-based management attests, legal recognition represents only one important aspect in promoting sustainable practices (Ostrom 1990; Gibson et al. 2000). Associated complex issues such as boundary definition, membership status and effective local institutions that have enforceable rules and appropriate dispute-resolution mechanisms are just some of the features that contribute to successful co-management arrangements involving common property regimes (McKean 2000; Kant and Cooke 1999). These and other matters will no doubt form the subject of negotiation and contested development over time. In the interim, this paper has simply sought to highlight something of the scope and strength of attachment among specific local Fataluku communities to a region of enduring and wider public interest.

References

Atkinson, Jane M. and Shelly Errington (eds). 1990. *Power and Difference: Gender in island southeast Asia*. Stanford: Stanford University Press.

Bellwood, P., J.J. Fox and D. Tryon. 1995. 'The Austronesians in History: Common origins and diverse transformations.' In Peter Bellwood, James J. Fox and Darrell Tryon, *The Austronesians: Historical and Comparative Perspectives*, Canberra: Department of Anthropology, Comparative Austronesian Studies Project, Research School of Pacific and Asian Studies, The Australian National University. pp. 1-16.

Fairhead, James and Melissa Leach. 1996. *Misreading the African Landscape: Society and ecology in a forest savannah mosaic*. Cambridge/New York: Cambridge University Press.

Fitzpatrick, Daniel. 2002. *Land Claims in East Timor*. Canberra: Asia Pacific Press.

Fox, James J. (ed.) 1997. *The Poetic Power of Place: Comparative perspectives on Austronesian ideas of locality*. Canberra: Research School of Pacific and Asian Studies, The Australian National University.

Fox, James J. and Clifford Sather. 1996. *Origins, Ancestry and Alliance: Explorations in Austronesian Ethnography*. Canberra: Research School of Pacific and Asian Studies, The Australian National University.

Gibson, Clark C., Margaret A. McKean and Elinor Ostrom. 2000. *People and Forests: Communities, Institutions and Governance*. Cambridge (Mass.) MIT Press.

Gomes, Francisco de Azevedo. 1972. *Os Fataluku*. Lisboa: Instituto Superior de Ciencias Socias e Politica Ultramarina, Universidade Tecnica de Lisboa.

Lameiras-Campagnolo, Maria O. 1972. 'Deux enquêtes à Timor Protugais chez les Fataluku de Lórehe.' *Asie du sud-est et monde insulienden*, 3 (3). pp. 35-52.

Lameiras-Campagnolo, Maria O. 1975. 'L'habitation des Fatuluku de Lórehe (Timor Portugais).' Paris: Thèse de doctorat de 3ème cycle, Université René Descartes, Sorbonne, Paris.

Hull, Geoffrey. 1998. 'The Basic Lexical Affinities of Timor's Austronesian Languages: A Preliminary Investigation.' In Geoffrey Hull and Lance Eccles (eds), *Studies in Languages and Cultures of East Timor*, Vol. 1, Macarthur (Aust.): Language Acquisition Research Centre, University of Western Sydney. pp. 97-198.

Hviding, Edvard and Tim Bayliss-Smith. 2000. *Islands of Rainforest: Agro-forestry, logging and eco-tourism in Solomon Islands.* Aldershot, Burlington, Sydney: Ashgate Publishing.

Kant, Shashi and Roshan Cooke. 1999. 'Jabalapur District, Madhya Pradesh, India: Minimizing conflict in joint forest management.' In Daniel Buckles (ed.), *Cultivating Peace: Conflict and Collaboration in Natural Resource Management*, Ottawa and Washington DC: International Development Research Centre and the World Bank Institute. pp. 81-97.

Kantor Statistik 1993. *Timor Timur Dalam Angka (East Timor in Figures).* Government of the Province of East Timor.

McKean, Margaret A. 2000. 'Common Property: What Is It, What It Is and, What Makes It Work.' In C. Clark, M. Gibson, A. McKean and E. Ostrom (eds), *People and Forests: Communities, Institutions and Governance*, Cambridge (Mass.): MIT Press.

McWilliam, Andrew. 2003. 'Timorese Seascapes: Perspectives on customary marine tenures in East Timor.' *The Asia Pacific Journal of Anthropology*, 3 (2). pp. 6-32

Ostrom, Elinor. 1990. *Governing the Commons: The Evolution of Institutions for Collective Action.* Cambridge, New York: Cambridge University Press.

Platenkamp, J.D.M. 1984. 'The Tobelo of Eastern Halmahera in the context of the Field of Anthropological Study.' In P.E. de Josselin de Jong (ed.) *Unity in Diversity: Indonesia as a Field of Anthropological Study*, Dordrecht-Holland: Foris Publications.

Platenkamp, J.D.M. 1988. 'Tobelo.' Unpublished PhD thesis Leiden University, Leiden.

Potter, Lesley and Simon Badcock. 2001. *The effects of Indonesia's decentralisation on forests and estate crops in Riau province: Case studies of the original districts of Kampar and Indragiri Hulu.* Bogor (Indonesia): CIFOR, ACIAR, DFID.

Smith, Joyotee and Sara J. Scherr. 2002. *Forest Carbon and Local Livelihoods: Assessment of Opportunities and Policy Recommendations.* Bogor (Indonesia): Centre for International Forestry Research, *Occasional Paper* No. 37.

Strathern, Andrew. and Pamela J. Stewart. 2000. *The Python's Back: Pathways of Comparison Between Indonesia and Melanesia.* Westport (Conn.) Bergin and Garvey.

Whistler, Art. 2000. 'Ecological survey and preliminary botanical inventory of the Tutuala Beach and Jaco Island protected natural areas, East Timor.' *Report to the United Nations Transitional Administration in East Timor.*

Vischer, Michael P. (ed.) Forthcoming. *Precedence: Processes of social differentiation in the Austronesian World*. Canberra: Pandanus Books.

ENDNOTES

[1] This paper was based on research undertaken in East Timor during 2001 and 2002 with funding from the Australian National University. Acknowledgment is extended to Umberto Rakupua, Arsio da Costa, Mario dos Santos Loyola and staff of the Directorate of Forestry in Timor Leste, Almeida Xavier, Mario Nunes and Fernandu Santana, for their assistance and advice.

[2] Exceptions to this general statement include the work of Gomes (1972) and Lameiras-Campagnolo (1972, 1975).

[3] The reputed biodiversity, however, is based on very limited biological or botanical inventories of species mix and composition.

[4] An area of 25,163ha was officially classified under this category of protection (Timor Timur Dalam Angka 1993).

[5] Bio-exploration refers specifically to the possibility for joint-venture exploration of flora and fauna biological resources in terrestrial and marine sites for prospective commercial applications (Maunsey, pers comm., 2002). Carbon-credit trading is a potentially exciting avenue for supporting forest conservation in East Timor following the agreement of the Clean Development Mechanism of the Kyoto Protocol. But it is one that requires further clarification and development to operationalise (see Smith and Scherr 2002).

[6] In the other subdistricts of Iliomar and Luro a range of other languages are used, all non-Austronesian. Macalero is the indigenous language of Iliomar, while in Luro the languages of Macassae and a dialect form known as Sa Ani predominate.

[7] Said by some to be a Portuguese transformation of the Fataluku phrase *los Pala*, meaning, 'fertile garden'.

[8] The other TNGP linguistic communities of note are the Bunak in central Timor and Macassae, the dominant language of Baucau, adjacent to Lautem District.

[9] Hull uses this example to support his hypothesis that the 'first Austronesians of Timor may well have been settlers from coastal New Guinea, and of mixed Austronesian and Papuan stock and culturally, but not linguistically Austronesian, (1998: 165).

[10] The language of Lovaia (Makwa) is currently restricted to a few speakers in the hamlet of Porlamano in Mehara village near Lake Ira Lalaru. Historical sources suggest the language was spoken much more widely in the past and is likely to have predated Fataluku settlement in this part of Timor.

[11] Most of these administrative units were converted to *desa* (villages) under Indonesian rule but have now reverted to the older term under the new National Government.

[12] Many Fataluku names inherited within *ratu* groups use the (Tetum language) qualifier *malae*, meaning 'foreign'. For example, the Opo *ratu* group uses names such as Ke *malae* (f.), Rusu *malae*, Pitino *malae*, Lavanu *malae*, while Loh Ratu has Iniku *malae*, Lelunu *malae* and so on. The use of this very Austronesian qualifier and its reference to external origins is an unusual cultural legacy among this 'indigenous' language community in East Timor. But it is consistent with the pervasive attention to seafaring mythologies of origin and the ancestral settlement of the island.

[13] Different *ratu* are said to possess unique powers and capacities to control natural elements, animals or spirit beings, which practitioners can utilise for protection or retribution (*kesino*, *loconu*).

[14] Caste is defined here as a rigid system of inherited social distinctions.

[15] A further category of people referred to as *acaru* (sorcerers, witches and shape-changers), who are feared for their malevolent activities. Like other social categories, descendants of *acaru* are also believed to take on this status.

[16] Significant variation in this form is, however, common. Other sites use carved timber posts such as banyan (*hama*) and ironwood (*fara*, *sauata*).

[17] These venerated figures were frequently subject to desecration and looting during the period of Indonesian rule, and consequently, many have been moved to locations within or close to present settlements for protection. *Ete-uru ha'a* can also take alternative forms, including carved wooden sacrificial posts.

[18] The remarkable number of these former fortified settlements, particularly in the forested eastern lowlands and hinterland, is suggestive of a possible significant depopulation of the area in historical times.

[19] *Aca* is a semantically rich term in Fataluku with multiple meanings including 'wood', and as a classifier for 'fowl', but here, the term *aca kaka* can be translated as 'elder hearth'. The 'sacred hearth' finds similar expression in the language of Tetum as *ahi matan*, literally, the 'eye of fire', which represents the 'origin hearth' of the affiliated group.

[20] See Campagnolo (1975: 77). Sacrificial posts are also known as *saka*.

[21] Ancestral invocations typically begin by calling on the *calu ho papu* (lit. 'grandfather and great grandfather'). These categories of ancestor represent more the immediate agnatic antecedents of the group; however, Fataluku also recognise two additional levels of male ancestors, *cuci ho macua* ('FFFF and FFFFF'). These terms also apply reciprocally and symmetrically to descending levels of progeny (grandchildren, great-grandchildren and so on). The names of origin ancestors may not be spoken.

[22] The house shrine contains the principal altar post sometimes referred to as *sikua lafai* (the great *sikua*). However, householders may also utilise subsidiary *sikua* protective devices for their crops or livestock. The use of *loho sikua* at buffalo corrals is a case in point. These protective devices fend off the potentially destructive interests of a variety of spirit beings (*ciapu*) and witches (*acaru*) as well as ordinary thieves.

[23] Women and young children of the *ratu* may not eat of the sacrificial meat because of its spiritual heat (*timine*). Younger daughters of the *ratu* are explicitly excluded because of their intended incorporation within their future husband's ritual group.

[24] *Horo* is a reference to the widespread stony coralline surface of land in this part of East Timor.

[25] Also referred to as the 'lord of the lontar and swidden garden' (*tua ocawa, pala ocawa*).

[26] Fernandu Santana of the Government Forestry Directorate has completed a survey of the proposed park boundaries including the number and extent of *ratu* claims within the area, which probably involve less than 10 principal groups.

[27] Like much of the population of Lautem at this time, they fled to the great mountains of Matebian in the neighbouring district of Baucau, and eked out an existence there until 1979 when the survivors surrendered to the Indonesian military and straggled back to Los Palos.

[28] Uses included sturdy timber trees for construction, medicinal trees, edible fungi, fruit and leaves as well as rattan, forest tubers and trees tapped for burnable oils.

[29] I am not able to identify this and many other tree species. However, based on matching survey data from preliminary work in the Vero River Valley to the east, commonly identified species include *apocynacae, sapotacae, ficus, anacadiaceae, Intsia bijuga* (ironwoods), *syzigiums* and *steculiacea*. The western Paichao Range is wetter than corresponding forest further east and consequently reflects a range of tree and plant species that are not identified in existing survey data as of 2003.

[30] Such trees traditionally may form part of the bride-wealth exchanges offered in the conduct of marriage.

[31] The original Muapitine is a forest settlement (*lata paru*) from where contemporary members of the community were relocated by the Indonesian Government. Mass resettlement of Timorese communities was a continuing feature of Indonesian occupation (see Fitzpatrick 2002: 135).

[32] The people of Vero supported the independence struggle despite the torching of their former settlement some distance away by Fretilin in 1978, as part of the campaign to undermine Indonesian claims of military success over the indigenous opposition. Former Falantil leader Konis Santana, from the local *ratu* group Kukulori, was one of many young Fataluku men of Tutuala who depended on the support of communities such as Vero to sustain their armed struggle.

[33] The mooted possibility of reopening a former rain-fed rice area on the Aleara Moko lowlands near the mouth of the Vero River is an example.

[34] His rights have devolved from his father, who married into the Kukulori *ratu* group from Iyoro settlement and gained access to the land.

[35] *Irinu ete taro on kesi kesi* ('forest tree vines still intact').

[36] Possibly cognate with the Austronesian term *teluk* (bay, cove or gulf).

[37] The Vekase River also separates the former political domains of Tutuala and Muapitine.

[38] Although originally settling with Paiuru *ratu*, it is said that the status of this group is subsidiary to Renu *ratu*. Paiuru *ratu* is referred to as the 'paddler' of the origin boat (*Loiasu matar*), while Renu *ratu*

commandeered the boat. Hence the group may be referred to as Paiuru Tirimana (from *paiuru*, 'paddle'). They maintain a younger/ elder (*noko kaka*) relation with Renu *ratu*.

[39] Pai *ratu* is said to have died out and its lands, centred on the former settlement site (*lata paru*) of Maiana, have reverted to Rene *ratu*.

[40] Under the former UNTAET Regulation 19/2000, which remains in force, sea turtles are a protected species and their consumption is not permitted. This regulation appears not to have had much effect in this part of East Timor where hunting and consumption of numerous protected species is common.

[41] The work of Hviding and Bayliss-Smith (2000) in the Solomon Islands offers an example of the kind of approach and detailed assessment that might be attempted for the proposed park area.

[42] As Fox (1997: 8) notes, topogenies take a great variety of forms among Austronesian populations. They may recount the journey of an ancestor, the migration of a group or the transmission of an object.

[43] The term *tahi* is cognate with the common Austronesian term *tasi* commonly used throughout Timor, which typically also adopts the male/female distinction. This refers on one level to the supposed 'calm' qualities of the Savu Sea to the north and the 'rough' Timor Sea to the south. However, the designation also speaks to a symbolic association of male and female to the east/south and west/north coordinates respectively.

[44] I note that the agreement also includes marine areas around Jaco Island and the culturally important freshwater Lake Ira Lalaru, to the north of the Paichao Range. Representatives from Mehara, one of the affected villages (*suco*), have strong traditional interests covering the lake and its shores.

[45] A prospect mooted by the village head (*Chefe do Suco*) on the basis of what, I assume, were previous discussions with government forestry staff.

Chapter 12. Self-Scaling the Earth: Relations of Land, Society and Body Among North Mekeo, Papua New Guinea

Mark Mosko

Introduction

The language spoken by the North Mekeo peoples of the Central Province of PNG has been classified by linguists (Jones 1998; Ross 1988) as one of three dialects of Mekeo in the Western Papua Tip cluster of Western Oceanic. Consequently, their language possesses many contemporary reflexes of Proto-Austronesian reconstructions. With regard to the topic of territorial categories and institutions, for Proto-Austronesian **banua* and **tanah* rendered as 'land', 'territory' or 'dwelling place', North Mekeo have *paunga* and *ango*, or 'village' and 'land', respectively. [1] Note that Proto-Oceanic for 'land' is **tanoq* (Pawley and Ross), *tana(q)* (Grace 1969a) or **panua*. In this chapter, I explore the meanings villagers themselves attribute to these notions, roughly extending to generalised understandings about space and time, particularly the contours of human society and the human body.

The last of these domains—the human body—might initially appear to fall outside the theme of this volume. However, as I have described about North Mekeo culture earlier (Mosko 1985), space and time, society and the body are conceived as homologous and interconnected. Moreover, in recent publications (Mosko 1992, 1997, 1998a, 2001a, 2000b, 2002), I have been investigating additional related dimensions of North Mekeo sociality, particularly the dynamics of personhood, chiefly agency and socio-cultural change, which may now shed considerable new light on North Mekeo notions of territoriality. I thus begin within some of the parameters of my original accounts of North Mekeo culture, social organisation and embodiment. First I locate North Mekeo notions of village and land in the local cosmology of the entire world, *ango faka*, as comprising two distinctive kinds of space, the village or human world, *paunga*, understood to be an 'outside' place, and the bush, *ango aonga*, or 'inside' land, an 'inside' place. In the temporal rhythm of daily human activities, however, the village/bush spatial duality is recursively crosscut by the inside/outside distinction to produce a fourfold totality of space-time relations—a structure of bisected dualities that I have characterised as distinctive to the culture generally.

Thus North Mekeo notions of land and village are first apprehended through temporal coordination of inside and outside spaces.

It is in accordance with these same dimensions of meaning that North Mekeo conceptualise the human body and society. In the second section, therefore, I attempt to summarise how indigenous classifications and processes involving the human body and social relations in analogous terms of inside and outside also conform to the dynamics of the bisected duality pattern. Borrowing the terminology of chaos theory, I argue that for North Mekeo, world, body and society are not merely formally analogous, they are fractally connected dimensions of one another, thereby constituting an instance of self-similarity or self-scaling (Gleick 1987; Stewart 1989; Mosko in press).

In the third section of this chapter, I introduce newly acquired ethnographic information suggesting that the lands, bodies and social relations of North Mekeo are understood to be *substantively* as well as structurally connected. In several field trips in the past decade, I have learned of a substance termed *ngaka*, which is thought to cycle between villagers' lands, bodies and social relations in the course of human life and death. Interestingly, North Mekeo can be seen here to qualify as a coastal Melanesian instance of the 'fluid ontologies' characteristic of non-Austronesian groups in the Highlands of PNG (Goldman and Ballard 1998; Stewart and Strathern 2001) and the 'flow of life' which has been reported widely for Austronesian-speaking societies of South-East Asia, particularly Indonesia (Fox 1980). In this context, I focus on the implications of processes and transactions involving *ngaka* in accordance with other writings concerning 'partible personhood', sociality and agency among Mekeo specifically and in Melanesia generally (Mosko 1985, 1992, 1995, 1998b, 2001a, 2002; Strathern 1988; Wagner 1986, 1991). In short, the critical element of interpersonal exchange and elicitation of which North Mekeo people and social relations are composed and decomposed is the substance, *ngaka* acquired originally from resources and beings of the territorial world, incorporated into the bodies and relations of human beings and, on death, returned to the ground in human burials. I regard this emendation of the North Mekeo ethnographic record to be itself of considerable ethnological value as it conjoins recent discussions of the dynamical fluid ontologies of the New Guinea Highlands and the flow of life across Indonesian societies with the supposedly distinctive Melanesian notions and processes of personal partibility and sociality.

With these points as ethnographic background, in the final section I focus on the intersection of North Mekeo notions of territoriality and personal agency with chiefly polity. Mekeo people have by now become one of the more well-documented examples of Austronesian-speaking 'chiefly' societies in Melanesia (see Seligmann 1910; Guis 1936; Hau'ofa 1981; Stephen 1974, 1995; Mosko 1985; Bergendorff 1996). Yet there remain in the recent ethnographic and historical literature of Mekeo (as for many other Austronesian-speaking societies in the Pacific) questions about the exact nature of 'chieftainship', and particularly the nature of chiefly agency (Mosko 1991a, 1992, 1995, 1997a, 1997b, 2001b; Hau'ofa 1971, 1981; Powell 1996; Hage 1998; Scaglion 1996; Peterson 1999; Stephen 1995, 1996, 1998; Bergendorff 1996; Rumsey 1999). With reference to the foregoing analysis of North Mekeo classifications of space, time, body, person and society, I attempt to clarify the nature and territorial extent of Mekeo 'chiefdoms'.

The Village and the Bush

The entire world, *ango faka* (lit.: 'great world'), for North Mekeo consists principally of two kinds of place, the village, *paunga*, and the bush, *ango aonga* (lit.: 'land inside'). As the label indicates, the bush is conceived as an inside place. Thus when passing from the village to the bush, people or things 'go inside' (*ke koko*). Correspondingly, the village is viewed as an outside place, and moving from bush to village is to 'go outside' (*ke pualai*). This nomenclature is in fact used quite regularly in villagers' discourse, as one often hears people remark, 'So and so has gone inside' (i.e. to the bush) or 'So and so is coming out' (i.e. returning from the bush to the village). And the existential experience of villages as relatively open places as compared with the enclosed, lushly vegetated, canopied spaces of the bush generally is consistent with the outside/inside designation.

Mekeo villages (*paunga*) are named and possess distinctive histories of their original settlement (see below). Stereotypically, villages are rectangular in layout, with a peripheral fence or hedge (*fangapu*, literally, 'skin place') of colourful crotons dividing the village from the surrounding bush. Domestic houses are arranged along the length of the village in parallel rows. Two clan clubhouses (*ufu* or *kofu*), each belonging to a different resident clan, stand facing one another at opposite ends of the village. The domestic dwellings and clubhouses, however, along with all other artefacts of daily life, are concentrated on the perimeter of the village, as the central promenade, termed the 'village abdomen' or 'womb' (*paunga inaenga*) is ordinarily kept entirely clear of all structures. [2] It is in the village abdomen that many of the most important rituals are performed, most significantly mortuary feasts, and in pre-colonial times it was in the ground underneath the abdomen that people buried the bodies of their dead relatives. The abdomen of every village thus served as the ritual focus for the human groups who resided there (Mosko 1985: Ch. 2).

While village and bush are thus opposed categories as outside to inside, human life is dependant largely on regular movements and transformations of objects between the two domains (Figure 1). A preponderance of things composing the village perimeter—the building materials for all types of human dwellings (domestic houses, chiefs' clubhouses, platforms)—are obtained from bush materials and are transformed into village resources. Garden foods and nearly all other things processed and consumed by human beings in the village are similarly obtained in untransformed states from the bush. Indeed, the very space constituting a Mekeo village was initially cleared 'out' of the inside space of the bush. This means that the outside village contains much that originated in the inside bush.

Figure 1: Village, bush and daily transfers between them (after Mosko 1985: 36)

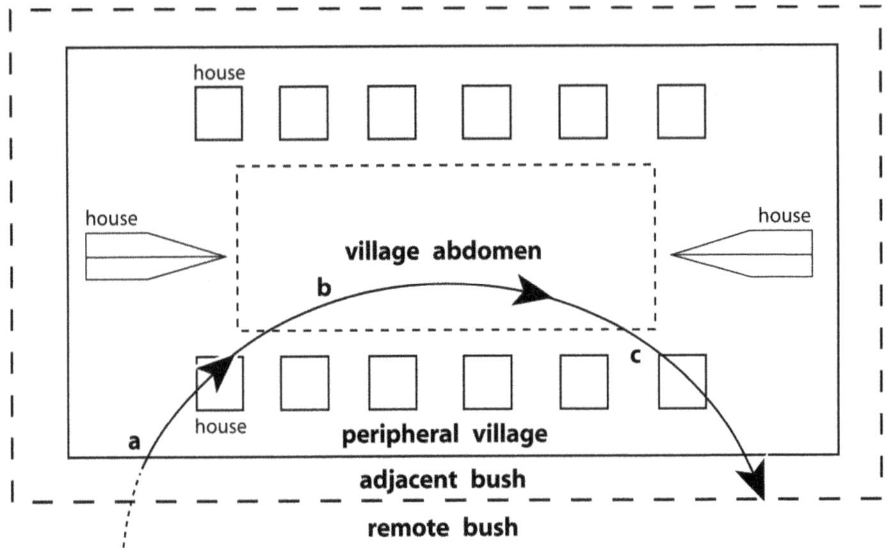

At the same time, the inside bush regularly receives contributions of essentially outside village products. In particular, it is in the region of the bush immediately surrounding the rectangular village where human beings deposit their waste products—their own bodily waste products and all the other detritus of their daily lives. Thus just as the village is inhabited by considerable amounts of transformed bush materials at the perimeter, a significant part of the bush contains large quantities of transformed village materials deposited in the bush adjacent to the village. But before village wastes are carried to the nearby bush, each morning they are swept and gathered into piles in the village's central abdomen.

So as a consequence of this temporal two-way transfer of materials between village and bush, each of the two zones is bisected. The peripheral zone of the outside village largely comprises bush materials transformed by human labour into village resources. In the *paunga*'s abdomen those things are accumulated once their usefulness has been exhausted. The remote bush is the source of materials for village resources, and it is in the adjacent ring of bush space surrounding the village that those things are redeposited once they have become wastes. In terms of inside and outside, the village contains one unambiguously outside place, the peripheral zone of transformed village resources, and an ambiguously *inner* part of the outside village, the village abdomen where wastes accumulate. Analogously, the bush contains one unambiguously inside place, the remote bush, and the ambiguously *outer* part of the inside bush adjacent to the village where human wastes are deposited. The North Mekeo world as a totality is thus constituted of an initial duality of inside bush and outside village, which is bisected by the same duality again to result in purely inside and outside spaces plus an 'everted inside' space of the bush adjacent to the village and an 'inverted outside' at the village's central womb. [3]

Following my own work (1985: 32), these relations can be characterised as:

inside	:	outside	::	inverted outside	:	everted inside
remote bush	:	peripheral village	::	village abdomen	:	adjacent bush

Within the Austronesian sphere, I do not believe that this classificatory patterning of village and bush is unique. Although cast in the different terms of the sea versus land, Sahlins has identified for Fiji, and thus for much of the remainder of Polynesia, basically the same structure of a bisected duality (Sahlins 1976; see also Hocart 1936; Valeri 1985).

The Human Body

The specific North Mekeo designations of the village and bush as outside and inside, respectively, may seem peculiar and counter-intuitive to many English speakers. For example, people live 'in town', and when they go to the countryside for holiday they get 'out of town'. However, the sense of North Mekeo inside and outside territorial designations and their inversions and eversions becomes perhaps more apparent in respect of analogous discriminations of the human body. This is implied strongly by the Mekeo word for outside, *fangai*, as applied to the world is a distinctively bodily metaphor meaning literally 'on the skin'. And similarly, as already noted, the term for the central village abdomen, *inaenga*, is also the word for bodily abdomen or womb. [4]

More importantly for present purposes, the human body, like the territorial world, contains unambiguously inside and outside regions and their ambiguous eversions and inversions resulting from temporal ingestion and excretion of resources and wastes, respectively. To North Mekeo villagers, the human body (*kumau*) is divided into inside (*aongai*) and outside (*fangai*) regions. The skin or *fanga* is the essential boundary between the two primary zones, just as the world has a category of 'skin' termed *fangapu* or *fanga apu* (or 'skin place') which demarcates the village from the bush—i.e. the fence or hedge of crotons mentioned above. And just as human life is dependent on regular transfers and transformations of things across the skin dividing village and bush, the life of the human body requires the movement of resources and wastes between its outside and inside regions.

Villagers are extremely diligent as regards the precise regulation of these flows, and with good reason. For if the appropriate sort of things are properly transferred from outside to inside and inside to outside, human life will continue. If inappropriate things from the outside are ingested or inappropriate parts of the inside are ejected, however, then the opposite of life, or death, is the result. Thus it is vital significance to every human being that the transfers and transformations between the inside and outside of his/her body are properly regulated. And in many ways it is possible to envision the entirety of Mekeo culture and social organisation as extenuations of these bodily ins and outs—from the processes of cooking, ingestion, digestion, excretion, sexuality and reproduction, generally, to ceremonial gift exchange, mortuary feasting, sorcery practice and the wielding of chiefly agency (Mosko 1983, 1985, 2001a). In this paper, I will have the opportunity to touch lightly on only a few of these embodied contexts of territoriality and sociality.

For present purposes, the regulated movements of things between the outsides and insides of human bodies result in an analogous classification of the body initially itself into four basic zones: unambiguous inside and outside regions, and ambiguously inverted and everted bisections of these. Much of the world at large consists of materials or things that have never been part of a human being (or human-like being; see below) and are hence unambiguously outside of the body, or part of the 'body outside'. Interestingly, these are predominantly things that originate from the unambiguously inside portion of the remote bush—wild animals and plants, the ground or soil of bush lands, waters flowing in the rivers and creeks, etc.—which are transported and transformed by human ingenuity or cleverness (*etsifa;* see below) for use in human life concentrated at the outside village. In contrast with the sector of the world that is external to the body is the body's own interior space, comprised of the bloody, fleshy parts, which, in a healthy state, remain inside and are never excreted. This includes the body's various organs, the bones, and in general all the bloody internal parts. Ordinarily in the course of life these bloody parts of the inside of human bodies remain there. They do not come out. Human life, however, is dependent on the transfers of different sorts of things, first from outside to inside and later from inside to outside, which result in ambiguously outside parts of the space inside bodies (i.e. outside inverted) and ambiguously inside parts of the space outside bodies (i.e. inside everted). On the one hand, ingested cooked foods can be taken to typify the former category. On ingestion, foods are transported to the abdomen whereon certain elements they contain (*ngaka;* see below) are assimilated into the inside of the body proper in the form of blood and tissues. The remaining wastes (faeces, urine), containing neither blood nor the constituents of blood, accumulate in the abdomen for eventual externalisation. Once excreted, they can be seen to occupy inside bodily space that has been everted, analogous with the waste deposit area of the bush surrounding the village. And it is no coincidence that it is in this same zone of the bush that the body's non-bloody wastes are normally deposited.

In trying to comprehend the patterning of these distinctions, I have developed an illustration (Figure 2) that has been inspired by Leach's (1961) famous discussions of topography. Think of a balloon, the skin of which demarcates an unambiguous boundary between inside and outside regions. Now with your thumb on the outside, push or fold the skin of the balloon inwards and then pinch it off at the point where it diverges from the balloon's spherical outline. The outside space occupied by your thumb would nonetheless appear to be inside, that is, outside space contained within a folding of the balloon's skin, thus analogous to an abdomen or womb—a portion of the space outside the body folded on itself. Now conceive as well of the reverse operation; that is, from the interior of the balloon extend the skin with your finger so that it protrudes beyond the otherwise spherical boundary of the balloon's skin, and fold or tie it off also. The result is a portion of inside space that is nonetheless outside the ordinary sphere of the balloon, analogous to excreted bodily wastes. Thus the duality of inside and outside spaces is stretched and twisted to produce four discernible spaces: simple inside, simple outside, inside everted, and outside inverted.

At a very broad level of generalisation, this interpretation of North Mekeo spatial categorisations is consistent with broader patterns of cultural integration. The Central Mekeo ethnographer Hau'ofa (1981) noted, for example, a consistent 'ambiguity' of indigenous Mekeo conceptual dualisms, such as senior and junior, male and female, as well as inside and outside, which I have elsewhere refined and formalised in terms of 'bisected dualities' (1985, 1991b). But this interpretation of North Mekeo spatial categorisations of the body is also useful for explaining an enormous range of specific ethnographic imponderabilia which otherwise appear to be inconsistent and/or inexplicable. For instance, human blood in all of its manifestations, including sexual fluids, is regarded as 'dirty' and 'hot' or dangerous when it is transferred from the inside of one body, where it ordinarily safely resides, to the inside of another human's body. If a human being should inadvertently ingest the blood of another human, especially a dead human, the ingested blood and the soul or spirit it embodies would act like a poison and lead to their death. Men's ejaculated semen, however, although it is dirty, hot and dangerous if orally ingested, does not cause sickness or death even though it appears to be deposited inside a woman's body during copulation.

This is because a woman's womb is not technically inside her body; rather, her womb is outside space folded inside, a process known in topography as invagination. So even though a man's semen would sicken a woman if she took it into her body orally, when deposited into her womb it remains contained within the inverted, invaginated *outside* space of her body. [5]

Figure 2: Body Space: inside, outside, inside everted and outside inverted

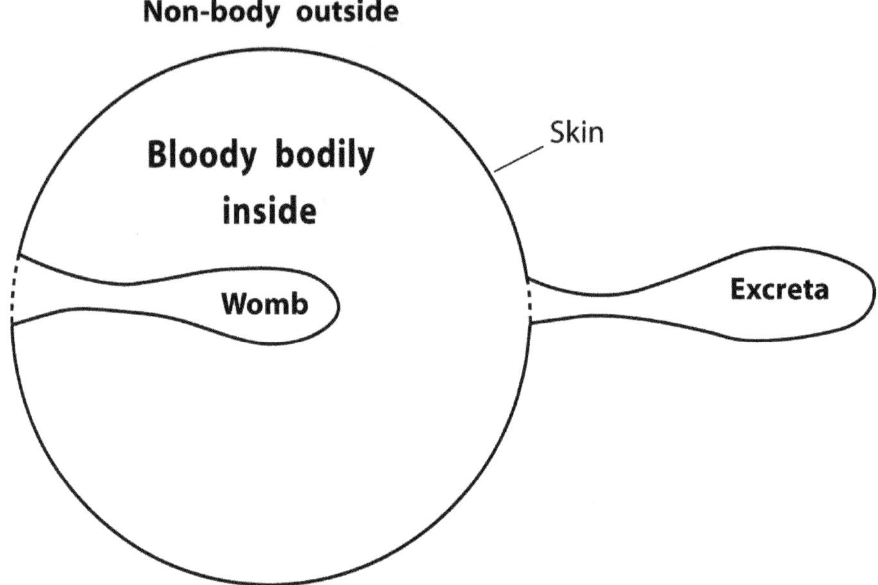

Thus the human body, like the territorial world, consists in an initial distinction of unambiguous inside and outside spaces, which, as a result of temporal transfers between the two zones, results in an analogous fourfold totality of inside, outside, inverted outside and everted inside spaces:

inside	:	outside	::	inverted outside	:	everted inside
remote bush	:	peripheral village	::	village abdomen	:	adjacent bush
bloody body	:	non-body things	::	bodily womb	:	bodily excreta

It is interesting that this particular classification of bodily space and process is not unique to North Mekeo among Austronesian speakers, for again it seems that the same pattern or structure is widespread in Polynesia, on the evidence of Gell's analysis of the logic of tattooing in the region: 'The basic schema of tattooing is thus definable as the exteriorisation of the interior which is simultaneously the interiorisation of the exterior' (1993: 39).

Society

The North Mekeo classification of society is homologous with villagers' classifications of the territorial world and the human body. From what can be reconstructed reliably on the basis of early post-contact information, however, North Mekeo society was organised at a number of different levels or scales: lineage, clan, moiety, village and tribe. I will do my best in this section of the paper to sketch the patterning of social organisation at all of these levels, which I hope to show is isomorphic with the bisected-duality-type patterning of bodily, land and territorial classifications discussed above. In this context, however, the village (*paunga*) is simultaneously a territorial and a social entity, and it is this relationship that I will be seeking to characterise in most detail.

The Mekeo-speaking peoples occupy the middle reaches of two adjacent river systems, the Angabunga and the Biaru. Those Mekeo who historically lived in village communities along the Angabunga have come to be known as Central Mekeo, or Mekeo proper, while those Mekeo living along the Biaru River generally are known as the North Mekeo. While all Central Mekeo speak a single dialect, North Mekeo speak two distinct dialects (Jones 1998). From before the imposition of colonial control to the present, the Central Mekeo have been organised politically into two 'tribes', the Biofa and the Ve'e (Seligmann 1910; Hau'ofa 1981; Stephen 1974; Bergendorff 1996). Similarly, the North Mekeo have comprised two tribal groupings, the Amoamo and the Kuipa. In pre-contact times, relations between members of different tribes tended to be hostile. Accordingly, tribal groups have been by rule endogamous.

While individual tribal groups were named in earlier times and continue to be so-named today, there does not appear to be in the language a generic term for 'tribe'. Among the Amoamo (North Mekeo) who I have studied most closely, the tribal unit consists of four dispersed patrilineal clans (*ikupu*) organised ideally into exogamous patrilineal moieties (*ngopu*). [6] Each clan is typically composed of more than one localised branch, and ideally each localised branch of a clan should contain a full complement of politically and ritually specialised lineages, relating to the well-documented fourfold division of Mekeo chiefly labour between 'peace chief' (*lopia*), 'war chief' (*iso*), 'war sorcerer' (*faika*) and 'peace sorcerer' (*ungaunga*) (Figure 3).

Figure 3: Classification of North Mekeo chiefly offices

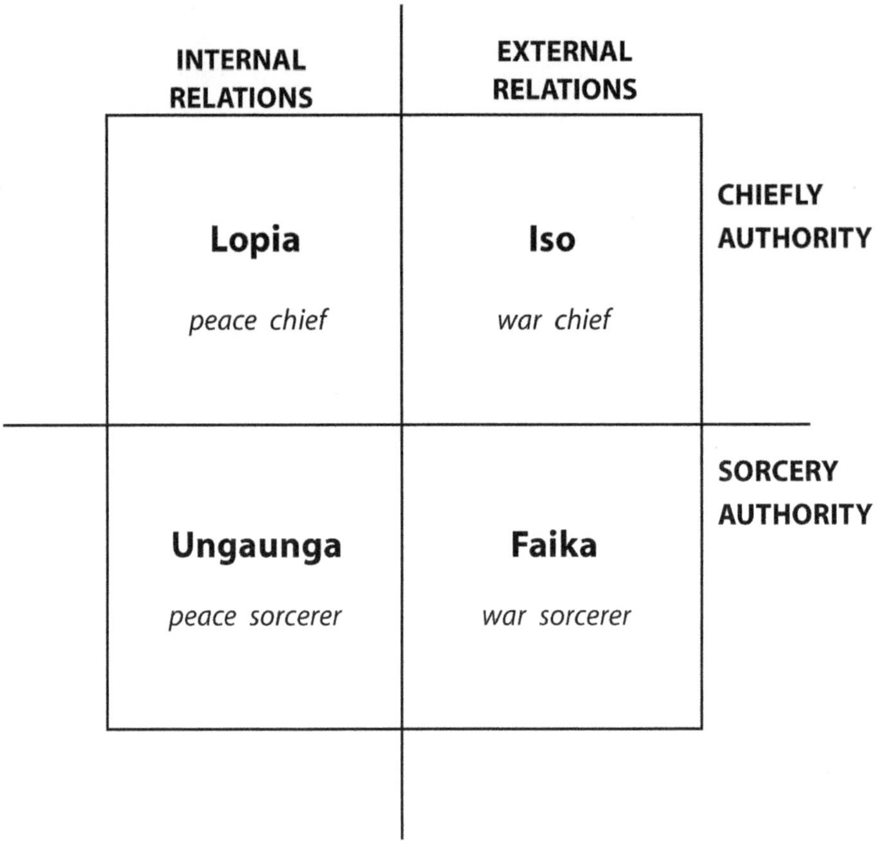

	INTERNAL RELATIONS	EXTERNAL RELATIONS
CHIEFLY AUTHORITY	**Lopia** *peace chief*	**Iso** *war chief*
SORCERY AUTHORITY	**Ungaunga** *peace sorcerer*	**Faika** *war sorcerer*

It is these 'residential clans' that are usually the main landowning groups. To the extent, then, that the territories of the residential clans composing a tribe are contiguous, as is usually the case, the tribe can be considered a territorial as well as a social entity.

There are several important qualifications to this generalisation, however, which must be noted. First, the decades preceding the establishment of colonial peace were marked by considerable migration of family, lineage and clan groups across the region. As a result, many lineage and/or clan groupings nowadays lay claim to parcels of land that lie outside their own village and tribal territories. Thus members of the Akaifu clan of Nganga village consider themselves 'owners' of land now occupied by members of other clans belonging to other villages. And some clans lay ancestral claim to lands that otherwise are now part of Biofa or Ve'e tribal territories. The exigencies of history have, therefore, greatly complicated the correlation of tribal groups with tribal lands. Secondly, related to this, as is common everywhere in PNG, practically every claim to ownership of land is contested by other individuals or groups either within the same village or tribe or in different tribes. It is, I believe, inherent in contexts of landownership that there is no one-to-one correspondence of a single group of owners with respect to a single parcel of land owned. And thirdly, to speak of the relation of people to land in simple terms of 'property' and 'ownership' seriously distorts the character of how villagers conceptualise their ties to land and, thereby, how they see themselves and their social relations (see Mosko 2002). This aspect of the problem invokes the distinctive sense of Melanesian personhood, agency and sociality on which I will focus later in this chapter.

Typically, the members of the several clans composing a tribal grouping do not live in a single location but reside in a number of nucleated villages, usually situated adjacent to a river or other water source. Ideally, each village is composed of members of the localised branches of two clans, one from each exogamous moiety. Thus the village of Nganga consists of members of the Pitoli and Akaifu clans plus the male members' wives and children, minus their married sisters (unless they married into the opposite clan in the same village). The nearest village, Ainapa, consists of another localised branch of Akaifu clan and the senior and junior clan branches of Ofuenge clan. It is the ceremonial clan clubhouses of these two clans that usually stand facing one another at opposite ends of the village abdomen (Hau'ofa 1981; Mosko 1985: 25), and it is the peace chief of the clan who nominally owns the clubhouse who is responsible for proceedings that take place there.[7] Adult male members of the clan meet in their clubhouse daily to discuss matters of common concern. And importantly, it is in their clan clubhouse that members entertain visitors from other clans, particularly those designated in special exchange relations, termed *kofuapie* (or *ufuapie*) and *pisaua* (see below).

Again, it is clan groups typically that are the collective owners of hereditary land—village house sites and surrounding bush lands used for gardening and hunting. It is usually the case also that villages have been established on the land owned by just one of the two (or more) clans resident there. This means that the peace chief of the landowning clan is the nominal owner of the village, but aside from his and his clan's special relationship with respect to the land itself, the peace chief's authority does not extend any further. That is, in all other contexts, the two peace chiefs of the two (or more) resident clans engage with one another as ritual 'friends' (*pisaua*) without any precedence of one before the other. There is, therefore, no such indigenous status as 'village' or 'tribal chief' (cf. Hau'ofa 1981; Stephen 1974; Bergendorff 1996). Peace chiefs, along with the other three types of hereditary officials I will describe below, are essentially *clan* functionaries. Aside from the local situation of the chief of one clan owning the land occupied or used by members of another clan, there is no chief who wields authority over members of other clans beyond in-marrying spouses when they attend mortuary feasts and the female members' offspring (*papie ngaunga*, or the 'women's children' of the clan).

Nonetheless, at the societal levels of village and tribe, which correspond roughly with territorial contiguities as noted above, there is an important coordination of functions that corresponds with the processes of inside/outside transfer in relation to classifications of territoriality and the human body. To illustrate this, I will describe the indigenous conceptualisation of clan groups as themselves analogous to human bodies of two gendered types, male and female, with certain kinds of interactions between them. For it is in these terms of interacting clan bodies that village and tribal entities or 'chieftainships' are constituted. Here, particularly, the relevance of the inside/outside classification of space/time and body domains for societal organisation becomes apparent.

The Clan as a Body

The term for 'clan' and its various subdivisions is *ikupu*. North Mekeo clans are patrilineal on the basis of continuous transmission of shared agnatic clan blood from fathers to children. It is the sharing of the same agnatic or male blood that defines the clan, for all of its members are regarded as 'one blood'. Literally translated, the term *ikupu* means 'closed', and the term is used frequently in reference to the ritual procedures whereby men and women restrict the flow of substances in and out of their bodies. Men close their bodies by fasting and various types of abstention when they engage in magical practices that require manipulation of dirty, bloody residues of dead humans—the basic category of substances employed in most types of sorcery. Women correspondingly close their bodies in the period between their weaning of one child and their resumption of sexual relations with their husbands (see Mosko 1983, 1985: Chapters 4 and 5). Clans, like bodies, however, are not entirely closed, for if they were this would imply that they are endogamous (Figure 4). By rule, clans are exogamous and, consequently, open to one another through marriage and the resultant exchange of cognatic bloods. So just as women and men periodically open their bodies to the flow of substances in and out, including the substances of one another's bodies, clans exchange parts of one another and thereby open their boundaries. Moreover, just as the inside and outside of the human body is bounded by the skin, a clan has a 'skin' too. It is commonly remarked that the women of a clan are the 'skin of the clan'. On marriage, they (or parts of them) go out and into other clans. The part of a woman's body that goes out of one clan and into another clan as a result of sexual intercourse and procreation is her blood, specifically into the bodies of her children.

Figure 4: The clan body and *kofuapie* relationships

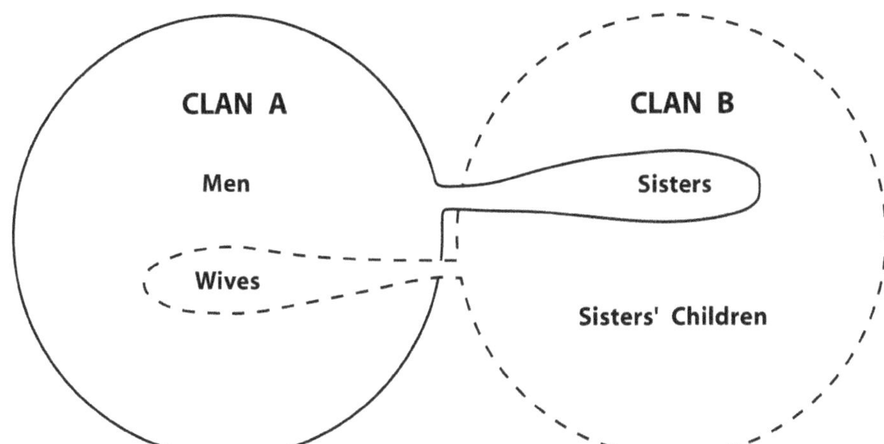

It may appear to be contradictory that clans that are open to one another through the exchange of women's or female blood are seen as being in some way closed. However, just as women and men periodically close their bodies, clans do the analogous thing by returning the blood previously incorporated into the bodies of their members through their mothers. This is accomplished in the context of reciprocal mortuary feasting. I have elsewhere (Mosko 1983, 1985) called this process 'de-conception'. By returning the female blood of other clans that had rendered their own clan temporarily open, members of a clan close their boundaries to one another. In the long term, then, clans are closed bodies. And it is because they periodically close their respective bodies to one another that clans can reopen their relations through future marriages.

In sum, just as human bodies have open and closed modes of interrelationship, clan bodies open and close their boundaries to one another. Moreover, it is through the opening of their bodies that life is generated and sustained, and it is in the closing or severing of their relations that death occurs.

Ngaka Vital Essence

The homologies that I have traced between the territorial world, the human body and society are not merely structural or even self-scaled fractal versions of one another, for these three contexts are also substantively linked. The key notion here is *ngaka*, which I will gloss in its positively valued or life-giving form as 'vital essence'.

I first learned from villagers of the existence of *ngaka* in their accounts of the relations between food and sexual bloods. Presumably, the critical life-giving element of ingested foodstuffs that are assimilated into the blood and tissues of human bodies is *ngaka*. Vegetable foods and meat foods each contain *ngaka*, but of distinct types, such that the human body requires both sorts in order to live. Analogously, human sexual bloods, semen and womb blood, which are required for procreation, contain or consist of complementary types of *ngaka*. Thus humans acquire life-giving *ngaka* from one another in procreative transmissions, and they acquire it as well from the foods they consume. Interestingly, the foods from which people acquire *ngaka* are obtained from resources that people extract from the remote inside bush. However, in their untransformed bush forms, the *ngaka* they contain is not utilisable by humans. Human labour and 'skill' or 'cleverness' (*etsifa*) is required to transform and combine the raw bush forms of *ngaka* in such a way that they can be absorbed into human life. Thus the contribution of human cleverness and labour is essential in the process of transforming bush resources into village ones. And to the extent that people usually exchange the products of their own bodily labours with other people rather than consume them themselves, even the food that people ingest for making the blood of life contains in effect the *ngaka* consequent to the actions of other human bodies. The *ngaka* that people produce in their labours and subsequently exchange thus contains the personal contributions of other people. It is almost as though the essence of human bodily blood and social relationship is to transmit in orderly fashion *ngaka* vital essence between people so that human life can continue. Moreover, to the extent that one's life is dependent on numerous prior exchanges and ingestions of *ngaka*, every person is constituted of the personal contributions of other people. Here you can detect the way in which my and other Melanesianists' discussions of personal partibility enters into the flow of *ngaka* vital essence throughout human life (Mosko 1985, 1992, 1995, 1998a, 2001a, 2001b, 2002, in press; Strathern 1988; Damon 1983; Battaglia 1986; Wagner 1986, 1991; Munn 1986; Foster 1995).

This implies, therefore, that human bodies and social relations including inter-clan transmissions of women's blood, are constituted and sustained by exchanges of *ngaka*—in effect, parts of other people. Moreover, to the extent that land is associated with particular people or groups of people (e.g. clans, villages, etc.), the world is itself a personalised universe. Every tract of village and bush land has the history of other people's contributions to it, and extractions from it. Thus through the extraction of *ngaka* originally from the land, people are not just part of one another, they are part of the land too. And so too are groups that occupy the land. The *ngaka* that they circulate in defining themselves as groups in their internal and external relations are also derivative of *ngaka* from the land—village and bush. So the continuity of the world as a territory, the human body and human sociality is not just formal, it is thoroughly substantive.

This continuity of world, body and society is also constituted by the recursive processes involving analogous crosscutting inside/outside relations. Expectably, the bodily excreta of human bodies contain no positively valued *ngaka*. With digestion, the 'good' *ngaka* of food is assimilated into the body. The wastes of human life, including the bloodless bodily excreta deposited in bush adjoining the village, are discarded because they have been depleted of their original good *ngaka*. Although they are classified as 'dirty' (*iofu*), and people avoid ingesting or otherwise using them in the pursuit of life, these non-bloody substances are not inherently dangerous; rather, they are inert, and only a crazy person would consume them.

There is, however, a second category of *ngaka*—*ngaka abala*, or 'bad' *ngaka*, which if consumed or otherwise ingested by human bodies leads to sickness and death. Villagers indicate that bad *ngaka* is the same substance as good *ngaka*, only it has died. Thus bad *ngaka* is found in its essential form in the bloody flesh of dead human beings. And just as consumed good *ngaka* leads to life in human bodies, bad *ngaka* produces sickness and death when ingested. It is the exploitation of precisely this capacity of bad *ngaka* to produce sickness and death that serves as the chief ontological and epistemological basis for the dangerous categories of sorcery, for which Mekeo are famous. Basically, sorcerers insert either physically or spiritually the bloody bodily residues of dead humans into their victims' bodies, so that bad *ngaka* does its work by reversing the transformations that support life. Rather than contributing to the formation of blood that stays inside the body, the victim's own bad blood containing bad *ngaka* is excreted to threaten still other people. And because every trace of bad *ngaka* is in effect part of another person—and if that person is dead already, it contains that person's soul or spirit—all sorcery is a social act on the order of personal partibility (Mosko 1992, 1997a, 2002; cf. Stephen 1998).

It is particularly noteworthy in this context that ideally the ultimate destination of all bad *ngaka* is underground in the village abdomen, for it is there that Mekeo in the past buried the corpses of their relatives. Wastes of human life that contain no *ngaka* vital essence are deposited above ground in the bush adjacent to the village, but the bad *ngaka* of human life is buried in the village abdomen, in the land, in the territory of that part of the world associated with those people and their social relations. People are connected with their land not only because they extract from it the good *ngaka* incorporated in their living bodies, they are connected with their land when the good *ngaka* of their bodies has died and become bad *ngaka*, whereon it is returned to the abdomen of the village where it resides forever. [8]

This general sort of cycling of life-giving substance is widespread among Austronesian-speaking peoples of island South-East Asia (Fox 1980) and non-Austronesian societies of the New Guinea Highlands (Goldman and Ballard 1998; Stewart and Strathern 2001). This cycling has not been heretofore reported for Mekeo or, as far as I am aware, other Austronesian-speaking peoples of Melanesia.

Village and Tribal Chiefdoms

I now turn to the relation of notions of land and village to the politico-ritual institution of North Mekeo chieftainship. For it is chiefs, and indeed the whole fourfold hierarchy of chiefly clan officialdom, who are instrumental in the regulation of these transmissions of *ngaka* among village and bush places, among people and their outside and inside bodily zones, and thereby among the social relations that define tribal groupings.

Basically, every named clan should have a full complement of four chiefly and sorcery offices, as noted above. The division of labour between the peace and war officials corresponds with the distinction of internal and external tribal relations, respectively. Thus peace chiefs and peace sorcerers are responsible for the regulation of the two main types of inter-clan exchange that I have described already: the transmission of exogamous bloods between clans of opposite moieties in procreation and the inverse exchange of bloods between clans in mortuary feasting and de-conception. These are, in fact, the essence of the *kofuapie* and *pisaua* exchange relationships that have received considerable attention in the various ethnographic accounts of the Mekeo peoples from Seligmann onwards. To the extent that the bloods of conception and de-conception embody the good and bad *ngaka* obtained originally from their own tribal territories, peace chiefs and peace sorcerers can be seen as the official regulators of life and death in the sphere of *intra*-tribal relations.

War chiefs and war sorcerers, in contrast, regulate life and death in the sphere of *inter*tribal relations. At the advent of the colonial era, Mekeo tribes were predominantly endogamous entities. Peaceful marital exchanges of life-giving blood occurred between clans of the same tribe. Even so, distinct tribes also exchanged blood and, through it, *ngaka*. Violent death in warfare, like death caused by peace sorcery, is dependent on the ritual insertion of bad *ngaka* into the open bodies of enemies so that they cannot effectively resist physical assault and the consequent excretion of bodily blood from inside to outside. In order to be capable of inflicting death in this way, tribal warriors had to ensure that their own bodies were effectively closed to the bad *ngaka* of enemy war ritual. It was the responsibility of war chiefs and war sorcerers to insert bad *ngaka* into tribal enemies' bodies and prevent its absorption in the bodies of members of their own tribe. Thus, complementary to the peace officials, war chiefs and war sorcerers regulated life and death in the context of exchanges of blood and *ngaka* between hostile tribal groups.

This implies that territorial tribal groups, like clans and human bodies, constituted collective bodies with internal and external dimensions; that a result of war exchange was to further bisect the internal and external dimension of tribal relations with inverted and everted extensions; that intertribal warfare, like intra-tribal marriage and feasting, involved processes of life and death; that life and death in the context of war, as in peace, involved the flow of good and bad *ngaka*; and that it was the war chiefs and war sorcerers of clan groups who regulated these processes.

In war and peace, chiefs and sorcerers acted only on behalf of fellow clan members. Ethnologically, this is a very important point. From pre-colonial times to the present, North Mekeo have been organised into tribal entities with territorial associations, as described above, but they have never possessed anything like a 'tribal chief' with authority over an entire tribal domain. As Godelier (1991: 303) has observed, among North Mekeo there are tribal 'chiefdoms' but no tribal 'chiefs'; that is, there are no politico-ritual functionaries whose dominion extends to an entire tribe. This contrasts in some respects with supposed chiefly societies elsewhere in Melanesia (e.g. the Trobriands; see Mosko 1995, 1997b; Powell 1997), Polynesia, Micronesia and Indonesia.

Conclusions

Much like the various flows of *ngaka* I have outlined here, my attempt to trace the relations of North Mekeo territorial categories to chiefly institutions has been hardly a direct one. In order to appreciate the meanings that villagers themselves attach to the categories *pangua* and *ango*, it has been necessary to consider them in relation to the broader spatio-temporal classification of the world or cosmos as a bisected duality of inside/outside plus their eversions and inversions as well as their fractal counterparts with respect to the human body and society. This, therefore, is my first conclusion: that in at least this one Austronesian setting, categorisations of land and territory must be seen in the context of indigenous self-scaled constructions of body and society. As I have already indicated, this conceptual scheme has been reported widely across many parts of the Austronesian-speaking Pacific.

Secondly, these analogies are not just formal associations inasmuch as the flows between village and bush, between the inside and the outside of bodies, and between exogamous clans and endogamous tribes involve the circulation of the one substance vital for life and death, *ngaka*.

Third, to the extent that it is elements of *ngaka* that are the critical components of the composition and de-conception of people and relations, North Mekeo agency and sociality as I have elsewhere analysed them in terms of personal partibility and the countervailing processes of conception and de-conception are encompassed thoroughly in the cosmic flows of *ngaka*. In this regard, the North Mekeo case provides an important point of convergence for some of the most convincing but heretofore separate models of the dynamics of Melanesian and Indonesian societies: partible personhood and fluid ontologies for the former, and the flow of life for the latter.

Finally, the system of North Mekeo clan chiefs and sorcerers provides another provocative example of what I have elsewhere argued pertains to the Austronesian sphere more generally: that there may be 'chieftainships' that are congruent with more or less territorially based tribal domains, but these domains nonetheless lack tribal 'chiefs'.

References

Battaglia, D. 1986. '"We feed our father": Paternal nurture among the Sabarl of Papua New Guinea.' *American Ethnologist*, 12. pp. 427-41.

Bergendorff, S. 1996. *Faingu City: A modern clan in Papua New Guinea*. Lund: Lund University Press.

Damon, F. 1983. 'Muyuw kinship and the metamorphosis of gender labour.' *Man*, (n.s.) 18. pp. 305-26.

Foster, R. 1995. *Social Reproduction and History in Melanesia: Mortuary ritual, gift exchange, and custom in the Tanga Islands*. Cambridge: Cambridge University Press.

Fox, J.J. (ed.) 1980. *The Flow of Life: Essays on Eastern Indonesia*. Cambridge. (Mass.): Harvard University Press.

Gell, A. 1993. *Wrapping in Images: Tattooing in Polynesia*. Oxford: Clarendon

Gleick, J. 1987. *Chaos: Making a new science*. New York: Penguin.

Godelier, M. 1991. 'An unfinished attempt at reconstructing social processes which may have prompted the transformation of great-men societies into big-men societies.' In M. Godelier and M. Strathern (eds), *Big Men and Great Men: Personifications of power in Melanesia*, Cambridge and Paris: Cambridge University Press Editions de la Maison des Sciences de l'Homme. pp. 275-304.

Goldman, L. and C. Ballard (eds). 1998. *Fluid Ontologies: Myth, ritual and philosophy in the Highlands of Papua New Guinea*. Westport (Conn.): Bergin and Garvey.

Guis, J. 1936. *La vie des Papous*. Paris: Dillen.

Hage, P. 1998. 'Austronesian chiefs: Metaphorical or fractal fathers?' *Journal of the Royal Anthropological Institute*, 4 (n.s.). pp. 786-9.

Hau'ofa, E. 1971. 'Mekeo chieftainship.' *Journal of the Polynesian Society*, 80. pp. 152-69.

Hau'ofa, E. 1981. *Mekeo: Inequality and ambivalence in a village society*. Canberra: Australian National University Press.

Hocart, A. 1936. *Kings and Counsellors: An essay in the comparative analysis of society*. Cairo: Paul Barbey.

Jones, A. 1998. 'Towards a Lexicogrammar of Mekeo (an Austronesian language of western central Papua).' *Pacific Linguistics*. Series C, No. 138. Canberra: Department of Linguistics, Research School of Pacific and Asian Studies, The Australian National University.

Leach, E. 1961. 'Rethinking Anthropology.' *London School of Economics Monographs on Social Anthropology*, No. 22. London: Althone.

Malinowski, B. 1965 [1935]. *Coral Gardens and Their Magic*, Vol. 1. Bloomington: Indiana University Press.

Mosko, M. 1983. 'Conception, de-conception and social reproduction in Bush Mekeo culture and social organisation.' *Mankind*, 14. pp. 24-43.

Mosko, M. 1985. *Quadripartite Structures: Categories, relations and homologies in Bush Mekeo culture*. Cambridge: Cambridge University Press.

Mosko, M. 1991a. 'Great men and total systems: Hereditary authority and social reproduction among the North Mekeo.' In M. Godelier and M. Strathern (eds), *Big Men and Great Men: Personifications of power in Melanesia*, Cambridge: Cambridge University Press. pp. 97-114.

Mosko, M. 1991b. 'The structure of myth and non-myth.' *American Ethnologist*, 18. pp. 126-51.

Mosko, M. 1992. 'Motherless sons: 'Divine kings' and 'partible people' in Melanesia and Polynesia.' *Man*, (n.s.) 27. pp. 697-717.

Mosko, M. 1995. 'Rethinking Trobriand chieftainship.' *Journal of the Royal Anthropological Institute*, (n.s.) 1. pp. 763-85.

Mosko, M. 1997a. 'Cultural construct *versus* psychoanalytical conjecture.' *American Ethnologist*, 24. pp. 934-9.

Mosko, M. 1997b. 'Trobriand chiefs and fathers.' *Journal of the Royal Anthropological Institute*, (n.s.) 3. pp. 154-9.

Mosko, M. 1998a. 'Magical Money: Commoditisation and the linkage of *maketsi* ('market') and *kangakanga* ('custom') in contemporary North Mekeo.' In D. Akin and J. Robbins (eds), *Money and Modernity: State and local currencies in Melanesia*, ASAO Monograph, Pittsburgh: University of Pittsburgh Press. pp. 41-61.

Mosko, M. 1998b. 'Austronesian chiefs: Metaphorical *versus* fractal fatherhood.' *Journal of the Royal Anthropological Institute*, (n.s.) 4 .pp. 789-95.

Mosko, M. 2001a. 'Syncretic people: Sociality, agency and personhood in recent charismatic ritual practices among North Mekeo (PNG).' In J. Gordon and F. Magowan (eds), *Beyond Syncretism: Indigenous expressions of world religions*, Special Issue No. 13 of *The Australian Journal of Anthropology*, 12. pp. 259-74.

Mosko, M. 2001b. 'Self-evident chiefs: 'Hereditary' chieftainship among the North Mekeo (PNG).' Presented at workshop on 'Making rights in indigenous property 'self-evident' in regimes of inheritance', *Property, Transactions and Creativity* colloquium, Cambridge University, December.

Mosko, M. 2002. 'Totem and transaction: The objectification of 'tradition' among North Mekeo.' *Oceania*. 73. pp. 89-109.

Mosko, M. In press. 'Introduction. A (re)turn to chaos: Chaos theory, the sciences, and Social anthropological theory.' In M. Mosko and F. Damon (eds), *On the Order of 'Chaos': Social anthropology and the science of chaos*, New York: Berghahn Press.

Munn, N. 1986. *The Fame of Gawa*. Cambridge: Cambridge University Press.

Peterson, G. 1999. 'Sociopolitical rank and conical clanship in the Caroline Islands.' *Journal of the Polynesian Society*, 108. pp. 367-410.

Powell, H. 1997. 'Trobriand chiefs and fathers.' *Journal of the Royal Anthropological Institute*, (n.s.) 3. pp. 154-6.

Ross, M. 1988. 'Proto Oceanic and the Austronesian languages of Western Melanesia.' *Pacific Linguistics*, Series C, No. 98. Canberra: Department of Linguistics, Research School of Pacific and Asian Studies, The Australian National University.

Rumsey, A. 2000. 'Agency, personhood and the "I" of discourse in the Pacific and beyond.' *Journal of the Royal Anthropological Institute*, (n.s.) 6. pp. 101-16.

Sahlins, M. 1976. *Culture and Practical Reason*. Chicago: University of Chicago Press.

Scaglion, R. 1996. 'Chiefly models in Papua New Guinea.' *The Contemporary Pacific*, 8. pp. 1-32.

Seligmann, C. 1910. *The Melanesians of British New Guinea*. Cambridge: Cambridge University Press.

Stephen, M. 1974. 'Continuity and Change in Mekeo Society 1890-1971.' Unpublished PhD thesis, Research School of Pacific Studies, The Australian National University, Canberra.

Stephen, M. 1995. *The Gift of A'aisa*. Berkeley: University of California Press.

Stephen, M. 1996. 'The Mekeo 'man of sorrow': Sorcery and the individuation of self.' *American Ethnologist*, 23. pp. 84-101.

Stephen, M. 1998. 'A response to Mosko's comments on "The Mekeo man of sorrow".' *American Ethnologist*, 25. pp. 747-8.

Stewart, I. 1989. *Does God Play Dice?: The mathematics of chaos.* Cambridge (Mass.): Blackwell.

Stewart, P. and A. Strathern. 2001. *Humors and Substances: Ideas of the body in New Guinea.* Westport (Conn.): Bergin and Garvey.

Strathern, M. 1988. *The Gender of the Gift: Problems with women and problems with society in Melanesia.* Berkeley: University of California Press.

Valeri, V. 1986. *Kingship and Sacrifice: Ritual and society in ancient Hawaii.* Chicago: University of Chicago Press.

Wagner, R. 1986. *Asiwinarong.* Princeton: Princeton University Press.

Wagner, R. 1991. 'The fractal person.' In M. Godelier and M. Strathern (eds), *Big Man and Great Man: Personifications of power in Melanesia,* Cambridge and Paris: Cambridge University Press/Editions de la Maison des Sciences de l'Homme. pp. 159-73.

ENDNOTES

1 'Village' in the Central Mekeo dialect is *pangua.*

2 That is, until Christian crosses were erected in the central abdomen of most villages after missionisation. The designation of the central space of the Mekeo village as an 'abdomen' or 'womb' compares interestingly with Malinowski's (1965) report that the centre of a Trobriand garden is referred to as its 'belly'.

3 This global scheme is further complicated by the presence of categorical 'holes' (*ine*) in each of the four primary zones as the consequence of the recursive intersection of an additional inside/outside dimension. For the purposes of this article, I merely refer interested readers to the original account (Mosko 1985: 29-35).

4 *Inaenga* also refers to 'mother' (*ina*); see Mosko (1985: 75).

5 When I first developed this interpretation of North Mekeo reproductive physiology and anatomy a number of years ago (Mosko 1991b), I ventured that the indigenous theory of human procreation has the appearance of marsupial anatomy and physiology. I can now report that subsequent inquiries in the field have verified this proposition. According to my research associates, the marsupial female's pouch is termed her *inaenga* ('abdomen' or 'womb'), and it is in that cavity that marsupial males are thought to deposit their semen and that marsupial foetuses are understood to be conceived. The chief difference between placental and marsupial mammals is that the breasts (*gugu*) of marsupials are contained on the external skin that has been enveloped by the womb, whereas the breasts of placental animals are placed on the body's external skin and are not enveloped by the womb. Even so, women's breasts are regarded as having a special connection with the womb, as women and men maintain that a man's semen deposited in a nursing mother's womb will spoil her milk and make the nursing infant sick. This compares interestingly with Seligmann's (1910) report that among Austronesian-speaking Motu in the area of Port Moresby, women's breasts are understood to be intimately connected with their wombs.

6 There is considerable ethnographic uncertainty as to the pre-colonial existence of these moieties as bounded groups. However, whether named, discrete moieties existed in the past is, for present purposes, irrelevant, as the relations between specifically intermarrying clans co-resident in the same village were conducted as though they were from different moieties; see Mosko (1985: Chapters 6-8).

7 If there are senior and junior branches of the same clan represented in the same village, their respective senior and junior peace chiefs take responsibility for the same clubhouse (see Mosko 1985).

8 Unless stolen by a sorcerer for insertion into the bodies of other human victims (see Mosko 1985).

Chapter 13. The Ways of the Land-Tree: Mapping the North Pentecost Social Landscape

John P. Taylor

On a sunny afternoon, in the shade of a canopy of corrugated iron, beside a smoking fireplace on which green bananas were slowly roasting, my *tama* (father) and *ratahigi* ('chief'), Ruben Todali, talked to me about the history of Pentecost Island. He told me that in the past, many centuries before the arrival of *tuturani* (whites, foreigners) like myself, the people of North Pentecost could not speak. They communicated by way of designs that they described into the ground with their fingers. Instead of people, the sentient and mobile rocks and stones were talkative. [1] The dark soil of the hills and valleys also spoke. So too did the winds, the rain, and the salt water that lapped against the sand and coral of the island's coast. But some time ago this situation reversed, so now it is people who talk, while the land, winds, rain and sea remain wordless. Nowadays, said Ruben, people sometimes said of their island, 'We must speak for the land, because the land cannot speak for itself' (from an interview with Jif Ruben Todali, Avatvotu, May 1999).

This intimate connection between people, land and language—of language as having somehow vacated the environment for the mouths of people—is echoed in the Raga words '*Sia Raga*'. Raga speakers (see below) use this pronominal phrase when they wish to express a shared identity of language, land and *alengan vanua* ('ways of the place'). The word '*sia*' means 'earthquake', and in this specific context refers to a seismic jolt known to have taken place many millennia ago, which caused the island's emergence from under the sea. '*Raga*' refers to the Raga language, and also, in that language, to the island of Pentecost itself. In this paper I use the term Sia Raga to designate the Raga speakers of North Pentecost, being those people who claim ancestral connections to *bwatun vanua* ('foundation places') in the Raga-speaking region of North Pentecost, and who express that connection through shared links of land, kinship, language and culture. [2]

Pentecost is a long narrow island stretching some 63 kilometres north to south and 12 kilometres across at its widest point. It is home to five distinctive vernacular languages (Tryon 1996: 170). The Raga language group has the highest number of speakers on the island—roughly 6,000. The area in which Raga is the defining language extends approximately 20kms southwards from the northern tip to Tasvarongo village, and also includes areas of South Maewo, the island immediately to the north of Pentecost. The least elevated part of the island, called Ahivo ('at down'), is the extreme northern tip. Here, more than 1,200 people reside in an area of about six square kilometres, making it the most heavily populated region of the island. The majority of other people live in villages of varying size, from as many as 2-300 to a single household. These are dotted mainly along the western coast, particularly within the Hurilau and Lolkasai districts, or across the inland central plateau of Aute. People also reside on the alluvial regions of the eastern coast at Aligu, either side of the main village of Renbura. Generally speaking, within the Raga-speaking region, hamlets are encountered with lessening frequency the further one travels southwards ('upwards', in local idiom), especially inland beyond the crescent-shaped west coast Bay of Loltong. Here, the terrain becomes increasingly rough, and overland travel more difficult.

As Lissant Bolton has observed, for ni-Vanuatu, the landscape is not considered a stable entity. Rather, she suggests, 'in a volcanic zone where islands rise and fall under the ocean, and where hurricanes, earthquakes and even volcanic eruptions frequently modify the landscape in small ways, places are understood to move' (1999: 44). Landscape is also shaped visibly through the movement of people. The whole of Sia Raga history, recent and 'deep', is characterised by a constant flux of people moving across the land. Physical evidence of abandoned village and ceremonial sites, in the form of old house foundations or the ancient *mwele* (cycad palms) that mark the location of ritual pig-killings, are discernible almost everywhere on the upper plateau of the North Pentecost landscape. Such evidence attests to a continuity with today's situation in which whole villages may sometimes take up roots, and set them down at new locations, often joining with or separating from larger villages.

In North Pentecost, physical space is transformed into meaningful place through continuing reformulations of locality—of house planting and replanting, crop planting and harvest. Through these processes, it becomes imbued with layers of memory that are etched into the landscape. Where individual and group identity is conceived as taken *from* the land and infused *into* it (Rodman 1985: 68), the ability of people to interpret the landscape thus becomes vitally important to the forging and strengthening of those identities. Knowledge of the memory of landscape—of houses built, gardens tended, or of ancestral connection ritually or otherwise affirmed—and an ability to retrace the tracks between known places help people to recognise their identity as a series of itinerant linkages. It is through such knowledge that people are able to legitimate their rights and ties to particular pieces of land.

In this chapter, I explore some central idioms by which the Sia Raga understand the relationship between people, place and landscape, particularly as these are articulated through the important concept of *vanua*. After briefly discussing the term *vanua* in relation to social practice, I do so initially through tracing the importance of North Pentecost founding ancestor Bwatmahanga. This is achieved through the presentation and analysis of a number of compelling images that were shown and explained to me by my North Pentecost father, mentor and *ratahigi* (in Bislama: *Jif*, or 'chief'), Ruben Todali. The arboreal nature of these 'land-tree' images provides insight into Sia Raga interpretations of landscape and habitation in terms of a dynamic historical emergence. Through such images, the relationship between people and place is conceptualised in terms of an itinerant cartography—stasis and growth built into the same image (compare with Patterson, this volume). In conclusion, the paper shows how the shape of this history is also made to incorporate important political issues within the neo-colonial present.

Atatun Vanua: The People of the Place

The term *vanua* intersects with numerous other Raga words in communicating ideas of location, space or place. In particular, *vanua* is closely related to the word *tano*, which may also be used in the identification or description of particular areas of land. In contrast with *vanua*, however, *tano* pertains more specifically to the physicality of the land, and in this way it can be used to mean 'ground' or 'soil', and appears in constructions such as *tanoga* (muddy) and *taniadu* (ashes). *Tano* also sometimes appears as a locative prefix—such as in *tanon alhuhuni* (west) and *tanon ha oha o* (handle). In this way, it overlaps with the more commonly used term, *ute*, such as in *ute maragasi* (hilly place) or *ute gogona* (restricted place). Unlike both of these terms, however, wherever the concept of *vanua* is used it always carries with it the profound sense of identity that the Sia Raga feel in relation to place and the importance of the experience of place as lived social space (for cognate Ambae terms, compare Allen 1969: 132, Rodman 1987: 35, Bolton 2003: 132; also Patterson, this volume).

Though *vanua* may also be used somewhat loosely to refer to any area of land, village or indeed to whole islands, in Raga it pertains more specifically to the hundreds of individually named pieces of land into which the whole region of North Pentecost is divided. Individual *vanua* are usually little more than an acre or two in size. Indeed, larger contemporary villages often span several *vanua*. These land segments provide a key category for the regulation of rights to utilise land as gardens (*uma*), household dwellings (*imwa*), or in any other capacity.

Although anyone may be granted rights to utilise the land within a particular *vanua*, these rights are usually maintained by the authority of individual descent groups. Just as the members of individual descent groups are somewhat dispersed across the Sia Raga population, each descent group retains custodianship of many individual *vanua* that are scattered throughout the North Pentecost landscape. Some *vanua* are, however, identified more specifically as *bwatun vanua* (literally 'source', 'foundation', 'head' or 'roots' of the *vanua*').[3] *Bwatun vanua* represent the specific origin places of individual descent groups, with which they share names, such as Anserehubwe, Gilau or Atabulu (see also Yoshioka 1988: 21). Each *Bwatun vanua* is characterised by the existence of a *bwaru* (ancestral grave site). These roughly circular stone piles contain the resting places of primordial and subsequent ancestors, the *atatun vanua* ('people of the place') from whom the people of Raga today descend.[4] *Atatun vanua*, who are described as 'ghosts' or 'devils' in Bislama, continually inhabit the *vanua* of their death.[5]

While many *vanua* do not contain any significant features, some are likewise distinguished by stones (*vatu*), cycad palms (*mwele*) or other significant historical markers that provide *dovonana* ('memorial' or 'proof') of the acts by which ancestors have in some way merged with the earth of that place, especially through the performance of pig sacrifice. Today, through the ritualised spilling of pigs blood and the subsequent appropriation of ancestrally defined 'pig names' (*ihan boe*), people continue to affect the absorption of essential ancestral qualities. Through this process, land, ancestors and people become merged. The ability to identify ancestral grave sites and other markers and to trace one's descent through the chronological recollection of those ancestors that they contain or represent is important in claiming rights to utilise land contained within individual *vanua*. Individuals are able to claim links to a great many *vanua*, and do so strategically.

Bwatmahanga: The Foundation Diverges

According to Sia Raga histories, the division of the land into *vanua* and *bwatun vanua* occurred as part of the same purposeful process and along the same tracks by which North Pentecost was colonised by their ancestors. This all began with Bwatmahanga, the 'first man' of Pentecost. According to Jif Ruben Todali, the appearance of Bwatmahanga defines the beginning of the third epoch or 'generation' (*tauva*) of Sia Raga cosmogony.[6] He was not the first sentient being to inhabit Pentecost, but he was the first person (*atatu*) to take fully human form, and, along with his siblings, was the apical ancestor of the people of Raga today. He is also remembered as the first 'chief' (*ratahigi*), the creator of the first household dwellings (*imwa*) and 'men's houses' (*gamali*), and pioneer of the road to *abanoi*. *Abanoi*, an invisible other world (or 'paradise', as it is referred to in Bislama), is woven through the material world of human experience (*ureure*), and is inhabited by ancestors (*atatun vanua*) and other spirit beings such as *tavalurau*, whose name—meaning literally, 'the other side of the leaf'—evocatively describes the relationship between the two realms.[7] Turning a leaf (*rau*) over merely renders the other side invisible. While both sides are always 'present' to consciousness, only one is accessible to the eye. As Jif Ruben Todali explained *abanoi* to me: 'You can't see it, but it is here with us anyway.'

Atmate, the 'spirits' or 'souls' of the dead, are also sometimes described by the related term *tavaltena*, or 'spirits of the other side'. Through these terms, the relationship between the two cosmological 'sides' of *ureure* and *abanoi* is pictured as simultaneously joined and separated. Bwatmahanga is the historical embodiment of key architectonic concepts. Two of the most important of these are present in his name: *bwat*, meaning 'source' or 'foundation' (see above), and *mahanga*, to 'branch' or 'diverge'. Bwatmahanga is the figure of the one that becomes two.

Bwatmahanga appears in many origin narratives throughout the northern islands of the archipelago, and wherever he does he is always accompanied and thwarted by his adversary, Tagaro. [8] In North Pentecost, part of the reason why narratives involving Bwatmahanga and Tagaro are so important is that they engage with the origin of human engagement with otherness. They thereby provide insight into the ambivalent dualism that has become the fundamental architectonic feature of the Sia Raga cosmological, metaphysical and social universe. As Battaglia (1990) found of the Sabbarl, the idea of dualism in Sia Raga ontology is not simply positive and productive, but has equally negative and destructive tendencies. In this way, the entangled careers of Bwatmahanga and Tagaro suggest a relationship fraught with productive potential and antagonism. Like the monster Katutubwai of Sabbarl children's stories, Tagaro's relationship to Bwatmahanga represents that of 'the spectre of the ambivalently valued Other that haunts the texts of human life—texts taken as interactional or 'dialogical' constructs, where the Other is historically an aspect of one's own life' (Battaglia 1990: 38). For Sia Raga, the processes of birth, growth, procreation, death and knowledge all depend on the continuing activation and engagement of that otherness, which contains the power to give and to take away. [9]

Tagaro's arrival marks the beginning of human violence and of an era in which peace (*tamata*) no longer constitutes the natural order of things, but must be constantly strived for and negotiated. Today, the search for *tamata* represents the ultimate stated goal of all Sia Raga ritual enterprise. In the course of striving for social and cosmological unity within their already divided world, division itself becomes a part of that strategy. Jif Ruben once explained to me that marriage (*lagiana*), funerals (*mateana*) and male rank-taking ceremonies (*bolololi*) all ultimately represent strategies or roads (*hala*) to the attainment of that same goal: peace (*tamata*). In all cases, these strategies involve the engagement of dynamic relationships struck between things divided, or 'sides' (*tavalu*), found for instance in the distinction between the two moieties (themselves called *tavalu*), the lived world (*ureure*) and the Other world (*abanoi*), and more recently between *alengan vanua* (local fashion) and *alengan tuturani* (the fashion of whites). As I hope will become more apparent throughout the course of this paper, *tamata* lies at the ideological centre of moiety division, the associated division of people and land into individual descent groups and *vanua*, as well as the networks of exchange by which these are bound together. As almost anyone from North Pentecost will tell you, peace is the true goal of all Sia Raga cultural endeavour.

Bwatuna: Foundations for the Land-tree

Figure 1 is a diagram that was drawn by Jif Ruben on a blackboard in the Avatvotu village *gamali*, and which I copied into my field notes in June 1999, a month after my arrival there. It is headed with the words, '*Vanua toto deti—bwatun touva*' ('Here is a tree of place—foundation of generations').[10]

Figure 1: Land-tree one

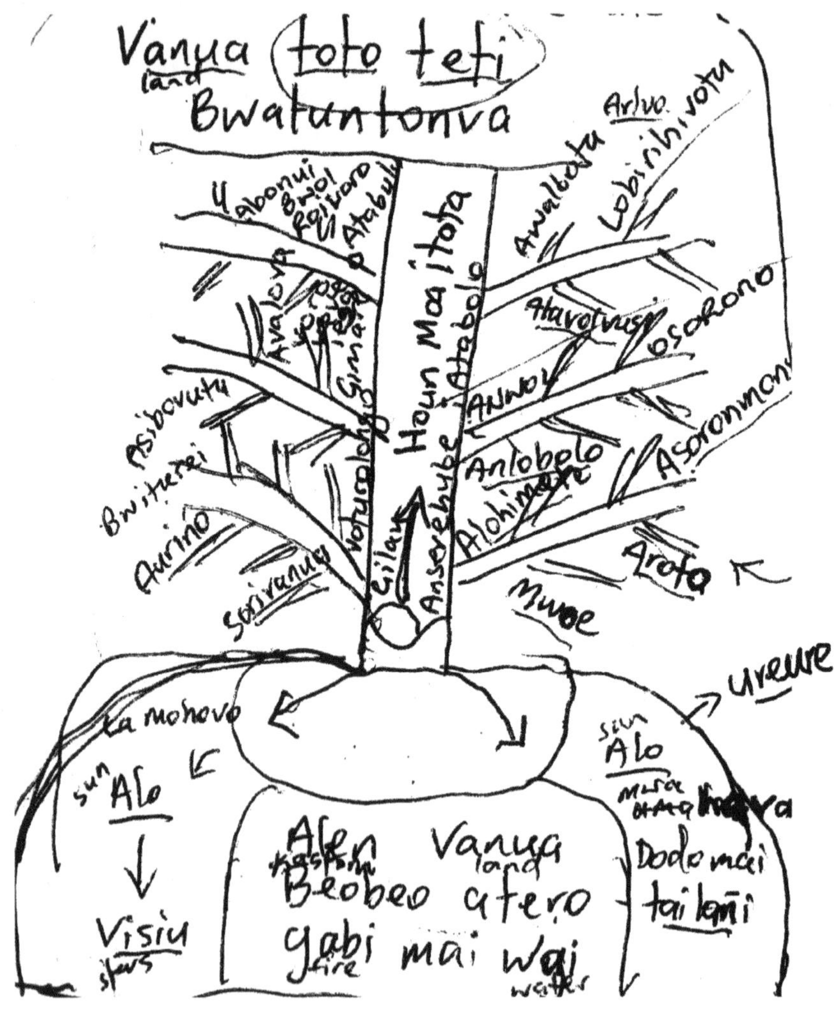

Blending cosmography with social topography, the image shows the emergence and presence of the differentiated cosmos that I have begun to trace above. It depicts the physical emergence of the island of Pentecost, and at the same time it traces the past and present distribution of *atatun vanua*, the 'people of the place', across that landscape. The island is imagined as a tree (*toto*), its branches ramifying on either side of a stout trunk. The tree grows from the soil of a unitary plenum, of land (*vanua*) and surrounding cosmos (*ureure*). This land is described as having formed during a cosmogonical episode in which fire and water met, reacted and affected the emergence of solid rock from the sea. Jif Ruben uses the words '*Alen Vanua beobeo atero gabi mai wai*' ('*kastom* land pushed from beneath by fire and water').[11] The land is enveloped by the stuff of *ureure*, the 'material' cosmos of lived experience—including '*alo, mahava, visui, dodo mai tailangi*' ('sun, air, stars, rain clouds and white clouds')—of which the land (*vanua*) is also a part.

Historical provenance for this remarkable land-tree image is the divisive turbulence of the early 20th century, its recent emergence being framed within the struggle for hegemony and the power to dictate cosmology by recent converts to the Anglican faith and those supporting *kastom*. Jif Ruben describes the 'inventor' of this technology—his father by birth, Vira Livlivu—as a man of questions, a man who needed to understand (*iloi*) everything. For this reason, while his attitude towards the growth of Anglicanism was essentially ambivalent, he was at the same time drawn to its novel spiritual ideas and to the new forms of knowledge that it was importing, and which were becoming increasingly popular throughout the region. As a result of his thirst for knowledge and his desire to further explore the ideas and teachings of the Anglicans, Vira Livlivu became a catechist, and thereby learned to read and write. In the evocative and ambivalent image with which Jif Ruben enjoys describing him, Vira Livlivu stands at the door of the local village church house, with one hand he rings the bell for Sunday service, in the other he holds a rifle.

As this image suggests, Vira Livlivu came to the conclusion that the knowledge and practices contained within church and *kastom* should be mutually maintained in Sia Raga society. He saw that those two apparently competing ideologies might be incorporated into a productive duality as new figures within the social and ontological framework of *tavalui* ('sides'). However fraught, this is a common sentiment today. In the context of the early 20th century, though, his position would no doubt have been quite novel, especially in consideration of the levels of conflict and violence that characterised the division (see Taylor 2003).

As a consequence of his interests, and in the hope that a fusing together of church and *kastom* might lead, ultimately, to *tamata* (peace), Vira Livlivu encouraged each of his two sons to pursue one of these divergent paths of knowledge. Today, Jif Ruben is the recognised *kastom* leader of Gelau, while his brother, Peter, was for many years catechist to the area. [12] On Sunday mornings, during my major field trip, Peter would read the Gospels to a smattering of local parishioners at the Lagaronboga church house. This was the time during which Jif Ruben, ten minutes walk up the hill, would habitually work with his exercise books, recording his knowledge of *kastom*. Utopian visions of *tamata* (peace) also provided the underlying reason why Vira Livlivu devised his 'land-trees' and passed them onto his son, Jif Ruben. Considering the continued importance of the knowledge that they systematise Jif Ruben has passed them to his own son, Kolombas.

Shortly after I arrived at Avatvotu—and before I encountered the land-tree on the blackboard—Jif Ruben spent one long afternoon picturing for me the shape and trajectory of Sia Raga cosmography. He began by describing to me the island's first creation as rock and its emergence from the sea. He went on to explain to me the processes of death and decay by which soil was formed from the moss (*lumute*) that settled on the rocks of the newly formed island, and of how that soil provided a substance in which a process of rebirth could occur, thus enabling that moss to diversify, eventually becoming the many plant and animal life forms that exist today. '*Lumute*,' he told me, 'is the basis of all life.'

Jif Ruben always provided caveats to these renditions, interspersing his narrations with statements such as this: 'I don't know if what I'm telling you is true or not. This is just what the old men from before believed. It may be true. I don't know.' Yet he would also contradict his modesties by pointing out that this *vevhurina* (history, or more literally, 'talk because of it') could nevertheless be authenticated beyond all others. Proof that humans are ultimately derived from *lumute*, through a process of incremental transformation, is retained in the physical characteristics of the first animal to appear on Raga, the *bebeure*. As Jif Ruben told me, if you tie one of these moths to a piece of string and ask it a question, such as 'Where is the rough sea?' or 'Which way is north?', it will attempt to fly off in that direction. 'It knows,' he said. 'That small piece of knowledge, that people emerged from it [the moth], is still here [retained in the moth]. This is apparent in that the knowledge that we have, this small knowledge, is shared by the small *bebeure*' (recorded at Avatvotu village, May 2000). Just as the existence of graves, cycads and rocks authenticate people's relation to place, so too the *bebeure* contains the *dovongana* (memorial, proof) of Jif Ruben's account of Sia Raga history, and, by extension, of the authority of the land-tree.

On a more pragmatic level, the land-tree operates as a central technological device whereby Jif Ruben is able to maintain his position as judicial negotiator at land-dispute meetings, which, given the considerable flexibility of the Sia Raga land-tenure system, are commonplace. Insofar as social identities in the present are seen to be crucially linked to the landscape through the foundational actions of ancestors, the land-tree is therefore made to function in a very practical and disciplinary way: to help settle land disputes by demonstrating the historical relationship between the land and its embodiment by the ancestors of disputants, and therefore by the disputants themselves.

During the time in which I lived with him, Jif Ruben was often called away to different areas of North Pentecost to help settle land disputes. He did not, however, display or refer to these images in such meetings. This does not mean that they constitute some sort of 'secret knowledge'. Rather, Jif Ruben was conscious that reference to written texts in such contexts is often viewed by others as undermining the authority of a speaker's arts of memory and of oration. Instead, in actual practice, the land-tree provides one of many mnemonic strategies by which named plots of land (*vanua*) are known and ordered—also apparent in house architecture and weaving patterns, for instance. It is usually referred to or rehearsed in private, on paper or the blackboard in the *gamali*. To my knowledge, only a handful of adult males draw them, and all of these are residents of Gilau.

Halana: The Ways of the Land-Tree

> The tree is already the image of the world, or the root the image of the world tree. (Deleuze and Guattari 1987: 5)

The primary function of the land-tree is to provide a map of relations between landholdings based on the history and colonisation of that land by ancestors. This is made more obvious in Figure 2, where the 'tree' is clearly the prime object of attention, and the more general cosmological elements are simply represented alongside the image of a globe, identified as such by the inclusion of lines of longitude and latitude.[13] As Jif Ruben explained it to me, the words that appear alongside the various branches and sub-branches of all of these land-tree images are the names of ancestral *bwatun vanua*, or the 'foundation places' of descent groups (see above). The collection of names is representative rather than exhaustive, and this mainly explains the significant differences between the two examples shown here. Some of the *bwatun vanua* appearing on these images are the names of contemporary hamlets, such as Asaola, Arevo, Atabulu and Amangao in Figure 1. Other names are said to represent the sites of hamlets long since abandoned.

Figure 2: Land-tree two

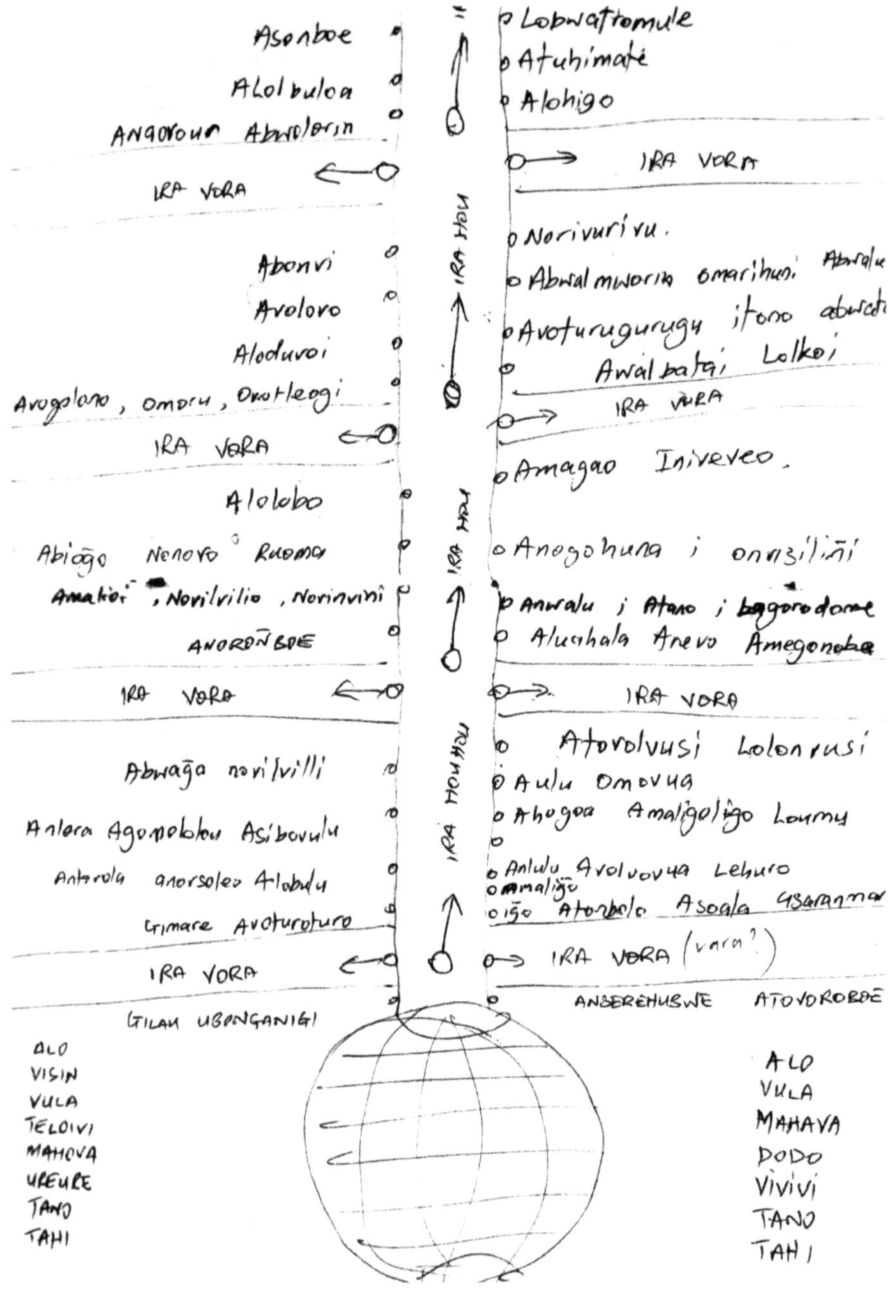

The land-tree very clearly demonstrates the centrality of itinerant principles, and especially of series and divergence, in Sia Raga interpretations of social topography. The analysis of these can readily be linked to recent appraisals in

Pacific anthropology of Deleuze and Guattari's distinction between rhizomic and arborescent models. [14] In apparent contradiction to Deleuze and Guattari's suggestion that Oceania, 'in particular', offers 'something like a rhizomic model opposed in every respect to the Western model of the tree' (1987: 18), their shape is clearly tree-like. Thus in Deleuze and Guattari's terms, and like the figure Bwatmahanga (discussed above), they may be seen to incorporate a certain 'tree logic' of 'tracing and reproduction'; something akin to an endless development of 'the law of the One that becomes two, then the two that becomes four' (Deleuze and Guattari 1987: 5).

Alan Rumsey (2001) has tested the application of Deleuze and Guattari's models of rhizome and tree to a variety of indigenous forms of 'topographic inscription', such as they are described in anthropological accounts from Australia and Melanesia. His discussion juxtaposes what he sees as the essentially 'rhizomic' nature of Aboriginal dreaming cartographies with several more ambiguously 'arborescent' examples from Melanesia. (The Moorhead River and Iatmul regions of PNG, and the island of Tanna in Southern Vanuatu, provide his main examples from Melanesia.) In the terms of this discussion, Rumsey notes the appearance of striking similarities across Melanesian cultures

> in the way the earth is interpreted as a surface of inscription, in the dense interconnectedness of named places along tracks established by the movements of protean creator figures, in the localisation of knowledge about these movements and the role that that knowledge plays in the reproduction and contestation of present-day people's rights to land. (Rumsey 2001: 32)

Rumsey's description of arboreal metaphor in the Moorhead River region of PNG, which draws mainly on the ethnographic work of Ayres (1983), is in many ways cogent to the form and movement of the images discussed here. For the Moorhead people and the Sia Raga, the tree seems to be the main figure by which people understand the spatiality of social relationships and the mapping of these onto the landscape. Indeed, this has also been noted as a common theme across the Austronesian language area (Fox and Sather 1996). Furthermore, in both cases the image of the tree as a fully formed object is not as important as an attendance to the nature and trajectories of its growth (Rumsey 2001:28). This final section is concerned with discussing the tree as just such an image, as a network of *hala* (ways, roads) by which the Sia Raga form an understanding of relationships to place, and also to each other, across space and time.

As is the case in Rumsey's (2001) discussion of Moorhead interpretations, the Sia Raga identify two places of original separation and dispersal for the formation of the cosmos and the island itself, and the peopling of the land. The first of these is the home of Mugarimanga, whose name, somewhat like that of Bwatmahanga (above), suggests the opening of 'sides', here being the two valves of a cockle shell—*mu* (mother), *gari* (cockle shell), *manga* (to open). Mugarimahanga's first-and second-born sons accidentally opened a hole in the ground from which issued a great flood of salt water, thus creating the sea that now divides Pentecost and Maewo, two islands that were previously joined. [15] Fleeing from the flood, Mugarimahanga's 12 children dispersed and embodied the natural environment, becoming the rain, wind, waves, tides and stones. [16] Some time after the embodiment of *ureure* (the cosmos) by these primordial *atatun vanua*, two of Mugarimanga's children met one day in the middle of the island of Pentecost at a place in the bush, somewhere above where the village of Bwatnapne is located today. [17] These were a woman called Mumate, who had become the 'quiet' western sea, and a man called Mauri, who had become the rough sea of the east. Without realising that they were in fact brother and sister, Mumate and Mauri met once again at Atabulu where they married and had children. [18] The first of these children, and therefore the 'first man' of Pentecost itself, was Bwatmahanga (the 'foundation diverges'), primogenitor of the Sia Raga today.

The second location is the home and place of death of Bwatmahanga. This is the starting point of human dispersal, but also of return, and it is with this location that Jif Ruben's land-tree image is primarily concerned. Anserehubwe is located at the extreme northern tip of Pentecost Island. Following Sia Raga directional orientation, in which to travel southwards is to go 'up' (*hae*), this point represents the very base of the island. It is thus located in the district called Ahivo ('at down'). The Sia Raga identify Anserehubwe as the pre-eminent *bwatun vanua* (foundation place), the unique place of origin and departure for the human settlement of Pentecost. It is also a place of merging (*hubwe*), for it is through this place that people at death 'return' to *abanoi* (the Other world) and become fully merged as *atatun vanua* (people of the place).

From Anserehubwe, the dispersal of the Sia Raga population across the land is reckoned to have followed specific patterned trajectories. As Jif Ruben's representations elegantly show, the image of the tree provides a binding metaphor by which this dispersal is traced, and eventually becomes a kind of cartography. Thus space and time are condensed within the same image. Attention to the manner in which the dispersal of people across the landscape is considered to have 'taken place'—the growth of the tree—is made clear by the presence of circles and arrows in the second of the figures presented. As Jif Ruben explained it to me, circles represent *bwatuna* (foundations, roots, places of settlement) and arrows represent *hala* (ways, roads, trajectories).

As Jif Ruben further explained, the land-tree demonstrates that dispersal took place in a series of departures divided into two successive phases. Each phase is characterised by a distinct pattern of movement, the first being a progression of what Rumsey describes as 'lineal segmentation from a unity' (see

Figure 3 [left], adapted from Rumsey 2001: 29), the second a mode of bifurcation from the points already established along that lineal segmentation (Figure 3 [right]). While obviously recognisable as a kind of 'branching', the latter kind of movement is clearly not identical to another mode described by Rumsey; rather than appearing as a somewhat rhizomic 'scattering or fragmentation from a starting point or centre' (Rumsey 2001: 29), what occurs here is serial bifurcation at specific nodal points (*bwatuna*) that are distributed evenly along a central 'trunk'. This pattern may be further imagined as recurring on subsequent branchings, and may be realised ultimately as an infinitely reticulating fractal (images not presented here, see Taylor 2003). The image of the tree is the image of the island, and it is also the image of the leaf.

Figure 3: Lineal segmentation from a unity (left, after Rumsey 2001: 29), and serial bifurcation at specific nodal points (right)

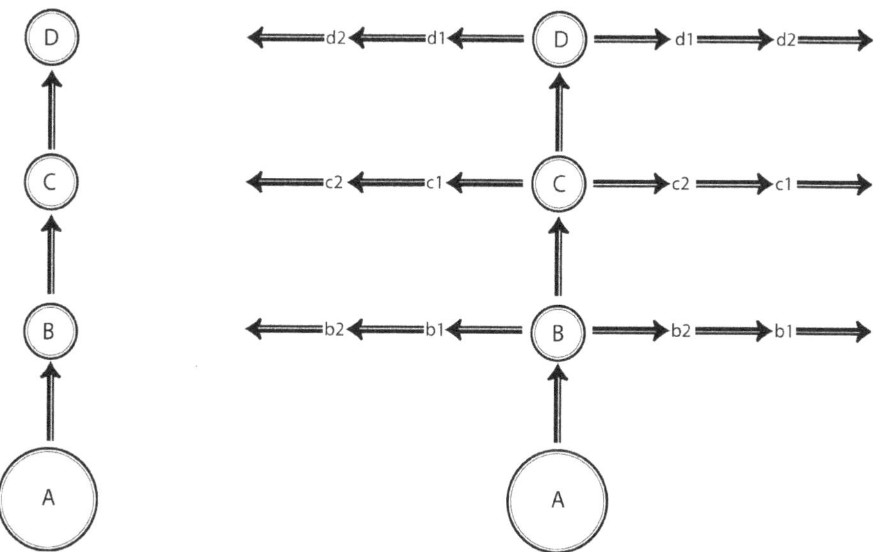

In explanation of these different itinerant modes, Jif Ruben told me that when the original departure from Anserehubwe occurred, the rules of marriage—the division of society into two exogenous moieties—had not yet been devised. Being devoid of the lateral dimension of 'sides' (*tavalui*), lineal movement was the only available option. While some people stayed at Anserehubwe a group of people moved upwards—or, in Western geographical idiom, southwards—to settle on a new point on the land. At a later stage, a division from this second group departed once again, continuing along the same trajectory, up the 'trunk' (*bwatun gai*) of the island. As this pattern of lineal segmentation continued, the children of those groups left behind formed their own new *bwatun vanua* (foundation places) at the places where they settled.

As Jif Ruben further explained to me, the main impetus for the succession of departures was fighting over land. Social tension was fuelled by the restrictive, linear nature of their pattern of movement and settlement. Nevertheless, throughout the course of their journeying, the people had been developing their knowledge. By the time they began to reach the 'end of the line', they came to a point where they were able to strategise new roads (*hala*) for the maintenance of peace (*tamata*). These roads, being the related rules of marriage and land tenure, were based on the designation of two moieties. These are known today as *Bule* and *Tabi*. With the division of the population into two *tavalui* (sides, halves, partners), successive generations began to move outwards rather than upwards, thus forming branches (*raran gai*) on either side of those previously established nodal settlements. With women moving across from one *tavalui* to the other in marriage, yet with land being retained within the matriline, the fair and equal distribution of land was ensured.

Tavalui: The Divided World

When Codrington first noted the pervasiveness of the idea of 'sides' as a socio-linguistic category linking the islands of northern Vanuatu, he argued that the extreme cultural and linguistic diversity that he found to be characteristic of the region must have emerged from a more unified source. [19] Thus he wrote of the Banks Islands:

> The identity of the language is conspicuous, however mutually unintelligible the dialects may be; and wherever a native of one of these islands may land he may find his due place in the *gamal*, the clubhouse of the *Suqe*. What is chiefly remarkable as showing how comparatively modern are these diversities, even of language, is the identity in all these Northern New Hebrides of the division of the population into two 'sides of the house,' which obtains in the Banks Islands. (Codrington 1881: 291; see also Wilson 1932: 65)

The notion of duality is also a pervasive feature of the Sia Raga conceptual universe in which it is considered that all things should have two 'sides' (*tavalu*), and that everything must have a 'partner' (also *tavalu*). [20] While in some instances such duality is considered in terms of hierarchical opposition—a person's strong, 'good' right side is distinguished from their left side, which is weak and 'bad'—it is more often the case that the two are seen to form an ambivalent yet productive complementarity. [21]

The division of the entire population into two exogamous matrilineal moieties, *Bule* and *Tabi*, provides the most powerful example of how dualism works as a productive organising principle within Sia Raga society. The two moieties are commonly referred to as *tavalu*, which has the basic meaning of 'opposite', 'side', 'half' or 'partner'. [22] An individual's sense of belonging to either one of the two major social divisions—of being either *Bule* or *Tabi*—is inscribed from birth as one of the most basic elements of social identity. Inclusion in either of the two moieties provides the basis of one's social categorisation, and for this reason strangers who arrive to stay in the area for only a few days are quickly defined accordingly. Conversely, to suggest that someone belongs to neither *tavalui* is considered the most serious of insults. One turn of phrase for such an accusation, *matan gai halhala*, is translated by Hardacre as 'son of a floating stick' (Hardacre n.d.: 40). This reflects the arboreal 'land-tree' images of kinship and social organisation described above. It also clearly resonates with Jolly's discussion of the privileging of different kinds of movement amongst the Sa speakers of South Pentecost. In North Pentecost, also, whereas rootedness and motivated movement are highly regarded, 'mere wandering or floating is deplored' (Jolly 1999: 284).

One of the many important characteristics of the distinction between one's own moiety members and those of the 'other' lies in the way it permeates the ceremonial and ritual duties that punctuate Sia Raga life. At such occasions, through performing those duties and obligations that are so important in the creation of the social identity of people, matrikin and patrikin 'become' interminably embroiled within a process of reckoning, delivering and receiving.

Like the role of hands in the making of string figures, *tavalui* construct the division across which meaningful *hala* (ways, roads, trajectories) can become linked. Indeed, tension and interplay between the moieties is considered to be essential to the maintenance of efficient and harmonious social relations and production. A strict rule dictating that a person may not marry a person of his or her own moiety is maintained, while major prestations in large part follow a cross-moiety trajectory. Intra-moiety marriages, called *bona*, are said to sometimes occur despite ridicule and ostracism. Such unions are, however, very rare, and only one was evident during my visit.

As Wagner found among the Barok people of New Ireland, the moieties contain their own and nurture the other, and thereby 'stand in a relation of asymmetrically and perpetually unresolved hierarchy to one another' (Wagner 1986: 49). In this way, Layard noted a 'creative tension between the moieties, which are at one and the same time necessarily opposed to one another and also essential to one another's existence' (Layard 1942:103). Whether performing transactions with the other world, *abanoi*, or in prestations between kin, all ritual action is concerned ultimately with the redefinition of differentiation and the relationship between *tavalui* (sides). The relationship between sides therefore appears as a separation and a binding together. Between them the Sia Raga, anxiously negotiate strategies by which to sustain a perilous equilibrium; to stop the sides from falling away from each other, but also from merging into confusion.

In North Pentecost, as the result of this creative tension, the two social divisions are perceived as entangled, or 'stuck' to one another. This 'entanglement' (cf. Thomas 1991) is described by the word *wasi*. Being *wasi* is itself considered a two-sided predicament, with good and bad qualities. It implies difficulty and costliness, but perhaps more importantly, strength, tenacity and security. For this reason, Sia Raga social life is considered to be inescapable, a situation that may give rise to feelings of resentment as well as assurance. In particular, like a severe case of 'tall poppy syndrome', the tension of otherness is seen to act in such a way as to negate assertions of individual difference. People complain that it is hard to get ahead, that they are constantly swallowed up by society. As one person told me, to be *man Raga* is like being trapped in the jaws of a clam shell. [23]

Alengan Tuturani: The Ways of Foreigners

Appearing in contradistinction to this appraisal of Sia Raga social organisation are widely held impressions of *alengan tuturani,* or the 'ways of whites/foreigners'. *Tuturani* has become an important oppositional category in the Sia Raga classification of their world, providing terminology for marking the otherness of introduced objects and styles. The concept of *tuturani* gives the Sia Raga a tag for most every plant, animal, artefact and *kastom* that has crossed their shores since contact with Europeans (cf. Dening 1980). People might speak of *ginau tuturani* (white man's things), including such things as *uhi tuturani* (fruit: *tuturani,* pawpaw) and *wai tuturani* (water: *tuturani,* alcohol). In this way, *alengan tuturani* (white man's fashion) is contrasted with *alengan vanua* (ways of the place) as two related but opposing 'sides' (*tavalui*) within Sia Raga classificatory idiom.

Once I told Jif Ruben that my parents were divorced, and that this was not an uncommon situation for children of my generation. In response, he suggested that together we write a book outlining the basic principles of Sia Raga kinship, and of moiety dualism in particular, and that we present this book to the New Zealand Government. The nationwide implementation of this social strategy in New Zealand would, he believed, put an end to the break-up of marriages.

When people say that there is no divorce on Pentecost they are articulating their faith in *alengan vanua* (ways of the place), and of a social cohesion bound up in the play between 'sides' (*tavalui*). [24] At the same time, Jif Ruben's proposal reflects the idea that, in contrast with Sia Raga sociality, the world of *tuturani* (whites) is 'free'. It is a society without structure, and devoid of the restraints formed by the webs of connectedness that bind the two moieties together. The price of this freedom, social chaos, is seen to extend beyond the family sphere. It is also made evident in negative images of theft, violence, self-advancement, and the gap between rich and poor in the West.

What follows is abstracted from a North Pentecost creation history that was narrated orally by the late Father Walter Hadye Lini in 1981. This history, which was transcribed and translated from Raga by Lini and David Walsh, is titled '*Veveven bwatun tauvwa, ata la Vanua Raga*', or 'A story about the beginning of creation, from Pentecost Island' (Walsh 1981). [25] After the emergence of the island from the sea, the story begins with the birth of a baby boy from a kind of shellfish. After the boy grows up, he meets a sea snake that later transforms into a woman:

> Thus the man and the woman came together and produced children. They two produced ten children while they stayed there, at Atano. They produced ten children, and they [the children] stayed there—and then they two moved on and went so that they would stay at the place of that woman. They both went and stayed there, at Anarasi. They stayed there until they produced some children there. Their children were many—they two arose from there and went up and stayed at Loltongo. They stayed at Loltongo and they produced some children there. They produced some children, and they [the children] stayed there—they two arose from there and went up and stayed at Bwatnapni. They stayed there and produced some children there also. They produced some children and they [the children] stayed there, and then they two arose from there and went up and stayed at Vat-tangele. They stayed at Vat-tangele and they produced children there also.
>
> It—all the children that they two produced—began at Ahivo and went up until it reached Vat-tangele; some were white people and some were black people. Today we call the white people *tuturani* and the black people *atatmato*. (Walsh 1981: 368-9)

The people then began quarrelling with a land snake, *teltele*, who eventually trapped them in their village by covering the entrance with a large rock. They then decided that the white people should try to escape by digging their way out of the village:

> The *tuturani* dug a hole—it went down underneath the fence of that village. They dug it—it went until it went down and came out on the coast; but on that coast stood various boats they had made—canoes and sailing ships. When the *tuturani* went down so that they would get away, they took those sailing ships and went with them, and those black people stayed and kept the canoes that lay there.
>
> The *tuturani* went—they went and stayed at other islands on which today *tuturani* are found; and the black people stayed at Raga—so today black people are found on Raga island ... Raga people today say that the *tuturani* went with those sailing ships and also with all the knowledge

and wisdom, and therefore today the black people stay back from certain knowledge and wisdom which the *tuturani* know today. (Walsh 1981: 370; all spelling is as it appears in the original text.)

This history differs from those that I was told on North Pentecost in several important respects. The unitary origins and kinship of *atatmato* and *tuturani*, along with the latter's departure from rather than arrival at Pentecost Island, represents a revision that bears relation to the political climate of national independence in which the story was told. [26] However, the narrative components provide a condensation of themes that recur frequently in Sia Raga histories. [27]

In particular, 'upward' (*hae*) colonisation of the land along a north to south itinerary followed by division or branching into 'sides' reinscribes the crucial orienting pathways by which the Sia Raga understand the emergent and present relationship of people to knowledge and place. Here, moving from the village of Atano in the far north (at Ahivo, 'at down'), then moving progressively southwards through a series of places—Anarasi (at Abwatuntora), Loltong, Bwatnapni (in Central Pentecost)—until eventually reaching Vatun Gele at the very south of the island, the peopling of the land occurs along a reverse trajectory to that which was forged by Bwatmahanga in his journey to *abanoi*. Significantly, histories recounting the 19th-century arrival of the Anglican Church and its spread across the island also follow this path (for instance, Leona n.d.). Likewise, the departure of *tuturani*, 'with those sailing ships and also with all the knowledge and wisdom' (Walsh 1981: 370), represents a splitting into ambivalently composed 'sides'. This is understood to exist within much the same kind of relationship as the two Sia Raga moieties, *Bule* and *Tabi*.

In this chapter, we have seen how the people of North Pentecost deploy metaphors based on arboreal imagery in order to explain ideas of origin, ancestry, historical emergence and social organisation. In the apical ancestor, Bwatmahanga, we saw how the concept of foundations or roots (*bwatuna*), coupled with that of bifurcation or branching (*mahanga*), constituted significant features of reference within these metaphors. The importance of trees as images of spatio-temporality rests not only in their shape, but in the manner of their growth. The becoming of the tree is seen to 'take place' along these two interrelated trajectories (*hala*), one appearing to take the form of lineal sequence, the second the form of divergence or branching. As the land-tree designs drawn by Jif Ruben and others demonstrate, the tree has the capacity to incorporate simultaneously an atemporal cartography or topography and a spatialised temporality and itinerant history.

Anyone familiar with the ethnography of Southern Asia and the Pacific will be aware that the employment of trees as metaphors for understanding social topography on historical terms are common throughout this region. [28] What is unusual about the Sia Raga example, and similar to the Moorhead people (Rumsey

2001: 28), is that although this topography is considered to have emerged in sequential fashion, it is not perceived to be hierarchically ordered, as so often appears to be the case elsewhere. The Sia Raga conceive of historical linearity as articulated with spatial divergence, and in terms of this articulation the past does not appear as a series of substitutions, but rather as layers of renewal. Histories produced within the rubric of this ontology entail a condensation of the language of time into that of space and place. In stressing the *presence* of historical location and movement, the past is not seen to be wholly 'gone'. Instead, the past might constitute a crucial path of action. For people in *ureure*, travelling such a path entails an overcoming of crises brought about through the passing of time. This pathway leads to the perfection of *abanoi*, where lies the truth of the people of the place.

References

Allen, M. 1969. 'Report on Aoba.' Edited by Caroline Leancy. *Incidental Papers on Nduindui District, Aoba Island, New Hebrides*, written for the British Residency in the New Hebrides, Port Vila.

Allen, M. 2000. *Ritual, Power and Gender*. Manohar: Sydney Studies in Society and Culture.

Allen, M. ed. 1981. *Vanuatu: politics, economics and ritual in island Melanesia*. Australia: Academic Press Australia.

Ayres, Mary 1983. 'This Side, That Side: Locality and Exogamous Group Definition in the Moorhead Area, Southwestern Papua.' PhD dissertation, Department of Anthropology. University of Chicago, Chicago.

Battaglia, D. 1990. *On the Bones of the Serpent: Person, Memory and Morality in Sabarl Island Society*. Chicago and London: University of Chicago Press.

Bolton, L. 1999. 'Women, Place and Practice in Vanuatu: a View from Ambae.' *Oceania*, 70. pp. 43-55.

Bolton, Lissant. 2003. *Unfolding the Moon: enacting women's kastom in Vanuatu*. Honolulu: University of Hawai'i Press.

Bonnemaisson, J. 1994. *The Tree and the Canoe: History and Ethnography of Tanna*. Honolulu: University of Hawai'i Press.

Codrington, R.H. 1881. 'Religious Beliefs and Practices in Melanesia.' *Journal of the Royal Anthropological Institute*, 10. pp. 261-316.

Codrington, R.H. 1891. *The Melanesians: Studies in their anthropology and folklore*. Oxford: Clarendon Press.

Crowe, P. 1990. 'Dancing Backwards?' *World of Music*, 32. pp.84-98.

Deleuze, G. and F. Guattari. 1987. *A Thousand Plateaus: Capitalism and Schizophrenia*. London and New York: Continuum.

Dening, Greg. 1980. *Islands and Beaches: discourse on a silent land: Marquesas 1774-1880*. Chicago: The Dorsey Press.

Fox, James J. and Clifford Sather. 1996. *Origins, Ancestry and Alliance: Explorations in Austronesian Ethnography*. Canberra: The Australian National University.

Goldman, L.R. and C. Ballard (eds). 1998. *Fluid Ontologies: myth, ritual and philosophy in the highlands of Papua New Guinea*. Westport (Conn.): Bergin and Garvey.

Hardacre, M. n.d. [c. 1910]. 'Raga Vocabulary.' Unpublished Manuscript.

Jolly, M. 1994. *Women of the Place: Kastom, colonialism and gender in Vanuatu*. Chur: Harwood Academic Press.

Jolly, M. 1999. 'Another Time, Another Place.' *Oceania*, 69. pp. 282-99.

Layard, J. 1942. *Stone Men of Malekula: The small island of Vao*. London: Chatto and Windus.

Leona, Richard. n.d. 'Uloilua mwa dau bwativuna Raga.' Unpublished Manuscript.

Morgan, L.H. 1964 [1877]. *Ancient Society*. Edited with an introduction by L.A. White. Cambridge: Harvard University Press.

Patterson, M. 1976. *Kinship, Marriage and Ritual in North Ambrym*. Sydney: Department of Anthropology, University of Sydney.

Patterson, Mary. 2002. 'Moving Histories: an analysis of the dynamics of place in North Ambrym, Vanuatu.' *The Australian Journal of Anthropology*, 13 (2). pp. 200-218.

Rival, Laura (ed.) 1998. *The Social Life of Trees: anthropological perspectives on tree symbolism*. Oxford and New York: Berg.

Rivers, W.H.R. 1914. *The History of Melanesian Society*. Cambridge: Cambridge University Press.

Rodman, M.C. 1985. 'Moving houses: residential mobility and the mobility of residences in Longana, Vanuatu.' *American Anthropologist*, 87. pp. 56-72.

Rodman, M.C. 1987. *Masters of Tradition: Consequences of Customary Land Tenure in Longana, Vanuatu*. Vancouver: University of British Columbia Press.

Rumsey, A. 2001. 'Tracks, Traces, and Links to Land in Aboriginal Australia, New Guinea, and Beyond.' In A. Rumsey and J. Weiner (eds), *Emplaced Myth: Space, Narrative, and Knowledge in Aboriginal Australia and Papua New Guinea*, Honolulu: University of Hawai'i Press. pp. 19-42.

Rumsey, A and J. Weiner. 2001. *Emplaced Myth: space, narrative, and knowledge in Aboriginal Australia and Papua New Guinea*. Honolulu: University of Hawai'i Press.

Taylor, John P. 2003. 'Ways of the Place: history, cosmology and material culture in North Pentecost, Vanuatu.' Unpublished PhD thesis, The Australian National University.

Thomas, Nicholas. 1991. *Entangled Objects: exchange, material culture, and colonialism in the Pacific*. Massachusetts and London: Harvard University Press.

Tryon, D. 1996. 'Dialect chaining and the use of geographical space.' In J. Bonnemaison et al. (eds), *Arts of Vanuatu*, Bathurst, N.S.W: Crawford House Publishing. pp. 170-81.

Wagner, Roy. 1986. *Asiwinarong: ethos, image, and social power among the Usen Barok of New Ireland*. Princeton: Princeton University Press.

Walsh, D. 1966. 'The Phonology and Phrase Structure of Raga.' Masters thesis, Auckland University, Auckland.

Walsh, D.S. and W. Hadye Lini. 1981. 'Veveven bwatun tauvwa, ata la vanua Raga: a story about the beginning of creation, from Raga Island.' In H.J. and A.K. Pawley (eds), *Studies in Pacific languages and cultures in honour of Bruce Biggs*, Auckland: Linguistics Society New Zealand.

Wilson, C. 1932. *In the Wake of the Southern Cross: work and adventures in the South Seas*. London: John Murry.

Yoshioka, M. 1987. 'The story of Raga: A man's ethnography on his own society (I) the origin myth.' *Journal of the Faculty of Liberal Arts* (Shinshu University), 21. pp. 1-66.

Yoshioka, M. 1985. 'The marriage system of north Raga, Vanuatu.' *Man and Culture in Oceania*, 1. pp. 27-54.

Yoshioka, M. 1988. 'The story of Raga: A man's ethnography on his own society (II) kin relations.' *Journal of the Faculty of Liberal Arts* (Shinshu University), 22. pp. 19-46.

Yoshioka, M. 1993. 'The Six-section System as a Model.' *Man and Culture in Oceania*, 1 (9). pp. 45-68.

ENDNOTES

[1] This is a common historical theme throughout all of Vanuatu, and, for instance, provided the title to John Layard's book, *Stone Men of Malekula* (1942: 18-19).

[2] My PhD fieldwork in this area took place over 15 months, from 1999 to 2000.

[3] The prefix '*bwat*' may be related to what Fox describes as 'the Proto-Austronesian term **puqun* meaning "tree", "trunk", "base" or "source"' (Fox 1993: 19), and the synonymous term **batang*.

[4] More recent graves are also usually constructed of stone piles, but now are typically rectangular in shape as in Christian graves.

[5] As Codrington noted, 'Ghosts haunt especially their burial-places, and revenge themselves if offended; if a man has trespassed on the grave-place of a dead chief the ghost will smite him, and he will be sick' (1891: 288). Unlike the other more ambivalent spirits that haunt the landscape, and even though they are similarly feared, the intentions of ancestral *atatun vanua* are ultimately considered just.

[6] *Tauva* was translated into Bislama as *jeneresen* ('generation') by Jif Ruben. It is probably related to the word *tau* ('to put, to make') (Yoshioka and Leona 1992: 33). This word appears in Hardacre's Dictionary as *dau*, with meanings including 'place', 'put', 'appoint', 'create', and 'bury'. Hardacre also lists the construction *dau bwatuna*, meaning 'begin' (Hardacre n.d.: 32). Note here the important connection between origin and location, or place. The appearance of Mugarimanga ('Mother clam gapes open') defines the first *tauva* (see discussion below). The second *tauva* is defined by the appearance of *tavalarau*—non-ancestral and invisible spirit beings (for further discussion, see Taylor 2003).

[7] As the destination (or habitation) of the dead, *abanoi* is presently somewhat ambiguously intertwined with the Christian concept of heaven.

[8] See Layard on what he calls the 'Tagaro-Qat complex' (Layard 1942: 224, 572). As Yoshioka notes (1987: 11), Bwatmahanga is clearly the North Pentecost equivalent of the Banks Islands' ancestral hero Qat. In current Raga orthography, the letters 'bw' have replaced 'q', as used by Anglican missionaries until the early to mid-20th century (see also Walsh 1966). After this change, 'Qat' should therefore appear as 'Bwat' ('source', 'foundation'). See also Codrington (1891: 156-7).

[9] In Tevimule's text, this burden is made apparent in the character of Bwatmahanga's follower Sumbwe, for whom knowledge gained through loyalty to Bwatmahanga is as easily taken away by Tagaro (Yoshioka 1987).

[10] Note that spelling employed by Jif Ruben is often inconsistent (and that there is no firmly established orthography for Raga).

[11] While the term *alengan vanua* (here spelt *alen vanua*) is typically translated as *kastom* in Bislama, most Raga speakers will ultimately suggest that the Bislama term is inadequate for describing the intimacy and full range of meanings contained within the term *alengan vanua*, or 'ways of the place' (see Taylor 2003).

[12] Peter sadly died at his home village of Lagaronboga in 2001.

[13] These are *alo, vula, mahava, dodo, vivivi, tano* and *tahi* (sun, moon, air, clouds, [unclear, but possibly meaning] rainbow, earth and sea).

[14] See especially Rumsey and Weiner (2001), Goldman and Ballard (1998), also Patterson (2002).

[15] Many Sia Raga people link this part of the history to the biblical flood.

[16] Somewhat like the more immediately ancestral *atatun vanua* (discussed above), these primordial *atatun vanua* also act as guardians of the land. Unlike the former, they are accorded with neither direct ancestral significance nor association with specific places and are thereby viewed in much more ambivalent terms—more 'devils' than 'ghosts'. Their punishments are meted on people who offend a more general 'spirit of the earth' (*vui tanonda*). Since such offences are also often meted with death, *atatun vanua* are likewise feared and highly respected.

[17] Bwatnapne appears to be an important focal point for Pentecost Island. For the Ambrymese, for instance, it is where their island was linked to Pentecost by a vine (Mary Patterson, personal communication).

[18] Codrington mentions a place called Atambulu as being 'the original seat of men' in Raga (1891: 169).

[19] On the small islands of Malakula, Vao and Atchin, Layard explored the topographical and conceptual divisions of society into the 'Sides' (*tosan*) of lodge, stone and island. He also found the linguistic category to be flourishing throughout the northern islands of Vanuatu (Layard 1942: 168). In the diffusionist style of his forebears, Morgan (1877), Codrington (1891) and Rivers (1914), he concluded that this provided further evidence for the theory of matrilineal primacy in the region (Layard 1942: 169; and

see Allen 1981, 2000). Patterson (1976) also discusses northern Vanuatu ideas of complementary opposition. She notes that the Ambrym term *tali viung* means 'one side of a bunch of coconuts'. Here the emphasis is patrilineal rather than matrilineal: 'a man and his father and a man and his son are '*tali viung*'. ... Likewise, a woman and her father's sister and a woman and her brother's daughter are '*tali viung*', but not a woman and her children.' She also makes the important point that such terms do not in fact pertain to the definition of categories or groups as such, but rather express the relationship *between* categories (Patterson 1976: 90-3).

[20] Hardacre's definition of *tavalui* is 'a side, one of two parts' (Hardacre n.d.: 87).

[21] See Crowe (1990: 89-95) for a discussion of left hand/right hand distinctions vis-a-vis what he describes as broader 'dualistic, twinning aspects of the Melanesian World', and northern Vanuatu in particular.

[22] Also noted by Rivers (1914 Vol. 1: 190).

[23] As we have seen, some creation histories recall that clams, *talai*, or other shellfish are the source of human origins.

[24] Marital separations do infrequently occur on Pentecost.

[25] Note here the different spelling of the word *tauvwa* from that given above (*tauva*).

[26] For instance, note the story's contemporaneity with John Leo Tamata's father's acquisition of the name Vira Lin Tuturani.

[27] See, for instance, the story of Bwatmahanga's death, as told by David Tevimule (Yoshioka 1987).

[28] See especially the collection of essays in *Origins, Ancestry and Alliance: Explorations in Austronesian ethnography*, and the association between topography and anthropological ideas of 'precedence' within Indonesian anthropology (Fox and Sather 1996). Also Rival (1998) and Rumsey (2001).

Chapter 14. Finishing the Land: Identity and Land Use in Pre- and Post-Colonial North Ambrym

Mary Patterson

Introduction

The first wave of scholars interested in the archipelago of Vanuatu, known as the New Hebrides before 1980, made frequent reference in their work to continuities and commonalities linking the region to its north-west, but it is in the work of linguists and archaeologists rather than in anthropology that Vanuatu's position in the Austronesian world has been recently established. In most of the work of the second wave of scholars working in the colonial period in Vanuatu, from the 1950s to the late 1970s, anthropologists were much more likely to refer to theoretical issues arising from work in Melanesia, for which PNG is frequently the metonym, or even to Australia, rather than to Austronesia.

Some of the work of that period focusing on land and place in Vanuatu, mostly published in the 1980s, brought out two master tropes of 'ethnoscapism': rootedness in place and mobility (Bonnemaison 1985). For Bonnemaison, Melanesian ethno-geography is characterised by reticulated space or networks, in which places are linked by alliances where there is no dominant centre, only foundation or primordial places (Bonnemaison 1996: 36-8). These notions seem eminently compatible with some of the core ideas identified by Fox as prominent and enduring features of Austronesian communities, such as concern with a multiplicity of origins, use of terms such as 'path' and 'road' as metaphors for important links between founder-focused groups and a concern that the blood or flow of life carried by female descendants of founders should be returned to the group of origin by means of some form of recursive marriage between descendants (Fox 1993, 1997; Fox and Sather 1996). All of these features are important in north Ambrym, an island in northern Vanuatu that is the focus of this chapter.

In foregrounding the importance of place and place-making in the Austronesian world, the Comparative Austronesian Studies Project offers the opportunity to consider the political dynamism involved in the local development and reinterpretation of old concepts in a region with a commonality of conflicts relating to land and identity. I begin with a brief overview of the vocabulary of 'place' in the national arena in Vanuatu since independence, then in the works of various authors writing about the north and north-central regions where various common usages are found that will be familiar to Austronesian scholars. I follow this with more specific detail on the somewhat different vocabulary in North Ambrym before proceeding to a discussion of the contemporary context in which land metaphors and the mythopoesis of earth and place have been played out in that island.

Land and National Consciousness in Vanuatu

Throughout Vanuatu, the words *'vanua'* and *'tan'* while having varied local salience, have entered the vocabulary of the nation state as part of indigenous political discourse about land and identity. In order to understand this local politics, we need to appreciate the importance of 'place-making' as an aspect of claims to precedence in an environment in which primordialism and movement into and out of place are valued and contested (Rodman 1992, 1994; Patterson 2002). Place-making at the national level, however, involved land in a rather different context that had emerged long before the colony of the New Hebrides became the Republic of Vanuatu in 1980. This is not surprising, of course, in an archipelago in which vast tracts of the most productive land had been alienated by Europeans. In consequence, the indigenous political groups that emerged in the 1970s saw land issues as the basis of their case for decolonisation and their rhetorical appeal to the varied populations of the islands (Lini 1980; Sope 1974; Van Trease 1987).

Two islands, Tanna and Vanua Lava in the Banks Graip, already incorporated the words we are investigating in their names, from the period of European exploration. When it came to a new name for the independent republic, the members of the first major political party were in no doubt about what should be the focus of such a name as they soon realised it should also be for the party they had formed. According to Walter Lini, who became the first Prime Minister of Vanuatu, the name of the party was changed from the New Hebrides National Party to the Vanua'aku Pati because 'we decided that the name of our country should become Vanua'aku' (Lini 1980: 26). I have so far searched in vain for anything that explains how the 'aku' in the Republic's name transmogrified to 'atu', but I suspect that the Vanua'aku Pati members were convinced by their opponents and friends that the name of the country should not be that of a political party. The details of this decision and the choice of word has not, as far as I know, been published. 'Atu' is translated from an unspecified language as variously 'has arisen' or 'stands up'. Walter Lini, and most of the other members of the proto-government (and later the elected government), came from islands in which *'vanua'* rather than *'tan'* featured as a polysemic word for land, domain, village site, and even men's house.

Two other political parties, both opposed to the Vanua'aku Party, incorporated *'tan'* in their name; one calling itself Natui Tano or 'the children of the land' was short-lived. [1] The other, Tan Union, a Francophone party, emerged in 1977 in opposition to the anti-Independence Francophones and the Vanua'aku Pati (Boulekone 1995: 198). Unlike Natui Tano, which, according to Van Trease, was merely

> an extension of the New Hebrides National Party shortly to be renamed as mentioned above, and ... relatively short-lived, fielding candidates at only one election, Tan Union remained a force in local politics until recently. (Van Trease 1987: 216)

At the local level, the vocabulary and discourse of land and place are also refracted through the struggle for independence and the coming to prominence of the ideology of *man-ples*, a Bislama (Vanuatu pidgin) term that is also deeply contextual with its meanings of 'indigenous person, primary landholder, recognised descendant of a founder of place'. These contexts frequently make local words extremely difficult to translate into a language such as English where the connection between people and places is overtly distinguished.

Preliminary inquiries into land and place categories in northern Vanuatu show a distribution that tends to feature one or the other of the *vanua* and *tan* terms. Although both words might be present, if '*vanua*' is prominent in local discourse then '*tan*' is not, and vice versa . In Ambrym and South Pentecost there appears to be no reflex of '*vanua*'. In Vao, one of the small islands off north-east Malakula, Layard gives *venu* and *vanu* as 'village' or 'place'—as in translation of the village name Togh-Vanu (Layard 1942: 75). In mainland Malakula, '*vene*' appears as part of clan names in a description of the *Nogho* rites but no translation is offered (Deacon 1934). In Malo, *tan* appears as part of clan names (Hume 1985). In East Ambae, '*vanue*' is important but '*tano*' less so. Writing of this region, Margaret Rodman says, '*Vanue* is not land (*tano*), it is lived space in which place and people are part of each other' (1987: 35). However, we do find both words in some places, as noted above, and other words with similar meanings but apparently different origins, in others. In the Banks Islands, according to Codrington the village site is referred to as '*vanua*' while house sites are called '*tano ima*' (Codrington 1957 [1891]: 65). Vienne, who worked in the Banks from the late 1960s to the early '70s, gives a more lyrical and nuanced account of the relationship between *vanua* and *tan*. He says:

> On the ocean float the islands: the *vanua*. The matter that constitutes the *vanua* is the *tano*, the earth, but also the place, the space, the land, the apparent and particular toponymic form of the '*vanua*'. The relations *lama/tas* (ocean/sea) and *vanua/tano* are in fact more complex than a simple opposition between space and matter. The two oppositions, taking into account the ensemble of their meanings, divide in a parallel manner, contrasting term by term from the general to the specific. (Vienne 1984: 69; my translation.)

He elucidates further:

> In this sense the *vanua* is also 'home', the free and appropriated space, dominated and known by those who belong to you and to whom you belong. The *vanua* is inscribed in the *'mot'* which is contained by and distinguished as uncultivated space, the wild, home of spirits and enemies, opposed to cultivated space, the domestic, home of men. The *'mot'* is the *Vanua gona*, the closed space—the territory of spirits. (Ibid.)

In West Ambae, Michael Allen noted the segmentary and polysemic character of the *vanua* term. While noting that the earth as substance is *tano*, *vanua*, according to context, can represent the whole island of Ambae, 'a district, a village, a village section or simply an individual's land' (Allen 1969: 132). But the definition of the maximal segment identified by Allen as the village or *ngwatu i vanua* (literally, the 'head of the land') is a function of local politics and shifting allegiances that were accentuated after the introduction of cash cropping before World War II.

Vanua, then, is a segmentary concept that is context dependent for its meaning. Used rhetorically to indicate the indivisibility of the land in Ambae, in situations where alienation is likely, the 'corporateness' of the concept was, according to Allen, easily overridden up to and during the time of his fieldwork in the late 1950s (Allen 1969: 132). In a summing up of linguistic evidence, in a recent work on reconstructions of Proto-Oceanic, Green and Pawley generalise these more specific instances to PMP (Proto-Malayo-Polynesian) and Poc (Proto-Oceanic), commenting that:

> although reflexes of PMP **banua* carry the meaning 'village' in a number of languages belonging to different high-order subgroups (or at least are given this gloss in dictionaries) a host of other evidence, summarised in Blust (1987: 94-5, 99-100) suggests that PMP **banua* and its reflexes referred primarily to an inhabited territory; not only to the land but to the human population and dwellings and all plant and animal life and other elements that contribute to the maintenance of the human community—a complex concept with no simple equivalent in European languages. … Indeed, the single word glosses that bilingual dictionaries give for reflexes of **banua* should generally be regarded not as accurate descriptions of their meaning in the source language but as shorthand translations designed to fit the categories of the target language. (Green and Pawley 1998: 63)

In the same volume from which this quote is taken, Osmond, in a chapter on horticultural practices, lists a third term, which we find distributed throughout central northern Vanuatu but which is not listed among the terms discussed in this volume. I have already quoted its Mota Lava reflex—namely *'mot'*. Osmond gives the Proto-Austronesian as **quCaN* and the Proto-Oceanic as **qutan*, where almost all the listed reflexes have lost the initial phoneme. The translation given for the Pan is 'fallow land'; for the Poc, 'bushland, hinterland'. Two of the local reflexes listed also give 'garden'—a meaning found in North Ambrym, which one might think indicates the opposite of Vienne's quoted definition of '*mot*' as wild and uncultivated land. Osmond comments that: this change of meaning is probably due to the fact that, in

> Melanesia gardens are often remote from the village and surrounded by bushland, so that to go to the garden is to go into the bush. (Osmond 1998: 119)

This would appear to be a similar problem of translation rather than contradictory meaning as noted above. This overview of north central Vanuatu foregrounds *vanua* as a place word; in the next section, I turn more specifically to North Ambrym, where other words are prominent in the discourse of land, place and precedence.

The Vocabulary of Place in North Ambrym

Place-dwellers know where they are and tend not to identify places in the same way that their neighbours do and certainly not as Europeans often insisted they should. While domains and specific areas in them are commonly named descriptively in North Ambrym, as, for example, 'on the beach' (*ranon*), 'by the *bulua* tree' (*lonlilibulua*), 'over the sea' (*fante*, the North Ambrym designation of Malakula), Ambrymese had no name for the entire island until Cook, in what is now a contemporary legend, named it for them. The explorer, who now stands for 'the first European', did indeed name the island though he did not land there. He is said to have misheard the phrase of those who offered a welcoming gift. '*Am rem*' ('your yam'), the men of Fona declared as they handed over the tuber, appropriately, though unwittingly, as the legend has it, conferring on their island the name of the cosmically iconic crop that stands for transformation, connection and life itself.

In North Ambrym, the three most important words used to refer to land and place are '*tan*', '*ot*' and '*vere*'. While there is no reflex of '*vanua*', the word '*vere*' has the broad connotations that we find elsewhere with *vanua* and its variants, for what Rodman refers to as 'lived space'. Its etymology is unclear but there are perhaps some clues in another Poc place term isolated by Green and Pawley (1998). They list Poc **pera*(?), translated as 'settlement, open space associated with a house or settlement', and some of the reflexes they list approximate the North Ambrym *vere*. However, they note that while

> [**pera* is] well attested in both major subgroups of Southeast Solomonic [it has] only one secure external cognate, in Manam. The range of

> meanings or glosses associated with this cognate set makes it impossible to make a firm semantic reconstruction either for Poc or for Proto Southeast Solomonic. Our best guess is that **pera* referred to some sort of settlement or space associated with this. (Green and Pawley 1998: 63)

Vere, like *vanua,* has a somewhat broader reference than the word *'ot'* discussed below, as when the people of West Ambrym refer to the north as *'vereha'* (which I would tentatively translate as 'the origin place', where *'ha'* has the connotation of staying forever). *Mweneng vere* could be translated as 'my island' or 'my place' in the general sense, where *mweneng* means 'my'. [2]

'Ot' in North Ambrym usually appears in a compound as an adverbial form. It seems to connote a more specific place where people have left their mark. So *lonor,* which translates literally as 'in the place', means 'garden' or cultivated land; when compounded with a named residential locality, it identifies the place, e.g. *ot* Fona- Fona village. It appears to me to be a more specific marker that we could translate as 'domain' and although it is presumably related to the Banks Island word *'mot'* that Vienne mentions, its connotations as noted above contain the sense of the wild and uncultivated and the specificity of inhabited space. It rarely, however, seems to be possessed. Specificity of place, as when one says *lonotgea,* 'in this place', seems to be the defining feature of this word. In its connotation of 'wild' space, we find the reference by the saltwater-dwellers to those of the hinterland as *'taot'*—the bush-dwellers. Nonetheless, there is semantic overlap between *'ot'* and *'vere'*; the period of ritual proscription during the major politico-religious rituals of the *mage* were referred to as *'otkonkon'* and *'vere' mokon'*: the first refers to the place as sacralised (being *kon*) and thereby proscribed—'the sacred place'; the second to the process of making the domain sacred— 'the place has been sacralised'.

Despite family resemblances in the three words for land and place, the major difference lies between *'ot'* and *'vere'* on the one hand and *'tan'* on the other. *'Tan'* which also connotes place, means more particularly and, as in the Banks and elsewhere in northern Vanuatu, 'earth', 'ground' and 'productive land'; its prime reference being to fertility, generativeness and transformative power. Moreover, this distinction is marked linguistically.

The 'Grounds' for Being

In many Austronesian languages, particularly those of Melanesia, we find interesting variations in the use of possessives. There is, for example, a major distinction between things such as body parts and kinsfolk that are inalienable and other things that are 'alienable'. In the former case, also referred to in the literature as 'direct' or 'zero possession' (Lynch 1982), the pronoun is suffixed to the noun root (or 'head nominal'). Two examples from North Ambrym to illustrate are *tabling,* 'my body' (where *tabli* is the root and *ng* the first person pronominal suffix), and *raheng*, 'my mother' (where *rahe* is the root and *ng* the suffix 'my'). In many Western Oceanic varieties of Austronesian, however, the alienable category is further divided according to the class of nouns referred to.[3]

The Ambrym case appears to be interesting in that the 'alienable' category is subdivided into a more than usual number of classes for the region. In the language of North Ambrym, there are six varieties of alienable possessive. Paton, the Presbyterian missionary linguist who published a grammar of Lonwolwol, the similar language of West Ambrym, distinguishes them as a 'common' set for ordinary things, and five other sets, which apply respectively to containers, fire and torches, liquids, maritime vessels and food. This last category, however, does not apply simply to food, as Paton notes (1971). Macintyre, in a paper on pigs in Tubetube, a community of Austronesian speakers in the Massim, notes that this category is often designated as indicating edibility but just as often contains 'a puzzling array of things', including, for example, appearance, height and enemies (1984). On the basis of the way in which these possessives are used in the Massim region, Macintyre suggests calling this a class of semi-alienable things that indicates mutability and transformation. Linguists have more commonly talked about this category as the one in which the food marker is used to indicate passive possession, such as 'actions over which the possessor has no control where he is the patient, target, or involuntary experiencer' (Pawley, cited in Lynch 1996: 96).[4]

In the anthropological literature on the use of possessives in Vanuatu in relation to land (such as it is), some distinctions have been made that appear not to be related to the linguistic arguments about possession. Margaret Rodman notes that in the Longana district of East Ambae, Vanuatu, 'land is not like other possessions. A distinction is made between things that move or grow, such as trucks, animals, or gardens under cultivation, e.g. *bulengu rivurivu* and land in general or uncultivated land, *nongo tano*, 'my land', and my unplanted garden'(Rodman 1989: 38-9). While the latter take the 'ordinary' possessive, the former takes the one Macintyre refers to as the 'semi-alienable'. In Ambrym, however, the words for garden and place, '*ot*' and '*vere*', take the ordinary possessive, while '*tan*' whether cultivated or not, takes the semi-alienable one. In a parallel way, individual items of food and food in general take the semi-alienable, or what we might better call the 'transformative', possessive, while vegetables, piled up in a composite heap called a *helat* to be displayed and then given away, take the ordinary alienable possessive.

The significance of the distinctive use of possessives lies, I would argue, in the properties of the earth, its transformative and generative potential. Classed together with those things that it transforms, such as the father whose dismembered body produced yams in all their variety that are fed to humans and tusked boars, the huge yams that represent men and are exchanged at all moments of life crisis, the sacramental boars that also transform into humans or indeed were human, the plants out of which autochthonous ancestors sprang, the land itself possesses and transforms the people who emerged from it and remain connected to it. There is no space here to document fully the mythopoetic nexus between people, land and its products including humans (but see Patterson 2002), a nexus that is commonly noted for Melanesia (see Weiner 1998: 139). But, as Weiner points out, invoking Heidegger, the 'ground' or 'earth' also represents the 'grounds for' or origin of being. The origin of things, in North Ambrym, *barite*, in Bislama, their *stampa*, or 'root', is frequently located in the material transformative power of the earth in particular places and indeed in 'placement' itself. [5]

Tan, then, in the Ambrym context, has a range of cosmological associations that are not so evident in the other place words. The French missionary Tattevin recorded a myth from South Pentecost, also known in North Ambrym, which has a cognate language, in which the first men, a group of six brothers, emerge from a coconut tree (1929-31). The eldest instructs the others to collect Tahitian chestnuts (*Inocarpus edulis* or *namambwe* in Bislama) and to roast them. Taking a roasted nut, the eldest throws it at the youngest to whose genitals it attaches. When he attempts to pull it off, his genitals come with it, transforming him into the first woman, called Sermorp, the split chestnut. [6] The brothers live together in a communal house and Sermorp in a separate dwelling. Barkulkul, the eldest, sends them in turn to request various items from their metamorphosed brother ostensibly in order to see what she will call them—each is addressed by one of the five categories of unmarriageable relative, until Balkulkul himself is revealed as the one she will marry when she addresses him as 'my dear sorcerer'. Apart from the establishment of the categorical elements of the kinship system, the myth isolates several categories of things that approximate—with a little creative interpretation—most of the alienable categories that are distinguished by noun markers in the language of North Ambrym: viz. fire (given to the one she addresses as 'brother'), sea shells, which we can equate to 'maritime vessels' (given to 'father'), vegetable food (given to the one she calls 'cross-cousin'), bamboo, which we can equate with 'containers' (given to 'mother's father'), salt water (given to her 'son') and fresh water (given to her 'husband'). The last two belong to the same general category (*mukuen*) from a woman's point of view and both are associated in the myth with liquids. [7]

Another curiosity of possessive marking in Ambrym that Paton found inexplicable is that the word for 'house' takes not the general possessive marker but the marker for liquids. The word for house is *'im'* but it also signifies, as is common in Austronesian societies, and indeed in many other parts of the world, an important descent group. In North Ambrym, this is the cognatic stock called the *buluim* or *bulufatao*, the 'doorway', rather than the house itself. This ancestor-focused descent group, I have argued elsewhere, symbolises 'flow' and 'flux'—one travels through it as women are sent forth and reclaimed in the recursive marriage pattern, also common in such societies (Patterson 1976, 2001). That the fixed abode should be marked by the possessive for 'flow' or liquid seems particularly appropriate.

The link between transformative ground, and the doorway to a house built on it, is the path or road, which also symbolically represents certain kinsfolk. Paths flowing through doorways, as women and some male kin are said to do, are aspects of association with the more fixed quality that characterises the primordiality of the named domain. The origin of these landscapes replete with signification lies in a myth we find widely, but variously distributed, in the Austronesian world. In North Ambrym, the creator spirit, Batgolgol (cf. Barkulkul in the kinship naming myth quoted above), already encountered in another mythic context as the creator of women, is now identified with the Christian deity and is credited with having 'produced all things'. On his creative path around the north of the island, however, he discovered several autochthonous beings already in residence (Patterson 2002a). He is said in one origin myth to have begun on the rugged east coast but when he arrived at the place called Barereo, he found an opposite-sex sibling pair who had hatched from the eggs of a small bird called *tilala*. Unimpressed by him, the man said to Batgolgol, 'I'm here, this is my place; you go and do your work somewhere else.' When he finally arrived on the east coast at Fona, Batgolgol found Bungyam, whose role is much more significant than the other autochthonous beings mentioned. In a series of apparently attenuated myths collected by the Catholic missionary in the vicinity of Olal, Bungyam and Batgolgol appear in another relationship commonly found in northern Vanuatu where one culture hero is clever, the other not. The significance of the 'stupid' hero lies in his connection to the earth. However nothing is as simple here as it may appear. In other myths known in North Ambrym and South Pentecost, Batgolgol is the great chief from whose dismembered body yams grow. In the version that I collected, the creator of yams is referred to simply as a great chief (*jafu*—a reflex of *ratu*). Sacrificing himself for his children, the father is killed, cut up and 'planted' by his youngest son. From his body spring forth all the varieties of yam that sustain his sons and all Ambrymese (Patterson 2002a).

Placement and Precedence

In their localised aspect, *bulufatao* somewhat resemble conical clans, with agnatic segments ranked in relation to their proximity to the apical or founding ancestor, but I did not find that any but the senior segments were differentiated, and then only by placename from the rest. Members of the senior segment keep the knowledge of the links to the founder and the narratives that link female descendants to other places. Old ceremonial grounds, where powerful rituals were performed in the past, are referred to as *ot hanglam* or 'tabu' grounds and every domain has at least one such dangerous site. Five of them are known to be so powerful that simply burying or even placing something that was in close association with someone in one of these will cause the person to die. Four of these domains, namely Hawor, Halhal, Fonteng and Metamli, feature in the narrative of Batgolgol's creative journey as origin sites of autocthonous beings, while the last, called Bulum'no (meaning the 'hole of sores'), is in an area now uninhabited in the vicinity of sulphurous springs.

In the Ambrymese landscape, every element is replete with signification; flora and fauna might be either or both sacred and utilitarian. Distinguished and identified in a hierarchy of inherited intellectual property rights, they are simultaneously pharmacopeia, and the means of daily sustenance. Senior members of a domain hold the knowledge of its sacred and dangerous places, and it is they who control access to its products. Edible or not, sequestered or free, the cosmoscape is created from the bodies of humans and is the very source of their being. The ground itself, that is, the '*tan*', is constitutive of the descendants of those who originated from it, absorbing the power of the ancestors who dwell in and around it, protecting its own and tormenting interlopers. In Fona, the domain of the demiurge Bungyam, where his descendants nurture the planting and harvesting of yams in an annual cycle, the spirit or *tegar* that inheres in this powerful place can afflict any non-descendants of the founder should they witness the planting of first yams by any of the founder's agnatic descendants, if they trip and fall into the hole of a harvested yam, or break a new yam from the Fona crop. Only recourse to exorcism performed by the yam master will prevent the interloper's death.

Another indication of the power of Bungyam's domain is the ritual divination of death performed by the yam master on the morning when the first yams are to be removed from the ground at Fona, inaugurating the northern harvest in a carefully timed sequence of domains that proceeds from west to east, in the direction opposite to that of the creator deity's journey. Taking the sacred sign of the yams (*muyune rem*) in his hand, the yam master sits in the *mel* (men's house) and sweeps it first to the right and then, changing hands, to the left. [8] He continues until he feels a sensation of cold on one side or the other, indicative of the location of the domain in which there will be a death. Although not caused by the yam master's action, the death is intimately connected to the power of the Fona domain *tegar* at this time of the removal of the iconic crop. While northern domains have clearly risen and fallen as sites of political eminence, or more recently been obliterated by depopulation, the precedence of the yam cycle remains embedded in the mythopoesis of contemporary life transforming the planting and harvesting sequence into a series of Christian first-fruits ceremonies where the crops are blessed in the sacred spaces of the church. Nonetheless, they must begin, as always, with Fona.

'Finishing the Land'

I want to turn now to the metaphor of my title, which is itself a title. *Tan Monong* means literally 'the ground is finished', but its sense is comparable with the English phrase 'known throughout the land' in the sense of 'renowned throughout the land' and can be translated as 'lord of the land'. It is a male title acquired by the performance of a rite called *mage ne kuman*, the significance of which is that it belongs neither to what I have referred to elsewhere as the indigenous *mage* of north Ambrym nor to the hierarchy of grades imported from Malakula known in the literature as the 'graded society' and also called *mage* (see Patterson 1981, 2002b). Although in some regions these rights are predominantly secular, in Ambrym the *mage* was, in its indigenous form, an instantiation of cosmology as well as the creative basis of status differentiation between individuals and groups.

Some time in the period before European contact, these rites were augmented by the apparently piecemeal acquisition of a similar but more hierarchical and elaborate complex from the neighbouring island of Malakula. The significant difference between the indigenous rites and the imported ones was that the former necessarily involved transactions between kin and those allied in marriage, whereas the imported ones were completely independent of such requirements. One could be inducted into one of the new 'grades' by anyone who had himself acquired it. The majority of the grades came into North Ambrym from the south-west bay area of Malakula via West Ambrym, but the two highest grades were imported from the small islands off the north-east coast. Somewhere in the hiatus between the acquisition of the two sets of rituals, the anomalous *mage ne kuman* arrived in Ambrym, according to legend, delivered by a woman from Ambae who came ashore at Ranon on the north-west coast, in a canoe made of coconut leaves. This rite, also called a *mage*, differs in almost all its elements from the imported kind but in the participation of female kin of both the initiate and the sponsor, it resembles the indigenous *mage*. And, like these latter rites, participation depended on having reached a certain level of the imported grades. The transfer of boars in the rite is unique. The sacrificial tusked boar that gives the right to the title *Tan Monong* must be given to the candidate by his father or a classificatory 'father' who then also acts as donor of the pigs that are exchanged with the sponsors for ritual insignia. In all of the imported *mage*, the candidate gives the pigs directly to the sponsors himself. In *mage ne kuman*, the candidates's mother or 'mothers' (the wives of his father[s]) rather than his own wife, then sacrifice[s] boars to receive the title *Jamarkon*. With the receipt of this title, such women must observe, like high-ranking *mage* men, the restrictions on commensality with those of lower grade. However, on completion of the rite, they could now share their food with boys who had made the first grade of the imported series.

Mage ne kuman, like the indigenous rites, may be repeated but unlike them must always be acquired from specified kin. It was available, however, only to a man who had already achieved the difficult upper grade of *meleun* or he could attempt it if he had reached the lesser (seventh) grade of *wurwur*, provided that his father had reached the highest imported grade of *mal*. But while its elements are specifically North Ambrymese, particularly in the involvement of kin, its provenance is just as specifically foreign and not just foreign but female. The Ambae woman who brought it is said to have been mistaken for a man because she was wearing a mat skirt and had 'the firm breasts characteristic of the women of her place' (Guiart 1951: 68). When a man noticed the damp spot on a stone that she had sat on, realised she was a woman and made advances towards her, she took a canoe at night and went back to Ambae, leaving her ritual with the people of Ranon. Like the other indigenous rites, *mage ne kuman* had not been performed in the north since just before World War II. The French ethnographer Jean Guiart, who was in Ambrym just after the war, was given an account of the rite by his informant, John Manu, who had performed it, and I was given an account by the yam master of Fona domain whose father had performed it.[9] Its memory lingers in ancestral names and in the frequently retold deeds of the hero Tan Monong Bariu –'Lord of the Land, the warrior'—whose exploits made him the archetypal *jafu gatlam* or great man of the past. I heard his story many times, particularly when I asked for the definition of 'a great man'. His story did not, however, concern his prowess as a fighter in battles against enemies. It concerned the murder of his father-in-law. [10] Compensating his affines with tusked boars after this shocking crime, he retrieved his wife from her natal place, and exchanged her for a 'sister' also visiting her birthplace, married, perhaps significantly, to a man of Fona and pregnant with that man's child. Proceeding to successfully complete a difficult ritual of the indigenous *mage* that required a great many tusked boars and access to a fund of metaphysical power, he invited the husband of the woman he had appropriated and to whom he had given his own wife, to contribute to the exchanges with kin at the birth of 'their' child. By these acts he became a truly great man who had 'finished the land'.

The story achieves mythic dimensions, I would argue, precisely because it ignores the ascendancy of the later imported rites, in favour of a thoroughly indigenised version of a foreign rite by whose title the hero is known, while demonstrating that what really makes a lord of the land is the ability to transform the inalienable ties of kinship. In appropriating the child of the descendant of another origin site with whom he does not share maternal origin, he demonstrates his supreme *helan* or power.

A man could thus 'finish the land' by achieving great renown, renown that had local and endogenous origins. There is, however, another way in which North Ambrymese speak of the land being 'finished'. The move to cash cropping that began in a small way along the coast between the two World Wars accelerated after World War II, so that many coastal domains had planted much of the flatter areas with coconuts. Ambrym, with active volcanoes at its core and much of the inland in the north steep rainforest, has a dearth of arable land in some areas and, in some depopulated domains, a plentiful supply. Nonetheless, in the rhetoric of the late Sixties, the deep division between the majority of Christian converts and their neighbours and kin in 'the bush' was expressed not only in the former's fear of the latter's sorcery but in the conviction of the bush-dwellers that Christian's were 'finishing' the land by cash cropping. The importance of yam cultivation went beyond subsistence, as will be clear from the previous section. The custodians of *kastom*, as the bush-dwellers saw themselves, complained bitterly about the declining varieties of yams, the curtailment of adequate fallow periods and the resultant poor crop quality and the encroachment of coconuts and coffee on land they felt should be reserved for yam gardens. Even more bitter and sometimes violent were the disputes over the bush-dwellers' pigs rooting out their Christian neighbours' coconuts or spoiling their unfenced gardens. Bush-dwellers fenced their gardens, leaving all but their valuable and cosseted tuskers to free range. The copra vs. pigs war was won when the Condominium Government decreed that all pigs must be fenced or tethered; marauding pigs could be shot with impunity when discovered destroying crops. It was no longer possible to keep pigs in the numbers required for a vigorous ritual life.

This hostility was increased by the growing perception in the 1970s that West Ambrymese refugees who had settled, intermarried and become prosperous after the disastrous 1913 eruption of the volcano that decimated their homeland, were avatars of an intrusive modernity linked to the British Government's introduction of local councils and to a perceived promotion of one of their leaders over those who espoused their role as guardians of *kastom* from the bush. In the decade before Independence, it was made increasingly clear to the West Ambrymese that the previous delicate balance between primordial and exogenous origins, in which their presence in the north had so far been unproblematic, was fast giving way beneath a torrent of external rhetoric about the alienation of land in Vanuatu. Leadership and its grounds were severely contested in a way that drew on earlier models and refracted them through novel discourses about worth and value (Patterson 2002, 2003).

Very little land had been alienated to Europeans in North Ambrym, and the sole plantation owned by a French company (SFNH) was abandoned at independence, leaving the various claimants to sort out their rights to it. Disputes over this land continue. Although there had been numerous European traders up and down the coast in the past, most of whom had small parcels of land, with a single exception, they were long gone by the '60s. Despite this apparent lack of motive, however, land issues loomed large in the late '70s. Writing in the 1990s on post-independence politics in Ambrym, two educated Ambrymese commented that the Vanua'aku Pati's campaign on land issues at the national level stimulated a local concern with the rights of immigrants who had moved out of their own domains in the colonial period (Alpi and Laan 1995: 325).

But just as *kastom* people did not reject aspects of modernity that suited them, Christians, particularly of the older generation, shared basic ontological assumptions with their *kastom* kin and neighbours. The *mage* was almost defunct but access to its titles was another matter. Although there is not space here to elaborate, a hereditary tendency in the acquisition of *mage* titles had clearly been developing for some time as is evidenced by the way, noted above, in which the *Tan Monong* title could be obtained by the son of a great man who was only relatively junior in *mage* rank himself. It was said that the highest grades of the *mage* could be attempted only by those who hailed from a 'great kindred', meaning one in which immediate ancestors were of high rank. It was also accepted that men could skip grades on the death of their high-ranking fathers and take their titles at the performance of the mortuary ceremonies. These tendencies then supported the claims of Christians whose ancestors had achieved high rank, contesting the equally important notion that all Christians in the *kastom* sense were 'unworthy' or 'profane'. In the late Seventies, the eclipse of the *kastom* leader by his Presbyterian rival was a bitter blow, particularly when the latter was elected in 1975 by the chiefs of the administrative district CD2 to be the representative of *kastom* on the new Representative Assembly set up by the Colonial Government (see Patterson 2002b). When the Council of *Kastom* Chiefs (later the Malvatumauri) was established in 1977 and Willy Bongmatur, an Ambrym Presbyterian, was elected its president, the *kastom* bush-dwellers felt they had been betrayed. As head of this important new body, Bongmatur needed to establish his credibility at home and abroad. He was a third-generation Christian and also 'from' West Ambrym, so establishing *kastom* bona fides now became a priority for him. He constructed ceremonial grounds at the mission village of Ranmuwuhu in the north and another at Fanu in West Ambrym. He donned a penis-wrapper and bark belt for the first time in his life, killed boars and erected slit drums. Recognition did not have to be local and, in fact, it was a longstanding practice throughout Vanuatu to gain prestige from introducing exogenous ritual forms and materials. Clearly attested by the ascendance of the imported *mage* in the north and the role of the rite that conferred the *Tan Monong* title, the 'foreign' means to local ends had an ancient provenance. In 1978, at the closing of the Council of Chiefs in Malakula, Bongmatur gave a pig to Chief Enoch of Unua in return for the title *Beranginvanu*, which is translated in one hagiography of Bongmatur as 'a huge stone in a large area of land' (Aaron 1981:98). *Berang* in North Ambrym is, however, the name for the sculpted tree-fern image set up in the *mage*. In a later account of Bongmatur's rise to fame, this time by an Ambrymese relative of his wife, this title has become 'one of the highest titles on Ambrym, *Peranginvanu* (means the man who stands on a high hill or stone looking out over the whole land' (Alpi and Laan 1995: 325). That he came to hold this title, the author comments, 'attests to the widespread support and influence he had among the whole island population, despite his close association with a single political party'(ibid.). [11]

Bongmatur has more recently enlisted the aid of anthropologists in what perhaps is the contemporary way in which 'finishing the land' can best be accomplished. When I returned to Vanuatu in 1992, he asked me to write his life story, which he wanted published. I agreed, gave him a dictaphone to use and recorded a lengthy preliminary interview. Not long after, he was approached by Lissant Bolton, who wanted to interview him about his involvement in the Cultural Centre. He gave her 13 hours of interviews, mostly about his life and rise to fame. He has also been interviewed by anthropologist Lamont Lindstrom (1997). Bolton recently published an account of Bongmatur's activities in this period in the *Journal of Pacific History*, which perhaps was not quite what Willy had in mind (Bolton 1998). Now retired and living between North Ambrym and Port Vila, where he frequently speaks out on local and global issues, he has constructed his own monument, a concrete church in his village in North Ambrym. One of the major ways in which he attempted to establish his right to become the President of the Council of *Kastom* Chiefs when his rival pointed out that he had never killed a pig, was to respond that while it was true that neither he nor his father had been involved in the *mage*, and that his grandfather had reached only a middle grade, his great-grandfather had sponsored his *kastom* rival's grandfather's accession to the grade *mal meurt*, the zenith of imported rites. Since it is generally known that the major sequence of grades called *mage* came to North Ambrym via the west, this seemed like a clinching argument. In the north itself, however, there were many who did not support Bongmatur who pointed out that the indigenous powerful rites involving kin, for which the imported grades were merely a preparation, as they were for the rite of *mage ne kuman*, conferring the *Tan Monong* title, were not performed by Bongmatur's ancestors. Within living memory, however, Bongmatur's *kastom* rival's father and grandfather had performed them and their ancestor was none other than *Tan Monong bariu*.

In the past, fame and renown were acquired through being established in an ancestral place, even though many became known to their descendants precisely because they had come from somewhere else and had connections to other places. But tracing one's primordial origins was not enough, one also benefited by demonstrating powerful connections to the wider world, through trade in material and intellectual property as well as prowess in giving tusked boars, frequently brought from elsewhere, to one's kin. Manoeuvring oneself and one's direct descendants closer to an apical ancestor was also a reason for keeping the knowledge of primordial connections and making claims to privileged access.

In the post-colonial period, these claims became more important in relation to access to land and rights of domicile.

When the yam master of Fona village was removed from his position, after Nagriamel, the land rights and secessionist movement, was defeated at independence, a member of a junior line in the village, and a Vanua'aku Pati supporter, was appointed in his stead. In the late 1980s, this man built himself a large new concrete well (actually a water tank) into the side of which he engraved the words 'Bungyam's well'. As village chief, he was now asserting a claim to precedence in the domain that was made possible by a totally novel situation: the obliteration of a person's once inalienable right to connection with their ancestors. His attempts to perform exorcism of those afflicted by Fona spirits were notably unsuccessful, according to the yam master's son. Once the Vanua'aku Pati lost power after an uninterrupted first decade, however, the Francophone Government was keen to see the rehabilitation of those who had been punished nationally and locally after the events of the Santo Rebellion. In 1998, the yam master received a distinguished service medal from the Government and the next year held an inauguration feast in which his eldest grandson was nominated as chief of Fona village, in an attempt to restore the position of his descendants to pre-eminence in the domain. In 1999, I was summoned to what I expected would be his deathbed, to find that he was hoping for the sort of anthropological donation given, he had heard, by the Norwegian researchers working in Ranon village in the early Nineties. With enough money, he could erect The Wilfred Koran Community Hall, a monument that would 'finish the land' in a thoroughly contemporary, yet perfectly precedented manner. He also wanted to revive the *mage ne kuman* ritual that confers the title *Tan Monong* before his death. But even if he does not succeed, the fame of this title has already broached the shores of Ambrym. John Manu, Guiart's informant of the 1940s, told the ethnographer that the ritual had been performed all over Ambrym and that his father had then taken it to Pentecost.

In February 2003, the *Pacific Islands Report* (http://pidp.eastwestcenter.org/pireport/2003/February/02-03-07.htm) documented the visit of the then Prime Minister, Edward Natapei, to central Pentecost to perform 'a custom peace ceremony' after several custom chiefs, 'some of whom are Tanmonoks (paramount chiefs)', were ill-treated by police causing the chiefs to cease performing their duties while banning law enforcement agencies from the island. Achieving the exogenous status of 'paramountcy', *Tan Monong* has indeed 'finished the land'.

References

Aaron, D.B. 1981. 'Chief Willy Bongmatur. National Council of Chiefs.' In B. Macdonald-Milne and P. Thomas (eds), *Yumi Stanap. Leaders and leadership in a new nation*. Suva: Institute of Pacific Studies, the University of the South Pacific and Lotu Pasifika Publications.

Allen, M.R. 1968. 'Report on Aoba.' Edited by Caroline Leaney. *Incidental Papers on Nduindui District, Aoba Island, New Hebrides*, written for the British Residency in the New Hebrides, Port Vila.

Alpi, B. and J. Laan. 1995. 'Ambrym.' In H. Van Trease (ed.), *Melanesian Politics. Stael Blong Vanuatu*, Christchurch and Suva: Macmillan Brown Centre for Pacific Studies, University of Canterbury, and Institute of Pacific Studies, University of the South Pacific.

Bellwood, P., J. Fox and D. Tryon. (eds). 1995. *The Austronesians: Historical and Comparative Perspectives*. Canberra: Department of Anthropology, RSPAS. The Australian National University.

Bolton, L. 1998. 'Chief Willy Bongmatur and the Role of Chiefs in Vanuatu.' *The Journal of Pacific History*, XXXIII. pp. 179-196.

Bonnemaison, J. 1985. 'The tree and the Canoe. Roots and Mobility in Vanuatu Society.' In M. Chapman (ed.), *Mobility and Identity in the Island Pacific* special issue of *Pacific Viewpoints*, 26 (1). pp. 30-62.

Bonnemaison, J. 1994. *The tree and the canoe: History and ethnogeography of Tanna*. Honolulu: University of Hawai'i Press.

Boulekone, V. 1995. 'Politics of Tan-Union.' In H. Van Trease (ed.), *Melanesian Politics. Stael Blong Vanuatu*, Christchurch and Suva: Macmillan Brown Centre for Pacific Studies, University of Canterbury, and Institute of Pacific Studies, University of the South Pacific.

Codrington, R.H. 1957 [1891]. *The Melanesians. Studies in their Anthropology and Folklore*. New Haven: HRAF Press.

Deacon, A.B. 1934. *Malekula: A Vanishing People in the New Hebrides*. Edited by Camilla Wedgewood. London: G. Routledge and Sons.

Fox, J.J. (ed.) 1993. *Inside Austronesian Houses: Perspectives on Domestic Designs for Living*. Canberra: Department of Anthropology, RSPAS, The Australian National University.

Fox, J.J. (ed.) 1997. *The Poetic Power of Place: Comparative Perspectives on Austronesian Ideas of Locality*. Canberra: Department of Anthropology, RSPAS, The Australian National University.

Fox, J.J. and C. Sather. (eds). 1996. *Origins, Ancestry and Alliance: Explorations in Austronesian Ethnography*. Canberra: Department of Anthropology, RSPAS, The Australian National University.

Guiart, J. 1951. 'Société, rituals et mythes du Nord-Ambrym.' *Journal de la Société des Océanistes*, 7 (7). pp. 5-103.

Green, R.C. and A. Pawley. 1998. 'Architectural forms and settlement patterns.' In M. Ross, A. Pawley and M. Osmond (eds), *The Lexicon of Proto Oceanic. The Lexicon and environment of Ancestral Oceanic Society. 1. Material Culture, Pacific Linguistics*, Series C-152, Canberra: RSPAS, The Australian National University.

Jolly, M. 1994. *Women of the Place. Kastom, Colonialism and Gender in Vanuatu*. Chur (Switzerland): Harwood Academic Publishers.

Layard, J. 1942. *Stone Men of Malekula*. London: Chatto and Windus.

Lynch, J. 1982. 'Towards a theory of the origin of the Oceanic Possessive Constructions.' In A. Halim et al. (eds), *Papers from the Third International Conference on Austronesian Linguistics*, Vol. 1, *Pacific Linguistics*, Series C-74, Canberra: Department of Linguistics, RSPAS, The Australian National University. pp. 243-68.

Lynch, J. 1996. 'Proto Oceanic Possessive Marking.' In J. Lynch and Fa'afo Pat (eds), *Oceanic Studies: Proceedings of the First International Conference on Oceanic Linguistics, Pacific Linguistics*, Series C-133, Canberra: Department of Linguistics, RSPAS, The Australian National University. pp. 93-110.

Macdonald-Milne, B. and P. Thomas. (eds). 1981. *Yumi Stanap. Leaders and leadership in a new nation*. Suva: Institute of Pacific Studies, the University of the South Pacific and Lotu Pasifika Publications.

Macintyre, M. 1984. 'The Problem of the Semi-alienable Pig.' *Canberra Anthropology*, 7 (1-2). pp. 109-121.

Paton, W.F. 1971a. 'Tales of Ambrym.' *Pacific Linguistics*, Series D-10. Canberra: Department of Linguistics, RSPAS, The Australian National University.

Paton, W.F. 1971b. 'Ambrym (Lonwolwol) Grammar.' *Pacific Linguistics*, Series B-19. Canberra: Department of Linguistics, RSPAS, The Australian National University.

Paton, W.F. 1979. 'Customs of Ambrym.' *Pacific Linguistics*, Series D-22. Canberra: Department of Linguistics, RSPAS, The Australian National University.

Patterson, M. 1976. 'Kinship, Marriage and Ritual in North Ambrym.' Unpublished PhD thesis. Anthropology Department, University of Sydney. Sydney.

Patterson, M. 1981. 'Slings and Arrows: Rituals of Status Acquisition in North Ambrym.' In M.R. Allen (ed.), *Vanuatu. Politics, Economics and Ritual in Island Melanesia*. pp. 189-236.

Patterson, M. 2001. 'Breaking the Stones: Ritual, gender and modernity in North Ambrym, Vanuatu.' In M. Patterson and R. Tonkinson (eds). *Special Issue: Gender, Power and Ritual in Cross-Cultural Perspective—essays in honour of Michael Allen, Anthropological Forum* 11 (1). pp. 39-54.

Patterson, M. 2002a. 'Moving Histories: An analysis of the dynamics of place and mobility in North Ambrym, Vanuatu.' *The Australian Journal of Anthropology*, 13 (2) pp. 200-18.

Patterson, M. 2002b. 'Leading Lights in the 'Mother of Darkness': Perspectives on Leadership and Value in North Ambrym, Vanuatu.' *Oceania*, 73 (2). p. 126-42.

Philibert, J.-M. 1992. 'Social Change in Vanuatu.' In A.B. Robillard (ed.), *Social Change in the Pacific Islands*, London and New York: Kegan Paul International.

Regenvanu, S. 1980. 'The Land.' *Vanuatu: twenty wan tintging long taem blong Independens*. Suva: Institute of Pacific Studies, University of the South Pacific, and the South Pacific Social Sciences Association.

Rodman, M. 1987. *Masters of Tradition. Consequences of customary land tenure in Longana, Vanuatu*. Vancouver: University of British Columbia Press.

Rodman, M. 1992. 'Empowering Place: Multilocality and Multivocality.' *American Anthropologist*, 94. pp. 640-56.

Rodman, M. 1994. 'Breathing Spaces: Customary Land Tenure in Vanuatu.' In R.G. Ward and E. Kingdon (eds), *Land, Custom and Practice in the South Pacific*, Cambridge: Cambridge University Press.

Ross, M., A. Pawley and M. Osmond. 1998. 'The Lexicon of Proto Oceanic. The Lexicon and environment of Ancestral Oceanic Society. 1. Material Culture.' *Pacific Linguistics*, Series C-152. Canberra: RSPAS, The Australian National University.

Sope, B. (ed.) 1974. *Land and Politics in the New Hebrides*. Suva: South Pacific Social Sciences Association.

Tattevin, E. 1929-31. 'Mythes et legends du sud de l'île Pentecôte.' *Anthropos*, 24: pp. 983-1004; 26: pp. 489-512, 863-6.

Tonkinson, R. 1968. *Maat Village, Efate: A Relocated Community in the New Hebrides.* Eugene (Oregon): Department of Anthropology, University of Oregon.

Tonkinson, R. 1982a. 'National Identity and the Problem of *kastom* in Vanuatu.' *Mankind,* 13 (4). pp. 306-15.

Tonkinson, R. 1985. 'Forever Ambrymese. Identity in a Relocated Community, Pacific Vanuatu.' In M. Chapman (ed.), *Mobility and Identity in the Island Pacific,* special issue, *Pacific Viewpoints,* 26 (1). pp. 30-62.

Van Trease, H. 1987. *The politics of land in Vanuatu. From colony to independence.* Suva: Institute of Pacific Studies, the University of the South Pacific.

Van Trease, H. (ed.) 1995. *Melanesian Politics. Stael Blong Vanuatu.* Christchurch and Suva: Macmillan Brown Centre for Pacific Studies, University of Canterbury, and Institute of Pacific Studies, University of the South Pacific.

Vienne, B. 1984. *Gens de Motlav. Idéologie et pratique sociale en Mélanésie.* Paris: Publication de la Société des Océanistes, No 42. Musée de l'Homme.

Weiner, J. 1998. 'Revealing the Grounds of life in PNG.' In S. Bamford (ed.), *Identity, Nature and Culture: Sociality and Environment in Melanesia,* special issue, *Social Analysis,* 42 (3). pp. 135-42.

ENDNOTES

[1] This was merely, according to Van Trease, 'an extension of the New Hebrides National Party' shortly to be renamed as mentioned above and it was relatively short lived, fielding candidates at only one election (Van Trease 1987: 216).

[2] When I left North Ambrym after my first period of fieldwork in 1969, the kind of song competition that accompanied boys' initiation was performed at my farewell feast. In one of the new songs, the composer described me as someone who 'has come to learn the language of my place', '*mame rongtane ral ne mweneng vere*'.

[3] There is some controversy among linguists here. Whereas earlier writers had seen the 'alienable' varieties of noun possession as a kind of gender system, by the 1970s, Pawley and Lynch in particular argued that they expressed the relationships of possession and were more comparable to verb-object relationships. It was recognised that 'possession with some nouns could be expressed by means of more than one construction, and that these nouns thus "belonged" to more than one class"'(Lynch 1996: 94).

[4] In a recent view, Lynch suggests that in Proto-Oceanic, passive possession might have been marked quite differently from food possession, by a now disappeared article (as found in some Polynesian languages –a/o) and that there were previously a greater number of possessive markers (Lynch 1996: 97).

[5] See Rodman (1995: 71-3) for an excellent overview of the ways in which connection to land has been documented in Vanuatu.

[6] In North Ambrym, the husks of Tahitian chestnuts symbolise female genitalia and feature in ribald joking between women.

[7] Salt water (*wekon*), which is referred to as '*kon*' or bitter/salt/sacred/tabu, is associated appropriately with a woman's son, who she calls by the same term that she uses for her father-in-law, i.e. the boy's father's father; these kin are for her members of an avoided ('*mokon*') category. Fresh water (*we*) is 'clear' and unrestricted as husbands must be after marriage and as mothers-in-law are made to be by the sacrifice of pigs.

[8] The *muyune rem* (literally, sign of the yam) was sold to a tourist by the yam master's son-in-law in the early 1970s. It was described as a small bundle of sticks bound together.

[9] The Presbyterian missionary Paton also records a description of the rite that appears to be somewhat muddled in relation to the identity of the protagonists (1979: 26-8). Paton does not mention the kinship relations between donor and sponsor and erroneously comments that women could take the title. While it is true that women participate in the rite, they could not initiate their participation nor participate on their own but only as mother of the candidate. Paton's description of the central act of the rite, where the husband and wife kneel covered with a red mat and are given water to drink from a vessel proffered by the sponsor who drinks first, then after they have drunk, pours water over their hands to 'wash' them, has a decidedly Christian resonance. It was not reported to me nor does it appear in Guiart's account. Paton, however, worked and lived among West Ambrymese refugees whose version of the rite might have contained these elements or they might have been added for Paton's benefit. In Paton's account the candidate takes a small pig and tosses it over the low fence that has been constructed around a section of the ceremonial ground, outside of which guests stand to observe the proceedings, rather like a bride tossing a bouquet. In fact, his account has a distinct 'wedding' quality to it. Whoever catches the pig may take it to eat with his grade mates. In Guiart's account, the water comes from a basin that is made of a leaf-lined depression in a canoe-shaped mound of earth constructed inside the coconut-leaf enclosure. At one end of the mound is a representation of a frigate bird or snake such as adorned seagoing canoes and which are also placed over the little shrines that cover the stone altars in the upper *mage* ranks. The candidate, who is surrounded by his classificatory fathers, must drink from the basin before sacrificing a boar and calling out his new title. His mother or 'mothers' (i.e. the wives of his fathers) then also kill pigs to take their titles, giving smaller pigs for pearl-shell armbands provided by the wife of the sponsor. This is one of the few occasions when some women were permitted into the ceremonial ground. All women other than the candidates had to participate in the accompanying dancing in the bush on the outskirts of the sacred space.

[10] In need of her labour because he was planning one of the important rituals involving his mother's origin place, he wanted her back. After arguing with his wife's father and shooting him, he proceeded to his mother's place, where he could expect sanctuary. He arranged with them to pay compensation of tusked boars to the murdered man's kin, retrieved his wife and took as well another woman, also visiting her birthplace, who happened to be married and pregnant to a man of Fona village. Sending word to the Fona husband that when his child was born he should come and contribute to the birth ritual exchanges for 'their' child, he went on with his preparation for the ritual, which he completed successfully. Descendants of the 'stolen child', who was brought up by Tan Monong Bariu, still claim descent from the Fona founder though their rights to land are unchallenged in Tan Monong Bariu's domain.

[11] This account also claims that he joined with Koran, the yam master of Fona, to kill a large number of pigs and take the title Molbaro, but according to Koran this was his initiative and did not involve Chief Willy.

Chapter 15. People and Place in Tonga: The Social Construction of *Fonua* in Oceania

Steve Francis

> Every Tongan adult has both a *fonua*, or island/village identity, and a *famili/kainga*, or kin set identity. (G. Marcus 1975: 37)

Introduction

Local Territory and Global Identity

This paper seeks to explore the social classification and territorial concept of *fonua* in the Pacific Island Kingdom of Tonga. A reflex of the reconstructed Proto-Austronesian territorial category **banua*, the word *fonua* as it is utilised in Tonga intimately connects the *people* of Tonga with the places that represent Tonga. [1] *Fonua* therefore constructs people and place as a bonded entity.

Although Tonga has been a Christian nation for more than a century, *fonua* invokes for Tongans an indigenous cosmology in which the environment is regarded as 'an extension of human society' (Mahina 1992: 57). As a result, human agency is integral to a physical landscape that includes the land, the ocean and the sky. In pre-constitution Tonga, the concept of *fonua* 'people of/and place' described a local territorial entity that incorporated the land and natural surrounds associated with a chiefly titleholding, and the people residing on that land. [2] For the residents of this territory, the outcomes of association with this bounded entity included participation in communal modes of agricultural production, intimate kinship connections, and subsumption within a chiefly titleholding hierarchy, which demanded surplus production as tribute.

Disassociated from this earlier societal framework, *fonua* is today employed in a national/political context. In contemporary Tonga, *fonua* embodies notions of Tongan nationhood and positive self-identification. By contrasting positive Tongan values with negative Western values, Tongans use the word *fonua* to denote a connection between the place(s) and people of Tonga, wherever and whoever they might be. While the contemporary version of *fonua* thus embodies a new formulation, it also continues to resonate with earlier meanings.

Fonua is therefore the embodiment of both local territorial belonging (a historicised rendering) and national self-identification (a contemporary rendering), simultaneously connecting Tongans to a mythological past and linking them with a globalised present. The category therefore conflates the physical and the metaphysical, the historical and the mythological, the political and the social, the local and the global.

Fonua, as a conjuncture of 'people and place', underpins primary social, economic and political relationships in Tonga. Accordingly, this paper will analyse how the people of Tonga employ this social category in varying political, economic and social contexts: political, in the sense of elite-commoner relations; economic, in the context of land use and landownership; and social, within the framework of village, island, regional and national identities. The paper will seek to make explicit the multiple roles of *fonua* in Tonga through an examination of myth, history, social relations and local boundaries within the Kingdom of Tonga.

Arrival: Austronesian-Speaking Peoples in Tonga

Incorporated within the final expansion of the Lapita pottery-making peoples into the South-West Pacific, the first human habitation of the Tonga Group has been recently dated at between 2850 BP (900 BC) and 2800 BP (850 BC) (Burley, Nelson et al. 1999: 63). [3] According to the evidence collected to date, the Lapita Period in Tonga conformed to many of the characteristics associated with the so-called Lapita 'cultural complex'. Archaeologists (Golson 1961; Green 1979) and anthropologists have identified a range of practices including characteristic agricultural techniques, coastal settlement and subsistence economies, which included reef and lagoon fishing and animal husbandry (pigs and fowl).

Linguistic analysis has also identified the languages spoken by the Lapita people as a subgroup of Oceanic (OC), itself a subgrouping of the major Malayo-Polynesian (MP) branch which derives from Proto-Austronesian (Blust 1980: 11). Proto-Polynesian (PN) is a further subdivision of Oceanic from which derives Proto-Tongic and Proto-Nuclear Polynesian (Kirch 1988:5; Pawley and Ross 1993: 440). The Tongan and Niuean languages have been identified as derivatives of Proto-Tongic (Kirch 1988: 5). Based on these linguistic conjectures, Blust has suggested that Tonga 'was the first (Proto-Polynesian) PN island group to be settled (by at least the late second millennium BC) and that Samoa was probably peopled from Tonga (by about 700-600 BC) in the second major PN movement' (Blust 1980: 27). [4]

The Tongan Island Group: A Local Geography

Centrally located in the Pacific Ocean, west of the International Dateline, south of Samoa and south east of Fiji, the Tonga Group is made up of more than 170 islands (only 43 of which are currently settled) extending in a north-south island chain. Covering a linear distance of 800 kilometres, the land area of 750 square kilometres contrasts with a claim to more than 362,500 square kilometres of ocean area (Maude 1965).

La Perouse first pointed out that

> [o]f the hundred and fifty islands which compose this archipelago, the greater number consists only of uninhabited and uninhabitable rocks. (La Perouse 1799: 173)

This rather harsh assessment notwithstanding, Tongans distinguish between four island 'clusters' within the kingdom, each with their own distinctive physical features and social normative attributes. These are the Tongatapu cluster incorporating Tongatapu and 'Eua, the dispersed Ha'apai cluster, the mountainous Vava'u cluster and the remote 'Niuas' (Niuafo'ou, Niuatoputapu and Taufahi) situated 400 kilometres north of Vava'u, physically closer to Samoa, Fiji, 'Uvea (Wallis) and Futuna than to Tonga. The inhabitants of each cluster are also ascribed idiosyncratic normative attributes by other Tongans and the residents themselves. These include stereotyping of personal characteristics, mannerisms and habits and accent differentiation as well as the assignment of social, economic and political status.

Fonua in Tongan Cosmology

> On the island there is hardly any mountain, spring, or large rock that does not refer to a myth. Between space and mythology, places and culture, the symbiosis is complete (Bonnemaison 1994: 113)

The concept of *fonua* 'people of/and place' was located centrally in the construction and organisation of the Tongan cosmological universe. In order to investigate *fonua* in the context of this mythological past, the discussion will focus on two examples of mythic storytelling. Cultural forms such as poetry, dance and mythic tales provide useful insights into the order and logic of the pre-contact cosmology. The first is an excerpt from the *Lau Langi*, 'The Skies', a version of the ancient Tongan dance form known as the *'Otuhaka*. The dance was performed for the *Tu'i Tonga* (the divine Kings of ancient Tonga) on ritual occasions. The second example utilised is a selection from the Tongan creation myth cycle, the *Talatupu'a*.

Lau Langi, 'The Skies'

Ke fanongo mai ho'o pulotu na,	Listen to us you composers
Kae fai 'emau talatupu'a,	Listen to us you composers
Ko e talanoa talu mei mu'a,	While we tell you a tale from long ago
Mei he'etau 'uluaki matua'a,	The story from the beginning
Na'e fakatapu hotau fonua,	From our first old men
'O fakapulonga mei 'olunga,	Our people/place was created [a]

Pea tau totolo hange ha 'unga,	Shrouded from above And we crawled like crabs. [b]

[a] In the translation, Kaeppler glosses *fonua* as 'land', however, I have replaced it with the gloss 'people/place' in order to maintain consistency of meaning in the context of this paper.
[b] This extract is taken from Kaeppler (1993: 64-5).

While the primary dance forms of contemporary Tonga, such as the *lakalaka,* begin with a *fakatapu,* 'sacred salutation', which pays respect to God, the King and his nobles, pre-Christian forms began with references to the creation of the world by the pantheon of Tongan gods. The *Lau Langi* is no exception as it proceeds to tell the story of the creation of the atmosphere, the sunset, the air and the stars.

The opening lines of the dance are particularly interesting in the context of the present discussion as they reflect the concept of *fonua* in the employment of images that intimately associate people with earth, with land, with place. The use of the word *'unga,* for example, is particularly evocative as it denotes a large form of hermit crab, which burrows into the ground at night. The association of crabs with the water is also emblematic of the importance of the ocean in the mythic imagination of the Austronesian people in Tonga and in the concept of *fonua* itself. [5]

Depicting the general populace (the *tu'a,* 'commoners') as tied to place or bound to place (i.e. a metaphor for low ranking) while associating the *hou'eiki* 'chiefs', with the sky (which is a metaphor for high rank) was a common practice. This was not surprising given that dance, poetry and myth-telling in general were written and performed with an *'eiki,* 'chiefly', audience in mind. As a result, emphasis was placed on symbolically reinforcing the longevity and strength of the existing hierarchical order of Tongan society in poetic form.

This symbolic separation was continued, even in the afterlife. For while the *'eiki* 'chiefs', were deemed to have souls, travelling to the Tongan paradise world of *Pulotu* upon death, the *tu'a,* 'commoners', without souls, were deemed unfit to enter *Pulotu.* In fact, they were designated as the *kau kai***fonua** , 'the people who eat place'. [6] This term, applied to commoners by the chiefs, starkly illustrates the connection made between the place and people of Tonga. In some versions of the story, the *tu'a,* 'commoners', ended their time by travelling to the *lalo***fonua** , 'the place below' (see Gordon 1988: 25).

The Talatupu'a: A Story of the Past

In the beginning there existed only *Vahanoa,* 'the endless open sea', and *Pulotu,* 'the home of the spirits and gods'. On the surface of *Vahanoa* drifted Seaweed (*Limu*) and Earth (*Kele*). But they were soon separated and between them emerged a huge rock, *Touia-'o-Futuna.* The rock shook angrily causing a series of tremors, which split open *Touia-'o-Futuna* and from it emerged four pairs of twins, male and female, *Piki* and his twin sister *Kele*, *'Atungaki* and his twin sister *Ma'imoa'alongona*, *Fonua'uta* and his twin sister *Fonua'vai*, and *Hemoana* and his twin sister *Lupe*. Incestuous sexual relations between each pair of twins resulted in a number of children. *Taufulifonua* and *Havealolofonua*, were the son and daughter respectively of *Piki* and *Kele*, while *Hemoana* and *Lupe* who produced a boy, *Tokilangafonua* and a girl, *Hinatu'aifanga*. [7]

In time *Taufulifonua* and *Havealolofonua* (brother and sister) produced a child, the Tongan goddess, *Havea Hikule'o*. They decided to create an island for her, called *Tongamama'o* (Distant Tonga). *Taufulifonua* then copulated with his cousin *Velelahi* producing the Tongan god, *Tangaloa 'Eiki*. He then coupled with another cousin, *Velesi'i*, producing another Tongan god, *Maui Motu'a*. When *Taufulifonua* was close to death, he set about dividing the universe among his children. **Tangaloa 'Eiki** was given *Langi* (the sky), *Maui Motu'a* was given the domain of *Maama* (the underworld) and *Havea Hikule'o* was given *Pulotu*, the world of the spirits, gods and demigods. [8]

As the island of 'Ata was still without vegetation, *Tangaloa 'Eiki* told one of his sons, *Tangaloa 'Atulongolongo*, to fly over (in the form of a *kiu* 'plover') and drop a seed. Eventually, a creeper covered the whole island and on returning *Tangaloa 'Atulongolongo* pecked a rotten branch out of which a huge worm crawled. He then pecked the worm into two pieces as instructed by his father. From the head of the worm, a man called *Kohai* 'Who', was formed. From the tail was formed a man called *Koau*, 'It is I'. A little piece was left over and this too became a man, *Momo*, 'fragment'. [9]

The *Talatupu'a*, meaning 'telling of the ancient/remote past', is a cycle of myths relating to the origin and creation of the Tongan world and its people by the gods. [10] It is similar to most Tongan (and other Polynesian) myths in that a basic story provides the framework on which, depending on the situation, occasion, audience, store of knowledge, locality, and politics of the event, the storyteller would add or subtract subplots or side stories. Although a mythic tale, the *Talatupu'a* is also a sociopolitical allegory in that it presents an ontologically ordered, Tonga-centred, elite-focused cosmogony. [11] As Mahina notes, the *Talatupu'a*

may be regarded as a cosmic representation of the social arrangement, where the environment is seen as merely an extension of human society. It follows that, as far as the *Talatupu'a* is concerned, the origin of the universe is socially connected. ... Literally, the universe is thus made

> social- and environmental-specific to the Tongan social world, and the universe, at least for the Tongans, is symbolically Tongan society. (Mahina 1992: 57-8)

In the *Talatupu'a*, as in the *Lau Langi*, *fonua* imagery underpins the connection of environment and place with people. According to the myth, the god *Tangaloa 'Atulongolongo* (in the form of a bird) pecked the first humans (depicted in the story as worms) out of a rotten creeper branch. This correlation with worms, who are literally dwellers in the earth, also recalls the designation of *tu'a*, 'commoners', as *kau kaifonua*, 'the people who eat place'. The association of worms and earth is further enhanced by reference to the rotten creeper branch, which brings with it images of deterioration and decay, but also of growth as the process of decomposition, facilitated by the worms, enriches the earth and promotes further growth. Again, these images recall the reference to crabs in the *'Otuhaka* discussed above.

These associations are also reflected in ancient agricultural terminology. For example, Tongans use the word *fonua* as a descriptive term for the soil that grips the roots of plants when pulled from the earth. Images of commoners in association with the earth are also employed in concepts of life and death. The old Tongan word for the placenta (an obvious symbol of birth) is *fonua*. According to ancient practice, the *fonua* was buried after birth. As Mahina has pointed out, 'according to the Tongan worldview, people are themselves the land' (Mahina 1992: 2). Similarly, the word for grave is a derivation of *fonua*. In Tongan, a grave is a *fonualoto*, which means literally 'centre or heart of place'. Death and burial are therefore symbolically linked with a return to the place from which the worm-like *kaifonua* first emerged.

Ocean and Sky

In the *Talatupu'a* myth, the *fonua* is intimately connected with the ocean and the sky. At the beginning of the tale, *Kele* (lit: 'earth/dirt') is found drifting in the ocean. Floating like the islands of Tonga, *Kele* connects the ocean (*tahi*, 'sea', or *moana*, 'deep sea') with *fonua*. The names of the gods in the story also reflect this theme. For example, *Fonua'vai*, 'place/people of the water', contrasts with *Fonua'uta*, 'place/people of the land'.

Intimate associations of *fonua* and the sky are also apparent in the story. While the apical gods are literally ejaculated from the *lalofonua*, 'the place below', by the volcanic fury of *Touia-'o-Futuna*, the creation of man is precipitated by a bird dropping a seed from the sky (*Tangaloa 'Atulongolongo*, son of *Tangaloa 'Eiki*, God of the Sky) (compare with Banda origin myths, cf. Winn, this volume). The names of the gods again reflect the subtext of the tale as ocean and sky are associated with the creation of the *fonua*, 'people of/and place'. In the story, *Hemoana* (lit: 'the ocean') and *Lupe* ('dove', i.e. a creature of the sky) produced a child named *Tokilangafonua*. The name of the god itself tells the story of creation of the *fonua* by the sky and the ocean. The name may be interpreted to mean 'newly created or newly built *fonua*'. The construction analogy (introduced by the word *langa*, 'build') is further enhanced through the double meaning of the word *toki*, which also means 'axe/adze'.

Fonua in Place: Connection and Separation

Tangaloa tu'u hake e Maui,	Tangaloa, arise Maui,
Ke fanongoongo hono 'otu muli	Harken his chain of foreign/exotic islands,
Katoa Tonga ni fakatefuli	All this place of Tonga [a]

[a] This is an excerpt from the *Poem of Tuku'aho* (Collocott 1928: 95) written in the early 1800s by Teukava, a chief of Hihifo, Tongatapu, who was an ally of the famous Ha'apai chief, Finau Ulukalala II, whose exploits were documented by the shipwrecked seaman William Mariner in his *Account of the Natives of the Tonga Islands in the South Pacific*.

The juxtaposition of earth, environment, ocean and sky in the stories examined above are reflective of Tongan notions of connection and separation. These epistemological precepts continue to inform contemporary ideas about the 'people/place' complex of the *fonua* and Tongan ideas of place-in-the-world. As can be demonstrated through an analysis of the *Poem of Tuku'aho* above, notions of connection and separation are essential in connecting Tongans to place and to each other.

Written in the early 1800s, the opening lines of the poem are an invocation by the poet to *Tangaloa 'Eiki*, God of the Sky, and *Maui Motu'a*, God of the Earth, Land and Underworld. This initial section of the poem captures a sense of Tonga as a physical sequence of linked islands and as a unified social 'whole'. The sequential use of the words *'otu* 'series, chain, row of islands', and *muli*, 'foreign', in the second line of the poem emphasises connection (*'otu*) and separation (*muli*). There are two primary agents central to the connection/association motif contained in the word *'otu*—the ocean (*lotomoana*) and the land (*uta*). [12]

As a source of sustenance, commerce, trade, decorative objects, sacred artefacts, spouses and, of course, as the agent that enabled travel over large distances, the life-giving and life-taking aspects of the ocean have been mythologised and incorporated into a lexicon of tradition and aspects of everyday life in Tonga (and other Pacific Islands) for many millennia (see, for example, Davidson 1977; Dickinson et al. 1996; Finney 1997; Goodenough and Thomas 1989; Green and Kirch 1997; Kaeppler 1978; Weisler and Woodhead 1995). It is the ocean, the Pacific Ocean, which creates a physical 'connection' between the islands of the Kingdom and to other islands of the Pacific. Of course, it is also the people of Tonga who create social 'connections' across the islands of the kingdom through kinship ties, religion and their associations with place and people (via *fonua*).

The connection theme associated with *'otu* contrasts strongly with the word *muli*, a separation/division motif that highlights the physical division of one island from another within the chain, as well as the distinct *fonua* identities of people and place associated with each Tongan island. These differences have in turn been enhanced and accentuated through myth, poetry and legend. The word *muli* as utilised in pre-contact times referred to Samoans, Fijians and people from other Pacific Islands such as 'Uvea, Futuna, Rotuma and Niue who lived in Tonga or with whom the Tongans had contact (Cummins 1977: 68). With the arrival of Europeans, the emphasis changed and today the word is often used to distinguish Tongans from Westerners in general, who are *kau muli*, 'foreigners'.

The third line concludes the introductory section of the poem with a pronouncement of unity as all the 'foreign' islands of the group are bestowed a collective identity and named 'Tonga'. The use of the word *katoa*, 'everything, whole, without exception', signals the all-inclusive intent (and hope) of the poet.

As will be demonstrated in the next sections, national discourse in Tonga today reflects the symbolism associated with these connection and separation motifs. In everyday speech, Tonga is referred to as a unified whole when comparing and contrasting Tonga with the rest of the *palangi* or 'Western' world, or with the other islands of Oceania. The separation motif also comes into play when Tongans discuss Tonga among themselves. At this point, local village and island identities will come to the fore.

Separation is also an issue for national identity in relation to the Tongan diaspora. As the dispersion and movement of the Tongan population has expanded in the contemporary era, separation and connection have become larger issues to do with cultural and ethnic identity, and thus have come to play a part in a larger debate between Tongans in Tonga and overseas (*muli*).

Having examined *fonua* as a manifestation of the mythological past, discussion now needs to move to an investigation of *fonua* as the principal local territorial division of pre-constitution (i.e. before 1875) Tonga.

Fonua in Tongan History

> Cultures are never static: they evolve through history. That is why the process of cultural reproduction is, in part, a process of cultural transformation. At any given time a group will inherit certain cultural institutions and traditions, but its acts of reiteration or repudiation, its

everyday interactions and its ritual practices will serve to select, modify, and transform these institutions. (Brah 1996: 18)

Locality and Lineage in Pre-constitution Tonga

In the context of pre-constitution Tonga, all land was held notionally by the Tu'i Tonga. The paramount spiritual ruler of the Tongan archipelago, the Tu'i Tonga traced direct patrilineal descent from the semi-divine *'Aho'eitu*, 'day-has-dawned', the son of *Tangaloa "*

'Eitumatapua, a god of the sky, and *Ilaheva*, a woman from Niuatoputapu also known as *Va'epopua* (Gifford 1924: 26). [13] In practice, custodianship of the land was vested in a large group of high-ranking titleholders controlling hereditary tracts as landlords rather than rulers (Maude 1971). The term used to describe these hereditary tracts and the people living on them was *fonua*.

Within each landholding, the populace tended towards dispersed settlement in local homesteads known as *'api*. Similar in composition to the *'api* of contemporary Tonga, these *'api* 'homesteads' or 'houses', often consisted of a parental couple, their married children and their families, unmarried children and wider kin. The oldest male member of the *'api* was known as the *'ulu* or 'head' (see Figure 1 below).

Several *'api* linked by patrilineal descent from a commonly acknowledged ancestor formed a *fa'ahinga*, 'kin group' (Gailey 1987; Grijp 1993; Maude 1965, 1971). [14] Each *fa'ahinga* was headed by a senior-ranking male, the *'ulumotu'a* or 'elder head'. [15] The *'ulumotu'a* often retained a minor title such as *matapule*, 'talking chief'. [16] Several *fa'ahinga* on a hereditary tract of land formed a corporate kin group called the *kainga*, 'kindred'. [17] The *kainga* was headed by an *'eiki si'i* or 'minor chief' related to the hereditary titleholder (who was the *'eiki* or *Tu'i* 'senior chief') (see Figure 1 below). In most cases, these chiefs were younger brothers or sons of the titleholders (Bott 1982: 68-9).

In many cases, the hereditary chiefly titleholders were absentee landlords based primarily in the ancient capital of Mu'a on the island of Tongatapu. As a result, chiefly titleholders often devolved everyday charge of their lands to associated patrilineal kin. In most cases, younger brothers or parallel cousins of the original titleholders, these patrilineal kin were often awarded titles of their own, known as *foha*, 'son', or *tehina*, 'younger brother', titles (Bott 1982: 68-9). These minor chiefs (*'eiki si'i*) were designated as *tauhifonua* or 'keepers or guardians of the land/people' or *motu'a tauhifonua*, 'the old one who looks after the land/people'. While only junior titleholders, the *tauhifonua* were still regarded as *'eiki* or 'chiefly'. [18]

Figure 1: Territorial/social divisions of *fonua*

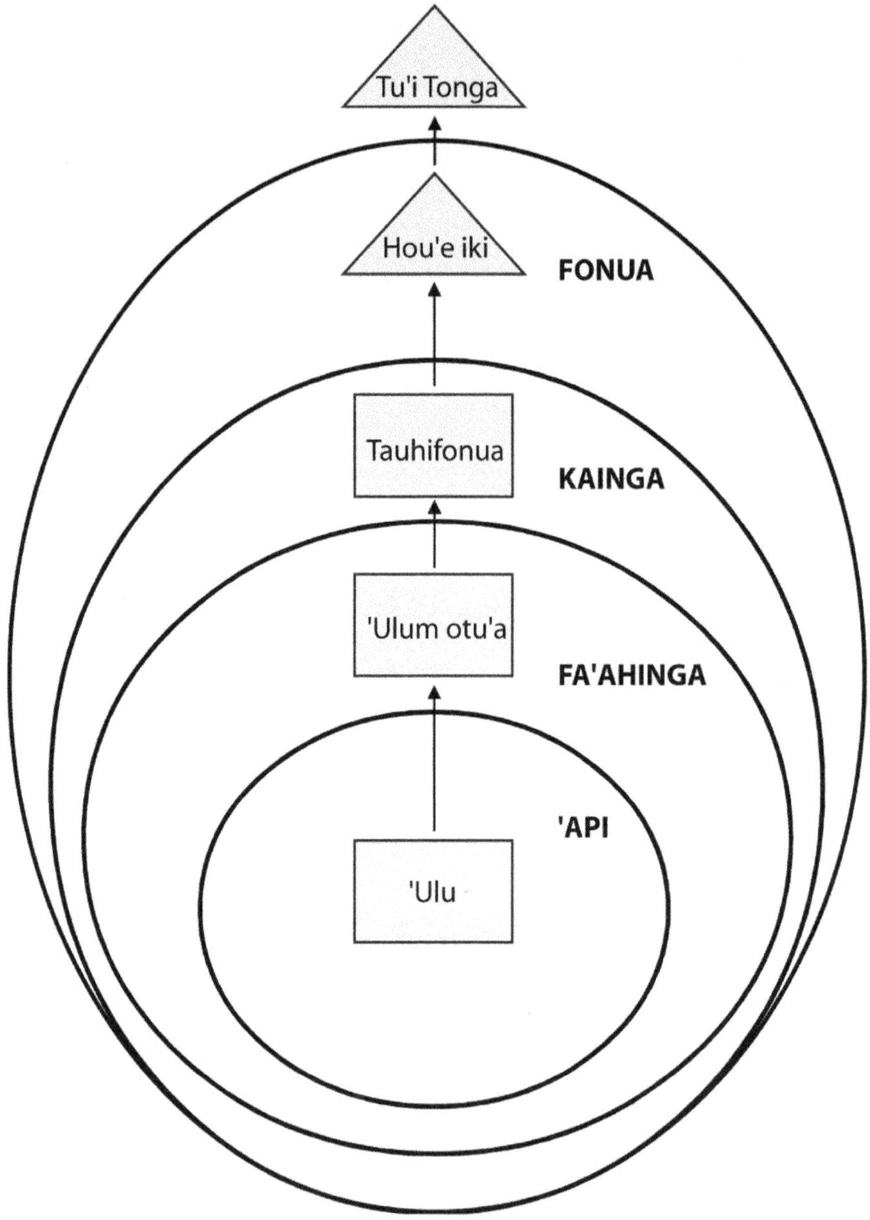

Guardians of the People/Place: Tauhifonua and Matapule

The role of the *tauhifonua* as the keeper or guardian of the *fonua* or 'people and place' in the absence of the titleholder is little discussed in the literature. In fact, many writers have conflated the role of *tauhifonua* with that of the *matapule*, 'talking chief'. A key difference between these positions is that while, as previously noted, the *tauhifonua* were most often connected patrilineally to the chiefly titleholder, and therefore *'eiki* or 'chiefly' themselves, the hereditary *matapule* occupied a ceremonial non-chiefly role. As a result, in the absence of the titleholder, for example, the *tauhifonua* would take the *'eiki* position (the *taumu'a 'olovaha* or 'head of the kava bowl') at kava ceremonies.

It should also be noted that the positions of *tauhifonua* and *matapule* were sometimes awarded to people of high standing or exalted deed. As Gifford noted:

> A warrior who killed ten men and brought the heads as evidence was highly regarded and might be raised to the rank of a *matapule* or a petty chief (*'eiki si'i*) and be given land; or again he might be given the privilege of drinking his chief's kava when it was called. (Gifford 1929: 126) [19]

Ironically, while the *matapule* still perform their ceremonial roles in contemporary Tonga, the position of *tauhifonua* does not exist in the formal sense. The position was not recognised in the Tongan Constitution introduced in 1875 by King Taufa'ahau Tupou I. While the guardian of the *fonua* thus lacks a role in the modern Tongan State, high ritual and ceremonial occasions often do reactivate older social roles such as the *tauhifonua*.

During my fieldwork period, I discovered that one of my informants was in fact a *tauhifonua* and continued to perform roles associated with the title, such as taking the chiefly role of *taumu'a 'olovaha*, 'head of the kava bowl', at most kava ceremonies in the village. This role became even more prominent with the death of the noble of the village, as my informant received tribute and other ceremonial honours during the mourning period observed by the village (and the nation) in respect of the deceased noble.

Former *tauhifonua* were 'honoured' during the reign of Queen Salote (1918-65) when she appointed many of them as *'ofisi kolo*, 'town officers', and *'ofisi vahefonua*, 'district officers'. *'Ofisi kolo* and *'ofisi vahefonua* today represent 'the hereditary estate holder in day-to-day affairs of the village [making] recommendations about allocation of farming and town allotments' (Wood-Ellem 1999: xv). These officers of the contemporary State perform roles that reflect the function but not the content of their former social and ritual status as *tauhifonua*.

Fonua and Agricultural Production

While social and ritual roles were key tasks performed by the *tauhifonua*, there was also an important economic imperative associated with the *fonua* of a titleholder. Agricultural production on and by the *fonua* formed an important component of the hierarchical social and political system of pre-constitution Tonga. Under the guidance and orders of the *tauhifonua*, who was in turn following the directions of the chiefly titleholder, the *'ulumotu'a* of a *fonua* directed the production and distribution of agricultural produce of the *fa'ahinga* (and associated *'api* 'homestead') under his auspices.

While subsistence farming was of course an important focus of *'api* activities, chiefs also required the production of a surplus in order to fulfil ritual and tributary obligations to higher-ranking chiefs including the Tu'i Tonga. The most famous example of this form of obligation was the *'inasi*, 'first fruits', ceremony, an annual tribute of yams (*'ufi*) to the Tu'i Tonga by the chiefs of all of Tonga. Of course, it was the 'commoners' (*tu'a*) working on the *'api* plantations who actually cultivated and harvested the produce by order of their chiefs. Captain Cook (1777), William Mariner (1817) and Rev. John Thomas (1879) all described the *'inasi* ceremonies as the distribution of a portion of the produce of the land 'to ensure the protection of the gods, that their favour may be extended to the welfare of the nation generally, and in particular to the productions of the earth, of which yams [were] the most important' (Mariner 1827, No. 162: 342). [20] It should be noted that while yams were the focus of the ceremony, other gifts designated as 'valued goods' (*koloa*), such as fine mats, were also included as tribute. Thus the *'inasi* served as a harvest prayer to the gods and as a staged demonstration on the part of the elites of their sacred and secular powers. In summary, the *fonua* was an integral component of the Tongan State.

Fonua in Contemporary Tonga

> This is tradition constructed in the present, however, not one that is glued to the past. (Flinn 1992: 45)

Constitutional Changes and the Individualisation of Land Tenure

Having outlined the localised practice of *fonua* in the pre-constitution period, the focus moves to *fonua* as it is utilised within the framework of contemporary national discourse. While today the concept still denotes place and people, the contexts in which the category is employed have changed. The primary changes relate to the fact that in post-constitution Tonga, *fonua* has been separated from the geographical context of local territory, the economic context of agricultural production and the social context of ritual obligation. *Fonua* has now become a symbol of national identity.

This transformation coincided with fundamental societal changes which occurred in Tonga during the 19th century. Codified in the 1875 Constitution, these changes included the unification of all the islands of the archipelago under one chiefly family and the installation of the contemporary monarchy; the abandonment of the ancient religion and adoption of Christianity; the dismantling of the chiefly system and the creation of a class of nobles; and the introduction of new land tenure arrangements.

While incorporating some elements of the *fonua* system, the new laws radically shifted emphasis away from a local communal organisation of production towards individual household production. Morton termed this individualising tendency of the new laws 'atomisation' (Morton 1987). While ensuring that all land in Tonga remained inalienable with ultimate title belonging to the King, the land was divided into 'estates' (*tofi'a*) controlled by a new class of 36 noble landholders. Nobles were allocated more than one tract of land, with most *tofi'a* incorporating numerous tracts of land on different islands. In most cases, individual holdings within these 'estates' conform to original *fonua* boundaries. The land encompassed within the *tofi'a* estates was then subdivided so that every male Tongan aged 16 years and over could access land. Two forms of landholding were designated: the *'api uta* or 'bush or plantation allotment', which incorporated eight and a quarter acres of agricultural land, and a *'api kolo* or 'tax/town allotment' on which to build a house (Maude 1971). Nobles were granted responsibility for the distribution of land on their *tofi'a* estate and, more importantly, discretion over title succession for heirs to town and bush allotments on the death of the landholder. Many nobles use these rights to their capital advantage in modern Tonga.

These land tenure changes, combined with the political and social upheavals of the 19th century, resulted in significant changes to the structure of social organisation and the focus of economic production. Although slow to be adopted (James 1995), the new land tenure arrangements had a profound effect on the *fonua* system. Individual landholding and production led to the demise of communal production directed by the *'ulumotua* and the *tauhifonua* on behalf of the titleholder. The position of *tauhifonua* was abolished, or, more correctly, was not recognised under the new system. The demise of homesteading as the primary settlement pattern also accelerated as commoners coalesced in villages, building houses on their *'api kolo* town allotments and growing crops for their *fāmili* and *kāinga* on their individually owned *'api uta* bush allotments. [21]

Needless to say, these changes profoundly altered the context in which *fonua* was utilised. A primary signifier of this change was the replacement of *fonua* with the concept of *tofi'a* ('estates') to denote a landholding. This transformation symbolically separated the people from the context of land. *Tofi'a* or 'estate' emphasises the connection between the noble and his land rather than the symbolic stress on a kinship connection between the chiefly titleholder, the guardian of place, and the people in the place (Evans 1996: 62) embodied in the notion of *fonua*.

Fonua and Contemporary National Identity

> 'The Tongan way' (*anga fakatonga*) is frequently invoked in everyday life in Tonga as both the defining element of Tongan identity and as the values and behaviours that comprise Tongan culture. *Anga fakatonga* is also rendered as *'ulungaanga o e fonua* or *anga fakafonua*: the way of the land and the people. (Morton 1996: 20)

Detached from the pre-constitution societal framework of communal production and direct connection to a titleholding hierarchy, *fonua* is today most often employed in a national political context. While transforming the circumstances in which the concept of *fonua* is invoked from the local to the national, the category continues to emphasise the connection between the Tongan people and Tonga as place.

During fieldwork, a recurring subject for discussion by my informants was a comparison between Western societies and Tonga. This was not particularly surprising given that a major focus of my work is movement and migration and that a significant proportion of the population now live and work in countries outside Tonga. In most cases, these discussions focused on a comparison of values. The positive value of *anga faka-Tonga*, 'the Tongan way', was contrasted with negative values attributed to Western societies. These negative values included the importance of a secular lifestyle above a spiritual relationship with God, and the privileging of money and work above family.

The positive value of *anga faka-Tonga*, 'the Tongan way', was emphasised continually as an integral and necessary component of adult Tongan behaviour. This concept is an embodiment of core Tongan values and consists of duty (*fatongia*) incorporating responsibility towards the fulfilment of kinship obligation, expressed symbolically through *'ofa*, 'love', and *faka'apa'apa*, 'respect'.

In contrasting positive Tongan values with negative Western values, my informants used the word *fonua* to denote the positive connection between the place and people of Tonga. *Fonua* would be invoked in phrases such as '*Ko e fonua a'aku eni*', which translates approximately as 'This place/people [Tonga/Tongans] are my land/people' or 'I am a component of this place/people known as Tonga.' These connections, made in the context of *anga faka-Tonga*, 'the Tongan way', are also embodied in the phrase '*kainga kakaifonua*', denoting 'the community/family group of the people of the nation of Tonga'. This statement incorporates the Tongan people as a unified, extended community/family. *Fonua* has therefore become the embodiment of a historicised national identity.

The importance of this symbolic utilisation of *fonua* is particularly significant given the establishment of numerous Tongan communities in the countries of the Pacific Rim. With second- and third-generation Tongans being raised in Western countries, issues of identity have become extremely salient for Tongans at home and abroad. As a result, *fonua* has come to embody values held as being core to Tongan identity, as well as representing a connection between the Tongan people (wherever they might be in the world) and the physical place of Tonga itself (both the nation of Tonga and the villages/islands/clusters from which individuals claim origin).

Fonua as Home

> The irony of these times, however, is that as actual places and localities become ever more blurred and indeterminate, ideas of culturally and ethnically distinct places become perhaps even more salient. It is here that it becomes most visible how imagined communities (Anderson 1983) come to be attached to imagined places, as displaced peoples cluster around remembered or imagined homelands, places or communities in a world that seems increasingly to deny such firm territorialised anchors in their actuality. (Gupta and Ferguson 1997: 10-11)

The mythological, historical and contemporary conceptions of *fonua*, 'people of/and place', explored in this paper incorporate mythic and locally connected aspects of 'home' as identified by Brah (1996).

In the first instance, Brah identifies home as a 'mythic place of desire in the diasporic imagination' (Brah 1996: 192). *Fonua* corresponds with this description when Tongans invoke the word as a signifier of identity, belonging and unity (of people and of place). The incorporation of *fonua* in the mythological storytelling of the past and the contemporary assertion of *fonua* as a representation of national identity are two examples of *fonua* in *mythic* mode. *Fonua* claimed in this way is a statement of connection (mutually understood), which all Tongans might make, whether they live in Tonga or in some other place, whether they were born in Tonga or in some other place. Through its association with the powerful declaration of Tongan cultural distinctiveness, *anga fakaTonga*, 'the Tongan way', *fonua* in this sense supports notions of belonging and unity among Tongans, wherever they are and whoever they are.

Through bonding *fonua*, the 'people and place', with *anga fakaTonga*, 'the Tongan way', in the contemporary context, Tongans place their national self-identification in contradistinction to an imagined set of *palangi*, 'Western', values and beliefs. In everyday discourse, Tongans define this contrast as a distinction between *fonua* (Tongan place and Tongan people) and *muli* (foreign places populated by foreign people and Tongans).

On the other hand, *fonua* is also grounded (literally) in the actuality of place and territory, hence *fonua* as the 'the lived experience of a locality. Its sounds and smells, its heat and dust' (Brah 1996: 192). *Fonua* invoked as local belonging intimately associates people with the place/s of their birth, childhood and journey to adulthood. These local places include the remembered chief-associated territory (*fonua*) and kinship (*'api/kainga*) groupings of local districts, the contemporary invitation to land use represented by the *toutu'u* and the shared histories and connections associated with villages, islands and island clusters (*'otu motu*).

In mythic mode, *fonua* may be seen to represent home as a unified, shared understanding that connects all Tongan people. In local mode, *fonua* invokes home as a local association, an association that privileges the few rather than the whole, exclusive in a sense to the individual. When examined from this perspective, *fonua* recalls the principles of separation and connection invoked in the *Poem of Tuku'aho* discussed above—separation in that both dimensions of *fonua*-as-home serve to distinguish Tongans from non-Tongans (the mythic) and individual Tongans from each other (the local). Connection in that the mythic and local dimensions of *fonua* connect Tongans in historical, cultural, economic and imaginary associations. *Fonua* therefore represents a powerful social construction, accommodating assertions of national unity (one people, one place) and a celebration of the diverse histories and distinct territories (many people, many places) that today comprise the Kingdom of Tonga.

References

Campbell, I. 1992. *Island Kingdom: Tonga Ancient and Modern*. Christchurch:

Canterbury University Press.

Beaglehole, J.C. 1967. *The Journals of Captain James Cook on his Voyages of Discovery*.

Cambridge: The Hakluyt Society.

Blust, R. 1980. 'Austronesian Etymologies.' *Oceanic Linguistics*, 19. pp. 1-189.

Bonnemaison, J. 1994. *The Tree and the Canoe: History and Ethnogeography of Tanna*.

Honolulu: University of Hawai'i Press.

Bott, E. 1982. *Tongan Society at the Time of Captain Cook's Visits: Discussions with Her Majesty Queen Salote Tupou*. Vol. 44. Wellington: The Polynesian Society.

Brah, A. 1996. *Cartographies of Diaspora: Contesting Identities*. London: Routledge.

Collocott, E.E.V. 1928. 'Tales and Poems of Tonga.' *Bernice P. Bishop Museum Bulletin*, Vol. 46. Honolulu: Bernice P. Bishop Museum.

Cummins, H.G. 1977. 'Tongan Society at the Time of European Contact.' In N. Rutherford (ed.), *Friendly Islands: A History of Tonga*, Oxford: Oxford University Press. pp. 63-89.

Davidson, J.M. 1977. 'Western Polynesia and Fiji: Prehistoric Contact, Diffusion and Differentiation in Adjacent Archipelagos.' *World Archaeology*, 9. pp. 83-94.

Dickinson, W.R., R. Shutler, R. Shortland, D.V. Burley, and T. Dye. 1996. 'Sand Tempers in Indigenous Lapita and Lapitoid Polynesian Plainware and Imported Protohistoric Fijian Pottery of Ha'apai (Tonga) and the Question of Lapita Tradeware.' *Archaeology in Oceania*, 31. pp. 87-98.

Evans, M. 1996. 'Gifts and Commodities on a Tongan Atoll: Understanding Intention and Action in a MIRAB Economy.' McMaster University, Ontario. unpublished PhD thesis.

Finney, B. 1997. 'Tongan Society at the Time of European Contact.' In N. Rutherford (ed.), *Friendly Islands: A History of Tonga*, Oxford: Oxford University Press. pp. 63-89.

Flinn, J. 1992. *Diplomas and Thatch Houses: Asserting Tradition in a Changing Micronesia.*

Ann Arbor: the University of Michigan Press.

Gailey, C.W. 1987. 'Kinship to Kingship: Gender Hierarchy and State Formation in the Tongan Islands.' *Texas Press Sourcebooks in Anthropology*, Vol. 14. Austin: University of Texas Press.

Gifford, E.W. 1924. 'Tongan Myths and Tales.' *Bernice P. Bishop Museum Bulletin*, Vol. 8. Honolulu: Bernice P. Bishop Museum.

Gifford, E.W. 1929. 'Tongan Society.' *Bernice P. Bishop Museum Bulletin*, Vol. 61: Bayard Dominick Expedition Publications. Honolulu: Bernice P. Bishop Museum.

Goodenough, W.H. and S.D. Thomas. 1989. 'Traditional Navigation in the Western Pacific: A Search for a Pattern.' *Expedition*. 29. pp. 3-14.

Gordon, T. 1988. 'Inventing Mormon Identity in Tonga.' Unpublished PhD thesis University of California.

Green, R.C. and P.V. Kirch. 1997. 'Lapita Exchange Systems and their Polynesian Transformations: Seeking Explanatory Models.' In M.I. Weisler (ed.), *Prehistoric Long-Distance Interaction in Oceania: An Interdisciplinary Approach*, Monograph 21, Auckland: New Zealand Archaeological Association. pp. 19-37.

Grijp, P.v.d. 1993. *Islanders of the South: Production, Kinship and Ideology in the Polynesian Kingdom of Tonga*. Leiden: KITLV Press.

Gupta, A. and J. Ferguson. 1997. 'Beyond "Culture": Space, Identity, and the Politics of Difference.' In A. Gupta and J. Ferguson (eds), *Culture, Power,*

Place: Explorations in Critical Anthropology, New York: Duke University Press. pp. 6-24.

Herda, P.S. 1988. 'The Transformation of the Traditional Tongan Polity: A Genealogical Consideration of Tonga's Past.' Unpublished PhD thesis. The Australian National University, Canberra.

James, K. 1995. 'Right and Privilege in Tongan Land Tenure.' In R.J. Ward and E. Kingdon (eds), *Land, Custom and Tenure in the South Pacific*, Cambridge: Cambridge University Press. pp. 157-89.

La Perouse, J. 1779. *A Voyage Round the World Performed in the Years 1785, 1786, 1787 and 1788 by the Boussole and Astrolabe*. New York: Da Capo Press.

Kaeppler, A.L. 1978. 'Exchange Patterns in Goods and Spouses: Fiji, Tonga and Samoa.' *Mankind*, 11. pp. 246-52.

Kaeppler, A. 1993. *Poetry in Motion: Studies of Tongan Dance*. Nuku'alofa: Vava'u Press.

Mahina, O. 1992. 'The Tongan Traditional History Tala-e-Fonua: A Vernacular Ecology-Centred Historico-Cultural Concept.' Unpublished PhD thesis. The Australian National University, Canberra.

Marcus, G.E. 1975. 'Alternative Structures and the Limits of Hierarchy in the Modern

Kingdom of Tonga.' *Bijdragen de Tot-Taal-en Volkenkunde*, 131. pp. 34-66.

Mariner, W. 1827. *An Account of the Natives of the Tonga Islands in the South Pacific. Compiled and arranged by John Martin*. Nuku'alofa: Vava'u Press.

Maude, A. 1965. 'Population, Land and Livelihood in Tonga.' Unpublished PhD thesis. The Australian National University, Canberra.

Maude, A. 1971. 'Tonga: Equality Overtaking Privilege'' In R. Crocombe (ed.), *Land Tenure in the Pacific*, London: Oxford University Press. pp. 106-28.

Morton, H. 1996. *Becoming Tongan: An Ethnography of Childhood*. Honolulu: University of Hawai'i Press.

Morton, K. 1987. 'The Atomisation of Tongan Society.' *Pacific Studies*, 10. pp. 47-73.

Pawley, A. and M. Ross. 1993. 'Austronesian Historical Linguistics and Culture History.' *Annual Review of Anthropology*, 22. pp. 425-59.

Reiter, P. 1907. 'Traditions Tonguiennes: De l'Origine de Diables ou Dieux.' *Anthropos*, 2. pp. 230-40, 438-48, 743-54.

Weisler, M.I. and J.D. Woodhead. 1995. 'Basalt Pb Isotype Analysis and the Prehistoric Settlement of Polynesia.' *Proceedings of the National Academy of Sciences*, 92. pp. 1881-5.

Wood-Ellem, E. 1999. *Queen Salote of Tonga: The Story of an Era 1900-1965*. Auckland: Auckland University Press.

ENDNOTES

[1] The use of the term *fanua*, the older form of *fonua*, was recorded by Evans (1996) on the island of Ha'ano (in the Ha'apai cluster) and during my fieldwork the term was sometimes utilised by people from the island of Foa (also in the Ha'apai cluster).

[2] This *fonua* territory also incorporated the sea.

[3] These dates were derived from charcoal samples taken at six sites in Ha'apai containing eastern Lapita and Polynesian plainware pottery.

[4] PN is an abbreviation of Polynesian.

[a] In the translation, Kaeppler glosses *fonua* as 'land', however, I have replaced it with the gloss 'people/place' in order to maintain consistency of meaning in the context of this paper.

[b] This extract is taken from Kaeppler (1993: 64-5).

[5] The poetic technique of *heliaki*, 'ironic discourse/double meaning', which is utilised extensively in Tongan poetry and dance, is also employed in the *Lau Langi*. For example, the use of the word *'unga* in the dance evokes for Tongans a multiplicity of mental associations including images of decay, rotting coconuts and the holes made by worms and grubs.

[6] This phrase is most commonly glossed as the 'earth eaters'.

[7] It is important to note that the paragraph breaks have been inserted to facilitate my discussion of the myth later in this section. Normally the story is presented as a complete block.

[8] These beings represent the three principal gods of the old Tongan religion.

[9] This version of the *talatupu'a* is a rendering based on a combination of accounts presented by a number of authors (Gifford 1924; Herda 1988; Mahina 1992; Reiter 1907).

[10] It is important to note that the term *talatupu'a* is also used to describe the telling of any 'ancient' Tongan myth.

[11] As Gunson (1993) has pointed out, received versions of the myth have been modified over the years to highlight and illuminate the divine origin of certain descent lines, particularly the current monarchy. As myth and legend have for centuries often been tools utilised by the elites, this practice is neither new nor surprising.

[a] This is an excerpt from the *Poem of Tuku'aho* (Collocott 1928: 95) written in the early 1800s by Teukava, a chief of Hihifo, Tongatapu, who was an ally of the famous Ha'apai chief, Finau Ulukalala II, whose exploits were documented by the shipwrecked seaman William Mariner in his *Account of the Natives of the Tonga Islands in the South Pacific*.

[12] *'Uta* connotes land without people and is often glossed as 'bush'. In this way, it can be distinguished from *fonua*, 'people of/and place'.

[13] Tangaloa 'Eitumatapua was a brother of Tangaloa 'Atulongolongo and son of Tangaloa 'Eiki and Tamapo'uli.

[14] In the literature, *fa'ahinga* is sometimes substituted with the term *matakali* (see Kaeppler 1971, for example). *Matakali* appears to have been derived from the Fijian *mataqali*. It should also be noted that neither of these kinship categories continue to be employed in the contemporary context.

[15] After the effective demise of the *fa'ahinga/matakali* (as noted above), the *'ulumotu'a* continues to play a minor role within Tongan families today as the coordinator of *kāinga*-(see above) focused activities for life-stage events.

[16] The *maapule* performed the role of attendant and spokesman for the *'eiki*, 'chief'.

[17] Kainga is an ancient kinship category that designates a unit larger than fāmili, covering an extended bilateral descent group in a cognatic network. Kainga has sometimes been described as an 'ideal ego-centred kindred' (Evans 1996: 110).

[18] It is difficult to estimate the number of *fonua* that existed in Tonga as they waxed and waned over time (a few hundred at the most). Estimating the number of people contained within a *fonua* is also difficult, although *fonua* could reasonably have incorporated at least 50 people, although more likely hundreds as whole villages could be subsumed within a *fonua*.

[19] 'Petty chief' is Gifford's phrase for the *tauhifonua* position.

[20] There is some conjecture about whether the ceremony that Cook witnessed was truly the *'inasi* ceremony or some other sacred event such as a Tu'i Tonga installation ceremony relating to power plays at the time. Also Thomas (1879) refers to two *'inasi* ceremonies, one in June and another in October (Beaglehole 1967: 145; Campbell 1992; Cummins 1977; Herda 1987).

[21] A Tongan translation of the English word family, *famili*, is a flexible modern concept that primarily denotes parents and their children, but also encompasses any extra lineal and collateral kin from several genealogical levels living on an *'api kolo* or 'town allotment'.

Postscript — Spatial Categories in Social Context: Tracing a Comparative Understanding of Austronesian Ideas of Ritual Location

James J. Fox

Introduction

This collection of ethnographic essays on different peoples within the Austronesian-speaking world represents a step in a comparative effort that is encouraging and frustrating. The papers in this volume engage in this comparative effort in fascinating and diverse ways but their very diversity only highlights the variety of approaches adopted within a comparative Austronesian framework. The papers speak to each other and to previous papers in earlier volumes in the series on Comparative Austronesian Studies but they represent no single viewpoint, nor do they espouse a consistent methodology comparable with that of the 'comparative method' in linguistics. The cumulative effect of the papers produces a strong resonance, but tracing relations among them can give rise to a variety of readings.

The initial question to be asked of this volume is straightforward. What contribution do these separate essays offer towards a comparative understanding of the Austronesians? Each paper deals with a different group of people located across a wide sweep of islands from Sumatra through Bali and eastern Indonesia to Melanesia and the Pacific. This scattered ethnographic coverage can be seen to represent a considerable social diversity yet it would be hard to argue the particular populations included in the volume offer comprehensive coverage of the Austronesian-speaking world or even a strategic selection of comparative case studies. In fact, one of the papers in the volume deals pertinently with a non-Austronesian population that has taken on many of the seemingly defining features of Austronesian societies.

Each paper focuses on local conceptions of land, territory and settlement but the approach taken to examine these conceptions varies significantly. While some of the contributors may share a similar background and operate with some common understandings, other contributors bring their own distinctive perspectives to bear on the issues set out for discussion in the volume. In each instance, an available ethnography is assessed in terms of general issues of the categorisation of land and its social implications and the problem at hand is redefined in each of these ethnographic iterations.

There is an implicit cross-referencing among the papers. Each separate inquiry, although focused largely on internal explication, offers multiple references to Austronesian concepts and practices noted and discussed in other papers. The comparative effort is thus indirect, partial and incomplete but nevertheless insightful. In each ethnographic analysis, some issues take on new dimensions while others appear to recede. Thus each paper offers its own ethnographic contribution but contributes cumulatively to a wider comparative perspective.

To understand the wider comparative thrust of this volume, it is essential also to recognise that this is the fifth volume in a series that has grown out of the original Comparative Austronesian Studies Project that began in the Research School of Pacific and Asian Studies in the late 1980s. The project began what could best be described as a continuing dialogue. As a consequence, in virtually all of the papers in this volume, there are references to other papers in preceding volumes. Various comparative notions developed and fashioned in these other volumes—ideas about origin, ancestry and precedence—continue to be applied in this volume as well as notions of complementarity and recursivity. From this perspective, the present volume is an extension of a continuing investigation and needs to be read within the context of an entire series.

Given this wider context, it is only at the end of the volume that one is in a position to comment upon its cumulative contribution. This postscript offers one such reading of the volume as a whole. One can consider the papers in this volume in a variety of ways. I have chosen to consider various papers in groups that together pose specific comparative issues and raise questions of significance and of interpretation.

Setting the Scene: The Idea of the Construct **Banua* and its Interpretation

An initial issue in this volume is posed most clearly in Thomas Reuter's paper on ritual domains in the highlands of Bali. The mountain Balinese or Bali Aga organise ritual relations among villages by means of networks known as *banua*, each of which is centred on a paramount temple (*pura banua*) whose ancestral deities insure the fertility of the land of the *banua*. A temple in each of the constituent villages of the *banua* is linked spiritually within the paramount temple and performs its own rituals for the land and people within bounds. Each *banua* is a dynamic creation whose core is of considerable antiquity. In his paper and previous publications, Reuter has described in detail precedence among villages in the large *banua* organised around the regional temple of Pura Pucak Penulisan. The paper raises a historical issue on the extent to which this organisational structure was once more pervasive throughout the whole of Bali. More broadly, the question arises of whether this particular structure reflects a heritage derived from earlier ritual modes in East Java.

Some of the earliest inscriptions in any Austronesian languages refer to the *vanua*. Thus the early seventh-century Sriwijaya inscriptions—in a form of Old Malay written with an adapted Pallava script—refer to the *vanua* as a constituent unit within the polity. Indeed, a single line from one of the earliest of the fragmented inscriptions found at Telaga Batu near the town of Palembang can be read as if it were modern Malay. It reads simply: *vihara ini di vanua ini*: 'This *vihara* [monastery] in this *vanua*' (Casparis 1956: 15). Various scholarly interpretations have been offered for the meaning of the term *vanua* in these inscriptions: proposed translations range from that of 'country' or 'kingdom' to that of the settled 'semiurban' area of a particular polity, the centre or nucleus of the realm (see Kulke 1993: 303-308; Manguin 2002: 82-3).

Similarly, some of the oldest surviving Javanese inscriptions refer to the *wanua/wanwa* as indigenous communities or settlements within a larger polity (Zoetmulder 1982, II: 1384). These communities were presided over by elders known as 'fathers' (*rama*) while all members were considered the 'children of the *wanua*' (*anak wanua*). Supomo, in an earlier volume in this series, has argued cogently that the three Austronesian terms *rama*, *rake* and *ratu*, all of which carry age connotations ('father'—'grandfather'—'ancestor/ruler'), defined three levels of early Javanese polities. Later inscriptions document the 'Sanskritisation' of these polities, as rulers (*ratu*) began to refer to themselves as *rajya* and their realms as *negara* (see Supomo 1995: 295ff.).

Critically for this volume, Graeme MacRae, in his paper, 'Banua or Negara?: The Culture of Land in South Bali', poses this contrast as a living reality in the cultural landscape of contemporary Bali. Popular accounts of the history of Bali credit the transformation of the island to ruling elites from the Kingdom of Majapahit on Java, who invaded in the 14th century, bringing with them new ideas of rule and religion; by contrast, the lesser-known but deeply held traditions of the Bali Aga look to the pre-Majapahit kingdoms of Kadiri and Singasari for the origins of their rituals and organisation. Thus the historical transformation that occurred on Java, it could be argued, is still under way in Bali. More generally, however, MacRae asks how the transformation based on this historical heritage can be related to a far more profound transformation that began with Dutch colonial rule and has been followed by Bali's incorporation as a tourist destination in a global economy.

The early historical references to *wanua* and the prominence of the *wanua* as a feature of some Austronesian polities prompts the question of the extent to which the Austronesian (or, more strictly, Proto-Malayo-Polynesian [PMP]) concept of **banua* has been—and continues to be—an important organising feature of societies throughout the region. As was originally noted in the first volume in the Comparative Austronesian Studies Project, *Inside Austronesian Houses*, reflexes of the term **banua* are found in most subgroups of

Malayo-Polynesian. In a few, the term is applied to house (Toraja: *banua*; Banggai: *bonua*; Wolio: *banua*; Molina: *vanua*; Wusi-Mana: *wanua*). More commonly, *banua* is glossed in general terms as 'land, country, place, settlement, inhabited territory, village' (see Fox 1993:12).

Thus, for example, in the first Austronesian volume, Clifford Sather (1993: 64-115) defined and described the *menoa rumah* as the 'territorial domain' of a longhouse among the Iban of Sarawak; while Michael Young interestingly described the situation on Goodenough Island (1993: 180-93), where *manua* refers to a house but connotes a village in the sense of a 'dwelling place'. This evidence alone indicates that some common ideas associated with the concept of **banua* were part of a social heritage that was transmitted by Austronesian populations in a wide area across the Indonesian Archipelago and into Oceania and that this heritage continues to inform local conceptions to this day.

In one of the initial chapters of the first volume of *The Lexicon of Proto-Oceanic*, dealing with the 'architectural forms and settlement patterns' of ancestral Oceanic society, Roger Green and Andrew Pawley examine the PMP **banua* (based on evidence in Blust 1987) and the equivalent construct, **panua*, in POc. In reviewing the range of reflexes for these terms, they conclude that 'PMP **banua* and its reflex in POc referred primarily to an inhabited territory; not only to the land but to the human population and dwellings and all plant and animal life and other elements that contribute to the maintenance of the human community—a complex concept with no simple equivalent in European languages' (Ross et al. 1998: 63).

In a separate paper, Andrew Pawley has focused on the 'meaning(s)' of **panua* to pose the fundamental question of semantic interpretation of any 'complex concept' associated with a particular lexical reconstruction. This is an essential question that underlies virtually all of the discussion associated with the reconstruction of proto-forms and their subsequent interpretation. Blust, for example, expounded the view that 'the atomistic chaining of glosses in association with PMP **banua* suggests an original semantic category for which no English equivalent exists, which has fragmented into various components in almost all daughter languages' (1987: 96). This view implies a chain of meanings that undergoes a fragmentation as an initial ancestral language divides and diverges: languages would thus preserve (and possibly extend) fragments of a whole while losing others.

By contrast (and in contradistinction to his earlier position), Pawley argues that instead of a single complex meaning, **banua/*panua* was 'genuinely polysemous' and in some contemporary languages of the Pacific, its current reflex retains this polysemy. He cites the case of Wayan Fijian where *vanua* has a 'semantic range' with at least eight senses, each of which can be shown to contrast by one or another criterion, thus forming 'a family of lexical units' with more central or more figurative senses: *vanua* as (1) 'land' as opposed to sea or sky; as (2) 'territory' or 'country', in which case it requires attributive modifiers; as (3) 'homeland', in which case it requires a possessive pronoun; as (4) 'community' or 'land-owning kin-group' in which case it can 'occur as the subject or object of a verb that requires this to be human or animate' (unlike *vanua* [1]); as (5) 'place' or 'area', where it is a near synonym of *tiki*; figuratively (6-8), in reference to the representative of the community, its living conditions and as a political federation of clans. By posing (but by no means answering) this question of the meanings of **panua*, Pawley points to the problematic nature of interpretative semantics in linguistic reconstruction. His proposed solution is much like that of the contributors to this volume. Recognising the historical significance of the category, he offers a careful examination of the use of this term in a wide variety of contexts in a single speech community. This knowledge of the category's usage offers a heuristic indication of its saliency and significance as an organising concept.

Tracing Ideas of the **Banua* (and **Taneq*/**Tanoq*) in Eastern Indonesia and the Pacific

In this volume, in addition to the paper on the Bali Aga, there are a number of other papers on societies in which some reflex of **banua* continues to be an important organising category: three societies in eastern Indonesia—the Keo of Central Flores, the indigenous Masarete-speaking population of Buru, and the Alune of the island of Seram—and two societies in the Pacific—the Raga of North Pentecost and the people of the Kingdom of Tonga. In each instance, reflexes of this category (*nua, fena, hena, vanua, fonua*) are embedded with other spatial categories and take their meaning, in relational terms, in a matrix of senses. It is possible to trace various comparative pathways among these cases. Interestingly, these pathways, signposted by reflexes of **banua*, intersect with other pathways, marked by reflexes of PMP **taneq* (POc: **tanoq*) which has similar meanings of 'earth, land'.

Philipus Tule's paper on the Keo of Flores offers an examination of the contextual significance of the **banua* category. In the case of the Keo, it is of interest that the reflex *nua* occurs with another recognisable widespread Austronesian term for 'land'—*tana*. The Keo identify themselves as 'children' of the land (*tana*) in both a spatial and a genealogical sense. The land is 'feminised' (*'ine tana*) as 'mother' and all Keo derive from this 'mother'. In ritual language, the male complement to this 'mother land' is 'father stone' (*'ame watu*)—all that surmounts the land. Figures of custodial authority are identified with the land and are referred to by the dual name 'mother land, father stone' (*'ine tana, 'ame watu*). Within this context, the term *nua* refers to the autonomous settlements, each with its own ritual leadership (*mosa daki*—or, in ritual language, *mosa nua,* *daki oda*) whose rituals are conducted through the origin houses (*sa'o pu'u*) that make up a village.

Crucially, among the Keo, there are two constituent categories of people: the *'ana tana*, an indigenous category of those whose origins are affirmed through their origin houses, and *ata demba mai*, incorporated 'migrants' of various sorts, whose origins are known to derive from outside the *tana* Keo. Ultimately, the constitution of Keo as a domain is based on an assertion of the knowledge of origins combined with the ritual acknowledgment and celebration of such origins. The *nua* serve as the named settlements in which the rituals of the origin of the land (*tana*) are grounded.

An examination of the use of reflexes of **banua* among the Keo of Flores with either the indigenous population of Buru or the Alune of Seram, who also structure their social worlds by means of this category, is one pathway of comparison, but it is also instructive to compare the Keo with the Sikka and related population of Tana 'Ai who live further east from the Keo on Flores.

For each of these societies, *tana* functions as the 'higher' category. It is the *tana* that Lewis defines as 'domain'—'the highest order of the classificatory categories of Tana 'Ai society'. A *tana*, Lewis writes, is 'a loosely organised region defined by a centre and whose peripheries form no clear boundary. A *tana*'s centre is defined ritually (if not geographically) by its *mahe*, the domain's central ceremonial site, and socially by the ceremonial office of the *tana pu'an* [its 'source of origin'].' The key to understanding a *tana*, in this context as in the case of the Keo, is its ritual definition and ceremonial continuity. In the case of the Keo, the head of a particular clan identified in relation to a specific *nua* is the local ritual celebrant; in Tana 'Ai, this celebrant is identified by clan affiliation alone.

In Central Sikka, where once there were more than 40 named *tana*, a political process of consolidation and redefinition has occurred. It is this historical process that Lewis sketches in his paper. At the heart of this process is an origin charter that transforms the basis of precedence allowing outsiders and other immigrants to establish their rule within an expanded domain. Similar myths by which an 'outsider' is installed 'inside'—the idea of the 'stranger king'—occur throughout eastern Indonesia and are, one could argue, a key epistemic component in the structuring of polities in the Austronesian-speaking world. [1]

In the comparison with Tana 'Ai, the rulers of Sikka have displaced the ceremonial figure of the *tana puang* as they established their own political centre at Sikka Natar. Thus in Sikka, the *natar* became a new ceremonial. In contrast with the Keo, where incorporated immigrants remain subordinate to the children of the land, in Sikka, the outsider has achieved political centrality.

Comparison with the cases from Maluku—Buru and Seram—reflects a different set of historical processes. Among the indigenous population of Buru, the reflex of **banua* is *fena*. As Barbara Dix Grimes notes, the *fena* constitutes an inhabited, domesticated territory whose ritual custodians are represented by particular clans (*noro*) within specific locations (*neten*). These custodians are the *geba neten duan*. Under a regime of shifting cultivation, the 'inside' of this territory (*fen-lale*) is not a fixed location and may shift in relation to changing patterns among clans. Named territories thus consist of an intersection of relations between clans and specific areas.

Among the Alune of Seram, the equivalent category to that of the *fena* on Buru is the *hena*. Where the population of Buru uses the term *noro* for 'clan', the Alune use *nuru*. The fact that the languages of the two islands are closely related makes comparison between their social systems the more interesting.

Among the Maluku Islands, Seram is considered the 'Mother Island' (*Nusa Ina*) and the source of some of its most profound ritual traditions. Christine Boulan-Smit, in her paper, provides a glimpse of this complexity. Her focus is on one *hena*, Ma'saman Uwei, of the Alune, who inhabit a segment of the territory known as the 'Three Large Rivers' ('Wele Telu Batai) in the western region of the island. In comparison with Buru, the *hena* is a more ritually circumscribed component involved in a wider range of social and spatial relationships. The ritual ordering of each 'domain' is assigned to particular clans that hold specifically named ceremonial positions—seven such positions in Hena Ma'saman Uwei—whose responsibilities are directed within and beyond the domain. This ceremonial system also involves an allocation of land based on the shifting precedence among the constituent clans of the domain.

In the discussion of these various societies from the mountains of Bali to the islands of Maluku in eastern Indonesia, the focus is not simply on inhabited land but on ritually defined, ceremonially ordered social space. Equally important to an understanding of this ordering of space is a social dynamic that defines the categories of 'inside' and 'outside' and their relationship to one another.

Here, the case of Banda, 'The Blessed Land' (*Tanah Berkat*), presented by Phillip Winn, offers an instructive contrast. Banda is remarkable in eastern Indonesia for the total displacement of its original population. In 1621, when the Dutch East India Company's (VOC) forces conquered the Banda Islands, they killed, enslaved, deported or drove into exile its entire population and then repopulated these islands as plantation with outside labour. As a consequence, Banda became a Malay-speaking social enclave witshin eastern Indonesia, a wholly immigrant society whose origin narratives link Banda to the foundations of Islam and as a 'blessed' land (*tanah*) directly to Mecca. In place of indigenous claims to origin, local sites imbued with 'past' significance are viewed as places (*keramat*) of 'hidden' meaning associated collectively with ancestral spirits (*datu-datu*). The discourse is that of the Malay world where religious sites, particularly tombs (*makam*), are the focus of veneration (Fox 1991, 2002). As a society of outsiders, the population of Banda treats the 'inside' foci of the land as spiritually powerful but vacant of any specific custodial claim. Yet, as Winn argues, through their 'ritually based engagement' with these sites, the population is able to 'become demonstrably local'.

It is this same theme that is carried forward in the discussion of *vanua* in North Pentecost and the *fonua* in Tonga. John Taylor begins his analysis in distinguishing the category of *vanua* from that of *tano*, a discussion that has its counterpart in eastern Indonesia. On the one hand, he notes that *vanua* are relatively small—an acre or two at most. This situation contrasts with all of the Indonesian cases, where *banua/nua/fena/hena* can encompass a substantial territory. On the other hand, he goes on to note that *vanua* are identified with what are called *bwatun vanua* (literally, the 'source', 'foundation', 'head' or 'roots' of *vanua*): '*Bwatun vanua* represent the specific origin places of individual descent groups.' These origin places are the sites of circular stone piles—grave sites associated with ancestors identified as 'people of the place' (*atatun vanua*). These ancestors are the invisible presence whom the living within each descent group must continue to propitiate.

Instead of holding a position of custodianship within a particular *banua/nua/fena/hena*, however, each descent group among the Raga 'retains custodianship of many individual *vanua* that are scattered throughout the North Pentecost landscape'. Thus, while local discourse resembles that in eastern Indonesia, the scale and scatter of social groupings is strikingly different. Particularly remarkable is the use of the 'land tree' as an image of differentiation—an image that is also common throughout Indonesia. Thus, for example, the mythical banyan tree, Nunusaku, at the centre of the 'Mother Island' of Seram, provides a similar metaphoric image of differentiation and distribution among all of the peoples of Seram.

Mary Patterson's paper on North Ambrym provides a counterpoint to John Taylor's paper on North Pentecost. Where Taylor discusses *vanua*, Patterson discusses *tan*. As Patterson indicates, in Vanuatu, the use of *vanua* or *tan* in local discourse tends to be mutually exclusive—even to the point of political identification: the Vanua'aku Pati versus the Natui Tano and the Tan Union. Yet her description of local *tan* resonates with aspects of Taylor's discussion of North Pentecost with its emphasis on origins and the ancestral spirits of the dead.

In the case of North Ambrym, *tan* refers to specific ancestral lands where custodial male kindred are described as the 'doorways' that provide access to local resources while women of the kindred are the 'roads' that 'go forth and return'. In this metaphoric world, men—when they die—are 'planted' by means of sacrifice and marked by the transfer of tusked boars to members of the mother's origin place.

Appropriately, Tonga offers a case study where the concept of *fonua* has undergone considerable social reconstruction but continues to figure prominently both nationally as well as locally. As Steve Francis points out, the *fonua* in contemporary Tonga embodies notions of nationhood. Whereas the *fonua* in pre-constitutional Tonga were territorial units under chiefly custodians ordered within a social and political hierarchy, the 1875 Constitution transformed this hierarchy and separated the *fonua* from 'the geographical context of local territory, the economic context of agricultural production and the social context of ritual obligation'. Interestingly, the process that Steve Francis sketches bears resemblances to the processes described by E. Douglas Lewis in the transformation of central Sikka under the rulers of Sikka Natar.

Comparative Excursions

Four other papers in this volume engage in implied comparisons on the theme of land as ritual location but without reference to either **banua* or **tana*. Although reference categories are different, the discussion in each of these papers relates to one or another of the themes broached in the earlier discussions.

Minako Sakai's paper deals with the Gumai, a Malay-speaking population in the highlands of South Sumatra among whom the word *tanah*, meaning 'land', occurs. Her concern is with *kute*, the term Gumai ritual specialists use, in preference to modern terms for village or hamlet (*desa* or *dusun*), to denote a 'residential territory' to which genealogically defined Gumai populations link their origins and celebrate their continuity with past generations. The term *kute*, which once implied a fortified centre, is derived from Sanskrit but has a long history of use in Old Malay. As in the case of the papers that discuss the ritual polities of Bali, understanding the Gumai requires some comprehension of the variety of political influences their region has been subject to since well before the time of the Sriwijayan Empire.

As a Muslim population, the Gumai retain non-Islamic ritual specialists (*jurai tue*) whose task is to link the present populations with the founding ancestors of the Gumai population. Sakai's paper is a brilliant exposition of just how these ritual specialists are selected in a society whose origin groups (*jungkuk*) rely on bilateral genealogical reckoning. As in other societies with similar forms of cognatic kin structures, residence—and the de facto inheritance of specific houses—provides the basis for a continuity of succession.

Although not central to her discussion, an interesting feature of her paper is the discussion of how Gumai incorporate 'stranger groups'—populations without genealogical links to the founder population of the *kute*. The Gumai case bears directly on the case of the Keo of Flores, but stands in contrast with that of Sikka.

My own paper, 'Contending for Ritual Control over Land and Polity: Comparisons from the Timor Area of Eastern Indonesia', is concerned with some of the same issues as the paper on the Gumai, particularly the idea of rule and the ritual custodianship of the land. It is in fact one in a succession of papers in which I have attempted to examine comparable aspects of various societies of Timor. The first of these compared houses and their significance (Fox 1993); the second, ideas of origin and the way in which 'progenitor lines' are defined and traced within Timorese societies (Fox 1996).

The paper is a comparison of three domains: Termanu on the island of Roti, Amanuban in south-west Timor and Wehali in south-central Timor. Termanu and Amanuban provide two cases where the contest for control of the land has resulted in the installation of an outsider—a 'stranger king'. As in Sikka in central Flores, this installation subordinated the local ceremonial custodianship over the land to a new political centre.

Wehali provides a contrasting case where such spiritual power has not been subordinated but in fact continues to emanate a vital authority to neighbouring domains. Thus Termanu and Amanuban have developed into polities—states with rulers—whereas Wehali has remained a ritual centre. The further interesting contrast among these cases is the valency given these different centres: Termanu is explicitly a 'male'-centred polity, Wehali is equally explicitly a 'female' centre, while Amanuban evidences elements of both valencies.

The two final papers in this reading—that by Mark Mosko on 'Self-Scaling the Earth' among the North Mekeo of PNG and that by Andrew McWilliam on forest tenures among the Fatuluku of East Timor—are the most challenging and provocative in the volume. Mosko's paper is an attempt to provide a bridge between the discourse currently being conducted in relation to the societies of eastern Indonesia and the distinct discourse on 'personal partibility' in Melanesia. His paper is an elaborate analysis of Mekeo land and society conceived on the model of a body, involving the two-way flow of substances from inside and out.

Andrew McWilliam's paper is particularly challenging in a volume on Austronesian comparison precisely because it deals with a non-Austronesian population who speak a Trans-New Guinea phylum language. As McWilliam makes clear, the Fatuluku have had 'a long-term engagement with Austronesian social and cultural ideas and practices' through contact with other Austronesian-speaking populations on Timor and, as a consequence, 'they have borrowed extensively from Austronesian registers and concepts over many generations'. (In fact, in another paper, McWilliam has referred to the Fatuluku as 'Austronesians in linguistic disguise'.) In his paper, he enumerates a range of conceptual features that the Fatuluku share with their Austronesian neighbours: similarly oriented spatial coordinates, an extensive use of common dyadic categories such as trunk/tip, male/female and elder/younger; landholding origin groups identified by the Austronesian term *ratu*; a clear recognition of progenitor lines among these *ratu* groups; myths of precedence based on a succession of boat arrivals from overseas; and the regular use of ritual language couplets.

Yet in considering Fatuluku society, there are also apparent differences coupled with an oblique untranslatability of concepts. Thus, for example, McWilliam refers intriguingly to 'the Fatuluku idea of a conceptual distinction between the "body" of the earth and its "skin"'—a distinction that is not known to be a salient feature of neighbouring Austronesian groups. It is perhaps interesting in this context that Mosko devotes attention to the notion of 'skin' as a critical feature of the 'body' of the earth among the Mekeo, some of whose cultural ideas might have derived historically from contact with neighbouring non-Austronesians.

Critical comparative issues raised by MacRae in relation to the Indic models that have contributed historically to the transformation of Bali are equally relevant but more elusive in the examination of the Austronesian/Non-Austronesian societies of eastern Indonesia, PNG and Melanesia that have, for millennia, been in regular contact. Fatuluku offers enormous potential for comparative Austronesian studies. The finer and the deeper McWilliam is able to develop his ethnographic understanding of the Fatuluku, the better we might be able to gauge what we mean by 'Austronesian'.

References

Blust, Robert. 1987. 'Lexical reconstruction and semantic reconstruction: the case of Austronesian "house" words.' *Diachronica*, 4. pp. 79-106.

de Casparis, J.G. 1956. *Prasasti Indonesia: Selected Inscriptions from the 7th to the 9th Century A.D.* Dinas Purbakala Republik Indonesia. Bandung: Masa Baru.

Fox, James J. 1991. 'Ziarah Visits to the Tombs of the Wali, The Founders of Islam on Java.' In M.C. Ricklefs (ed.), *Islam in the Indonesian Social Context*, Clayton (Vic.): Centre for Southeast Asian Studies, Monash University. pp.19-38.

Fox, James J. (ed.) 1993. *Inside Austronesian Houses: Perspectives on Domestic Designs for Living*. Canberra: Department of Anthropology, Research School of Pacific and Asian Studies, The Australian National University.

Fox, James J. 1993. 'Memories of Ridgepoles and Crossbeams: The Categorical Foundations of a Rotinese Cultural Design.' In J.J. Fox (ed.), *Inside Austronesian Houses: Perspectives on Domestic Designs for Living*, Canberra: Department of Anthropology, Research School of Pacific and Asian Studies, The Australian National University. pp.140-79.

Fox, James J. 1996. 'Transformation of Progenitor Lines of Origin: Patterns of Precedence in Eastern Indonesia.' In J.J. Fox and C. Sather (eds), *Origin, Ancestry and Alliance: Explorations in Austronesian Ethnography*, Canberra: Department of Anthropology, Research School of Pacific and Asian Studies, The Australian National University. pp.130-153.

Fox, James J. (ed.) 1997. *The Poetic Power of Place: Comparative Perspectives on Austronesian Ideas of Locality*. Canberra: Department of Anthropology, Research School of Pacific and Asian Studies, The Australian National University.

Fox, James J. 2002. 'Interpreting the Significance of Tombs and Chronicles in Contemporary Java.' In A. Reid and H. Chambert-Loir, *The Potent Dead: Ancestors, Saints and Heroes in Contemporary Indonesia*, Sydney: Allen & Unwin. pp. 160- 172.

Kulke, Hermann. 1993. *Kings and Cults: State Formation and Legitimation in India and Southeast Asia*. New Delhi: Manohar Publishers and Distributors.

Manguin, Pierre-Yves. 2002. 'The Amorphous Nature of Coastal Polities in Insular Southeast Asia.' *Moussons*, 5. pp. 73-99.

McWilliam, Andrew. 2004. 'Austronesians in Linguistic Disguise: Fatuluku Cultural Fusion in East Timor.' unpublished manuscript, The Australian National University (available online at http://faculty.washington.edu/plape/pacificarchwin06/readings/mcwilliam-austronesians%20in%20ling%20disguise.pdf

Pawley, Andrew. 2005. 'The meaning(s) of Proto Oceanic *panua.' In Claudia Gross, Harriet D. Lyons and Dorothy A. Counts (eds), *A Polymath Anthropologist: Essays In Honour of Ann Chowning*. Research in Anthropology and Linguistics, Monograph No. 6. University of Auckland, Department of Anthropology.

Ross, Macolm, Andrew Pawley and Meredith Osmond (eds). 1998. *The Lexicon of Proto Oceanic: The Culture and Environment of Ancestral Oceanic Society. Vol. I: Material Culture. Pacific Linguistics*, C-152. Canberra: Research School of Pacific and Asian Studies, The Australian National University.

Sather, Clifford. 1993. 'Posts, Hearths and Thresholds: The Iban Longhouse as a Ritual Structure.' In James J. Fox (ed.), *Inside Austronesian Houses: Perspectives on Domestic Designs for Living*, Canberra: Research School of Pacific and Asian Studies, The Australian National University. pp. 64-115.

Supomo, S. 1995. 'Indic Transformation: The Sanskritization of Java and the Javanization of the Bharata.' In Peter Bellwood, James J. Fox and Darrell Tryon (eds), *The Austronesians: Historical and Comparative Perspectives*,

Canberra: Research School of Pacific and Asian Studies, The Australian National University. pp.291-313.

Young, Michael. 1993. 'The Kalauna House of Secrets.' In James J. Fox (ed.), *Inside Austronesian Houses: Perspectives on Domestic Designs for Living*, Canberra: Research School of Pacific and Asian Studies, The Australian National University. pp.180-93.

Zoetmulder, P.J. (in collaboration with S.O. Robson). 1982. *Old Javanese-English Dictionary*. 2 Volumes. 'S-Gravenhage: Martinus Nijhoff.

ENDNOTES

[1] I embarked on a comparative study of this mythic charter in a paper entitled 'Installing the "Outsider" Inside: The Exploration of an Epistemic Austronesian Cultural Theme and its Social Significance', which was presented at a session of the First European Association for Southeast Asian Studies Conference, 'Local Transformations and Common Heritage in Southeast Asia' (Leiden University, June 29 to July 1, 1995). I have since continued to add to this initial paper, which has now taken on monographic proportions.

Contributors

Christine Boulan-Smit

Christine Boulan-Smit (PhD, The Australian National University) is a Visiting Fellow in the Resource Management in Asia Pacific Program (RMAP), at the Research School of Pacific and Asian Studies, The Australian National University, and also works as a senior consultant anthropologist. Her current research interests in applied anthropology include social impact assessment and monitoring of significant industrial developments (mining) in rural South-East Asia and Latin America.

James J. Fox

James J. Fox was educated at Harvard (AB 1962) and Oxford (B Litt. 1965, DPhil. 1968). He is Professor of Anthropology in the Research School of Pacific and Asian Studies at the Australian National University where he has served as Director from 1998 to 2006. He has edited several of the previous volumes in the Comparative Austronesian Project series, the most recent of which was *The Poetic Power of Place: Comparative Perspectives on Austronesian Ideas of Locality* (1997). His research continues to focus on Java and Timor and on issues in Austronesian studies.

Steve W. Francis

Steve W. Francis was educated at Monash University (B Arts. Hons 1990, M. Arts. 1991) and the University of Melbourne (PhD 2003). He is the Policy Co-ordinator for the Centre for Multicultural Youth Issues and a Fellow with the School of Anthropology, Geography and Environmental Studies, University of Melbourne. His research interests focus on homeland and movement in Oceania and the settlement needs of young refugees. Recent publications include a review of *Voyages in Pacific Studies* (2006) and *Participation for All?: Searching for Marginalised Voices: The Case for Refugee young people in Children, Youth and Environments ((2006)*.

Barbara Dix Grimes

Barbara Dix Grimes is an anthropologist (PhD, 1994 The Australian National University) who has worked in eastern Indonesia with Universitas Hasanuddin in Sulawesi, Universitas Pattimura in Ambon, and, more recently, Universitas Kristen Artha Wacana in West Timor. She currently lives in Darwin and makes frequent trips to consult on community development issues and church-based multilingual education and translation programs in Timor.

Douglas Lewis

E. D. Lewis was educated in San Antonio, Texas, and studied at Rice University (BA 1971), Brown University (AM 1975), and the Australian National University (PhD 1983). He is Senior Lecturer in Anthropology in The University of Melbourne and is author of *People of the Source: The Social and Ceremonial Order of Tana Wai Brama on Flores* (1988), co-producer the film *A Celebration of Origins* (1994), editor of *Timothy Asch and Ethnographic Film* (1994), and author of a number of papers on the ethnology of eastern Indonesia. His current research aims at the development of a neurobiological theory of culture.

Graeme MacRae

Graeme MacRae teaches anthropology at Massey University in Auckland, New Zealand. His PhD (Anthropology, Auckland, 1998) was on economics, ritual, history and tourism in Bali. Since then he has been researching on a range of topics in Bali and South India including architecture, landscapes and agriculture. Recent publications include 'Negara Ubud; the theatre-state in twenty first century Bali' (in *History and Anthropology* 16:4) and 'Growing Rice after the Bomb: Where is Balinese agriculture going?' (in *Critical Asian Studies*. 37:2).

Andrew McWilliam

Andrew McWilliam completed his Phd (1990) in the Department of Anthropology of the Research School of Pacific and Asian Studies at the Australian National University. He is currently a Research Fellow in the Department with continuing interests in island Southeast Asia, especially eastern Indonesia and Timor. He is the author of *Paths of Origin, Gates of Life: A study of place and precedence in southwest Timor* (KITLV Press, 2002), and numerous papers on Timorese ethnography and the anthropology of natural resources management.

Mark S. Mosko

Mark S. Mosko is Professor and Head of the Anthropology Department in the Research School of Pacific and Asian Studies at the Australian National University. Over three decades he has conducted several ethnographic field studies of the North Mekeo peoples of Papua New Guinea and written comparatively on numerous other societies including hinterland Madang, Trobriands, Tikopia, ancient Hawaii, caste India, and the Mbuti of Zaire. His theoretical interests have covered a wide range of ethnological issues, from social organisation, structuralism, historical process and gift exchange theory to hierarchy and chieftainship, personhood and agency, body decoration, commodification, and hristian syncretism and symbolism. In addition to numerous journal articles and book chapters, he is author of *Quadripartite*

Structures (1985) and co-editor of *Transformations of Hierarchy* (1994) and *On the Order of Chaos* (2005).

Thomas Reuter

Thomas Reuter completed his PhD in anthropology on the indigenous highland people of Bali, Indonesia, at the The Australian National University's Research School of Pacific and Asian Studies in 1996. After teaching for two years at the University of Heidelberg in Germany, Thomas returned to accept a Postdoctoral Research Fellowship from the Australian Research Council, at the University of Melbourne. In 2001, he was awarded a Queen Elizabeth II Fellowship to study 'Revivalism and Religious Conflict in Javanese Society'. He is currently employed as a Senior Research Fellow in Anthropology at Monash University. Theoretical interests include social organisation, change, conflict, movements, religion, ethnicity, kinship, marginality, architecture, cross-cultural epistemology, communication, and the politics of representation. Recently published books include: T.A. Reuter (ed.) 2003, *Inequality, Crisis and Social Change in Indonesia: The Muted Worlds of Bali*, London: Routledge-Curzon Press; T.A. Reuter, 2002, *The House of Our Ancestors: Precedence and Dualism in Highland Balinese Society*, Leiden: KITLV Press; T.A. Reuter, 2002, *Custodians of the Sacred Mountains: Culture and Society in the Highlands of Bali*, Honolulu: University of Hawai'i Press.

Mary Patterson

Mary Patterson completed undergraduate studies and a PhD in anthropology at the University of Sydney, and then taught at the University of Sydney. She took up a postdoctoral fellowship at the University of Melbourne in 1991, and is now a Senior Lecturer in Anthropology in SAGES at Melbourne. Her fieldwork in Vanuatu spans three decades; her research interests extends to the Pacific region in general. She is currently working on issues of globalisation and the politics of aid in the Pacific and the intersection of politics and the occult. Her theoretical interests are in kinship, gender and social organisation, the occult and its political effects, and political anthropology.

Minako Sakai

Minako Sakai obtained her PhD in Anthropology from the Research School of Pacific and Asian Studies at The Australian National University in 2000. She is a senior lecturer in the Indonesian Studies at the School of Humanities and Social Sciences, University of New South Wales at ADFA campus. She is the editor of Beyond Jakarta: Regional Autonomy and Local Societies in Indonesia (Crawford 2002) and has published articles on Islamic identity and local politics in Sumatra. Currently she is completing a book on globalised Malay identity and regionalism in Southeast Asia.

John Taylor

John Taylor is an ARC Postdoctoral Fellow at the Gender Relations Centre of the Research School of Pacific and Asian Studies at the Australian National University. His current research explores gender relations and male subjectivities in northern Vanuatu, particularly through the social, economic and symbolic context of kava *bisnis*. This represents the initial component of a more extensive project that aims to expand knowledge of island Melanesian communities, sexuality and gender through the study of masculinities. John holds a BA in English Literature and Anthropology and a MA in Social Anthropology from the University of Auckland. Research for MA resulted in the monograph *Consuming Identity: Modernity and Tourism in New Zealand* (1998). His PhD was carried out at the Australian National University and the thesis "Ways of the place: History, cosmology and material culture in North Pentecost, Vanuatu" (2003) won the inaugural prize for a doctoral thesis awarded by the Australian Anthropological Society in 2004. He is currently revising this for publication as a book.

Philipus Tule

Philipus Tule was born in Kolinggi, Flores. He is a member of the Society of the Divine Word Missionaries (SVD) and studied at the seminary in Ledalero in Flores from 1975-1984. In 1988, he obtained an MA in Islamology from the Pontifical Institute of Arabic and Islamic Studies, Rome; in 2001, he obtained his PhD in Anthropology from the Australian National University, Canberra. He is currently Rector of St Paul's Major Seminary in Ledalero. His publications include *Longing for the House of God, Dwelling in the House of the Ancestors: Local Belief, Christianity and Islam among the Kéo of Central Flores.* (2004)

Phillip Winn

Phillip Winn is a Lecturer in the School of Archaeology and Anthropology at the Australian National University, Canberra. His PhD (Anthropology, Australian National University, 2002) analyzed the interrelation of place, identity and community in the Banda Islands of central Maluku, Indonesia – a locale historically transformed by expansive trade and by colonial violence. In previous publications he has explored aspects of Muslim ritual practice and social life, inter-communal conflict, moral discourse and resource use, and cultural tourism. His current research interests include local visions of Islam in Southeast Asia, the cultural dynamics of state formation, and violence.

Index